W9-BCB-084

WHEN ALL ELSE FAILS

For my daughters, Julia and Emily

WHEN ALL ELSE FAILS

Government as the Ultimate Risk Manager

David A. Moss

HARVARD UNIVERSITY PRESS

Cambridge, Massachusetts

London, England

2002

Copyright © 2002 by David A. Moss
All rights reserved
Printed in the United States of America

Library of Congress Cataloging-in-Publication Data

Moss, David A., 1964–
    When all else fails : government as the ultimate risk manager /
    David A. Moss.
        p. cm.
    Includes bibliographical references and index.
    ISBN 0-674-00757-3
    1. Risk management—United States.   2. Risk management—Government
policy—United States.   3. Insurance, Government—United States.
4. Disaster relief—United States.   I. Title.

HD61 .M63 2002
338.5—dc21   2002017111

Contents

Preface

It has been said that "[h]istory in the making is a very uncertain thing."[1] And so it is. I finished writing this book nearly five months before the tragic events of September 11, 2001. By the time the book was edited and ready to go to press, the United States was at war in Afghanistan and the federal government was struggling mightily to restore security and stability at home.

The attacks themselves—on four commercial aircraft, the World Trade Center, and the Pentagon—had no precedent in American history. Yet in many ways the response from Washington proved remarkably familiar. Like their predecessors who faced other plagues, including financial panics and natural disasters, federal policymakers quickly capitalized on the government's special strengths as a risk manager. And this was not just in the realm of national defense or macroeconomic policy. In the wake of the attacks, federal officials moved to manage a broad array of risks. They immediately introduced legislation, for example, to compensate victims and their families, to bail out the airlines, and to bolster the insurance market.

Confidence in the private sector's capacity to manage terror-related risks deteriorated rapidly in the aftermath of September 11. Even many business leaders admitted that they could no longer handle these risks on their own. Reflecting the prevailing sentiment, a prominent insurance executive announced two weeks after the attacks that the insurance industry "cannot insure risks that are infinite and impossible to price."[2] Government involvement, he suggested, was simply essential. Nor was there any serious debate among political leaders about whether the government ought to serve as the nation's insurer of last resort. Republicans and Democrats argued over how—but not whether—to write the relevant legislation.

Foreign observers, meanwhile, were astonished to witness such extensive government intervention in the U.S. economy. As one French economist put it, the Americans who had long "been teaching the gospel of free markets" had, in the aftermath of the attacks, suddenly seemed "to forget the universal laws of the market."[3] Weren't the Americans violating their own hallowed creed of laissez-faire?

This book provides an answer to that question, suggesting that deep government involvement in the management of private sector risks is really nothing new in the United States, despite the nation's reputed commitment to laissez-faire. Throughout the country's history, lawmakers have enacted a wide array of risk management policies, particularly in times of crisis when they most doubted the capacity of the private market to get the job done. The response to September 11 was no exception.

This book addresses neither the attacks themselves nor the frenetic policymaking that followed. It is a study in historical political economy, not current events. But by tracing the history of American risk management policy, the book should help to elucidate why federal officials responded the way they did. Above all, it should reveal the government's critical role as a risk manager, which—for the most tragic of reasons— has lately assumed new prominence in American life.

David A. Moss
Boston, Massachusetts
November 25, 2001

1

Introduction

This book is about the government's role as a risk manager. As I will show, risk management constitutes a potent and pervasive form of public policy in the United States. Our economy would be unrecognizable in its absence. It is even possible that the economy would not function at all. Without limited liability law, bankruptcy law, government-printed money, and unemployment insurance—just to name a few pivotal risk management policies—it is doubtful that a modern industrial economy could have taken root in America.

Strangely, risk management is not generally viewed as a function of government.[1] Perhaps this is because risk management is less tangible than most other governmental functions. When a government builds roads or schools or military bases, pursues criminals, or imposes tariffs on foreign goods, the results are obvious. Risk management policies typically exert subtler effects. Yet these policies touch every American every single day. Whenever you deposit money in an FDIC-insured bank or observe the speed limit on a public road or buy shares in a limited liability corporation, you are (whether you know it or not) the beneficiary of a risk management policy.

So what is risk management policy? It comprises any government activity designed either to reduce or to reallocate risk. Product liability law provides a good example of the latter. Every consumer faces the risk of injury from an unsafe product. The existence of product liability law shifts part of this risk onto the manufacturer by allowing injured consumers to sue for damages. Similarly, workers' compensation laws shift the risk of workplace accidents from employees to employers and, in

1

most cases, to their insurers. Federal deposit insurance, meanwhile, safeguards individual depositors by spreading the risk of bank failure across all depositors. And federal disaster relief shields victims of natural catastrophes by diffusing part of the financial burden over the entire tax-paying public.

In addition to reallocating risks away from the most vulnerable parties, state and federal governments also try to *reduce* risks through a variety of devices. Examples include consumer product safety laws, minimum banking standards, workplace safety regulations, and even the construction of flood levees. Life would be considerably more dangerous in the absence of such protections, and these examples reveal only the tip of the iceberg.

Risk management policies have now proliferated to such an extent that it is hard to think of any greater governmental responsibility. When a dispute between President Bill Clinton and the Republican-controlled Congress ended in a government shutdown in early 1996, Secretary of Labor Robert Reich explained the impact, first and foremost, in terms of the increased risks individuals would face. "You know," he said, "much of what the federal government does in the United States . . . is to provide what is almost a large insurance policy for people. And it's only when you get into trouble . . . that you realize that the insurance policy has effectively been cancelled. And that is what's happened now."[2]

The federal shutdown of 1996 lasted only a short time. But the secretary's words serve to remind us that risk management is indeed a central function of government and one with far-reaching implications. Even in a country well known for its hostility to government, policymakers have emerged as aggressive risk managers. The purpose of this book is to explain both how and why this has come to be.

Public Risk Management in Historical Perspective

In recent years, nearly all of the attention that risk management policies have attracted has been negative. Countless critics have charged that government attempts to shield citizens from adverse risks are turning America into a nation of ninnies, devoid of courage and personal responsibility. One writer complained in the *New Republic* in 1989 that the "desire for a risk-free society is one of the most debilitating influences in America today."[3] Several years later, after the famous McDonald's hot coffee case, another pundit lamented that America had "devolved from a country of pioneers to a nation of plaintiffs."[4]

Budget hawks, meanwhile, continually remind us just how expensive these policies can be. The major social insurance programs—Social Security, Medicare, unemployment insurance, and workers' compensation—alone cost well over $500 billion per year.[5] And the maximum potential liabilities associated with deposit insurance, pension insurance, and other federal financial guarantees easily exceed $6 trillion.[6] As early as 1991, President George H. W. Bush's budget director, Richard Darman, warned that each of these federal liabilities was "like a hidden Pac-Man, waiting to spring forward and consume another line of resource dots in the budget maze."[7] All by itself, the savings and loan fiasco of the late 1980s and early 1990s is estimated to have cost the federal government more than $150 billion.

While such criticisms have considerable merit, they create the impression that public risk management is a luxury we cannot afford—the product of overindulgent and weak-willed policymakers. Attacking the U.S.-led bailouts of ailing Asian economies in 1997 and 1998, an op-ed piece in the *New York Times* announced that the nation's leaders were "emotionally incapable of accepting capitalism's inherent risks."[8] But the truth is that the markets themselves have not always proved capable of managing capitalism's inherent risks in an acceptable manner.

Some years ago the Nobel economist Kenneth Arrow explained that missing and incomplete markets for risk represented one of capitalism's greatest failings. "Perhaps one of the strongest criticisms of a system of freely competitive markets," he wrote in a 1970 article with Robert Lind, "is that the inherent difficulty in establishing certain markets for insurance brings about a sub-optimal allocation of resources."[9] Elsewhere Arrow suggested that it was up to the government to take up the slack, to "undertake insurance in those cases where [a private market for insurance], for whatever reason, has failed to emerge."[10]

A close look at American history reveals that state and federal policymakers had been heeding Arrow's "advice" long before he gave it, at least since the dawn of the Republic. Yet most accounts in the popular press foster the opposite impression—that government "meddling" with private sector risks is of recent vintage. Articles on the subject often hark back to some earlier time, when America was full of vigor and individualist spirit and when every citizen faced his own risks with a sense of stoic independence and pride. But such a time never really existed. While government involvement in risk management has certainly changed and expanded over the years, it is impossible to locate a moment in history when policymakers were not wrestling with a variety of nettlesome risks. One cannot understand public risk management in the United States without first coming to terms with its history.

Phase I: Security for Business (to 1900)

Broadly speaking, American risk management policy has passed through three phases, the first of which was already under way when the Constitution was ratified in 1789. In the late eighteenth and early nineteenth centuries, when the United States was itself a developing country, policymakers focused particular attention on risks that were thought to undermine trade and investment. Contrary to today's conventional wisdom, the historical record strongly suggests that well-conceived risk management policies can foster economic development and growth. Although risk taking lies at the heart of capitalism, the experience of this early period indicates that certain types of risk may be dysfunctional in a developing-country context.

A good example involves the problem of unlimited liability for passive investors. Before Americans began to develop a significant manufacturing base in the early nineteenth century, the vast majority of investors were active investors, meaning that they owned and managed their own companies and farms. But the emergence of large-scale enterprises (including some textile factories and other manufacturing operations) required the participation of a new type of investor, the passive investor, who would buy shares but would not be directly involved in managing the firm. Passive investors emerged as an increasingly vital source of capital as the nation industrialized.

The problem in the early nineteenth century was that many passive investors were reluctant to part with their savings so long as they faced unlimited liability. If a firm collapsed, its bankers and other creditors were entitled to seize the personal assets of any investor, whether active or passive. This meant that every single investor risked personal financial ruin—and potentially even incarceration in a debtor's prison—if his investment went bad. Such extreme liability seems almost unimaginable today, but it was the norm two hundred years ago.

Although active investors had long been willing to tolerate unlimited liability, economic policymakers soon learned that passive investors were less adventurous. "The business of manufactures requires, for its successful prosecution, the employment of large capital," Governor Levi Lincoln of Massachusetts stated in 1830. "The contributions of many individuals are necessary to the creation of the fund. But men, with the admonitions they have had, will no longer consent, for the chance of profit upon a share in a concern, to put their whole property at the hazard of circumstances, which they neither can foresee, nor over which they can have any control." Unless limitations on shareholder liability were promptly established, the governor warned, "the manufacturing interest, to a great extent, must be abandoned in Massachusetts."[11] Without the enactment of limited liability laws in the first half of the nineteenth century, the development of American manufacturing might well have been impeded.

Significantly, limited liability laws required no new taxes or spending, nor did they create any new regulatory bodies. All they did was shift a portion of corporate default risk from shareholders to creditors. Several students of the subject have astutely characterized limited liability as "an implicit, creditor-provided form of insurance of the risks of business failure."[12] Amazingly, this one simple risk-shifting device was likely responsible for preserving and accelerating industrialization. "Insofar as one associates economic progress with economies of scale," the economist Sir John Hicks wrote, "it must be regarded as a major achievement of limited liability that it has made much of our economic progress possible."[13]

Though exceedingly important, passive investment risk was not an isolated problem in the nineteenth century. The emerging American economy was full of energy but also teeming with risks that threatened to undermine growth. Even money was far from secure as a means of payment, forcing policymakers to engage in a perennial battle to solve the problem of "money risk." Senator Robert Strange of North Carolina complained in 1840 that "the paper [money] system has drawn everyone irresistibly into its vortex." It had, he said, "made itself the precarious basis of all employments; it had undermined the firmest foundations, so that no man is now secure against those unforeseen accidents which were once peculiar to the trader."[14]

While policymakers recognized the need to manage a wide range of business risks, from bankruptcy to bank runs, most also understood that they operated on a razor's edge. This was particularly true in the case of money risk. Had government officials clamped down too hard on the banks (which were the primary suppliers of the nation's currency at the time), they would have strangled the burgeoning economy, depriving it of vital credit and liquidity. And yet to leave this risk entirely to the market threatened to submerge the whole business community in a frenzy of speculation and fear.

By the end of the nineteenth century, American lawmakers had enacted a wide range of risk management policies, all intended to promote trade and investment. Most notable among them were limited liability, banking regulation, bankruptcy law, a fixed exchange rate, and the predictable enforcement of property rights.[15] These policies are relevant now not only because they laid the institutional foundations of America's economic success, but also because today's developing economies face many of the very same problems. How to manage economically dysfunctional risks without stopping up the wellspring of economic progress is one of the most difficult challenges facing policymakers in every developing country. The recent financial crises in Latin America, Southeast Asia, and Russia testify to this fact. Nineteenth-century America, struggling to develop its own economy, demonstrated at least one successful path through a minefield of risks on the way to industrial affluence.

Phase II: Security for Workers (1900–1960)

The dawn of the twentieth century brought an entirely new set of risks to the attention of U.S. policymakers. Industrial workers, who had once constituted but a tiny fraction of the nation's labor force, had by now grown into a large and powerful social group. Although wages had increased substantially in the late nineteenth century, most workers' financial positions remained precarious. In the new industrial economy, the loss of a job—whether because of a workplace injury, illness, old age, or an economic downturn—could easily land a worker and his family in poverty. Extensive family support networks had helped to spread individual risks in older agricultural communities, but rapid urbanization left these traditional safety nets in tatters.

Progressive reformers worried that widespread worker insecurity could provoke unrest and even rebellion. After all, the Russian Bolshe-viks had proved the viability of a workers' revolution in 1917. John R. Commons, an academic economist and the intellectual father of Amer-ica's Social Security system, warned ominously that "unless the cap-italistic system begins to take care of the security of the laborer, begins to make jobs as secure as investments, then there is a serious question . . . whether that system can continue to exist."[16]

The focus of risk management policy thus shifted from business to la-bor in the early twentieth century. Workers' compensation laws, which mandated on-the-job accident insurance, were enacted in just about ev-ery state between 1911 and 1920; and compulsory unemployment and old age insurance were introduced a generation later as part of the Social Security Act of 1935.

The man who signed the Social Security bill into law, President Frank-lin Roosevelt, fully appreciated the transformation that his signature helped set in motion. "Beginning in the nineteenth century," he ob-served in a speech about Social Security, "the United States passed pro-tective laws designed, in the main, to give security to property owners, to industrialists, to merchants and to bankers." This was the first phase of risk management policy in the United States. But while business-oriented policies had been sufficient in the nineteenth century, FDR in-sisted that the growing complexity of industrial society in the early twentieth made it "increasingly difficult for individuals to build their own security single-handed." Government, he concluded, "must now step in and help them lay the foundation stones, just as Government in the past has helped lay the foundation of business and industry. We must face the fact that in this country we have a rich man's security and a poor man's security and that the Government owes equal obligations to both."[17] With that, America's welfare state was born, and Phase II of American risk management policy was definitively under way.

At the time, many critics inveighed against the inevitable expansion of government authority, warning that these new social programs would choke off the dynamic spirit of American capitalism. In 1916, Ralph Easley of the powerful National Civic Federation dismissed social insur-ance as "largely saturated with the virus of socialism."[18] Two years later, the president of a New York trade association characterized compulsory insurance as an "absolutely un-American and paternalistic" device that would transform American workers into "spineless creatures dominated by the will of an autocracy."[19] Similarly, in 1935, one congressman bitterly attacked the Social Security bill as "simply one more step toward sovietizing our distinctive American institutions, devitalizing the self-reliance and enterprise of our people, and mortgaging our future."[20]

Despite such rhetoric, social insurance programs proved popular with the electorate—perhaps because the government appeared to be succeeding where the private market had failed. Workers' compensation and unemployment insurance grew substantially over the years, and Social Security (once so reviled by the right) appeared to become a political sacred cow. Today, Americans spend considerably more on social insurance than on any other budget item, including national defense.

Phase III: Security for All (since 1960)

The shift in emphasis from business risk to worker risk in the transition from Phase I to Phase II exerted a profound effect on the American economy and on American society. Not only did it utterly transform the nation's social welfare policy, but also, for the first time, it brought a great many citizens face-to-face with the risk management function of government. Within a relatively short period, nearly every member of the labor force came under the nation's social insurance umbrella. This ultimately had the effect of lowering the bar on new risk management policies. If the government was going to protect businesspeople and workers against a variety of hazards, why shouldn't it also protect consumers and homeowners and countless other groups from potentially ruinous risks? This was the question that opened a third phase of public risk management in the United States beginning in the early 1960s.

Risk management policy expanded suddenly and dramatically under Phase III. Federal disaster policy is a good case in point. Whereas federal disaster relief covered just 6 percent of uninsured losses from a major catastrophe in 1955, the figure had surged to nearly 50 percent by 1972.[21] In his memoirs Herbert Hoover looked back nostalgically to the 1920s, when the government's role in disaster relief had been small. "[T]hose were the days," he wrote, "when citizens expected to take care of one another in time of disaster and it had not occurred to them that the Federal Government should do it."[22] By the 1970s, those days were long gone.

Meanwhile, state and federal policymakers had launched an all-out assault on personal risk. Health, safety, and environmental regulations multiplied rapidly; and lawmakers created a broad new array of federal insurance programs and financial guarantees. Congress even established liability caps on credit cards—a sort of limited liability for consumers. First enacted in 1970, these rules required credit card issuers to act as implicit insurers, guaranteeing all cardholders against losses stemming from unauthorized use of their cards.[23]

Not to be outdone, the nation's judges turned product liability law upside down, converting it from a producer promotion program into a powerful consumer protection device. As successful product liability suits became more and more common, manufacturers discovered that the doctrine of *caveat emptor* had been completely inverted. Now sellers, rather than buyers, had to "beware" every time a good was sold.

One of the architects of the new liability regime, Justice Roger Traynor, acknowledged as early as 1965 that America's risk management policy was maturing along with the economy itself. "We have come a long way," he remarked in a law review article. "The great expansion of a manufacturer's liability for negligence . . . marks the transition from an industrial revolution to a settled industrial society. The courts of the nineteenth century made allowance for the growing pains of industry by restricting its duty of care to the consumer."[24] After 1960, however, the imperatives of personal security rivaled, and perhaps even exceeded, those of economic growth in the United States. This shift was clearly reflected in the simultaneous transformations of statutory and common law approaches to risk management. It was also becoming increasingly evident in everyday life. Phase III had arrived.

Learning from History

As should be clear even from this brief historical survey, American lawmakers have utilized risk management tools to achieve a range of social objectives over a long period of time. From an economic standpoint, the full spectrum of risk management policies might be viewed simply as a series of responses to risk-related failures in the private sector. A great many interventions have been necessary precisely because these sorts of failures are pervasive in a free-market economy like ours.

Although economists have thought deeply about why markets for risk frequently fail, most of their conclusions remain abstract, revolving primarily around the problem of asymmetric information between buyers and sellers of risk. Their tendency has been to privilege theoretical models over real-world examples. While this approach has proved enormously productive in many regards, it has also had the unfortunate effect of insulating theory from the slings and arrows of reality. The historical approach offered here may help to address this shortcoming.

The history of risk management policy in the United States brings the subject to life, revealing an epic drama about the gradual taming of the American economy. Along the way it spotlights the ongoing efforts of policymakers and other social reformers to understand precisely the sorts of private failures that have intrigued modern-day social scientists. These historical figures have a lot to teach us, and we ought to listen to them if we truly want to understand the risk management function of government. History—or, more precisely, historical political economy—represents a vital complement to economic theory in the study of capitalism's institutional foundations. Nowhere is this more true than in the field of public risk management.

Risk-Related Failures in the Private Sector

To begin with, the historical record suggests new insights about why risk-related failures are so common in the private sector. These failures are troubling because they mean that Adam Smith's invisible hand is missing a finger or two. Ideally, well-functioning markets would move risks to those parties best able to handle them. Most homeowners, for example, pay to shift their fire risk to insurance companies, which are well positioned to assess and diversify the risk of houses burning down. Yet in a great many other cases, well-functioning markets for risk simply do not exist. You cannot buy insurance against declining housing prices, even though a significant drop in the price of your home might affect you much more than a fire in your basement.[25] Nor can you buy insurance against a decline in the average wage in your industry, or against the possibility that a key member of your team at work will come down with the flu the day before a big presentation. In a world of perfect markets, all of these risks and countless others would be tradable in the marketplace. Because they are not, our collective well-being is less than it should be. Risk is being borne inefficiently. The key question is why.

Economic theorists have traditionally blamed risk-related failures in the private sector on asymmetric information problems such as adverse selection and moral hazard, which will be treated at some length in the next chapter. But a careful review of the relevant legislative history reveals that policymakers and reformers have attributed these failures to a broader array of causes, including not only information problems but also perception, commitment, and externalization problems. Although these too will be taken up in the next chapter, the basic point is this: even if complete information about a particular risk were equally available to all potential buyers and sellers, the market still might not allocate it in an acceptable way. This could occur if one side systematically *misperceived* the risk, if no buyer (insurer) could credibly *commit* to compensate future losses, or if some third party managed to *externalize* the risk, imposing it on others without having to bear the attendant costs.

As we will see, many reformers and lawmakers paid particular attention to perception problems. The Columbia economist Henry Seager observed in 1907, for example, that workers in hazardous industries tended to view themselves as immune to injury. "[E]ach individual," he said, "thinks of himself as having a charmed life."[26] If true, this charmed life phenomenon surely could have undermined or even destroyed the market for private accident insurance. Why would workers want to buy insurance if they didn't expect to get hurt? Confident that this was in fact a problem, Seager aggressively championed workers' compensation laws, which *required* employers to insure their employees against on-the-job accidents.

More than a half-century later, the Yale law professor Guido Calabresi emphasized precisely the same problem as a justification for imposing strict manufacturer liability in product injury suits. Catastrophic injuries, he explained, "always happen to 'the other guy,' and no amount of statistical information can convince an individual that they could happen to him." From this Calabresi concluded that "someone other than the individual, someone who *can* make a rational evaluation of the risk involved, is better suited to decide the optimal degree of loss spreading. This someone can be thought of as 'society.'"[27]

Arguments like these concerning individual misperception are intriguing because they run contrary to the standard economic justifications for compulsory insurance. Economists have typically attributed the failure of private insurance markets to individuals' having better information than their insurers.[28] But Seager and Calabresi suggested almost exactly the opposite. In their view, insurance markets may have failed to develop because individuals effectively had *too little* information, owing to their inability to process correctly that which was actually available.

Naturally, we cannot say for sure whether contemporary policymakers and policy advocates such as Seager and Calabresi were right or wrong in their assessments. Just because they were around at the time is no guarantee that they truly understood the problems they were trying to solve. Yet their interpretations deserve considerable weight. Unlike subsequent generations of scholars, they had the opportunity to examine how private markets worked—or failed to work—*prior* to the government interventions that they helped engineer. They also had the unique ability to ask questions both of other relevant analysts and of the key economic actors involved. In trying to figure out why so many workers were uninsured against on-the-job accidents, Seager spoke with employers, insurance executives, and laborers. His opinions should count with modern-day economists because he was exceptionally well positioned to study many of the very same questions they are interested in today.

The main historical focus of this book is thus on those moments when key risk management policies were first debated and introduced, whether by legislatures or courts. Anyone interested in understanding government's role in addressing market failures ought to view these moments as excellent sources of data. Through court decisions, legislative debates, and other primary documents, lawmakers and social reformers have left us an invaluable record—a detailed account of how and why private markets were thought to fall short and the ways in which public policy might be used to remedy these weaknesses.

This record is far from pure, of course. It is full of the distortions, machinations, and miscues that are the stuff of politics. Politicians prepared their speeches not to teach us about political economy, but rather to get their bills passed and to get themselves reelected. Yet many of them were also problem solvers of the first order, chosen by the electorate to address the nation's ills. The fact that many of the policies to be reviewed here have stood the test of time only adds to these policymakers' credibility as effective problem solvers. It is in this special context that their words become data for the political economist.

Although the chapters that follow track both politicians and social reformers, the politicians are of special interest. This is because political leaders serve a vital, if underappreciated, role as filters of information. Mediocre politicians are like flypaper for ideas, indiscriminately picking up just about anything that comes along. This is rather easy to do, because "experts" of almost every variety are often eager to share their views with those in power. One quality that distinguishes superior politicians from inferior ones is the ability to cast off weak arguments, to save only the strongest, and especially those with the ring of truth. By the time a discriminating politician gets to the floor of a legislature for debate, he has filtered out all but the best insights and interpretations—drawn from all quarters—and is ready to present them as his own. This is why moments of policy inception are so valuable and serve as the empirical foundation of this book. Ultimately, these moments tell us a great deal about the sources of risk-related failures in the private sector and about the government's capacity to respond.

Evolution of Social Priorities: From Growth to Security

The historical record also makes clear that the formation of risk management policy has been about much more than mere market failures. In fact, it is impossible to explain government intervention in the allocation of private sector risks as a response to market failure alone. The number of risks that legislators could theoretically justify addressing on technical grounds—that is, because private markets for risk were incomplete or nonexistent—is simply staggering. Instead, prevailing social priorities have played a crucial role in determining which risks have provoked government action at particular moments in time. Perhaps most fascinating of all, the evolution of risk management policy in the United States reflects an unmistakable shift in social priorities from growth to security over the past two centuries.

Until about 1900, it appears that the main factor guiding American lawmakers in their choice of risk management policies was an interest in stimulating sustainable economic growth. If technical market failures had been their only concern, they could easily have started elsewhere. The market for worker risks (such as workplace accidents and unemployment) was far from complete in the nineteenth century, and no market for consumer risks existed at all. Lawmakers overlooked these sorts of failures because they were more concerned about forms of insecurity that inhibited growth than about insecurity in general. The absence of corporate default insurance and money-risk insurance were of special interest in the early 1800s because these failures seemed to be deterring businesspeople from engaging in trade and investment. As the legal historian James Willard Hurst observed, the overriding goal of nineteenth-century policy was the "release of energy," which included a "desire to achieve greater certainty or definition of risks for men venturing property."[29] Uninsurable workplace risks would not become a salient political issue until after 1900, and uninsurable consumer risks until after 1960. Social priorities, not the mere existence of market failures, are what set the nation's policy agenda.

But what accounts for the stunning shift in priorities that drove the three phases of risk management policy? There are many possible explanations, but perhaps the most intriguing one relates to America's success in raising personal incomes over time. Back in 1820, per capita income was just under $1,500 (in 1999 dollars). That was pretty good at the time, ranking fifth among the world's industrializing nations, but still pitiful by current standards. Today, a single person in the United States is defined as living in poverty if her income is below $8,500, and a family of four is said to be living in poverty if its combined income is less than $17,000 (or $4,250 per person). By 1890, per capita income in the U.S. approached $4,500 (in 1999 dollars), now ranking third in the world. And by 1913, the United States had surpassed all other nations with a per capita income of nearly $7,000. By the time John Kenneth Galbraith published *The Affluent Society* in 1958, per capita income in America had passed $13,000 (in 1999 dollars), and today the figure stands at about $35,000.[30]

As average income departed ever further from the poverty line through the late nineteenth and twentieth centuries, more and more Americans came to feel that they had something worth protecting. The prospect of additional income as a result of economic growth naturally remained welcome, but protection against the loss of existing income (security) apparently emerged as an increasingly significant social objective. This is entirely consistent with Kenneth Arrow's hypothesis that individuals' relative risk aversion increases with wealth—that is, they become more fearful of losing what they have as they get richer.[31] It is also consistent with the historical fact that private insurance markets began to develop rapidly in the United States during the late nineteenth and early twentieth centuries, extending for the first time beyond economic elites.[32] John Kenneth Galbraith has written that in industrial nations, "most people, when employed, are not primarily preoccupied with the size of their income. They seek to increase it . . . but inadequacy of income is not their first concern. . . . Their principal worry is the danger of losing all or most of their income."[33]

Over the extraordinarily affluent twentieth century, security thus came to rival growth as a major social priority. As it did, the target of risk management policy gradually shifted from the businessperson to the worker and, ultimately, to the citizen at large. Whether the third phase represents a natural extension of the other two or a dangerous departure is a matter of considerable dispute these days. But this question can be meaningfully answered only after a thorough examination of all three phases. The oft-heard charge that Americans have become obsessed with security should not be evaluated in isolation. A proper historical perspective—including an understanding of changing social objectives and major policy developments—is essential.

A New View: Government as Risk Manager

History thus provides a vital window on the government's role as a risk manager. Perhaps most important, the historical record brings into full relief both the breadth and the depth of this governmental function. The story to be told is not just about product liability gone mad, as some would have it, or about the excesses of federal disaster relief, but about limited liability law and banking regulation and bankruptcy law and social insurance as well. In an economy defined by risk, public risk management is simply unavoidable, particularly given the pervasiveness of risk-related failures in the private sector.

Unfortunately, relatively little is known about public risk management because it has not generally been recognized or studied as a function of government. Some of the individual policies have received considerable attention, but the broader governmental function has remained obscure. The basic premise of this book is that a careful survey of its history will make public risk management unignorable and, in so doing, will help us to understand government and its role in the economy in a new way.

The Book's Scope

Precisely because this book addresses such a large subject, it has been necessary to limit its analytic scope along a number of different dimensions. One choice has been to consider a single country, the United States, rather than to adopt a broader cross-national perspective. Another choice has been to focus mainly on policies designed to reallocate risk (whether by shifting it or spreading it), rather than on those designed to reduce risk straightaway. Perhaps the most important choice of all has been to highlight ideas and values, as opposed to political pressures and interests, in telling the story of American risk management policy. Although the implications of these choices should become evident as the account unfolds, it may be helpful to provide a little in the way of explanation at the outset.

Focus on America

Although the United States makes considerable use of public risk management, it is certainly not the only country to do so. To varying degrees and in varying ways, every government manages risk. Some even employ it as a central tool of national economic policy.[34] A cross-national study of the subject would clearly be of tremendous value. The problem, however, is not simply that such an undertaking would likely require several volumes, but that it might well be premature, since individual country studies have yet to be written. Fortunately, the United States has much to recommend it as an initial specimen.

First, relevant historical documents on the development of risk management policies are plentiful and largely accessible in the United States, greatly simplifying the task of the historian. Although the record is obviously thinner for the early nineteenth century than for the late twentieth, the most vital documents are available for nearly all of the key policies, from limited liability law to federal disaster relief.

Second, the United States represents a particularly compelling subject for a case study because of its success in generating high levels of growth over a long period of time. Lawmakers who enact economic policy generally suggest they are addressing various sorts of private failures, and they sometimes try to articulate the nature of those failures as part of the policymaking process. Naturally, they may be mistaken, either in their identification of private failures or in their diagnoses of the causes. If the U.S. economy had run out of steam in the nineteenth century, many observers would likely have blamed bad public policy. But given the continued strength of the American economy and the long life and fundamental character of some of the policies to be examined here, the original assessments of the policymakers who envisioned them cannot easily be brushed aside. So the legislative history takes on special significance in a U.S. context.

Finally, risk management policies seem to occupy an unusually prominent place in America's political economy. A nation widely known for its anti-statist sentiments and its faith in limited government ("laissez-faire, anti-statist, market-oriented," in the words of Seymour Lipset),[35] the United States is nonetheless up to its elbows in risk management policies. There are many reasons for this. But part of the appeal of public risk management could be that it often proved nearly invisible. Limited liability law, for example, required no new bureaucracy nor any new taxes. Policies such as workers' compensation and deposit insurance demanded a more noticeable institutional presence, but were still much less invasive than publicly run health care systems and state-owned banks, which were common elsewhere. Product liability and medical malpractice law, meanwhile, have imposed stringent regulations on companies, hospitals, and doctors with virtually no government bureaucracy other than the courts themselves.

Less visible than other forms of government intervention in the economy (such as wealth redistribution or direct government ownership), risk management policy may be particularly well suited to the distinctive political and ideological character of the United States: statism for anti-statists, so to speak. The fact that pervasive risk regulation has spawned a considerable bureaucracy since the early 1960s only goes to show that America's special attraction to risk management policy has now taken on a life of its own, moving beyond its original anti-statist logic.[36] Clearly, few countries could provide such a fascinating venue for an inaugural investigation of public risk management as the United States.

Risk Reallocation versus Risk Reduction

The next big question concerns the types of risk management policies to be examined. In the United States, as in every country, there are two basic categories of public risk management. Policymakers may attempt to *reduce* risk outright by prohibiting or otherwise controlling risky activity. Or they may seek to *reallocate* risk, either by shifting it from one party to another or spreading it across a large number of people. In some cases, risk reallocation can lead to risk reduction, but not always.

Although policies that reduce risk directly (such as safety regulations) are no less important than those that reallocate it (including social insurance and liability law), the latter are of particular interest here. Most of the policies to be examined in this book are ones that either shift or spread risk. This focus on risk reallocation provides a convenient way of narrowing a potentially unwieldy subject. It also serves to complement the existing public policy scholarship, which has taken up risk reduction as a policy category but not risk reallocation.

A careful history of risk-reduction policies would, at the very least, require a separate volume, since the number of public policies designed to reduce risk is exceedingly large. Lawmakers impose quarantines to reduce the risk of contagious disease, set maximum speed limits to reduce the risk of accidents on the road, restrict the use of known carcinogens to reduce the risk of cancer, and so forth. Indeed, this list could be extended almost indefinitely.[37]

Fortunately, there is already a substantial literature in the social sciences devoted to the subject of "risk regulation," which focuses mainly on health and safety rules.[38] Although this literature is not particularly historical, it boasts a compelling mix of theoretical and empirical analysis. Perhaps most important, contributors to this literature have managed to place a diverse set of risk-reduction policies under a common conceptual umbrella.

The same cannot be said of risk reallocation, however, which has received far less attention as a policy category.[39] This is surprising, since risk-reallocation policies have been employed to address many of the same problems as risk-reduction policies. And because programs that reallocate risk tend to be broader in coverage, they are also fewer in number. A single workers' compensation law, for example, covers workers against a wide array of risks on the shop floor—risks that would require a great many separate regulations if dealt with piecemeal through a risk-reduction approach.[40]

Risk-reallocation policy thus proves especially tractable from a historical standpoint. Although we cannot examine the origins of every risk-reallocation policy in the pages that follow (or even every major one), we are able to take a close look at a substantial subset, including many of the most important initiatives at both the state and federal levels.[41]

It should be noted that despite some superficial similarities, risk-reallocation policies are conceptually distinct from policies designed to redistribute income or wealth. The difference is roughly analogous to that between private insurance and charitable giving. Both insurance and charity ultimately direct funds to individuals in need. In the case of insurance, however, the eventual beneficiaries are not in need (or even known) when the insurance contract is written. In fact, all of the participants in an insurance pool face approximately the same chance of falling victim to the insured hazard. Unlike charity, insurance is not normally viewed by those who purchase it as a means of assisting the poor, but rather is seen as a means of protecting themselves.

Another way of understanding this difference is to recognize that insurance and charity affect expectations in fundamentally different ways. Whereas charity necessarily *changes* the level of income or wealth that individuals can expect to have at the end of a given year (lowering that of donors and increasing that of recipients), insurance aims to *limit deviations* from expected levels of income or wealth. Indeed, precisely the same distinction applies in the realm of public policy. Whereas redistributive policies are enacted to *change expected outcomes* (by transferring resources from rich to poor), risk-reallocation policies are put in place to *make individuals' expected outcomes more certain* (often by pooling resources among those with comparable levels of risk). This distinction is no doubt sharper in principle than in practice, since many risk-reallocation policies involve at least some degree of income redistribution. But it still remains exceedingly useful in analyzing real-life policies and, particularly, in understanding the diverse arguments used to justify them. It helps to distinguish, for example, between the food stamp program (income redistribution) at one extreme and workers' compensation (risk reallocation) at the other.[42]

The analogy just offered also suggests another reason why the focus of this book is on policies that reallocate risk as opposed to those that reduce risk outright. An emphasis on risk reallocation puts a finer point on the question of why government efforts to manage risk were viewed as necessary in the first place. After all, risk-reallocation policies often bear a striking resemblance to private market solutions, including private insurance. Given the private sector's obvious competence at shifting and spreading a wide range of risks, what exactly did government policymakers expect to add to the mix? As will become clear from our historical investigation, key advocates of risk-reallocation policies often attempted to address this question themselves.

All this is not to say that risk-reduction policies will be ignored completely over the remainder of this volume. They show up now and again, particularly in Chapter 4, which examines a variety of attempts to stabilize a volatile money supply in antebellum New York. But there is no chapter devoted exclusively to a risk-reduction strategy, such as the ongoing effort to reduce consumer risks through product safety regulation. Although this choice brings with it some cost in terms of breadth of coverage, it allows for a far more cohesive and, I hope, readable treatment of public risk management in the United States.

The Power of Ideas and Values

Finally, it is essential to emphasize that this book is not a political history, even though it features a large number of political decisions and political actors. The purpose of each chapter is not to explain why a particular bill became law, which would require a careful examination of competing interests and factions. Rather, the purpose is to expose the conceptual frame of reference and the implicit social values underpinning particular policy initiatives. The larger goal is to demonstrate that a wide range of seemingly unrelated initiatives—from limited liability law to federal disaster relief—actually had far more in common than a standard political history would suggest. All shared a common economic logic, the logic of risk management. And although specific policy objectives varied dramatically from case to case, broader social objectives appear to have been far less volatile, as reflected in the three phases already discussed.

Instead of asking what interests policymakers were trying to serve, therefore, this book asks what problems they were trying to solve. This approach may strike some readers as rather unusual, since it is now fashionable to dismiss lawmakers as opportunists, driven by little more than their own unquenchable desire for power and wealth. But the truth is that while opportunism matters a great deal in the policymaking process, so too do ideas and values. (Look closely at the records of just about any major policy debate and you will find corroboration for this "hopelessly naïve" view of the process.) A sustained focus on the problems policymakers were trying to solve—and on the ideas and values that they drew on—is of vital importance here because it ultimately reveals the hidden coherence of American risk management policy.

We will begin this historical journey shortly, surveying major policy developments across the three phases in Chapters 3 through 9 and wrapping up with a summary of key findings in Chapter 10. But first, by way of background, the next chapter offers a brief digression on the underlying concept of risk and *its* history.

2

A Primer on Risk and Its History

Risk is an intuitive subject. All of us have a sense of what risk is and how nervous or excited it makes us feel. At the most basic level, risk exists whenever more than one outcome is possible. Homeownership is risky because a house may be worth more or less tomorrow than it is today. It is even possible that it will be worth nothing at all, since it might burn down in a fire or get carried away in a flood. Although the term "risk" is commonly associated with bad events (such as illness and financial loss), bad contingencies cannot exist in the absence of favorable ones (such as good health and financial gain). It is our uncertainty about what the future will bring—rather than bad events per se—that makes our lives full of risk.

But that is not all there is to it. Risk is also a highly technical subject, the focus of textbooks and academic articles. This chapter aims to make the technical side of risk more accessible, employing intellectual history as a bridge between the technical and the intuitive. A variety of concepts developed over the past four hundred years—from expected value and risk aversion to adverse selection and moral hazard—will come in handy as we examine government efforts to manage risk in subsequent chapters.

Expected Value and Risk Aversion

One of the first serious studies of risk dates from the mid-1500s, when an Italian physician and mathematician named Girolamo Cardano turned his attention to gambling. Before this time, perhaps no one had thought about chance events in such a systematic way. Cardano's breakthrough was in discovering that the likelihood of rolling a particular sum with two dice exactly equaled the number of ways that sum could be obtained, divided by the total number of possible rolls. The probability of rolling a five, for example, was 4/36—that is, four possible ways to roll a sum of five (1 + 4, 2 + 3, 4 + 1, 3 + 2) divided by thirty-six possible rolls (1 + 1, 1 + 2, 1 + 3, 1 + 4, and so on down to 6 + 6).[1] Whereas a gambler at the time surely would have known from experience that throwing a seven was more likely than throwing a five, Cardano could say with precision that the probability of throwing a seven was 6/36 (16.7 percent) as compared to 4/36 (11.1 percent) for a five. (See Figure 2.1.)

The broader notion of *expected value* (or *mathematical expectation*) emerged over the next hundred years. Cardano's work itself was not published until 1663.[2] In 1657 the Dutch physicist Christiaan Huygens had proposed a precise method for determining the expected value of a game, which was simply the weighted average of all possible outcomes. He observed that in a lottery with two equally likely payoffs, *a* and *b*, the "fair" price of a ticket was ½(*a*) + ½(*b*). So if a lottery ticket had a fifty-fifty chance of paying $0 or $1,000, then its expected value was ½($0) + ½($1,000), or $500. (Note that in Figure 2.1, the expected value of the game of dice—the sum of all eleven outcomes multiplied by their respective probabilities—is exactly seven.) This insight marked an enormous conceptual advance in the budding field of probability theory.[3]

At about the same time, the French mathematician Blaise Pascal went so far as to use the notion of expected value to demonstrate the wisdom of believing in God. The core of his argument was that the value of any bet equaled the likelihood of winning times the size of the potential payoff. Since the payoff from being a believer was infinite if God existed, then it was definitely worth believing, even if one thought the probability of God's existence was very small. Pascal seemed to acknowledge that the alternative of not believing in God also involved a payoff, in the form of additional worldly pleasure from sinning. But since the value of worldly pleasure remained finite, the *expected value* of being an atheist could never be as great as that of being a believer.[4]

All of these early students of probability theory assumed that expected value was the same as "fair price" in the marketplace. The fair price of a game with a fifty-fifty chance of paying $0 or $1,000, they be-

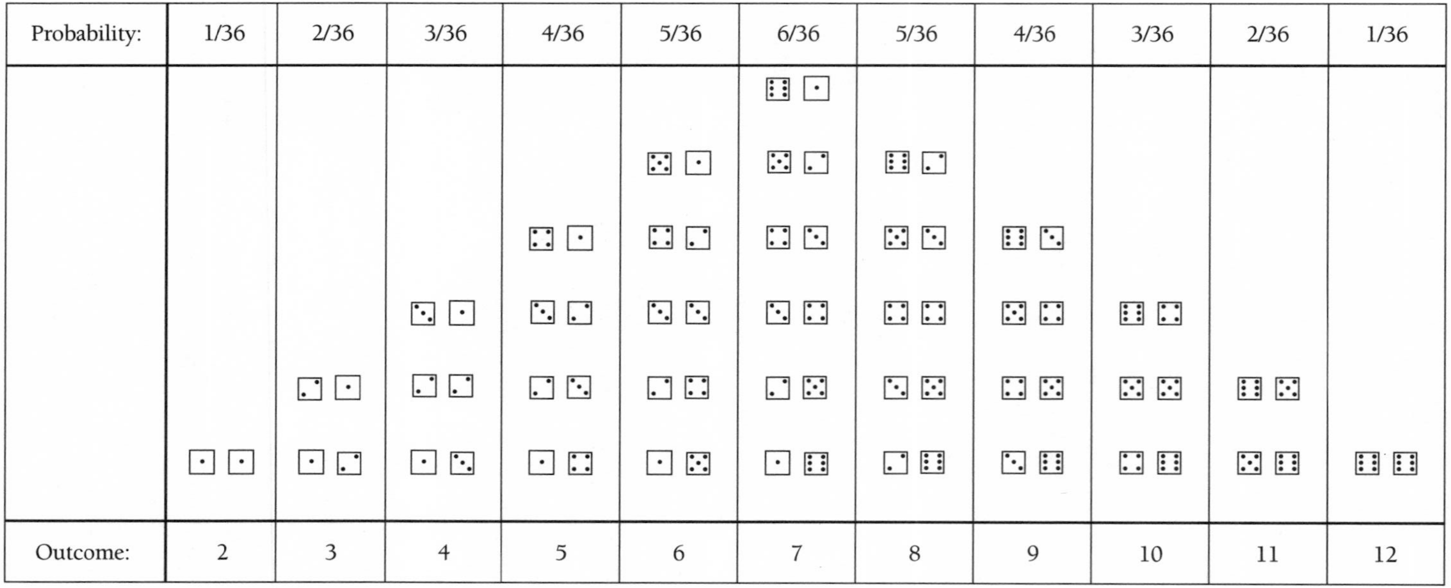

Probability:	1/36	2/36	3/36	4/36	5/36	6/36	5/36	4/36	3/36	2/36	1/36
Outcome:	2	3	4	5	6	7	8	9	10	11	12

Figure 2.1 Early probability theory: Finding order in random rolls of the dice. The 36 pairs shown represent all of the possible combinations from a single throw of two dice. The "outcome" is simply the total number of dots that appear on any given throw, while the "probability" is the likelihood that a particular outcome will occur. Since there are 36 possible ways that the dice can be thrown (combinations) but only one way to throw a two (i.e., "snake eyes"), the probability of throwing a two is 1/36. Since there are two ways to throw a three (either 1–2 or 2–1), the probability of throwing a three is 2/36. And so on. Expected value is simply the probability-weighted average of all the outcomes. In this case it equals $(2 \times 1/36) + (3 \times 2/36) + (4 \times 3/36) + (5 \times 4/36) + (6 \times 5/36) + (7 \times 6/36) + (8 \times 5/36) + (9 \times 4/36) + (10 \times 3/36) + (11 \times 2/36) + (12 \times 1/36)$, which sums exactly to 7. In rolling two dice, therefore, the expected value is 7, which is also intuitively evident from the illustration.

lieved, was exactly $500. This implied that the owner of a $100,000 house should pay no more than $10,000 for insurance when the probability of loss was 10 percent. One of the most fascinating discoveries in the history of economics was that most people are willing to pay *more* than the expected value of a hazard in order to eliminate it. In our example, the homeowner would be willing to pay in excess of $10,000 to insure her home. Economists call this *risk aversion,* a deeply rooted human characteristic that defines a substantial part of the economic world as we know it. In its absence, much of the financial sector (and especially the insurance industry) would have little reason to exist.

The first clear recognition of risk aversion can be traced to 1738, when a Swiss mathematician named Daniel Bernoulli published a pathbreaking exposition on risk.[5] Writing in Latin, Bernoulli claimed that scientists such as Huygens and Pascal had been wrong to equate expected value with fair price in the marketplace. To emphasize his point, he recalled a puzzle introduced twenty-five years earlier by his esteemed cousin Nicolas Bernoulli. Nicolas had put the following question to another famous mathematician, Pierre Rémond de Montmort, in 1713:

> Suppose Peter tosses a coin and continues to do so until it lands on heads. Peter promises to pay Paul one dollar if it lands on heads on the first throw, two dollars if heads on the second throw, four dollars if heads on the third throw, eight if on the fourth, and so on (i.e., $\$2^{n-1}$ if heads on the nth throw). How much should Paul be willing to pay Peter for the opportunity to play this game?[6]

Although Montmort did not appreciate it at the time, this was an exceptionally difficult problem. It would ultimately become known as the St. Petersburg Paradox. The trick was that although no reasonable person would pay more than about $20 to play the game, its expected value was infinite: $(1/2 \times \$1) + (1/4 \times \$2) + (1/8 \times \$4) + (1/16 \times \$8) + \ldots = \infty$. How could this be?

Daniel Bernoulli believed he had the solution. In his view, people determined how much to pay for the game on the basis not of expected value (or mathematical expectation) but rather of *expected utility*—that is, the amount of pleasure they expected to derive from the game. Each potential payoff (whether $1, $2, $4, or even $1 billion) would generate a specific amount of utility. Expected utility simply represented the probability-weighted sum of all possible utilities—that is, 1/2 times the utility from $1 *plus* 1/4 times the utility from $2 *plus* 1/8 times the utility from $4, and so on. The reason this sum never got anywhere near infinity, according to Bernoulli, is that individuals derived a progressively smaller amount of utility from each additional dollar. In other words, they valued every new dollar a little less than the one before, which explains why a rich person typically values a dollar less than a poor person does.

In modern economic parlance, Bernoulli was describing the diminishing marginal utility of wealth. One critical implication of this notion is that individuals will place a higher value on losses than on equal-sized gains, and thus will generally avoid taking mathematically fair risks. Anyone "who bets any part of his fortune . . . on a mathematically fair game of chance acts irrationally," Bernoulli wrote.[7] Here, in just a few words, was his definition of risk aversion. It was an extraordinary contribution, but he did not stop there.

Assuming that the steady decline in utility from each new unit of wealth followed an exact logarithmic formula, Bernoulli calculated the amount a person ought to pay for the opportunity to play Peter's game. He determined, for instance, that a person worth $1,000 should pay no more than $6 to play, even though the expected value of the game was infinite. Although economists have since dispensed with Bernoulli's notion of a precise logarithmic relationship between money and utility, his core insight—that individuals typically value each additional dollar less than the previous one—remains the dominant characterization of risk aversion.[8] His analysis also formed the basis of expected utility theory in economics, which was ultimately established in modern form by John von Neumann and Oskar Morgenstern in the 1940s.[9] Though by no means perfect, expected utility theory constitutes the most widely accepted framework we now have for modeling human decisionmaking under uncertainty.

The Power of Diversification

Quite independent of all this theory, the modern insurance business had already begun to emerge by the time Daniel Bernoulli wrote his landmark article. Merchants meeting in Lloyd's coffeehouse in London began underwriting marine and other risks in 1688. Before long, Lloyd's had developed into an important and very active insurance exchange.[10] And that was only the beginning. At least four fire insurance companies were operating in England by 1700.[11] Across the Atlantic, the first American fire insurance company (the Friendly Society for Mutual Insuring of Houses Against Fire) was founded in Charleston in 1735.[12]

Of course, the origins of insurance go back much further. References in the Hammurabi Code suggest that Babylonians were entering into primitive insurance contracts at least as early as the eighteenth century B.C., and it is likely that these early forms of insurance were present in Babylon as far back as the fourth millennium B.C.[13] Bottomry contracts, as they came to be known, specified that loans to shippers should be forgiven whenever their shipments were lost in transport.[14] These contracts spread rapidly until finally prohibited by the Catholic Church as an illicit form of usury in 1227 A.D.[15]

Additional forms of insurance and other financial guarantees emerged in ancient Greece and Rome, including a number of early exercises in public risk management. As part of a military support operation around 215 B.C., the Roman government assumed "all risk of loss by reasons of perils of the sea or capture" for any private trader willing to ship supplies to the republic's allies in Spain.[16] Some years later, Emperor Claudius (10 B.C.–A.D. 54) directly underwrote merchants' losses resulting from storms, apparently in an attempt to accelerate growth in the grain trade.[17] Cicero (106–43 B.C.) had earlier suggested the use of private sureties to protect government funds in transport; and primitive annuity contracts were described in both Ulpian's table (third century A.D.) and the Digest of Justinian (sixth century A.D.).[18]

Perhaps the most fascinating development up to the seventeenth century was the widespread practice of private risk spreading through friendly societies and guilds. Reaching all the way back to ancient times, friendly societies in China, India, Greece, and Rome typically provided a rudimentary form of life insurance that covered burial expenses for their members. Some offered limited coverage against sickness and other hazards as well.[19] The insurance function of mutual associations and guilds expanded significantly in Europe during medieval times, with some offering coverage against losses from marine and fire risk and even legal liability.[20]

The underlying logic of all of these early efforts at risk spreading was that the burden of any given risk (that is, the unexpected variation) declined sharply when distributed among a large number of people. The preamble to the first English insurance act, passed in 1601, explained that marine insurance was advantageous because "upon the loss or perishing of any ship, there followeth not the undoing of any man, but the loss lighteth rather easily upon many than heavily upon few."[21]

Even though Jacob Bernoulli (still a third Bernoulli, Daniel's uncle) did not formalize the *Law of Large Numbers* until the late seventeenth or early eighteenth century, the essential idea had long been understood by practitioners. In Bernoulli's words, "even the most stupid of men, by some instinct of nature . . . is convinced that the more observations have been made, the less danger there is of wandering from one's goal."[22] What Jacob Bernoulli ultimately proved, in a manuscript published posthumously in 1713, was that the mean of a sample would approach its expected value as the sample size tended toward infinity. More precisely, he demonstrated that as samples grew ever larger, the difference between the sample mean and the theoretical mean (i.e., the expected value) would shrink ever further, eventually reaching an infinitesimally small level. This principle implied that large-scale risk sharing could reduce individual risks close to zero while leaving aggregate risk unchanged.

To illustrate, consider an individual merchant who organized one major shipment each year.[23] If the shipment arrived safely, the merchant could count on earning $10,000. But if the shipment was lost in transport (because of theft, storms at sea, or any other hazard), he earned nothing. If we assume that the probability of loss was 20 percent, the merchant faced an earnings distribution with an expected value of $8,000—that is, an 80 percent chance of $10,000 and a 20 percent chance of $0. Naturally the merchant would worry about the possibility of having no income at all. And because he was risk averse, he would much rather have had a certain income of $8,000 than an uncertain one with an $8,000 expected value. Fortunately, the Law of Large Numbers offered him a way of reducing his uncertainty.

If the merchant could find other traders with identical profiles whose risks of loss were independent of his, then he and his colleagues could dramatically reduce their individual levels of risk simply by agreeing to share their earnings equally. Since the sample mean would approach the true expected value as the sample size grew, each participant could count on earning close to $8,000 (regardless of what happened to his individual shipment), so long as the number of merchants participating in the sharing arrangement was sufficiently large.

The power of *diversification*, implicit in this example, is presented graphically in Figure 2.2. With only two participating merchants, there are but three possible outcomes: both merchants will lose their shipments (4 percent probability), or just one will lose his shipment (32 percent), or neither will lose a shipment (64 percent).[24] From a risk-based perspective, this already marks a big improvement for the original merchant. Although his chance of receiving $10,000 has fallen from 80 to 64 percent as a result of the sharing arrangement, his chance of earning nothing at all has fallen even more sharply—from 20 percent when he was operating on his own to just 4 percent now. Nor are $0 and $10,000 the only possibilities anymore. If one of the ships is successful and the other is not (the odds of this being about one in three), the two merchants will split the proceeds and end up with $5,000 each.

Sharing between just two merchants, therefore, significantly reduces each merchant's uncertainty. A favorite statistical measure of risk, which gauges the spread within a distribution, reveals precisely the same thing. The *standard deviation* of each merchant's prospective income declines from $4,000 before sharing to $2,828 after. With ten merchants participating, the standard deviation falls to $1,265; and the probability of anyone's receiving under $5,000 drops to just 3.3 percent. With three thousand merchants participating, the standard deviation tumbles all the way to $73; and each trader can feel confident that the probability of receiving between $7,800 and $8,200 at the end of the year now exceeds 99.9 percent.

Convergence toward the expected value of $8,000 becomes ever more obvious with each successive increase in the number of participants. Although this is the central point of the example, a few other points are also worth mentioning. As portrayed in Figure 2.2, convergence toward expected value implies not only the elimination of bad outcomes (such as zero earnings), but also elimination of better-than-average outcomes (such as $10,000 earnings). The only reason this trade-off appears desirable to our merchant is because he is risk averse.

It is also important to recognize that although risk is now being distributed more efficiently through the sharing arrangement, the aggregate amount of risk has not been affected. Numerous shipments will still be lost, and no one can say for sure how many. Only *individual* risk declines as a result of risk spreading. The *total* risk of loss is naturally much greater with three thousand shipments than with just one. Therefore, in sharp contrast to individual standard deviation, which falls with sample

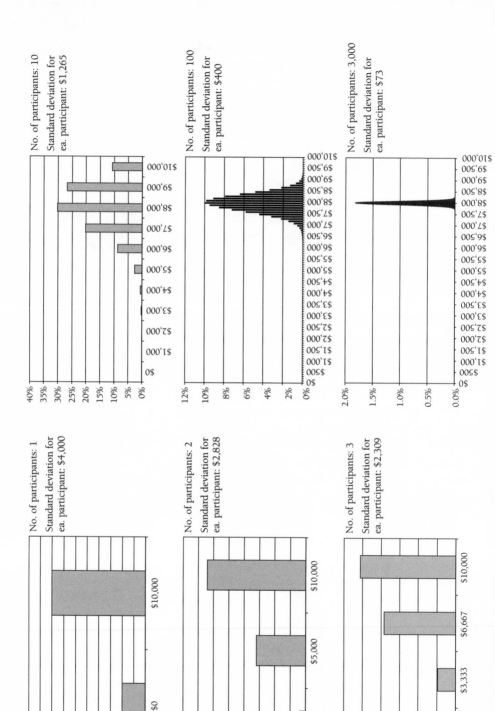

size in the presence of sharing, aggregate standard deviation steadily rises with sample size, regardless of whether there is any sharing or not. In our example, aggregate standard deviation rises from $4,000 when there is only one merchant to $219,089 when there are three thousand. The merchants' pooling arrangement, in other words, does not reduce uncertainty about aggregate losses (about how many ships will sink and so forth). But it does sharply reduce each individual merchant's uncertainty about his own personal losses and thus about the size of his future income.

In this stylized example, diversification involves the pooling of identical risks, since every merchant faces precisely the same set of payoffs and the same odds of failure. Yet diversification remains an effective way of reducing individual risk (while preserving expected returns) even when the various risks being pooled are not identical. As compared to one who holds a single stock, the individual who holds a diverse portfolio of stocks can potentially achieve the same expected return with much lower risk, even though the risk profiles of the various stocks in the portfolio are *not* identical.

The one truly vital prerequisite for diversification is that the risks being pooled are independent (or at least largely independent) of one another. To return to our merchant example, imagine that one of the hazards contributing to each merchant's 20 percent risk of loss was faulty ship construction. There would be no problem so long as all of the ships were built at different shipyards. But if they were all built at the same shipyard, then faulty construction in one could mean faulty construction in all. Under these circumstances, there might well be no earnings left to share at the end of the year because *all* the ships might have sunk. Clearly, our mutual arrangement would be useless if all the individual risks being shared were perfectly correlated in the first place.

Risks of this type are referred to as *catastrophic* or *systematic* risks. Wars, economic downturns, and natural catastrophes are some of the most obvious examples. They are said to be catastrophic risks because they can be expected to affect just about every member of a large population at the same time, which renders them largely immune to diversifica-

Figure 2.2   The power of diversification. The distribution of possible outcomes for each participant in a mutual agreement, when each can expect to earn either $10,000 (80%) or $0 (20%) and the various participants agree to share all earnings equally.

tion and thus very difficult to manage. As we will see, government has often played a leading role in helping to address these sorts of risks. But this is getting ahead of ourselves. The central point of our merchant example is that in most cases diversification *can* work magic—dramatically reducing personal risk (and anxiety) so long as the individual risks are independent of one another and the pool is sufficiently large.

Although the example is obviously contrived, it has many real historical analogues. Even before the emergence of functioning financial markets, family and community members commonly spread a variety of risks among themselves on the basis of informal agreements. If one member of a clan was somehow debilitated, the other members would be expected to provide for her. Such arrangements have long been prevalent in agricultural communities, and they probably represented the most important form of social provision in the United States at least until the early twentieth century. As one historian of insurance has noted, "In . . . a self-contained [agricultural] society there was little need for insurance of any kind, for the head of a family left to his survivors a means of livelihood, and misfortunes were alleviated by mutual aid."[25] Such arrangements remain common in many developing countries today.[26]

An even more striking resemblance to our merchant example may be found in the formal risk-sharing schemes of friendly societies, guilds, and numerous incorporated towns in medieval Europe. From the eighth to the eleventh centuries, the guilds of Flanders offered coverage against losses stemming from fire, shipwreck, and other misfortunes. Writes another historian of insurance, "They were, in short, clubs or societies for the purpose of the mutual insurance of members."[27] In 1070 the Charter of the Charitable Brotherhood of Valenciennes specified that if one member's merchandise were lost, all the others were to compensate him, assuming the victim himself was not to blame. By the first half of the thirteenth century, numerous towns provided that if a house burned down, the owner "was to be indemnified without delay by the whole village for his loss."[28] Our merchant example, in other words, was not far from reality.

Markets for Risk in Theory and Practice

Market-based arrangements to shift risk became increasingly common as the Middle Ages gave way to modern times. Derivative markets tied to foreign exchange rates are said to have existed in sixteenth-century Antwerp.[29] Although the trades were probably more akin to gambling than to deliberate risk management, one observer noted in 1542 that this "sort of wager seems to me to be like Marine Insurance."[30] By the end of the century, some Dutch whalers were known to sell their catches even before setting sail, thus engaging in a very early use of forward contracting.[31] A futures market for rice apparently emerged in Japan around 1650,[32] and futures markets for other agricultural products arose in Europe a little more than a half-century later.[33]

Although organized stock trading can be traced back to seventeenth-century Amsterdam or even twelfth-century France,[34] several of the now familiar exchanges first appeared in the late eighteenth century. The London Stock Exchange dates from 1773 and the New York Stock Exchange from 1792. Since stocks constitute claims on assets of uncertain future value, these exchanges created fantastic new opportunities for the trading of risks. As for insurance, it had even deeper historical roots, as we have seen. But it began to emerge in modern form in the late seventeenth and early eighteenth centuries in Britain and the United States.

In each of these cases, the essential reason for trading risk in the marketplace was to move it to an optimal risk manager—that is, to someone for whom the risk represented the smallest possible burden. A simple analogy may help to clarify this point. Although it may sound strange, a market for risk turns out to be a lot like a market for garbage. When there is competitive bidding for sanitation services, you will generally agree to "transfer" your garbage to the lowest bidder. Unlike the market for almost any other good, where the buyer pays the seller, here the seller pays the buyer to take the product (the garbage) away. The lowest bidder should, in most cases, be the most efficient waste management firm. A working market for garbage thus allows you to transfer your refuse to the optimal waste manager. Essentially the same holds true in the case of risk. A working market for risk facilitates its transfer to the most efficient *risk* manager.

But what makes one person (or entity) a better risk manager than another? In our earlier merchant example, the collective merchant association managed transport risks better than any individual merchant because it enjoyed the ability to diversify. Today, most of us shift numerous risks onto insurance companies for about the same reason. The power of diversification is not limited to insurance carriers, however. Commercial banks, in particular, are well positioned to provide risky small business loans because they can diversify their lending across a large number of small businesses. Part of the interest that a bank charges on every loan is equivalent to an insurance premium—a payment necessary to induce the lender to bear a portion of the borrower's default risk. Bigger banks frequently can offer lower premiums (and thus lower interest rates) because they can spread the risk of default that accompanies each and every loan across a larger number of borrowers.

Diversification provides an important rationale for economic actors to buy and sell risks, but it is not the only rationale. Another important one is that different people have different tolerances for risk. Some are extremely averse to risk, others less so. Still others may actually derive pleasure from taking risks. Given these differences, one would expect considerable potential for welfare-enhancing trade. A highly risk-averse owner of a piece of land, for example, might try to find less risk-averse partners (or simply sell them the land) before undertaking a bold development plan. The fact that we all harbor differing degrees of risk aversion thus creates countless opportunities for productive exchange in the marketplace.

Yet another reason why risks often are bought and sold is that some parties are better than others at actually reducing risks. In fact, this represents one of the standard justifications for health maintenance organizations (HMOs). Proponents argue that HMOs are ideally suited to assume health risk because they are superior risk reducers—more capable than either their patients or other traditional insurers at identifying and providing the right types of preventive care. Under the best of circumstances, effective preventive measures would end up reducing health risk outright, not just spreading it across a large number of people as traditional health insurance does. Ideally, both aggregate *and* individual standard deviation would be brought down. (Whether HMOs can actually succeed at reducing health risk remains to be seen, but at least the possibility is there.)

Two final motivations for risk trading are *differential risk assessment* and *portfolio balancing*. Suppose that one of those Dutch whalers from the sixteenth century went out on a voyage in April with the goal of selling his catch in July. One reason why he might have wanted to write a forward contract before leaving was that he was particularly pessimistic about what the price of whales would be when he was ready to sell. He knew the April price, but there was no way he could be certain about the

July price. Yet if he could find someone else (such as a merchant) who was more optimistic about the July price than he was, there might be room for a deal. The optimistic merchant might agree to pay now for delivery in July, presumably at a price somewhere between the optimistic and pessimistic forecasts. By entering into this *forward contract*, the pessimistic whaler would be shedding the price risk that so worried him, and the optimistic merchant would stand to make a tidy profit in July if his optimism about high prices proved accurate. In this case, differential risk assessment creates the basis for trade.

Even if the merchant was no more optimistic than the whaler, however, there still might be room for a deal if the merchant saw the forward contract as a good way to balance his overall portfolio. Suppose that the merchant had already contracted to deliver whale carcasses to a third party in July but had accepted payment at the current price. Any increase in the whale price before July would prove painful to the merchant because it would raise the cost of what he had promised to deliver. Under these circumstances, the prospect of entering a forward contract with the whaler might look especially attractive since it would balance his portfolio. By locking in the current price, the merchant would effectively eliminate (or *hedge*) his price risk on the existing delivery contract.

The point of these examples is that there are lots of good reasons for economic actors to trade risks with one another. And, indeed, they do it all the time, through insurance contracts, stock transactions, derivative contracts, just about all forms of lending, and in a thousand other ways. Standard economic models actually envision a world of *complete contingent markets*, where any risk—no matter how small or unusual—can be bought and sold in the marketplace. If such a world existed, social welfare could always be optimized through market transactions; and there would be much less justification for government intervention in the allocation of private sector risks.[35] Kenneth Arrow and Gerard Debreu formally demonstrated the efficiency of a system of complete contingent markets in the 1950s in what has become known as the Arrow-Debreu general equilibrium model, one of the crowning achievements of modern economics.[36]

Complete contingent markets do not exist in reality, however. Although markets for risk may sometimes appear almost limitless, given the great diversity of financial instruments, they are in fact notoriously incomplete, failing for all sorts of reasons. Arrow himself acknowledged that "the bulk of meaningful future transactions cannot be carried out in any existing present market."[37] As we will see, this failure within the private marketplace represents one of the core justifications for public risk management.

Limits of Private Risk Management:
Adverse Selection and Moral Hazard

As noted in the introduction, economists have identified two problems of asymmetric information, *adverse selection* and *moral hazard,* as the primary sources of risk-related failures in the private sector. Both terms date back at least to the nineteenth century.

Adverse selection occurs when individuals know more than their insurers about their own levels of risk. People who suffer from terminal diseases, for example, are likely to want to buy plenty of life and health insurance, so long as their insurers remain unaware of their medical condition and thus fail to raise their premiums. People who know themselves to be unusually healthy, meanwhile, are likely to purchase less insurance. By skewing the insurance pool toward ever-higher levels of risk, such *self-selecting* behavior has the potential to distort and even to destroy insurance markets.

The earliest use of the term "adverse selection" is not known, but it was explicitly identified as a problem for the life insurance industry in the 1890s. For some time, life insurers had struggled with the question of surrender values. When a client prematurely canceled his whole-life policy, how much of the equity should he be allowed to collect? Most insurers agreed that some penalty was necessary, and, in the mid-1890s, an actuary named Miles Dawson published an article explaining why. "The practice," he wrote, "is principally defended upon the ground that withdrawals from an [insurance] office tend to lower the average vitality of the lives insured. . . . The more robust lives are likely to withdraw, the less vigorous to remain at all hazards. The premiums of the office are calculated upon certain mortality assumptions which may be vitiated by such adverse selection."[38]

Whereas Dawson expressed concern about good risks (i.e., healthy individuals) leaving the insurance pool, life insurers also have to guard against too many bad risks entering it, as we have seen. This is why applicants for life insurance are frequently required to pass medical examinations before receiving coverage. In the absence of such screening, high-risk applicants would likely enter the pool disproportionately, driving aggregate benefit payments higher than expected and cutting sharply into profits. Where screening proves difficult or impossible, the provision of insurance may not be viable—which is why insurers have long worried about the problem of adverse selection.[39]

Moral hazard is also a very serious problem, though it has been of less concern in life insurance than in other parts of the industry. Some of the earliest uses of the term show up in the context of fire insurance in the mid-nineteenth century. A fire insurance guide published in the 1860s defined moral hazard as "the danger proceeding from motives to destroy property by fire, or permit its destruction."[40] Ever since the 1840s, fire insurers had identified bad character on the part of some policyholders as a type of hazard facing their companies. Immoral clients could increase company loss ratios by engaging in arson, fraud, or "interested carelessness."[41] As an economist writing in 1895 explained, the "[l]ack of moral character gives rise to a class of risks known by insurance men as moral hazards. The most familiar example of this class of risks is the danger of incendiary fires. Dishonest failures, bad debts, etc. would all fall in this class."[42]

According to one student of the subject, nineteenth-century insurers actually highlighted the problem of moral hazard as a means of increasing popular acceptance of insurance, which constituted a new and rather questionable branch of business at the time. To combat the prevalent perception of insurance as a vehicle for evading personal responsibility, insurers insisted that moral hazard could be distinguished from other, more natural hazards. They also maintained that it could be screened out altogether. For these insurers, identification of moral hazard was a necessary first step toward eliminating it, which was in turn a prerequisite for legitimizing their industry in the eyes of the public.[43]

In other contexts, however, practitioners—and especially government policymakers—have viewed moral hazard as an almost inevitable byproduct of risk shifting, tempting even the most virtuous of citizens. Whenever someone retains control of an activity after having shed the downside risk (by shifting it to an insurer, for example), he has a strong incentive to try to increase the overall riskiness of the activity. After all, he will reap all the gains, while the other party (the insurer) will have to bear the losses. This is essentially how economists conceive of moral hazard today, though the original sense of moral outrage has been largely abandoned.[44]

Back in 1841, when federal lawmakers were debating whether to establish a discharge in bankruptcy (which would erase a bankrupt's former debts at the end of the legal process), many congressmen worried about moral hazard, though without exactly using the term. One representative suggested that with a discharge in place, the debtor "was a man above all men exposed and tried. His morals were at stake. By passing such a bill Congress exposed him to such a temptation as ought never voluntarily to be encountered by man. . . . [A discharge] would naturally lead to extravagance in living, and to all sorts of wild undertakings and hazardous enterprises; men would have nothing to restrain the spirit of speculation but the inward restraints of honor and honesty."[45] In the upper house, Senator James Buchanan of Pennsylvania (the future president) wholeheartedly agreed, declaring that the "present bill would stimulate the spirit of speculation almost to madness."[46] As these quotes make clear, a fairly modern conception of moral hazard was already evident by the 1840s.

Indeed, the problems of adverse selection and moral hazard (like so many other insurance concepts) were familiar to practitioners long before they were named and defined in published sources. In the case of moral hazard, the Charitable Brotherhood of Valenciennes had, already in the eleventh century, explicitly proscribed coverage of losses stemming from the negligence of the victim. The authors of the Brotherhood's charter recognized the problem of moral hazard, even if they did not take the trouble to give it a name.

As we have seen, the first known uses of the terms "adverse selection" and "moral hazard" date from the second half of the nineteenth century. But the underlying concepts were not formalized in economics (under the general heading of asymmetric information problems) until almost a hundred years later. Kenneth Arrow is generally credited with offering the first systematic treatment of moral hazard in a 1963 article on uncertainty in the provision of medical care.[47] The problem of adverse selection was injected into the emerging field of information economics seven years later, when George Akerlof published his now famous article on the market for "lemons" (used cars).[48] Economists' understanding of risk-related failures—and especially the vital role of information—was advancing by leaps and bounds at this time and has since exercised enormous influence within both academic and policy circles.

Beyond Asymmetric Information

Today, "adverse selection" and "moral hazard" are still almost always the first words to roll off the tongues of economists in response to any sort of incomplete or missing market for risk. But economists' confidence in these explanations may be excessive. Just because an explanation is logically consistent does not mean it is necessarily descriptive of reality; and this disconnect has long been a problem in economic treatments of adverse selection and moral hazard. As early as the 1890s, Miles Dawson conceded that "[c]omparisons of the mortuary experience of [insurance] companies which allow liberal [surrender] values and companies which are less liberal have so far not yielded any support to the theory of adverse selection."[49] Although both moral hazard and adverse selection represent highly compelling explanations for most risk-related market problems, corroborating evidence has sometimes been hard to find.

There are, of course, other possible explanations, including other sorts of *information problems*. In some cases, a market for risk may function poorly or fail altogether, not because one party has better information than the other (asymmetric information), but because neither party can obtain sufficient information about the risk in question. This might occur either because the relevant information simply does not exist or because it is prohibitively expensive to acquire. Recent declines in the availability of private disaster insurance, for example, have sometimes been attributed to a growing belief among insurers that they simply do not understand the underlying risks, having only limited historical information about major natural catastrophes.[50]

A wide variety of other explanations for shaky or even nonexistent markets for risk can be classified under three additional headings: *perception problems, commitment problems,* and *externalization problems.* Compared to adverse selection and moral hazard, these three problems have received much less attention from economists. But they are of special interest here because they appear to have played a significant role in the formation of American risk management policy over the past two hundred years. Subsequent chapters will explore this historical record, detailing how policymakers justified government intervention on the basis of precisely these sorts of problems. First, though, we will examine them from a conceptual standpoint over the remainder of this chapter.

Perception Problems

Primarily the domain of cognitive psychologists, the study of *perception problems* has gradually (if somewhat reluctantly) been taken up by economists as well. The pressure to do so has come from a long series of attacks on their discipline's traditional approach to risk. Its rather strong assumptions about human rationality and consistency have come in for especially harsh treatment.

One of the earliest of these attacks targeted a critical assumption in Daniel Bernoulli's expected utility theory, which required that the probabilities of all possible outcomes be known. Recall that the St. Petersburg Paradox identified a specific probability and payment for each potential outcome. Yet in the real world, it is unusual to know the *precise* probability of almost anything. How do we determine expected value, expected utility, or degree of risk aversion when the probabilities of future outcomes are not well defined? Will individuals or firms behave any differently under such circumstances? The economist Frank Knight first grappled with these questions in the early 1920s, and the result was a pivotal distinction between *risk,* on the one hand, and *uncertainty,* on the other.

According to Knight, risk involves measurable probabilities, whereas uncertainty involves unmeasurable (and perhaps unknowable) probabilities.[51] The possibility that a fifty-five-year-old non-smoking woman might die this year falls under the heading of risk, since the probability of this event is well known among life insurance actuaries as a result of substantial historical experience. By contrast, the possibility that the United States might find itself at war sometime next month or next year is a matter of uncertainty, since there are precious few historical cases on which to base a prediction or to estimate a precise probability. Knight suggested that while risk could be managed by insurance companies and other bureaucratic organizations, uncertainty was the special domain of the entrepreneur.[52]

Despite its intuitive appeal, Knight's distinction has fallen into obscurity, with modern economists generally dismissing it as irrelevant.[53] Building on the pioneering work of Frank Ramsey and others, Leonard Savage argued in 1954 that precise probabilities were not needed for expected utility theory to work. All that one had to assume was that individuals concocted *subjective* probability estimates in their heads and then treated them as if they were objective facts.[54] Subjective-expected-utility theory (SEU) offered a defense not only against the problem of Knightian uncertainty but also against the more mundane problem that individuals are not always aware of objective probabilities even when they exist. As a result of Savage's work and that of his compatriots, the expected-utility fortress once again felt secure—that is, until an audacious young scholar named Daniel Ellsberg arrived on the scene.

Best known for leaking the Pentagon Papers concerning the Vietnam War in 1971, Ellsberg had already inaugurated a war of his own against the so-called Savage Axioms in the early 1960s. He simply did not believe that people behaved in reality the way Savage had them behave in his models. Central to this critique was a clever game that has since become known as the Ellsberg Paradox.[55] To play the game, you must imagine an urn containing ninety balls. Thirty are red; and the other sixty are either black or yellow, but in unknown proportion. Just before a ball is drawn at random, you are asked to choose one of the following two payoff plans:

	Red	Black	Yellow
I	$100	$0	$0
II	$0	$100	$0

(This matrix should be read as follows: Under payoff plan I, you will be paid $100 if a red ball is chosen, $0 if black, and $0 if yellow. Under payoff plan II, $0 if red, $100 if black, and $0 if yellow.)

"Which would you prefer?" Ellsberg inquires. You are then asked to choose from another set of payoff plans:

	Red	Black	Yellow
III	$100	$0	$100
IV	$0	$100	$100

"Which of these do you prefer?" Ellsberg now asks. He adds playfully, "Take your time!"[56]

If you chose I and IV, you are in good company. So did many of the most famous economists of the time, including (it seems) Savage himself. But it also turns out that if you chose I and IV, you violated one of the Savage Axioms. Admitted Howard Raiffa, a distinguished professor at the Harvard Business School who submitted to the test, "I was found wanting. I was inconsistent."[57] How could this be?

In Ellsberg's clever game, the participant's choice in the first round reveals important information about his subjective probability assessment of the black-to-yellow ratio. A choice of payoff plan I implies (according to SEU analysis) that he believes there is a higher probability of drawing a red ball than a black one. Yet a choice of payoff plan IV in the second round implies precisely the opposite: that the odds of picking a black ball are higher than the odds of picking a red. From the standpoint of the Savage Axioms, it is fine to believe either one of these things, but not both. Those who would choose I and IV, Ellsberg insists, "are simply not acting 'as though' they assigned numerical or even qualitative probabilities to the events in question."[58]

The device of having sixty black and yellow balls in unknown proportion was a way of simulating Knightian uncertainty. Consistent with Knight's position, Ellsberg found that most people do not treat risk and uncertainty the same way. They are not only risk averse but also *ambiguity averse,* to use Ellsberg's phrase. The reason they choose I and IV, he suggested, is that they wish to avoid ambiguous (or unknowable) probabilities. Since the ratio of black to yellow balls is unknown, they avoid payoff plans II and III, for which the ratio matters. If they had followed the SEU approach and simply inferred a probability for picking a black ball, their choices would have been "rational." If the odds of selecting a black ball were subjectively viewed as greater than $33\frac{1}{3}$ percent, then II and IV would be the optimal choices. If less than $33\frac{1}{3}$ percent, then I and III. But never I and IV (unless perhaps one thought the red and black probabilities were exactly the same). Ellsberg's finding of ambiguity aversion struck at the heart of expected utility theory, even in its modified SEU form. Ellsberg himself concluded that "in the situations in question, the Bayesian or Savage approach gives wrong predictions and, by their lights, bad advice."[59]

Since the appearance of Ellsberg's article in 1961, researchers in psychology and economics have identified all sorts of other peculiarities in the way people make decisions about future contingencies.[60] Some, following Knight and Ellsberg, have focused on seemingly irrational behavior in the face of unknowable probabilities. Others have identified biases in the way we casually estimate probabilities when precise probabilities are not available. Still others have examined inconsistencies in the way we make use of probabilities, even when precise ones are available. In one way or another, all of these studies raise suspicions about the social optimality of market-based transactions involving risk.

The problem of biased estimation techniques burst onto the academic scene in the early 1970s, when Daniel Kahneman and Amos Tversky began publishing their seminal work on heuristics. Until then, as the economists George Akerlof and Janet Yellen have recalled, "it was widely believed that in most cognitive judgments, people acted as intuitive scientists."[61] Kahneman and Tversky soon stunned the economics profession, mounting a serious challenge to this conventional view. On the basis of numerous experiments involving human subjects, these two Israeli psychologists concluded that most cognitive judgments were far from scientific and that people frequently used little tricks (heuristic devices) to help them estimate hard-to-pin-down probabilities. Though extremely useful in reducing "the complex tasks of assessing probabilities . . . to simpler judgmental operations," these heuristics sometimes produced systematic biases that could severely compromise decision making.[62]

Under the *availability heuristic,* for example, people estimating a probability tend to overweight the most available or memorable information that seems pertinent. "Availability is a useful clue for assessing frequency or probability," Kahneman and Tversky explain, "because instances of large classes are usually recalled better and faster than instances of less frequent classes." At the same time, however, the availability heuristic leads people to rely excessively on especially striking information, regardless of whether it is representative. "It is a common experience that the subjective probability of traffic accidents rises temporarily when one sees a car overturned by the side of the road."[63]

Numerous other sources of systematic bias have been documented as well. As described in the introduction to this book, Henry Seager's early twentieth-century observation about workers in hazardous industries living a "charmed life" (believing themselves virtually immune to accidents) would today be described as a case of *optimistic bias.* Empirical studies have shown that the vast majority of drivers believe they face lower-than-average odds of getting into automobile accidents.[64] In fact, psychologists have found that optimistic bias colors perceptions of a wide variety of hazards ranging from asthma to unemployment.[65] No less an authority than Adam Smith wrote of "the natural confidence which every man has, more or less, not only in his own abilities, but in his own good fortune." He even attributed the widespread interest in lotteries to this optimistic bias, which he characterized as an "absurd presumption."[66]

In all of these cases, and many more, individuals display a tendency to misestimate certain probabilities in a systematic way. But even when precise probabilities are given to them, their decisions do not always reflect the sort of rationality that is taken for granted in economics. Once again, Kahneman and Tversky were trailblazers in this area. One source of trouble, they observed, is that individuals often think very differently about a given set of probabilities depending on the context, or *framing,* of the problem.

Perhaps the most famous example of a framing inconsistency is their "Asian flu" experiment. Subjects (college undergraduates) were told to imagine that an unusual Asian disease was expected to kill six hundred people and that one of two possible programs could be chosen to combat it. One group of subjects was then presented with the following two choices:

A: A health program that will save 200 people, or
B: A health program where there is a 1/3 probability that 600 people will be saved and a 2/3 probability that no one will be saved.

Given this choice, 72 percent of respondents chose A, and only 28 percent chose B. But when conceptually identical options were simply framed differently (in terms of lives lost rather than lives saved), a second group of subjects showed the opposite preference. In this round, the choices were:

C: A health program where 400 people will die, or
D: A health program where there is a 1/3 chance that no one will die and a 2/3 chance that 600 people will die.

Now only 22 percent of respondents chose C, while 78 percent chose D. In an effort to explain this extraordinary result, Kahneman and Tversky suggested that the initial point of reference matters a great deal. People are apparently more risk averse when choices are framed in terms of gains, and less risk averse (and perhaps even risk seeking) when they are framed in terms of losses.[67]

In other experiments, Kahneman and Tversky observed that people often have difficulty making sense of extreme probabilities, that "highly unlikely events are either ignored or overweighted, and the difference between high probability and certainty is either neglected or exaggerated."[68] This may help to explain why individuals confronting extremely low-probability events (ranging from rare diseases to natural catastrophes) frequently either fail to insure or seem to overinsure. There is considerable evidence of "irrational" behavior either way.[69] Indeed, all of the various perception problems described here (as well as numerous others) challenge standard rationality assumptions in economics and suggest reasons why private exchanges of risk may not always be socially optimal.[70]

Commitment Problems

Yet another source of trouble for private risk management is a class of obstacles that I have called *commitment problems*. Perhaps the most obvious of these arises when the government itself has a hard time committing not to compensate victims, which sometimes occurs when especially devastating hazards are involved. In 1988 two Harvard economists characterized this as a "dilemma of government responsiveness."[71] Knowledge that government compensation is likely tends to discourage individuals from purchasing insurance, thus undermining a private market solution. Representative Fred Grandy of Iowa observed in the aftermath of a massive Mississippi River flood in 1993, "We're basically telling people, 'We want you to buy insurance, but if you don't, we'll bail you out anyway.'"[72] In fact, relatively few victims of the flood had purchased flood insurance on their own.

Although this particular commitment problem emerges out of a government failure, at least three other kinds of commitment problems have their origins in the private sector. In each case, markets for risk are compromised by the inability of private actors to commit definitively to future courses of action.

Perhaps the most intriguing of the three emanates from the *inalienability of human capital*. Human capital is the productive power that resides within each of us, allowing us to generate streams of income over our lifetime. Under most circumstances, human capital is inalienable (unable to be sold) because individuals cannot credibly commit to turn over their future income to others. This is true not only because slavery is illegal but also because every individual enjoys a nonwaivable right to protection in bankruptcy.[73] Human capital thus constitutes a nontradable asset because private transfers of it cannot be enforced in a court of law. Even if you sign a contract promising to pay someone a large amount of money several years hence, you can always shield your *future* income (though not your current assets) by filing for bankruptcy.

One consequence of all this is that human-capital risk cannot be diversified in the private market because claims on human capital cannot be bought and sold. Robert Merton, who has since won a Nobel Prize, first highlighted this failure in a 1983 paper on Social Security. Without government intervention, he observed, private parties are unable to diversify what is, for many, the most valuable component of their "portfolios." Most young people have little or no financial capital (stocks, bonds, and so on) but plenty of human capital. Most of the elderly, by contrast, have built up stockpiles of financial capital but have long since depleted their human capital, having retired from active work. Given the power of diversification, it would be advantageous for the elderly to trade some of their financial capital for some of the young's human capital. That way, both the young and the old would end up with more diverse—and thus less risky—portfolios. But the law simply does not allow such a trade because it prohibits citizens from committing their own human capital to others. The young, therefore, have no choice but to hold too much human capital while the old are forced to hold too little.[74]

A second private commitment problem stems from the impossibility of committing future generations to current risk-sharing arrangements through private contracts. This problem is mainly relevant to the phenomenon of systematic risk. By definition, systematic risk cannot be diversified at any moment in time. It would not be feasible to insure property against damage in a massive nuclear war, for example, because almost everyone who survived would file a claim at precisely the same time, overwhelming the resources of any private insurance company. Macroeconomic booms and busts also represent systematic risk because they affect just about everyone at the same time and generally in the same basic way. The vast majority of people are richer in booms and poorer in busts.

Although systematic risk cannot be diversified at any moment in time, it might be diversifiable across time. Over long enough periods, ups and downs in the economy could tend to balance each other out. The problem is that complete intergenerational risk sharing is not feasible in the private sector because current market participants cannot write binding contracts with generations of people who have yet to be born. Writes Joseph Stiglitz: "[T]here is, in the life cycle model [of economics], an implicit market failure. Individuals in one generation cannot trade with those of another generation; in particular, they cannot engage in the sharing of risks. (Of necessity, then, the set of Arrow-Debreu contingent claims markets must be incomplete.)"[75] Significantly, Stiglitz goes on to assert that government alone "provides the mechanism by which this kind of risk sharing can occur" because government enjoys the exclusive authority to bind future generations through its taxing and monetary powers.[76]

A related commitment problem stems from the fact that no private entity can credibly commit *not* to default on its future obligations. As is well known, all private entities are liable to fail. Fortunately, this problem is manageable in most transactions. Yet in some, even minimal amounts of default risk can prove debilitating. One of the original justifications for establishing Social Security in 1935 was that individuals of modest means feared investing their lifetime savings in private pension funds that could end up failing before they retired. This was apparently a concern even when the probability of failure was very small.[77]

Similarly, a long series of attempts by private banks to provide a general means of payment—money—have broken down as a result of this type of commitment problem. Irreducible levels of risk in private monetary arrangements can prove highly corrosive because, as Milton Friedman has observed, the "very performance of its central function requires money to be generally acceptable and to pass from hand to hand."[78] So long as private banks can fail, private (bank-issued) money can never represent a perfect means of payment. In fact, this is one of the main reasons why the government now issues all of our currency and why it backs both checking and savings accounts with federal deposit insurance. Privately issued money, we have learned through hard experience, is never completely reliable, since private institutions—even conservatively managed banks—cannot always make good on their commitments.

Externalization (and Feedback) Problems

One final glitch in the market mechanism that sometimes undermines the efficacy of private risk management is the problem of externalization. This is actually a generic source of market failure which boasts a long and distinguished history. As the economist A. C. Pigou explained as early as 1912, the free market will fail to maximize social welfare whenever some of the costs or benefits of a particular economic activity are *externalized* and thus not fully reflected in the price of the product.[79] Pollution is often cited as a classic externality. Factory owners who do not have to pay for the pollution they emit will likely go on emitting it even when the social costs of their pollution exceed the social benefits of the final goods they produce.

Although externalities are clearly not limited to circumstances involving risk, they nonetheless constitute an important source of risk-related failure in the private sector.[80] When companies dump toxic waste, for instance, they often impose significant risks on local communities without having to bear the attendant costs. In fact, part of the logic of the so-called Superfund legislation of 1980 was to *internalize this externality* by holding toxic waste dumpers fully liable for the costs of cleaning up hazardous sites.

Another good example of an externalized risk involves automobile accidents. Since every vehicle on the road is liable to cause an accident, every driver—even the best intentioned among us—heightens the risk of injury facing other drivers and pedestrians. Part of the justification for making automobile insurance mandatory was to force drivers to assume responsibility for this risk.

Under very special circumstances, externalized risks also have the potential to induce dangerous feedback loops, which occasionally threaten individual companies and even entire economies. A standard explanation for financial panics, for example, is that fear can be contagious. But a financial panic is not just a psychological phenomenon. It is also an economic one, rooted fundamentally in the problem of externalization. When anxious individuals begin withdrawing funds from a bank, their behavior may undermine the bank's financial integrity, even if the bank was perfectly sound to begin with. An externality is involved because these nervous depositors have inflicted a cost on every other depositor. Their own insecurity about a particular risk—the risk of bank failure— has led them to behave in a way that actually increased the overall level of risk (i.e., the likelihood that the bank in question would fail). If enough people began acting this way, then even the most economically rational depositor would be inclined to join the herd, since her own bank deposits could easily become worthless as a result of the emerging panic. And of course, once she joined the herd, she would implicitly place pressure on others to join, and so on, until the bank finally collapsed.

This sort of feedback externality is of particular interest because it seems to violate one of the cardinal rules of risk management, namely, that insurance can reduce individual risk but not aggregate risk. We saw this principle illustrated in our merchant example. Each individual merchant faced a dramatically lower risk of loss as a result of pooling, but the aggregate risk of loss remained unchanged.[81] In the presence of a feedback externality, however, insurance (or pooling) actually has the potential to reduce aggregate risk. Deposit insurance offers a good example. At a conceptual level, deposit insurance promises to make depositors feel more secure, rendering them less likely to withdraw funds unexpectedly and thus less likely to provoke a panic. The overall risk of bank failure should decline as a consequence—a truly stunning result.

Yet private deposit insurance has never proved particularly stable in practice. In this case as in so many others, private risk management seems to fall short. Having reviewed some of the best explanations for this pervasive weakness in the private sector, we are now ready to ask whether the government can possibly do any better. Can policymakers overcome the information problems, perception problems, commitment problems, and externalization problems that seem to wreak so much havoc in the marketplace? As will become clear, the answer is a resounding "yes" in theory, but only a tantalizing "maybe" in practice.

Government as the Ultimate Risk Manager

Though by no means a perfect risk manager, the government does enjoy certain advantages over private entities. The most important of these— out of which all the others flow—is its power to compel. Lawmakers can compel current citizens and even future generations of citizens to participate in insurance programs and other risk management schemes. This means that the government can spread risks extremely broadly, even when many citizens would opt out if left to their own devices. Because of its powers to tax and to print money, the government may command a near-perfect credit rating. In most cases, its credibility regarding both current and future financial commitments is simply unequaled. The state's monitoring capabilities are also without parallel in the private sector. It boasts a long and powerful investigative arm (the police); and it can demand truthful disclosure of information from its citizens, backed by the threat of civil and criminal penalties for noncompliance. These are truly awesome powers that stand far outside the reach of private risk managers.

There is no need to review these advantages in any detail here. Concrete examples emerge in each of the historical chapters, and a full summary appears at the end of the book. But a quick sketch showing how these advantages pertain to the government's role as a risk manager may help to map out the basic terrain.

Perhaps the most widely recognized justification for public risk management relates to adverse selection. It has become almost conventional wisdom among policy-oriented economists that lawmakers can "solve" adverse selection problems by compelling broad participation in either private or public insurance. While this is not strictly true, the government can moderate the consequences of adverse selection through the application of carefully constructed policies. Compulsory insurance is especially effective because it prevents anyone—even the lowest-risk individuals—from opting out of the pool.[82]

The case for government intervention to address moral hazard is not as strong as that for adverse selection; but neither is it negligible, as some analysts have suggested. There are a number of techniques available to both public and private insurers for controlling moral hazard. Both, for example, can impose substantial deductibles and coinsurance, which may discourage unwanted behavior by shifting some of the risk back onto the insured. But the government enjoys a considerable advantage over private insurers when it comes to monitoring and controlling moral hazard directly as a result of its unparalleled investigative and enforcement capabilities. In the extreme, government officials can use the long arm of the law for monitoring purposes and can even punish false statements and other forms of misbehavior with civil and criminal penalties.

The gap between public and private capabilities is even wider when it comes to addressing perception problems. About the only way private insurers can overcome broad-based underestimation of a risk, for example, is through an aggressive campaign to inform the public. An insurer or an insurers' association can try to convince potential customers that the risk in question is real and that they are neither immune to it nor above it.[83] Government officials, however, have a far more powerful weapon. They can compel citizens to buy insurance. The logic supporting compulsion is that policymakers may know more about individuals' true interests than do the individuals themselves. If workers in hazardous industries decide not to buy insurance on the mistaken belief that they are immune to injury, policymakers have the potential to improve the workers' long-term prospects by forcing them to insure. This sort of paternalism may raise some hackles, but it is commonplace in the policy arena. It also represents a decisive advantage of the government over the private sector.

The government's inherent advantages in dealing with commitment problems are equally impressive. Its taxing and monetary powers not only provide it with the deepest of all financial pockets but also allow it to spread risks across multiple generations. Citizens can therefore feel confident that the government has the capacity to cover even the most extraordinary events, such as a nuclear disaster or a financial collapse, and to distribute the costs in the widest possible fashion. The taxing power also gives the government the unique ability to spread human capital risk by taxing earnings and redistributing the proceeds. No private entity can do this.[84]

Finally, the government alone can "internalize" externalities by levying taxes or imposing liability on the culprits. A company that is held legally liable for damages stemming from its toxic waste, for example, is likely to exercise considerably more care in the way it disposes of hazardous substances than it would in the absence of such liability. Policymakers also have the ability to contain feedback externalities by mandating broad insurance coverage when necessary. As we will see, both unemployment insurance and deposit insurance were originally justified on this basis—as a way of tempering a very pernicious sort of fear that seemed to feed a dreadful underlying risk.

Before we move on to the next chapter, it is worth repeating that in spite of all these advantages, the government is still not a perfect risk manager. Far from it. Governments, like all human institutions, make mistakes. Bad policies can easily make things worse, and often have. Even the best-conceived policies face all sorts of natural constraints. They also may foster an unhealthy public perception that government compensation will always be forthcoming in the aftermath of losses.

But the point of this discussion is to make it very clear that the government does enjoy several critical powers—to compel, to tax, to print money—all of which private risk managers lack. How policymakers have tried to use these powers, given the various principles and problems highlighted here, is the subject of the rest of this book. We begin in the next chapter with the intriguing case of limited liability.

3

Limited Liability

Of all the risk management policies we will examine, limited liability is the most celebrated and the most mysterious. The illustrious president of Harvard University, Charles Eliot, characterized it as "by far the most effective legal invention for business purposes made in the nineteenth century."[1] The president of Columbia University, Nicholas Murray Butler, went even further, declaring in 1911 that "the limited liability corporation is the greatest single discovery of modern times. . . . Even steam and electricity are far less important than the limited liability corporation, and they would be reduced to comparative impotence without it."[2]

Drawing top billing above steam and electricity is certainly impressive. The mystery is how this simple legal device could possibly have achieved such status. Its only function is to shield the owners of corporations from personal liability in the event of corporate default. Limited liability does not make default risk disappear, but merely transfers a portion of it from shareholders to creditors. From an economic standpoint, one has to wonder why a corporation's creditors—including bankers, bondholders, suppliers, workers, and even successful litigants against it—should be any better at managing this risk than the shareholders themselves. Nor is it obvious why the government has to intercede to facilitate the transfer.

The editors of the *Economist* magazine addressed the latter question as early as 1854. In their view, a limited liability law then under consideration in Britain would be "of little practical importance." Since shareholders and creditors were already free to transfer risks any way they pleased through private contracts, they could negotiate the best arrangements on their own. Government intervention, the editors suggested, would prove superfluous.[3]

By this time, however, many of Britain's former colonies across the Atlantic had already enacted limited liability laws, and the United States was well on its way to challenging Britain as the world's leading industrial power. Apparently impressed by the American experience, the British Parliament went ahead and enacted limited liability the very next year.

Although the *Economist*'s interpretation soon fell out of favor (with even the magazine's own editors heaping praise on limited liability in 1926), its original laissez-faire view has since made a comeback in academic circles.[4] Numerous professors of law and economics now write confidently about the irrelevance of limited liability law or, worse, about its deleterious effects. A few have even called for its repeal.[5] But just as real-world developments pushed the *Economist*'s original assessment to the sidelines, the early history of limited liability in America casts considerable doubt on these modern critiques. To most of the policymakers who debated this issue in the nineteenth century, limited liability was anything but irrelevant.

The concept itself can be traced at least to Roman times. But the world's first limited liability statutes were enacted in the United States in the early nineteenth century. New York lawmakers led the way. Hoping to catch up with the British, as well as with their more industrialized neighbors in New England, they viewed limited liability as a vital means of mobilizing capital for manufacturing purposes. Legislators in neighboring states soon followed suit, fearful of being left behind.

Limited liability law thus represented an exceptionally pure form of Phase I risk management policy. The overarching objectives were business development and economic growth. In retrospect, it probably ranks as one of the most valuable pieces of industrial policy ever enacted in the United States, fostering large-scale enterprise which in turn powered the American economy through much of the nineteenth and twentieth centuries. Limited liability surely constitutes a critical foundation of our capitalist economic system. The purpose of this chapter is to explore the ideas and the values that helped bring it into existence.

The Dawn of Limited Liability in America

Given America's current preeminence in the world economy, it is strange to think that the United States was once a developing country. But that is exactly what it was at the beginning of the nineteenth century. In economic terms, the nation was largely dependent on foreigners. Domestic capital was scarce. Output was mainly agricultural. And a small industrial sector, while full of promise, was struggling desperately to become competitive and to grow.

For about a quarter-century after winning independence in 1783, the former colonists had reluctantly relied on Britain for most of their manufactured goods. But the economic environment changed rapidly as international tensions mounted, leading up to the War of 1812. Trade collapsed almost immediately after Congress imposed an embargo on shipping in late 1807. Exports fell from $108 million that year to just $22 million in 1808, while imports dropped from $139 million to $57 million over the same one-year period. By the close of the war, in 1814, total exports stood at just $7 million and imports at $13 million.[6]

With British competition largely excluded, American entrepreneurs saw enormous new opportunities in domestic industry, and policymakers came under intense pressure to cultivate domestic manufacturing capabilities.[7] Until 1809, the year Congress passed the Nonintercourse Act, state legislatures had only rarely granted corporate charters to manufacturing companies—and even then usually without limited liability. But 1809 marked a turning point. After incorporating only ten manufacturers over the previous twenty years, Massachusetts now incorporated eleven manufacturing firms in a single year. New York followed a similar pattern, incorporating eight manufacturing companies in 1809.[8] Only two years later, Albany lawmakers undertook a bold new experiment with limited liability, aiming to mobilize scarce capital for its emerging manufacturing sector. Though not the most industrialized state at the time, New York consistently led the pack in legal innovation, which served it well in this highly fluid economic environment.

Promoting Manufactures in New York State

New York lawmakers exhibited a decidedly entrepreneurial bent at the dawn of the nineteenth century, determined to promote rapid economic growth through innovative policy initiatives. "New Yorkers fashioned a distinctive political economy," writes one historian, "the most notable feature of which was the commitment to large-scale, pragmatic state intervention to stimulate and direct the course of economic development."[9]

The state government had obtained shares in the nascent New York Manufacturing Society as early as 1790, and it inaugurated a broad program to encourage internal manufactures fifteen years later. But this policy of industrial promotion expanded dramatically in response to the embargo of 1807. The legislature immediately authorized a new $450,000 fund in support of household textile production and established cash awards for the highest-quality textiles produced statewide. Six years later, with the country now embroiled in war, state lawmakers chartered a special corporation, capitalized at $600,000, for the purpose of extending loans to manufacturers. These sorts of initiatives were necessary, the legislature acknowledged, because of "the difficulty in inducing persons to invest their money in untried enterprises."[10]

Integral to this nascent industrial policy was the world's first general incorporation law for manufacturing companies, enacted in Albany in 1811.[11] Until that time, citizens wishing to incorporate had been required to make special appeals to the legislature. Lawmakers enjoyed complete discretion over the process, often wielding their authority with all the subtlety of a sledgehammer. Special favors, connections, and payoffs frequently made the difference in a rough-and-tumble political system where successful appeals were more the exception than the rule.

The new law, by contrast, guaranteed that every applicant who met certain minimal standards would be granted a corporate charter. Budding manufacturers across the state wasted no time in exploiting this unprecedented opportunity. Between 1811 and 1815, more than a hundred manufacturing firms successfully obtained corporate status under the new law, outpacing the rate of incorporation in almost any other state.[12]

The corporate form offered many advantages over partnership, which was the only alternative form of business organization at the time. Each and every member of a partnership had the authority to sign contracts binding the whole firm, meaning that a single dissenting partner could cause considerable trouble for the others. Having a corporate charter allowed investors to select a management team to operate the firm on their behalf, thereby avoiding the dissenting-partner problem. Whereas a partnership was required to dissolve upon the death of any member, a corporate entity could survive any and all of its original members. In theory, it could even live in perpetuity, though the corporations established under the 1811 act were limited to durations of twenty years.

Finally, an incorporated firm had the unique ability to sue and be sued and to own and convey property as a discrete entity rather than as a group of legally distinct partners.

The famous eighteenth-century legal commentator Stewart Kyd characterized the corporation as "a collection of many individuals, united into one body, under a *special denomination,* having perpetual succession under an *artificial form,* and vested, by the policy of the law, with the capacity of acting, in several respects, as an *individual.*"[13] Chief Justice John Marshall described it as "an artificial being, invisible, intangible, and existing only in contemplation of law."[14]

Although limited liability did not become synonymous with incorporation until at least the late nineteenth century, New York's 1811 statute did include a limited liability provision. The law specified that shareholders "shall be individually responsible to the extent of their respective shares of stock in the said company, and no further."[15] At the time, many observers viewed this limitation on liability as the single greatest benefit of incorporating under the act. As Chief Justice Ambrose Spencer of New York's highest court explained:

> [t]he object and intention of the legislature . . . was, in effect, to facilitate the formation of partnerships, without the risks ordinarily attending them, and to encourage internal manufactures. . . . The only advantages of an incorporation under the statute over partnerships . . . consists in a capacity to manage the affairs of the institution by a few and select agents, *and by an exoneration from any responsibility beyond the amount of the individual subscriptions.*[16]

Limited liability was thus granted as a special privilege to manufacturing corporations, on the grounds that it would induce additional investment in this small but increasingly vital sector of the economy.

The limitation on liability written into the 1811 statute was ultimately reinterpreted in the courts—and in a surprisingly restrictive manner. Spencer's 1822 opinion, just quoted, seemed to suggest a single liability rule—that is, limited liability as we know it today.[17] But only four years later, Justice John Woodworth ruled unequivocally that the statute imposed *double liability* on all shareholders. "Every stockholder," Woodworth asserted, "incurs the risk of not only losing the amount of stock subscribed, but is also liable for an equal sum, provided the debts due and owing at the time of dissolution, are of such magnitude as to require it."[18] Sharing this interpretation, Senator John C. Spencer (the former Chief Justice's son) observed: "Surely the legislature did not mean to declare, that the stockholders should be liable, as they had already agreed to be liable, and as they were liable at common law. Something more was intended."[19]

Though obviously less favorable to shareholders than what has since become the standard, double liability still placed a definite limit on the losses a shareholder might face in the event of corporate default. But it was a bit like changing the rules after the game had begun. The biggest burst of incorporations came in the early years of the act, when investors were likely under the impression that the law offered single, not double, liability for shareholders. By the time of Woodworth's reinterpretation, fifteen years *after* the law was enacted, over 160 manufacturing firms had already used it to incorporate. In fact, New York had now chartered more business corporations than any other state, and it was rapidly gaining strength as an industrial power.[20]

Despite these advances, some analysts have judged the 1811 act harshly because a substantial number of corporations chartered under its provisions failed in short order. The problem was especially pronounced among those founded during the initial burst of chartering activity.[21] But such criticism neglects the original purpose of the law, which was to encourage the deployment of risk capital in manufacturing. Limitations on liability were required, one must presume, precisely because the targeted ventures were seen as unusually risky. A high failure rate was to be expected—a natural consequence of trying to accelerate the flow of capital into unfamiliar manufacturing operations. By this logic, the large number of failures may actually have been indicative of the law's success, not its failure, in mobilizing the capital of otherwise timid investors.

Halting Capital Flight from Massachusetts

As in New York, lawmakers in Massachusetts began granting considerably more corporate charters for manufacturing enterprises amidst mounting hostilities with the British. Eighty-eight charters were granted to textile firms between 1809 and 1814, as compared to just four over the previous twenty-one years.[22] Unlike their counterparts in New York, however, they chose to put no floor on shareholder liability. On the contrary, the Massachusetts legislature explicitly mandated unlimited liability for the shareholders of all newly incorporated manufacturing firms beginning in early 1809.[23]

Had the state's legislators simply remained silent on the liability issue, the courts would likely have established a limited liability regime on their own. Over a series of cases from 1808 to 1824, the Massachusetts high court made clear that a corporation's shareholders enjoyed limited liability unless its charter explicitly stated otherwise.[24] But the legislative branch remained adamant. Its very deliberate decision to impose unlimited liability on manufacturing corporations made the contrast with New York all the more curious.

By 1809, Massachusetts was already far ahead of New York as a manufacturing power, especially in the crucial textile industry.[25] Though unwilling to grant limited liability protection, policymakers in Massachusetts had no reservations about promoting manufacturing through other means. In fact, the New England states—especially Massachusetts and Rhode Island—had long been more aggressive than any others in subsidizing and otherwise cultivating their infant manufacturing sectors.

Massachusetts lawmakers had extended a land grant to the Lynn ironworks as early as 1644, and they gave three thousand acres to John Winthrop four years later in return for his commitment to establish a saltworks and to produce at least a hundred tons of salt annually. Besides giving away land, Massachusetts also provided loans and even cash grants to promising manufacturers. Robert and Alexander Barr received £200 from the state government in 1786 to help them build new machinery for the production of wool and cotton textiles.[26]

Another fascinating technique employed in the promotion of manufactures was the granting of lottery privileges. Firms that the state wished to support were authorized to hold lotteries and to retain the proceeds. The technique dated back a long way. As early as 1612, King James I granted the Virginia Company the right to sell lottery tickets in England in order to support the Jamestown settlement in America.[27] In Massachusetts, lotteries were authorized for the construction of a paper mill in Milton in 1782, for the establishment of a glassworks in Boston in 1783, and for a cotton factory in Beverly in 1791—to name just a few examples from manufacturing.[28]

Clearly, Massachusetts policymakers were not averse to promoting manufactures, having already proved themselves leaders in the field.

They had simply not made limited liability a standard part of their arsenal. Even outside of manufacturing, Massachusetts lawmakers had traditionally shown little interest in granting limited liability protection to corporate enterprises. From the time of the Revolution, policymakers in just about every state had experimented with limited liability, granting it as a special privilege to corporations that were thought to serve the public interest, such as canal and turnpike companies. Although such grants were emphatically the exception rather than the rule, they were more common in New York than in Massachusetts until well into the nineteenth century.[29] All this meant that by 1809, the Commonwealth had far less experience with limited liability than its budding rival, New York.

Another important distinction between these two states is that they fared quite differently as a result of the congressionally imposed trade disruptions with Europe. Although the embargoes of 1807 and 1809 created new opportunities for domestic manufacturing in both states, they inflicted substantially more pain in Massachusetts. Tightly tied to foreign commerce, the Massachusetts economy soon buckled as trade was choked off. The resulting economic crisis severely depressed demand for the state's textiles.[30]

Stunned by a series of failures in their leading manufacturing industry, Massachusetts lawmakers found little reason to encourage additional risk taking through the introduction of limited liability. Their goal in 1809 was to resurrect the state's manufacturing base while being careful to discourage recklessness on the part of investors. There seemed to be sufficient capital available, since many of the rich Boston merchants victimized by the trade disruption were now eager to find new outlets for their funds. Unlimited liability would help to ensure adequate financial discipline, especially by constraining those investors who had little capital of their own. Some time later, a proponent of limited liability in the Massachusetts Senate explained the state's long commitment to unlimited liability in precisely this way—as a sincere, albeit misguided, attempt to prevent reckless speculation. "The principle had been introduced from the best motives," observed Senator John Pickering, "to guard the public against losses from adventurous speculators without capital."[31]

By the mid-1820s, however, the bedrock principle of unlimited liability—that every debt ought to be repaid no matter what—was beginning to feel like a millstone around the neck of the state's economy. Large-scale textile operations had begun to appear in the early 1810s. Integrating every aspect of the production process, these new factory complexes "marked a radical departure from all that had gone before."[32] Not surprisingly, those who ran them exhibited a voracious appetite for capital. Petitioning the legislature for a corporate charter in 1813, the founders of the very first of these "Waltham-style" factories (the Boston Manufacturing Company of Waltham, Massachusetts) insisted that "a great capital, always at the command of the manufacturer, is essential to his success."[33]

But while the shareholders of Massachusetts corporations continued to face unlimited personal liability, shareholders in neighboring states were beginning to receive more favorable treatment. As we have seen, New York lawmakers had limited the liability of their manufacturing corporations beginning in 1811. And just eleven years after that, in another legal first for the nation, they created a new form of partnership, which extended limited liability protection to all passive partners.[34] Meanwhile, New Hampshire, Connecticut, and Vermont had begun granting limited liability on a regular basis to their incorporated manufacturers in the late 1810s; and Maine, just recently separated from Massachusetts in 1820, enacted a broad rule of limited liability for its manufacturing corporations in 1823.[35] With limited liability now available in every adjacent state except Rhode Island, policymakers and business-people in Massachusetts began to worry that their unlimited liability regime might be undermining the industrial competitiveness of the Commonwealth.

Governor Levi Lincoln identified unlimited liability as a problem for Massachusetts almost immediately after taking office in 1825. Particularly given his political background, the new governor was clearly someone to be reckoned with. His father, Levi Lincoln, Sr., had served in the cabinet of President Jefferson and as governor of Massachusetts from 1808 to 1809. Following in his father's footsteps, Levi Jr. was elected to the state Senate as a Jeffersonian Republican in 1812, at a time when the Federalists largely controlled the state's political machinery. Despite ongoing and often vicious partisan attacks against him, Lincoln entered the state's House of Representatives two years later, and he ultimately rose to become Speaker of the House in 1822. After receiving and then declining the nomination of the Jeffersonian Republicans to run for governor in 1825, Lincoln decided to campaign for the office on his own, without any party endorsement. Running unopposed, he won over 90 percent of the votes cast that year and emerged as a potent political force in Massachusetts.[36]

Committed to strengthening the state's industrial base, Governor Lincoln worried that its liability regime was itself a liability for the Commonwealth. His primary concern in 1825 was that the existing law held shareholders *jointly and severally* liable. This allowed creditors to sue any individual shareholder or any group of shareholders for the full amount due. Though convenient for creditors who wished to collect unpaid corporate debts, the joint-and-several rule proved extremely unsettling for shareholders. Creditors could not literally extract a pound of flesh, but many shareholders must have viewed the rule with about as much alarm.

Massachusetts law also dictated that shareholders should remain liable forever, even after they had disposed of their shares. An individual who had once bought but a single share of stock could theoretically be held liable for many millions of dollars in unpaid corporate debts long after he had sold the share to someone else. The "persons and private estates of the stockholders are holden untimely liable, *without limitation of time,* and *to the full extent of the contracts,* however small may be the proportion of stock," Lincoln lamented. "In a government professing a deep interest in the prosperity of domestic manufactures . . . the policy of requiring that each proprietor of stock shall personally guarantee the responsibility of every other, and they severally, the credit of the corporation . . . cannot be maintained."[37]

At this stage the governor stopped short of asking for limited liability. Instead, he proposed that unpaid corporate debts be apportioned according to ownership share, rather than jointly and severally, and that all personal liability cease soon after one's shares were sold. In this way, someone who owned 1 percent of a corporation could not be held liable for more than 1 percent of its debts (i.e., proportional liability); and an investor who sold his shares would not remain liable beyond a reasonable period of time, such as a year. "In this age of great undertakings and of strenuous competition for pre-eminence in local advantages and influence," Lincoln intoned, "it is surely wise to regard with care, the permanent resources of the Commonwealth."[38]

Although New York had already experimented with proportional liability in the late eighteenth century, the Massachusetts legislature refused to enact it for Governor Lincoln in 1825.[39] Two years later, the state Senate and House finally did agree that liability should cease one year after shares were sold.[40] But this was too little, too late, for Governor Lincoln. Now he and his growing circle of allies wanted to go all the way and adopt a true limited liability regime, though they continued to attack the joint-and-several rule with particular zeal.

By 1830, the reformers' leading argument was that unlimited liability was driving capital from the Commonwealth. So long as manufacturing corporations retained unlimited liability, they insisted, prospective investors would remain insecure and would anxiously search for opportunities in more accommodating jurisdictions. The authors of a propagandistic pamphlet on the subject estimated that the Commonwealth's liability policy had diverted "more than *Eight Millions* of capital" to other states.[41] Numerous politicians claimed much the same thing. "Since 1820," Senator William Hastings maintained, "it is computed that not less than twenty millions have been sent from [Boston] alone to build up Manufacturing villages in the country, giving wealth and employment to the surrounding population. Of this sum not less than six or seven millions have been expended in New Hampshire and Maine, where more liberal laws upon this subject exist."[42] Governor Lincoln warned ominously that if limitations on shareholder liability were not enacted, "the manufacturing interest, to a great extent, must be abandoned in Massachusetts."[43]

The capital flight problem would not have been nearly as serious in a modern context. Besides the obvious fact that limited liability currently exists in every state, firms can now incorporate in one state and freely do business in another. If Maine had a more attractive liability regime, but Massachusetts had a superior place to locate a textile factory, a group of investors could simply incorporate in Maine and build their factory in Massachusetts. But this was not clearly an option in the early nineteenth century. Although a series of cases decided between 1813 and 1830 established that a foreign (out-of-state) corporation had the power to sue in state court, the question of whether a corporation could hold property and otherwise do business in another state received remarkably little attention before 1839. And even then the relevant rules remained fuzzy.[44] If investors preferred a particular state's liability regime in 1830, they most likely had to locate their operations there if they wished to take advantage of it. Here, then, were the roots of the capital flight problem plaguing Massachusetts.

Proponents of limited liability insisted that the problem had grown increasingly serious as the scale of manufacturing operations grew ever larger. Bigger factories demanded bigger sources of capital and, ultimately, the support of passive investors. As Senator Pickering observed, unlimited liability "might not have produced any injurious effects at a time when a small number of individuals were concerned in small establishments chiefly upon credit; but the case is widely different, since there has been an abundance of capital waiting only an opportunity for safe investment, which renders such restrictions burdensome and unnecessary."[45]

Although limited liability would protect both active and passive investors from personal liability, passive investors were of particular interest. With little or no control over the day-to-day affairs of their corporations, passive investors were largely at the mercy of the corporate directors who managed their companies. "It is not reasonably to be expected," Governor Lincoln had observed in 1825, "that prudent men, except under particular circumstances of personal confidence in their associates, should be ready to incur even the possible risk of utter ruin, for the chance of profit, in the joint stock of a manufacturing concern."[46] It was one thing for an investor to stake his entire future and fortune on his own decisions, but apparently quite another to stake them on somebody else's.

The governor well understood the potential cost of a serious business mistake—particularly at a time when debtors' prisons were still a fact of life. As Lincoln himself had made clear in his 1825 speech, unlimited liability meant that both "the persons and private estates of the stockholders are holden untimely liable." The local sheriff could literally seize the "person" of the stockholder and hold him in prison, in some cases at the discretion of the creditor. It was not uncommon for imprisoned debtors to live a long time—even the rest of their lives—behind bars, since repayment often became considerably more difficult once incarceration commenced.

With so many passive investors loath to put their homes and assets— and even their own bodies—at risk unnecessarily, proponents of limited liability were confident that a favorable change in the law could make a big difference. The Supreme Judicial Court of Massachusetts emphasized precisely this point in an 1809 case involving a turnpike corporation. Defending the common law rule of limited liability for corporations, the court declared:

> Persons not interested in having the turnpike, either from their situation or private property, may be requested to associate and become corporators. They may not be able to judge of the probable expenses or profits. But if they know, that if the assessment becomes grievous, they may abandon the enterprise by suffering their shares to be sold, they may on this principle join the association.[47]

Many manufacturers agreed. In an 1826 petition to the state legislature, the directors of one Massachusetts corporation complained that the Commonwealth's policy of unlimited liability for manufacturers had retarded their ability to attract adequate investment. According to the petition, the members of the Salem Mill-Dam Corporation "find in the existing provisions of the Laws relative to manufacturing corporations, obstacles which prevent many persons from aiding the proposed establishments. . . . These obstacles . . . will not be effectually removed . . . unless the Laws . . . shall be essentially modified . . . to relieve the individual stockholders in manufacturing corporations from those liabilities to which they are now subjected."[48]

Governor Lincoln advanced a nearly identical argument in 1830. "The business of manufactures requires, for its successful prosecution, the employment of large capital," he noted. "The contributions of many individuals are necessary to the creation of the fund. But men, with the admonitions they have had, will no longer consent, for the chance of profit upon a share in a concern, to put their whole property at the hazard of circumstances, which they neither can foresee, nor over which they can have any control."[49] Although the context was quite a bit different from that of New York in 1811, the focus on capital mobilization was very much the same.

Naturally, proponents of limited liability offered a variety of other arguments as well. One of the reformers' favorites was that unlimited liability was undemocratic, giving wealthy citizens a substantial advantage in gaining access to capital. "Shall a few favored monopolists reap the fruit of our pleasant fields, and turn out of doors the children of the inheritance?" asked Representative John Lowell. "I insist not. If this event must come, let it come by the operations of nature not by that of law."[50]

Representative John Brooks put an even finer point on the issue, claiming that "[y]oung men of skill in business having but a small capital, are driven from the State."[51]

Another such argument was that unlimited liability (especially of the joint-and-several variety) encouraged fraud and deception, providing shareholders of manufacturing corporations with a strong incentive to try to hide their assets. According to a group of manufacturers who petitioned the legislature, this left "payment of the corporate debts to fall with double severity upon the more honest or less wary of their associates—or amid this general ruin leave the creditor unable *to procure payment at all*."[52]

Equally troubling, the law was said to wreak havoc on the credit rating of anyone associated with a manufacturing company, disrupting a wide range of normal business transactions.[53] Several lawmakers also insisted that the resulting fear unduly depressed manufacturing shares, in some cases rendering them unexchangeable. "The stock of the corporation is discredited and depreciated," Governor Lincoln maintained, "because it attaches personal liabilities to proprietors."[54] Senator Pickering added that manufacturing stock "had been completely divested" of the "essential quality of all property known in society—its exchangeable character."[55] These arguments no doubt resonated especially well in 1830, with Massachusetts again in the midst of a short but sharp recession.[56]

One final argument, also well suited to the recessionary environment, was that unlimited liability offered creditors too much security, or perhaps a false sense of it. Either way, the effect was to make credit abundantly available to corporate managers, allowing (and even encouraging) them to borrow recklessly and engage in wild speculation. This is precisely the opposite of what had been argued in 1809, when lawmakers figured that unlimited liability would help to rein in reckless investing. Said Representative Lowell:

> Friends of the old system . . . asserted that this individual liability would make each member of a manufacturing company so watchful over its shoulders that it could not enter into great or ruinous speculation. Experience has completely refuted this proposition. We find corporation after corporation leveled in ruin by the eagerness of its managers, and the unlimited credit that these managers could control; and hundreds have been deeply injured or ruined by the operation of debts of whose existence they had no definite information.[57]

In full agreement, Senator Hastings maintained that it "requires no argument to prove, that a great facility in obtaining credit is a source of ruin and insolvency both to individuals and Corporations." The implication was that when it came to default risk, creditors were better monitors—better risk managers—than the shareholders themselves. "Limit . . . liability to corporate property," explained Senator Hastings, "and you limit the credit of the Corporation to its corporate means of payment; you thereby abridge and diminish its capacity of incurring debts and of creating ruinous losses either to stockholders or creditors."[58]

In modern parlance, the introduction of limited liability would raise the cost of borrowing, since lenders—who now faced additional default risk—would want to embed additional risk premiums in the interest rates they charged. Lowell and Hastings were no doubt right about this. The critical question, though, was whether the new inflow of equity capital from passive investors would be sufficiently large to drive down the *overall cost of capital,* even as the cost of borrowing increased. This would occur only if limited liability proved more of an attraction to shareholders than a deterrent to creditors.

Whereas the proponents' core arguments about capital mobilization suggested that the overall cost of capital would fall, Lowell's and Hastings' arguments about "limit[ing] the credit of the Corporation" so as to diminish "ruinous losses" vaguely suggested the opposite. Strangely, this tension was never addressed, even by opponents of the proposed legislation.

Leading opponents did offer a variety of counterarguments, however. Representative William Sturgis, himself a large shareholder in several manufacturing corporations, disputed the proponents' core claim that capital was leaving the state in search of limited liability elsewhere. "Sir, I am incredulous on this point," he said on the floor of the state House of Representatives. "I am not convinced that this property has been driven out, in consequence of your laws. It has gone from far different causes. . . . It has gone, sir, because it could find a more eligible location; a better rent, supplies more accessible, labor more cheap. . . . As I well know, the mention of liability, in this State, was never dreamt of by these individuals."[59]

Another common counterargument was the traditional one: that limitations on liability would encourage reckless behavior. This represented an early articulation of the moral hazard principle, though the term itself was not used. "Men who are restrained only by the limits of their capital stock," Representative Sturgis maintained, "do not and cannot feel under the apprehension of those who are restrained, each one by his own personal jeopardy, to the amount of all his means: to the extent of his very livelihood. . . . Your best security always is in the apprehension of your debtor."[60]

In the end, though, the proponents' arguments carried the day. The state legislature reversed its 1809 law in early 1830, explicitly introducing a regime of limited liability for the shareholders of new manufacturing corporations. "[N]o member of such Corporation," the law read, "shall be liable to have his person or property taken on any writ or execution against such Corporation, except in the manner and for the causes herein provided."[61] This was not a general incorporation law. Each group of investors that wanted a corporate charter would still have to make a special appeal to the legislature. But from this time forward, every charter granted to a manufacturing firm in Massachusetts would extend limited liability to its owners. Governor Lincoln had scored a major political victory.

Limited Liability Law since 1830

In subsequent years, two trends were visible across a large number of states: the enactment of general incorporation statutes that included limited liability, and the extension of such privileges to an ever larger circle of industries. New York lawmakers introduced a new general incorporation statute for manufacturing firms in 1848, which provided shareholders with limited liability protection against all creditors (other than employees) once capital had been fully paid in.[62] Over time, more and more industries were brought into the fold: ice companies in 1855, printers and publishers in 1857, and so on.[63] Even many erstwhile opponents of corporate charters and limited liability came to favor general incorporation laws on the grounds that they would eliminate preferential treatment and thus help to level the economic playing field.[64]

Massachusetts adopted a general incorporation policy in 1851, and New Hampshire did the same in 1866.[65] As in New York, subsequent laws and rulings extended the right to incorporate with limited liability to nearly every industry. Most other states followed roughly the same pattern.[66] The biggest exception was California, which maintained a regime of proportional unlimited liability from the year of its establishment as a state in 1849 until 1931, when it finally fell into line and adopted a policy of limited liability.[67]

The onward march of limited liability law did not stop there, however. Professional services, one of the few industries to be excluded from limited liability protection in just about every state, was finally brought into the mainstream in the 1960s and 1970s. Once given the chance, doctors, lawyers, and many other professionals rushed to form professional service corporations, which protected them from most liabilities, though not those stemming from their own malpractice.[68] The limited liability company, another new legal entity, emerged not long after, appearing for the first time in Wyoming in 1977 and soon spreading to all fifty states. A hybrid structure with roots in New York's Limited Partnership Act of 1822, the limited liability company offered corporation-style protection to owners but had the advantage of being taxed as a partnership under the federal tax code.[69]

Limited liability law thus remains a work in progress. Across American history, it has moved inexorably forward, reaching into every jurisdiction, every industry, and even beyond the corporation itself. Historians have nevertheless found it difficult to demonstrate a clear connection between limited liability and economic performance. As yet there is no definitive evidence demonstrating that states which adopted limited liability first consistently outperformed their economic rivals. This is mainly because detailed data on pre–Civil War industrial performance and capital flows are scarce, and because the two undisputed industrial leaders of the early nineteenth century, Massachusetts and Rhode Island, were both relatively late in adopting limited liability for manufactures. Massachusetts waited until 1830 and Rhode Island until 1847.

Still, there are scattered pieces of evidence suggesting that limited liability did make a difference. After adopting limited liability policies in the late 1810s, New Hampshire and Connecticut experienced an increased rate of incorporation relative to Massachusetts, which retained unlimited liability. When New Hampshire temporarily abandoned limited liability for manufactures in 1842, incorporations plummeted until it was reintroduced in 1846.[70] Three other states—Michigan, Wisconsin, and Pennsylvania—also dropped limited liability for a time, only to return to the fold in short order.[71] The fact that every single state ultimately adopted limited liability is perhaps the strongest evidence of all, particularly given the highly competitive economic environment of the nineteenth century.

The examples of Massachusetts, Rhode Island, and even Great Britain clearly demonstrate that early industrialization *was* possible without limited liability law, particularly when other promotional policies were in place. Most nascent manufacturing operations were owned by a relatively small number of shareholders, who frequently managed their own companies. The larger manufacturing firms that relied on passive investors typically turned to successful merchants, whose financial sophistication likely allowed them to view limited liability more as an inducement than as a necessary condition for investing.[72] Nonetheless, the early adoption of limited liability in New York and other states probably did channel capital into manufacturing and may well have helped them to catch up with the industrial leaders. It certainly appears that Massachusetts lawmakers were feeling increasingly nervous about this by the late 1820s.[73]

Limited liability is thought to have played an even more pivotal role later on, with the onset of heavy industrialization.[74] Because nearly every state had adopted limitations on liability by the late nineteenth century, it is impossible to know whether unlimited liability would have hindered the development of major railroads, steel and chemical companies, and the like. But the consensus among most economic and business historians is that limited liability was vitally important to the progress of the so-called second industrial revolution.[75]

Two financial historians have written, with perhaps a touch of hyperbole, that the railroads "needed so much [capital] and needed it so badly that railroad promoters went from house to house peddling stock for pennies."[76] Would such broad-based capital mobilization have been possible in the absence of limited liability? Given the tremendous debts taken on by these new mega-corporations and the growing gulf separating ownership from control, it seems hard to believe that many a small investor would have been willing to risk it all—everything he had—in return for a handful of shares. "Insofar as one associates economic progress with economies of scale," posits the British economist Sir John Hicks, "it must be regarded as a major achievement of limited liability that it has made much of our economic progress possible."[77] Indeed, it was precisely this logic that led President Butler of Columbia University, speaking in 1911, to rate the importance of limited liability above that of even steam and electricity in the history of civilization.[78]

More recently, limited liability law has taken on new significance as sizable jury awards have become increasingly common in America's courts. Whereas the total amount of money owed to a corporation's *voluntary creditors* (its bankers, bondholders, and so forth) can be known with certainty, the amount of money potentially owed to *involuntary creditors* (victims of the corporation, such as injured consumers and polluted communities) is simply immeasurable. Even relatively small corporations can be sued for enormous sums, rendering limited liability all the more valuable to their shareholders.

Protection against the claims of involuntary creditors is certainly nothing new. Even in the early nineteenth century, adverse court judgments sometimes exhausted the resources of otherwise solvent corporations, or were levied against corporations already in default. If the shareholders in these cases were lucky enough to have limited liability, they could walk away, leaving involuntary creditors with little or nothing in the way of compensation.

In 1809, for example, the shareholders of the Blue-Hill Turnpike Corporation successfully shielded their personal assets against the claim of an exceptionally worthy involuntary creditor. Blue-Hill had exercised its power of eminent domain to take the plaintiff's land, a remarkable power that the state sometimes granted to canal and turnpike companies at the time. Although the law simply required that Blue-Hill pay the former owner fair value (which in this case a jury determined to be $1,850), Blue-Hill fell into insolvency before paying. The former owner, whose property had literally been expropriated without compensation, sued for damages. Not surprisingly, a sympathetic county court sided with the plaintiff, ordering a warrant of distress levied on the private property of Blue-Hill's shareholders. But the Supreme Judicial Court of Massachusetts disagreed, overturning the lower court order to the great delight of Blue-Hill's shareholders.[79] "In *Commonwealth v. Blue-Hill Turnpike Corporation*," writes one legal historian, "the court directly addressed the issue of limited liability in its harshest light and did not flinch."[80]

What has changed since then is the volume and magnitude of these sorts of judgments, particularly in the realm of tort law. Tort suits certainly existed in the early nineteenth century; but they were much less common than they are today, and they only rarely involved questions of negligence. In the words of the legal scholar Lawrence Friedman, "Negligence was the merest dot on the law."[81] No longer. As a result of extraordinary developments in the law of product and environmental liability since the early 1960s, involuntary creditors have emerged as a realistic threat to just about every corporation in America. We will return to the remarkable story of product liability law—and its curious transformation—in Chapter 8, and then to environmental liability law in Chapter 9. But for now it is enough to note that the meaning of limited liability has itself been transformed as a result.

Unraveling the Mystery of Limited Liability Law

Although much has changed since the nineteenth century, the early debates over limited liability law leave little doubt that the primary objective then was capital mobilization. New York legislators hoped that its introduction in 1811 would channel resources into manufacturing, helping to close the gap with several more advanced industrial powers, both foreign and domestic. Policymakers in Massachusetts subsequently sought to stem an apparent outflow of capital—and thus preserve their impressive lead in manufacturing—by copying their neighbors and enacting a limited liability law of their own.

This interest in capital mobilization, so evident in New York and New England, ultimately drove policy innovation in most other states as well. Even in Minnesota and California, where standard limitations on liability came unusually late, the arguments for adopting limited liability statutes were much the same. The Supreme Court of Minnesota explained in 1889 that the "purpose" of the state's 1873 law to extend limited liability to manufacturing corporations "was to encourage manufacturing enterprises by exempting those investing their capital in that business from personal liability."[82]

The story was similar in California. Finally abandoning unlimited shareholder liability in 1931, California was the very last state to do so. Yet policymakers charged with modernizing the state's corporation law still echoed arguments advanced in Massachusetts a full century earlier. The Committee on Revision of the Corporation Laws, appointed by the state bar of California in 1928, determined that the state's unlimited liability policy "discourages, to an important extent, the investment of outside capital in the stock of California corporations. It also makes impossible the stock structures demanded in modern corporate financing, and so drives California enterprises to incorporate in other States."[83]

Although the committee itself was made up of lawyers, its members interviewed numerous business leaders before issuing their report to the state bar. According to Colonel Allen G. Wright of the California Development Association, "Business interests believe that California is being handicapped by stockholders' liability in attracting capital." Another business representative "pointed out that investors object to taking stock in California corporations, and this is a serious disadvantage in selling stock in the East."[84] Although times had changed since the original legislative debates over limited liability during the antebellum period, the underlying arguments remained very much the same. A simple change in the law, proponents maintained, would dramatically improve the climate for capital investment.[85]

Given this history, one might conclude that the case for limited liability law is clear. Naturally, most individuals will want to invest more of their funds once a floor is placed beneath their downside risk. As one Californian put it in 1929, "Most investors wish to risk only a definite sum in any given enterprise, and are unwilling to risk all they have."[86] What could be more obvious?

On closer inspection, however, the economic logic linking limited liability law and capital mobilization turns out to be far from obvious. Some scholars have even questioned whether any such logic exists at all. As already noted, limited liability does not eliminate default risk but merely shifts some of it from shareholders to creditors. Creditors face an increased chance of loss under a limited liability regime because they can no longer seize shareholders' personal assets when a corporation proves unable to cover its debts. Since a simple transfer of risk is all that limited liability accomplishes, why should we expect net investment to rise? Nervous about their increased level of risk, creditors will likely demand some sort of compensation from shareholders in the form of higher interest rates. This would tend to reduce corporate borrowing and might even discourage shareholders from investing in the first place, effectively defeating the underlying goal of capital mobilization. So what exactly is the lure of limited liability; and what benefits, if any, does it bring to the economy?

A related set of questions concerns the government's role in all this. Even if we assumed that limited liability was advantageous—generating benefits for shareholders that outweighed the inevitable costs for creditors—wouldn't we expect the relevant parties to negotiate appropriate arrangements on their own? Indeed, this is precisely the question the editors of the *Economist* magazine posed back in 1854. The private market generally works well when there are gains to be had from trade. Why was government intervention required in this case?

The Lure of Limited Liability

The first set of questions turns out to be considerably more tractable than the second. Limited liability is attractive to shareholders precisely because it eliminates, in Governor Lincoln's words, the "risk of utter ruin."[87] Although an increased *chance* of loss is shifted onto creditors, each creditor's *maximum possible loss* remains unchanged. The most a creditor ever stands to lose is the amount of his loan, whether under a limited or an unlimited liability regime. An unlimited liability shareholder, by contrast, always stands to lose everything he owns. In the early nineteenth century, as we have seen, he could even lose his freedom, since delinquent debtors were often consigned to debtors' prisons.

The introduction of limited liability thus implies a trade-off between the magnitude and the probability of loss. The shareholder's maximum possible loss (magnitude) is capped at a much-reduced level, while the creditor's probability of loss is simultaneously increased. As it turns out, there is good reason to believe that the overall effect of this trade-off may be positive, with the benefit to shareholders exceeding the cost to creditors. To understand why, we need only recall Daniel Bernoulli's famous solution to the St. Petersburg Paradox.

Bernoulli's key insight was that people tend to value each additional dollar less than the one before. Almost anyone would love to win $1 million in a lottery, and most of us would be even happier about winning $100 million. But Bernoulli's principle implies that the pleasure derived from winning $100 million would be less than one hundred times as great as that from winning $1 million. It also suggests that we would prefer a 0.01 chance of winning $1 million to a 0.0001 chance of winning $100 million.

The same logic applies in reverse in the case of losses. People tend to dislike large losses disproportionately more than small ones. So losing all of one's net worth—say, $100,000—would be more than one hundred times as painful as losing 1 percent of it, or $1,000. Similarly, most of us would be more afraid of a 0.0001 chance of losing $100,000 than a 0.01

chance of losing $1,000, especially if the bigger loss would wipe us out financially. When it comes to losses, therefore, magnitudes generally carry disproportionately more weight than probabilities, particularly in the extreme. And this is why limited liability is likely to deliver a net benefit—because shareholders may well gain more satisfaction from the sharp reduction in their maximum possible loss (their "risk of utter ruin") than creditors lose from the corresponding increase in their probability of a more limited loss.[88]

The implication for net investment is equally positive. If the reasoning just outlined is correct, net investment should rise with the introduction of limited liability since risk will now be allocated more efficiently. Of course, creditors will demand compensation in the form of higher interest rates for their increased probability of loss. But most shareholders, delighted by the sharp reduction in their maximum possible loss, are likely to be more enthusiastic about investing, even after the interest rate hikes.

Somewhat perversely, shareholders derive an additional bonus at the expense of tort claimants and other involuntary creditors. Unlike their voluntary counterparts, involuntary creditors have no way of exacting compensation for the increased risk that limited liability forces on them. A pedestrian struck by a runaway train, for example, might well become an involuntary creditor by successfully suing the railroad company. But the pedestrian would have had no way of exacting a risk premium—in advance of the accident—to compensate for the possibility that the railroad might fail before paying the court-awarded damages. Limited liability law thus permits shareholders to shed (or *externalize*) a portion of their default risk for free—again increasing the appeal of equity investment, though this time at the expense of involuntary creditors.

One additional factor, which I have labeled the *lottery impulse,* may enhance the lure of limited liability still further. Lotteries, of course, have always proved seductive. As Alexander Hamilton observed in 1793, "Every body, almost, can and will be willing to hazard a trifling sum for the chance of a considerable gain."[89] The point here is that the same basic logic may apply to limited liability stocks as well. This is because lottery tickets and limited liability stocks share two critical features in common. Both allow "investors" to choose the precise amounts they wish to put at risk (with no additional liability attached), and both allow virtually unlimited upside potential.

The "universal success of lotteries," as Adam Smith put it, suggests that many people find something particularly attractive about this sort of payoff structure. So long as the downside is clearly delimited, people seem to derive a sizable thrill from the knowledge that they could end up rich—sizable enough, that is, to outweigh the negative expected return on the lottery ticket itself. Back in the 1830s, when lotteries were all the rage, the *Ladies Companion* ran a story featuring an avid French lottery player. "Every time I give my five franc piece for a quarter ticket," says the character, "I receive more satisfaction than if I had spent it at the Restaurateur, for I purchase the privilege of raising air castles for the next twenty-four hours."[90] Smith himself characterized this thrill as the product of an irrational optimistic bias, a very significant (and pervasive) *perception problem*. "The vain hope of gaining some of the great prizes is the sole cause of this demand [for lotteries]," he insisted.[91]

Part of the appeal of a limited liability stock may be that its distinctive combination of limited downside and unlimited upside creates a lottery-type thrill, while presumably offering a positive expected return at the same time. Although the link between limited liability and lotteries is not widely recognized, it has some intuitive appeal. It also has a fair bit of circumstantial historical evidence behind it.

When the United States was still a developing country in the eighteenth and early nineteenth centuries, both lotteries and limited liability were employed to mobilize capital for various purposes, including the promotion of manufacturing. Alexander Hamilton's early fascination with lotteries stemmed mainly from his interest in financing a model manufacturing community, the Society for Establishing Useful Manufactures, in the 1790s. Successful in obtaining from the New Jersey state legislature both lottery privileges and limited liability protection for his new corporation, Hamilton actually used the same term, "adventurers," in referring both to lottery participants and to limited liability investors.[92]

In many states, limited liability laws were being adopted on economic grounds at just about the same time that lotteries were being eradicated on moralistic grounds (in the 1830s and 1840s). Indeed, a considerable number of nationally organized ticket brokers quickly converted themselves into securities brokers and bankers. Both the First National Bank of New York and the Chase National Bank had their roots in lottery brokerage. Even Jay Cooke and Company, which helped to finance the Union's war effort, had links to the lottery business.[93]

Years later, John Maynard Keynes observed that investment in early manufacturing firms and other small-scale enterprises was "partly a lottery," particularly since there was no precise way of estimating future profits. "If human nature felt no temptation to take a chance, no satisfaction (profit apart) in constructing a factory, a railway, a mine or a farm," Keynes suggested, "there might not be much investment merely as a result of cold calculation."[94] Milton Friedman and Leonard Savage subsequently wrote in a seminal 1948 article on risk, "Rents and interest are types of receipts that tend to be derived from investments with relatively little risk, and so correspond to the purchase of insurance, whereas investment in speculative stocks corresponds to the purchase of lottery tickets."[95]

More recently, in 1999, the nation's chief central banker, Alan Greenspan, acknowledged that a "lottery premium" was probably embedded in the share prices of some of America's hottest high-tech stocks. "What lottery managers have known for centuries is that you could get somebody to pay for a one-in-a-million shot more than the value of that chance," he noted. "And what that means is that when you're dealing with stocks—the possibilities of which are either it's going to be valued at zero or some huge number—you get a premium in that stock price which is exactly the same sort of price evaluation process that goes on in a lottery." Although there was surely a lot of "hype and craziness" in the process, Greenspan conceded, it turned out to be an enormously successful way of "ferret[ing] out the better opportunities and put[ting] capital into various different types of endeavors prior to earnings actually materializing. That's good for our system."[96] The original authors of limited liability would hardly have disagreed.

Of course, this is not to say that stocks are merely lottery tickets in disguise. Far from it. The expected returns are presumably positive in the former case and definitely negative in the latter. Unlike participants in a lottery, moreover, equity investors may reasonably expect that good judgment in the selection of stocks will be rewarded in the long run. But in each case, the asset's distinctive payoff structure of limited downside and unlimited upside may generate a certain thrill for the buyer—a lottery impulse, so to speak, which may heighten its appeal even beyond its true expected return. The lottery impulse may thus be one more factor explaining the lure of limited liability, proving particularly relevant during periods of rapid industrial change like the early nineteenth century.

The lottery impulse may also help to explain why nineteenth-century policymakers ended up enacting a regime of limited rather than proportional unlimited liability. In recent years a number of prominent scholars have argued that the main problem with an unlimited liability regime is not really unlimited liability per se but rather the joint-and-several rule with which it is almost always associated. Under joint-and-several liability, every single shareholder in a corporation is always potentially liable for all of its debts. This not only greatly magnifies the maximum potential loss facing each shareholder but also destroys the logic of diversification.[97]

It is well known that by purchasing a small number of shares in a large number of companies, an investor can effectively insulate herself against the consequences of any one company failing. A diversification strategy dramatically reduces the investor's overall level of risk, leaving her vulnerable only to downturns in the market as a whole. The old advice about not putting all your eggs in one basket captures the basic idea. With joint-and-several liability, however, owning a small number of shares in a large number of companies would be exceedingly perilous, since the investor would become potentially liable for *all* of the debts of *all* of the corporations.[98] Instead of putting her eggs in many baskets, as traditionally recommended, she would be wiser to put all her eggs in one basket and then to watch it like a hawk.

A regime of proportional unlimited liability, say its supporters, would solve these problems by making shareholder liability far more predictable. An individual who owned 1 percent of a corporation could be held personally liable for no more than 1 percent of its unpaid debts. Such a regime, they argue, would dramatically reduce the maximum possible loss facing any given shareholder and would ensure the feasibility of diversification, just as limited liability does. At the same time, a proportional regime would discourage corporations from taking risks at the expense of helpless involuntary creditors—a vicious incentive that constitutes an inevitable by-product of limited liability law. In short, the proponents of a proportional regime insist that it would offer just about all the benefits of limited liability without the attendant costs for involuntary creditors.

Although Governor Lincoln originally endorsed a proportional regime in 1825, he soon championed limited liability as a better remedy. Policymakers in every other state ultimately came down the same way. The lone holdout, California, finally abandoned its unique regime of proportional unlimited liability in 1931. Naturally, the key question is why: Why did limited liability beat out proportional unlimited liability in every single state? The historical record suggests several possible answers.

Given the immaturity of financial markets, thorough diversification would have been almost impossible in the early nineteenth century, regardless of the liability regime. Industrial shares were only rarely traded on public exchanges before the 1890s.[99] Involuntary creditors, moreover, remained a relatively minor concern for most policymakers and corporate managers until at least the 1950s. Within this context, proportional liability offered no real advantages over limited liability but still entailed several important disadvantages. First, the cost of having to collect payments from hundreds, thousands, or even tens of thousands of shareholders might well have discouraged even the most energetic of creditors.[100] Limited liability does away with these costs altogether by abolishing post-default collection from shareholders.

Second, a proportional regime almost surely would have undermined the lottery impulse. Part of the attraction of playing a lottery is that there is nothing to lose besides the price of the ticket itself. The possibility of additional losses beyond the ticket (or stock) price might well dampen the thrill that comes with imagining the big prize. Even more troubling in a modern context, the strategy of diversification—so central to the logic of proportional liability—is simply incompatible with the lottery impulse. After all, diversification will tend to eliminate all sharp departures from the mean, including not only devastating losses but fantastic windfalls as well. This may be one reason why, even today, many people choose not to diversify their holdings fully, despite the ready availability of mutual funds that would allow them to do so.[101] Unlike a diversified portfolio, an individual stock always offers the remote chance of a fantastic gain. And with limited liability, there is no potential downside beyond its original cost, which enhances the thrill all the more.

Finally, as compared to proportional unlimited liability, limited liability leaves the shareholder certain about her maximum possible loss. This is important because people are often willing to pay surprisingly large amounts to eliminate the final increment of doubt about an especially devastating hazard. Consider a thought experiment first conceived by the economist Richard Zeckhauser. As the story goes, Zeckhauser wondered how much an individual who had been forced to play Russian roulette would pay to remove one bullet from a loaded six-chambered gun. Although economic theory would predict that a rational person should pay more to reduce the number of bullets from four to three than from one to zero (because his money is worth less in the first scenario, given the higher probability of death), most people surveyed say just the opposite—that they would pay more, and likely much more, to remove the last bullet.[102] Almost all of us would probably pay an even larger sum to reduce the number of bullets from six to five, thereby avoiding certain death. But the relevant point here is that eliminating that last increment of doubt turns out to be worth an awful lot. If the same holds true when the penalty is personal financial destruction rather than death, then the case for limited liability becomes all the stronger.

Fixing a Risk-Related Failure in the Private Sector?

The problem with all of these explanations regarding the lure of limited liability is that they only compound the mystery about why government intervention was needed in the first place. If the prospect of eliminating personal liability was indeed so appealing to shareholders, why didn't they simply contract with creditors directly to cap their liability, even before lawmakers established limited liability by statute?

The 1854 piece in the *Economist* claimed that such liability-limiting deals were actually being consummated in Britain at the time. Under this sort of arrangement, "all the partners contract with each other, and the company contracts with every person it deals with, that all claims shall be confined to the subscribed fund of the company. Every person with whom it deals entering voluntarily into the contract, the principle of limited liability is, by common consent, fully carried out, whatever the law may say to the contrary."[103] Yet, despite these assertions, it remains unclear how widespread this practice was in Britain. Nor is there much evidence of such contracts being written on any regular basis in the United States.

So what sorts of obstacles might have impeded private limited liability deals? In theory, involuntary creditors might have gotten in the way. By their very nature, involuntary creditors come into existence suddenly and unexpectedly, often as the result of some sort of accident. It is thus virtually impossible for a corporation to contract with involuntary creditors in advance, because no one (including the involuntary creditors themselves) know who they are until it is too late. Whereas limited liability law offers shareholders comprehensive coverage against the claims of both voluntary and involuntary creditors, privately negotiated limitations on liability can extend only to voluntary creditors. And this means that even the best private arrangements could never be airtight. Limited liability law was required to complete the seal.

At the time these laws were enacted in the early nineteenth century, the most astute policymakers probably did understand the implications for involuntary creditors. Prior ad hoc grants of limited liability had already generated a bit of relevant case law. Handed down in 1809, for example, the *Blue-Hill Turnpike* decision not only demonstrated that limited liability shareholders were immune to the claims of involuntary creditors, but also poignantly illustrated just how unfair such immunity could be in real life.[104] Lawmakers apparently decided that a small amount of scattered suffering was a price worth paying to gain the full capital-mobilizing effect of airtight shareholder protection.[105] It is thus conceivable that the involuntary creditor problem contributed to the enactment of limited liability law. But it is hard to believe that it could have made much of a difference, since involuntary creditors remained such a minor concern throughout this early period.

A second possible explanation for the absence of private limited liability arrangements—and thus the need for limited liability law—revolves around transaction costs. Perhaps the cost of actually writing all the necessary contracts was simply too high. A great many contracts would have been required—between all the various owners, and with every banker, bondholder, vendor, and worker who functioned, even temporarily, as a creditor of the corporation. But again, it seems doubtful that simple contracting costs could have been the primary obstacle that necessitated limited liability law. As several students of the subject have noted, "[s]uch contracts would quickly emerge as standard forms costing only a few pennies to print and sign."[106]

A related explanation shows considerably more promise. Under a legal regime of unlimited liability, creditors may well have been suspicious of corporate managers who sought to limit their shareholders' liability by contract. Why would a corporation's managers request such an extraordinary grant of immunity unless they knew the corporation's risk of default was greater than it appeared? The fact that business was not normally conducted this way would only have added to the creditors' suspicion. Bankers had long enjoyed legal claims on shareholders' personal assets, while vendors and workers often extended credit informally, with no written contracts at all. The very act of asking for contractual limited liability, therefore, might have signaled a corporation's creditors that some sort of trouble was afoot. In theory, such an adverse selection problem could easily have impeded the efficient transfer of default risk from shareholders to creditors.

The next question, though, is why limited liability law would be expected to solve this sort of problem. According to economics textbooks, the standard government solution for adverse selection is compulsory coverage. Yet limited liability law has always been more or less voluntary. Even under a legal regime of limited liability, shareholders retain the ability to opt out by pledging personal security to their creditors. Bankers often refuse to lend to small, closely held corporations, for example, unless such pledges are forthcoming from the major owners. The fact that shareholders and voluntary creditors can opt both in and out of any liability regime has led many academics to question whether limited liability law "has any significant impact at all."[107]

In theory, a "voluntary" limited liability law, like the ones enacted in the United States, might be expected to have little effect on an adverse selection problem. For it would simply shift the creditor's frame of reference. Instead of having to be suspicious of any corporation whose shareholders asked for limited liability, the creditor would now have to be suspicious of any corporation whose shareholders refused to opt out by pledging personal security.

In practice, however, the way decisions are framed often matters a great deal. Recall, for example, Kahneman and Tversky's Asian flu experiment described in the previous chapter. Subjects were far more likely to endorse a solution that was sure to save two hundred (out of six hundred) lives than one that would guarantee four hundred deaths, even though the two solutions were identical. A similar sort of perception problem may apply in the case of limited liability. Creditors may well worry more about a corporation that asks for limited liability when the prevailing regime is unlimited than about a corporation that is reluctant to accept unlimited liability under a legal regime of limited liability. In other words, departures from the starting position may be interpreted as sending especially strong signals of trouble. So by changing the starting position from unlimited liability to limited liability, the new laws may have helped to solve both a serious adverse selection problem and a perception problem that together hindered the formation of private limited liability arrangements.[108]

The truth is that despite all this speculation, there is no way to know for sure exactly why limited liability law was necessary. The existing historical record offers but scant clues about the failure of private solutions to emerge on their own. But the record is abundantly clear on one point: something was standing in the way. After all, every single state legislature ultimately felt the need to jump aboard the limited liability train. If limited liability truly had no "significant impact at all," it seems likely that at least one state—and probably several—would have retained unlimited liability, only to discover that it made no difference. The fact that this never happened strongly suggests that limited liability did matter— that the lawmakers' fear of being left behind was real rather than imaginary.

Conclusion

For all the mystery surrounding it, limited liability law is actually a remarkably simple risk management device. All that it does is shift a portion of default risk from shareholders to creditors—in many ways, mimicking an insurance policy. Unlike many of the other risk management policies to be explored in subsequent chapters, limited liability law involves nothing in the way of supplementary regulation, taxation, or expenditure. It is a risk management policy through and through.

Limited liability law also represents an exceptionally pure component of Phase I. The fundamental goal was to promote economic growth by mobilizing capital for nascent manufacturing operations. The fact that certain individuals or families would be saved from financial destruction was occasionally mentioned as a residual benefit.[109] But by far the most common and most powerful arguments of the day were forward-looking. By removing the possibility of extreme personal losses, limited liability law would encourage prospective shareholders to invest more freely, liberating them from that all-consuming fear of financial catastrophe and perhaps even tapping into a hidden lottery impulse. Limited liability was viewed, first and foremost, as a means of accelerating investment rather than as a device for bailing out losers.

Although the enactment of limited liability laws ended up shifting additional default risk onto creditors, the voluntary ones (especially bankers and bondholders) were presumably better positioned to bear it, since they could never be held liable for more than they had lent. In all likelihood, these voluntary creditors exacted compensation for their additional risk by hiking up their interest rates. But the net effect on investment was probably still positive. For those passive shareholders who had previously lived in fear of colossal losses, the attraction of limited liability would outweigh the deterrent of slightly higher interest rates on corporate loans. Freed from the "risk of utter ruin," these passive investors would inject new capital into the mix, thereby lowering its overall cost in the marketplace.

Just about the only real losers from limited liability law were involuntary creditors, who were forced to assume additional default risk without compensation of any kind. This meant that a tiny bit of additional risk fell on every member of society, since just about anyone could become the victim of a corporation in one way or another. Although the problem of involuntary creditors was hardly noticed in the nineteenth century, it has taken on new significance with the transformation of tort law since the 1960s (the subject of Chapter 8). Two prominent legal scholars from Yale and Harvard have even called for the abolition of limited liability protection against the claims of tort victims. Such protection, they insist, "encourages excessive entry and aggregate overinvestment in unusually hazardous industries."[110]

How times have changed. In the early nineteenth century, when the United States was still a developing country, the terms "excessive entry" and "aggregate overinvestment" would likely have been viewed as rather peculiar ways of describing the order of the day—rapid and sustained capital mobilization for industrial enterprises. Amazingly, a simple risk-shifting device called limited liability proved powerful enough to move mountains of capital, one investment at a time.

4

Money

Monetary policy represented yet another vital domain of public risk management in nineteenth-century America. Confronting a crippling financial panic in 1819, Governor DeWitt Clinton of New York blamed the crisis on an overabundance of paper money. "The vast excess of paper above metallic money . . . and the constant demand for the latter," he declared, "have produced a state of alarm and anxiety, and have created great distress."[1] With citizens desperately trying to convert bank-issued currency into gold, their bankers responded by calling in overdue loans and sharply curtailing the supply of new credit. Some even closed their doors altogether. The dynamism that had characterized the state's economy for more than a decade now gave way to depression with terrifying speed. By October 1820, the president of the Genesee Agricultural Society of western New York, Samuel Hopkins, announced that he was "aghast at the prospect of families naked—children freezing in the winter's storm." The state's horrendous economic conditions were simply "without . . . parallel."[2]

Although the downturn of 1819 proved unusually severe, it was hardly an isolated event. An ongoing cycle of economic boom and bust traversed the entire nineteenth century and part of the twentieth as well. Panics and recessions struck with disturbing regularity. Etched into the minds of historians, the dates of the most spectacular crises (1819, 1837, 1857, 1873, 1893–1896, 1907, and 1929–1933) have come to represent natural break points in the long narrative of America's economic and social development. At the time, however, each of these crises was regarded first and foremost as a vital problem to be solved, as a foe to be vanquished.

Like Governor Clinton, many contemporary observers blamed the recurring panics on mismanagement of the money supply. Although there were plenty of other possible explanations for these crises, the monetary system came in for particular scrutiny. Indeed, monetary questions sparked some of the most dramatic political conflagrations of the nineteenth century. Especially memorable are President Andrew Jackson's fierce battle against the Second Bank of the United States in the early 1830s and William Jennings Bryan's passionate crusade against the gold standard six decades later. Until the Civil War, debates over banking policy often assumed comparable intensity at the state level. Supplying the bulk of the nation's currency, private (state-chartered) banks occupied a pivotal position in the monetary system; and questions about how best to manage them provoked bitter controversy in state legislatures all across the country.

Already by 1819, privately issued bank notes were the most common form of money in the United States. The now familiar green bills issued by the Federal Reserve did not yet exist. The federal government minted coins out of precious metals, which citizens often used to pay for goods and services and to settle debts. But bank notes proved far more convenient and enjoyed broader use.[3] Resembling modern-day traveler's checks, these notes (issued by state-chartered banks) were probably what most people had in mind when they talked about paying for something with "money" during the early nineteenth century.

To a large extent, banks were willing to issue these notes because they generated an important source of loanable funds. Individuals and firms commonly accepted bank notes in lieu of gold or silver (specie) because paper notes were easier to carry and store than coins. Although a bank's notes were supposed to be redeemable for full payment in specie at any time, in practice these notes often circulated from hand to hand for long intervals before making their way back to the bank of issue. In the meantime, the bank could use the underlying funds as the basis for additional loans, which were typically paid out in bank notes as well.

At any given moment, therefore, most banks had many more notes in circulation than specie in reserve. This practice greased the wheels of commerce, allowed for the expansion of bank credit, and generated profits for the banks themselves. But it also created the potential for crisis, promising to throw banks into default if a large portion of their notes returned for payment simultaneously. Just as fire insurance was based on the assumption that not all covered structures would burn down at the same time, banking was based on the assumption that not all note holders would demand specie at the same time. As we will see, banks provided a special form of insurance to their customers.[4] The problem was that the demand for specie tended to be contagious, threatening at any moment to infect otherwise healthy banks and to bring the whole financial system to its knees.

Policymakers were thus caught in a bind. Rapid economic growth demanded abundant bank credit and money, while monetary and financial stability seemed to require just the opposite. An anonymous New Yorker declared in an 1816 petition, "WE WANT CAPITAL—WE WANT ALSO, A WHOLESOME CIRCULATING MEDIUM. If we must be deprived of one, it is difficult to say, which ought to be sacrificed."[5] Here, in stark terms, was the fundamental trade-off that both puzzled and captivated American lawmakers for more than a century. It was a risk management problem of the first order. The great challenge was how to achieve safety and security in the banking sector without clamping down so hard on individual banks as to choke off vital credit and liquidity. Remarkably, lawmakers in antebellum New York experimented with all of the classic risk management tools—shifting, spreading, and reduction—in their ongoing efforts to solve this most vexing problem.

Money Risk in Theory and Practice

Money risk—or, to put it another way, uncertainty about the value of money—has existed ever since people began using money to facilitate exchange. Government attempts to manage this problem go back a long way too, though not quite as far. As Milton Friedman once noted, "monetary arrangements have seldom been left entirely to the market."[6]

Adam Smith explained in his *Wealth of Nations* that one of the reasons governments began stamping coins in the first place was to reduce the uncertainty that arose when precious metals were used as a medium of exchange. Unless some portion of a traded metal was properly melted and assayed, "any conclusion that can be drawn from it, is extremely uncertain." To reduce the residual doubt (and to enrich the public coffers), governments took over this function, stamping precious metals into coins and marking each one with its official value. The goal, according to Smith, was to "facilitate exchanges, and thereby to encourage all sorts of industry and commerce."[7]

Times have changed since Smith's day, but his emphasis on reducing uncertainty remains remarkably current. The British economist and central banker Charles Goodhart has observed that the very essence of money—the quality that distinguishes it from other assets—is its certainty as a final means of payment. He argues that "the main function of money . . . is to meet and alleviate problems of exchange under conditions of uncertainty."[8] The local café owner prefers that I pay for my coffee with a dollar bill (rather than a comparably priced share of stock or a pound of copper or a candy bar or even an oral promise to pay in the future) because he is certain that someone else will accept the dollar when he is ready to make a purchase or settle a debt. He is also fairly confident about what the dollar will buy in the future (whether later today, tomorrow, or next year) and pleased that it fits neatly into his cash register.

Back in the eighteenth century, the American colonists were already beginning to embrace paper money as an acceptable substitute for specie when they declared their independence from Britain in 1776. The colonial governments had been issuing small amounts of paper for some time, and the Continental Congress proceeded to print paper bills in enormous quantities during the Revolution—so much, in fact, that the new U.S. currency quickly depreciated in value. Private bankers had also recognized the appeal of paper notes and chose to issue them despite the failure of the "Continental," as the wartime currency was known.

As a result, the American economy gradually moved from a commodity standard of money (based on precious metals) to a fiduciary standard (based on paper promises to pay). The replacement of coins with bank notes, which were themselves payable in specie, marked an important step in this transition. Coins made from precious metals were heavy and awkward, and they wore down over time. Even more important, there never seemed to be enough specie in circulation to satisfy the public's growing demand for money. Increased economic specialization and growth necessitated more and more transactions, which in turn required ever more money to accommodate them. Once the federal government stopped issuing paper currency after the Revolution, state-chartered banks soon stepped into the breach.

The shift toward a fiduciary standard allowed for a far more flexible money supply, since the volume of bank notes could now expand and contract with demand, even when the supply of precious metals remained fixed. This shift also transformed the function of money, permitting it to serve as a source of liquidity *and* credit simultaneously. When people stored gold coins in their pockets and purses, they gained liquidity (that is, the ability to spend their wealth anytime or anywhere they pleased), but they also immobilized precious capital. No one else could use this wealth for productive purposes if it was rattling around in someone's pocket. Bank notes were quite different, however. So long as individuals held onto these notes, banks could lend out most of the underlying funds to worthy borrowers. It was a neat trick. Although the notes were technically redeemable in specie, the real backing was the loans themselves.

Unlike commodity money, bank money was based on the principle of insurance.[9] Bankers expected that loans would sometimes go bad (default risk) and that note holders and depositors would occasionally demand specie for their notes (liquidation risk). But just as long as large numbers of defaults and liquidations did not occur all at once, bankers could use the very same funds to back liquid notes and deposits on the one hand, and to finance illiquid loans on the other. As already noted, fire insurers extend coverage far beyond their ability to pay—on the grounds that not every covered structure will burn down at the same time. Antebellum bankers did much the same thing, promising specie far beyond their ability to pay—on the grounds that not every note holder and depositor would demand specie at the same time. They also loaned out much more than they could afford to lose—again assuming that a large proportion of borrowers would not default simultaneously. On the basis of these simple insurance principles, money was liberated to do double duty, so to speak, injecting new liquidity *and* credit into the American economy.

Naturally, though, the new reliance on bank money had a downside as well, since it greatly intensified the problem of money risk. As Henry Thornton observed in his classic 1802 text on money and credit in Britain, "all . . . promises to pay money [proceed] not on any principle of moral certainty, but on that of reasonable and sufficient probability."[10] Bank notes had no inherent value like gold coins; and they were not legal tender, meaning that creditors were not required by law to accept them in payment of debts. At root, they were merely paper promises to pay, which were only as sound as the banks that issued them. A bank's notes would immediately plummet in value if its loans went bad. And even when its loans were performing well, it could still get caught short if its note holders and depositors somehow were spooked into exercising their claims on specie all of a sudden, causing a bank run.

Because bankers could not always make good on their promises, bank money was plagued by a serious *commitment problem*, which distressed policymakers no end. Ideally, money was supposed to be perfectly secure, a certain and final means of payment. But, of course, nothing is perfectly certain in real life. In the early nineteenth century, New York bank notes typically traded at small discounts, which meant that a $1 bank note generally could purchase only about 99 cents worth of goods. While discounts of less than 1 percent were common, questions about a bank's solvency could quickly drive discounts much higher, leaving unlucky note holders with considerable losses. Discount rates were recorded on a regular basis in newspapers and specialized bank note reporters. Writing near the end of the century, one monetary expert recalled "the old complexity and uncertainty in [pre–Civil War] bank-note circulation, when every man doing business had to consult the bank-note detector for every transaction."[11]

Many astute policymakers in the nineteenth century recognized, as Adam Smith had, that uncertainty about the medium of exchange could undermine trade. In New York, Governor William H. Seward announced in 1840 that "commerce is only an exchange of productions" and that to "effect this exchange, a currency or medium is indispensable, and it should every where have the highest attainable uniformity of value."[12] Some years earlier, Governor Martin Van Buren had declared how imperative it was that in exchanging their wares and services for bank notes, "the farmer . . . the mechanic . . . the merchant . . . and all other classes of the community . . . may rest contented as to its value."[13] Although lingering uncertainty about the medium of exchange was no doubt important, many policymakers expressed even greater concern about the pain that ensued in the wake of actual bank failures.[14] Like just about every other risk, money risk exerted both ex ante and ex post effects; and policymakers were mindful of both.

Another concern was that excesses in the issuance of bank notes could provoke inflation and instability in the real economy. While most banking experts recognized that bank-supplied paper money saved the nation "the cost, interest, wear and waste . . . of metallic currency," they also worried about the consequences of its not being "kept in just proportion to the necessities of business."[15] The author of the nation's first bank insurance law, Joshua Forman, warned in 1829 that a "too abundant" supply of bank notes would raise "the price of commodities by competition in the market," ultimately damaging the balance of trade and triggering an outflow of specie.[16] Once individuals realized that they had more bank notes than seemed either necessary or safe, they would begin returning them for payment, possibly sparking a macroeconomic downturn. Banks would be forced to "press their debtors" (that is, they would refuse to roll over their short-term loans), which in turn could "cause the ruin of multitudes of enterprising men."[17]

Perhaps most worrisome of all, every element of money risk was made worse by the threat of contagion in the banking sector. Even a single bank failure had the potential to trigger many others. Once note holders and depositors began to question the soundness of their banks (whether for good reasons or not), they might demand repayment en masse, conceivably bringing down the whole banking system. A full-fledged banking panic was the worst of all financial nightmares—simultaneously choking off credit, collapsing the money supply, immobilizing the payments system, and demolishing public confidence.

Money risk was thus an extremely serious problem that provoked a long series of policy responses at both the state and federal levels. The ultimate fix would have been to prohibit bankers from converting liquid liabilities (notes and deposits that were payable on demand) into illiquid assets (such as long-term loans to small businesses). In the extreme, banks could have been required to back their notes 100 percent with specie, retaining the requisite amounts of gold and silver on reserve in their vaults. But this would have been a little like trying to eliminate automobile accidents by reducing the speed limit to zero.[18] Banks were a vital part of the economy, and intermediation between liquid notes and illiquid loans constituted one of their most important functions.

There was an enormous demand for credit in the burgeoning American economy. Budding entrepreneurs of all sorts relied on credit—and especially bank credit—to maintain and expand their business operations. These included farmers who wanted to buy seed or equipment or new land, shopkeepers who sought to increase their inventories or to expand their storefronts, manufacturers who needed working capital to keep small factories running or, in some cases, long-term capital to build larger ones. As the historian Bray Hammond has put it, antebellum Americans were "tortured with a thirst for credit."[19]

Because individuals with excess funds saved in all sorts of ways, there were many potential sources of credit. Some wealthy merchants lent directly to businesses in need of funds. But much of the time, banks served as critical intermediaries between savers and borrowers. "Banks' contribution to the takeoff of [this] capital-hungry economy," writes the historian Charles Sellers, "can hardly be exaggerated."[20] Many savers chose to buy stock in the banks, which in turn extended loans to just about every sort of enterprise.[21] Another route was for savers to invest in liquid bank notes or deposits, which together accounted for another sizable fraction of the banks' total liabilities—often for about a third but sometimes considerably more. By converting these highly liquid liabilities (bank money) into far less liquid loanable funds according to insurance principles, banks maximized the resources available to entrepreneurs who were almost literally crying out for credit.

Like limited liability corporations, therefore, banks helped mobilize capital for productive purposes. And the creation of bank money (through the provision of notes and demand deposits) was an important part of the process. The problem was that this very same process, which expanded the money supply as well as the supply of credit, also tended to intensify money risk, rendering bank money ever less secure. Although policymakers continually sought to optimize this trade-off, finding just the right balance proved exceedingly difficult.

The next section of this chapter focuses on a series of attempts to manage money risk in New York State before the Civil War. As was true in the case of corporation law, New York legislators proved remarkably innovative in the field of banking policy. But their story is not unique, since the policies adopted in New York ultimately showed up, in one form or another, all across the country. The problem of money risk was pervasive, and so too were the policies created to combat it.

Managing Money Risk in Antebellum New York

As we have seen in earlier chapters, policymakers enjoy three broad options for addressing risk management problems. They can *reduce* risk directly by restricting or prohibiting risky behavior. They can *shift* risk from one party to another by transferring the financial burden, either through liability law or tax policy. And they can *spread* risk across a large number of individuals by providing public insurance or mandating private insurance coverage.

By way of illustration, American policymakers have employed all three of these risk management tools in addressing the problem of automobile risk. First, they have sought to reduce the risk of accidents by licensing drivers, establishing minimum safety standards for automobiles, and setting maximum speed limits. Second, they have shifted a certain portion of the risk—namely, that arising from substandard automobiles—by allowing accident victims to sue manufacturers for damages whenever product defects are thought to be responsible for losses. Finally, policymakers have spread much of the remaining risk as broadly as possible by mandating that all drivers carry automobile insurance.

One of the most fascinating things about antebellum banking policy is that state lawmakers experimented with these very same risk management strategies—one after the other—in addressing the problem of money risk. Early on, they engaged in a concerted policy of *risk reduction* by rationing bank charters. No individual or group was permitted to operate a bank without first obtaining a charter from the state legislature, which specified precisely what the bank could and could not do. Just as the licensing of drivers is designed to reduce accident risk, the chartering of state banks was designed to reduce money risk. The policy proved highly reactive, however, with legislators granting new charters when the economy seemed stable and withholding them whenever signs of trouble appeared. (It also proved highly conducive to political manipulation, cronyism, and corruption, given the considerable value of the charters that lawmakers were entitled to dispense.)

An important modification of the chartering strategy came with the introduction of double liability for bank shareholders. This change constituted a new exercise in *risk shifting,* transferring additional default risk from creditors (including note holders and depositors) to shareholders. The goal was to enhance incentives for self-regulation on the part of the bankers themselves. Much as in modern tort law, the idea was to shift risk onto the parties best positioned to monitor and minimize risky behavior—the "cheapest cost avoiders," in the words of two modern scholars.[22]

But after only a short time, the state legislature again changed strategies, enacting the nation's first bank insurance law in 1829. A bold new experiment in *risk spreading,* the New York Safety Fund was designed to diffuse individual risks across the entire banking system. Like mandatory automobile insurance, the Safety Fund pooled risks to prevent any one person from suffering a disproportionate loss. A unique added benefit of bank insurance was that it promised to reduce systemic risk (in the form of contagious bank runs) by boosting creditor confidence throughout the system.

After the panic of 1837, however, the Safety Fund fell into disrepute, and mounting demands for a system of "free banking" finally carried the day. New York's Free Banking Act of 1838 was a general incorporation law, eliminating the requirement that every bank obtain its own special charter directly from the legislature. The law required that all free bank notes be backed one-for-one with high-grade bonds or mortgages deposited with the state's comptroller. This represented an extreme form of *risk reduction,* since the primary source of money risk—the connection between liquid bank notes and illiquid bank loans—was simply abolished. It was almost as if the government had in fact decided to clamp down on automobile accidents by reducing the speed limit to zero, or at least into the single digits. If not for an important loophole in the law, this radical step might well have ended in disaster, undermining credit creation all across the state. Ultimately, though, New York's experience with free banking proved reasonably successful. As is so often true, the devil (or, in this case, the angel) was in the details.

Regulation by Charter: An Early Exercise in Risk Reduction

The first step in this extended process of experimentation with risk management strategies came in 1791, when New York chartered its very first bank, the Bank of New York.[23] For the next thirty-eight years, until the establishment of the Safety Fund system in 1829, lawmakers in Albany regulated money and banking primarily through the chartering process. Their control of bank charters allowed them to limit the number of banks in operation and to constrain the range of permissible banking activities.

The chartering process represented a powerful, if not particularly delicate, risk-reduction device. The charter of the Bank of New York came to serve as a basic model for most others until the end of the 1820s.

The standard charter required a bank to redeem its notes for specie (or, until 1816, for other banks' notes) upon request. It also limited total debt "over and above money deposited in the vaults" to three times capital; fixed the capital at a specified dollar amount; prohibited trading in stocks or any goods; and specified the location where the bank could conduct business.[24] All of these provisions were intended to reduce banking risk and, in turn, the riskiness of bank notes.

One problem that state lawmakers soon confronted was the fact that chartered banks faced competition from unchartered banks. To address this, the legislature passed the Restraining Act of 1804, which forbade unincorporated associations from performing banking operations such as issuing notes.[25] The Restraining Act strengthened the state's control over the industry, ostensibly to protect note holders. It also bolstered the market power of existing banking corporations, many of which had formed close alliances with elected representatives in Albany.[26]

Having solidified their control over the provision of banking services, the state's lawmakers pursued a highly reactive strategy. They chartered many new banks when times were good, only to clamp down tightly when times turned bad. In some cases, legislators attempted to expand banking services and reduce banking risk at the same time by granting more charters but on less favorable terms.

As shown in Table 4.1, by the end of 1810, the state government had chartered ten banks, including the Bank of New York.[27] Nine more were incorporated in rapid succession in 1811 and 1812. Although legislators ignored Governor Daniel Tompkins's warning that there were already too many banks operating in the state, they did add several new clauses to the standard charter to remedy obvious abuses. The 1811 charters, for example, restricted the amount bank directors could borrow from their own institutions.[28]

Four more banks were chartered in 1813, but by this time the system was showing signs of strain. The War of 1812 provoked a deterioration of the nation's trade balance as well as a sharp decline in its gold stock. By the end of 1814, most banks were no longer able to redeem their notes on a regular basis.[29] As the U.S. treasury secretary observed in October, "There exists at this time no adequate circulating medium common to the citizens of the United States."[30]

Most states other than New York responded to these conditions by chartering even more banks, which dramatically increased the quantity

Table 4.1   The formation and extinction of chartered banks in New York State
(excluding Safety Fund and free banks), 1791–1860

Chartered banks	1791–1800	1801–1810	1811–1820	1821–1830	1831–1840	1841–1850	1851–1860
Created	4	6	23	11	0	0	0
Failed	0	0	2	7	0	0	0
Expired	0	0	0	15	13	5	0
Total	4	10	31	20	7	2	2

Source: Adapted from L. Carroll Root, "New York Bank Currency: Safety Fund vs. Bond Security," *Sound Currency,* 2, no. 5 (February 1895), 3, 6–7; William H. Dillistin, *Historical Directory of the Banks of the State of New York* (New York: New York State Bankers Association, 1946), p. 105.

Note: "Total" indicates the total number of banks in December of the terminal year of the range. That is, there were four chartered banks in December 1800, ten in December 1810, and so on.

of notes in circulation.[31] In 1815, meanwhile, the U.S. Treasury issued $9 million in small, non–interest-bearing notes—the very first federal experiment with paper money since the Constitution was ratified in 1789.[32] The net result of these monetary expansions was inflation and a loss of confidence in bank money.[33] Even in New York, where lawmakers had pursued a relatively conservative policy during these years (creating only two new banks between 1814 and 1816 and with more restrictive charters), typical bank note discounts ranged between 10 and 15 percent.[34]

Specie payments resumed in early 1817, largely as a result of pressure exerted on state banks by the Second Bank of the United States, a newly chartered federal institution which functioned somewhat like a central bank.[35] New York lawmakers took the opportunity to ease up on the reins once again, chartering four new banks that year and another four the following year. Aware of Governor Clinton's concerns about laxity in the banking sector, they also tightened a number of rules.[36] But by 1819, the accuracy of Governor Clinton's repeated warnings about excessive paper money was becoming increasingly clear.[37] Once the Second Bank of the United States initiated its now famous contraction, many state banks suddenly found themselves overextended. The collapse of the Bank of Niagara in 1819 was the first bank failure in New York since the period of chartered banking began twenty-eight years before. A second bank, the Bank of Hudson, went under soon thereafter.[38]

The response from Albany was, by this point, predictable. The legislature chartered no new banks until 1821 and incorporated just one more that year. It also significantly tightened the chartering process. The New York constitutional convention of 1821 mandated that henceforth a two-thirds majority in both the Senate and the Assembly would be necessary to charter a bank.[39] Part of the justification for this reform was to make the chartering system less vulnerable to abuse, but some critics charged that it ended up having precisely the opposite effect. Said one observer, the two-thirds rule increased "the evil by rendering necessary a more extended system of corruption."[40] Whatever the case, six banks were eventually chartered over the next three years, including the New York Chemical Manufacturing Company (Chemical Bank). After this brief expansion, three bank failures in 1825 signaled Albany that it was again time to tap the brakes. Although new banks were established that year, several received unusually restrictive charters.[41]

The sensational "conspiracy trials" of 1826 (in which several well-known and highly regarded New York City residents were tried for financial fraud), along with a new round of bank and insurance failures in 1827, reignited public hostility against the "moneyed institutions" and set the stage for major new reforms of New York's banking system. Governor Clinton urged the legislature to establish general laws to restrain note issues and provide "adequate security" for their redemption, and the legislature denied all forty-two applications for new bank charters and charter renewals that it received in 1827. State lawmakers also enacted a tough new set of banking reforms, including the so-called double liability rule, to which we now turn.[42]

Double Liability: The Promise (and the Pitfalls) of Shifting Risk

New York legislators had inserted double liability clauses into bank charters for the first time in 1817, in the wake of the financial turbulence arising from the War of 1812. In fact, double liability was imposed on all four banks chartered that year.[43] (What this meant was that if any of these banks failed, its shareholders could be held personally liable for losses up to the amount of their original investments.) Over the next ten years, double liability clauses were written into bank charters just three more times, once in 1824 and twice in 1825.[44] In 1827, however, the legislature mandated that double liability apply to all new and rechartered banks, a strategy which would reach almost every bank in the state within just a few years.[45]

Double liability marked a significant departure from existing policy because banking corporations—commonly viewed as quasi-public enterprises—had traditionally enjoyed limited liability protection.[46] Presumably this was one of the reasons why bank stock was such a popular investment in the early nineteenth century. But proponents of double liability believed that limited liability had made investing in banks (and especially risky banks) a little too attractive.

As compared to limited liability, double liability would shift a larger portion of default risk from creditors to shareholders. Ideally, this would encourage shareholders to demand more prudent behavior from their bank managers, and it would assure creditors of more complete reimbursement in the event of bank failure. Albany's existing approach to banking policy, dating all the way back to 1791, had required constant intervention on the part of the legislature. The attraction of double liability (risk shifting) was that it might lead to a greater degree of self-regulation by the bankers themselves.[47]

The choice of liability regime was particularly important in the case of banks, since their primary creditors were vast numbers of note holders and depositors. Given the relatively small claim that each of these microcreditors held against a bank, it is doubtful that many of them would have had sufficient information or incentive to monitor bank activities effectively. Evaluating the riskiness of a bank's balance sheet would have been tough in any event. There were no standard reporting requirements, and bank portfolios were typically filled with nonmarketable loans whose values were opaque to outsiders. The fact that discounts on the various banks' notes demonstrated exceedingly little independent variation in New York, rising and falling almost in unison, reinforces the idea that individual bank performance was not in fact being monitored very closely.[48] (See Table 4.2.)

The presumption that double liability would lead to better shareholder monitoring and safer banks finds some corroboration in a recent study of postbellum banking from 1865 to 1935. According to the study, double and triple liability banks tended to hold less risky portfolios than ones with limited liability.[49]

Table 4.2   Bank note discounts and failures, 1823–1829: Aggregate statistics for all chartered banks in New York State

Year	Average discount (percent)	Median discount (percent)	75th percentile discount (percent)	Maximum discount (percent)	Coefficient of variation	Total number of banks	Bank failures	Banks created
1823	0.49	0.0	0.88	5.0	1.71	32	0	1
1824	0.08	0.0	0.00	2.5	4.62	33	0	5
1825	0.33	0.0	0.00	50.0	9.20	38	3	4
1826	3.23	0.0	1.00	75.0	4.01	39	0	0
1827	3.39	0.5	0.50	100.0	4.19	39	1	0
1828	6.11	0.5	0.75	100.0	3.63	38	0	0
1829	9.57	0.5	0.75	100.0	2.72	38	2	11

Source: New-York American, 1823–1829, various issues of the weekly and semiweekly editions; L. Carroll Root, "New York Bank Currency: Safety Fund vs. Bond Security," *Sound Currency,* 2, no. 5 (February 1895), 3.

Note: The bank note tables from which this table was derived list discounts for each bank on a weekly basis. "Average discount" represents the unweighted average of all weekly observations for all banks for a given year. The minimum discount and even the 25th percentile discount were always zero over these years. "Total number of banks" indicates the total number of chartered banks in New York State as of January of each year. But because distinct discounts were occasionally listed for bank branches in the bank note tables, branches were treated as separate banks for calculating the various discount statistics. With regard to "Banks created," twenty-six banks received Safety Fund charters in 1829, but only eleven were new banks. The average discount of banks that did not join the Safety Fund system was 16.72 for the second half of 1829, whereas the average Safety Fund discount was only 0.61.

Yet a number of prominent and well-informed critics of double liability suggested just the opposite in the late 1820s, predicting that a more stringent liability rule would actually increase the riskiness of bank portfolios. Their argument was that double liability would discourage responsible businesspeople from participating in banking and instead attract reckless speculators. "No prudent man—no honest man—will or ought to engage in it," observed the Speaker of the Assembly. Before unincorporated banks were abolished under the Restraining Acts, he recalled, the notes of these banks had often been far from secure, despite the unlimited liability of their owners.[50]

The failure in 1825 of two of the four double liability banks chartered in 1817 only strengthened the critique of double liability.[51] Perhaps most damning of all, one of the failed double liability banks, the Bank of Washington and Warren in Hudson Falls, had been taken over and apparently mismanaged by the notorious adventurer Jacob Barker.[52] The legislature's refusal to grant any of the more than thirty charter and charter-renewal applications it received in 1828 may well have stemmed at least in part from an undercurrent of dissatisfaction with the double liability rule.[53]

By the time Martin Van Buren was sworn in as governor in early 1829, the seriousness of the state's banking problems was becoming obvious. Average discounts on state bank notes had risen substantially since 1824, in large measure because of four bank failures; and lawmakers had chartered no new banks since 1825 (see Table 4.2). Over the next four years, thirty-one of the state's forty banks would expire if the legislature did not find an acceptable way to renew their charters.[54] Recalling the urgency of the situation and "the hopelessness . . . of putting a stop to the improper increase of banks," Van Buren later said that he had begun to consider "the most effective measures to protect the most helpless against losses by their failures."[55]

Skeptical of the double liability rule and unwilling to return to the old system of chartered banking, Van Buren turned to Joshua Forman for advice. In response, Forman recommended a radical plan for mandatory bank liability insurance, the first of its kind in America and probably the world. Known as the Safety Fund system, Forman's scheme was extraordinary because it aimed to manage money risk through an unprecedented combination of compulsory *risk spreading* (bank insurance) and *risk reduction* (ongoing bank supervision), a surprisingly modern approach for the 1820s. Since banks functioned like insurance companies, what was needed was a solid *reinsurer* to insure the insurers. This was the essential logic of the Safety Fund, which would serve as the final reinsurer of banking activities all across New York State.

The Safety Fund System: Spreading (and Mitigating) the Risk

Joshua Forman was a natural choice to overhaul the state's banking system at the end of the 1820s. He was widely recognized not only as a person who could envision great things, but also as someone who could effectively translate his dreams into reality. Forman was perhaps the earliest promoter of the Erie Canal as well as the founder of the city of Syracuse.[56] Particularly as a result of his work on the canal, he had developed considerable experience with the state's banks. He agreed with Van Buren that the existing banking system was failing and that far-reaching reform was essential.

Forman also shared Van Buren's skepticism about the effectiveness of double liability as a remedy, predicting that the "ownership and management of such [double liability] banks would soon come into the hands of needy adventurous men," that "failures would be frequent," and that "the public would lose all confidence in bank paper."[57] The fact that individual bank failures might lead the public to "lose all confidence" reflected a market failure which, in Forman's view, necessitated state intervention. The trick was how to fashion a government remedy without unduly compromising banking services, which were so vital to the "increasing commerce of New York, and the new field of business opened along the line of the canals."[58] Forman aimed, in short, to optimize the money risk trade-off, furnishing a secure money supply without unduly constricting credit and liquidity. According to Van Buren, the goal was to establish not a perfect safeguard but rather a *more efficient* safeguard."[59]

Forman and Van Buren may also have sought to undercut the Second Bank of the United States. A major risk management institution in its own right, the Second Bank disciplined the state banks by regularly returning their notes for specie, particularly after 1823, when Nicholas Biddle took the helm.[60] One of the bank's primary objectives, in the words of one historian, was to create "an instrument responsible for the maintenance of a uniform national currency."[61] But the Second Bank operated under a federal charter; and its headquarters were located in Philadelphia, not New York, much to the chagrin of Manhattan's budding financial community. An ancillary purpose of the Safety Fund, therefore, may have been to demonstrate that New York State could ensure a safe money supply on its own, without any interference from a federally chartered bank in Philadelphia.[62]

At the heart of Forman's proposal lay two new governmental functions, bank insurance and bank supervision. Under the insurance provision, banks would be required to contribute a small percentage of their capital to a common fund, which would be used to pay off the debts of failed banks. Although contributions would be mandatory, the fund would technically "remain the property of the banks."[63] Forman insisted that the Safety Fund would prevent bank runs by guaranteeing full compensation to the creditors of failed institutions.[64]

Of equal importance were the provisions for ongoing bank supervision, which (like the insurance provisions) had no precedent in the history of American banking.[65] Believing that regulations would not work effectively "without being occasionally adjusted," Forman proposed a permanent board of commissioners, which would have the authority to inspect and regulate the banks on an ongoing basis.[66] Ideally, increased supervision and regulation would help to control the moral hazard that could be expected to arise out of the insurance scheme. His plan, in other words, was comprehensive.

As Bray Hammond has observed, Forman's proposal reflected his "intelligent understanding that banks constitute a system, being particularly sensitive to one another's operations, and not a mere aggregate of free agents."[67] Of crucial importance was the fact that weakness in one bank could easily undermine confidence in others. Well aware of this, Forman claimed that a credible state insurance fund would quell the fear that drove bank runs and contagious panics. Although he did not say so explicitly, his insurance fund also promised to reduce the proportion of specie that each bank needed to keep in reserve to fend off bank runs, thus increasing the efficiency of the overall system.

Forman readily acknowledged that mandatory insurance was not the only conceivable solution to the problems he sought to address. Another possibility would have been to encourage branch banking. At the time, most banks were unit banks, meaning that they had no branches at all. And even those that did have branches never had more than a few. Much like Forman's insurance scheme, extensive branching promised to spread the two key risks facing individual banks: the risk of loans going bad and the risk of note holders and depositors suddenly demanding specie. Governor Van Buren suggested in 1829 that he might actually have preferred a quasi-public branch system had he been creating a new banking regime from scratch.[68]

But Forman strongly disagreed, insisting that his Safety Fund proposal would be "as perfect and more beneficial for the public than that of a general bank over branches." Under a branch system, he stressed, misjudgment at the top "might ruin the whole concern." The mutual nature of his proposed Safety Fund would, in his view, increase the security of the whole system without obliterating individual freedom of action, the great strength of unit banking. As part of the Safety Fund system, the various unit banks would form "a kind of community something after the model of our federal union," he suggested hopefully, where "the right of self government in each [state], constitutes the security of the whole."[69] Bank insurance, in other words, promised to spread risk broadly while avoiding a frightening concentration of financial power in a small number of very large banks.

Forman's proposal was quickly taken up in the Assembly Committee on Banks and Insurance Companies, which recommended a bill incorporating most of his ideas. The committee seemed to like the Safety Fund proposal because it promised to protect note holders while allowing for the creation of substantially more banks.[70] Risk pooling, they hoped, would foster a more efficient use of resources, improving both the quality and the quantity of banking services.

When the bill finally reached the full Assembly in mid-March, however, it met with considerable skepticism.[71] The Speaker of the Assembly, Peter Robinson, wondered how a fund of $500,000 could possibly guarantee note issues that were authorized to reach nearly $75 million.[72] Another representative, Walter Hubbell, worried about the problem of moral hazard, claiming that a bank insurance program would weaken the "public scrutiny and watchfulness which now serve to restrain or detect mal-conduct."[73] John Dickson objected to the "compulsory partnership" aspect of the fund, reasoning that it "was improper, because it required the stockholders of one bank to become . . . responsible for all the rest."[74] Representatives of banking interests in Albany and New York, meanwhile, opposed the bill on the grounds that the proposed tax on capital would unfairly penalize the city banks, since their note-to-capital ratios were much smaller than those of the rural banks.[75]

In spite of these objections, the Safety Fund bill gradually gained strength in the Assembly. The public wanted banking reform. After some debate and much political machination, the Assembly finally passed the bill on March 18, and the Senate followed suit two weeks later. Governor Enos T. Throop, who had replaced Van Buren after the latter departed for Washington in early March, signed the bill into law on April 2, 1829.[76]

As enacted, the statute required all banks obtaining new or renewed charters to participate in the Safety Fund system. Each bank would be required to contribute 0.5 percent of paid-in capital each year until it had deposited a total of 3 percent of capital into the fund. In the event of a bank failure, creditors (including both depositors and note holders) would be entitled to full compensation from the fund once the bank's liquidation was complete. The three Safety Fund commissioners were authorized both to settle the affairs of insolvent banks and to regulate all solvent ones on an ongoing basis.[77]

The adoption of the Safety Fund law set off a rush for new banking charters, particularly because none had been granted since 1825. By the end of 1829, the state legislature had chartered eleven new banks and rechartered fifteen existing ones. Nine more banks were chartered the following year, and eight New York City banks joined the fund in 1831.[78] Forman's experiment was now safely under way. Indeed, Vermont paid New York the highest of compliments that year when it created a bank insurance scheme of its own, patterned closely after the New York model. (In all, six states adopted bank insurance schemes during the antebellum period: New York, Vermont, Indiana, Michigan, Ohio, and Iowa.)[79]

Although New York's Safety Fund system was always the subject of some controversy, it functioned relatively well until the panic of 1837. The state legislature chartered more banks in the first eight years under the Safety Fund law than it had over the previous thirty-eight years. From January 1829 to January 1837, the number of New York banks increased by 161 percent—noticeably greater than the national figure of 98 percent.[80] Although aggregate balance sheet data from the period are far from perfect, it appears that nominal notes in circulation in New York more than doubled from December 1830 to December 1836 (see Table 4.4, pp. 110–111), as did note circulation of state banks nationwide. Yet the failure rate among Safety Fund banks remained remarkably low. Even with a note-to-specie ratio higher than that of the non–Safety Fund banks in New York (and about the same as the national average for state banks in 1836), the Safety Fund experienced no failures before the panic of 1837 and only one failure during the system's first ten years of operation.[81] Certainly, by the beginning of 1837, the insurance model appeared to be working.

Some financial conservatives, however, continued to worry about excessive note creation and sought to go considerably further in controlling money risk.[82] The Safety Fund commissioners suggested in early 1833, for example, that it was simply inappropriate for banks to issue liquid bank notes at the same time that they were extending illiquid, long-term loans. "The legitimate use of banks is not for the purpose of loaning capital," they announced, "but for the purpose of furnishing a currency to be used instead of specie, in facilitating the exchanges of property. . . . If loans of capital are required, it is better for the community as well as the borrower, that they should be made of individuals or corporations not having the power of issuing currency, than of banks which have."[83] To prevent the overextension of irredeemable notes, they advocated separating banks of deposit, which might lend funds deposited for longer periods of time, from banks of issue, whose notes should be backed only with short-term loans and preferably trade credits.[84] Forman had advanced a similar proposal back in 1829.[85] On neither occasion, however, did the legislature pay much attention to the idea of prohibiting banks from extending long-term credit.[86]

In fact, even as the commissioners were advising caution, the state's lawmakers went ahead and chartered more banks. After approving eleven new bank charters in 1829, the legislature granted between seven and nine additional charters each year from 1830 to 1834 and twelve more in 1836.[87] (See Table 4.3.) With each passing year, the public's demand for additional banks seemed only to intensify, and nowhere was this more evident than in the western regions of the state. An editorial in the *Geneva Gazette* stated plainly, "We want more banking capital."[88]

Although many citizens were constantly calling for more banks, this was hardly the only source of public frustration with the banking system. Many also feared that the relationship between the Albany Regency and the banks it chartered had grown far too cozy, and that the banks themselves had amassed too much power. The Regency, an association of Democrats that had controlled the legislature for many years, no doubt profited from their exclusive authority to grant bank charters. Numerous critics (both at the time and since) charged that members of the Regency supported the Safety Fund Act only as a way of preserving the charter system and their control over it. The rise of the Locofoco movement in 1835 epitomized these anti-monopoly sentiments as well as mounting anxieties about the perils of paper money.[89]

By 1837, demands for banking reform were growing ever louder, and the notion of "free banking" was becoming increasingly popular. Some advocates of free banking hoped that the Safety Fund system could be expanded to include an unrestricted number of banks.[90] An editorial in the *Ballston Spa Gazette* demanded, "STRENGTHEN THE SAFETY FUND SYSTEM *by enacting a General Law, throwing open the doors to fair competition.*"[91] On March 18, a Senate select committee explicitly endorsed free banking, denouncing both chartered banking and the Safety Fund for neutralizing "free competition . . . the only safe and salutary regulatory of all pecuniary dealings."[92] The two legislative houses voted in favor of a modified free banking bill—with a safety fund feature—soon thereafter, but they did not deliver the requisite two-thirds majorities necessary for enactment.[93]

Despite this legislative defeat for free banking, a sharp financial crisis

Table 4.3   The formation and extinction of Safety Fund banks, New York State, 1829–1860

Safety Fund banks	1829–1830	1831–1840	1841–1850	1851–1860
Created	35	57	0	0
Failed	0	3	10	4
Expired	0	0	8	41
Total	35	89	71	26

Source: L. Carroll Root, "New York Bank Currency: Safety Fund vs. Bond Security," *Sound Currency,* 2, no. 5 (February 1895), 3, 6–7.

Note: "Total" indicates the total number of banks in December of the terminal year of the range. That is, there were 35 chartered banks in December 1830, 89 in December 1840, and so on. Banks that were rechartered as Safety Fund banks were counted as new Safety Fund banks.

in May almost immediately transformed the political environment. In early May, New York City's Dry Dock Bank (not a member of the Safety Fund) as well as three Safety Fund banks in Buffalo suspended payments, which helped trigger a nationwide panic. Banks across the state suspended specie payments beginning May 10, and the legislature legalized the suspension for one year on May 16.[94]

In retrospect, it appears that Safety Fund officials managed the crisis reasonably well. Although the law technically precluded them from reimbursing creditors of an insolvent bank until all of the bank's assets had been liquidated, they obtained permission from the legislature to grant immediate reimbursement to both note holders and depositors.[95] They also succeeded in resurrecting the embarrassed Buffalo banks as well as the Sacket's Harbor Bank, whose charter had been repealed by the state legislature on May 12. These institutions soon repaid their withdrawals from the Safety Fund with 7 percent interest. In the end, only one Safety Fund bank, the Lockport Bank, was permanently closed down.[96]

Although the fund's financial capital was not seriously compromised, its stock of political capital was now depleted. The Safety Fund could easily have been integrated with a free banking system; and, as has been noted, there were numerous proposals to do just that. But by this point, the fund was too closely aligned with the detested system of chartered banking to be included in any new reform legislation.[97] The political tide had turned.[98]

The Dawn of Free Banking: A Novel Approach to Risk Reduction

The dawn of free banking marked a sharp change in strategy. Signed into law on April 18, 1838 (less than six months after the Whigs captured control of the New York Assembly), the Free Banking Act was a general incorporation statute for banks.[99] Entry into the banking industry would no longer be contingent on specialized grants of approval from the legislature. Rather, the right to establish a free bank was open to anyone meeting two basic criteria. First, the law imposed a minimum capital requirement of $100,000.[100] No free bank could open or remain in operation with capital below this amount. Second, the law required that all free bank notes be fully backed with high-grade bonds or mortgages deposited with the state's comptroller.[101] If a bank failed to convert any of its notes into specie on demand, the comptroller would be entitled to liquidate *all* of the bank's deposited securities to reimburse note holders. The bank would also be required to pay damages equivalent to 14 percent annual interest on unredeemed notes.[102]

Not surprisingly, free banking has often been viewed as a radical market-based approach to banking and monetary policy. By eliminating the need to obtain legislative permission to establish a bank, policymakers had thrown open the doors to competition, ensuring that the provision of banking services would be driven by the dictates of economic supply and demand rather than political give-and-take. In this sense, it was a solution grounded in the philosophy of laissez-faire.

Yet at the same time, one might just as fairly characterize free banking as a heavy-handed government response to the problem of money risk. Instead of imposing additional restrictions on the practice of issuing liquid bank notes as a source of funds for illiquid loans, the legislature simply prohibited the practice altogether. According to the statute, the notes of free banks had to be fully backed with high-grade securities. If note holders demanded more specie than a free bank had on reserve, the bank (or the state comptroller) could always sell its bonds to make up the difference. Both Forman and the Safety Fund commissioners had previously suggested, without success, that banks of issue be prevented from extending long-term loans. But the idea that bank notes should be completely divorced from the provision of bank credit was considerably more extreme.

From a risk management perspective, the requirement that bank money be backed with high-grade securities constituted an extraordinary risk-reduction technique. Whereas double liability was intended to shift risk and the Safety Fund to spread it, the state's free banking rules were designed to reduce risk straightaway by eliminating the underlying source of bank note volatility. As one representative explained at the time: "There may be *over-issues*, I can well see, but never of *irredeemable* paper. The issues may be beyond the actual or necessary wants of the people, but not, I repeat, *irredeemable*. . . . These bills are signed or endorsed by your Comptroller, founded on an equal amount of State or United States Stock, pledged . . . for their redemption."[103]

But if risk reduction was really this simple, why had lawmakers taken so long to settle on this strategy? After all, the risk-reduction concept at the heart of free banking had been circulating for some time.[104] The political answer is that leaders of the Albany Regency had grown attached to the system of chartered banking because it vested considerable power and financial resources in their hands. From an economic standpoint, moreover, the logic of free banking was by no means flawless, and the benefits came with considerable costs. Two shortcomings are of particular interest here.

First, a free banking system could not guarantee complete convertibility even if all of its notes were fully backed by high-grade government bonds. Were a large proportion of note holders to demand payment in specie simultaneously, the specie price of bonds would likely collapse as banks or the state comptroller frantically tried to sell bonds for specie. In fact, a sudden decline in the market value of bonds could itself spark a banking panic by undermining public confidence in the value of the bank notes they backed. The point is that although New York's free banking law sharply reduced the risk that notes would ever become irredeemable, it did not eliminate this risk altogether, since the bonds which served as collateral were themselves liable to fall in value.[105] One of Forman's advisers, Isaac Bronson, seemed to recognize a similar problem within the context of the Safety Fund. "Let it be remembered that this fund is not specie," he cautioned.[106]

A second—and more profound—problem had to do with credit creation. Lying at the very heart of the discussion in this chapter is the fact that bank-issued notes and deposits (bank money) provided banks with an important source of loanable funds. At the beginning of 1828, for example, the liabilities of twenty-one New York banks reporting to the state totaled $26.6 million, which included $6.7 million in notes (25 percent), $5.5 in deposits (21 percent), and $14.2 million in paid-in capital (53 percent). Lending by these banks to the non-financial sector totaled $22.9 million that year.[107] (Table 4.4 provides balance sheet data for other selected years.) The big question was how credit creation would be effected once notes were eliminated as a source of funds for non-mortgage lending in the private sector, as the Free Banking Act required.

Proponents probably hoped that alternative sources of funds would soon materialize as people rearranged their portfolios. Some individuals who had previously held sizable volumes of bank notes might decide to invest more of their savings in the stocks and bonds of individual companies, or they might choose to buy more bank stock. The problem with these scenarios, however, is that they assume away one of the main reasons for having banks in the first place.

As we have seen, banks provide two critical services that sometimes come into conflict. First, they satisfy the public's demand for liquidity by pooling the risk facing every individual saver that he might need access to his funds sooner than expected. "In this role," write economists Douglas Diamond and Philip Dybvig, "banks can be viewed as providing insurance that allows agents to consume when they need to most."[108] Second, banks extend non-marketable loans to parties that do not always enjoy access to credit on the open market (that is, through bond issues). "In this latter context," Bank of England governor Eddie George explained in a 1997 address, "banks have traditionally played a key role in financing the corporate and household sectors, earning their return by gathering information about, and assessing and monitoring, the creditworthiness of private sector borrowers, especially those who do not or cannot cost effectively provide the comprehensive, public information that would allow them to access the capital markets."[109] *A critical function of banks, therefore, is to intermediate between savers who demand complete liquidity and borrowers who require illiquid (non-marketable) loans.*[110]

The question, to repeat, is whether the advent of free banking constrained credit creation in New York State. Did the prohibition on issuing bank notes to fund small business and other non-marketable loans sharply reduce the availability of credit in New York State? The answer appears to be no, but perhaps only because free banks effectively cir-

Table 4.4 Aggregate balance sheets for banking corporations in New York State, 1791–1860

Year	Banks	Capital (employed)	Notes	Demand deposits	Other liabilities	Specie	Loans and discounts	Other assets
Panel A: Chartered banks								
1791[a]	1	$1,000,000	—	—	—	—	—	—
1818	33	$20,488,933	$12,500,000	—	—	$2,000,000	—	—
1830	20	$15,028,860	$4,526,606	—	—	—	—	—
1836	8	$4,600,000	$2,132,877	$4,333,683	$6,780,495	$994,653	$12,052,020	$4,800,382
1839	5	$3,850,000	$692,452	$2,838,068	$2,333,631	$893,826	$5,542,110	$3,278,215
1860	2	$2,250,000	$366,857	$3,527,317	$3,238,628	$1,335,207	$5,636,048	$2,929,052
Panel B: Safety Fund banks								
1830	29	$6,294,600	$5,870,935	$1,608,096	$4,341,400	$443,384	$11,155,026	$6,516,622
1836	90	$32,501,460	$22,065,123	$15,009,015	$38,343,468	$5,562,367	$67,261,168	$35,095,531
1839	91	$32,951,460	$9,937,062	$13,213,323	$14,284,988	$4,970,808	$47,246,096	$18,169,929
1846[b]	80	$30,241,460	$16,033,125	$22,112,826	$16,028,749	$6,340,513	$54,938,836	$23,136,811
1860	25	$8,205,660	$3,973,044	$8,256,504	$4,272,464	$1,571,701	$18,443,824	$5,901,381

Panel C: Free banks

1841	43	$10,731,993	$2,187,229	$2,808,388	$1,782,276	$686,170	$7,306,925	$9,516,791
1846	70	$12,783,198	$6,235,397	$9,317,762	$5,388,539	$1,707,871	$17,363,144	$14,653,881
1860[c]	240	$99,513,410	$22,075,060	$96,324,065	$50,048,937	$23,437,185	$174,167,263	$79,546,278

Source: L. Carroll Root, "New York Bank Currency: Safety Fund vs. Bond Security," *Sound Currency,* 2, no. 5 (February 1895), 3 (for the 1791 data); *Annual Report of the Comptroller of the Currency in the Second Session of the Forty-Fourth Congress of the United States,* December 4, 1876 (Washington, D.C.: GPO, 1876), p. lxxxiv (for the 1818 data); *Report of the Bank Commissioners,* January 25, 1831, Assembly Document 59, pp. 8 and 39; *Annual Report of the Bank Commissioners,* January 27, 1837, Assembly Document 78, pp. 58–59; *Annual Report of the Bank Commissioners,* January 24, 1840, Assembly Document 44, pp. 52–53; *Annual Report of the Comptroller,* January 6, 1847, Assembly Document 5, pp. 52–53; *Annual Report of the Superintendent of the Banking Department,* January 6, 1862, Assembly Document 4, pp. 63–82.

Note: The number of banks listed here does not exactly correspond with Table 4.1. This is because the balance sheet information (and thus the number of banks that it was based on) was derived from different data sources. The category "Demand deposits" excludes corporate, governmental, and interbank deposits (all of which were captured in the "Other liabilities" category). Although the official reports used as sources only began employing the label "due depositors on demand" in 1846, it was assumed that the deposits listed in prior years (usually as "deposit" or "individual deposits") were mostly or exclusively demand deposits.

a. Capital in 1791 represents authorized capital rather than employed capital.

b. The data for 1846 (from November) cover both chartered banks and Safety Fund banks. Safety Fund banks represented 77 of the 80 banks and probably accounted for 80 to 90 percent of combined assets and liabilities.

c. Because of imperfections in the aggregate data, assets are not exactly equal to liabilities in 1860 (all three panels).

cumvented the constraint, relying increasingly on demand deposits (checking accounts) rather than bank notes as a major source of funds for their non-marketable lending operations. It is as if the legislature decided to curtail highway accidents by reducing the speed limit for cars to just 5 miles per hour, while leaving the speed limit for trucks unchanged at 55. Just as one would expect to see a dramatic shift from the use of cars to the use of trucks under such a scenario, one would expect to see an equally dramatic shift from bank notes to checks (demand deposits) under the free banking scenario. And this is precisely what happened.

Both deposits and the ratio of deposits to notes surged under free banking in New York, far outpacing comparable figures for the nation as a whole (see Table 4.4 and Figure 4.1). From 1841 to 1860, New York's free bank deposits grew over thirty-four-fold, from $2.8 million to $96.3 million, whereas notes grew about tenfold, from $2.2 million to $22.1 million. As a consequence, the ratio of deposits to notes issued by the state's free banks increased from 1.3 to 4.4 over this period.[111] Among non-free banks in New York, by contrast, the deposit-to-note ratio remained considerably lower throughout this period, increasing from 1.2 in 1841 to just 2.7 in 1860.[112] Although New York City banks led the way by attracting the most deposits, rural banks followed a similar pattern.[113] The state's superintendent of banking acknowledged at the beginning of 1860 that checkable deposits had overtaken bank notes as the dominant means of payment in New York. "[T]he business of the country has, in a measure, ceased to be transacted through the medium of bank notes," he conceded.[114] Meanwhile, the deposit-to-note ratio for state banks across the country (excluding New York) had risen only modestly from about 0.7 in 1841 to 0.8 in 1860.[115] (Table 4.5 outlines the growth of free banks during this period.)

According to Harry Miller, an authority on antebellum banking theory, the recognition that demand deposits constituted a form of money came rather early in America. Alexander Hamilton acknowledged this in his 1790 *Report on a National Bank,* as did Gallatin in his *Considerations* (1831). A Pennsylvania legislative committee reported in 1821, moreover, that the "right to draw a check upon a bank, *payable on demand,* is as much a part of the currency as a bank note."[116] Even so, New York policymakers did not appear to have appreciated fully the close connection between demand deposits and bank notes when they enacted the Safety Fund law in 1829 or the Free Banking Act nine years later.

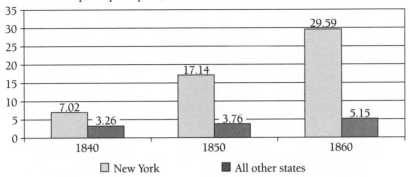

Panel A: Deposits per capita (dollars)

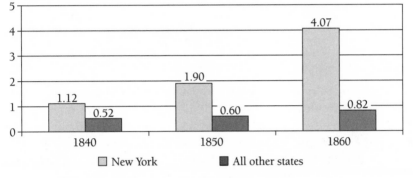

Panel B: Ratio of deposits to notes

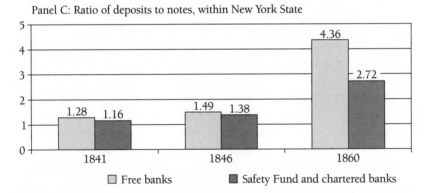

Panel C: Ratio of deposits to notes, within New York State

Figure 4.1 The growth of demand deposits, 1840–1860. From *Annual Report of the Comptroller of the Currency in the Second Session of the Forty-fourth Congress of the United States,* December 4, 1876 (Washington, D.C.: GPO, 1876), pp. xlv and cii; U.S. Department of Commerce, Bureau of the Census, *Historical Statistics of the United States, Colonial Times to 1970* (Washington, D.C.: GPO, 1975), ser. A7, p. 8, and ser. A195, p. 32; *Annual Report of the Bank Commissioners,* January 26, 1842, Assembly Document 29, p. 90; *Annual Report of the Comptroller,* January 6, 1847, Assembly Document 5, pp. 52–53; *Annual Report of the Superintendent of the Banking Department,* January 6, 1862, Assembly Document 4, pp. 63–82.

Table 4.5   The formation and extinction of free banks in New York State, 1838–1860

Free banks	1838–1840	1841–1850	1851–1860
Created	82	103	237
Closed	5	45	95
Total	77	135	277

Source: Iftekhar Hasan and Gerald P. Dwyer, Jr., "Bank Runs in the Free Banking Period," *Journal of Money, Credit and Banking,* 26, no. 2 (May 1994), 273; L. Carroll Root, "New York Bank Currency: Safety Fund vs. Bond Security," *Sound Currency,* 2, no. 5 (February 1895), 3, 6–7, 19.

Note: "Total" indicates the total number of banks in December of the terminal year of the range. That is, there were 77 chartered banks in December 1840, 135 in December 1850, and so on.

Whereas the Safety Fund for a time covered both notes and deposits (allegedly the result of a mistake in the original legislative drafting process), the Free Banking Act covered notes alone—an intriguing choice given the lawmakers' stated goal of ensuring a safe money supply.[117]

The deposit "loophole" in New York's free banking law allowed banks to continue serving their special intermediary function—that is, transforming liquid (monetary) liabilities into illiquid assets (non-marketable loans). It also guaranteed that bank money would remain much less secure than lawmakers had hoped. In 1857, the failure of the Ohio Life Insurance Company to honor its debts to New York banks set off a nationwide panic. This time it appears that depositors, rather than noteholders, led the charge in New York. "[D]epositors," Governor John A. King explained the following year, "made the run upon the banks which forced them into suspension."[118] New York City banks suspended specie payments on October 13, precipitating suspensions statewide and across most of the nation.[119] Although the crisis proved short-lived, it did drive eight free banks and three Safety Fund banks into insolvency.[120] Clearly, the problem of money risk remained formidable, even after the introduction of free banking.[121]

The Logic, Limits, and Legacy of Antebellum Banking Policy

Although lawmakers in antebellum New York had failed to eliminate the scourge of banking panics and the uncertainty surrounding bank money, they had made considerable headway in addressing the problem of money risk. From the 1790s through the 1830s, they cycled through a series of major policy initiatives, including chartered banking, double liability, bank insurance, and free banking. Each of these initiatives was rooted in a classic risk management tool: risk reduction, risk shifting, risk spreading, and, finally, risk reduction again.

Ultimately, with passage of the Free Banking Act of 1838, New York lawmakers came close to eliminating the problem of irredeemability that had plagued the state's primary form of money, bank notes, for nearly fifty years. They did this by requiring that all free-bank notes be fully backed with high-grade securities, which ensured that the notes would trade at par virtually all the time. But while the problem was largely solved in this one arena, it soon migrated to another, as uncertainty about bank notes gave way to uncertainty about demand deposits. It was as if the legislature had successfully plugged the hole in a leaky pipe, only to discover that increased pressure caused the pipe to burst in another spot.

Still facing the problem of money risk, state and federal lawmakers continued experimenting with new variations on the same basic risk management tools for nearly a hundred years after the enactment of New York's free banking statute. Like many other states, New York reintroduced double liability in 1850—though this time primarily for the benefit of depositors rather than note holders.[122] Thirteen years later, when the federal government sought to create a more uniform national currency, it adopted a free banking system of its own for federally chartered banks. Federal bank notes quickly emerged as the nation's dominant form of hand-to-hand money, particularly after Congress levied a prohibitive federal tax on state bank notes that wiped out the competition.[123] Under the new system, federal bank notes were required to be fully backed by government bonds (risk reduction). They also carried the explicit guarantee of the federal treasury (risk spreading).[124] To top it all off, federal bank shareholders were required to bear double liability in the event of default (risk shifting). Aggressive risk management, in other words, was still very much in evidence.

As the nineteenth century wore on, banking panics continued to strike on a fairly regular basis. Only now, deposits rather than notes were typically at the heart of the problem. The same transformation of the money supply that we saw under free banking in antebellum New York was occurring nationwide in the final decades of the nineteenth century.

By 1890, the comptroller of the currency estimated that fewer than 10 percent of transactions (by value) involved either notes or specie as the means of payment. Most payments were now made with checks rather than notes.[125] Although citizens no longer had to worry about their bank notes becoming irredeemable, they did have to worry about their demand deposits (their checking accounts) becoming worthless if their banks failed. As the critical locus of money risk thus shifted from notes to deposits, the merry-go-round of risk management responses continued.

Following an especially severe financial panic in 1907, Congress established the Federal Reserve System in 1913. This was the first American central bank since the demise of the Second Bank of the United States in the 1830s. In fact, the Federal Reserve System comprised not just one bank but rather twelve separate reserve banks, each operating under the supervision of a central Federal Reserve Board in Washington. The reserve banks were authorized, among other things, to issue the green bills (Federal Reserve notes) that we all carry around in our pockets and now take so much for granted.

One of the main reasons for creating the Federal Reserve System was to allow greater flexibility in the provision of credit. Often described as "bankers' banks," the twelve reserve banks had the power to lend directly to commercial banks (by purchasing short-term assets at a discount). This promised to enhance the banking system's capacity to accommodate sudden changes in the demand for credit, including the highly seasonal fluctuations so common in rural areas. As the House Banking and Currency Committee reported on September 9, 1913, the central objective of the Federal Reserve bill was the "[c]reation of a joint mechanism for the extension of credit to banks which possess sound assets and which desire to liquidate them for the purpose of meeting legitimate commercial, agricultural, and industrial demands on the part of their clientele."[126]

At the time, it was widely believed that this new institution would also eliminate the terrible problem of banking panics. The Federal Reserve's unique ability to lend cash to commercial banks when they needed it—to serve as a "lender of last resort"—offered a sort of implicit insurance against bank runs. If a large proportion of depositors suddenly demanded their balances in cash, their bankers now had the ability to turn to the Federal Reserve banks for assistance. Emergency loans from the Federal Reserve promised not only to satisfy depositors' frantic demands for cash in moments of crisis but also, more broadly, to restore public confidence in the nation's banks.[127]

Numerous state legislatures, meanwhile, had already begun addressing the problem of banking panics on their own by enacting explicit bank insurance programs. Between 1907 and 1917, eight states—Oklahoma, Kansas, Nebraska, Texas, Mississippi, South Dakota, North Dakota, and Washington—passed bank insurance statutes. In most cases these statutes mandated that all state-chartered banks contribute to a common fund, which would be used to compensate losses in the event that any banks were unable to make good on their commitments to customers. Though resembling New York's Safety Fund system from 1829, these twentieth-century schemes were designed to protect deposits rather than notes. All of the state funds failed in relatively short order, however—an indication that individual state governments were perhaps too small to manage this sort of risk on their own.[128]

Congress and the president finally stepped in to establish *federal* deposit insurance in June 1933, following the most severe banking panic in the nation's history. This marked the climax of more than a century of legislative wrangling over the problem of money risk. The panic itself, which spread like wildfire in late February and early March, was largely under control by April. Franklin Roosevelt had managed to stem the crisis by declaring a national "bank holiday" and then gradually reopening banks that his officials identified as sound. But although the worst of the financial crisis was soon over, both the banking system and the economy as a whole remained in a terrible state. Speaking on May 20, the chief sponsor of banking reform in the House, Alabama's Henry Steagall, declared: "Agriculture is prostrate. Industry is crushed. Trade and commerce, both foreign and domestic, have been paralyzed. Bank credit has been destroyed. Confidence has vanished. . . . These conditions culminated in the complete collapse of the banking system of the Nation, and the measure of recovery so far attained is by no means satisfactory."[129]

Convinced that full economic recovery was contingent on comprehensive reform in the banking sector, Representative Steagall joined Senator Carter Glass of Virginia in proposing a two-part remedy. What became known as the Glass-Steagall bill mandated the complete separation of commercial from investment banking and, at the same time, authorized the establishment of federal deposit insurance for commercial banks. Steagall and his allies believed that once commercial banks were prohibited from engaging in investment banking activities (which they regarded as excessively risky), the introduction of deposit insurance could safely reinvigorate the system.

By bolstering public confidence and thus sharply reducing the threat of bank runs, deposit insurance promised to help optimize the transformation of money into credit. "We cannot have a normal use of bank credit in the United States," Steagall declared on the House floor, "until people are willing to put their deposits into banks. Deposits constitute the basis for bank credit, and bankers can never be free to extend credit . . . until they are permitted to retire at night without fear of mobs at their doors the next morning demanding cash for their deposits." The confidence that deposit insurance would instill, he concluded, "is indispensable to the support of business and the successful financing of the Treasury."[130]

Although the exigencies of the Great Depression drove a good deal of the debate in 1933, longer-term considerations were also very much in evidence, with supporters reiterating (and often clarifying) many of the key arguments that had been circulating ever since 1829. At the heart of their case was the relatively simple idea that insurance constituted a natural response to a highly unpredictable (and uncontrollable) hazard—bank loss. "I have seen insurance extended in every direction," proclaimed Representative Robert Luce of Massachusetts, "and I fail to understand why the depositors in a bank, persons who have no opportunity to know, who have in fact no knowledge about the interior affairs of the bank . . . should not be insured against mischance that they cannot guard against and prevent."[131] Steagall added that "[e]very banker applies the principle of insurance in every other line of his activities. He requires insurance at the hands of employees. He insures himself against his own negligence and mistakes. . . . This bill simply sets up a system of mutual insurance. Bankers should have been first to advocate it."[132]

As always, critics warned that mandatory insurance could trigger a severe moral hazard problem. Since insured depositors would no longer have any incentive to discriminate between sound banks and unsound ones, "a reputation for high character would be cheapened and recklessness would be encouraged."[133] Proponents, however, doubted whether small depositors truly had the ability to discriminate in this way, even when they had every financial incentive to do so. Implicit in Representative Luce's comments, this notion was repeated again and again in both the House and the Senate. "[T]he vast majority of depositors can never be expected to be so informed as to understand which bank is absolutely safe," declared Ohio's junior senator, Robert Bulkley. "The necessary measure of safety will not come without definite and decisive government action."[134]

Echoing Joshua Forman's arguments about the Safety Fund, the bill's supporters in Congress claimed that federal deposit insurance would actually improve the monitoring of bank risk along two different dimensions. First, they insisted that it would bring the government in as a more aggressive regulator, correcting many "of the abuses of the past . . . so that failures . . . will be cut to the irreducible minimum."[135] Second, they assumed that a well-designed insurance program would create powerful incentives for bankers to monitor one another. As Senator Bulkley put it: "[T]he mutual responsibility and mutual liability of all bankers for all banking losses will have a strong tendency to bring about better banking, through more complete cooperation among bankers and through the creation of a definite selfish motive on the part of each banker to be active in preventing unsound banking practices by neighboring banks."[136]

Perhaps most important of all, proponents viewed public insurance as the best possible protection against the scourge of bank runs, which put every depositor "at the mercy of his fellow depositors" and every strong bank at the mercy of every weak one.[137] "Let me say . . . that this is not a provision altogether for the weak banks; not by any means," exclaimed Carter Glass, the bill's chief sponsor in the Senate. "It is an insurance to the entire banking community of the United States, because when weak banks begin to topple there takes place a disastrous psychology in the whole country that precipitates runs on strong banks that break them down."[138] Although one would normally expect insurance merely to spread aggregate risk but not reduce it, the proponents of federal deposit insurance felt confident that it would dramatically reduce the risk of bank failures, both by improving the monitoring of banking risk and by countering the vicious psychology of fear that drove bank runs.

Finally, proponents argued that it was absolutely imperative that this sort of insurance be provided by the federal government. A federal insurance program, they maintained, would prove far more stable than had the various state funds because it would spread banking risk in a much broader fashion.[139] Supporters were quick to point out, moreover, that the federal government had the unique ability to restore public confidence because of its unparalleled financial credibility. One congressman from New York even suggested that the credibility of the federal government was perhaps the last tether still holding the country back from a terrifying descent into communism.[140]

The odd thing about these last lines of reasoning is that the proposal to establish federal deposit insurance did not include any explicit guaranty from the federal government. In fact, Senator Glass, who had long feared that a federal guaranty on bank deposits would end in disaster, repeatedly denied that his bill included any such guaranty. Instead, under his proposal, banks would be required to contribute to a fund that would be used to compensate losses. If the fund ever ran dry and losses continued to mount, the federal government would bear no legal responsibility to cover the shortfall.[141] In spite of Glass's unequivocal statements on the subject, however, there remained a pervasive sense on Capitol Hill—and very likely in the country at large—that a *federal* insurance program would carry the unique financial credibility of the federal government.[142]

With the exception of these last arguments about federal financial prowess, much about the struggle for deposit insurance in 1933 was reminiscent of Joshua Forman's original campaign for the Safety Fund in 1829. Most of the justifications given were remarkably similar, though several of them (especially those regarding monitoring) were articulated with considerably greater clarity and precision during the later campaign. There were also a number of other parallels. In both 1829 and 1933, for example, the introduction of bank insurance (risk spreading) was associated with the termination of a preexisting double liability rule for bank shareholders (risk shifting).[143] And in both cases, public bank insurance was offered up as a way of preserving and strengthening that uniquely American institution, unit banking.[144]

The main reason for these similarities was that the underlying problem being addressed in 1933 was essentially the same as in 1829. Although bank money now took the form of checks rather than notes, policymakers were still searching for the best ways to make credit and liquidity simultaneously safe *and* abundant without abandoning the nation's decentralized banking system. Insurance was not the only weapon that they sought to employ in their assault on money risk. But in 1933 as in 1829, they viewed it as a necessary addition to the arsenal. Deposit insurance, they believed, promised to fortify not only the banking system itself but also "the gigantic economic life of this great Nation."[145]

Conclusion

Today, most Americans take the quality of their money for granted. Not only would it be inconceivable for local merchants to refuse to honor paper currency, but it would be almost equally unthinkable for local banks to "suspend payments," barring customers from withdrawing cash or from writing checks on valid accounts. Bank runs and bank suspensions have all but disappeared in the United States, even as bank money and credit have continued to grow at a brisk pace.

This favorable state of affairs, unprecedented in American history, rests on an elaborate set of risk management institutions. Ever since the dawn of the Republic, there has been an almost universal consensus that private banks could not be left to create and disseminate money on their own.[146] The risks were simply too high and the stakes too great. Because average citizens were thought to be incapable of assessing these risks without assistance, government assumed a very prominent role in managing the problem of money risk.

Much of the conceptual groundwork for the monetary institutions we now have was laid during the antebellum period. As we have seen, lawmakers in New York, like their counterparts in other states, faced a vexing trade-off. They recognized that a growing economy required plenty of liquidity to grease the rails of commerce and plenty of credit to accelerate innovative investment projects. But the lax banking policies that would have ensured abundant liquidity and credit (at least in the short run) also promised to undermine faith in the security of the money supply. To address this trade-off, New York lawmakers experimented with a variety of methods for shifting, spreading, and reducing risk. These included the nation's very first bank insurance scheme as well as one of the earliest attempts to back bank notes with government bonds.

Eventually, these ideas found their way to the federal level. Congress's decision during the Civil War to create federally chartered banks—and to require that all federal bank notes be fully backed with U.S. government bonds—produced a truly uniform national currency, with federal bank notes consistently trading at par all across the country. (Federal bank notes ultimately gave way to Federal Reserve notes with the founding of the Federal Reserve System in 1913.) The establishment of federal deposit insurance in 1933, moreover, solidified demand deposits as another secure form of money, while at the same time eliminating once and for all the terrible scourge of banking panics that had wracked the nation's economy for well over a hundred years. Although money risk remains a live issue even now—primarily as a result of volatility in international exchange rates and the domestic price level—it is not nearly as extensive or as dramatic a threat as it once was. A relatively small number of risk management policies designed to safeguard the nation's money supply appear to have made a very big difference.[147]

In enacting these policies, lawmakers highlighted a variety of motivations. Part of the appeal was simply in protecting citizens from loss. But there was also a more fundamental objective involved. Unlike most other types of risk, which inevitably threatened individual victims with loss, money risk also threatened the economic system itself. "When a bank fails there is not only serious loss to the depositors," said one congressman in 1933, "but the general business of the community suffers."[148] Again and again, lawmakers emphasized that their broader goal was to promote trade and investment by fashioning a more secure business environment.[149]

Indeed, this was the battle cry of Phase I. It drove not only the introduction of banking policies from double liability to deposit insurance, but also the enactment of limited liability laws and (as we will see in the next chapter) the creation of a federal bankruptcy code, which redefined the risks of entrepreneurship in a rapidly changing economy. Shaping institutions from money to bankruptcy, public risk management was emerging as a truly pivotal feature of American capitalism.

5

Bankruptcy

Like so many risk management policies, bankruptcy law was formed against the backdrop of economic crisis. Congress passed four separate bankruptcy statutes during the nineteenth century—three temporary ones in 1800, 1841, and 1867, and finally a permanent one in 1898. In each case, federal lawmakers acted at a moment of severe economic distress, hoping to extricate multitudes of failed debtors from beneath an avalanche of bad debts.

The Bankruptcy Act of 1841, for example, was passed during the long depression that followed the panic of 1837, the same storm that had brought down Joshua Forman's Safety Fund system in New York State. Writing in June 1840, a former mayor of New York City, Philip Hone, observed that business "of all kinds is completely at a stand . . . and the whole body politic sick and infirm, and calling aloud for a remedy."[1] By the time President William Henry Harrison summoned an extra session of Congress a year later, it was said that 500,000 debtors had succumbed to the crisis, having proved unable to pay their debts.[2]

The newly elected Whigs, who had swamped the Democrats in the elections of 1840, moved quickly to exploit their momentum. Topping their agenda were proposals for a national bank to stabilize the country's money supply, a higher tariff to raise revenue and promote domestic investment, and a federal bankruptcy law to provide relief and facilitate recovery. Amidst all the economic turmoil, however, the bankruptcy bill assumed particular urgency. As Nathaniel Tallmadge, a New York Democrat, proclaimed on the floor of the Senate: "Sir, this extra session was called for the purpose of adopting measures for relief of the present distressed and embarrassed condition of the country. What measure would give greater, and more extensive, and more instantaneous relief than passage of a bankrupt law?"[3] A new federal bankruptcy statute was finally enacted on August 19.

At the heart of the 1841 law was its discharge provision, which allowed debtors who filed for bankruptcy to be "discharged" from their debts after surrendering most of their physical and financial assets. Often called a fresh start, the bankruptcy discharge allowed failed debtors to begin anew, free of the financial burdens that had overwhelmed them in their prior business dealings. By the time the law was repealed in 1843, more than thirty thousand bankrupt debtors had obtained discharges under its provisions.

At the time, many of the law's critics found the notion of a legal discharge utterly shocking. Allowing individuals to escape debts that they themselves had contracted, opponents argued, would inevitably provoke a horrendous moral hazard problem, encouraging reckless speculation and otherwise undermining personal responsibility. The future president of the United States, Senator James Buchanan of Pennsylvania, warned that such a right would erode "the morals of the people," would "stimulate the spirit of speculation almost to madness," and would serve as an open invitation to "wild and extravagant" business dealings.[4]

Other critics claimed that the 1841 law constituted little more than a giveaway to failed debtors, an exercise in popular sentimentality rather than sound economic reasoning. A retroactive discharge, they emphasized, would require the abrogation of existing debt contracts, a profound and potentially insidious departure from the nation's traditional commitment to property rights. Even Daniel Webster, a leading advocate of the new bankruptcy bill, acknowledged that it would "impair the obligation of contracts."[5]

The pivotal question, then, is why such an extreme remedy was necessary. Why did lawmakers feel compelled to grant debtors a nonwaivable (and retroactive) right to discharge? Over the past several decades, a number of academics have suggested that the economic purpose of bankruptcy law was essentially the same as that of limited liability: to encourage risk-averse savers to invest in risky ventures by providing them with a form of insurance against extreme loss. Discharge, writes one prominent legal scholar, "enables the venturer to limit his risk of loss to his current assets; he is not forced to hazard his entire earning capacity on the venture. Incorporation performs the same function of encouraging investment by enabling the risk averse to limit their risk of loss to their investment."[6] Says another, "Discharge may be viewed as a form of limited liability for individuals—a legal construct that stems from the same desire, and serves the same purposes, as does limited liability for corporations."[7]

From a conceptual standpoint, there can be little doubt that the discharge provision in bankruptcy (much like limited liability) creates a form of implicit insurance, transferring risk from debtors to creditors. According to one of the nation's leading students of bankruptcy, "[a] right to a fresh start . . . is a kind of insurance. All debtors pay a higher rate of interest at the outset and, in return, the creditor bears part of the loss that arises when a particular debtor falls on hard times."[8] The analogy to insurance was even recognized by some lawmakers in the nineteenth century. As Representative Joseph Trumbull of Connecticut observed in 1841, "the creditors stood in the nature of an insurer."[9]

Significantly, though, insurance can serve two very different purposes. On the one hand, by providing a sense of security, insurance may encourage risk-averse individuals to undertake activities that might otherwise strike them as too risky. This may be characterized as the *ex ante* benefit of insurance, since it is of value to the insured regardless of whether a loss ever occurs. On the other hand, by providing compensation in the aftermath of loss, insurance also plays a critical role in allowing victims to escape financial catastrophe and to get on with their lives. For obvious reasons, this may be characterized as the *ex post* benefit of insurance.

As we have seen, state limited liability law was justified almost exclusively on ex ante grounds during the nineteenth century, as a way of encouraging passive investors to buy stock in risky enterprises. What should become clear in this chapter is that federal bankruptcy law was justified very differently—on the basis of ex post, rather than ex ante, arguments. In each of the congressional debates over bankruptcy, but especially in 1841 and 1898, the main objectives that lawmakers cited were to relieve and to resurrect failed entrepreneurs (i.e., active investors). Amazing as it may sound, the idea of trying to stimulate risk-averse savers to invest in risky projects—the central argument for limited liability—was hardly ever mentioned within the context of bankruptcy.

The establishment of a right to discharge thus constituted a distinctive Phase I policy. Like limited liability, it was supposed to bolster investment and enlarge productive capacity by transferring default risk from debtors to creditors, forcing the latter to act as implicit insurers against business failure. But whereas limited liability was designed to increase investment incentives before any failure occurred, bankruptcy discharge was created to revive entrepreneurs—and to resurrect their precious human capital—in the aftermath of failure. One was an ex ante policy, the other an ex post. Though largely overlooked now, this simple distinction proved exceedingly important in the nineteenth century, casting bankruptcy law as a novel form of public risk management designed for the active (rather than the passive) investor.

The American Tradition of Debtor Protection

Before we turn to the legislative debates themselves, it is first necessary to recognize that U.S. bankruptcy law was not conceived in a vacuum. Even before the enactment of the first federal bankruptcy statutes in 1800 and 1841, Americans had long displayed a penchant for forgiving or otherwise relieving distressed debtors, particularly in the midst of economic crises. Although the motivations and mechanisms of debtor protection have evolved considerably over the years, the American tradition of shifting default risk away from borrowers has exceptionally deep historical roots. Indeed, the United States has long distinguished itself as a nation with a special fondness for debtors.

Protecting the Debtor in Early America

The thirteen colonies had experimented with a wide array of debtor-protection devices even before the Revolution. Although debtors' prisons were still a fact of life in most places, numerous colonies (such as New Jersey in 1755) permitted confined debtors to be discharged from prison on the condition that they assign whatever property they had to unpaid creditors.[10] Several colonies (including Massachusetts, New York, and South Carolina) also sought to discharge cooperative debtors from existing debts, though such provisions were typically overturned by the British Privy Council.[11] Contemporary observers commonly distinguished between laws discharging the debtor's body from prison, which were broadly accepted, and laws discharging the debt itself, which were not.

Some of the more creative debtor-protection techniques of the colonial period included so-called valuation and replevin laws. By authorizing insolvent debtors to have their assets valued by independent assessors rather than through auctions, valuation laws allowed debtors to avoid selling assets at sharply depressed prices in the midst of economic downturns. Instead, they could simply turn over real assets to creditors at something like book value. Under replevin laws, debtors could trigger stays of execution by issuing personal "replevy" bonds to their creditors. The General Court of Massachusetts adopted a valuation law as early as the 1640s (during a sharp recession), and Virginia had a replevin system in place from 1748 to 1817.[12] Two additional methods of debtor relief practiced in colonial times involved the enactment of stay laws, which temporarily blocked creditors from seizing debtor assets, and the adoption of inflationary policies, which permitted debtors to repay their loans in depreciated paper currency.

The climax of eighteenth-century debtor-protection policy came just after independence, during the severe economic crisis following the Revolutionary War. The inability of the new central government to repay its wartime debts, combined with the breakdown of trade with Britain, had set off a chain reaction of failures. The U.S. finance minister, Robert Morris, resigned in 1782, acknowledging that "it can no longer be a doubt . . . that our public credit is gone."[13] Farmers who had fought in the war and had patriotically accepted government obligations as payment were especially hard hit. With the financially crippled central government unable to make good on its wartime promises, many farmers fell short on their own mortgage payments and risked losing their farms.

In most of the newly independent states, lawmakers moved quickly to ease the pain. Numerous states enacted stay laws in the early 1780s, and many also experimented with inflationary policies, issuing paper currency in unusually large quantities.[14] All across the country—and especially in Rhode Island, where the policy of inflation was pushed further than anywhere else—creditors charged that their property was being confiscated. James Madison agreed, warning that paper money "affects the Rights of property as much as taking away equal value in land."[15]

Other debtor-protection devices that came into common use at this time included installment and commodity payment laws. A Virginia installment law, enacted in 1786, permitted debtors to delay loan servicing, offering the possibility of payment in three annual installments. James Madison was again dismayed, this time by the action of his own state. "[S]uch an interposition of the law in private contracts," he noted in a letter to his father in December, "is not to be vindicated on any legislative principle within my knowledge."[16] Commodity laws, meanwhile, effectively made certain goods (other than specie) legal tender, allowing debtors to repay their loans in officially overvalued commodities.[17]

Given the severe economic conditions and the relative impotence of the new central government under the Articles of Confederation, state lawmakers feared civil unrest.[18] In Massachusetts, where legislators apparently showed less interest in debtor relief than in most other states, a former Revolutionary War captain led 2,500 men in a small-scale rebellion beginning on August 29, 1786. The captain, Daniel Shays, sought to prevent officers of the court from seizing the property of delinquent farmer-debtors in western Massachusetts. Rumors circulated that Shays and his men planned to overthrow the state government, but nothing of the sort ever happened. Although Shays' Rebellion was put down the following year, the newly elected Massachusetts legislature heard his message loud and clear. State lawmakers quickly passed a variety of debtor relief measures including a far-reaching moratorium on debts.[19]

Though these measures offered solace to distressed debtors, a growing number of the nation's founders viewed them with alarm—as evidence that their precious experiment in democracy was coming apart. "I am mortified beyond expression," declared the hero of the Revolutionary War, George Washington, "that in the moment of our acknowledged independence we should by our conduct verify the predictions of our transatlantic foe, and render ourselves ridiculous and contemptible in the eyes of all Europe."[20] In combination, the federal government's inability to pay its debts, Shays' Rebellion in Massachusetts, and widespread state interference in private debt contracts played a critical role in motivating the Constitutional Convention of 1787.[21] Many prominent figures such as Madison and Washington came to believe that a stronger central government was simply imperative and that tighter rules would have to be imposed on the states, which had shown themselves woefully unable to resist popular demands for redistribution and the wholesale violation of property rights.

Finally ratified in 1789, the new U.S. Constitution offered a direct response to many of the most extreme debtor-relief measures of the previous decade. Article 1, section 10, prohibited the states from coining money and barred them from "impairing the Obligation of Contracts." One convention delegate, Charles Cotesworth Pinckney of South Carolina, declared optimistically that "in the future we shall be free from the apprehensions of paper money, pine barren acts [commodity payment laws], and installment laws."[22] But to the great consternation of federalists like Pinckney, paper money soon returned in a new guise (state bank notes) and state debtor-protection laws proved more popular and tougher to eliminate than almost anyone had anticipated.

The Constitution was apparently not quite as powerful a constraint on state action as its framers had hoped. In addition to chartering private banks with the authority to issue bank notes (which were not legal tender but nonetheless widely circulated as money), the states continued passing stay laws, installment laws, and numerous other infringements on existing debt contracts during times of economic distress. Pennsylvania enacted a stay law at the turn of the century that allowed debtors owing less than $100 to delay legal collection efforts for up to nine months. Many other states (including North Carolina, Georgia, Virginia, Rhode Island, and Vermont) also permitted stays of various forms in the years following ratification.[23]

New York went even further, enacting a full-fledged bankruptcy law in 1788, and reenacting it in 1801. Among its many provisions, the New York statute permitted a debtor to be discharged from all his debts with the consent of three-fourths of his creditors (by value). This meant that up to a quarter of a debtor's obligations could be discharged without creditor consent, and the figure was later raised to one-third in 1813.[24]

The U.S. courts ultimately struck down or circumscribed many of these state initiatives. Ruling on the New York bankruptcy statute in 1819, Chief Justice John Marshall reasoned that a state discharge, applying retroactively to debts already in force when the law was passed, impaired the obligation of contracts and was thus "contrary to the constitution of the United States."[25] Eight years later the Supreme Court determined (now over the objection of Marshall) that each state *was* entitled to enact a prospective discharge, applying exclusively to debts contracted after passage of the law. But even here, the Court imposed a formidable constraint. A state discharge, the justices concluded, could legitimately protect debtors against creditors from the same state but not against out-of-state creditors, all but eliminating its value when cross-border transactions were involved.[26]

Nevertheless, debtor-protection laws remained popular and continued to be enacted at the state level all across the country. In many cases, constitutional caution was thrown to the winds. Never was this more true than after the devastating financial panic of 1837. One contemporary observer lamented that from everywhere "comes rumor after rumor of riot, insurrection, and tumult."[27] Facing truly desperate circumstances, Alabama, Illinois, and Virginia all enacted various sorts of stay laws for ailing debtors; and Ohio, Indiana, Michigan, Mississippi, and Illinois passed appraisal laws, mandating that the property of delinquent debtors could not be sold at auction for less than a fixed proportion (often two-thirds) of its appraisal value. Passions ran so high that some Illinois residents promised defiance when the Supreme Court struck down the state's appraisal law in 1843.[28] In the end, the Court's verdict was honored, but only reluctantly.

Part of the appeal of these debtor-protection measures through the mid-nineteenth century may have been that they helped compensate for some rather harsh legal penalties. Creditors, after all, were entitled to seize not only the personal assets of delinquent debtors but their actual bodies as well. The threat of being condemned to debtors' prison loomed large throughout this period. In Britain, which had a similar system in place, Charles Dickens immortalized the trauma of seeing his own father arrested and imprisoned for failing to pay his debts in the novel *David Copperfield*. In real life, young Charles and his family visited his father frequently in prison through the terrible year of 1822.[29]

Back in America, it has been said that as many as 75,000 persons were still being imprisoned for debt annually by about 1830.[30] Nearly 2,000 debtors were confined in New York City jails alone from January 1826 to November 1827, allegedly "without either food, fuel or bed, except a quart of soup each twenty-four hours."[31] Although such accounts probably exaggerate the severity of debtor confinement in America, the system was no doubt brutal.[32] Tales of suffering debtors, imprisoned and defeated, were commonplace in the early nineteenth century.

To be sure, citizens sometimes relished the punishment of a reckless speculator or a debtor who had defrauded his creditors; but they often expressed sympathy for the "honest" debtor (perhaps like Dickens' father) who found himself incarcerated as a result of economic events beyond his control.[33] Growing public dissatisfaction with the debtors' prison system led to its gradual dismantling through the antebellum period. New York lawmakers finally ended the practice of imprisoning female debtors in 1828 and males in 1831, except in cases of fraud. Massachusetts was one of the last states to abolish the notorious institution, in 1857.[34] Even before abolition, however, public hostility to the practice was often so intense that "some lenders gave up their power to seize defaulters rather than be thought grasping and inhuman."[35]

Although the existence of debtors' prisons almost surely increased the popularity of debtor-relief measures through the mid-nineteenth century, state lawmakers continued to show a remarkable commitment to debtor protection long after debtors' prisons had been abolished. Writing in the midst of the Great Depression of the 1930s, bankruptcy historian Charles Warren noted with some amazement that states had continued to enact stay laws in almost every recession, "in spite of the Constitutional prohibition against laws impairing obligations of contract." Repeated court rulings striking down these stay laws seemed to have had "little effect in preventing their enactment."[36] America's fondness for its debtors ran deep; and though the nation's politicians frequently waxed eloquent about the sanctity of debt contracts, they were surprisingly quick to abrogate them in times of economic crisis.

Besides passing temporary stay laws on an ad hoc basis—often just one step ahead of the courts—state lawmakers also figured out a variety of constitutional means for relieving their debtors. These included prospective discharge laws and, far more prevalent, homestead exemptions. The Republic of Texas passed the first homestead exemption in 1839, six years before it was admitted into the Union. The exemption offered substantial protection to delinquent debtors by removing up to fifty acres, as well as a home worth up to $500, from the reach of grasping creditors. The Texas exemption was increased just a few years later to two hundred acres and up to $2,000 in home value.[37] Almost every other state followed suit over the next thirty years, though often with less generous exemption provisions than those enacted in Texas.[38] Unlike stay laws, these exemptions were neither temporary nor unconstitutional, surviving in modified form just about everywhere down to the present day. Over 150 years later, Texas is still well known for its unusually generous exemption rules.

To some extent, the various debtor-protection devices invented and implemented at the state level in the eighteenth and nineteenth centuries may be viewed as early antecedents to Phase III risk management policies. They were generally created for the benefit of all citizens, including consumers, rather than just for businesspeople or workers. Stay laws, for example, were often targeted at petty debtors, who in many cases borrowed solely (or mainly) for consumption purposes. Homestead exemptions and discharge provisions, moreover, typically covered everyone, not just traders or other sorts of entrepreneurs.

But even in these cases, nineteenth-century proponents of debtor-protection policies typically advanced powerful Phase I justifications, claiming that such measures were essential for promoting trade and investment. Already in 1817, for example, the federal justice Brockholst Livingston wrote a decision upholding New York's bankruptcy law (which he called an "insolvent law") based in part on "a conviction that the encouragement of trade required it." Admittedly, he showed little tolerance for ad hoc debtor relief policies like stay laws and installment laws, which he dismissed as dangerous knee-jerk responses to economic hard times. These sorts of policies arbitrarily impaired the obligation of contracts, he insisted, leading to the "decay of commerce, the ruin of public credit, and the almost entire extinction of confidence between individuals." A permanent bankruptcy law, by contrast, would promote economic activity as well as extend to debtors "that mercy and forbearance which, in similar circumstances, [their creditors] would wish and expect to have extended to themselves."[39] Although the U.S. Supreme Court soon ruled the other way on one element of the New York law (retroactive discharge), Livingston's early argument about encouraging trade remains highly significant.

Similar justifications, emphasizing economic development and business promotion, were employed in support of homestead exemptions as well. One of the main reasons why the Republic of Texas adopted a homestead exemption in 1839 was to try to attract settlers from the neighboring United States. Four decades later, Texas lawmakers created a novel business "homestead" exemption, once again with the intention of promoting entrepreneurial activity within the state. "Developmental purpose figured prominently in Texas [exemption] policy," writes the leading historian of the subject. "Texans rejected the contention of conservatives that homestead exemption weakened moral fiber, coddled the weak, cheated creditors, and subverted the free market."[40]

Commenting on the "profound wisdom of our homestead law," Justice Abner Lipscomb of the Texas Supreme Court proudly declared in 1852 that it allowed individuals to "commence again, Anteus-like, with renewed energy and strength and capacity for business . . . [as] more practical and useful members of society."[41] Far-reaching debtor protection, in other words, was justified on economic grounds, not just humanitarian ones. Lipscomb believed that the homestead exemption would enrich the whole society by helping to resurrect otherwise wasted human capital. Significantly, numerous members of Congress advanced precisely the same argument in support of a federal discharge for bankrupt debtors, which ultimately emerged as the most potent debtor-protection policy of them all.

Creating a Federal Bankruptcy Law, 1800–1898

As we have seen, colonial lawmakers had begun experimenting with bankruptcy laws and discharge provisions even before there was a United States. In these early years, however, bankruptcy was far less favorable to debtors than it has since become. The first bankruptcy legislation on record in America was enacted in colonial Massachusetts in 1714. Patterned after an earlier British bankruptcy statute from 1705, this law was intended mainly for the benefit of creditors. Although a discharge was granted at the end of the bankruptcy process, it was regarded primarily as an inducement for bankrupt debtors to reveal and convey all of their assets. The overriding public policy goal was to increase collection rates, rather than to relieve failed debtors.[42] Similar bankruptcy provisions were enacted in other colonies, including South Carolina in 1721, Rhode Island in 1746, North Carolina in 1749, and New York in 1755. But these laws were short-lived, in most cases lapsing after just a few years.[43]

When the Constitution was ratified in 1789, it authorized Congress to "establish . . . uniform Laws on the subject of Bankruptcies throughout the United States."[44] Congress passed the first federal bankruptcy statute eleven years later. Like the British law on which it was modeled, the Bankruptcy Act of 1800 applied exclusively to traders and other intermediaries; and it permitted only creditors, not debtors, to initiate bankruptcy proceedings. The focus on traders arose out of the belief that individuals engaged in commerce were unusually dependent on credit and, at the same time, subject to considerably more risk than those in other professions, such as farmers, manufacturers, and artisans.[45] As for the rule that creditors alone could launch bankruptcy proceedings, it probably stemmed from concerns about debtor misbehavior. A law allowing debtors to file for bankruptcy voluntarily, most lawmakers apparently assumed, would quickly become an invitation for fraud.[46] Overall, the act of 1800 was widely viewed as a creditor-oriented statute. As one congressman observed in 1799, the "bill [was] calculated, upon the whole, to benefit the creditor."[47]

At root, federal bankruptcy law was thought to provide creditors with a superior method of collection as compared to that available under state law. One problem for creditors who had to rely on state rules was that legal procedures varied considerably from region to region. In 1799, Congressman Harrison Otis expressed his "regret for the discordant and inconsistent system of the debtor laws of the several States." Since "commerce is a general concern," he insisted, uniformity was essential; and uniformity could be achieved only through the enactment of a federal bankruptcy statute.[48]

Even beyond the problem of regional variation, many state laws tended to produce grossly unequal distributions of debtor assets in the aftermath of default. In the New England states, in particular, collection from delinquent debtors was run strictly on a first-come, first-served basis. Unpaid creditors were entitled to place liens on debtor property to cover the amounts they were owed. But in practice, the first few creditors to take legal action often emptied the till, seizing all of the debtor's tangible assets. This had the unfortunate effect of depriving slower-acting creditors from recovering much of anything, which in turn encouraged a bank run mentality, whereby every creditor wanted to be the first to take legal action for fear of being left empty-handed.

Sadly, an otherwise sound business venture that missed a payment or two because it was temporarily short on cash risked being shut down altogether by a run of fearful creditors. Although a little patience on the part of lenders might have been sufficient to get the venture back on track, future repayment would be virtually impossible following a run, since just about all the firm's equipment, machinery, and other assets would have been attached. The first-come, first-served principle embedded in state law thus created a perverse incentive for creditors to rush for the exit at the first sign of trouble, potentially killing off viable enterprises and quite possibly reducing overall debt repayment in the process. As Congressman Otis put it, "an individual, upon an impulse of resentment or jealousy, might destroy his debtor root and branch, by taking out an attachment against his property, and securing himself to the exclusion of all other creditors."[49]

Federal bankruptcy law was designed to solve these problems. Once a bankruptcy proceeding was initiated, all other payment and collection efforts were immediately superseded. According to the act of 1800, the debtor's assets were to be turned over to bankruptcy commissioners, who would safeguard and manage them until an equitable distribution of the debtor's property could be worked out. The debtor had the possibility of earning a discharge at the end of the proceeding, but only after two-thirds of the creditors (by number and value) gave their consent to the arrangement and after the bankruptcy commissioners certified that the debtor had been fully cooperative in every aspect of the process.[50]

Because under federal bankruptcy law creditors were no longer penalized for being patient (or even inattentive), the bank run psychology was effectively eliminated. Healthy debtors who found themselves temporarily short on cash now had a better chance of surviving, which meant that creditors might have a better chance of being repaid in the long run. Nor did creditors have to worry about variation across states, or about coming out on the losing end of an arbitrary distribution of assets based on the first-come, first-served principle. Even apart from the discharge provision, therefore, bankruptcy law represented an important risk management mechanism, dramatically reducing the risk of runs on cash-poor debtors as well as the risk to creditors of receiving less than their fair share from a failed enterprise.

In time, of course, the discharge would emerge as a powerful risk management device in its own right, shielding debtors from considerable downside risk by forcibly shifting it onto creditors. But this was not the goal from the beginning. The original purpose of granting a discharge, particularly under eighteenth-century British bankruptcy law, was to facilitate the discovery process for creditors. Debtors who knew that full cooperation would be rewarded with a certificate of discharge at the end of the proceeding were more likely to be truthful in revealing their assets. Discharge was but a means to an end. In fact, to this day, numerous bankruptcy laws around the world retain a powerful creditor orientation.

Yet in America, where notions of debtor protection enjoyed unusually strong support, discharge quickly became an end in itself. The traditional logic of bankruptcy was inverted. Concern for the creditor loomed largest in the act of 1800. But even in the congressional debates over this early bill, many lawmakers devoted considerable attention to the goal of relieving and resurrecting failed debtors. Representative Thomas Pinckney of South Carolina, for example, "could conceive of no measure more desirable than a law which shall prevent the hopes of an unfortunate but fair trader from being forever blasted, because the hand of misfortune had reached him; which should restore him to society, and enable him again to provide for himself, and perhaps a large family."[51]

The Bankruptcy Act of 1800 was ultimately repealed in 1803, two years before its scheduled termination. Opposition arose in large measure because the law came to be viewed as excessively favorable to debtors, especially "fraudulent debtors" who managed to take "refuge in [its] provisions."[52] Although debtors lost this particular battle, they seemed to enjoy an increasing edge in the broader war. By the time the next federal bankruptcy law was enacted in 1841, debtor protection had emerged as a primary objective. It was now at least as important as creditor protection, and probably even more so.

With as many as 500,000 debtors said to have been overwhelmed in the financial panic of 1837 and its aftermath, Congress was determined to extend a lifeline. Whereas the earlier act of 1800 had covered only a few select classes of debtors (traders, retailers, and financial intermediaries), the 1841 law covered every individual debtor, regardless of profession. And whereas the first law prohibited debtors from filing for bankruptcy voluntarily, the 1841 act introduced the availability of voluntary bankruptcy for "[a]ll persons whatsoever." It also limited creditor-initiated involuntary filings exclusively to merchants, retailers, and financial intermediaries "owing debts to the amount of not less than two thousand dollars."[53] This meant that farmers, manufacturers, artisans, and wage earners could choose to file for bankruptcy voluntarily, but were shielded from involuntary proceedings instigated by hostile creditors. Finally, whereas the act of 1800 had made a debtor's discharge contingent on the explicit approval of two-thirds of his creditors, the 1841 statute ensured discharge unless at least half the creditors filed written dissents. The effect was to make discharge all but certain at the end of each bankruptcy proceeding. For all of these reasons, the Bankruptcy

Act of 1841 was widely regarded as pro-debtor in orientation and has since been characterized as the first modern bankruptcy law in the United States.

Once again, however, Congress repealed the 1841 statute less than two years later. Especially after the economic crisis had eased, opposition seemed to emerge from all sides. Creditors complained bitterly about the excessive generosity of the law, which ultimately released nearly 33,000 bankrupts from almost $400 million in debts. Many debtors, too, were apparently unhappy, having lost some of their favorite exemptions and other protective measures previously available at the state level. Indeed, the votes for repeal were overwhelming: 32 to 13 in the Senate and 140 to 71 in the House.[54]

The next federal bankruptcy statute, enacted in 1867, combined many of the features of the two prior ones. It was more generous to debtors than the act of 1800, but considerably less debtor-friendly than the act of 1841. The authors of the 1867 law reintroduced both voluntary and involuntary bankruptcy, but they excluded debtors owing less than $300 from filing voluntarily and placed many fewer restrictions on creditors wishing to initiate involuntary proceedings.[55] The 1867 law survived longer than either of its predecessors, though it too was repealed after just eleven years. In this case, opposition grew out of the law's extreme complexity, its "unbearable fees and delays," and the hostility "a lot of irresponsible carpetbag Judges" engendered in the South.[56]

Congress eventually passed a fourth bankruptcy law at the end of the century. In almost every way, the Bankruptcy Act of 1898 was the most debtor-friendly of them all. Said one contemporary observer, "[T]he principal object of the law appears to be to make discharges easy, inexpensive and certain."[57] Representative Robert Burke of Texas captured the spirit of the discussion in Congress when he announced that relief for debtors should be the chief priority of any bankruptcy legislation, and the "preservation and protection of the just rights and interests of their honest creditors" only a secondary objective.[58] Under the new law, any qualified person, regardless of debt level, could file for voluntary bankruptcy. Debtors were almost assured of being discharged at the end of the process, even if their creditors objected. The statute also exempted wage earners, farmers, and state and federal banks, as well as any person or partnership owing less than $1,000, from involuntary bankruptcy proceedings, which were initiated by creditors.[59]

All in all, the 1898 act laid the foundation for American bankruptcy law in the twentieth century.[60] Unlike the previous three statutes, this one was not repealed after only a few years. It was amended on several occasions, and it was technically repealed and replaced in 1978. But ever since 1898, a debtor-friendly bankruptcy system—arguably the most debtor-friendly system anywhere in the world—has remained a permanent and vital feature of American capitalism.[61]

The Case for Bankruptcy Discharge

Like most of the debtor-protection devices fashioned at the state level, all four federal bankruptcy laws were enacted—at least in part—as emergency relief measures for failed debtors. Each one was passed in the wake of a major economic crisis.[62] Unlike the states, however, the federal government faced no constitutional constraints in releasing debtors from existing contractual obligations. The Constitution explicitly authorized Congress to enact bankruptcy laws (Article 1, section 8), and its prohibition on impairing contracts (Article 1, section 10) applied only to the states, not to the federal government. Federal bankruptcy law thus emerged as a particularly potent means of relief.

Congress passed the Bankruptcy Act of 1800 following two financial panics in 1792 and 1797, which left prostrate a great many debtors, including some very prominent ones. The New York speculator William Duer actually died in a debtors' prison in 1799; and Robert Morris, who had helped finance the American Revolution, ended up spending three years in one in the late 1790s.[63] Each of the next three federal bankruptcy laws was enacted under similar circumstances. The Bankruptcy Act of 1841 followed the economic turmoil of the late 1830s and early 1840s. The act of 1867 was provoked, in large measure, by the massive economic dislocation resulting from the Civil War. And the 1898 law followed several notable financial panics (especially those of 1893 and 1896) as well as a generation of ongoing deflation.[64] In fact, by the 1890s, the pattern of enacting bankruptcy statutes after periods of crisis, and soon repealing them, seemed so well established that numerous congressmen wanted nothing more than a temporary law.[65] But in 1898, the advocates of a temporary program were distinctly in the minority.

Ever since the early nineteenth century, a growing number of federal lawmakers had sought to create a permanent bankruptcy system. Senator Tallmadge insisted in 1841 that in a "commercial community," a "bankrupt law . . . is one of the most important features in a system of political economy." Such a law, he predicted, would "keep in constant employment the activity, energy, and enterprise of the whole people." But to "accomplish these ends, it must be the permanent law of the land."[66] Tallmadge's wish, denied in 1841 and again in 1867, was finally granted in 1898, when Congress succeeded in enacting a permanent bankruptcy law with an exceedingly liberal discharge provision. The critical question was whether such a measure would foster anything more than a permanent means of relief for debtors. Confident that it would, proponents like Tallmadge pinned their hopes on the idea that a well-structured bankruptcy law would also help to conserve precious human capital.

Resurrection of Failed Entrepreneurs

At least by 1841, this notion of conserving human capital had emerged as one of the main objectives—and perhaps *the* main objective—in creating a permanent right to discharge. Supporters insisted that the availability of a discharge in bankruptcy would prevent entrepreneurial talent (human capital) from going to waste as a result of crippling, overhanging debt. Compassion dictated assorted measures of relief, but sound political economy apparently demanded strategies for rehabilitation as well. Indeed, this theme was present in all of the major bankruptcy debates of the nineteenth century. Although the debates were by no means identical, one can still detect a strong and largely common argument about the economic role of discharge, particularly in the discussions leading to the acts of 1841 and 1898.

Cognizant of the importance of predictable property rights, even some proponents of discharge acknowledged that a retrospective law impairing existing debt contracts had the potential to do great harm. "It is true, indeed, sir, that a power like this should be most cautiously exercised," Representative William Fessenden of Maine admitted in 1841. "As a general rule, the obligation of contracts should be held inviolable." But sometimes the rights of the individual citizen "must yield to high considerations of public policy." Emergency relief—or, in Fessenden's words, "sympathy for human suffering"—was not a sufficient justification. Rather, "[l]egislation of this kind must be founded upon higher views . . . which look to the general weal—to national objects."[67]

Collectively the supporters of a federal discharge constructed a compelling case that the reform they desired would indeed "look to the general weal." Their overall argument, spread out across the nineteenth century, began with the simple observation that business failure often resulted from factors and forces beyond the control of individual entrepreneurs. Federal action was especially warranted, they declared, in the wake of severe economic crises, since most recession-related failures could not be blamed on the victims themselves. Representative John Bell of Colorado, a Populist who opposed the House bill in 1898 as being too tough on the unfortunate debtor, offered one of the strongest renditions of the economic crisis argument:

> Many and many of our people who were once buoyant, energetic, and prosperous men of business, whose "words were as good as their bonds," are now loaded down with hopeless, helpless debt, from the burdens of which they can never expect to be extricated except through legislative relief. In multiplied instances their unhappy situation can not justly be ascribed to mere improvident speculation, nor culpable management, nor reckless indiscretion and disregard of usual business methods, but may rather be attributed to the general environment, phenomenal shrinkage in values, abnormal monetary conditions, unforeseen inability to make collections . . . and universal dislocation.[68]

Not surprisingly, numerous proponents of the bill argued along similar lines, implicitly invoking the problem of systematic risk in support of a permanent bankruptcy law.[69]

To stress the unpredictability of panics and depressions, many lawmakers drew analogies to natural disasters, another familiar form of catastrophic risk. "In 1893," Representative Jesse Strode of Nebraska observed, "a great financial panic swept like a mighty, wide, extended, and destructive hurricane over the whole country and left in its wake a vast number of honest, energetic, and enterprising men hopelessly insolvent."[70] Strode supported the House bill in 1898, but even many critics of the bill offered similar analogies. Representative Oscar Underwood of Alabama, a leading opponent of the House bill, noted that all previous federal bankruptcy laws had been enacted "after panics had swept down great numbers of business men, as a cyclone levels the trees in the forest, through no fault of their own, but because they found themselves facing the unforeseen danger and had not opportunity to get out of the way."[71]

The reason why supporters and opponents often seemed to be arguing along similar lines in 1898 is that, as we have seen, they tended to disagree more about the proper duration of a federal bankruptcy law than about whether one should be enacted at all. Almost everyone agreed that some sort of legislative remedy was necessary. But many opponents of the proposed legislation, mainly from the highly indebted southern and western states, believed that the law should apply solely to victims of the depression. In all earlier times, Underwood recollected, "[a]s soon as the storm had passed and the debris had been removed . . . the [bankruptcy] laws were repealed."[72] Southern and western opponents apparently feared that a permanent law would cut through state protections, allowing northern creditors to oppress debtors from every other region. Supporters of a permanent law vehemently disagreed, however. Continuing to highlight advantages for debtors from all regions, they insisted that a permanent bankruptcy system was essential because insolvencies—even ones that could not be blamed on the victims—often occurred outside of economic downturns. "Unmerited failures," declared Representative Richard Parker of New Jersey, "are not occasional but constant."[73]

Central to this argument was the question of what types of events could not reasonably be anticipated, or perhaps insured, by the debtor. The original Bankruptcy Act of 1800 was limited mainly to merchants, since "so great and inevitable were the risks attendant on commerce, that no human prudence could guard against them."[74] When a new bankruptcy bill was being considered by Congress in 1818, Representative Ezekiel Whitman of Massachusetts carried this point several steps further, focusing in particular on the problem of uninsurability. "Every effort of the merchant is surrounded with danger," he noted, "the very basis on which he stands is every moment liable to be swept away. Gentlemen have said that the merchant may insure. . . . He may insure against sea risks and capture. But are these all the risks to which the merchant is liable? Indeed they are not. The risks which overwhelm him are more frequently and almost always, those against which he can have no insurance."[75]

By the early 1840s, some congressmen still claimed that traders alone deserved special treatment on the grounds that only they faced truly extraordinary hazards.[76] But most leading voices in the debate now maintained that virtually all businessmen faced such risks and thus deserved protection in bankruptcy. Representative Jacob Howard of Michigan asked pointedly, "Why, sir, are not all alike liable to misfortune? the doctor, the lawyer, the farmer, as well as the merchant? A thousand casualties await every class, every interest."[77] Lawmakers identified a wide range of causes for these unmerited failures, from wars to ill-advised government meddling in the economy. Senator Robert Strange of North Carolina, for example, spoke passionately about the terrible risks associated with paper money, which "has drawn everyone irresistibly into its vortex . . . so that no man is now secure against those unforeseen accidents which were once peculiar to the trader."[78] This notion that risk was pervasive, that it affected all types of business and at all times (not just during depressions), was emphasized repeatedly—even after the Civil War, when paper money was no longer regarded as a major source of uncertainty in the business world.[79]

For supporters of a liberal bankruptcy law, the emphasis on blameless misfortune was vital, since it would have been much tougher to justify discharging and rehabilitating failed debtors who had deserved to fail. Rehabilitating "losers" would all but guarantee a waste of social resources in the future. Indeed, opponents of a permanent bankruptcy law in 1898 frequently adduced a survival-of-the-fittest argument. Entrepreneurs who failed because of a "widespread and far-reaching epidemic of financial distress" should be rehabilitated through a temporary bankruptcy law, Representative Elijah Lewis of Georgia suggested, but those who failed in good times (and thus who likely deserved to fail) merited no special treatment.[80] One of the most prominent business opponents of a national bankruptcy law in the late nineteenth century, Marshall Field, observed in 1895 that without a bankruptcy law, "the debtor can be driven out of business and kept out."[81]

In countering this line of reasoning, supporters of a permanent law asserted again and again that most debtors who failed—whether in good times or bad—were worth rehabilitating and that a properly written bankruptcy statute would liberate enormous entrepreneurial energy. This claim, in fact, constituted the very heart of their case for bankruptcy discharge. One senator, reading from a circular of the New York Merchants' Exchange in 1840, announced that a bankruptcy law "is warmly advocated" and was seen "as the only means by which a large body of our most meritorious, intelligent, and enterprising fellow citizens can be extricated from embarrassments which the keenest vigilance could not have foreseen, nor the strictest prudence have prevented." A constructive bankruptcy system, the circular continued, "would operate greatly to the advantage of the country at large, by reviving its business and commercial enterprise, in bringing once more into active and successful operation the latent energy, skill, and experience of intelligent and industrious men, who have been prostrated by misfortune, and who look to this source alone for aid."[82]

Nearly identical arguments were adduced at the end of the century. Discharging the honest but unfortunate debtor would advance the national interest by allowing him to reenter the business world, contributing those special energies and skills that he had to offer. Naturally, many insolvent debtors would refrain from working in the absence of a discharge, since every penny earned would immediately be seized by their creditors (under state debtor-creditor law). One congressman, who preferred the more debtor-friendly Senate bill to the House bill in 1898, was greeted with applause on the House floor when he declared, "Let us build up our country by renewing the energies of those in distress and not further retard it by extending Government aid to those [creditors] grinding on the resources and muscles of the toilers."[83]

In both 1841 and 1898 a number of congressmen carried this idea even further, suggesting that a great many bankrupts likely exceeded non-bankrupts in terms of entrepreneurial talent. "Many of those who become victims to the reverses," declared Representative Eugenius Nisbet of Georgia in 1841, "are among the most high-spirited and liberal-minded men of the country—men who build up your cities, sustain your benevolent institutions, open up new avenues to trade, and pour into channels before unfilled the tide of capital." Nisbet went on to describe how two of the entrepreneurs who had helped build the town in which he lived, after becoming very wealthy, ultimately succumbed to the economic crisis of the late 1830s. What should be done with such people? "Viewing this subject in the light of political economy," he answered, "the public will be great gainers by discharging the bankrupts, because thereby you throw into activity a large amount of intellectual and professional capital, which otherwise would be forever lost."[84]

Similarly, Congressman Fessenden estimated in 1841 that when bankrupts were "freed from the shackles that bind them, their labor is not to be estimated by the ordinary standard of day labor." Claiming that they were "[a]s a class . . . the most intelligent and enterprising in the community," he declared that these were the "men that give employment to labor—that pioneer in the enterprises of commerce and manufactures, as well as in mechanical and agricultural pursuits."[85] In 1898, Representative William Sulzer of New York maintained that "[w]ithout such a [bankruptcy] law, properly guarded against frauds, tens of thousands of the most useful men of this generation will be unable to reestablish themselves again in business, and the country will lose the benefit of their energy, their enterprise, their experience and business activities."[86]

Even one of the leading opponents of a permanent law in 1898, Representative Underwood, justified a temporary bankruptcy law along essentially the same lines:

> We all recognize that that class of men who invest their money in bonds and clip their coupons are not our most useful citizens. . . . Our best citizens are those men who invest their money in the development of our country's resources, who build the railroads, open the mines, start the furnaces, factories, and foundries. . . . These are the . . . men . . . who have made us the greatest nation on the globe. . . . [T]hese are the men for whose benefit the sentiment had grown up that a bankrupt law should be passed.[87]

Interestingly, Underwood's implicit preference for active over passive investors was echoed by Representative George Ray of New York, the leading House proponent of a permanent law in 1898.[88]

What is so striking about all of these arguments regarding the advantages of providing a discharge in bankruptcy is their undeniable ex post perspective. The central question in each and every debate was what to do with the debtor once he had failed. Exceedingly little attention was devoted to the potential benefits of encouraging ex ante risk taking—in stark contrast to the limited liability debates, where this was the pivotal argument.[89] Especially from 1840 on, congressional consideration of a discharge provision revolved mainly around the ex post notions of relief and rehabilitation for the "honest but unfortunate debtor." As Representative Fessenden announced on the House floor in 1841, "By the passage of this bill, Mr. Chairman, we raise a very numerous body of our fellow-citizens to a position in which their intelligence and powers of labor are at once made available. Their active services are restored to the community in which they live. The nation is enriched exactly in proportion to their number."[90]

Bankruptcy Discharge versus Limited Liability

Curiously, congressional proponents of bankruptcy discharge never drew explicit comparisons to limited liability, even though both policies were designed to shift a portion of default risk from debtors to creditors. In fact, as we have seen, the original legislative sponsors of bankruptcy discharge and limited liability employed radically different economic logic to justify these two risk management devices. Whereas limited liability was enacted primarily on the basis of ex ante arguments (that it would encourage passive investors to commit their funds to risky projects *before* any failure took place), bankruptcy discharge was passed mainly on the basis of ex post arguments (that it would relieve and resurrect entrepreneurs in the *aftermath* of failure). What accounts for this remarkable divergence in economic reasoning?

One possible answer is that state lawmakers were more inclined to view limited liability from an ex ante perspective because they lacked the constitutional power to limit liability on existing contracts. Yet state lawmakers expressed little if any disappointment at the time about their inability to apply limited liability retroactively. Even more telling, the federal authors of bankruptcy discharge—who did have the power to legislate retroactively—applied their ex post logic of relief and rehabilitation not only retrospectively (to existing debtors) but prospectively as well. Indeed, this is why so many advocates of discharge, particularly in 1898, demanded a permanent statute. They wanted the rehabilitation of failed debtors to become an enduring feature of American law. State legislators who supported limited liability could easily have applied the same ex post logic with respect to future defaults (claiming that limited liability would "rehabilitate" the shareholders of failed corporations), but they rarely did so.

A better explanation stems from the distinction between passive and active investors. As described in Chapter 3, state lawmakers believed that if they did not offer limited liability protection for shareholders, many passive investors would withhold capital from manufacturing corporations located in their states. The underlying logic of this ex ante approach to limited liability was that stop-loss protection would encourage passive investors to "experiment" with some portion of their available funds. Just as the availability of marine insurance encouraged commercial activity, the existence of limited liability would presumably encourage manufacturing activity by attracting additional equity capital from passive investors who were, by nature, risk averse.

But this powerful line of reasoning was hardly ever employed in support of bankruptcy discharge, perhaps because it seemed inapplicable to entrepreneurs, who constituted active rather than passive investors. Experience through the nineteenth century demonstrated that entrepreneurs had been willing to place both their financial and their human capital at risk even in the absence of default insurance or protection in bankruptcy. There was simply no evidence that a discharge was needed to encourage this sort of investment. If anything, entrepreneurs seemed almost too willing to invest in risky projects in the absence of any sort of personal financial safety net. Observing in an 1895 journal article that "over 90 per cent. of those who go into business become bankrupts," John Haynes concluded that this statistic revealed "the great extent to which men go into business when the real probability of loss exceeds the probability of gain."[91] Comparable statistics were also occasionally cited in the congressional bankruptcy debates of the nineteenth century.[92]

Perhaps the problem was that entrepreneurs were susceptible to overoptimism in their business dealings. The legal scholar Thomas Jackson has observed that one possible justification for providing a discharge in bankruptcy is the existence of "incomplete heuristics" (which "makes individuals overly optimistic about the future") as well as the need for "impulse control" to be exerted by cautious creditors.[93] By this reasoning, the creation of a nonwaivable right to discharge would effectively force debtors who might be overly optimistic about their future prospects to buy at least a minimal amount of insurance against the possibility of failure. Such insurance would not only help facilitate recovery in the aftermath of default but also encourage creditors (the implicit insurers) to exercise greater care in monitoring their debtors' undertakings in the first place.

As it turns out, many of the sponsors of a permanent right to discharge seemed to adopt a similar outlook in the nineteenth century. Although they obviously never spoke about "incomplete heuristics," much of their rhetoric was profoundly paternalistic. Central to their case was the idea that entrepreneurs had to be safeguarded against their own mistakes and misfortune—not simply for their own benefit but for that of their creditors and for society as a whole. A discharge, they argued, represented just such a safeguard.

Even before any failure took place, the availability of discharge would encourage better monitoring on the part of creditors. This was one of the only ex ante arguments introduced in support of discharge in the nineteenth century. Objecting to critics who claimed that the law would *"encourage a wild spirit of speculation,"* Senator John Berrien of Georgia maintained that "precisely the opposite must follow from its continued operation." Since the law would *"diminish the security of the creditor,"* he asked, "is it not then most obvious, that it will *increase his caution?* that it will render the creditor more careful *with whom* he deals? *how,* and to *whom* he gives *credit?* . . . This does not seem to me to present any very strong temptation to wild speculation. No sir: the natural effect of a bankrupt law is, to *diminish the amount* of dealings *on credit,* while it renders *those dealings more secure."*[94]

While this argument about monitoring was raised on numerous occasions (particularly during the 1841 debates), considerably more attention was devoted to the implications of discharge in the aftermath of failure. Lawmakers remained acutely aware that in the absence of discharge, entrepreneurs who had defaulted on prior debts were often disinclined or unable to get back in the game. Under most state laws, unpaid creditors had the right to seize almost any new income that their debtor generated, imposing an effective tax rate on the hapless debtor of nearly 100 percent. Facing such a confiscatory tax on new earnings, failed debtors had a strong incentive to reduce their (visible) work effort to zero.[95]

Ideally, the various parties to a debt contract would overcome this sort of stalemate themselves by renegotiating a mutually beneficial arrangement, whereby the debtor could keep some portion of his future earnings and the creditors would be assured of receiving the remainder— that is, something rather than nothing. In practice, however, such arrangements proved exceedingly difficult to negotiate since the consent of every single creditor, from the largest to the smallest, was required. Gamesmanship on the part of individual creditors apparently terminated many negotiations before they ever reached fruition.

Reformers believed that a well-crafted bankruptcy law would help to solve this vicious incentive problem. The establishment of a right to discharge, it was hoped, would increase post-insolvency work effort by eliminating the confiscatory tax on new earnings. Proponents argued that creditors would lose little if anything (because they had little to lose), while debtors would end up getting their lives back. "An enlightened public policy," announced Representative Thomas Ball of Texas in 1898, "demands that a debtor loaded down with debts impossible to be [repayed], with his productive energies so paralyzed that his business undertakings are conducted without profit to himself or creditors, should be permitted to surrender his estate, and, divested of debt, begin anew the race of life."[96]

Again and again, federal lawmakers highlighted how important many of these failed debtors were to the nation's economy and how much society would benefit from their rehabilitation. "Free these chafed and bowed spirits," urged Representative Nisbet in 1841, "let them tread again the land and traverse the sea—give wing to their ardent enterprise—and, my word for it, in most cases, they will pay their debts, and enrich the State by the creation of capital."[97] A little over a half-century later, proponents of a permanent discharge advanced the very same argument. "When you look . . . over this land," exclaimed Congressman Ray in 1898, "and count the thousands of active, energetic, and brainy men who are now tied down, bound hand and foot by a load of debt they never can pay and who, if this law is enacted, will come again to the front and become active, energetic, and useful business men in the community, it seems to me impossible that any man should seek to prevent its speedy enactment."[98]

Whereas limited liability was all about mobilizing the *financial capital* of passive investors, bankruptcy discharge promised to free the precious *human capital* of active ones. Once passive investors had lost their financial capital, society no longer needed them. Subsequent to failure, they had little social value. But active investors, who contributed human as well as financial capital to their investment projects, remained precious even after failing. These entrepreneurs were, in the words of Representative Tallmadge, members of "the most enterprising, intelligent, and active portion of the community."[99] At root, this is why limited liability was justified mainly on ex ante grounds while bankruptcy discharge was justified mainly on ex post. Both policies were forward-looking in that they would affect future economic outcomes, but one focused on mobilizing financial capital *before* failure and the other on releasing human capital in its *aftermath*.

Human Capital, Slavery, and Discharge

Before moving on, we should consider one final explanation for the ex post appeal of bankruptcy discharge that struck a particularly sensitive chord in nineteenth-century America. The establishment of a federal discharge had long been viewed by proponents as a humane step away from the tradability of human capital. Naturally, the abolition of slavery coming out of the Civil War represented the most important step in this direction. But the elimination of debt servitude—first through the abolition of debtors' prisons and now through the provision of discharge in bankruptcy—was also regarded as necessary to carry this policy to its logical conclusion. The creation of a full legal discharge would render unenforceable all private claims on human capital, including contracts that relied on the borrowers' future earnings as collateral for current debts.[100]

As early as 1819, Chief Justice Marshall had observed that in the absence of bankruptcy law, human capital should be as liable to attachment by deserving creditors as physical capital. "Industry, talents, and integrity," he explained, "constitute a fund which is as confidently trusted as property itself." Creditors could reach this human capital through claims on their debtors' "future acquisitions."[101] But this was precisely the practice that opponents of debt servitude wished to end. As Representative James Connolly of Illinois declared in the 1898 debates: "The insolvent trader—the trader unable to pay his debts—is today a slave absolutely to every creditor that he owes. He is as thoroughly within prison bars as any man who is actually there. He is no longer a free man." Harkening back to the days of Lincoln, he asked, "If it was good policy to emancipate the slave of the South . . . why is it not equally proper to lift up the white brother, to strike off the shackles from him, and let him also stand in God's pure sunlight a free man, and begin again the manly struggle for subsistence?"[102] Representative Burke of Texas set off enthusiastic applause on the House floor when he urged his fellow lawmakers, "Let Congress . . . declare by the passage of this bill that . . . financial bondage shall cease in this land."[103]

Even before the abolition of slavery in the 1860s, proponents of bankruptcy law had condemned debt servitude (and thus the legal impairment of human capital) as a violation of constitutional principles. Insolvent debtors, Daniel Webster intoned, "find themselves bondsmen, because we will not execute the commands of the Constitution [to enact a bankruptcy law]; bondsmen to debts they can not pay, and which all know they can not pay, and which take away the power of supporting themselves. Other slaves have masters charged with the duty of support and protection; but their masters neither clothe, nor feed, nor shelter; they only bind."[104] Providing anything less than a full and complete discharge would have amounted to an acceptance of debt servitude and a violation of the sanctity of human capital.[105] On both economic and moral grounds, therefore, the protection of human capital proved central to the enactment of bankruptcy discharge in the nineteenth century.

Conclusion

Clearly, bankruptcy is a complex institution serving a variety of different purposes. One of its most basic functions, however, is to shift a portion of default risk from debtors to creditors (via the discharge provision). Designed with the goal of fostering investment and economic growth, nineteenth-century federal bankruptcy law constituted a classic Phase I risk management policy.

To be sure, the logic underlying bankruptcy law was distinctive, revolving around the ex post benefits of relieving and rehabilitating failed entrepreneurs. In sharp contrast to limited liability law, bankruptcy law was designed to liberate human—rather than financial—capital. But the broader objective of promoting economic development through the reallocation of risk was common to each of the major Phase I initiatives, including not only bankruptcy law but limited liability and banking regulation as well. It is no accident that all three of these policies have come to be viewed as vital institutional pillars of the nation's capitalist economic system.

Although the twentieth century saw the dawn of a new phase in American risk management policy, geared more toward worker security than economic growth, it is not as if the change was absolute or that it occurred all at once, at the stroke of midnight on December 31, 1899. Landmark Phase I policies such as limited liability and bankruptcy remained very much alive in the new century, and lawmakers continued to introduce some significant Phase I innovations, including federal deposit insurance in 1933. Even within bankruptcy law, new provisions for business reorganization were codified in the years 1933 to 1938, designed to facilitate the rehabilitation of distressed corporations just as discharge provisions in earlier acts were designed to rehabilitate distressed entrepreneurs.[106]

Nevertheless, a considerable change in the tenor and scope of risk management policy *was* evident in the early twentieth century. The traditional goal of promoting trade and investment (Phase I) was increasingly rivaled by the newer goal of promoting security for the nation's workers (Phase II). This change was visible across a wide range of issues, from unemployment to old age security. But nowhere was the change more striking than in the law of accidents, where a long-standing judicial strategy of diverting risk away from business (to encourage industrial investment) was almost completely inverted. As will become clear in the next chapter, the enactment of workers' compensation laws in the 1910s represented a critical first step in this remarkable transformation of American risk management policy.

6

Workers' Insurance

As the nineteenth century gave way to the twentieth, worker insecurity was fast becoming a major political issue. The economist John Commons observed in 1894 that the "seriousness of the problem of poverty today is not that there are greater numbers of poor . . . than ever before, but that greater numbers are constantly on the verge of poverty."[1] For the typical worker, now almost completely dependent on money wages, even a temporary loss of income could prove catastrophic.

The five leading hazards facing every American worker were accidents, illness, premature death, unemployment, and disability and old age.[2] Although none of these risks was new at the turn of the century, a growing band of reformers believed that rapid industrialization had rendered them more destructive than ever before. "[They] fall with crushing force on the families which suffer from them," remarked Columbia University professor Henry Seager, "and only too often reduce such families from a position of independence and self-respect to one of humiliating and efficiency-destroying social dependency."[3]

Beginning in the early twentieth century, reform-minded social scientists like Commons and Seager championed government-mandated insurance as the most appropriate solution to this festering problem. Their colleague at the American Association for Labor Legislation, John Andrews, declared in 1915, "Since the efforts of individual workmen have proven so futile, it seems time for the state to step in."[4] In spearheading a national campaign for social insurance, these reformers—the vanguard of Phase II—ended up exerting an enormous impact on the country. The shift in emphasis from business security to worker security which they helped bring about was itself profound, as was the expansion of government authority that ultimately went along with it.

By the mid-twentieth century, workers' compensation, unemployment insurance, and old age insurance had all emerged as permanent fixtures of American life. Government had become a major insurer in its own right, changing forever public expectations about its place and purpose in society. Today, at the dawn of the twenty-first century, Americans spend more on social insurance than on any other type of government program, including national defense. Largely taken for granted now, this degree of government involvement in the lives of everyday workers was almost unimaginable at the dawn of the twentieth century.

Social insurance remained highly controversial at least through the 1930s. Critics regularly attacked the idea as un-American and socialistic. Facing proposals for compulsory public health insurance in 1916, the president of the Great Eastern Casualty Company urged everyone in the insurance industry to "do all in your power . . . to combat this pernicious un-American idea of State Insurance."[5] Until the Great Depression, even many of the nation's top labor leaders, such as Samuel Gompers, fiercely opposed compulsory unemployment and health insurance as antithetical to the principles of personal liberty and voluntarism.[6] Although organized labor ultimately changed sides during the 1930s, not everyone underwent the same conversion. A vocal member of Congress bitterly denounced FDR's social security bill in 1935 as "simply one more step toward sovietizing our distinctive American institutions, devitalizing the self-reliance and enterprise of our people, and mortgaging our future."[7]

As some of the more discerning critics of social insurance pointed out, a broad range of insurance coverage was already available in the private sector, through commercial carriers, fraternal orders, unions, and employers. With all of these private options, they asked, why was it necessary for the government to intervene?[8] This was the single most important question that social insurance proponents had to answer. They had to explain to a skeptical public why, in Andrews' words, it was "time for the state to step in." Indeed, advocates of compulsory health insurance have continued to struggle with precisely the same question ever since.

During the Progressive Era (roughly 1900 to 1920), leading reformers regularly highlighted large holes in the nation's private insurance umbrella. Prior to the enactment of social insurance laws, most workers had managed to insure themselves for little more than funeral expenses through industrial life insurance or fraternal societies. Although some union members enjoyed more extensive coverage, only a relatively small minority of America's workers actually belonged to unions. The majority had little or no coverage against industrial accidents, illness, unemployment, or permanent loss of income owing to disability or old age.

Even more damning, many reformers charged that the costs of industrial hazards were being systematically misallocated in the private labor market. Effectively insulated from the worst industrial risks, employers were said to be underinvesting in both preventive measures and commercial insurance coverage. Social insurance laws that penalized employers exhibiting unusually high rates of unemployment, illness, or any other hazard would help shift industrial risks from workers onto employers. Such laws, the reformers argued, would not only ensure adequate compensation for the victims but also maximize employer incentives for prevention, thus helping to reduce the overall level of risk facing the nation's workers. This was the logic that dominated social insurance debates through the second decade of the twentieth century.

The Rise of Worker Insecurity

Though by no means unknown in earlier years, worker risks such as accidents, illness, and unemployment began to assume new prominence in the late nineteenth and early twentieth centuries. The increasingly sharp contrast between a burgeoning national economy and a growing cadre of broken-down workers heightened awareness. "Notwithstanding the remarkable economic progress of the nineteenth century," lamented Henry Seager in 1907, "the civilized world enters the twentieth century with the problem of poverty seemingly as far from a solution as ever." Seager, a future president of the American Association for Labor Legislation (AALL), was quick to blame the destitution of a great many workers on "the contingencies which drag them down."[9]

As Seager's words suggest, rapid industrialization seemed to intensify worker risks even as it generated fabulous increases in national income. While millions of workers headed for the cities in search of higher wages, many were leaving behind the traditional security of agricultural life. The urban industrial worker no longer enjoyed immediate access to food on the farm in hard times. Urbanization also disrupted vital family support networks. The extended family had long served as a critical risk management device in rural communities. When one family member fell sick or was otherwise incapacitated for a lengthy period, others often lent a hand to support him and his dependents. Rural neighbors frequently filled in as well. Having separated from family and farm, however, the typical industrial worker was left entirely dependent on his wages, which meant that a sudden decline or cessation of income could easily impoverish him and his family.[10]

Urbanization, moreover, was but one part of the growing problem of worker insecurity. The increased pace and intensity of work on railroads, in mines, and in energy-intensive manufacturing operations sharply raised the risk of accidents on the job. Railroad work and mining were especially dangerous. For the nation as a whole in 1910, almost 5 percent of the labor force worked in the railroad industry, about 3 percent in mining, and 31 percent in agriculture. (See Table 6.1.) Yet in Minnesota, a state which produced unusually detailed accident data in 1910, railroads accounted for 26 percent of fatal accidents (20 percent of nonfatal), mining for 24 percent (43 percent of nonfatal), and agriculture for only 3.5 percent (0.5 percent of nonfatal).[11] During the first six months of 1914 in California, 13 percent of fatal accidents occurred in the railroad sector, 10 percent in mining and smelting, and 9 percent in agriculture.[12]

No doubt there was a tendency—especially among reformers—to exaggerate the increased risk stemming from modern industry. High accident rates on the railroads were well documented, but gruesome stories

Table 6.1   The transformation of the U.S. labor force, 1840–1930

| Year | Labor force | Employment in selected industries as a percent of total labor force | | | | | |
		Agriculture	Construction	Trade	Manufacturing	Mining	Railroads
1840	5,660,000	63.1	5.1	6.2	8.8	0.6	0.1
1880	17,390,000	51.3	5.2	11.1	18.9	1.6	2.4
1910	37,480,000	31.4	5.2	14.2	22.2	2.8	4.9
1930	48,830,000	21.6	4.1	16.6	20.2	2.1	3.4

Source: U.S. Department of Commerce, Bureau of the Census, *Historical Statistics of the United States, Colonial Times to 1970* (Washington, D.C.: GPO, 1975), ser. D 167–181, p. 139.

about workers getting crushed to death while trying to couple cars or decapitated while passing beneath low bridges made the risks of railway work seem even higher than they actually were. Horrifying examples from other industries produced the same effect. One expert warned in 1915 that "our practice of declaring nearly or quite all branches of manufacturing . . . 'especially dangerous' or 'extra hazardous' . . . is a transparent subterfuge." The risk of accident in agricultural work, he suggested, was much higher than commonly thought.[13]

Nevertheless, heavy industry probably did introduce a greater degree of accident risk in employment; and there is no doubt that this was widely believed to be true at the time. I. M. Rubinow, the noted actuary and social reformer, announced in 1904, "Year in and year out industrial workers will give a larger percentage of injured than agricultural workers, and railroad and mine employees a larger percentage of injured than any other branch of industrial activity."[14] Similar arguments were advanced about occupational disease as well. Industrial laborers were thought to face an increased risk of illness compared to agricultural workers. This was due not only to the prevalence of specific toxins such as lead and phosphorous in industrial processes, but also to more general unhealthful conditions, such as poor ventilation, which were common in America's factories and mines.[15]

Although Europeans were moving rapidly into many of the same industries as the Americans, injury rates were apparently much higher in the United States. One commonly cited statistic was that American railroads employed twice as many workers as their British counterparts but killed four times as many of them.[16] Higher accident rates in the United States were frequently attributed to the more vigorous pursuit of industry—"the incomparable energy, restlessness and fearlessness of American workingmen, of the relatively high intensity of work in American shops and factories, and of the vastly greater use that our people make of machinery."[17]

Even apart from the intensity of industrial work, it was thought that the advance of ever more sophisticated industrial enterprises increased worker insecurity by disempowering the worker and depersonalizing the underlying employment relationship. The rise of large-scale industry, the bureaucratization of employer-employee relations, and the divorce of wage earners from the tools of production tended to sever any personal connection between owners and workers and to reduce the control individual laborers exercised over the production process. At the AALL's First American Conference on Social Insurance in June 1913, its president, William F. Willoughby, directly attributed the worldwide movement for social insurance to the fact that rapid industrialization had left workers alienated and insecure. "They have become almost literally but parts of a great impersonal mechanism," he noted poignantly. "Their relation to this mechanism differs but little from that of the inanimate agencies employed. When disabled through old age or failing powers, and when not needed through a reduction in the scale of operations, they are discarded as other useless parts."[18]

Closely associated with these industrial developments were changing ideas about fault. Particularly in the case of industrial accidents, fault seemed increasingly difficult to identify and assign with any accuracy. "It must be clear, upon reflection," observed Adna Weber, a statistician at the New York State Department of Labor, "that the conditions under which modern industry is carried on preclude the possibility of explaining every accident by somebody's negligence."[19] This point was highlighted again and again in the late nineteenth and early twentieth centuries, not only by academics and reformers but by legislators and judges as well.[20] One of the most frequently cited studies was the Pittsburgh Survey of 1907–8. Crystal Eastman concluded from the Pittsburgh data that out of 410 work-accident fatalities for which sufficient information was available, employers were partly or solely responsible for 147, foremen for 49, fellow workers for 56, and the victims themselves for 132 (of which only 68 were due to the fault of the victim alone). Perhaps most striking of all, she classified 117 accidents, or 28.5 percent of the total, as unavoidable because there existed no basis for assigning any blame at all.[21]

Assumptions about the causes of another major hazard, unemployment, appear to have been moving in the same direction. There was an increasing tendency beginning in the late nineteenth century to blame unemployment on the industrial system rather than on the jobless themselves. "The funny-paper jokes about Weary Willy and Ragged Rufus," observed William Hard at the AALL's fifth annual meeting in 1911, "have passed their meridian and now for some time have been declining into twilight and oblivion. Unemployment has ceased in America to be a joke." Instead, "[u]nemployment begins to be considered, even in the most popular of magazines, as a characteristic of that sponge which we call industry . . . a process in which control lies rather with the sponge than with the water."[22] Borrowing a phrase from the British unemployment expert William Beveridge, others at the AALL commonly referred to joblessness as a "problem of industry."[23] How successful these reformers were in transforming public opinion about unemployment is a matter of some debate.[24] But at the very least, it seems that the public had gradually come to accept the possibility—particularly during sharp economic downturns—that a substantial fraction of unemployed workers had lost their jobs through no fault of their own.[25]

This notion of blameless misfortune helped to distinguish social insurance from poor relief. So long as the public believed individual workers were primarily to blame for their own accidents or unemployment, "insurance" would be viewed as little more than a transfer payment from "good" workers to "bad" ones. Evolving attitudes about fault thus represented an important development. Combined with the deterioration of traditional family safety nets and the increased riskiness of industrial work, these changes in the public's conceptions of blame and responsibility dramatically increased the attractiveness and the apparent feasibility of broad-based workers' insurance.

Indeed, a crude form of life insurance, known as industrial life insurance, had begun to spread among American wage earners in the late nineteenth century. Originating in Britain in 1850, industrial life insurance arrived in the United States in 1875, courtesy of the Prudential Insurance Company. Covered workers typically paid between 5 and 25 cents per week for policies valued in the vicinity of $100. The insurance was remarkably expensive in actuarial terms, and the average payout hardly sufficient to support a family for very long. But many workers took comfort in the idea that funeral expenses would be covered and that their families would enjoy small financial cushions in their time of need. Indicative of the mounting demand for economic security, industrial life insurance spread rapidly after its introduction in the United States. Between 1876 and 1910, the value of industrial life insurance in force increased from $400,000 to over $3 billion, and the number of policies exploded upward from just 8,416 to 22.3 million over the same years.[26]

Family budget studies from the early twentieth century indicated that wage earners were typically spending between 2 and 4 percent of their modest incomes on insurance of various kinds.[27] Industrial life insurance premiums absorbed the lion's share of these expenditures, but workers also bought insurance against a wide range of other hazards—from accidents to illness to unemployment—through casualty companies, fraternal societies, trade unions, and company funds. The diversity of policies and coverage available was truly remarkable, and a good deal of experimentation was going on all the time.[28]

Well aware of these trends in the private sector, many progressive reformers still believed that government intervention was required. Industrial life insurance, they insisted, was absurdly expensive, in large measure because of the high cost of weekly door-to-door premium collections. In 1904, fourteen industrial life insurance providers collected $110 million in premiums on 15.6 million policies, but they paid out only a little over $31 million in claims.[29] When "people of wealth" discovered that they had paid too much for a policy, the sociologist Charles Richmond Henderson suggested, "their business training enables them to discover legal means of redress and correction. But the majority of wage-earners are not in like situation."[30] Industrial life insurance thus struck many of these reformers as exploitative. Nor were they much happier with the insurance programs of fraternal societies and labor unions, since most of them rested on extremely shaky financial foundations. Short on reserves, these funds often provided far less security than participants were led to believe.[31]

Above all, social insurance advocates protested that few workers participating in private plans enjoyed comprehensive coverage against the full array of industrial hazards. Private coverage was spotty at best; and private benefits, when they were paid at all, were often inadequate to keep insured families out of poverty. As two of the leading students of compulsory health insurance, John R. Commons and Arthur J. Altmeyer, wrote in 1919, "Advocates of compulsory health insurance believe that existing voluntary insurance carriers cannot take care of the problem, because not enough people are insured and those who are insured as a rule carry only enough to provide funeral expenses."[32] Henry Seager stated flatly that "experience everywhere has shown that voluntary insurance will not reach the classes which need it most."[33]

Worker insecurity had clearly emerged as a major social problem by the early twentieth century. The fact that workers were paying a small fortune for the feeble private coverage to which they had access was evidence enough for many contemporary observers. Although no political consensus had yet developed in the United States on how to deal with the problem, a small group of reformers (including Commons, Seager, and others at the AALL) believed that the answer lay just across the Atlantic, where government-mandated insurance had already been widely adopted. It was time, they believed, for the new world finally to catch up with the old.

The United States as a Social Insurance Laggard

European legislatures had begun establishing public insurance for their workers in the late nineteenth century. Germany led the way, adopting compulsory health insurance, workers' compensation (workplace accident insurance), and old age and invalidity insurance between 1883 and 1889. Britain followed a bit later, enacting workers' compensation in 1897, old age pensions in 1908, and health and unemployment insurance in 1911. In fact, almost every country in Europe had erected one or more forms of compulsory workers' insurance by the first year of the new century.[34] "When we come to study the status of labor insurance in this country," Rubinow lamented in 1904, "we cannot help feeling somewhat abashed at the comparison [to Europe]."[35]

The causes of America's tardiness in enacting social insurance laws seemed plain enough at the time. Most striking of all was what Adna Weber characterized as the nation's "prevalent individualistic philosophy."[36] Americans had long viewed big government as distasteful and threatening. Not only were most citizens fully capable of looking after themselves, the standard argument ran, but also they were generally at their best when doing so. Paternalistic public policies threatened to foster dependency and demoralize the recipients. Although advocates of social insurance worked hard to distinguish public insurance from public relief, it was a tough sell in the United States, especially in the early years.[37]

Reinforcing these anti-statist attitudes were numerous constitutional constraints, which often proved even less forgiving than public opinion. In 1915, Henry Seager characterized due process as the "constitutional rock" on which most progressive reforms foundered in the United States. "If New York state and other American states are today behind progressive European countries in the field of social and labor legislation," Seager insisted, "it is chiefly because of this constitutional barrier."[38] The so-called liberty-of-contract doctrine and the constitutional prohibition on class legislation also proved to be major obstacles on the road to labor legislation. Having already stuck down numerous state statutes regulating wages, hours, and other working conditions, the courts were quick to overturn state social insurance laws as well.

The very first workers' compensation law in the United States, enacted in Maryland in 1902, was declared unconstitutional just two years later, as were the next two laws, passed in Montana and New York in 1910.[39] Ruling on the New York law, which was the most comprehensive of the three, Judge William Werner declared unequivocally that "the liability sought to be imposed upon the employers enumerated in the statute before us is a taking of property without due process of law, and the statute is therefore void."[40] Due process had struck again. Although social insurance advocates would ultimately find ways around these legal barriers, and the courts themselves would later relax many of their restrictions, constitutional constraints loomed large in the early twentieth century.

Complicating the legislative situation still further was the reality of competition among the states. State lawmakers were always wary of enacting new pieces of labor legislation—including social insurance—for fear of placing their firms at a competitive disadvantage relative to rivals in other states.[41] A Massachusetts bill modeled on the British Compensation Act of 1897 failed in 1904 after manufacturers claimed "that the indemnities required of them would cripple them in competing with manufacturers of other states."[42] The very same argument was used repeatedly against unemployment and health insurance as well. "[S]uch legislation," complained the author of a 1916 article in the trade journal *Iron Age*, would compel "manufacturers to move their works out of State."[43]

Though discouraged by these obstacles, many social reformers persevered year after year, absolutely convinced that industrial hazards represented a social problem of enormous proportions and that social insurance was the best possible solution. More than any other organization or interest group, the American Association for Labor Legislation led the campaign in the United States during the 1910s. Composed mainly of social scientists, social workers, and a few business and labor leaders, the AALL helped set the legislative agenda in numerous states, while carefully identifying and publicizing the most compelling arguments for each form of social insurance. Its leadership focused first on the problem of industrial accidents and the promise of workers' compensation laws.[44]

Workers' Compensation

During the first decade of the twentieth century, perhaps 15,000 worker deaths were attributable to industrial activity each year.[45] Coal miners and railroad employees, as we have seen, were especially vulnerable. Of the 4 million bituminous coal miners employed in the United States from 1899 to 1908, 13,717 (or almost 1,400 per year) died as a result of industrial accidents. The fatality rate was even higher among certain classes of railroad workers. Between 1898 and 1907, 17,924 of the nation's 2.35 million railway trainmen were killed in job-related accidents.[46]

Although workers injured on the job had always been able to sue their employers for damages, reformers claimed that the nation's employer liability system was deeply flawed. Consistent with the basic logic of Phase I risk management policy, nineteenth-century judges had created a set of employer defenses that made it exceedingly difficult for injured employees to recover anything unless their employers were entirely at fault. Although these defenses probably bolstered investment in hazardous industries such as railroads and mining, they also left workers with little recourse or support in the aftermath of accidents. According to one legal historian, the employer liability system was best characterized as "a noncompensation system or a system for discouraging claims."[47]

The three most important employer defenses in the nineteenth century were contributory negligence, the fellow-servant rule, and assumption of risk. Under contributory negligence, an employer could avoid all damages if the injured worker had been in any way negligent himself. Even if the court found that the employee was only 5 percent to blame for the accident, he was not entitled to any damages whatsoever. The fellow-servant rule, meanwhile, barred recovery if another worker, rather than the employer himself, had caused the accident. Finally, if an employer could show that the injured employee had known the dangers associated with the job—had "assumed the risk"—when she accepted employment, then the employer could escape all liability. According to Massachusetts Chief Justice Lemuel Shaw in a landmark decision of 1842, "[H]e who engages in the employment of another for the performance of specified duties and services, for compensation, takes upon himself the natural and ordinary risks and perils incident to the performance of such services."[48]

A number of state legislatures began paring back these employer defenses around the turn of the century. Still, successful employee recovery remained more the exception than the rule. As late as 1911, Henry Seager described the employer liability system as "a complete failure."[49] The whole idea of basing the system on fault, reformers insisted, was simply anachronistic in the modern industrial era, since blame was often impossible to determine in individual cases and culpability could only rarely be attributed to one party alone. Against this backdrop, the contributory negligence defense struck them as particularly unfair.

Reformers challenged the fellow-servant rule as well, characterizing it as a curious and unwelcome exception to mainstream liability law. Under the doctrine of *respondeat superior*, principals were normally held responsible for the negligence of their agents. If the driver of a delivery wagon negligently ran down a pedestrian on the road, the latter could sue the owner of the delivery service (not just the driver) for damages. But the fellow-servant rule broke this chain of responsibility in the workplace. When a worker was injured on the job, his employer was not responsible for the misdeeds of fellow workers.[50] Dissenting from an 1880 decision of the New York Court of Appeals, Judge Robert Earl cautioned that this particular limitation of employer responsibility had "no foundation in abstract or natural justice, and all attempts to place it upon any other foundation than that of public policy will prove unsatisfactory when brought to the test of careful and logical analysis."[51] By the early twentieth century, this sort of critique had become commonplace. Once lauded as a bulwark of both industrial justice and business promotion, the fellow-servant rule was now the target of almost constant criticism.

Many reformers showed even more contempt for the assumption-of-risk doctrine. Although assumption of risk was a powerful employer defense in its own right, it was also frequently put forth as a justification for the fellow-servant rule.[52] Adna Weber dismissed the doctrine out of hand in 1902 as "legal fiction [with] no basis in fact."[53] Judge Earl had used precisely the same word, "fiction," when discussing assumption of risk in 1880.[54] By 1910, a New York State commission set up to investigate the problem of industrial accidents concluded, much like Weber and Earl, that "under modern industrial conditions the individual workman consents and assumes the risk only because in the ordinary case he has no option to do anything else."[55]

Even beyond these defenses, the employer liability system was roundly criticized for its inefficiency in compensating victims. Of all the money collected through employer liability insurance premiums, surprisingly little was actually paid out to injured workers. In 1887, insurance companies collected $203,132 in premiums and paid out only $32,924 in losses. By 1908, the payout rate had increased considerably, as had the total amount of coverage. But insurers were still paying only $10 million in losses on premiums of nearly $28 million.[56] "As a rule," Commons and Andrews observed, "the insurance companies act as if their duty under employers' liability law is not to compensate the injured, but to defeat their claims."[57]

Employer liability law thus seemed especially ill suited to the needs of the nation's workers. It was heavily biased against them in many respects. Yet the system ultimately provoked the ire of employers as well as employees. Though uncommon, large court judgments in favor of injured workers did occur from time to time—a fact which generated considerable anxiety among employers. "The always threatening possibility of having to pay heavy damages as the result of an accident," Crystal Eastman reported, "puts [the employer] to the expense of maintaining a special claim department and hiring expert attorneys, although he rarely pays a verdict."[58] Some employers offered to provide accident insurance for employees who voluntarily waived their right to sue, but these arrangements were not generally recognized as valid in court once an accident actually occurred.[59]

The best solution, reformers at the AALL insisted, was for the states to enact workers' compensation laws. These laws would compel employers to buy or provide accident insurance for all their workers and, at the same time, would largely eliminate the employer liability system. Because injured workers would no longer have the right to sue for damages, huge awards—which were already rare—would disappear altogether. Every injured worker, meanwhile, would now be entitled to compensation according to a state-determined schedule of benefits, regardless of fault. Proponents maintained that with a workers' compensation system in place, families would no longer have to fear falling into poverty as a result of industrial accidents.

Nor was guaranteed compensation the only advantage. Adding a distinctively American twist to the standard European arguments for social insurance, reform-minded economists like Commons and Andrews claimed that well-structured workers' compensation laws would create powerful employer incentives for prevention, dramatically reducing the total number of accidents.[60] Characterizing workers' compensation as a special type of tax, Commons explained in 1919, "We tax his accidents, and [the employer] puts his best abilities in to get rid of them."[61] Elsewhere, he described workers' compensation "as a kind of social pressure brought to bear upon all employers in order to make them devote as much attention to the prevention of accidents and to the speedy recovery from accidents as they do to the manufacture and sale of the products."[62]

At the heart of the prevention argument was one simple idea: that the private market failed to locate the consequences of accident risk in the proper place. Most leading reformers believed that the burden ought to have been shifted onto the employer and then finally onto the consumer (via higher prices), since employers and consumers were the ultimate beneficiaries of production. "It is for the benefit of consumers that production is carried on," said Seager, "and they should be made to pay—so far as this can be measured in money—what goods cost in maimed bodies and shortened lives as well as what they cost in hours of work and used-up raw materials."[63] As it turned out, however, the cost of accidents was generally borne by the workers themselves. This implied that employers faced an inadequate incentive to prevent accidents and, by extension, that thousands of workers were being killed and maimed needlessly.

The employer liability system surely exacerbated this problem, since the various employer defenses made successful worker suits exceedingly difficult. But even if workers had enjoyed no right to recovery at all, a well-functioning labor market should have shifted the costs of industrial accidents onto employers (and ultimately onto consumers) through the mechanism of compensating wage differentials. As Adam Smith observed in his *Wealth of Nations* in 1776, "[t]he wages of labour vary with the ease or hardship, the cleanliness or dirtiness, the honourableness or dishonourableness of the employment."[64] Smith's reasoning suggested that in an unusually dangerous industry like coal mining, workers should have received a higher than normal wage to compensate for the extra risk involved. In this way, the market would prod employers in dangerous industries to invest in safety equipment and other preventive measures. Employers who reduced their accident rates would be rewarded with lower wage bills, since workers would no longer require such high risk premiums.

According to Seager, speaking at the first annual meeting of the AALL in 1907, the theory of compensating wage differentials "is so plausible that it might still be accepted if it were not completely disproved by the facts. Wage statistics show, however, that wages in dangerous trades are little, if at all, higher than in comparatively safe employments."[65] Although several recent academic studies have cast some doubt on Seager's observation, suggesting the existence of modest compensating differentials in the late nineteenth and early twentieth centuries, Seager's view was widely accepted at the time.[66] He certainly appears to have convinced New York's Wainwright Commission on industrial accidents, which concluded that the "theory does not work out. Wages are not relatively higher in the most dangerous trades."[67]

In Seager's view, this failure in the private market grew out of two interrelated problems. Like Adna Weber, who dismissed the assumption-of-risk doctrine as a "legal fiction," Seager doubted that meaningful labor contracts always existed in reality. "[T]he unequal bargaining power between employer and employe [sic] and the resulting absence of a free and voluntary contract between them in the determination of labor conditions is being more and more recognized," he wrote in 1915.[68]

A second problem, according to Seager, was that even when such labor contracts did exist, many workers so underestimated their odds of getting hurt that they failed to demand appropriate risk premiums for hazardous employment. While some workers were simply ignorant of the true hazards involved in their jobs, countless others seemed to give little thought to the future or to view themselves as immune to injury, regardless of the hazards they faced.[69] Each individual worker, Seager suggested in 1907, "thinks of himself as having a charmed life."[70] Three years later, he explained that the "average workman, whatever his employment, is an optimist. He may know that a certain proportion of his fellow-workmen is likely to be killed every year and a larger proportion injured, but he personally does not expect to be either injured or killed."[71] Modern psychologists would characterize this as a problem of optimistic bias. But whatever its appellation, it may well have undermined market pressure for accident prevention in the early twentieth century.

In search of a solution, many state legislatures moved to weaken the traditional employer defenses. But a growing number of critics claimed that employer liability law would never provide an optimal means of preventing accidents, regardless of how it was structured or whom it favored. As one of the chief purveyors of this argument, John Commons cleverly differentiated between the legal liability associated with accidents and the accidents themselves. Employer liability law, he argued in 1909, created an employer interest in minimizing the former but not necessarily the latter. The distinction meant that an employer might invest in expensive legal services instead of safety devices in order to avoid liability. Under a system of workers' compensation, by contrast, expensive legal advice would be of little help, since automatic payments to accident victims would supersede negligence law. The employer's only means of lowering costs when confronted with a workers' compensation law, advocates insisted, would be to lower the number and severity of accidents and related medical costs.[72]

At the same time, compulsory accident insurance promised to spread the residual risk of accidents across the entire workforce, thereby reducing worker anxiety and averting impoverishment. Although the compensation side of workers' compensation was obviously important, reformers at the AALL consistently emphasized prevention as an even more fundamental objective. As Andrews once told a staff member at the association, "Prof. Commons and I in all of the work we have done together have thought first of prevention and second of relief in dealing with each form of social insurance in this country."[73]

Supremely confident in their arguments, progressive reformers continued to campaign aggressively for workers' compensation even after their humiliating defeat at the hands of Judge Werner in New York. Seager later recalled that the *Ives* decision striking down New York's compulsory workers' compensation law in 1911 was "doubly disappointing. Our act was maimed and twisted so that it might commend itself to the judges, and, notwithstanding our efforts, those judges unanimously condemned it as unconstitutional."[74] Although many lawmakers across the country took *Ives* as a signal that they had better enact elective rather than compulsory workers' compensation laws, reformers at the AALL decided to redouble their efforts in support of compulsory legislation.[75] If the state constitution was the obstacle, they reasoned, then it was their "clear and manifest duty" to amend it.[76] And that is precisely what they set out to do.

Even though the road ahead looked long and hard, victory turned out to be closer than almost anyone had anticipated. Workers' compensation was less controversial than it appeared because a considerable number of influential employers supported the basic idea, if not all the details, of the proposed legislation.[77] The AALL reformers finally saw their constitutional amendment ratified and a new, compulsory workers' compensation law inaugurated in New York in the concluding weeks of 1913. "The enactment of the Glynn Workmen's Compensation Act by the New York legislature on December 12th," wrote Andrews in a letter to AALL members, "marks the culmination of a long struggle in which this Association has played an honorable part." The New York statute, he noted with obvious pride, represented "the best and most carefully drawn compensation law that has yet been passed by any American state."[78]

Strangely, when the New York Court of Appeals ruled on the new law's constitutionality two years later, the decision seemed almost to suggest that a constitutional amendment had never been required in the first place. Compulsory insurance, the court now announced, was perfectly legitimate so long as a vital public purpose was involved. As precedent, the New York court cited a recent U.S. Supreme Court opinion upholding—of all things—a compulsory deposit insurance statute in Oklahoma. "A compulsory scheme of insurance to secure injured workmen in hazardous employments and their dependents from becoming objects of charity," the court concluded, "certainly promotes the public welfare as directly as does an insurance of bank depositors from loss."[79] The essential connection between these two powerful forms of public risk management, deposit insurance and workers' insurance, could not have been clearer.

In any case, just as defeat in 1911 had led to the enactment of numerous elective laws, success in 1913–1915 helped accelerate the enactment of mandatory workers' compensation laws all across the country. By 1920, the vast majority of states had enacted some form of workers' compensation, and many of these laws were compulsory. Seven states mandated exclusive state insurance funds, but all the rest permitted commercial carriers to provide the requisite coverage.[80] Although few state laws were as generous as New York's (which included a compensation scale set at two-thirds of wages for total disability), many gravitated in this direction over subsequent years.[81] The nation's first major experiment with social insurance was now well under way.

Compulsory Health and Unemployment Insurance

The leaders of the AALL turned their attention to compulsory health and unemployment insurance beginning in 1914. Still basking in the glow of their constitutional and legislative victories in New York, they were utterly confident, especially about health insurance. "It is coming. It is inevitable, and you, I am sure, will help bring it about," said John Andrews at the association's annual meeting in 1916.[82] Since their workers' compensation strategy had been so successful, all that seemed necessary was to apply it again—with perhaps just a few modifications here and there. Obstacles would no doubt pop up from time to time, but the direction of change seemed clear. American workers, leading reformers predicted, would soon enjoy the benefits of comprehensive social insurance coverage.

Although proponents at the AALL were quick to highlight the advantages of assured compensation for workers who fell sick or were laid off, their key arguments for compulsory health and unemployment insurance again revolved mainly around prevention. Just as workers' compensation was expected to create powerful incentives for the prevention of industrial accidents, compulsory health and unemployment insurance were supposed to induce employers to fight occupational disease and to minimize layoffs. "It is amazing what business can accomplish when it has a sufficient inducement," Commons remarked some years later. Once the financial costs were located in the right place, the worst hazards facing America's workers would be greatly reduced.[83]

As early as 1910, an AALL committee on occupational disease estimated the economic cost of sickness in the United States at $773 million annually, of which one-fourth ($193 million) was thought to be preventable.[84] At the time, the organization was still struggling to combat worker hazards through direct risk-reduction techniques, rather than through risk shifting or risk spreading. In their campaign against phosphorus poisoning in the match industry, for example, AALL reformers sought to reduce the risk to workers by prohibiting use of a key toxin, white phosphorus.[85] Their battle against lead poisoning was also based on the introduction of risk-reducing sanitation regulations, just as early campaigns for workplace safety revolved mainly around the promulgation of specific safety codes.[86] Even in the case of unemployment, reformers believed that direct risk reduction could be achieved through the adoption of "regularization" procedures in industrial hiring and firing as well as the introduction of countercyclical government spending on public works.[87]

Increasingly, however, leaders in the fight against worker insecurity came to view risk shifting (via social insurance) as a superior means to the same end. As Andrews once recalled with regard to occupational disease, "Gradually we realized that the best way to protect health in industry was not to attempt to forbid a shifting catalog of specific acts, but in some way to bring pressure to bear upon the employers so as to make them personally keen to keep down sickness."[88] The pressure Andrews had in mind was experience-rated public health insurance.

Central to social insurance theory in the early twentieth century, *experience rating* required employers with higher than normal losses to pay correspondingly higher premiums. A firm that lost one out of every one hundred workers to sickness would have to pay more in premiums than a firm that lost one out of every two hundred. Once in place, an experience-rated social insurance system would provide employers with powerful monetary incentives to reduce the hazard in question. Andrews commented to a friend at the Life Extension Institute in late 1915 that "varying insurance rates with the incidence of sickness will offer the same incentive toward prevention which has been offered by workmen's compensation in the field of accident prevention."[89]

The very same shift in focus—from direct risk reduction (regulation) to indirect risk reduction via risk shifting (experience-rated social insurance)—eventually drove the AALL's unemployment agenda as well. Commons and Andrews stressed repeatedly that although private employers were in the best position to reduce joblessness, they were unlikely to adopt far-reaching regularization procedures on their own until encouraged to do so through the financial incentives of experience-rated unemployment insurance. As Commons observed at a conference of employment managers in 1919, "We know that employers can prevent unemployment and will do it if they can make money by doing it."[90]

Commons and Andrews defined social insurance in their textbook on labor legislation as a method of risk *spreading*—"a settled policy of cooperative action to distribute among a group the losses suffered by individuals arising from their inability to work and thereby earn a livelihood." But they also stressed that experience-rated social insurance would indirectly reduce risk by *shifting* it onto employers. "[It] furnishes a kind of cooperative pressure on employers," they wrote, "which can be utilized effectively in the elimination of risks in so far as they are preventable."[91] Their decision to emphasize prevention over compensation (and thus risk shifting over risk spreading) in all their public campaigns for social insurance would ultimately provoke bitter dissension within the ranks of social reformers. At least through the Progressive Era, however, such conflict remained almost imperceptible. Prevention was widely heralded as the first priority, though nowhere more than at the AALL.[92]

As for the hazards themselves, there was nearly universal agreement during the Progressive period that disease was a far more serious problem for workers than unemployment. "America presents no exception to the finding of Sidney and Beatrice Webb," Andrews once wrote, "that 'In all countries, at all ages, it is sickness to which the greatest bulk of destitution is immediately due.'"[93] When the association's first president, Richard T. Ely, was asked in 1909 what subject was of greatest importance to his organization, he responded decisively, "Industrial hygiene, without question."[94]

Nevertheless, from the end of 1913 through 1915, the problem of unemployment took on special prominence as a result of a short but sharp economic downturn. Although national unemployment statistics were not yet being collected, subsequent estimates suggested that the annual unemployment rate peaked at 8.5 percent in 1915. Labor union reports from across the country indicated an even more serious problem at the time. Near the middle of 1915, Massachusetts unions reported that 17.2 percent of their members were unemployed, while joblessness among New York State's union members was alleged to have reached 32.7 percent.[95] Sensing an opportunity, the AALL issued a "Practical Program for the Prevention of Unemployment" in 1914, which prominently featured unemployment insurance among its short list of recommendations.[96]

A group of Massachusetts reformers associated with the AALL managed to draft a model unemployment insurance bill over the next year. The bill was introduced into the Massachusetts House of Representatives on January 14, 1916. This marked the very first time unemployment insurance had been taken up by any legislature anywhere in the

United States. The bill itself was patterned closely after the British unemployment insurance provisions of 1911. Like Britain's National Insurance Act, the Massachusetts bill promised to make unemployment insurance compulsory for certain trades and to subsidize trade associations that ran voluntary plans. Compulsory insurance benefits, which were reserved for persons both willing and able to work, were to be jointly funded by employers, employees, and the state. As an inducement for prevention, employers and employees who demonstrated better than average employment records were entitled to special refunds—annually in the case of employers and in a lump sum at age sixty in the case of employees.[97]

The bill never got very far, however. Once interest in unemployment insurance began to fade with the improvement of economic conditions in late 1915, support quickly evaporated. The proposal died quietly in the Massachusetts legislature the following year. As we will see in the next chapter, John Commons reintroduced unemployment insurance legislation in Wisconsin in 1919 and all through the 1920s; and insurance against unemployment ultimately rose to the top of the national agenda during the Great Depression. But for the remainder of the 1910s, compulsory health insurance easily eclipsed unemployment insurance as the association's highest legislative priority.[98]

Convinced that it was the form of social insurance workers needed most, the leaders of the AALL devoted enormous energy to their health insurance campaign. Today, the vast majority of health insurance plans in the United States are purchased voluntarily from private entities and cover medical costs exclusively. During the Progressive Era, however, AALL reformers sought to introduce legislation that would make health insurance mandatory for a large portion of the industrial labor force, exclude private insurance companies, and compensate sick workers for lost wages as well as medical costs.

Although scattered forms of private, voluntary health coverage already existed at the time, leading reformers had little confidence that private plans would reach the majority of workers anytime soon.[99] Lack of standardization across insurance plans generated considerable confusion, fostering a chaotic market environment that was ripe for abuse. Many workers ended up buying into schemes that offered precious little coverage—such as plans indemnifying against individual diseases that were notorious but rare. Paternalistic reformers also worried that a large fraction of industrial workers lacked "sufficient cultural status for the appreciation of the advantages of the insurance principle," were too shortsighted about the future to obtain appropriate coverage, or simply had insufficient disposable income to purchase adequate insurance on their own.[100]

Existing policies only rarely covered medical costs *and* wage loss, but most reformers insisted that both forms of protection were necessary. Many viewed wage replacement as even more important than medical coverage, since lost wages stemming from sickness often proved more devastating to working families than the medical costs themselves. As Miles Dawson, a noted actuary and active AALL member, explained to the Massachusetts Special Commission on Social Insurance in 1916, "sickness insurance is primarily for the purpose of maintaining families when the bread winners are unable on account of sickness to maintain them."[101]

Having begun the process of drafting a model health insurance bill at the end of 1913, the association's Committee on Social Insurance finally completed its work two years later, as the campaign for unemployment insurance was rapidly winding down. In sharp contrast to its unemployment insurance bill, which was largely copied from the relevant British statute, the committee's health insurance bill was truly an original creation. Most of the committee's members preferred the German model, which relied on local mutual funds as underwriters, over the English model, which relied on friendly societies that were often national in scope and open to the involvement of large commercial carriers. But even the German model did not dominate completely.[102]

The AALL's model bill envisioned a health insurance system that would be obligatory for all manual workers and all others earning under $100 per month. Financing would come from employers (40 percent), employees (40 percent), and the state (20 percent), on the theory that all three had a role to play in preventing and bearing the costs of illness. In most cases, mandatory contributions were to be paid to local mutual funds, managed jointly by workers and employers. Other types of funds, including those run by unions, fraternal orders, and even individual firms, would be allowed to participate so long as they met certain eligibility criteria. In all cases, experience rating was permitted and encouraged. Covered hazards included any sickness, injury, or death that was not insured through workers' compensation. Covered workers could count on cash benefits of up to two-thirds of wages, medical and surgical care (including maternity care) for all family members, and funeral benefits in the event of death.[103]

The AALL introduced its health insurance bill in the New York, Massachusetts, and New Jersey state legislatures in 1916. Through that year and into the next one, victory seemed almost assured. Opponents raised the same arguments about competitive disadvantage that they had introduced without success in the workers' compensation debates. During a legislative hearing in New York, both Rubinow and Dawson claimed that employers were obviously bluffing when they threatened to leave the state if a health insurance law were enacted. "Gentleman, the same threat was made years ago, on the Workmen's Compensation [bill]," Rubinow reminded lawmakers, "and I have still to hear of a single firm that had to move."[104] In Massachusetts, Carroll W. Doten of the AALL's social insurance committee marveled at "how mild and how weak" the bill's opponents seemed to be, noting that they no longer "thundered their opposition" as they had during the fight over workers' compensation.[105]

Although representatives of big business and big labor at the National Civic Federation (including Ralph Easley and Samuel Gompers) made their opposition known, the National Association of Manufacturers at first seemed surprisingly receptive to health insurance.[106] Even the American Medical Association appeared ready to cooperate, with one official informing Andrews toward the end of 1915 that the AALL's agenda was "so entirely in line with our own that I want to be of every possible assistance."[107]

The state legislatures in California and Massachusetts created social insurance commissions in 1916, and the governors of those states officially endorsed public health insurance early the next year. Although neither commission explicitly supported the AALL's model bill, both ended up endorsing the concept of compulsory health insurance in short order. Twelve state legislatures ultimately took up health insurance bills in 1917. In California, meanwhile, lawmakers and voters were busy debating a constitutional amendment put forth by the state's social insurance commission that would have removed all legal obstacles to the enactment of compulsory health insurance. Rubinow noted in December 1916 that it was "impossible to escape the conclusion that we are on the very eve of constructive legislation."[108]

It was not long, however, before the AALL's carefully crafted health insurance campaign started coming apart. Problems began popping up everywhere, like leaks in a rotting ship. Years later, Rubinow would acknowledge that the leading proponents of compulsory health insurance had been infected with "over-enthusiasm, over-confidence . . . and last but not least failure to recognize the various class and group interests involved." Almost every major interest group ultimately lined up in opposition. "And who was for it?" he asked. "An energetic, largely self-appointed group, which could compensate by its enthusiasm and literary ability what it lacked in numbers and which carried with it the profession of social work, to some extent the university teaching groups, the economic and social sciences, and even the political progressive organizations, but very little support beyond these narrow circles."[109] He was writing, of course, about the AALL.

The National Association of Manufacturers soon turned against the proposed legislation, largely on the grounds that it would be too expensive and that it would violate the American principles of free contract and voluntarism. One representative of the organization insisted that while its leadership had always supported voluntary health insurance, "the principle of direct legislative mandatory compulsory insurance is a horse of a different color."[110] The American Medical Association executed a similar 180-degree reversal in 1917. Indeed, the official who had originally pledged full cooperation with the AALL now denied that he had ever supported compulsory health insurance in the first place. Many doctors feared that under a public system, the physician would "professionally cease to be an individualist and will be but a cog in a great medical machine."[111] Others worried that health insurance would turn out like workers' compensation, "which puts the physician and patient at the mercy of the insurance company—the most unjust provision ever enacted."[112]

The opposition to compulsory health insurance that emerged in 1917 turned out to be remarkably diverse, including not only manufacturers and doctors but also less prominent interest groups from druggists to Christian Scientists. By far the most powerful resistance, however, came from the insurance industry. Just as the political tide was beginning to turn against his cause, John Andrews estimated that "nine-tenths of the opposition to social health insurance progress comes directly from men who are in the hire of private insurance companies."[113] Indeed, front organizations for the insurance industry regularly attacked health insurance and its supporters. Red-baiting was especially popular. "When Compulsory Health Insurance enters the United States," proclaimed the Insurance Economics Society of America, "Socialism will have its foot upon the throat of the nation."[114] Even one of the AALL's strongest allies during the workers' compensation campaign, Frederick L. Hoffman of the Prudential Insurance Company, turned bitterly against the association once it began campaigning for compulsory health insurance.[115]

The insurance industry no doubt had good reason to fear the association's model bill. Not only would it effectively lock commercial carriers out of the market for workers' health coverage, but also it threatened to usurp one of the industry's core lines of business, industrial life insurance. The funeral benefit provision in the AALL's proposal would have rendered most industrial life insurance superfluous, since workers typically bought it mainly to ensure coverage of their own funeral expenses. Collecting approximately $230 million in industrial life premiums in 1917, the insurance industry had a powerful incentive to protect this line of business; and it spared no expense in working to defeat the AALL's proposal.[116] "By including the funeral benefit," Rubinow later conceded, "the health insurance movement signed its own death warrant."[117]

The truth is that the AALL had few friends on the issue of compulsory health insurance. Even organized labor was sharply divided over the issue and far from helpful until very late in the campaign. Like Samuel Gompers of the AFL, many union leaders fiercely opposed every form of compulsory insurance other than workers' compensation. Having suffered numerous defeats as a result of unwelcome government intervention, particularly by the courts, they had developed an understandable aversion to active state involvement in their affairs.[118] Perhaps even more important, compulsory health insurance would have competed with the unions' own benefit funds, which protected members against various hazards (including illness) and which represented one of the distinctive perks of union membership.[119] The AALL thus emerged as a threat as soon as it took up compulsory health insurance, leading Gompers to rename it the "American Association for the Assassination of Labor Legislation."[120]

Naturally, not all union officials were as hostile as Gompers. In New

York, representatives of the AALL finally persuaded the State Federation of Labor to sign on to their health insurance initiative in 1918, after carefully modifying their model bill to meet labor's demands.[121] Although Gompers and the AFL continued to oppose the legislation, the state federation's endorsement breathed new life into the AALL's campaign. Obviously frightened by the alliance, an upstate trade association proclaimed frantically in its official journal, the *Monitor*, that if labor succeeded in getting the bill passed, it "would absolutely have every manufacturer, merchant, or other employer in this State by the throat and could enforce any demand that any business agent desired to make."[122]

Ongoing opposition—particularly from employers, doctors, and insurance representatives—helped defeat the health insurance bill for a third straight time in the New York legislature in 1918. But reformers at the AALL, emboldened by their new alliance with the State Federation of Labor, were by no means ready to give up. By the beginning of 1919, they had also secured the support of the Women's Joint Legislative Conference (comprising five prominent women's organizations) and the endorsement of Governor Alfred E. Smith. "Nothing is so devastating in the life of the worker's family as sickness," Governor Smith told the state legislature on New Year's Day. "The incapacitation of the wage earner because of illness is one of the underlying causes of poverty. Now the worker and his family bear this burden alone. The enactment of a health insurance law, which I strongly urge, will remedy this unfair condition."[123]

To almost everyone's surprise, the movement for compulsory health insurance reached a sudden climax on April 10, 1919, when the New York State Senate finally passed the bill by a vote of 30 to 20. It was a major victory for the AALL—the first time any legislative body in the United States had ever passed a compulsory health insurance bill.[124] In the state Assembly, however, the bill never even came up for a vote. Speaker Thaddeus C. Sweet, himself an upstate manufacturer and a major power broker in Albany, persuaded his fellow Republicans to keep it (as well as a broader package of reform legislation) from ever reaching the Assembly floor. The health insurance bill officially died at adjournment. According to an editorial in the *Monitor*, "Every employer in the state who followed the trend of events heaved a sigh of relief when the

Legislature of 1919 adjourned, sine die, on the evening of April 19."[125] Although proponents continued to hope for the best, the condition of the health insurance movement was now terminal.

The association's bill had failed in every state legislature in which it was brought up; and the proposed constitutional amendment in California had been overwhelmingly rejected by a vote of 358,324 to 133,858 on election day in 1918.[126] The association's bill was introduced one last time in the New York State legislature in 1920, but it was hardly taken seriously. As an editorial writer at the *Monitor* observed in November, it was "a little bit like trying to resurrect the dead to keep talking about compulsory health insurance."[127] The association's five-year campaign was finally over.

Conclusion

From a legislative perspective, social insurance advocates were only partly successful during the 1910s. Their focus on misplaced risks in the marketplace and the gruesome costs of industrial accidents helped drive the enactment of workers' compensation laws in just about every state in the nation. They failed, however, in their two subsequent campaigns for social insurance. Economic recovery in late 1915 knocked the wind out of their drive for unemployment insurance; and the combined efforts of insurance companies, employers, doctors, and many other interest groups easily trumped their reasoning about health risk in the battle over health insurance.

Still, these reformers achieved a great deal—perhaps more than they realized—since the nation's policy agenda was fundamentally transformed during these years. The focus of risk management policy shifted decisively from business security to worker security. The transition from Phase I to Phase II is, in retrospect, simply unmistakable. In sharp contrast to the nineteenth century, when the primary objective of risk management policy was to stimulate trade and investment, the early twentieth century saw an entirely new emphasis on the worker and the problem of industrial hazards. Instead of worrying about how best to allocate default risk among debtors and creditors, leading reformers and policymakers now pondered how best to allocate worker risk. They contemplated how much of it should come under government management, how much should be spread across the entire labor force (through social insurance), and how much should be shifted from workers to employers (through experience rating). The range of risk management tools remained remarkably stable from the nineteenth century to the twentieth, but the nation's underlying policy objectives most certainly did not.

As we will see in the next chapter, Progressive Era arguments about risk shifting and risk spreading rapidly reemerged as the American movement for social insurance came roaring back to life during the Great Depression. Unemployment insurance and old age insurance were hotly debated and ultimately enacted at the state and federal levels. Yet compulsory health insurance remained conspicuously absent—the one glaring exception to the rule that otherwise defined Phase II risk management policy through the first half of the twentieth century.

7

Social Security

The second phase of American risk management policy reached its apogee on August 14, 1935, the day President Franklin D. Roosevelt signed the Social Security bill into law. The Social Security Act represented a sweeping response to the problem of worker insecurity. Not only did it mandate federal old age insurance for the vast majority of America's workers, but also it effectively forced the states to enact compulsory unemployment insurance. "We can never insure one hundred percent of the population against one hundred percent of the hazards and vicissitudes of life," said FDR at the signing ceremony, "but we have tried to frame a law which will give some measure of protection to the average citizen and to his family against the loss of a job and against poverty-ridden old age." Fully aware of the bill's significance, he added, "If the Senate and House of Representatives in this long and arduous session had done nothing more than pass this Bill, the session would have been regarded as historic for all time."[1]

The motivations behind Social Security were not altogether different from those driving workers' compensation in the 1910s. Social insurance advocates continued to blame widespread worker insecurity on the forward march of industrialization. FDR himself observed that "startling industrial changes" had "tended more and more to make life insecure."[2] The increased pace and intensity of industrial work, the extreme cycle of economic boom and bust, and the breakdown of traditional family support networks all contributed to the problem, leaving workers with razor-thin margins of safety. "When earnings cease," the President's Committee on Economic Security concluded, "dependency is not far off for a large percentage of the people."[3] Like their predecessors in the Progressive Era, New Dealers heralded compulsory social insurance as an ideal remedy.

But the similarities between the social insurance campaigns of the 1910s and the 1930s go only so far. The onset of the Great Depression transformed the political landscape. Like a powerful winter storm, the depression was relentless, affecting almost every aspect of the policy-making process. Hard-headed logic about hazard prevention, which had so captivated Progressive Era proponents of social insurance, had less appeal in the 1930s, particularly on the crucial subject of unemployment. The idea that a small financial incentive stemming from experience-rated unemployment insurance could deter employers from laying off workers en masse struck many policymakers as downright ridiculous in the depths of the depression. Faith in the private sector was badly bruised. Even the survival of large private insurance companies could no longer be taken for granted. At another time, policymakers intent on mandating old age insurance might have thought about compelling coverage through private insurers, just as workers' compensation laws did. But with the nation's financial system now in tatters, reliance on private agents seemed unnecessarily dangerous.

Public risk management thus achieved new prominence during the Great Depression. In the halls of Congress, risk was treated more explicitly and more exhaustively than it ever had before. The limits of private risk management became painfully obvious amidst all the turmoil of collapsing companies, record unemployment, lost nest eggs, and widespread privation. Numerous issues that had previously been viewed as mere subtleties or fine points in the rhetoric of risk now emerged as pressing public policy questions in their own right. The once esoteric distinction between risk shifting and risk spreading in social insurance theory proved pivotal in the unemployment insurance debates of the 1930s. And previously obscure notions like work-duration risk assumed new prominence in the detailed deliberations over old age insurance.

Although the core objective of Social Security remained relatively simple—to protect working families against income-destroying hazards—the means chosen were anything but. Public risk management achieved a new level of sophistication in the United States during the 1930s, and President Roosevelt's New Dealers seemed determined to lead the way.

Unemployment Insurance

The primary motivation behind the renewed campaign for social insurance was the scourge of unemployment. The annual unemployment rate peaked at 25.2 percent in 1933, meaning that nearly 13 million workers were out of a job and actively looking for work. By 1935, almost 11 million workers remained unemployed, generating an annual unemployment rate of 20.3 percent.[4] Joblessness was widely characterized as the most devastating problem facing the nation; and it was within this context that public unemployment insurance began to look like an absolute necessity.

Wisconsin and Ohio (Risk Shifting versus Risk Spreading)

As the issue gained strength in Washington in the early 1930s, it was natural for federal policymakers to look to Wisconsin for guidance. Wisconsin was still the only state to have enacted an unemployment insurance law (in early 1932), and it boasted more than its share of experts on the subject. John Commons had been theorizing about unemployment insurance since the mid-1910s, and he and his political allies had begun introducing model bills in the Wisconsin state legislature as early as 1921.

With each passing year, Commons seemed to become ever more infatuated with the logic of prevention. His original argument, expounded at length during the Progressive period, was that experience-rated social insurance would induce employers to try to prevent industrial hazards such as workplace accidents, illness, and unemployment by shifting part of the risk their way. He carried this notion considerably further, however, in the early 1920s, now claiming that experience-rated unemployment insurance would actually smooth the business cycle by imposing a cost on employers who overhired and on the bankers who lent to them. "The overexpansion of credit is the cause of unemployment," he wrote in 1923, "and to prevent the overexpansion of credit you place an insurance liability on the business man against the day when he lays off the workmen."[5]

Although Commons' unemployment insurance bill was defeated in every session of the Wisconsin legislature in the 1920s, it was resurrected by two of his students, Harold Groves and Paul Raushenbush, at the beginning of the next decade. Similarly enthralled with the preventive power of experience rating, Groves and Raushenbush took the idea to its logical extreme. Instead of simply requiring experience-rated employer contributions to a general insurance pool, the Groves-Raushenbush bill mandated the creation of individual employer reserve accounts. Tacitly acknowledging that this was no longer insurance, supporters began using the term "unemployment compensation" to describe their special system of segregated employer reserves.[6]

As finally enacted on January 28, 1932, the Wisconsin Unemployment Compensation Act obligated every employer with ten or more workers to deposit 2 percent of payroll annually into his own reserve account at the state treasurer's office until it averaged $55 per worker. At that point, the required annual contribution would drop to just 1 percent, and it would finally disappear altogether once the accumulated fund reached $75 per worker. Further contributions would become necessary only if workers were laid off and benefits commenced (or if new workers were hired), since the employer's reserve account would then fall below the requisite $75 per worker. Benefits were to be paid only after a two-week waiting period and were set at half of weekly wages, though they were never to exceed $10 per week.[7]

Groves and Raushenbush believed that their scheme would maximize employers' incentives for prevention, since the full cost of unemployment benefits would now fall directly on the offending employers themselves.[8] Commons apparently agreed, boasting several months later that the Wisconsin law "appeals to the individualism of American capitalists, who do not want to be burdened with the inefficiencies or misfortunes of other capitalists, and it fits the public policy of a capitalistic nation which uses the profit motive to prevent unemployment."[9] The concept of compulsory employer reserves received an additional boost in 1932 when it garnered the tacit endorsement of the Interstate Commission on Unemployment Insurance, a body established by Governor Franklin Roosevelt of New York and the governors of six other eastern states.[10]

The individual reserves approach pioneered in Wisconsin had obvious advantages, placing pressure on each employer to stabilize employment while at the same time preserving his sense of independence. The Wisconsin plan also had a few key weaknesses, however. Critics emphasized that an unemployed worker might receive little or nothing under the Wisconsin law if his employer's reserve fund were somehow depleted. This could occur if a large number of workers were laid off all at once or, even worse, if the employer himself failed and was thus unable to replenish the fund. Particularly when unemployment rates were high and when joblessness was unevenly distributed across firms and industries, individual reserves were likely to deliver lower average benefits than a single pooled insurance fund.[11]

Perhaps most damning of all was the question whether individual employers were capable of preventing much unemployment on their own, especially during a depression. Leading opponents of the reserves approach—including Paul Douglas, Abraham Epstein, I. M. Rubinow, and William Leiserson—doubted that an incentive equal to 2 percent of payroll could have any significant effect. They were "decidedly skeptical," said Douglas, "about the degree to which individual employers or even an entire industry could stabilize employment, and [they] did not believe that the proposed system of plant reserves would stimulate any very dynamic drive in this direction."[12]

The primary alternative to the Wisconsin approach emerged in Ohio—the product of a special commission on unemployment appointed by Governor George White in late 1931. Under the leadership of Rubinow and Leiserson, the Ohio commission crafted an innovative unemployment insurance plan that differed from its Wisconsin counterpart in two critical ways. First, it based benefit financing on pooled rather than individual reserves; and second, it offered a considerably more generous benefit package for unemployed workers.

The Ohio plan, as it came to be known, required both employers and employees to contribute to a single state insurance fund. Workers were obliged to pay 1.5 percent of wages, while employers were to devote between 1.5 and 3.5 percent of payrolls, depending on their firms' past records of unemployment and those of their industries. As with the Wisconsin plan, benefits were supposed to replace up to 50 percent of prior wages and were to commence after a moderate waiting period (three weeks in Ohio, two in Wisconsin). But the Ohio plan set its maximum weekly benefit at $15, 50 percent higher than Wisconsin's; and it permitted benefits to be paid for up to sixteen weeks, 60 percent longer than what its rival allowed.[13]

The Ohio commission's report to the legislature was surprisingly blunt in its criticism of the Wisconsin approach. "There is no pooling of risks," the commissioners wrote about the Wisconsin plan, "no purchasing of insurance. . . . [T]he reserves of each employer would be locked up, so to speak, and the amount that each employer could afford to set aside in this way would be too small to provide anything like adequate benefits."[14] While the Ohio commissioners sought to encourage employment stabilization (unemployment prevention) through experience rating, their primary goals were to provide adequate compensation for unemployed workers and to attack joblessness at the macro level by sustaining aggregate purchasing power.[15] This represented an entirely new vision of unemployment insurance in the United States. Rubinow was so pleased with what the commission had produced that he gleefully announced to Leiserson at the end of 1932, "The Wisconsin plan is dead."[16]

As it turned out, Rubinow's obituary for the Wisconsin plan was a bit premature. Lawmakers in the various states considered at least fifty-six unemployment insurance bills in 1933, the year after the American Federation of Labor finally endorsed compulsory unemployment insurance.[17] None of these bills were actually enacted. But according to one study, eighteen were based on the Wisconsin plan and only sixteen on the Ohio plan. Seven others involved industry reserves, six provided for pooled funds but without experience rating, and six more were characterized simply as "radical" bills.[18]

Still, Rubinow's comment about the death of the Wisconsin plan accurately reflected the severity of the rift between the two schools. The once harmonious movement for social insurance had broken into feuding clans. Over the strong objections of John Andrews at the AALL, Rubinow and Epstein (both members of Andrews' organization) had created the American Association for Old Age Security in 1927. The group later changed its name to the American Association for Social Security (AASS) in 1933, presumably to accommodate its new focus on unemployment insurance during the depression. In forming the organization, Epstein and Rubinow had sought to reinvigorate the movement for social insurance, which they believed was suffocating under the leadership of the AALL.[19] "Of course, Dr. Andrews does not like us," Epstein wrote to a correspondent in the middle of 1933, "but a little more hate cannot hurt."[20]

There were many reasons why the movement ruptured. The leaders of the AASS leaned further left than most of their counterparts at the AALL. Accordingly, they exhibited less faith in the private market and a greater commitment to income redistribution. At a conceptual level, however, the core disagreement between these organizations proved to be surprisingly technical, relating to the relative merits of two different methods of risk management. Key reformers at the AALL preferred risk *shifting*, while their rivals at the AASS favored risk *spreading*. The inherent conflict between these two approaches had been conveniently papered over during the Progressive period, but it could no longer be covered up, especially not during the Great Depression.

Whether in the form of individual employer reserves or experience rating, risk shifting was designed to move risk from worse to better risk managers. Reformers such as Commons and Andrews believed that employers constituted superior risk managers as compared to workers, because they generally had greater financial resources and because they were better positioned to prevent the industrial hazards in question. As we have seen, members of the Wisconsin school focused particularly on this latter point. Again and again, they claimed that effective risk shifting from workers to employers would create powerful employer incentives for prevention, ultimately leading to the reduction of aggregate risk.

Risk spreading, by contrast, had an entirely different purpose. It was designed to ease the financial consequences of individual hazards, not to create incentives for prevention. By spreading the financial risk of joblessness across the entire workforce, an unemployment insurance program based on pooling would leave each individual worker with a relatively stable stream of income, regardless of whether or not he lost his job. Compared to risk shifting, moreover, risk spreading had the advantage of making more resources available to hazard victims at any given moment in time. This is because risk shifting effectively dispersed reserves (in the extreme, creating as many "insurance funds" as there were employers), whereas risk spreading concentrated reserves in a single pooled fund, making it far less vulnerable to unexpected shocks.

Proponents of risk spreading also advanced another, rather astonishing argument about risk reduction. Normally, risk spreading can be counted on to reduce individual risk but not aggregate risk. Fire insurance, for example, sharply reduces the suffering of the individual fire victim, but is unlikely to reduce the total number of fires or the resulting financial losses. If anything, risk spreading has a tendency to increase aggregate risk as a result of moral hazard (such as greater carelessness on the part of insured homeowners). In the case of unemployment insurance, however, leading members of the Ohio school claimed that risk spreading would actually *reduce* aggregate unemployment risk (prevent unemployment) by sustaining workers' purchasing power. The Ohio commission had suggested this argument in its 1932 report, and numerous economists continued to develop it in subsequent years.[21]

The underlying logic was that depressions were caused, at least in part, by unexpected shortfalls in consumer spending, and that such shortfalls could result from workers losing their jobs or fearing the prospect of job loss in the future. By increasing worker security and stabilizing workers' incomes over time, unemployment insurance thus had the potential to prevent depressions. As in the case of deposit insurance, risk spreading promised to reduce aggregate risk because both the hazard itself (unemployment) and especially the fear of its occurrence (worker insecurity) generated behavior (reduced consumer spending) that increased the likelihood of the hazard. "The provision of self-respecting unemployment benefits," Paul Douglas explained at an economics conference in the darkest days of the depression, "would diminish the fears which the employed workers would entertain towards the prospect of unemployment and hence would lessen their frantic personal savings at such times and increase the amount which they would spend upon consumers' goods. There would be a better balance between spending and saving and less unemployment would be created."[22]

This was truly an extraordinary argument. One could hardly imagine that greater personal security about other types of risk, such as fires and automobile accidents, could possibly reduce the likelihood of these hazards. Unemployment, it seemed, was a very special sort of risk.

The result of all this economic reasoning was that the Ohio school ended up championing prevention just as the Wisconsin school did. But unlike the Wisconsinites, who highlighted the positive effect of risk *shifting* on employer incentives, leaders of the Ohio school emphasized the favorable effect of risk *spreading* on individual workers and on their spending habits. Unemployment was largely a systemic problem, they argued, beyond the control of individual employers. Never did this seem more true than in the depths of the Great Depression. Although the Wisconsin plan was not dead yet, it was no doubt rapidly losing strength.

Finding Common Ground: The Logic of a Federal Solution

Despite the deep division between the Wisconsin and Ohio schools, progress was still possible because both sides agreed on two basic points: first, that private initiatives to address the problem of unemployment would inevitably fall short; and second, that individual states would find it exceedingly difficult to enact unemployment insurance laws on their own as a result of interstate competition. On the subject of private solutions, reformers at both the AALL and the AASS maintained that private unemployment insurance was all but unworkable. As early as 1904, Rubinow had highlighted a severe moral hazard problem stemming from the fact that insurers would have a hard time distinguishing voluntary from involuntary unemployment.[23] Developing this point in a subsequent article, Rubinow wrote: "Unemployment often is and still oftener may be claimed to be the result of the individual's effort or lack of effort. It may easily be simulated. In other words . . . it is a bad 'moral hazard,' and sound insurance business avoids bad moral hazards."[24] Reasoning along similar lines, Paul Douglas noted in 1932 that private insurance companies would find it almost impossible to determine "whether the claimant was genuinely unemployed."[25]

Consistent with this argument, commercial experience with unemployment insurance was extremely limited in the United States. One private insurer in Chicago apparently began offering such coverage in 1897, and two others in Michigan are said to have entered into the business on a very small scale during the 1910s. But next to nothing is known about how many policies they wrote or what ultimately happened to them.[26] During the 1920s, the president of the Metropolitan Life Insurance Company, Haley Fiske, showed considerable interest in writing unemployment insurance; yet he consistently ran up against New York insurance law, which prohibited commercial carriers from selling it.[27]

At least one legal scholar has argued that private unemployment insurance would have blossomed on its own but for the existence of adverse laws like the one in New York.[28] But the historical record is far from clear on this point. Attempts to modify the New York law failed in

1919, 1924, 1926, 1927, and 1931.[29] The state's superintendent of insurance helped stymie the very first effort, warning that this untested line of insurance could "endanger policyholders' money."[30] Indeed, initial support for the change came primarily from railroad companies rather than major insurers. Although Fiske entered the fray as early as 1919, he does not appear to have enjoyed much support within the insurance industry—or even within his own firm. One executive at Metropolitan Life, Louis Dublin, later recalled that "there were within the organization specialists on the subject whose studies convinced them that unemployment insurance was not an insurable risk within the framework of sound actuarial practice."[31] When Fiske died in 1929, his dream died with him, since no other champion of private unemployment insurance ever emerged, either at Metropolitan Life or at any other major insurance company.[32]

The only forms of private coverage against unemployment that ever developed beyond infancy involved union and company funds, which sometimes offered jobless benefits to their members. Unlike third-party insurers, employers and especially unions were well positioned to detect and punish moral hazard. Rubinow once noted that the "'moral hazard' of malingery is naturally reduced to a minimum" within a labor union, in part because it "is almost impossible for a refusal of a reasonable offer to remain a secret."[33] By 1931, approximately 45,000 workers were covered under union plans, and roughly another 50,000 came under company plans (though most of these were at one firm, General Electric).[34] Some estimates ran even higher. Paul Douglas suggested that as many as 200,000 workers may have participated in these sorts of plans, though he viewed even this as just a drop in the bucket. If private unemployment insurance continued to grow at its historical rate, he noted sarcastically in 1932, the attainment of universal coverage would have taken upwards of two thousand years.[35]

Douglas's skepticism was widely shared at both the AALL and the AASS. Commons and Andrews observed that "only a few unions were known to pay out-of-work benefits. [T]he cost borne by the workers alone proved a heavy burden on them; comparatively few were able or willing to insure; and adequate benefits could seldom be paid."[36] Beyond all of these problems, the plans themselves were often far from secure. Company plans could be terminated by employers at any time; and both union and company plans were, as a rule, severely underfunded.[37]

Rubinow recognized in 1913 that "the problem of accumulating sufficient reserve in order to meet the sudden increase in unemployment during an acute panic or prolonged depression can seldom be met successfully."[38] The funds' failure to diversify widely across industrial sectors only exacerbated the weakness of their financial position.[39] Not surprisingly, their numbers had dwindled considerably by the late 1930s as a result of persistently high unemployment.[40]

For all of these reasons, social insurance advocates agreed that private solutions to the problem of unemployment would never be sufficient. They also agreed that securing state legislation—whether on the Wisconsin or the Ohio model—was going to be enormously challenging as a result of fierce interstate competition. Many state lawmakers were simply unwilling to impose any special burdens on their employers for fear of driving them away. Believing that the "'interstate competition' argument against state labor legislation is undoubtedly overworked," Harold Groves nonetheless acknowledged in an article with Elizabeth Brandeis that "its political significance is considerable, whatever its economic validity."[41] True, reformers had secured an unemployment insurance law in Wisconsin, but only after a decade of painstaking work and unending compromises with business interests. Even after enactment, the Wisconsin law was put on hold for more than two years, in large measure because of the ongoing resistance of anxious employers.[42]

Curiously, the man who was supposed to run Wisconsin's unemployment compensation system, Paul Raushenbush, found himself temporarily out of work in 1933 as a result of the law's postponement. With extra time on his hands that summer, Raushenbush decided to take a vacation with his wife, Elizabeth, and his father-in-law, Supreme Court Justice Louis Brandeis. Frustrated that none of the other states had followed Wisconsin's lead or seemed inclined to do so, he asked Justice Brandeis one day whether there was any way around the interstate competition obstacle. Brandeis replied in the form of a question: "Have you considered the case of *Florida vs. Mellon?*"

The 1926 Supreme Court decision to which Brandeis referred had upheld a federal tax imposed for the sole purpose of forcing the states to adopt uniform inheritance laws. Some years earlier the state of Florida had eliminated its inheritance tax altogether, with the goal of attracting rich elderly citizens from other states. Intent on foiling Florida's scheme, Congress enacted a special inheritance tax that included a tax-offset feature. The federal statute levied an inheritance tax on all citizens but offered credits of up to 80 percent of the total to citizens who paid state inheritance taxes. Effectively nullifying Florida's mischievous policy, the federal tax-offset program removed once and for all the lure of dying tax free in the Sunshine State.[43]

Brandeis's not-so-subtle question in the summer of 1933 thus alerted Raushenbush to the promise of the federal taxing power as a weapon in the campaign for state unemployment insurance laws. Inspired and excited, Raushenbush soon set to work with Associate Solicitor Thomas H. Eliot in drafting a model federal statute, which was introduced in Congress as the Wagner-Lewis bill on January 5, 1934.[44] The Wagner-Lewis bill levied a 5 percent payroll tax on the vast majority of the nation's employers; but those who participated in a satisfactory state unemployment insurance program would be allowed to deduct the full amount of their state contributions from the federal tax. As Andrews observed at the time, "The Wagner-Lewis bill is an ingenious device to remove the 'interstate competition' obstacle to state legislation while giving a compelling economic incentive to state action." Although the bill soon died in Congress (mainly because of weak support from President Roosevelt), the logic of the tax-offset method remained very much alive.[45]

The President's Committee on Economic Security

The main reason President Roosevelt allowed the Wagner-Lewis bill to die in 1934 was that he wanted more time to draft his own social security legislation. Accordingly, on June 29, he issued an executive order creating the Committee on Economic Security (CES), which was supposed to "study problems relating to the economic security of individuals" and to report its findings and recommendations no later than December 1, 1934.[46] FDR selected his secretary of labor, Frances Perkins, to chair the CES; and he rounded out the committee with Treasury Secretary Henry Morgenthau, Jr., Agriculture Secretary Henry A. Wallace, Federal Emergency Relief administrator Harry L. Hopkins, and Attorney General Homer Cummings.

The president's executive order authorized the CES to appoint both a Technical Board ("consisting of qualified representatives selected from various departments and agencies of the Federal Government") and an executive director and associated staff (to "have immediate charge of studies and investigations . . . under the general direction of the Technical Board").[47] The committee picked Arthur J. Altmeyer, second assistant secretary of labor, to head the Technical Board. Before coming to Washington to work with Perkins, Altmeyer had served as secretary of the Wisconsin Industrial Commission and, years earlier, as John Commons' research assistant.[48] Edwin Witte, the chairman of the economics department at the University of Wisconsin, became the staff's executive director. Members of the Ohio school could hardly have been pleased to see two Wisconsinites elevated to the upper reaches of the CES, which was now fully in charge of Roosevelt's social security initiative. But they were helpless to do anything about it since the CES was, by this point, virtually the only game in town as far as social insurance was concerned.

INSURING AGAINST UNEMPLOYMENT

Although the phrase "social security" would eventually become almost synonymous with old age insurance in the United States, this was emphatically not the case in the mid-1930s. At the time, the term was used almost interchangeably with "economic security." Indeed, the administration's Economic Security bill became the Social Security bill in the House Ways and Means Committee in early 1935.[49] Both terms were used to describe a broad package of policies designed to protect the worker, of which unemployment insurance was probably the most important in the middle of the Great Depression. According to Altmeyer, "the President and his committee both felt that unemployment insurance should have top priority."[50] The head of the CES's old age staff, Barbara Nachtrieb Armstrong, later complained of feeling left out, noting that "not only did [Perkins] never see me but she *refused* to see me."[51] With the national unemployment rate still over 20 percent in 1934, the Committee on Economic Security was unwilling to give precedence to anything else. As Representative Robert Doughton of North Carolina declared on the floor of the House the following year, "No greater hazard confronts the American worker today than that of losing his job."[52]

Naturally, the CES was forced to wrestle with many of the same issues that had motivated and divided proponents of unemployment insurance over the previous two decades. On the crucial issue of federalism, the committee ended up endorsing the federal tax-offset method as a way of forcing the states to enact unemployment insurance laws.[53] This step was taken with considerable reluctance, however. There was a good deal of interest among CES members and staff in developing a purely federal unemployment insurance system, since a national program promised to spread the risk of unemployment in the broadest possible fashion. "We thought we had proved it again and again," Armstrong later recalled, "that . . . it was absurd to try to do something by political units [the states] which had nothing to do with economic units and didn't give any fair distribution of risk."[54] But in the end, concerns about the opposition of states' righters in Congress, about the sensitivities of Wisconsin lawmakers, and, especially, about the possibility of an adverse ruling from the Supreme Court proved decisive.[55]

On the pivotal question of pooled versus individual employer reserves, most CES members and staff seemed to favor pooling, despite the committee's strong ties to Wisconsin. Even Edwin Witte, a former student of Commons, had long since acknowledged shortcomings in his teacher's logic. Prevention, he had asserted as early as 1921, "is not the only argument in favor of unemployment insurance. . . . [It] is a method for better distribution of losses. Fluctuations in employment due to business conditions, I feel, are largely beyond the control of the individual employer."[56] Concerns about systematic risk and the inability of individual employers to do anything about it became even more pronounced during the Great Depression. As Secretary Perkins remarked at the Senate hearings in 1935, "We have come to realize that no local government and no individual employer can be held responsible for the unemployment which accrues during these world-wide depressions, that that is really a situation over which he individually has no control."[57] The CES also adopted the purchasing power argument, which was again closely associated with the Ohio school.[58]

Despite these leanings, the president's committee decided against requiring the states to adopt any particular model of unemployment insurance. On almost every contentious issue (including pooled versus individual reserves, experience rating, and the relative contribution rates of employers, employees, and the state), the committee simply left it up to state lawmakers to choose for themselves.[59] Although many CES members and staff personally identified with the Ohio plan, powerful proponents of the Wisconsin approach—including leaders of the AALL and representatives of big business, such as Gerard Swope of General Electric and Walter Teagle of Standard Oil—could not be ignored.[60] The best thing to do, it seemed, was to put the tax-offset scheme in place and then trust the states to find the right answers on their own.

"EMPLOYMENT ASSURANCE"

Another reason why the CES was willing to grant the states so much freedom was that state-run unemployment insurance constituted only half of its battle plan against joblessness. The other half involved the notion of "employment assurance," and here the committee insisted on maintaining strict federal control. Though long forgotten, the employment assurance proposal was probably the most original of all the recommendations to come out of the CES. The basic idea was that unemployed workers should have access to federally provided jobs once their state unemployment insurance benefits ran out, typically after just a few months.

The reasoning behind this proposal was that state unemployment insurance programs would be suitable for covering only short-term unemployment. Longer bouts of joblessness, resulting from severe economic downturns, were thought to be the responsibility of the federal government, since it possessed the deepest of all financial pockets.[61] One additional assumption was that the long-term unemployed would be better served through work relief than cash awards. The committee therefore recommended that workers who exhausted their state unemployment insurance benefits before finding a job "be given, instead of an extended benefit in cash, a work benefit—an opportunity to support themselves and their families at work provided by the Government."[62] This was employment assurance—guaranteed public employment for the long-term unemployed. The journalist Walter Lippmann was so impressed when he heard about the idea that he immediately shot off a letter to John Maynard Keynes, describing the proposed "right to a job" in detail and characterizing it as "an extremely interesting experiment."[63]

But the experiment never actually got under way—at least, not the way the CES had intended. After receiving the committee's preliminary report at the end of December 1934, President Roosevelt agreed with his acting budget director that the proposal for employment assurance ought to be severed from the CES's economic security bill and instead incorporated into Harry Hopkins' public works program.[64] The public works legislation of 1935, known as the Emergency Relief Administration Act, earmarked $4.8 billion for work relief, and it was commonly characterized as establishing a "right-to-work" guarantee. But the truth is that it was only a temporary measure, not a permanent right-to-work law.[65]

This defeat was naturally disappointing for the CES. As it turned out, however, employment assurance proved to be the only major piece of its economic security package that did not make it to Capitol Hill intact. The rest of the committee's recommendations, including the tax-offset scheme for unemployment insurance, arrived safely in the halls of Congress on January 17, 1935.[66]

Compulsory Unemployment Insurance: The Final Act

The hearings and the debate over unemployment insurance in the U.S. House and Senate presented relatively few surprises. Some rather remarkable alternatives were introduced here and there, including proposals for a shorter workweek, the establishment of a legal right to work, and even a tax on new technology (a so-called technotax).[67] But none of these propositions gained any serious support. There was a good deal of wrangling over various details of the tax-offset plan and a limited amount of outright criticism. In the end, however, the unemployment insurance provisions Congress passed in the summer of 1935 were nearly identical to those the CES had proposed back in December.[68]

Along the way, the legislation's supporters in the House and Senate highlighted just about all the key arguments that reformers had developed over the previous years. They began by observing that private attempts to provide unemployment insurance had failed miserably and that the states were constrained from intervening as a result of interstate competition. The bill's proud sponsor in the Senate, Robert F. Wagner, insisted that federal compulsion was necessary because "[l]ess than one-half of 1 percent of the workers in this country are covered by the much-heralded private and voluntary plans for their protection. And so paralyzing has been the fear of unfair competition by backward States that only Wisconsin dared to proceed in splendid isolation by enacting an unemployment-insurance law."[69] Both of these problems were emphasized repeatedly in the congressional debates.[70]

Proponents in Congress were also quick to stress the advantages of insurance over relief. One of the legislation's two co-sponsors in the House, Robert Doughton, explained that social insurance "does not carry with it the stigma of charity with its devastating effect on the morale of our population and its loss of self-respect. The protection afforded by social insurance comes to the worker as a matter of right." And because only those laborers with a demonstrable work history would be eligible for benefits, "social insurance will do nothing to break down the sacred American tradition of self-reliance and initiative."[71]

Like the membership of the Committee on Economic Security, leading advocates of unemployment insurance on Capitol Hill were careful to identify both compensation and prevention as critical objectives, though often with a slight tilt toward the former.[72] By this point, however, the word "prevention" was no longer merely shorthand for the Wisconsin logic of risk shifting and employer incentives. The House bill passed on April 19 explicitly excluded state unemployment insurance schemes based on individual employer reserves. Although Representative Harry Sauthoff had protested that this exclusion would force Wisconsin "to scrap its unemployment compensation law," the House refused to budge.[73] Experience rating was still permitted under the House bill, but many representatives expressed far more enthusiasm about the preventive potential of enhanced purchasing power—that is, a macro rather than a micro approach to unemployment prevention.[74] Without any question, Ohio had trumped Wisconsin in the House of Representatives.

Although the CES remained officially neutral in the conflict between the two schools, Secretary Perkins made perfectly clear to the Senate Finance Committee that she personally supported the Ohio model. "If I were voting in the State legislature I would vote in favor of a pooled fund rather than plant reserve funds," she explained, "as I think it is more secure, more sound, less troublesome, and on the whole would have better results." Yet she was quick to add, just as she had in her testimony before the House Ways and Means Committee, that "very conscientious citizens in some States are in favor of reserve funds" and that it would be best to let the state legislatures decide for themselves.[75]

At the insistence of Wisconsin's senator Robert M. La Follette, Jr., the Senate Finance Committee ended up accepting Perkins' recommendation for tolerance. A clause permitting the states to adopt individual employer reserve plans was restored in the Senate version of the bill.[76] Once the proposed legislation arrived on the Senate floor, La Follette inserted a long statement into the record outlining the many advantages of the Wisconsin plan and highlighting the ability of individual employers to prevent unemployment if given the proper incentives.[77]

La Follette was certainly not the only senator to articulate the old logic of risk shifting. Senator Wagner himself noted that because the federal bill permitted and encouraged experience rating, it provided a "specific incentive to business men to diminish the volume of unemployment."[78] Still, most of the major supporters in the Senate (including Wagner) focused considerably more attention on the favorable effects of automatic compensation, both for individual workers struggling to stay out of poverty and for the American economy as a whole.[79] Here, too, the Ohio approach had the upper hand.

The full Senate finally passed its version of the bill on July 19 by the lopsided vote of 77 to 6 (12 not voting). The vote in the House had been similarly unbalanced (372 to 33, with 2 voting "present" and 25 not voting). But the two bills were not identical. House and Senate conferees spent more than a month trying to reconcile their differences. Although the question of whether to permit individual employer reserves proved to be a major sticking point, the House conferees finally yielded after obtaining one of the items on their wish list: an agreement to establish an independent social security board.[80] Once complete, the reconciled bill was passed by voice votes in the House on August 8 and in the Senate the very next day.

Even after President Roosevelt signed the bill into law, however, the fight for unemployment insurance was still not quite over, since the Social Security Act simply pushed the battle down to the states. But given the pressure of the federal government's new tax-offset scheme, state legislators had good reason to move quickly. Four states (New York, New Hampshire, California, and Massachusetts) had already adopted unemployment insurance in the final months leading up to passage of the federal bill. All the remaining states followed suit within just two years. Illinois was the last state to do so, enacting a compulsory unemployment insurance law on June 30, 1937.[81]

After an extended federal campaign, therefore, the long-standing contest between the Wisconsin school and the Ohio school—between advocates of risk shifting and advocates of risk spreading—was decided just where it began, in the states. Initially, all but six established unemployment insurance systems based on pooled funds; and two of the six that allowed individual reserves also required some pooled contributions as a sort of safety net. Just eleven states decided against experience rating, and all but two of these called for further investigation of the technique. The combination of pooled funds and experience rating was clearly a favorite. Eventually all of the states converged toward this standard. Individual employer reserves were gradually abandoned everywhere, even in Wisconsin; and experience rating was universally adopted as well.[82]

The message seemed to be that experience rating (risk shifting) was likely to prevent a little unemployment by tweaking employer incentives, but that most of the residual risk ought to be spread as widely as possible to ensure adequate compensation for those who still lost their jobs. The primary objectives were to assist deserving workers and to sustain their purchasing power to help stabilize the macro economy. The essential logic of the Ohio plan had triumphed in the end.

Old Age Insurance

Like unemployment, old age dependency was a perennial problem that became much worse during the 1930s. There were 6.5 million people over the age of sixty-five at the beginning of the decade, making up 5.4 percent of the population. The Committee on Economic Security estimated that by 1934, between 30 and 50 percent of senior citizens were dependent on others for economic support and that roughly a million were receiving at least one form of public charity. State old age pensions covered only about 180,000 people, and private pensions available through employers and unions covered even fewer, approximately 150,000.[83]

None of the existing remedies seemed remotely adequate. Employer-provided pensions came in for particular criticism. Senator Wagner complained that besides being limited in scope, employer plans typically offered workers a false sense of security: "In many cases men are discharged in the middle of life and never receive the benefits." Another problem was that most industrial pensions could be terminated at any time at the discretion of the employer. The result, Wagner suggested, was that "only about 4 percent of the workers covered by such plans actually draw benefits upon retirement."[84] The states, meanwhile, were simply overwhelmed by the magnitude of the problem. "The care of the old cannot be left indefinitely to the miserably weak pension laws which exist in only 33 states," Wagner warned.[85]

While there was widespread agreement that some sort of federal response was necessary, the big question was what form it should take. The adoption of old age insurance was by no means a foregone conclusion when President Roosevelt appointed the Committee on Economic Security in the middle of 1934. Although the insurance model ultimately prevailed, captivating both policymakers and the public at large, it actually emerged rather late in the game. For a long time, old age assistance (not insurance) was the policy of choice.

Insurance and Assistance

Although old age had always been recognized as a major source of poverty, old age insurance had not been considered as a serious policy option in the United States prior to the 1930s.[86] Even most of the leading proponents of social insurance during the Progressive Era had shown little interest in the idea. At the AALL, this may have been because the notion of insuring against old age or even old age dependency was inconsistent with the logic of prevention.[87] Some social reformers also worried that contributory old age insurance would prove impractical from an administrative standpoint, particularly as a result of substantial labor migration across state lines.[88]

The result was that noncontributory public pensions for the elderly—rather than contributory old age insurance—emerged as the preferred solution to the problem of old age dependency during the 1910s and 1920s.[89] Because these pensions were to be funded out of general revenues and strictly means-tested, proposals for their enactment constituted calls for income redistribution, not social insurance. By 1934, twenty-eight states had old age pension laws on the books, not one of which was contributory. Pension benefits varied widely, from an average of 69 cents per month in North Dakota to $26 per month in Massachusetts. All but five states paid average monthly benefits of less than $20, and thirteen paid less than $10.[90]

Even at the Committee on Economic Security, there may have been some support for an exclusively noncontributory system, particularly in the committee's early months of operation. Barbara Nachtrieb Armstrong later suggested that Secretary Perkins "definitely wanted not to have old age insurance; she wanted old age assistance."[91] Ultimately, though, the committee recommended both insurance and assistance, while making abundantly clear its predilection for the former. "Contributory annuities are unquestionably preferable to noncontributory pensions," the CES declared in its report to the president. Noting the "disastrous psychological effect of relief upon the recipients," it lauded contributory old age insurance as "a self-respecting method through which workers make their own provision for old age."[92] Some measure of noncontributory relief would also be necessary, the committee explained, to "meet the problem of millions of persons who are already superannuated or shortly will be so and are without sufficient income for a decent subsistence."[93] It thus recommended federal matching grants to encourage the states to enact and expand noncontributory, means-tested pensions for the elderly.[94] But there was no question that federal old age insurance constituted the centerpiece of the committee's overall plan for old age security.

According to the CES proposal, the insurance program would cover nearly all manual workers as well as all others earning less than $250 per month. After an initial startup period, covered workers and their employers would be required to pay a special tax equal to 5 percent of payroll, to be divided equally between them. These payments were thought of as social insurance premiums. In return, covered workers would be entitled to lifetime annuities as soon as they reached age sixty-five and retired from gainful employment. The families of workers who died before age sixty-five or before receiving the nominal value of their contributions back in benefits would be entitled to a lump sum death benefit. Such a system, the CES concluded, "will enable younger workers . . . to build up gradually their rights to annuities in their old age."[95] The contractual insurance model, which would transform old age benefits from a privilege into a "right," proved to be a major selling point.

Most of the committee's proposals regarding old age security ultimately found their way into the Social Security Act, though often in modified form.[96] Although the statute was widely recognized as a landmark piece of legislation, the act itself was never held up as a thing of beauty. Thomas Eliot, who drafted the administration's version of the bill, remembered that "[p]eople called it a 'hodge-podge.'"[97] Perhaps the most peculiar thing about the act was that the benefit and tax sides of the old age insurance program were written into nonconsecutive titles almost as if there were no connection between the two: whereas Title II carried the heading "Federal Old-Age Benefits," Title VIII bore the nondescript label "Taxes with Respect to Employment."

The purpose, it turns out, was to try to head off opposition from the courts. Always fearful that a federal old age insurance program would be struck down as unconstitutional, those who drafted the legislation did their best to disguise the proposal. They carefully avoided using the word "insurance," and they cleverly suggested through their titling maneuver that their applications of the federal spending and taxing powers were entirely distinct and in no way novel. Of course, federal social insurance *was* novel in 1935, and the New Dealers knew it. But it was only after the Supreme Court upheld their legislation in 1937 that they could finally admit it, often with a bit of self-deprecating humor about their futile efforts to perpetrate this transparent subterfuge. "We could have called it an insurance system," Armstrong later conceded; "we could have called it anything we liked."[98]

Four Functional Pillars of the Old Age Insurance Program

Regardless of what the program was called, the contributory portion of Social Security's old age provisions may be thought of as resting on four functional pillars. These were economic stabilization, redistribution, forced savings, and risk management. Although our primary focus here is on the last of these, a quick review of the other three should help to set the stage.

The first, *economic stabilization,* stood apart from the others because it was the only one not directly associated with old age security. Although the argument has long since lost its appeal, the notion that old age insurance might help stabilize the economy was raised frequently during the depression. Proponents claimed that it would reduce the likelihood and severity of economic downturns by freeing up jobs for younger workers and by enhancing the purchasing power of the elderly.[99] Focusing particularly on the promise of additional purchasing power, Senator Wagner confidently predicted that "a flood of benefit payments . . . will have an incalculable effect upon the maintenance of industrial stability."[100]

The second pillar, *redistribution,* was sometimes obscured and even diminished by the contractual rhetoric associated with the insurance model. But redistribution—both across and within generations—nonetheless remained a vital objective for many policymakers. Although FDR himself eventually demanded an exceedingly tight connection between the contributions and benefits of each participant (as in a private annuity contract), most of his advisers and many of the leading advocates in Congress appeared to believe that a degree of redistribution was both necessary and appropriate. As Armstrong insisted in her influential book on social insurance in 1932, many lower-income workers simply did not have sufficient disposable income to save adequately for retirement on their own.[101] This view was widely shared among social insurance experts and frequently advanced in the congressional debates. Indeed, the populist Huey Long declared on the Senate floor that it was "mighty hard to understand how a man can lay up very much for his old age when during his useful years he is making less than it takes to live in the barest poverty."[102]

Public support for redistribution to the elderly was evident in the popularity of the Townsend plan, which promised a monthly pension of $200 for each citizen over the age of sixty. Although the authors of Social Security typically dismissed the Townsend plan as thoroughly irresponsible, many of their own proposals stemmed from a similar impulse. There was broad agreement at the Committee on Economic Security that a contributory scheme based exclusively on payroll taxes would not be sufficient. Federal funds would have to come into play, and the linkage between contributions and benefits would have to be somewhat flexible. Not only did the committee recommend noncontributory old age assistance for citizens who were already retired or on the verge of retirement, but also it explicitly acknowledged that early participants in the contributory program would have to receive disproportionately large benefits. Even more striking, the committee recommended that the federal government "guarantee to make contributions" in the future, supplementing those that the employers and employees made themselves.[103]

President Roosevelt was so incensed by this last proposal that he demanded it be qualified in the final hours before the report was transmitted to Congress. With the help of the Treasury Department, he subsequently eliminated even the hint of future federal contributions by accelerating the phase-in of the payroll tax and by increasing the final tax rate.[104] Even so, the old age insurance provisions retained a modest redistributive tilt. As finally enacted, the benefit formula was progressively scaled according to lifetime taxable wages. Retired workers were entitled to monthly benefits equal to one-half of 1 percent of the first $3,000 of wages on which they had paid Social Security tax, plus one-twelfth of 1 percent on the next $42,000, plus one-twenty-fourth of 1 percent on everything beyond $45,000.[105] This guaranteed that older workers who retired soon after the program was inaugurated would receive an unusually large return on their contributions, and that the lowest-wage workers would forever after receive a proportionately greater return than their higher-wage counterparts.

Many of the legislation's initial authors at the CES were clearly disappointed.[106] Armstrong later protested that the "extra amount for the lowest paid groups should have been a United States government general funds subsidy. It should not have come out of what the middle workers and the better paid workers were getting."[107] The Social Security Amendments of 1939 took some of the edge off, temporarily freezing scheduled tax increases, raising benefits for the lowest-paid workers as well as for those retiring in the program's early years, and introducing new benefits for dependent family members. But even after these changes, many friends of the legislation continued to complain about insufficient redistribution.[108] Such disappointment was probably unavoidable, given the inherent conflict between popular redistributive goals and the equally popular contractual model of social insurance. In the end, the Social Security Act could offer but a crude compromise between the two.

The contractual model found its fullest expression in the last two pillars, *forced savings* and *risk management*. The contributory portion of the old age program was very often characterized as the public analogue of a private savings plan or an insurance policy. The savings analogy was especially attractive. In his testimony before the House Ways and Means Committee, J. Douglas Brown, a Princeton economics professor and a member of the CES's old age staff, said: "It is our belief that to the employee this plan of old-age insurance will look virtually like a savings plan. It is, of course, compulsory. But to the employee the contributions, placed in the fund and matched by the employer, are equivalent to a savings account."[109]

Although the savings analogy obviously helped sell the program to the public, it was more than mere PR. Many of the leading advocates of old age insurance took for granted that a large proportion of the nation's citizens would fail to save sufficiently for their own retirement. As we have seen, part of this failure was blamed on low wages, which in turn justified a degree of redistribution. But another piece of the problem seemed to be inadequate foresight or discipline on the part of the workers themselves. The old age insurance program, said Secretary Perkins, would make "almost compulsory a habit of a slight saving every month, which has long been thought of as desirable, but which I think most of us find very difficult unless there is some rather systematic way by which we can compel ourselves to do so."[110] To some extent, therefore, the framers of old age insurance conceived of it as a means of forcing savings.[111]

Intimately associated with this logic was the idea that individual workers, if left to their own devices, were liable to squander their savings through poor investment strategies or just plain bad luck. In an interchange with Senator Long, Senator George Norris of Nebraska observed that "it could be said, as an objection to [a compulsory program], 'If you would let me handle the money, I would have made more out of it.' Sometimes that would be true, but we all know, from our own experience that, as a general rule, it has not been so." Long apparently agreed, interjecting "I admit all that" as Norris continued with his line of reasoning.[112]

Arguments for forced savings thus blended almost seamlessly into arguments for public risk management. Besides requiring considerable self-discipline over the long term, investing for one's own retirement was risky business. Failure always remained a distinct possibility. And because the consequences of failing to build a sufficiently large nest egg for retirement could be so devastating, proponents of compulsory old age insurance insisted that these "savings [be] safeguarded by the government."[113] Of the four pillars, risk management may well have been the most important. "I am sure we all agree," Senator Wagner announced toward the end of the congressional debate over Social Security, "that one of the fundamental purposes of government is to give security to its people; and I do not think any greater contribution could be made to the happiness of our people than to give them security in old age."[114] His message was surprisingly simple, but the risks to be managed were actually as complex and elusive as any the federal government had ever confronted.

Managing Retirement Risk

Of the roughly 3 million citizens that the CES classified as elderly dependents, some had never prepared for their old age at all. Others had tried and failed. Saving for one's retirement was no easy task. The risks involved were many and varied. Not all of these risks were fully apparent to the average citizen, and several could not be covered in the private

market in any case. Well aware of these difficult risk management problems, a growing number of policymakers concluded that a large federal
role in retirement planning was simply a must.

LONGEVITY RISK

The first risk to be considered, and the one most easily managed privately, was longevity risk. Because individuals could not know precisely
how long they (or their dependents) would live, it was simply impossible for them to know how much to save for retirement. Individuals who
lived longer than expected would find that they had saved too little,
while those who died before retiring or soon thereafter were liable to
have saved too much. Whereas today most people expect to live well beyond age sixty-five, the average life span was only about sixty-two years
in 1935, and so even the prospect of reaching old age was itself highly
uncertain.[115]

Private annuities offered a good solution to the challenges posed by
longevity risk. Through the purchase of an annuity, an individual obtained the right to a stable stream of income for the remainder of his life,
regardless of how long he lived. Annuities were simply insurance products that pooled longevity risk across a large number of people, and they
were freely available from many insurance companies. The problem was
that few people actually bought them. A publication put out by the U.S.
Department of Labor in 1929 offered two explanations: that annuities
were "much more costly than ordinary life policies" and that young people tended "to discount the future and to delay taking out such insurance."[116]

Economists have since suggested that the high cost of annuities may
be due to an adverse selection problem. Assuming that individuals have
a better sense of their own longevity than do the providers of annuities,
the latter would want to charge far above average actuarial cost to control for the possibility that short-lived people would opt out of the risk
pool.[117] This was not a common argument in the 1930s, however. At that
time, social insurance proponents focused more attention on the problem of inadequate foresight and overconfidence. As Rubinow pointed
out, the "successful businessman," who might have the means and the
wisdom to buy annuities, often thinks "that in this country of unlimited
possibilities he can do better by himself by handling his own problem of
saving and investment." The "masses," meanwhile, failed to buy or save

for annuities because old age seemed too "remote and uncertain" when they were young.[118]

The Social Security Act solved these problems by offering what amounted to a federal annuity program and by making participation mandatory. Indeed, the CES titled the relevant section of its report "Contributory Annuities (Compulsory System)."[119] Section 202 of the act promised monthly benefits for every "qualified individual" beginning when "he attains the age of sixty-five . . . and ending on the date of his death." (The 1939 amendments effectively converted this individual annuity into a joint-survivorship annuity, guaranteeing continued benefits for the elderly widows of fully insured workers.) Compulsory participation not only overcame the problems of inadequate worker foresight and overconfidence but also eliminated any selection bias in the risk pool, thus avoiding the ratcheting up of costs.

WORK-DURATION RISK

A closely associated risk, which the original old age provisions did not address nearly as well, was work-duration risk. The main reason why careful retirement planning was necessary in the first place was that most people became dramatically less fit for employment after a certain age. But this age varied from person to person and could not be predicted with much accuracy for any given individual very far in advance. Work-duration risk thus arose out of the impossibility of knowing precisely when one's human capital—one's capacity to generate a future stream of earnings—would be depleted. Whereas longevity risk could potentially be covered through the purchase of annuities, this was not the case for work-duration risk. Other than disability insurance (which was sold during the 1920s), there were no private means of covering a longer than expected retirement as a result of a shorter than expected duration of work.[120] Most likely, this was because of the enormous potential for moral hazard arising from the near impossibility of verifying the exact moment when a person's human capital was finally depleted.[121]

The problem of work-duration risk was certainly well understood during the New Deal. The CES's old age staff explained that "the date and conditions of the ultimate interruption of . . . earning power, when the head of a family or a single person must face the fact that he is no longer able to earn a living, is unpredictable for an individual."[122] Yet the old age provisions of the Social Security Act offered only a modest response, namely, the denial of benefits to workers over age sixty-five who remained gainfully employed. A seventy-year-old who continued to earn a living would not be entitled to benefits under the program since he had obviously not yet depleted his human capital. As J. Douglas Brown later explained, "[t]he contingency to be covered by old age insurance is not age alone but insufficient earnings from current employment *because of old age*."[123]

Lawmakers expanded Social Security's coverage of work-duration risk in subsequent years. Federal disability insurance was incorporated into the program beginning in 1956. Early retirement was introduced in 1961, allowing eligible workers who so elected to begin receiving slightly discounted benefits at age sixty-two. Eleven years later, Congress authorized a delayed retirement credit for those workers who remained employed after the age of sixty-five. All of these legislative changes from the 1950s through the 1970s helped workers better manage their own work-duration risk.[124]

In 1935, however, policymakers' concerns about the unpredictability of each individual's work duration still took a back seat to the larger problem of declining *average* work duration. Noting in his congressional testimony that the "trend of employment among the aged has been downward for 40 years," Murray Latimer predicted that this trend was likely to continue in the future and ultimately reach well beyond the elderly. "[I]t is likely," he suggested pessimistically, "there will be a large amount of permanent unemployment among the middle aged."[125] Combined with ever-increasing life spans, declining work duration promised to extend the average length of retirement and thus greatly exacerbate the threat of old age dependency. Legislators interpreted this as an unfortunate but inevitable consequence of ongoing industrialization. "[T]he situation is being constantly aggravated," said Senator Wagner, "by the lengthening span of the average life . . . and by the technological changes driving the elderly worker from the factory."[126]

Under these circumstances, the enactment of compulsory old age insurance was viewed as absolutely essential. Since a great many workers would deplete their human capital before they died, they would need some sort of financial backstop, which is precisely what Social Security was meant to provide. And since the cost of supporting the elderly would inevitably rise in the future (as work duration fell and life span increased), the contributory nature of the program would ensure its continued fiscal viability.[127] In the minds of its supporters, therefore, contributory old age insurance constituted an ideal solution to a social problem of truly enormous proportions.

INVESTMENT RISKS

There were many justifications for establishing a large government role in retirement planning. But one of the most important was that individuals, on their own, could never be sure that their investment strategies would be successful. Owing to a variety of investment risks, there was always the possibility that retirement savings—whether placed in the stock market, in commercial banks, or even in private pension funds— could perform worse and perhaps far worse than expected.

Naturally, the threat of underperformance plagued all types of investment, but it was especially worrisome in the context of retirement. This is because individuals who reached old age could no longer rely on their own earning power in the event of severe financial trouble, since their human capital was very likely depleted. As Representative William Sirovich of New York observed: "If, unfortunately, their income did not permit them to save for old age, or they lose their money through unfortunate investments, then modern industry throws them back upon the community as human driftwood and wreckage that is useless because of life's wear and tear. Thus we behold our wage earners transformed from a group of hopeful, independent citizens into a class of helpless poor."[128] Because the elderly no longer held a diversified portfolio of both financial and human capital, they found themselves unusually vulnerable to volatility in the financial markets.[129]

In thinking about this, lawmakers identified several different types of investment problems affecting retirement. One was simply poor judgment—or perhaps irresponsibility—on the part of individual savers. Senator Norris suggested that workers often lost funds "in some plan by which they expected to make a lot of money," and Representative Sirovich reminded his colleagues in the House that "[u]nfortunate business investments, alluring advertisements, high-pressure salesmen have ruined many an old father and mother."[130] A related problem was that countless citizens were "unfamiliar in the ways of money and finance."[131] The average worker, Senator Wagner once observed, "is not an actuary. He is not a mathematician. He is just a plain worker."[132]

But even when individuals invested wisely and responsibly, perhaps on the basis of expert advice, there were still no guarantees. Markets could crash, as they had in 1929. Employer pension plans could fail, or simply be terminated unilaterally by employers, as was common in the 1930s. Even banks and insurance companies could collapse unexpectedly, as evidenced in the panic of 1933. Senator Royal Copeland of New York lamented the plight of "thousands of families, I suppose millions, who thought they had prepared for the rainy day, but by reason of the depression, and the circumstances involved in it, they have come to be almost as bad off as many who were born and have lived all their lives in poverty."[133] The horrendous consequences of the financial downturn for individual savers were highlighted again and again—not only in the congressional debates but also in the committee hearings, the work of the CES, and most of the leading scholarly treatments of social insurance.[134] Investment risk was viewed, quite understandably under the circumstances, as a vicious and vexing problem that was liable to frustrate every conceivable private solution.

Government-run old age insurance was thus held up as an ideal institutional remedy. Unlike private firms and individuals, the federal government was virtually immune to market and default risk. This insight came through with particular clarity at the hearings of the House Ways and Means Committee. "[W]e have the credit of the Government as the real underlying reserve," Secretary Perkins explained in her testimony. "That is what gives this stability." According to J. Douglas Brown, the insurance proposal "affords a facility for saving for old age which, provided by the Government itself, avoids the dangers of bank failures, of losses on securities and real estate, or of other means of investment or of hoarding." W. R. Williamson, an actuarial consultant for the CES, added that "the Government expects to be a going concern indefinitely."[135]

PUBLIC VERSUS PRIVATE RISK MANAGEMENT

Running against this logic of public risk management was a proposal that emerged in the Senate to carve out a zone of private pension coverage within the Social Security system. Senator Joel Clark of Missouri suggested that employers providing pension plans that met certain minimum standards and promised benefits at least as favorable as the government plan ought to be exempted from the public program. Responsibility for certifying, monitoring, and decertifying these private plans would be vested in the Social Security Board itself. Finally, if a participant in a private pension plan ended his involvement for any reason (either because the plan was terminated or the worker changed jobs), the employer would be required to pay all back taxes plus 3 percent interest to the federal government, and the worker would gain full coverage under the public plan.[136]

Clark and his allies argued that this exemption was necessary to prevent overcentralization of old age insurance under government auspices, to encourage private initiative, and to avoid inadvertently shutting down private plans that already offered more generous benefits than what the government was prepared to provide.[137] Although the amendment passed by a vote of 51 to 35 in the Senate, it proved terribly unpopular in the House and never made it into the final legislation. The Clark Amendment had also provoked the fierce opposition of every major sponsor of the Social Security bill, including Senator Wagner, Representative Doughton, and President Roosevelt himself.[138]

There were many reasons for such hostility. Besides believing that the nation's private pension system had already fallen short, most of the leading proponents of compulsory old age insurance feared that a private opt-out clause would end up crippling the public system they were trying to build. Again and again, critics highlighted the problem of adverse selection. "The only people who would be covered by private plans," Representative Doughton predicted, "would be the younger workers. Thus the Government plan would be left with all the 'bad risks', while all the strong contributors would be exempt. Very soon the Government fund would be insolvent, and the entire insurance principle would be destroyed."[139] Opponents of the Clark Amendment also worried that by emphasizing the link between the tax and benefit provisions in the Social Security Act, it might increase the odds of the legislation being struck down as unconstitutional.[140]

Perhaps most intriguing of all, the debate over the Clark Amendment placed concerns about default risk in the sharpest possible relief. Senator Pat Harrison of Mississippi warned that "if there is a private industrial institution with a private pension system, and it should go bankrupt . . . the responsibility would be placed on the Government, and it would have to pay the pension and not the private institution, because there would be nothing left of that institution."[141] Senator Henrik Shipstead of Minnesota shared Harrison's concern, reminding his colleagues that private plans had often failed to make good on their promises in the past. "I have had, in recent years, complaints from people who supposed that they were the beneficiaries of private retirement systems," he said, "but who found that the reserve funds invested to carry on the retirement plan had been so badly invested that when the time came for them to receive the benefits which were anticipated, and which they expected to receive annually, the condition of the fund was such that the amount received by them, in many cases, was very little."[142]

Although Clark and his allies insisted that such failures would be extremely unlikely since the amendment authorized the Social Security Board to monitor the private plans as necessary, critics claimed that such monitoring would inevitably prove inadequate. "A [federal official] could not be sent in every week or every month to make an investigation as to how the funds were being administered," Senator Wagner protested. When Clark reminded him that his amendment would permit precisely this sort of inspection, Wagner shot back, "I am addressing myself more to the physical impossibility of doing it."[143] Perfect monitoring of private funds, he believed, was simply an impossible task for the government, suggesting that the best solution to the nagging problem of default risk was a purely public program with no private involvement whatsoever. If the government was going to assume all the risk anyway, it might as well run the program itself.

ROADS NOT TRAVELED?

Ideas about risk management thus played a vital role in the original debates over federal old age insurance. Even a private defined-benefit pension plan—which was designed to manage both longevity risk and market risk by promising a stable benefit throughout retirement—was itself liable to fail as a result of default risk. Only the government, proponents suggested, could provide a perfectly secure defined-benefit plan since only it was expected "to be a going concern indefinitely." The federal government was thus put forth as the ultimate risk manager.

Still, of all the plausible risk management arguments that might have been advanced in support of old age insurance, a few were noticeably absent from the discussion. Perhaps most striking from a modern perspective was the lack of any sustained treatment of intergenerational risk spreading. Those who lived through the depression were surely aware that some generations got hit harder than others as a result of economic downturns and other calamities. "The aged of this decade," one congressman sadly declared, "have not only been deprived of a just share of the fruits of their labor but of employment. They have been stripped of their savings by years of unsound economic conditions, by the dust storms of speculation that swept our country and the consequent failure of banks, building and loan associations, and kindred institutions."[144] Concerns of this sort were nearly universal. Almost everyone wanted to help those unlucky enough to have reached old age during the depression. Yet proponents of compulsory old age insurance stopped short of characterizing the program as a means of spreading extraordinary (systematic) risks across multiple generations.[145]

The Committee on Economic Security did acknowledge that disproportionately large payments to workers who retired in the early years of the program would involve "the creation of a debt upon which future generations will have to pay large amounts annually." But this was portrayed as a one-time transfer rather than as a precedent for future crises. As the committee went on to explain, "[T]he plan we advocate amounts to having each generation pay for the support of the people then living who are old."[146] No special escape hatches were written into the legislation allowing especially unlucky cohorts to pay smaller than normal taxes or to receive larger than normal benefits. Indeed, President Roosevelt insisted on pushing the program in the other direction, raising taxes and trimming benefits in the early years so as to remain more faithful to the contractual model. It was only with the Social Security Amendments of 1939 that the pay-as-you-go principle became operative; and even then, the potential for intergenerational risk spreading was left vague at best.[147]

Another risk that was only barely addressed amidst the establishment of federal old age insurance had to do with inflation. The real value of monthly pension benefits (whether public or private) could easily be eroded as a result of unexpected increases in the consumer price level. Because there was no private market for inflation risk (meaning that no financial instruments were being sold allowing one to insure or hedge against inflation), the government potentially had a special role to play in managing this risk.[148] Although several scholars, a number of CES staff members, and a few congressmen clearly recognized the problem, precious little attention was devoted to the idea of indexing monthly benefits to the consumer price index.[149] In all likelihood, this was because most policymakers were far more concerned about deflation than about inflation during the 1930s. Once inflation actually did emerge as a serious problem in American economic life (several decades later), Congress quickly authorized automatic cost-of-living adjustments for old age insurance recipients as part of the Social Security Amendments of 1972.

One final risk that played little role in the original formulation of Social Security policy involved unexpected changes in the average standard of living. Even in the absence of rising consumer prices, larger than expected increases in real per capita income could compromise the perceived value of otherwise stable monthly pension benefits. This is because individuals generally evaluate their standards of living in relative as well as absolute terms. The problem was largely overlooked during the New Deal, however. Other than the fact that monthly benefits were to be calculated as a percentage of lifetime taxable earnings, there was no meaningful attempt to address relative standard of living risk in the Social Security Act of 1935.

In subsequent decades Congress ended up covering this risk, more or less, by approving ad hoc benefit increases that exceeded cost-of-living adjustments. Particularly since 1960, the ratio of Social Security's average annual retirement benefit to per capita GDP has remained remarkably stable at approximately 30 percent.[150] As in the case of inflation risk, therefore, the old age insurance program emerged as an even more far-reaching risk management tool than many of its authors had originally intended. Clearly, the public management of retirement risk has retained considerable economic and political appeal.

Conclusion

In laying the rhetorical groundwork for what would become the Social Security Act, President Roosevelt declared that the people "want some safeguard against misfortunes which cannot be wholly eliminated in this man-made world of ours."[151] The Committee on Economic Security quoted this passage back to the president in the very first sentence of its report, and then refined it, noting that "[m]ost of the hazards against which safeguards must be provided are similar in that they involve a loss of earnings."[152] This idea—that workers' earnings had to be protected against a variety of hazards—was at the core of the committee's recommendations and of the Social Security Act itself. It also neatly summarized the primary objective of American risk management policy under Phase II.

Social Security addressed two of the leading hazards facing nearly every worker: unemployment and insufficient income in old age. Specifically, it inaugurated federal-state systems of unemployment insurance and old age assistance as well as a strictly federal system of old age insurance. It appropriated funds for a number of other purposes as well, including aid to dependent children (which would ultimately evolve into AFDC), various maternal and child welfare programs, a range of public health services, and aid to the blind. But the two insurance programs were by far the most important features of the legislation, dominating the debate in Congress and quickly capturing the imagination of the American people.

The act was far from complete, however—even from a risk management perspective.[153] Not only were certain aspects of unemployment and retirement risk left uncovered, but several other major worker risks were left out altogether. Arthur Altmeyer later described the absence of mandatory health and disability insurance as the "great gap" in Social Security coverage.[154] Already in 1935, most of the legislation's architects were acutely aware of these structural deficiencies, even as the final plans for Social Security were being drawn up and approved.

Compulsory health insurance actually came surprisingly close to becoming a part of the draft legislation Roosevelt submitted to Congress in 1935.[155] There was considerable support for the idea among the members of the CES; and even FDR had indicated on several occasions that any comprehensive program of economic security would ultimately have to include health insurance.[156] Although the committee avoided making any firm recommendations on the subject in its first report to the president, it ultimately endorsed compulsory health insurance after receiving a favorable recommendation from its key medical advisers. A draft report to the president was quickly drawn up in March calling for the establishment of a federal-state system, which would cover both wage loss stemming from illness and the costs of essential medical care. But the process was soon aborted as a result of fierce opposition from physicians and especially the American Medical Association. Fearing that the inclusion of compulsory health insurance "would spell defeat for the entire bill," Roosevelt and his top advisers reluctantly let it go. The committee's report on health insurance was hidden from public view and its official transmission to the president was delayed until November, long after the Social Security bill had already been enacted into law.[157]

Although all subsequent attempts to resuscitate compulsory health insurance came to naught, coverage against a related risk—disability—was eventually incorporated into the Social Security program beginning in the 1950s. The Social Security Amendments of 1956 established monthly benefits for totally and permanently disabled workers between the ages of fifty and sixty-five. Disability benefits, which commenced after a six-month waiting period, were intended to replace a portion of lost earnings—precisely in line with the logic of Phase II. The amendments of 1960 extended the program to workers of all ages, and the amendments of 1965 allowed benefits to be paid to workers whose disabilities were not expected to last beyond twelve months. The 1965 amendments also created Medicare, another monumental social insurance program in its own right, which provided public health insurance for the elderly and, some years later, for the disabled as well.[158]

By this time, however, the heyday of Phase II had already come and gone. Worker security remained an important policy objective, as exemplified by passage of the Employee Retirement Income Security Act (ERISA) in 1974. ERISA authorized extensive regulation of private pension funds and required defined-benefit plans to purchase government insurance from the newly created Pension Benefit Guaranty Corporation.[159] But this sort of income security measure was now more the exception than the rule. As we will see in the next two chapters, a great many of the new risk management policies introduced after 1960 no longer focused on the problem of unexpected wage loss. Instead, they seemed to address an ever-widening array of risks that threatened consumers, homeowners, pedestrians—indeed, citizens in almost every conceivable role and guise. Phase III had arrived.

8

Product Liability Law

The third phase of American risk management policy reshaped a wide range of government activities and responsibilities. No longer were businesspeople and workers to be the primary beneficiaries of public risk management. Security for the citizen at large quickly emerged as a leading social priority. The dawn of Phase III was visible in areas as diverse as public disaster relief, insurance guaranties, and environmental policy. But perhaps nowhere was the change more evident than in the transformation of product liability law.

New ideas about consumer protection and producer liability swept through the courts like a tidal wave beginning in the 1960s, demolishing much of the traditional legal doctrine on the subject. Manufacturers and their insurers were stunned to discover that within just a short time, the familiar notion of *caveat emptor* (buyer beware) had given way to *caveat venditor* (seller beware). The old logic of liability law, which seemed to protect producers at almost every turn, had been the target of criticism and reform for some time. But now, rather suddenly, it was being overturned altogether.

In many ways, the story was similar to that of workers' compensation at the beginning of the century (Phase II). Once again, the key question was how best to allocate accident risk. Just as early proponents of workers' compensation believed that existing law was biased against injured workers, early proponents of product liability reform believed that existing law was biased against injured consumers. In both cases, reform-minded academics played a pivotal role. And in both cases, leading advocates of change argued that the proper allocation of accident risk

216

would work wonders, not only promising compensation for victims but actually preventing a great many accidents from happening in the first place.

For all of these similarities, however, the differences between the two campaigns were equally notable. The academics who helped to orchestrate the overhaul of product liability law were legal scholars, not economists; and their focus was on the consumer rather than the worker. Having chosen liability law as their central risk management tool, they appealed mainly to judges instead of legislators. As they well understood at the time, their choice of policy instruments was of enormous significance. Unlike social insurance, liability law was primarily a device for shifting risk, not spreading it. It was also a much blunter implement than social insurance—a legal sledgehammer, of sorts, which promised to get the job done but not without leaving some rough edges.

The essential argument that underlay the transformation of product liability law was that producers, not consumers, were best positioned to manage product injury risk. This is why advocates of reform insisted that accident risk ought to be shifted aggressively onto their shoulders. By holding producers strictly liable for consumer injuries, they maintained, the courts would induce manufacturers to make safer products, thereby reducing the overall injury rate. They also believed that producers were ideally positioned to spread the remaining risk, since they could pass the cost of injuries on to all of their consumers in the form of slightly higher prices.

Even more than the early proponents of workers' compensation and Social Security, the legal scholars and judges who championed strict liability for consumer products were steeped in the language and the logic of risk management. One of the seminal articles, for example, was Guido Calabresi's "Some Thoughts on Risk Distribution and the Law of Torts," published in the *Yale Law Journal* in 1961. Ideas about optimal risk management were absolutely central to the whole project. At the same time, however, the campaign for strict liability also suggested a new set of social priorities, though often under the guise of devising more efficient means of allocating risk. To the extent that there was a trade-off between economic growth and personal security, the advocates of strict liability seemed to place considerably greater emphasis on the latter than did their predecessors in the nineteenth and early twentieth centuries.

The purpose of this chapter, therefore, is to explore both the logic and the passions driving the transformation of product liability law, a truly pivotal risk management policy. Precisely what problems were proponents of product liability reform aiming to solve, and exactly how did they expect their proposed solution to work? Because the answers to these questions come into particularly sharp focus when placed in a proper historical context, the chapter starts with a brief survey of product liability law through the nineteenth and early twentieth centuries. It then homes in on the extraordinary changes that unfolded some years later as part of Phase III. By all accounts, there was a "revolution in liability law."[1] The goal here is to understand how and why this came to be.

The Early History of Product Liability Law

Producer Protection and the Pursuit of Growth

Product liability law exhibited a powerful producer orientation in the nineteenth century. The story may be said to begin with *Winterbottom v. Wright,* a British case from 1842 that quickly became ruling precedent on both sides of the Atlantic.[2] The plaintiff in the case, Winterbottom, was injured while driving a mail coach that collapsed as a result of defects in its construction. He sued Wright, the coach manufacturer and repairman who had contracted with the postmaster general to keep the coach in good repair. As was typical at the time, the suit alleged breach of warranty. Such a case would almost surely fall under tort law today, but suits involving parties to commercial transactions were nearly always handled under contract law in the nineteenth century. Winterbottom thus charged that Wright had violated his contract to maintain the coach.

Although the coach was certainly not in good repair when it collapsed, and although Winterbottom was most definitely injured as a result, the Court of the Exchequer ruled that no cause of action existed, citing an absence of *privity of contract* between the driver and the repairman. Winterbottom had been hired by an independent contractor rather than by the postmaster general himself; and Wright had contracted exclusively with the postmaster general. As Lord Abinger, the Chief Baron, declared: "There is no privity of contract between these parties; and if the plaintiff can sue, every passenger or even any person passing along the road, who was injured by the upsetting of the coach, might bring a similar action. Unless we confine the operation of such contracts as this to the parties who entered into them, the most absurd and outrageous consequences, to which I can see no limit, would ensue." Baron Alderson added in a concurring opinion, "The only safe rule is to confine the right to recover to those who enter into the contract: if we go one step beyond that, there is no reason why we should not go fifty." Naturally, no one could deny that it was "a hardship upon the plaintiff to be without a remedy." But as Baron Rolfe concluded in another concurring opinion, "[B]y that consideration we ought not to be influenced. Hard cases, it has been frequently observed, are apt to produce hard law."[3]

In America, the powerful legal principle that Lord Abinger articulated in *Winterbottom* was confirmed again and again in the courts, and its application was certainly not limited to stagecoach accidents.[4] Since nearly all manufactured goods were sold through intermediaries, the privity doctrine effectively insulated manufacturers against the vast majority of defective-product suits. "It is a long established general rule," a Massachusetts court explained as late as 1921, "that the manufacturer of an article is not liable to those who have no contractual relations with him for injuries resulting from negligence in its manufacture."[5]

As was discussed in an earlier chapter, injured workers had also faced tremendous obstacles in recovering from employers during the nineteenth century, even when the employer himself or one of his agents was found to be negligent. Once again Lord Abinger played a pivotal role, writing a forceful decision in the case of *Priestly v. Fowler* five years before *Winterbottom*. The case involved a butcher's servant who was severely injured when an overloaded meat wagon suddenly collapsed. Sounding the same conservative tone as in *Winterbottom,* Abinger declared, "If the master be liable to the servant in this action, the principle of that liability will be found to carry us to an alarming extent."[6] Just a few years later, in the landmark case of *Farwell v. Boston & Worcester Railroad Corporation,* Chief Justice Lemuel Shaw of the Massachusetts Supreme Court defined the assumption-of-risk doctrine and the fellow-servant rule, further clarifying the legal logic that shielded employers against worker suits.[7] Contributory negligence soon emerged as yet another powerful employer defense against the claims of injured workers in the nineteenth century.[8]

On the basis of differing legal rationale, therefore, the American courts severely constrained both consumers and workers from obtaining compensation for accident-related injuries. Strangely, whereas consumers were barred from recovery for being contractually too distant from negligent manufacturers, workers were blocked for being too close to negligent employers or fellow workers, ostensibly on the grounds that they had assumed the risks of their own employment. In both cases, however, the end result was the same. As Oliver Wendell Holmes declared in 1881, the "general principle of our law is that loss from accident must lie where it falls."[9] Chief Justice Shaw had made almost precisely the same observation in his *Farwell* opinion back in 1842, and it remained one of the pillars of American law throughout the nineteenth century.[10]

EXCEPTIONS TO THE RULE

Naturally, numerous exceptions emerged with the passage of time, particularly for consumers. The New York high court ruled in *Thomas v. Winchester* in 1852 that privity was not essential for recovery from negligent producers when inherently dangerous goods, such as poisons, were involved. In *Thomas,* the defendant had actually mislabeled a poison as medicine, leading the court to hold him liable for damages despite the absence of privity.[11] Nearly a quarter-century later, the Supreme Court of Pennsylvania similarly determined that a manufacturer would remain liable for injuries stemming from the use of dangerous lamp oil even after the product had passed through many intermediaries. The manufacturer who had sold this "death-dealing fluid," the court declared, could "plead nothing in defence of this wilful, terrible wrong done to a confiding community."[12]

Under extreme circumstances like these, nineteenth-century judges frequently recognized the claims of injured consumers even in the absence of privity. Manufacturers in these cases were said to have violated some fundamental duty of care, and thus came under the law of negligence rather than contract. The challenge, as Judge Francis Black of Missouri stated in 1892, was "to fix upon the dividing line between those cases where the duty begins and ends with contract, and where the law imposes a duty to third persons notwithstanding contract."[13]

One federal judge, Walter H. Sanborn, attempted to specify such a demarcation in 1903, identifying three broad categories of exceptions to the privity defense. The first involved injuries from inherently dangerous goods or goods designed "to preserve, destroy, or affect human life." These goods included poisons, weapons, some combustibles, drugs, and foodstuffs. The second category of exceptions (and the only one that did not typically affect consumers) stemmed from injuries resulting from defective equipment used upon the owner's invitation, such as faulty scaffolding or loading chains. Finally, a third class of exceptions involved injuries arising out of the failure of sellers to warn of known dangers or defects that could result in severe harm. A California woman who broke her arm using a defective folding bed purchased by her landlords, for example, was allowed to recover from the furniture dealer despite the absence of privity. But this was only because the dealer, "knowing [the] folding bed to be defective and unsafe, sold it to a Mr. Apperson [the landlord] without informing him of the fact."[14]

Given these wide-ranging exceptions to the privity rule, a number of legal scholars have essentially denied the existence of producer bias in nineteenth-century injury law, arguing that the obstacles to consumer recovery generally proved modest in practice. Gary Schwartz has suggested that nineteenth-century "tort law exhibited a keen concern for victim welfare," while Peter Karsten concludes that "those injured by defective products in eighteenth- and nineteenth-century England and America had generally been able to obtain redress under the law."[15]

No doubt there were a great many cases of successful consumer recovery, even in the nineteenth century. To paraphrase Karsten, judges often ruled from their hearts as well as their heads. Exceptions like the ones Schwartz and Karsten have highlighted demonstrate the limits of simple historical classifications, including the three phases of risk management policy suggested here. They also reveal that not all nineteenth-century policymakers were blind to the needs of workers and consumers, nor to the many risks that they faced. But when all is said and done, one has to be careful not to become so intrigued with the various exceptions as to lose sight of the rule around which they all revolved.

THE HARD LOGIC OF AMERICAN LIABILITY LAW UNDER PHASE I

The truth is that the essential *rule* of product-injury law remained heavily biased in favor of producers throughout most of the nineteenth century and into the twentieth. The judges who ruled on these cases—including those who ultimately awarded damages to injured plaintiffs—had no trouble distinguishing the exceptions from the rule itself. As Judge Sanborn explained when he identified the three basic categories of exceptions: "The general rule [of privity] is that a contractor, manufacturer, or vendor is not liable to third parties who have no contractual relations with him for negligence in the construction, manufacture, or sale of the articles he handles. . . . But while this general rule is both established and settled, there are, as is usually the case, exceptions to it as well defined and settled as the rule itself."[16]

Many nineteenth- and early twentieth-century judges were equally explicit about the Phase I logic that lay behind the general rule of privity. The Pennsylvania high court warned in 1891 that without the privity rule, it would be "difficult [for the contractor or manufacturer] to measure the extent of his responsibility, and no prudent man would engage in such occupations under such conditions. It is safer and wiser to confine such liabilities to the parties immediately concerned."[17]

Similarly, the Supreme Judicial Court of Massachusetts predicted in 1907 that if

> extended liability attached where no privity of contract exists . . . manufacturers as a class would be exposed to such far reaching consequences as to seriously embarrass the general prosecution of mercantile business. In the usual course of trade upon making a sale, as the article passes from the ownership and control of the maker, it is held that when these cease his liability also should be considered as ended.[18]

Lord Abinger himself had speculated in *Winterbottom* that without a privity rule, "the most absurd and outrageous consequences, to which I can see no limit, would ensue." Some sixty years later, Judge Sanborn attributed the privity doctrine, above all else, to the dictates of "wise and conservative public policy," which required that "there must be a fixed and definite limitation to the liability of manufacturers and vendors for negligence."[19]

Before revisionists like Schwartz and Karsten began advancing their critiques, the consensus view among legal historians was that nineteenth-century judges had bent over backward to favor business. Willard Hurst wrote of the desire to "encourage entrepreneurs by reducing risks," noting that the courts' rulings in tort cases "evidenced . . . caution against creating indefinite risks of liability, especially during the rise of new industries in the first half of the century."[20] Similarly, Lawrence Friedman observed in a pathbreaking history of American law that absolute liability was rejected in the nineteenth century—"more accurately, it was never considered"—on the grounds that "it might have strangled the economy altogether." The fear was that if "railroads, and enterprise generally, had to pay for all damage done 'by accident,' lawsuits could drain them of their economic blood. . . . Capital had to be spared for its necessary work."[21] He added a few pages later that "the concept of spoon-feeding enterprise, the blind desire for economic growth, [was] responsible for a good deal of 19th-century callousness."[22] Refining this argument and extending it still further, Morton Horwitz declared in his survey of early American legal history that "common law doctrines were transformed [during the antebellum period] to create immunities from legal liability and thereby to provide substantial subsidies for those who undertook schemes of economic development."[23]

Historians such as Hurst, Friedman, and Horwitz may well have exaggerated the pro-business bias of nineteenth-century accident law; and there is no question that they overlooked many of the pro-consumer exceptions that speckled the legal landscape.[24] The implications of *Winterbottom* were so extraordinarily harsh for injured consumers that many judges looked for ways to escape the logical straitjacket Lord Abinger had imposed on them. Even so, they proved resolute in their commitment to the general rule that *Winterbottom* established. Economic imperatives surely loomed large.[25] Along with the three employer defenses ("the unholy trinity of common law defenses," in the words of one critic), the privity defense against consumer suits strongly favored the producer. Unless one focuses almost exclusively on the exceptions, it is difficult to escape the impression that nineteenth-century judges did indeed insulate industry from at least part of the burden it was imposing on society in the form of accidents.

Perhaps the strongest evidence for this conclusion may be found in the remarkably slow development of product liability insurance. Whereas fire insurance emerged after the great London conflagration of 1666, the various forms of liability insurance came much later.[26] Employer liability insurance found a market in Britain only after passage of the Employers' Liability Act of 1880, which sharply limited the fellow-servant defense. Similarly, in America, employer liability insurance caught on toward the end of the century as numerous state legislatures began paring back the "unholy trinity" of employer defenses.[27] Product liability insurance, by contrast, failed to emerge in the United States until the early twentieth century; and there remained relatively little demand for it until after World War II. Although one investigator found that "most manufacturers were carrying employers' liability and many carried general public liability [insurance]" by the 1920s, the vast majority of companies still refused to give in "to the entreaties of buyers and brokers for products coverage." When asked about product liability coverage in 1939, an insurance company representative conceded that "product liability lines have not been sought after by many companies," an admission that the interviewer characterized as "a masterly understatement."[28]

Cracks in the Wall of Producer Protection

It was no coincidence, of course, that "adequate products liability policies first began to be written" in the 1920s.[29] The rule established in *Winterbottom* had just recently suffered its first major defeat, when the New York Court of Appeals handed down the landmark *MacPherson v. Buick Motor Company* decision in 1916.[30] The case itself was an interesting one. Donald C. MacPherson was injured on being thrown from his car after the wooden spokes in one wheel suddenly splintered. The spokes were later determined to have been defective. Although Buick had bought the spokes from another manufacturer, there was evidence that the defects "could have been discovered by reasonable inspection [by Buick], and that inspection was omitted." The key question in the case was whether MacPherson had a right of action against Buick, since he had purchased the car through a retail dealer rather than from Buick directly.[31]

Writing for the majority, Justice Benjamin Cardozo recognized the principle established in *Winterbottom* but suggested tactfully that "[p]recedents drawn from the days of travel by stage coach do not fit the conditions of travel to-day." He thus carefully worked his way around the privity doctrine. Articulating a new test for product liability actions, he wrote,

> If the nature of a thing is such that it is reasonably certain to place life and limb in peril when negligently made, it is then a thing of danger. Its nature gives warning of the consequences to be expected. If to the element of danger there is added knowledge that the thing will be used by persons other than the purchaser, and used without new tests, then, irrespective of contract, the manufacturer of this thing of danger is under a duty to make it carefully.

In a strongly worded dissent, Justice Willard Bartlett complained that the majority's decision (along with the lower court decisions it affirmed) "extend the liability of the vendor of a manufactured article further than any case which has yet received the sanction of this court." Indeed, Cardozo himself acknowledged that the majority decision represented a significant departure, treating an injury resulting from a commercial transaction as a subject of tort law rather than as a contractual issue. "We have put aside the notion," he wrote with obvious feeling, "that the duty to safeguard life and limb, when the consequences of negligence may be foreseen, grows out of contract and nothing else. We have put the source of the obligation where it ought to be. We have put its source in the law."[32]

MacPherson was clearly a pivotal decision, dramatically expanding the exception originally carved out in *Thomas v. Winchester* (1852) so that it applied not just to inherently dangerous items but to all things that threatened to become hazardous when negligently made. Some sixty years later, Justice Richard Jones of the Alabama Supreme Court noted that with *MacPherson*, "the exceptions [finally] consumed the rule."[33]

As it turned out, however, the rule of privity was not consumed all at once. The new doctrine articulated in *MacPherson* spread rather slowly to other jurisdictions; and privity still remained applicable in a number of related areas, including the law of implied warranty.[34] As a result of *MacPherson*, tort law did increasingly replace contract law as the appropriate legal domain for product liability suits against manufacturers. But even so, recovery remained difficult in most cases because of the need to prove negligence. Justice Jones observed, "While *MacPherson* was a major advance in consumer protection, the . . . difficulty of proving a manufacturer's lack of due care . . . still plagued plaintiffs."[35] This is very likely the reason why there remained precious little demand among manufacturers for product liability insurance even after a number of commercial carriers began offering such coverage in the 1920s. Despite *MacPherson*, manufacturer liability in product injury cases appears to have remained relatively low for many years to come.

The changing treatment of workers injured in on-the-job accidents offered a stark contrast. At the same moment that *MacPherson* was being decided in 1916, numerous state legislatures were enacting workers' compensation laws, which mandated no-fault insurance for workplace accidents. Under these statutes, injured workers were entitled to compensation even in the absence of employer negligence. Whereas workplace injuries were now quickly coming under a standard of strict liability, consumers still had to adjudicate product-related injuries under negligence law. What mattered was not the nature or the severity of the accident but rather the status of the victim. The essential worker orientation of Phase II could hardly have been clearer.

The first signs of an equivalent transformation of product injury law—that is, toward strict liability in consumer cases—came considerably later. Justice Roger Traynor of the California Supreme Court first injected the strict liability idea into the judicial record in a concurring opinion to the now famous *Escola v. Coca Cola* case of 1944. The California court ruled that a waitress who was injured when a bottle of Coca-Cola exploded in her hand could recover damages from the bottling company on the grounds that it had acted negligently. But Traynor maintained that proof of negligence should not have been required for recovery. "I concur in the judgment," he wrote,

> but I believe the manufacturer's negligence should no longer be singled out as the basis of a plaintiff's right to recover in cases like the present one. In my opinion it should now be recognized that a manufacturer incurs an absolute liability when an article that he has placed on the market, knowing that it is to be used without inspection, proves to have a defect that causes injury to human beings. . . . Even if there is no negligence . . . public policy demands that responsibility be fixed wherever it will most effectively reduce the hazards to life and health inherent in defective products that reach the market. It is evident that the manufacturer can anticipate some hazards and guard against the recurrence of others, as the public cannot. . . . [T]he risk of injury can be insured by the manufacturer and distributed among the public as a cost of doing business. . . . Against such a risk there should be general and constant protection and the manufacturer is best situated to afford such protection.[36]

This powerful argument for liability without fault carried no legal weight because it was expressed in a concurring rather than a majority opinion. But the fact was that traditional ideas about negligence were already on the defensive in the nation's leading law schools; and it would not be long before the doctrine of strict liability was spreading through the courts as well.

New Life in the Ivory Tower

Academic interest in the promise of strict liability began growing in the 1920s and 1930s, blossomed in the 1950s and early 1960s, and ultimately bore fruit in the courts over the next twenty years. Beneath these scholarly and judicial developments were two sturdy conceptual roots. One was historical. Leading proponents of strict liability, particularly at the Yale Law School, claimed that a product injury regime based either on privity or negligence was no longer appropriate in the twentieth century. Special protections for producers may well have been necessary to sustain nascent industrialization in the nineteenth century, they conceded, but were strangely out of place now that the industrial economy had matured.

The other conceptual root, branching off from the historical one, was more philosophical in nature. The core idea here was that the concept of risk was superior to fault in the assessment of liability. Believing this, several of the nation's most brilliant and daring legal scholars attempted to craft an entirely new analytic framework for product injury law. Whereas the nineteenth-century regime was designed to allocate blame, this one—the legal regime of the future—would allocate risk as efficiently and as humanely as possible.

John Maynard Keynes once suggested that "the power of vested interests [to influence public policy] is vastly exaggerated compared with the gradual encroachment of ideas."[37] Though Keynes was writing mainly about economic policy, his observation also aptly characterizes the development of tort law in the United States—particularly during the second half of the twentieth century. The ideas of legal scholars proved pivotal in the courts' adoption of strict liability after 1960. Indeed, in writing their opinions, many judges were quick to acknowledge their intellectual debts to academic luminaries such as Fleming James (Yale Law School), Friedrich Kessler (Yale Law School), William Prosser (Berkeley Law School), and Guido Calabresi (Yale Law School). By the late 1960s, life had definitely begun to imitate art in the realm of product liability law.

Fashioning Rules for a "Settled Industrial Society"

The leading authorities on American liability law had no trouble explaining the origins of the existing fault-based system. It was, they thought, a natural outgrowth of nineteenth-century laissez-faire individualism. Given the enormous contemporary emphasis on personal responsibility, it seemed only natural that nineteenth-century judges would have chosen to assign liability on the basis of fault and to allow losses to lie where they fell when blame could not be pinned solely or definitively on the defendant.[38]

Proponents of strict liability also argued that the existing liability regime—based on the principle of privity as well as negligence—had been consciously conceived in the nineteenth century as a means of promoting industrialization. As early as 1905, the legal scholar Francis Bohlen began questioning whether the producer orientation of American liability law was perhaps too extreme. "To encourage commerce and industry by removing all duty and incentive to protect the public," he wrote, "is to invite wholesale sacrifice of individual rights at the altar of commercial greed. . . . It would appear to be high time to consider whether this price is not too high to pay for industrial expansion, and whether those who profit by the operation of a business should not bear at least the burden of exercising reasonable competence and care therein."[39]

This view was highlighted repeatedly over the first half of the twentieth century and gained even greater currency in the fifties and sixties. Charles Gregory of the University of Virginia Law School wrote in 1951 that nineteenth-century judges "believed that the development of this young country under a system of private enterprise would be hindered and delayed as long as the element of chance exposed enterprisers to liability for the consequences of pure accident, without fault of some sort." Speaking more specifically about the standard defenses in employer liability law, Gregory added that "[j]udicial subsidies of this sort to youthful enterprise removed pressure from the pocket-books of investors and gave incipient industry a chance to experiment on low-cost operations without risk of losing its reserve in actions by injured employees. Such a policy no doubt seems ruthless; but in a small way it probably helped to establish industry, which in turn was essential to the good society as Shaw envisaged it."[40] Gregory singled out Chief Justice Lemuel Shaw of the Massachusetts Supreme Court simply because he had been the first American judge to articulate the assumption-of-risk doctrine and the fellow-servant rule back in 1842.[41]

In their seminal text on tort law published in 1956, Fowler Harper and Fleming James (both of the Yale Law School) observed incisively: "Much affirmative activity is dangerous. In an industrial age, this is perhaps especially true. . . . It is the very gist of the fault principle to privilege the entrepreneur to take this toll [on others], so long as the activity is lawful and carried on with reasonable care." It was not by chance, therefore, "that this development [of the fault principle] coincided with the industrial revolution." The origins of the nation's negligence-based liability regime, Harper and James insisted, was deeply rooted in the economic imperatives of the nineteenth century.[42]

Although this argument about the growth orientation of nineteenth-century liability law was typically expressed in rather general terms, a young assistant professor at Yale attempted in 1961 to add some specificity and to place it on a firmer economic footing. Guido Calabresi, who would eventually rise to become dean of the Yale Law School and later a federal judge, noted that in the "early days of the industrial revolution many industries were operating on a decreasing cost basis." This suggested that "if an industry could expand sufficiently its costs would fall as a result of that expansion," and thus that "a subsidy to that industry [would] probably help, rather than hinder, proper allocation of resources." It may therefore have been efficient in the nineteenth century, Calabresi speculated, for American judges to subsidize industry by sparing industrialists "from paying hidden accident costs." He also noted that as a result of this logic, "the allocation-of-resources theory could in the 19th century justify a result we would deem outrageous today," namely, that injured workers and consumers should "subsidize industrial expansion" by bearing the costs of accidents themselves.[43]

The reason why advocates of strict liability placed so much emphasis on the pro-growth (Phase I) logic underlying nineteenth-century liability law was that they hoped to demonstrate its obsolescence in the twentieth century. Justice Roger Traynor, for example, stressed "the transition from an industrial revolution to a settled industrial society."[44] Somewhere along the way, the idea of promoting industry by pushing accident costs off onto consumers had apparently lost its appeal. Numerous legal scholars insisted that the economy's extraordinary complexity had transformed the privity and negligence standards into unreasonable bars to recovery. Indeed, the proliferation of mass production itself had rendered negligence almost impossible to prove in many cases.[45]

The most important argument of all, however, was simply that consumer protection had emerged as an increasingly vital social priority as America's industrial economy matured. "The 'humanitarian' social conscience of today is apparently much more concerned with the poor devil who gets injured by our modern devices than was the social conscience of the Victorian period," wrote Lester Feezer on the state of manufacturer liability in 1930. "So it is that the social concept of what is the end or purpose of the law seems to be changing." Feezer went on to characterize the change as "in part a reaction to representative government, to more widespread education, and to general prosperity. . . . There is a general sense of well-being and an expansiveness of spirit that wants to share the general prosperity with the other fellow, rather than leave him unaided after an accident."[46]

Over the next thirty years, this argument emerged as a staple in the campaign for product liability reform—initially as a justification for individual exceptions to the negligence standard and for the abandonment of the privity requirement, and ultimately for the wholesale adoption of strict liability in all product injury cases. In 1956, Harper and James wrote of the "ever-growing pressure for protection of the consumer." Four years later, in one of the most influential law review articles ever written, William Prosser, dean of Berkeley Law School, declared that "the 'emotional drive' and the public demand that has sprung from it have centered in the consumer."[47] That the old regime was obsolete—inconsistent with twentieth-century social priorities—appeared altogether obvious. The tougher question now was how best to craft and justify a new one.

The Emerging Logic of Strict Liability

In retrospect, it seems clear that a handful of law professors, including both James and Prosser, helped orchestrate a silent coup to overthrow the nation's fault-based liability regime. Waged mainly in leading law journals and other legal publications, the campaign was essentially invisible to the public at large and probably to the vast majority of elected officials. But it proved to be a major coup nonetheless. Fault was toppled from its commanding position as the unifying principle of American accident law, and the more technical notion of efficient risk management was installed in its place.

Karl Llewellyn of the Columbia Law School observed in the *American Economic Review* as early as 1925 that lawyers "have been turning to economics for light on the nature and function of law." One of the leaders of the so-called Realist school of American jurisprudence, Llewellyn suggested that "legal institutions fix and guarantee the presuppositions on which the economic order rests" and that the "law's machinery is increasingly put to revealing unheeded costs of production, and thereby shifting the whole basis of bargaining." In a wide-ranging article, he devoted more than a page to the "displacement of *caveat emptor*" and to the exotic notion of "liability for damage, without reference to fault." Although the general rule of strict producer liability was still many years off, Llewellyn believed that a trend in this direction was already visible; and he seems to have done his very best to help nudge it along. Alluding to *MacPherson*, Llewellyn highlighted the "growing common law tendency to force an insurer's liability on the manufacturer of articles which, like automobiles, are dangerous if improperly made." He also emphasized the "dependence of laborer, bystander or consumer on an industry with which as an individual he cannot cope." Revealing an incipient risk management perspective, he wrote approvingly of the "legal tendency to throw risks of industrial civilization in the first instance upon the industry to which they are chargeable as costs."[48]

One of Llewellyn's former colleagues at Columbia, William O. Douglas, carried this analysis considerably further in a 1929 article titled "Vicarious Liability and Administration of Risk." The future Supreme Court Justice had just recently joined the faculty of the Yale Law School after concluding a bitter confrontation with Columbia University president Nicholas Murray Butler. An intellectual maverick, Douglas boldly focused on risk (rather than fault) in determining an appropriate basis on which to assign liability. In fact, the traditional notion of fault was barely even mentioned in his article.[49]

Douglas divided risk management into four categories: avoidance, prevention, shifting, and distribution. An economic actor could "avoid" risk by refraining altogether from the risk-inducing activity. He could "prevent" risk even while engaging in the activity by devoting more resources to safety devices and precautions. He could "shift" risk by paying someone else (such as an insurer) to assume it. And he could "distribute" risk by embedding the injury costs associated with the activity in the price of the product he sold, thus spreading it over a large number of consumers.[50]

A key question in assigning legal liability, Douglas suggested, was which party could achieve these four aspects of risk management at the lowest possible cost. If parties A and B were equally well suited to avoid, shift, and distribute a particular risk, but B could prevent it more cheaply, then it would seem reasonable to assign the liability to B. Douglas implicitly conceded that in cases that were not so clear-cut, it would be a difficult problem to decide whether "to weight risk prevention more than, less than, or equal to risk distribution." But at least "the issue would be clearly stated, the misplaced emphasis would disappear, the social and economic factors involved in the decision would receive careful consideration, and the articulation would be more definite and clear cut."[51]

Not surprisingly, purveyors of this logic offered frequent analogies to social insurance. As in the campaigns for workers' compensation in the 1910s and unemployment insurance in the 1920s and 1930s, the movement for strict liability revolved around two critical questions: What type of liability regime would lead to the most efficient pursuit of risk prevention? And what regime would distribute the remaining risk in the broadest possible fashion? As James explained in 1957, "[t]he accident problem calls for two things: (1) steps which will cut down accidents; (2) administration of losses that do happen in such a way as to minimize the individual and social burden of them."[52] Although the legal scholars who championed strict liability ended up relying on a very different policy mechanism (common law liability) than did the economists who championed social insurance earlier in the century, the reasoning that these two groups of academics employed proved remarkably similar.[53]

PREVENTING ACCIDENTS THROUGH EFFICIENT RISK SHIFTING

Just as economists at the American Association for Labor Legislation had insisted that experience-rated social insurance would encourage employers to prevent industrial hazards, most of the law professors who championed strict liability assumed that it would facilitate accident prevention. Llewellyn, for example, suggested in 1930 that the law ought to "place the loss where the most pressure will be exerted to keep down future losses."[54] Just over a quarter-century later, James declared that "the manufacturer is in a particularly strategic position to improve the safety of his products, so that the pressure of strict liability could scarcely be exerted at a better point if accident prevention is to be furthered by tort law."[55] Guido Calabresi and Jon Hirschoff subsequently refined and popularized this idea, advising judges to determine "which of the parties to the accident *is in the best position to make the cost-benefit analysis between accident costs and accident avoidance costs and to act on that decision once it is made.* The question for the court reduces to a search for the cheapest cost avoider."[56]

Although the phrase "cheapest cost avoider" was new (and was destined to achieve spectacular currency among legal scholars and social scientists in the future), the underlying idea of utilizing liability law to minimize accident costs went back a very long way. As early as 1842, in the landmark *Farwell* decision, Chief Justice Shaw had highlighted "the expediency of throwing the risk upon those who can best guard against it."[57] Shaw, however, was convinced that the injured railroad employee (the victim in this case) and his fellow railroad workers were far better positioned than their employer to prevent accidents on the job. The enactment of workers' compensation laws during the early twentieth century, by contrast, was based on precisely the opposite assumption: that employers were better positioned than their workers to prevent accidents. Similarly, twentieth-century proponents of strict liability in product injury cases felt certain that producers should be held liable for the costs of accidents since they promised to be far more effective than their consumers in fostering prevention.

Central to the twentieth-century view was the concept of enterprise liability, which suggested that firms ought to be fully accountable for the consequences of their profit-making activities. One legal scholar writing in 1916 characterized it as a "doctrine which seeks to throw upon the undertaker the full responsibility for harm arising from his enterprise."[58] Gradually refined over the years, the idea had achieved broad acceptance within academic circles by the mid-1950s.[59] The concept was justified on many different grounds, though prevention definitely figured into the mix. Producers who were forced to bear (or internalize) injury costs would work to prevent accidents whenever doing so proved cost effective. As Llewellyn had explained in 1925, the effect of "this legal risk shifting" was that "unheeded real costs [are] forced to the . . . investor's attention . . . through his pocket."[60] The notion of enterprise liability was thus inseparable from the logic of accident prevention via cost internalization.

Reinforcing their position still further, a number of strict-liability proponents highlighted current research on "accident proneness," which contradicted the traditional view that fault-based liability would inevitably discourage dangerous behavior. In their 1956 treatise on tort law,

Harper and James cited numerous studies suggesting that some people were simply more accident prone than others. The effect of this research, they explained, "has been to cut down the importance of personal moral shortcoming as a factor in causing accidents." With hardly even a hint of skepticism, Harper and James interpreted the research on accident proneness as constituting yet another nail in the coffin of fault-based liability. Since "the individual may be quite helpless to prevent some of his own accident-producing behavior . . . it would be altogether idle to expect the fear of paying damages to deter it." A strict liability regime, by contrast, would tend "to increase the pressure toward accident prevention on large groups and enterprises, where we have seen it will do the most good, rather than on the individual, where it will do relatively little good."[61]

DISTRIBUTING RISK TO ALL CONSUMERS

Although the promise of improved accident prevention represented an important rationale for the adoption of strict liability in product injury law, it nonetheless appears to have ranked a distant second behind the goal of improved risk distribution in the minds of many proponents. Most of the leading legal scholars who championed strict liability devoted more attention to this latter objective. And a few, including Fleming James, explicitly identified broad-based risk spreading as their highest priority.

Llewellyn posited in 1930 that liability law ought to "shift the immediate incidence of the hazards of life in an industrial society away from the individual and over to a group which can distribute the loss."[62] Not surprisingly, business enterprises were regarded as especially useful vehicles for this task, since they could spread accident costs across all of their consumers in the form of slightly higher prices. "By industry's assuming the burden," Gregory observed in 1951, "the cost is spread in tiny contributions over all the community."[63] Nine years later, Prosser not only extolled the "'risk-spreading' argument" but also insisted that it was "[e]ntitled to more respect" than the case for prevention, which he dismissed as "specious and unconvincing."[64]

Many of these scholars simply took for granted that broad-based risk spreading would prove socially beneficial. James, however, was careful to spell out the essential logic, which was grounded on the concept of risk aversion. "It is true," he conceded in 1941, "that the total cost of

[an] accident . . . cannot be diminished by its distribution." But, as he proceeded to explain, "[s]ocial gain accrues, nevertheless, since consistent distribution of losses over a large group tends to substitute . . . a certain and calculable cost for the uncertain risk of ruinous losses to individuals. This removal of risk and uncertainty, moreover, eliminates fear inhibiting desirable enterprise, activity, and progress."[65] In fact, James was so impressed with the advantages of risk spreading that he seemed to support strict liability in product injury cases simply as an intermediary step on the path to universal social insurance for all accidents. "The full blessings of distribution," he wrote in his 1941 article, "can best be attained by comprehensive social insurance."[66]

SHIFTING VERSUS SPREADING: THE WISCONSIN-OHIO DEBATE REVISITED

Taking a fresh look at the distribution argument twenty years later, Calabresi acknowledged that scholars like James "who have been concerned primarily with risk spreading or 'deep pocket' have tended to view enterprise liability as, at best, a half way house on the road to social insurance."[67] While it was true that risk *shifting* via liability law would generate considerable secondary risk *spreading* (through higher consumer prices), a strict liability regime would never distribute risk as effectively or completely as a true social insurance program.[68] If risk spreading were the only objective, Calabresi suggested, "the most desirable plan would be some sort of government accident relief program spread over the population through taxes."[69]

The truth was, though, that Calabresi viewed risk spreading as only one of several major objectives—and by no means the most important one of the bunch. He explicitly warned that mandatory accident insurance, if financed out of general revenues, would distort incentives and ensure a suboptimal allocation of resources. By insulating manufacturers from any variation in injury costs, such a program would inevitably encourage the producers of especially dangerous products to make and sell too many of them.[70] The problem, as Calabresi well understood, was that optimal resource allocation required that risk be shifted onto producers, whereas optimal risk distribution required that risk be spread in the broadest possible fashion through an insurance pool. Conflict between these two objectives was simply unavoidable.[71]

Indeed, this was precisely the tension that had broken the movement for unemployment insurance into two feuding clans some years before. There was, on the one hand, the Wisconsin school, which favored employer reserves (risk shifting) as a means of achieving optimal resource allocation; and, on the other, the Ohio school, which favored pooled insurance (risk spreading) as a means of achieving optimal distribution of risk. The Ohio school ultimately prevailed in the unemployment debate, but only after a long and bitter fight.

Perhaps not surprisingly, the very same conflict—between risk allocation and risk distribution—ended up dividing legal scholars as well, for it was here that Calabresi parted company with James. "On the basis of the discussion in this Article," Calabresi concluded, sounding very much like a member of the old Wisconsin school, "enterprise liability is superior to social insurance in that it promotes proper allocation of resources."[72] For good measure, the young professor added that the concept of enterprise liability was profoundly consistent with America's free enterprise system, and that, as a consequence, it was "unlikely to be relegated to the role of a stop-gap measure on the road to social insurance."[73] Whatever the explanation, Calabresi's prediction has certainly proved accurate so far. While strict liability was ultimately adopted in the courts, James's dream of universal accident insurance never even found its way into the nation's public discourse, let alone into its public policy.

WEAK CONSUMERS, WEAK MARKETS

One final link in the logical chain used to support strict liability related to the problem of private market failures. Although this issue was not typically discussed at great length, it was of paramount importance from a conceptual standpoint. After all, if private markets worked perfectly on their own and consumers always acted rationally, the adoption of strict liability would have had little if any effect. By demanding appropriate price deductions for dangerous products, consumers theoretically could have shifted accident costs onto producers on their own, thus ensuring an optimal allocation of resources regardless of the liability regime. And by purchasing adequate and actuarially fair accident insurance, they could have ensured an optimal distribution of risk as well. As Calabresi rightly observed, "[I]n the economist's world [of perfect markets] it often makes no difference whether [the legal regime places] the cost of an injury [on one party or the other]."[74]

With regard to private accident insurance, however, many legal scholars stressed that consumers frequently failed to buy adequate coverage on their own. "Many of these losses may be guarded against—*theoretically*—by insurance of one kind or another which the injured man himself has taken out," James noted. "Accident insurance, blue cross, and medical insurance are available for this purpose. But the studies show that very few accident victims are in fact protected in any material degree against such losses. Moreover the poorer the victim is, the less likely he is to be insured."[75]

Although this fact was widely recognized, much less attention was devoted to the existence or absence of compensating price differentials for hazardous products. Friedrich Kessler had suggested fairly early on that the rise of standardized contracts had increasingly chipped away at consumers' bargaining position, leaving them in an inferior position and denying them the opportunity to demand much of anything at all.[76] Calabresi subsequently speculated about a number of other potential problems, including high information costs. "[I]n the real world not all parties evaluate losses equally," he wrote in 1961, implying that not everyone had equal access to information about risk or was equally able to process the information that was available.[77]

Calabresi also emphasized the possible existence of a problem resembling optimistic bias. Focusing initially on the issue of workplace injuries, he posited that before the adoption of workers' compensation laws, "the individual worker simply did not evaluate the risk of injury to be as great as it actually was. He took his chances. . . . The result—apart from some individual tragedies—was that wages and prices in certain industries simply did not reflect the losses those industries caused."[78] This was precisely the same logic that Henry Seager had advanced back in 1907 to justify the enactment of workers' compensation laws. The individual worker, Seager maintained, fails to demand an adequate compensating wage differential because he "thinks of himself as having a charmed life."[79]

Significantly, Calabresi ultimately extended this analysis to consumers as well. In his 1970 book *The Costs of Accidents*, he suggested that even if consumers "had adequate data for evaluating the risk" of potentially dangerous products, they might be "psychologically unable to do so." In the extreme, one might conclude that "people cannot estimate rationally their chances of suffering death or catastrophic injury. Such things always happen to 'the other guy,' and no amount of statistical information can convince an individual that they could happen to him."[80] Calabresi also emphasized that high transaction costs of various sorts could compromise the optimal allocation of resources in a free market, which suggested still more potential justifications for strict liability in product injury cases.[81]

The central point of all this was simply that the private market could not always be counted on to move risk to the optimal risk bearer—in large measure because of various weaknesses on the part of consumers. Liability law could thus make a real difference. Although Calabresi was considerably more precise in his treatment of these issues than most of his predecessors, the essential notion of market imperfection was implicit in much of their earlier work. The adoption of strict liability, they maintained, would ultimately allow the market to work better, improving overall social welfare through the more efficient allocation and distribution of accident risk.

The Search for a Pathway Back to Strict Liability

For all the emphasis on newness and change coming out of the academy, strict liability was itself not a new concept in the twentieth century. It actually appears to have been the standard rule for allocating accident losses prior to the first industrial revolution. "The notion [at that time]," Harper and James explained, "was . . . that he whose affirmative act directly caused the harm should ordinarily pay for it."[82] Even after the emergence of a fault-based system in the nineteenth century, moreover, there were some notable exceptions where liability was assessed without fault. The most obvious one was workers' compensation, which imposed strict liability for workplace accidents by statute. But this was neither the only nor the earliest exception to the fault principle.

Within the common law, the most famous exception arose out of *Rylands v. Fletcher*, a British case from 1868.[83] In *Rylands*, the defendants were forced to pay damages after dammed-up water on their property unexpectedly escaped and flooded a neighbor's property, even though the accident was not a result of the defendants' negligence. A lower court had actually found for the defendants on the grounds that there was no negligence.[84] But two higher courts went the other way. In explaining the final verdict for the plaintiff, Lord Cairns stressed that building a reservoir on an abandoned shaft of a coal mine constituted a "non-natural use" of the land. "[I]t appears to me," he concluded, "that that which the defendants were doing, they were doing at their own peril; and if in the course of their doing it the evil arose . . . then for the consequence of that, in my opinion, the defendants would be liable."[85]

Over the remainder of the nineteenth century and into the twentieth, American judges applied the *Rylands* rule of strict liability intermittently in cases involving high explosives, dangerous animals, poison sprays, and the like.[86] In a 1931 case involving a defendant who had stored dynamite not far from another's home, Judge Augustus N. Hand ruled that dynamite "is of the class of elements which one who stores or uses in such a locality, or under such circumstances as to cause likelihood of risk to others, stores or uses at his peril. *He is an insurer, and is absolutely liable if damage results to third persons.*"[87]

Rylands offered an intriguing (if highly controversial) means of skirting the standard negligence rule, but it was not the only trick in the book. Another favorite was the newer notion of implied warranty. Under this rule, which evolved as part of contract law rather than tort law, sellers were held strictly liable to their immediate customers for injury-inducing defects in the products they sold. Neither negligence nor any explicit warranty was required for an injured plaintiff to recover.[88]

Equally important was the doctrine of *res ipsa loquitur* (the thing speaks for itself), which was used with increasing frequency in the first half of the twentieth century. In injury cases where the accident would not ordinarily have occurred in the absence of the defendant's negligence, the doctrine excused plaintiffs from actually having to prove such negligence. "Thus where a human toe is found in chewing tobacco, or a worm in a bottle of soda," wrote Harper and James, "it is hard indeed to escape the imputation of negligence somewhere in the process used by the manufacturer or bottler." By creating a rebuttable presumption of fault, the doctrine of *res ipsa loquitur* thus lowered the bar on recovery in numerous cases.[89]

The problem for reformers was that in spite of these various tricks, recovery remained far from certain for a large fraction of product injury victims. Because implied warranty was part of contract law, most manufacturers remained effectively insulated from suits of this sort, since privity was required. The theory of implied warranty did permit injured consumers to hold retailers strictly liable for defective products, but these retailers typically had only the shallowest of pockets. "The difficulty here," explained one expert on the subject, "is that, from the consumer's viewpoint, the action against the retailer is a hollow right if the retailer is not financially able to satisfy the judgment."[90] The doctrine of *res ipsa loquitur,* meanwhile, was applicable only against presumably negligent defendants. To make matters worse, even when the nature of an accident permitted an inference of negligence, plaintiffs often found it difficult to identify the presumably negligent party. Was the original manufacturer to blame or perhaps someone else in the distribution chain—a wholesaler, jobber, or retailer? Unless the plaintiff could answer this question to the court's satisfaction, recovery would be denied, irrespective of *res ipsa loquitur.*[91]

One of the more popular academic proposals for patching these holes—and thus for establishing a true strict liability regime in product injury cases—was to eliminate the privity requirement from the theory of implied warranty. This way, all parties along a distribution chain— from the manufacturer to the wholesaler to the retailer—would be held strictly liable for defects in the products they sold. Noting that implied warranties were "imposed by law as vehicles of social policy," Harper and James insisted that "the courts should extend them as far as the relevant social policy requires. The interest in consumer protection calls for warranties by the maker that *do* run with the goods, to reach all who are likely to be hurt by the use of the unfit commodity for a purpose ordinarily to be expected."[92] Elsewhere, James called for "strict liability on the part of the manufacturer, upon an implied warranty, for unreasonable dangers lurking in any kind of product. All limitations imposed by the doctrine of privity should go."[93]

Writing in 1960, however, Prosser disagreed vehemently with this approach. He, too, sought to establish strict liability in product injury cases; but he thought that it bordered on the bizarre to rely on the notion of implied warranty, a legal contrivance of questionable origins. "The adoption of this particular device," he reminded his readers, "was facilitated by the peculiar and uncertain nature and character of warranty, a freak hybrid born of the illicit intercourse of tort and contract."[94] Continuing the argument, he suggested that "as a device for the justification of strict liability," implied warranty "carries far too much luggage in the way of undesirable complications, and is leading us down a very thorny path." Why depend on a suspicious concept from contract law? he asked. "If there is to be strict liability in tort, let there be strict liability in tort, declared outright, without an illusory contract mask."[95]

The notion of imposing strict liability through implied warranty had been criticized before, but never as forcefully or as convincingly as Prosser did in his 1960 article in the *Yale Law Journal*.[96] His proposal—to establish strict liability in tort by removing the negligence standard in product liability cases—constituted the most direct line of attack. Tellingly, he titled his article "The Assault upon the Citadel (Strict Liability to the Consumer)." It would not be long before the courts took notice. In fact, the wholesale departure from a negligence standard in product injury cases was already under way.

From Theory to Practice

The Adoption of Strict Liability: Henningsen *and* Greenman

Almost simultaneously with the publication of Prosser's article (but certainly before it arrived in law libraries and law offices across the country), the Supreme Court of New Jersey rendered a landmark strict liability decision on May 9, 1960.[97] One of the plaintiffs in the case, Claus Henningsen, had purchased a Plymouth automobile from Bloomfield Motors on May 7, 1955. Claus apparently bought the car as a Mother's Day present for the other plaintiff, his wife, Helen. Unfortunately, Helen sustained serious injuries on May 19 when she lost control of the vehicle while driving to Asbury Park. Although experts believed the accident was probably caused by a defect in the steering wheel, mechanics could not determine this with certainty since the front end of the car had been almost completely destroyed. The Henningsens subsequently sued both the dealer and the manufacturer (Chrysler), claiming breach of warranties as well as negligence. In the end, the trial court threw out the negligence counts, submitting the case to the jury solely on the grounds of breach of implied warranty. The jury found for the plaintiffs and against both defendants.[98]

Ruling on the inevitable appeal, the New Jersey Supreme Court unanimously upheld the trial court verdict. With numerous citations to Harper and James (as well as a number of other prominent scholars of strict liability), the high court announced that privity should no longer stand as an obstacle to recovery in implied warranty cases.[99] The opinion not only articulated a new standard of strict liability in product injury suits but also explicitly highlighted the risk management logic that lay behind it. Strict liability, running from the manufacturer all the way to the retailer, would shift risk onto those parties best able both to ensure safety and to distribute the costs of accidents that were not preventable. As Justice John Francis wrote for the court:

> Thus, where the commodities sold are such that if defectively manufactured they will be dangerous to life or limb, then society's interests can only be protected by eliminating the requirement of privity between the maker and his dealers and the reasonably expected ultimate consumer. In that way the burden of losses consequent upon use of defective articles is borne by those who are in a position to either control the danger or make an equitable distribution of the losses when they do occur. As *Harper & James* put it, "The interest in consumer protection calls for warranties by the maker that *do* run with the goods, to reach all who are likely to be hurt by the use of the unfit commodity for a purpose ordinarily to be expected."[100]

Several years later, Prosser declared triumphantly that "the date of the fall of the citadel of privity [in products liability] can be fixed with some certainty. It was May 9, 1960, when the Supreme Court of New Jersey announced the decision in *Henningsen v. Bloomfield Motors, Inc.*"[101]

Prosser could not have been wholly satisfied with *Henningsen,* however. Although the New Jersey high court articulated a standard of liability requiring neither negligence nor privity, it still relied on the theory of implied warranty which Prosser had earlier dismissed as a "freak hybrid." But this problem, too, was corrected in 1963, when the Supreme Court of California not only established a strict liability rule in product injury cases but also grounded it firmly in tort law. Writing for a unanimous court in the case of *Greenman v. Yuba Power Products, Inc.*, Justice Roger Traynor declared unequivocally that a "manufacturer is strictly liable in tort when an article he places on the market, knowing that it is to be used without inspection for defects, proves to have a defect that causes injury to a human being."[102]

The plaintiff in the case, William B. Greenman, was injured when the

Shopsmith power tool that his wife had bought him for Christmas, along with the attachments that he had subsequently purchased, suddenly malfunctioned, shooting out a piece of wood which struck him on the forehead. Even though Greenman had failed to give the manufacturer notice of breach of warranty as quickly as the law required, the court concluded that breach of warranty was not the relevant issue. The "liability is not one governed by the law of contract warranties, but by the law of strict liability in tort."[103] Negligence, moreover, was no longer a requirement for recovery. "To establish the manufacturer's liability," Traynor declared, "it was sufficient that plaintiff proved that he was injured while using the Shopsmith in a way it was intended to be used as a result of a defect in design and manufacture of which plaintiff was not aware that made the Shopsmith unsafe for its intended use."[104]

Significantly, Traynor claimed that it was unnecessary to "recanvass the reasons for imposing strict liability on the manufacturer." Insisting that these reasons were well known, he simply cited Harper and James's 1956 treatise, Prosser's 1960 article "Assault upon the Citadel," and his own concurring opinion in *Escola*.[105] The logic of strict liability that Traynor had so eloquently expressed in 1944 had now finally become law in California.

Section 402A and the Spread of Strict Liability

Even as Traynor was writing the *Greenman* decision in 1963, Prosser was hard at work crafting the products liability section (402A) of the American Law Institute's second Restatement of Torts. Restatements such as this one allowed legal scholars to articulate the current state of the law in particular areas and to suggest trends that appeared to be emerging. Although they were drafted under private auspices and had no legal force, they were often enormously influential within the legal profession and the judicial community. The first Restatement of Torts, drafted in the early 1930s, revealed considerable confusion on the subject of product injury law. Some thirty years later, Prosser hoped to offer greater clarity by specifying the reach of strict liability. In an initial draft completed in 1961, he recognized strict liability in food cases only. Next, in a second draft written in 1962, he claimed that it applied to any product designed for "intimate bodily use." Ultimately, he extended strict liability to all products.[106]

Prosser's final draft, approved by the American Law Institute in 1964, held all manufacturers and dealers strictly liable for injuries resulting from any defective products they sold, irrespective of negligence or privity. According to the Restatement:

> [P]ublic policy demands that the burden of accidental injuries caused by products intended for consumption be placed upon those who market them, and be treated as a cost of production against which liability insurance can be obtained; and that the consumer of such products is entitled to the maximum of protection at the hands of someone, and the proper persons to afford it are those who market the products.

The document emphasized that the proposed rule would "not preclude liability based upon the alternative ground of negligence of the seller," but that it would permit the seller to be held liable "even though he has exercised all possible care in the preparation and sale of the product."[107]

Ultimately released in 1965, section 402A of the second Restatement played a very significant role in fostering acceptance of strict liability all across the country.[108] Prosser reported in 1966 that already eighteen states had adopted strict liability via high court rulings, six more had done so on the basis of statute, and numerous others had begun moving in this direction.[109] Twenty-eight states had adopted strict liability by the time Prosser died in 1971, and forty-one had done so by 1976.[110] The speed with which product liability law was transformed in the United States was simply astounding. The academics' "assault upon the citadel" had ended in victory.

Impact of a Doctrinal Revolution

Perhaps not surprisingly, product liability cases soon began to mount. Between 1974 and 1985, the number of product liability cases filed in federal courts surged from 1,579 to 13,554—an increase of more than 750 percent. Over the same period, all other tort cases filed in federal courts increased by only 25 percent (from 22,652 to 28,610), and total civil filings in federal courts increased by about 140 percent.[111] Although the cost of product liability insurance as a fraction of sales remained relatively stable over the late 1960s and early 1970s, it increased sharply in the mid-1970s—by 40 percent in 1975 and another 27 percent in 1976. One student of the subject characterized these as "catch-up increases."[112]

Overall, it is difficult to avoid the conclusion that the doctrinal revolution which began in the early 1960s exerted some very significant effects. George Priest concluded in an influential article in 1985 that as a result of the "conceptual revolution" in product liability law (which he dated mainly to the years 1960–1964), the "liability of manufacturers for product-related losses was vastly increased and the obligations of consumers vastly diminished."[113] The available evidence strongly suggests that he was correct.

EXTENDING STRICT LIABILITY TO DESIGN AND WARNING DEFECTS

As Priest himself was well aware, however, the original doctrinal shift holding manufacturers strictly liable for product defects was not the only development contributing to the radical expansion of manufacturer liability. The later extensions of strict liability to cases involving defective design and defective warnings were at least as important and perhaps considerably more so.[114] As a result of these extensions, an injured plaintiff could often recover even if the defect in question was not the consequence of a manufacturing error, such as an unusually weak bolt or a faulty hinge.

In a 1967 case, for example, a child was burned after tripping over the electrical cord of a steam humidifier. This particular humidifier had not been defectively produced, but the Minnesota high court ruled against the manufacturer anyway, claiming that the product design was inherently defective (the top should not have been so loose) and that the company had failed to warn consumers about the potential for this sort of mishap.[115] The famous Ford Pinto case, in which Ford was found liable for a defectively designed gas tank, provides another good example.[116]

There remains some question about whether the early academic proponents of strict liability intended their doctrinal shift to apply to anything other than manufacturing defects.[117] But whether the ultimate inclusion of design and warning defects was intended or not, it was certainly a logical extension of the original idea that scholars like Llewellyn, James, and Prosser had introduced. And it was justified once again on the grounds of optimizing the allocation and the distribution of risk.[118]

AN EXPLOSION OF PUNITIVE DAMAGES?

Yet another factor contributing to the expansion of manufacturer liability since the early 1960s was the rise of punitive damages. Numerous observers and critics have characterized the increased willingness of juries to impose punitive damages as triggering a virtual explosion of liability in product injury cases, placing an enormous burden on business and perhaps on the economy as a whole. Justice Sandra Day O'Connor sounded precisely this theme in a widely quoted dissenting opinion from 1989. "Awards of punitive damages are skyrocketing," she exclaimed. "As recently as a decade ago, the largest award of punitive damages affirmed by an appellate court in a products liability case was $250,000. . . . Since then, awards more than 30 times as high have been sustained on appeal. . . . The threat of such enormous awards has a detrimental effect on the research and development of new products."[119]

Of course, punitive damages were themselves not a new phenomenon. In the United States, the first punitive damages case dates to 1784. (The practice went back even further in England.) Nor are public campaigns to abolish punitive damages unprecedented in American history. Simon Greenleaf of the Harvard Law School, for example, launched just such a campaign in the nineteenth century, insisting that damages "should be precisely commensurate with the injury, neither more nor less."[120]

The use of punitive damages certainly expanded in the twentieth century, but the change does not appear to have been nearly as profound or as far-reaching as the doctrinal shift to strict liability. Whereas punitive damages in the nineteenth century were awarded almost exclusively as punishment for malicious acts, they were increasingly used in the twentieth century to punish extremely negligent behavior as well. But the expansion stopped there. Although strict liability emerged as the standard for awarding compensatory damages in product injury cases after 1960, it never became the standard for assessing punitive damages—a fact which remains true even today.[121]

As it turns out, the available data on punitive damages in product injury cases suggest that the increased use of this device has been far less dramatic than is commonly thought. To be sure, there are plenty of mind-boggling stories—the woman who was awarded $2.7 million in punitive damages from McDonald's after spilling hot coffee on herself at a drive-through, or the man whose displeasure with a surreptitiously repainted automobile cost BMW $4,000 in compensatory damages plus $4 million in punitive damages.[122] Given jury awards like these, it is no wonder that punitive damages in product liability suits are widely viewed as being out of control.

But the truth is that such cases are exceedingly rare. Surveying product liability suits over the years 1965 to 1990, Michael Rustad was able to identify a grand total of only 355 cases in which juries awarded punitive damages. Ninety-five of these involved asbestos-related injuries. Although the number of punitive awards increased over time (from just 7 in the period 1965–1970 to 151 in the period 1986–1990), the total was never very large. Punitive awards in non-asbestos product liability cases, moreover, actually appear to have peaked in the mid-1980s, reaching 119 in 1981–1985 before falling to 78 in the years 1986–1990.[123]

Indeed, the vast majority of punitive awards in the nation's courts arise not out of product liability cases but rather out of intentional tort and business contracts cases, such as the monumental *Penzoil-Texaco* case (which involved a $3 billion punitive award). According to one study conducted by the RAND Institute for Civil Justice, punitive awards in product injury cases accounted for just 4.4 percent of all punitive awards.[124] As already suggested, a related fact is that punitive damages are assessed in only a very small proportion of product injury cases. Estimates vary, but most empirical studies reveal that plaintiffs prevail in nearly half the cases that go to trial, while only about 2 to 10 percent of successful plaintiffs end up receiving punitive damages.[125]

In an extensive Justice Department study of tort cases in 1992 (summarized in Table 8.1), juries in the seventy-five largest counties in the United States received 360 product liability cases. They ruled for the plaintiffs in 142 of these, but awarded punitive damages in just three cases. Punitive damages, in other words, were assessed in only 2.1 percent of the successful product liability suits—far less often than in almost any other type of tort action. In the overall Justice Department sample, punitive damages were awarded to 4 percent of successful tort plaintiffs. Even at this higher rate, punitive damages (in dollars) still accounted for just 5 percent of total damages awarded. The ratio of punitive to total damages was considerably greater in toxic-substance cases

Table 8.1 Punitive damages in civil cases, 1992

Type of case	Civil cases initiated	Jury trials	Plaintiff victories	Punitive awards (no. cases)	Punitive award cases as percentage of plaintiff victories	Total damages awarded ($)	Punitive damages as percentage of total damages
Tort cases	377,421	9,532	4,584	190	4.1	1,869,699,000	4.89
Product liability	12,763	360	142	3	2.1	103,346,000	0.04
Toxic substance	6,045	287	202	13	6.4	106,306,000	24.85
Automobile	227,087	3,915	2,280	55	2.4	502,602,000	7.07
Premises liability	65,372	1,991	845	15	1.8	196,207,000	0.65
Medical malpractice	18,396	1,370	403	13	3.2	598,148,000	0.52
Intentional tort	10,879	448	199	38	19.1	105,466,000	10.36
Professional malpractice	6,827	187	92	15	16.3	97,308,000	6.25
Slander/libel	3,159	66	27	8	29.6	6,284,000	21.34
Other tort	26,891	909	393	30	7.6	154,032,000	4.38
Contract cases	365,263	2,217	1,322	169	12.8	820,098,000	20.67
Seller plaintiff	188,761	610	417	24	5.8	88,368,000	1.38
Buyer plaintiff	44,592	593	363	47	12.9	173,965,000	15.78
Fraud	15,917	317	173	38	22.0	117,209,000	6.26
Employment	8,064	311	170	46	27.1	249,206,000	53.27
Rental/lease	20,587	133	85	11	12.9	159,734,000	0.25
Other contract	87,342	252	113	2	1.8	31,616,000	1.15
Real property cases	19,235	277	43	5	11.6	13,886,000	49.50
Total civil cases	761,919	12,026	5,949	364	6.1	2,703,683,000	9.91

Source: U.S Department of Justice, Office of Justice Programs, "Civil Jury Cases and Verdicts in Large Counties" (Civil Justice Survey of State Courts, 1992), *Bureau of Justice Statistics Special Report* (July 1995), tables 1, 2, 6, and 8.

Note: This table is based on civil case loads in state courts from the 75 largest U.S. counties during 1992. Cases that did not go to jury trials ended either in agreed settlements (460,000), default judgments (108,000), dismissals (82,000), transfers (29,000), summary judgments (28,000), or in bench trials, arbitration proceedings, or directed verdicts (33,000).

(25 percent), but dramatically smaller in non–toxic-substance product liability cases (0.04 percent).[126] As in numerous other studies, the overall effect of punitive damages in the product liability arena appeared remarkably limited.[127]

Contrary to the conventional wisdom, moreover, there seemed to be a fairly tight correlation between punitive and compensatory damages in civil cases, suggesting that the size of punitive awards was not randomly determined as in a lottery. Even when juries did seem to get carried away, their punitive awards were very often overturned or reduced on appeal.[128] Indeed, a judge subsequently reduced punitive damages in the McDonald's hot coffee case from $2.7 million to $480,000. The plaintiff, who had suffered roughly $200,000 in actual damages, later settled with McDonald's for about $600,000. Even more striking, the Alabama Supreme Court ultimately scaled back BMW's punitive damages in the infamous repainting case from $4 million to just $50,000.[129] Overall, the evidence suggests that punitive awards in product liability cases did increase after the mid-1960s and that they did contribute to rising manufacturer liability.[130] But while the potential for huge punitive awards could hardly have been ignored in the nation's boardrooms, the fact is that punitive damages seem to have accounted for well under 10 percent of total damages in all product liability cases. From a business standpoint, therefore, the broader doctrinal shift in product injury law appears to have been a far more important determinant of liability than the oft-discussed "explosion" in punitive awards.

Conclusion

As we have seen, the wholesale shift to strict liability was inaugurated in the 1960s on the basis of powerful risk management logic. Although the legal reform itself was ultimately executed in the nation's courts and in a few state legislatures, the true engine of change was a small group of legal scholars who sought to replace the traditional principle of fault with a much newer logic of risk in the adjudication of product injury suits.

The adoption of strict liability has often been characterized as marking a revolution in both legal thought and business practice, and this is no doubt an accurate depiction in many respects. Still, a few caveats are in order. To begin with, it is important to note that even under the new regime, manufacturers did not become liable for *all* product-related injuries. To recall one of James's favorite examples, "a book placed strategically at the top of a long dark flight of stairs" could surely become "an instrumentality of serious injury." But no judge or jury would ever find the book manufacturer liable for any resulting injury since the "quality or condition of the product [was not] unreasonably dangerous either for a use to which the product would ordinarily be put, or for some special use which was brought to the attention of the defendant."[131] Similarly, as Traynor later observed, "[a] knife manufacturer is not liable when the user cuts himself with one of its knives. When the injury is in no way attributable to a defect there is no basis for strict liability."[132]

A second caveat concerns the magnitude of the impact on manufacturers. There is no question that the advent of strict liability proved devastating for the makers of a number of different products, including the Dalkon Shield contraceptive device, silicone breast implants, and asbestos insulation. Asbestos manufacturers alone faced many billions of dollars in damages as a result of product liability suits, and at least one major asbestos producer (Johns-Mansville) was forced into bankruptcy.[133] For the vast majority of manufacturers, however, the risk of product liability damages was not nearly as disruptive. Although insurance rates did tend to rise after the introduction of strict liability (and occasionally increased very sharply), commercial coverage for all but a few especially hazardous products remained available without interruption— even through the so-called liability insurance crisis of the mid-1980s.[134]

Significantly, policymakers moved to limit liability in several of the areas where disruptions occurred. Since a certain fraction of all transfused blood inevitably and unavoidably proved "defective" (in that it carried undetectable disease), lawmakers in forty-eight states enacted legislation explicitly insulating hospitals and blood banks from strict liability in cases involving blood. In most jurisdictions, recipients of infected blood could still sue when there was negligence, but not in its absence.[135] Similarly, in 1994, Congress placed a limit of eighteen years on the liability of non-commercial aircraft manufacturers, ostensibly to help keep the industry alive.[136]

A third caveat about the strict liability revolution is that compensation for product-related injuries remained far from automatic. In sharp contrast to a system of workers' compensation, in which recovery was virtually assured and benefit levels well defined for a wide range of potential accidents, the new product liability system still required injured consumers to sue for damages in courts of law. This implied, on the one hand, that many victims would fail to pursue their claims (or receive far less than actual damages) on account of high transaction costs; and, on the other, that jury-awarded damages would likely show considerable variation even across roughly comparable cases. For all their precision in discussing optimal risk management and efficient resource allocation, the champions of strict liability ended up relying on a remarkably blunt legal instrument.

One final caveat is that although plaintiffs under the new regime no longer had to prove negligence in most product liability suits, concerns about negligence definitely did not disappear altogether. As we have seen, findings of negligence (indeed, extreme negligence) remained exceedingly important in the assessment of punitive damages. Equally significant were comparative and contributory negligence rules, which continued to exist in one form or another in all fifty states.[137] In the McDonald's hot coffee case, for example, the victim was found to have suffered $200,000 in actual damages as a result of severe burns. Although the jury originally awarded her all $200,000 in compensatory damages (along with $2.7 million in punitive damages), the compensatory component was later reduced to $160,000 on the grounds that the victim herself was 20 percent at fault for the accident.[138] More generally, the Justice Department's study of civil cases in 1992 found that compensatory damages were reduced as a result of plaintiff negligence in 13 percent of successful suits.[139] The point is that negligence often remained a relevant issue in product injury cases, though far less so than before the advent of strict liability.

Perhaps the best way to understand the transformation of accident law, therefore, is in terms of what Chief Justice Shaw once described as a "pure accident," in which neither the plaintiff nor the defendant was obviously to blame for the injury.[140] In the nineteenth century, liability for pure accidents almost always landed on the victims. As Shaw put it, "it must rest where it first fell."[141] In combination, the negligence standard, the privity doctrine, and the "unholy trinity" of employer defenses made accident law a classic Phase I risk management policy, protecting business and broadly favoring economic growth over personal security.

In the early twentieth century, however, Shaw's formula was reversed for America's workers. With the enactment of workers' compensation laws in the 1910s, most of the liability for pure accidents (and, indeed, for almost all accidents) that occurred in the workplace was shifted onto employers and ultimately onto their insurers. The financial burden no longer came to rest "where it first fell"—at least, not as far as workers were concerned. Phase II had arrived.

Finally, with the transformation of product injury law in the 1960s and 1970s, liability for pure accidents resulting from defective products could now be shifted from consumers onto manufacturers (and typically onto wholesalers and retailers as well). Where obvious negligence existed on one side or the other, awards might be pushed up or down. But in the case of pure accidents arising out of defective products, victim-consumers could generally expect to obtain compensatory damages so long as they were willing to sue. This was the essence of the product liability revolution. Reflecting as it did the increasing societal emphasis on personal security, this revolution not only transformed the law of accidents but also helped mark the dawn of a vital third phase in American risk management policy.

9

Security for All

When Henry Fairlie wrote in the *New Republic* in 1989 that the "desire for a risk-free society is one of the most debilitating influences in America today," he was criticizing not only a frame of mind but also an ever-expanding array of public policies designed to operationalize it.[1] Strict liability for product injuries was surely one such policy, but there were many others, ranging from credit card liability caps to consumer safety legislation. The vast majority of these policies had been introduced or significantly expanded after 1960 and may be thought of as coming under the umbrella of Phase III. In each case, at least one important goal was to alleviate risk facing individuals. Although businesspeople and workers were sometimes beneficiaries as well, they were no longer the exclusive or even the primary ones. Security for consumers and plain old citizens had now emerged as a dominant social priority in the United States.

This chapter explores three distinct manifestations of Phase III policy-making: the rise of federal disaster relief, the creation of state-level insurance guaranty funds, and the dramatic expansion in environmental liability. Although these three areas are by no means exhaustive, they do reflect the enormous breadth of the transition under Phase III, in terms of both policy objectives and risk management tools employed. As will become clear, there was no master plan behind all of these policies. But the basic notion of shifting risks away from individuals and onto firms and governments guided lawmakers in all of these areas and in many others as well. Indeed, this notion was at the very heart of Phase III.

Federal Disaster Policy

The transformation of federal disaster policy offers an intriguing case study.[2] Just as natural disasters have always been a part of American history, so too has federal disaster relief. But until the middle of the twentieth century, Congress granted such relief only occasionally on an ad hoc basis. The first major legislative change came in 1950, when Congress finally authorized the creation of a permanent disaster relief fund. Even then, however, federal resources were reserved exclusively for the repair of local government facilities. Only later—particularly in the sixties and seventies—was federal disaster policy extended to cover losses sustained by private citizens. Clearly reflecting the transition to Phase III, the federal government now emerged as a pivotal manager of catastrophe risk—not just for major institutions and local governments but for individual Americans all across the country.

Toward Implicit Public Insurance for Natural Disasters

The first known instance of federal disaster relief dates to 1803, when Congress granted the victims of a fire in Portsmouth, New Hampshire, an extension on the repayment of custom house bonds. Between 1803 and 1947, various floods, earthquakes, fires, and other disasters prompted at least 128 specific legislative acts offering ad hoc relief. In most cases, the acts authorized the purchase and distribution of provisions and medical supplies.[3]

Despite the frequency of such legislation, policymakers did not typically view disaster relief as an ongoing federal responsibility. More often than not, the federal government provided no assistance in the aftermath of catastrophes.[4] In the mid-1880s, for example, President Grover Cleveland vetoed a bill that would have appropriated $10,000 for the distribution of seed to the victims of a severe drought in Texas. "I can find no warrant for such an appropriation in the Constitution," he explained, "and I do not believe that the power and duty of the General Government ought to be extended to the relief of individual suffering which is in no manner properly related to the public service or benefit." He added that "though the people support the Government, the Government should not support the people. . . . Federal aid in [cases of misfortune] encourages the expectation of paternal care on the part of the Government and weakens the sturdiness of our national character."[5]

Congress took a small step away from President Cleveland's dictum in 1905, when it designated the American National Red Cross as the official agent of the federal government in providing essential disaster-related assistance. Ever since its founding in 1881, the Red Cross had raised and distributed private funds to aid disaster victims. But now these services became the organization's legal responsibility. Although Congress had appropriated no new resources, it had begun the process of institutionalizing disaster relief by officially charging this volunteer association with the task of collecting private funds and distributing them to those in need.[6]

The Red Cross retained primary responsibility for disaster relief in the United States over the next several decades; but the public-private balance had already begun to shift by the 1930s. In the wake of several natural catastrophes that struck during the Great Depression, the Federal Relief Administration and the Federal Civil Works Administration received authority from President Franklin Roosevelt to distribute surplus federal property to states and local governments and to repair damaged roads and bridges. Congress formalized this practice in 1947, when it passed the first general disaster relief act. In the event of a disaster, local governments could turn to the War Assets Administration or the Federal Works Administration for much-needed help. Three years later Congress passed the Federal Disaster Act of 1950, creating a permanent relief fund and granting the president broad discretionary power to decide what constituted a disaster eligible for federal aid. While the Red Cross continued to manage the distribution of relief to private citizens and businesses, the federal government now assumed responsibility for the repair and restoration of local government facilities.[7]

Through the 1950s and early 1960s, the federal government broadened and refined the contours of the 1950 law—in most cases with little debate or controversy. The 1951 Kansas-Missouri flood provoked Congress to authorize emergency housing for disaster victims. Over the next several years, rural communities, unincorporated towns, and state facilities also became eligible for federal assistance, as did Guam, American Samoa, and the Trust Territory of the Pacific Islands. Relief acts in 1964 and 1965, passed in response to major disasters in several states, increased federal contributions to highway reconstruction and expanded federal loan programs, such as those of the Small Business Administration (SBA) and the Farmers Home Administration (FmHA).[8] In this way, step by step, the federal role in disaster relief was greatly enlarged. Whereas in 1953 Red Cross assistance still outpaced federal spending on disasters by a ratio of 1.6 to 1, by 1965 federal disaster aid exceeded Red Cross spending on disasters by nearly 8 to 1.[9]

The pace of federal disaster policy accelerated even more sharply during the late 1960s and early 1970s. "As we move into a new decade," President Nixon announced in a message on disaster assistance in 1970, "one of the nation's major goals is to restore a ravaged environment. But we must also be ready to respond effectively when nature gets out of control and victimizes our citizens."[10] The country had experienced twenty-nine major disasters in 1969, requiring an allocation of roughly $150 million from the President's Disaster Relief Fund. Although this was the largest appropriation for disaster relief since passage of the Federal Disaster Act nineteen years earlier, it marked the beginning of a new trend rather than a one-year anomaly.[11]

Motivated in particular by Hurricane Camille, which claimed 248 lives and inflicted $1.5 billion in damages in five southern states in 1969, Congress passed a new Disaster Relief Act in 1970.[12] This landmark legislation established a permanent and comprehensive program of federal assistance, covering both public and private losses. Through the 1960s, federal disaster relief had gradually expanded to include funding for the repair of damaged higher education facilities, debris removal from private property, and unemployment compensation and food coupons for hard-pressed disaster victims. The federal government had also increased the availability of SBA and FmHA disaster loans. The 1970 act not only codified this diverse disaster legislation but charted new territory as well. Strongly emphasizing relief for individual victims, it mandated grants for temporary housing and legal services. Subsequent amendments, especially in 1974, further expanded the assistance available to both public and private disaster victims.[13]

Indeed, by the mid-1970s, an entirely new model of federal disaster relief was rapidly taking shape. A number of important policy innovations still lay in the future, including the establishment of the Federal Emergency Management Agency (FEMA) in 1978.[14] But the essential features of the new regime—providing what amounted to implicit public insurance against natural catastrophe losses—were already clear. Although private property-and-casualty insurance continued to play a critical role in covering some of the largest disaster-related risks, the federal government was increasingly emerging as an insurer of last resort, offering limited compensation for a wide range of uninsured and uninsurable risks affecting public entities, firms, and (most notably) individual citizens. As explained in a Senate committee report on the 1970 bill: "Not only do private individuals who are suddenly and totally deprived of the means of providing themselves the basic necessities of life require emergency assistance—food, clothing, shelter, and medical care—but also longer-term recovery assistance must be provided to such individuals, the sources of their employment and the communities in which they live."[15] One of the key sponsors in the House, Representative Harold T. Johnson of California, added that even though neighbors had always sought to help disaster victims in America, federal relief was necessary to achieve the same objective in "a complex twentieth century such as we now live."[16] Ideas about federal disaster policy had certainly come a long way since the days of Grover Cleveland.

Clarifying the Federal Role in Disaster Relief: 1927 versus 1993

The full extent of this transformation becomes plain through a direct comparison of two of America's most devastating natural catastrophes— the great Mississippi floods of 1927 and 1993. In 1927 the river swelled to about sixty miles in width, inundating over 16.5 million acres (a land area roughly the size of Ireland) in 170 counties of the lower Mississippi Valley. Several hundred people lost their lives that year; over half a million were left temporarily homeless; and damages were estimated at $300 million, or almost $3 billion in 1993 (inflation-adjusted) dollars.[17] Sixty-six years later, an estimated 20 million acres flooded along the upper Mississippi, leading the Soil Conservation Service to state that "it was as though a sixth Great Lake, centered around northern Iowa, had sprung up in the Midwest." The 1993 flood inflicted considerably less human misery than its predecessor in 1927. Thirty-eight lives were lost and 55,000 persons displaced. Yet the economic impact of the 1993 flood was even greater, with overall damages estimated at between $12 and $16 billion, including about $2.5 billion in agricultural losses.[18]

Despite the similarity of the events themselves, the way government officials managed the two crises turned out to be radically different, revealing a dramatic change in both public policy and public expectations. In 1927 the federal government and the American National Red Cross organized the biggest disaster relief effort in U.S. history to that time. As was customary, Calvin Coolidge, president of the United States, was also president of the American National Red Cross. On April 22, 1927, he announced:

> The Government is giving such aid as lies within its power. Government boats that are available are being used to rescue those in danger and carry refugees to safety. The War Department is providing the Red Cross with tents for housing refugees. The National Guard, State and local authorities are assisting. But the burden of caring for the homeless rests upon the agency designated by Government charter to provide relief in disaster—The American National Red Cross. For so great a task additional funds must be obtained immediately.
>
> It therefore becomes my duty as President of the United States and President of The American National Red Cross to direct the sympathy of our people to the sad plight of thousands of their fellow citizens, and to urge that generous contributions be promptly forthcoming to alleviate their suffering.[19]

As Coolidge suggested, the federal government and the Red Cross worked together in the relief effort, but the latter carried most of the financial burden. Federal assistance remained limited mainly to lending government equipment and personnel and to placing the "bully pulpit" of the presidency at the disposal of private fundraising efforts.

Although President Coolidge refused to call a special session of Congress as some representatives from the affected states urged, he did direct his commerce secretary, Herbert Hoover, to help run the relief effort and ordered the rest of his cabinet to assist when necessary. Through various agencies, the federal government spent about $10 million (or 3.3 percent of total damages) on relief. The Red Cross, by comparison, collected $17.5 million in cash donations as well as another $6 million of in-kind contributions. It also provided emergency services, including food and shelter, to more than 600,000 flood victims over a fourteen-month period.[20]

Herbert Hoover viewed the efforts of the Red Cross in 1927 as enormously successful. By today's standards, the reimbursement rates were small. Together, the states, the federal government, and the Red Cross covered only about 13 percent of total damages. But by the standards of the time, the effort was Herculean. Hoover declared that the Red Cross had "become the one guarantee to the American people that loss of life shall be prevented in calamity and that suffering shall be mitigated to the utmost degree."[21] Writing his memoirs a decade later, he expressed particular pride in the fact that private sources had provided the bulk of all assistance in 1927. "[T]hose were the days," Hoover recalled nostalgically, "when citizens expected to take care of one another in time of disaster and it had not occurred to them that the Federal Government should do it."[22]

By 1993, however, those days were definitely gone, since just about everyone now expected that the federal government would help to bail out the victims of that year's great Mississippi flood. President Clinton quickly declared all of Iowa and multiple counties in eight other midwestern states federal disaster areas, and he asked Congress for a large emergency supplemental appropriation. With no significant opposition to a massive federal relief effort in either the House or the Senate, the most contentious issue on Capitol Hill was how the bailout should be financed.[23]

A few lawmakers raised deeper questions. Robert Byrd, chairman of the Senate Appropriations Committee, repeatedly cautioned his colleagues against fiscal excess, asserting that "disasters are not spending opportunities."[24] Others complained that knee-jerk federal relief policy rewarded personal irresponsibility. As Representative Fred Grandy of Iowa observed, "We're basically telling people, 'We want you to buy insurance, but if you don't, we'll bail you out anyway.'"[25] By this logic, the federal government was contributing to a potentially enormous moral hazard problem.

But politicians from the affected states showed little patience for such speculation. "This is not a time for debating the fine points of long-term policy," exclaimed Governor Mel Carnahan of Missouri. "We have acted in other disasters, whether they be hurricanes, whether they be earthquakes, whether they be other floods. We even acted to help Kurdistan and the savings and loans." Victims of the Mississippi flood, he maintained, deserved no less.[26] Echoing these sentiments, Governor Jim Edgar of Illinois asserted that the great flood was "just as serious a problem for the country as war. I don't think anyone is expecting 100 percent reimbursement, but it has to be adequate."[27]

In the end, warnings about fiscal excess and moral hazard proved no match for the politics of relief in the middle of a catastrophe. Said one congressman, "If you ask the American in the Midwest who is paddling towards his living room or watching his business go down the drain whether he wants us to sit here today and have a budget discussion or whether he wants to pass disaster aid, I submit he would say, 'I want disaster aid.'"[28] Sure enough, the massive appropriation was passed overwhelmingly in both houses of Congress. Although the final package had swelled from President Clinton's initial $2.5 billion request to $6.3 billion, the president did not hesitate for a moment when given the opportunity to sign it.[29]

Clearly, then, federal disaster policy had undergone a profound change sometime between 1927 and 1993. Figure 9.1 helps to pinpoint the timing. Federal coverage of disaster losses had begun creeping upward before the 1960s, but the most dramatic surge came in the late 1960s and early 1970s, just as Congress began to assume ongoing responsibility for assisting individual disaster victims.[30] In the absence of long-term public opinion polls on the subject, it is impossible to offer direct empirical evidence regarding changes in public expectations about the government's role in time of disaster. But it seems clear that public expectations had increased enormously. The federal government covered 3.3 percent of total damages after the Mississippi flood of 1927, 6.2 percent of damages after Hurricane Diane in 1955, 12.8 percent of damages after the Pacific Northwest floods of 1964, and 48.3 percent of damages after Tropical Storm Agnes in 1972.[31] Although federal lawmakers subsequently scaled back several of the most generous forms of relief for private individuals and firms (though not for farmers), federal disaster assistance for state and local governments continued to increase.[32] Overall, federal disaster spending from 1977 to 1993 averaged $7 billion per year (in 1993 dollars), and federal expenditures following the great Mississippi flood of 1993 covered about half of total estimated damages. Without a doubt, the federal government had come to assume a pivotal role in the overall management of natural catastrophe risk.[33]

Fitful Steps toward Explicit Public Disaster Insurance

One final twist in the story concerns an ongoing debate about the merits of disaster relief versus explicit (contractual) public catastrophe insurance. As we have seen, lawmakers treated federal disaster policy almost

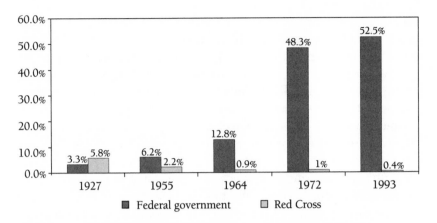

Figure 9.1   Approximate coverage rates on five major disasters, federal government and the Red Cross. Coverage rates computed as a ratio of disaster spending to total estimated damages, in percent. From David A. Moss and Julie Rosenbaum, *The Great Mississippi Flood of 1993,* case no. 9-797-097 (Boston: Harvard Business School, 1997), exhibit 3. Reprinted by permission. The sources used to produce this figure are also described in David A. Moss, "Courting Disaster? The Transformation of Federal Disaster Policy since 1803," in Kenneth A. Froot, ed., *The Financing of Catastrophe Risk* (Chicago: University of Chicago Press, 1999), fig. 8.2.

as an implicit form of insurance, emphasizing that it provided limited coverage against an unavoidable natural hazard. Representative William Cramer noted in 1966 that "no one knows when or where a national disaster will strike. Nobody knows whose home or whose income may be destroyed, or whose life will be jeopardized by an act of nature." Because everyone was exposed to disaster risk all the time, he concluded, "it appears to me . . . that it is justified that all people in America should have the same Federal Government relief available to them on a uniform basis."[34]

But if implicit insurance was good, wouldn't explicit insurance be even better? Proponents of this approach claimed that explicit public insurance would more accurately reflect varying levels of disaster risk in different parts of the country and parcel them out in a more fair and rational manner. President Roosevelt had inaugurated federal crop insurance in the late 1930s; but this covered only farmers and, at the outset, only selected crops in selected counties.[35] A much bigger step on the path to federal disaster insurance involved the establishment of a federal flood insurance program, which was first proposed in the early 1950s and which finally came to fruition nearly two decades later.

Flood insurance was of particular interest to policymakers because private insurers generally excluded flood damage from their property and casualty policies. This was the result of hard experience. Private experiments with flood insurance had failed in the 1890s and again in the 1920s. In the latter case, the extraordinary flooding of 1927 proved especially devastating. According to a contemporary report, "Losses piled up to a staggering total which was aggravated by the fact that this insurance was largely commonly treated in localities most exposed to flood hazard. . . . By the end of 1928 every responsible company had discontinued this insurance."[36] Having learned that individual flood risks were often highly correlated in specific regions, insurers had apparently decided that the prospect of catastrophic flooding rendered this particular risk uninsurable. Two experts on the subject wrote in 1955 that floods "are almost the only natural hazard not now insurable by the home- or factory-owner, for the simple reason that the experience of private capital with flood insurance has been decidedly unhappy."[37]

It was against this backdrop that President Truman championed national flood insurance in 1951 and 1952. Frustrated that so little of the damage from the great Kansas-Missouri flood of 1951 was privately insured, he decided that a federal solution was necessary. Congress rejected the idea, however, and it lay dormant until President Eisenhower again put forth a federal flood insurance plan in 1956. Although Eisenhower's bill was enacted that year, the program itself was stillborn because Congress never approved the necessary funds. In both cases, opposition from the insurance industry had played an important role in scuttling the idea.[38]

Federal flood insurance finally became a reality twelve years later, this time with some crucial support from the insurance industry. Proponents claimed that a federally backed insurance program would succeed where private insurers had failed by spreading flood risks nationwide and providing the necessary financial backing. They also hoped it would curb the expensive supplemental relief appropriations that now inevitably seemed to follow natural disasters. Equally important, they believed that a true insurance program would inject a greater degree of personal responsibility into federal disaster policy, requiring citizens to buy insurance in advance of catastrophes rather than simply expecting government largesse afterward. As one Senate committee report stated: "Insurance protection against the risk of destruction caused by tornadoes and other natural catastrophes is generally available, but it is not available against the risk of flood loss. . . . These facts underline the need for a program which will make insurance against flood damage available, encourage persons to become aware of the risk of occupying flood plains, and reduce the mounting Federal expenditures for disaster relief assistance."[39]

The National Flood Insurance Act of 1968 offered coverage for residential and business properties. It also emphasized prevention by extending coverage only to those floodplain communities that enacted and enforced suitable hazard mitigation measures, such as zoning regulations and building codes. For the most part, insurance premiums were supposed to cover expected costs. Exceptions were made, however, for structures erected before an area's identification as a flood zone, in which case subsidized rates applied.[40] Although the original plan envisioned a public-private partnership (which had helped win much-needed insurance industry approval), the federal government ended up dominating the program and bearing virtually all of the risk once it got under way.[41]

Even before passage of the act, many scholars and policymakers found the idea of public insurance so compelling that they were prepared to look beyond floods to disasters more generally. Two experts, Douglas Dacy and Howard Kunreuther, wrote at the time, "It is our hope that the flood insurance bill before Congress will be swiftly passed and eventually extended to cover other natural hazards, enabling the federal government to withdraw from its paternalistic role in relation to the private sector."[42] Such enthusiasm continued after enactment, despite lower than expected participation in the National Flood Insurance Program. Senator Quentin Burdick maintained in 1974 that there was "[c]onsiderable interest . . . in the possibility of developing nationwide, comprehensive insurance for all kinds of major disasters. Most of the suggestions contemplate an all-risk type policy, partially subsidized by the Federal Government, to provide compensation for damages caused by all natural hazards." Supporters, he suggested, believed that most citizens would prefer to purchase this sort of coverage than "to depend on receiving possible public or private assistance" in the wake of a catastrophe.[43]

In the end, however, such a scheme was never enacted. As Senator

Burdick noted in 1974, the Ninety-Third Congress saw at least a dozen bills introduced in the House and two in the Senate designed "to establish a national system of major disaster insurance, but as yet no action has been taken."[44] The idea continued to surface from time to time, making a particularly strong showing in the wake of several colossal disasters in the early 1990s.[45] But no matter how much proponents of public disaster insurance complained about the unwieldiness and the expense of the existing approach, their proposals for reform consistently failed.[46]

For all its crudeness as a risk management device, unilateral disaster assistance had emerged as an extremely popular Phase III policy. Indeed, it always seemed to achieve its most spectacular public support just when the nation's politicians were paying closest attention to the issue, in the immediate aftermath of a catastrophe. Like many other Phase III policies, therefore, federal disaster relief proved surprisingly well entrenched as the twentieth century came to a close.

The Rise of State Guaranty Funds

A less visible—but no less important—facet of the transition to Phase III involved the rise of state guaranty funds, which established public coverage against the insolvency of private insurance companies. In creating these funds, lawmakers once again acted as insurers of last resort. Unlike federal disaster policy, however, state guaranty laws established explicit (rather than implicit) public insurance. The goal was essentially to insure insurance, guaranteeing that policyholders' claims would be paid even if their carriers went bust. Although a handful of guaranty funds came into existence well before 1960 (mainly in New York State), the vast majority began to emerge in the late 1960s—at almost precisely the same moment that the nation's courts were adopting strict liability in product injury cases and lawmakers in Washington were radically expanding federal disaster relief.

The notion of guaranteeing private insurance policies was sometimes likened to deposit insurance, since the basic idea was to compensate the customer-creditors of failed financial institutions. But the analogy never proved very useful because although there were some obvious similarities, the differences turned out to be even more significant. Unlike the nation's deposit insurance system, which was established as part of FDR's New Deal in 1933, guaranty funds were enacted at the state rather than the federal level. The guaranty funds, moreover, were generally financed on the basis of post-assessments rather than advance premiums. Whereas banks had to contribute to the Federal Deposit Insurance Corporation year in and year out, insurance companies had to pay into their state guaranty funds only *after* one or more of the insurance companies doing business in the state actually failed. In contrast to the FDIC, therefore, the state guaranty funds were frequently empty. Perhaps most important of all, the core objective in creating guaranty funds was not to safeguard the money supply or the financial system (as in the case of deposit insurance) but simply to protect the consumer. The guaranty funds were Phase III risk management policy through and through.

Significantly, the man mainly responsible for drafting the states' model guaranty fund legislation, Spencer Kimball, later suggested that the extraordinary emphasis on consumer security which motivated these laws would have been unimaginable much earlier than the 1960s. "A society only gradually and recently becoming security-conscious in the contemporary sense would not have . . . felt a need to 'insure insurance' through the recently appearing guaranty funds," he wrote in 1986. "Apparently, only in the last few decades has achieving the riskless life become a consuming personal and social goal."[47] Here, in abbreviated form, was precisely the reasoning that drove American risk management policy in so many new directions—including into the business of insuring insurance—after 1960.

Coming to Terms with Failure in the Insurance Industry

The threat of insurer insolvency had always been a significant concern for American policymakers. From its inception, the insurance industry had been regulated more than most—in large measure because it was viewed as serving a vital public purpose. During the antebellum period, this regulatory authority was exercised mainly though the imposition of charter restrictions. Direct administrative oversight began to appear in some states near the middle of the nineteenth century and was firmly in place everywhere by the middle of the twentieth. At each stage, concerns about insolvency proved pivotal.[48]

Naturally, this long tradition of insurance regulation in the United States bears directly on the history of risk management policy. It strongly reinforces the idea that American lawmakers have historically shown a special willingness to intervene in the economy to address risk-related problems. According to one authority on insurance regulation, government intervention has long been justified on the grounds that policyholders "lack easy access to information regarding the future solvency of insurers" and tend to "make irrational decisions" even when such information "is fully and freely available."[49] There are, to be sure, numerous other justifications for the regulation of insurance, including the notion that scale economies in the industry may stifle competition and generate vast inequalities of bargaining power between insurers and their customers.[50] But the alleged inability of individual consumers to grapple with complex risk-allocation contracts is of special interest here because it has arisen in a variety of other policy contexts as a serious argument for government intervention. The history of insurance regulation thus complements the broader story of public risk management.

But it also presents a problem, since the early emphasis on consumer protection seems to violate the timing of Phase III. After all, lawmakers had begun working to reduce consumer risk in the insurance industry long before 1960. The small policyholder was already an important beneficiary of legislative action by the mid-nineteenth century.[51] No doubt, consumer protection was only part of the story. The regulatory emphasis on insurer solvency also served powerful developmental goals, particularly since a large portion of insurance was written for commercial clients, and since major insurers accumulated huge pools of precious investment capital. As Kimball once observed, "[t]he preservation of the integrity of these 'trust funds' became a major problem of public policy, for such enormous sums of money tempted the venal, the ambitious, and the foolish."[52] Still, there is little doubt that nineteenth-century insurance regulation was motivated not only by standard Phase I objectives but by nascent Phase III objectives as well.

Whatever the case, it is now clear that these early impulses for consumer protection reached an entirely new level of intensity in the twentieth century, and particularly after 1960. (Though imperfect, the three-phases framework thus remains relevant.) The most striking development in this regard was the idea of directly compensating the victims of insurance company insolvencies, which was written into law for the first time in New York State in 1935. That year, legislators in Albany enacted the Workmen's Compensation Security Funds Law, which guaranteed that every injured worker would receive appropriate benefits even if his employer's insurance company failed. Financing for the measure was based on mandatory premiums that were assessed on all insurers writing workers' compensation policies anywhere in the state. The failure of two out-of-state carriers in 1933, which deprived numerous injured workers of the benefits to which they were entitled under the state's workers' compensation law, were the main provocations for the enactment of the nation's first guaranty fund law two years later.[53]

The 1935 law itself presents no problem for our periodization of the three phases, since it was clearly designed to advance worker security and thus fits neatly into Phase II. The same cannot be said, however, of three subsequent guaranty fund laws enacted in New York over the next twelve years. The first of these was the Public Motor Vehicle Liability Security Fund. Established in 1939, it guaranteed liability insurance on taxicabs and other public conveyances.[54] Next, in 1941, New York lawmakers created the Life Insurance Guaranty Corporation, which was designed to cover claims against failed life insurers.[55] Finally, the state legislature passed the Motor Vehicle Liability Security Fund Act in 1947, extending the earlier guaranty on taxicab liability insurance to all automobile liability policies.[56]

Only a handful of other states enacted comparable laws before 1960; and all but one of these laws (New Jersey's 1952 Motor Vehicle Liability Security Fund Act) applied exclusively to workers' compensation insurance.[57] For the most part, therefore, the basic idea that risk management policy enacted between 1900 and 1960 tended to focus on the worker holds even in the context of guaranty fund legislation. The coverage of automobile liability insurance in New York and New Jersey in the 1940s and 1950s, and particularly New York's coverage of life insurance in 1941, constituted the only true exceptions to the rule.

In fact, as Table 9.1 makes abundantly clear, the extension of guaranty funds beyond workers' compensation moved with extraordinary speed beginning in the late 1960s, just as one might have expected under Phase III. All fifty states created funds covering property and casualty policies between 1969 and 1981, and all fifty had created similar funds for life and health insurance by 1991. The distinctive logic and timing of consumer-oriented risk management policy was once again evident.

Explaining the Rapid Enactment of Insurance Guaranty Laws

The main impetus for the onslaught of state guaranty legislation was the threat of federal action in the second half of the 1960s. Ever since 1945,

Table 9.1   The spread of insurance guaranty funds

Year	States establishing property and casualty guaranty funds	States establishing life and health guaranty funds
1941	—	New York
1969	California, Michigan, New York, Wisconsin	Wisconsin
1970	Alaska, Delaware, Florida, Georgia, Idaho, Iowa, Kansas, Louisiana, Maine, Mississippi, Ohio, Pennsylvania, Rhode Island, South Dakota, Vermont, Virginia, West Virginia	—
1971	Colorado, Connecticut, Hawaii, Illinois, Maryland, Massachusetts, Minnesota, Missouri, Montana, Nebraska, Nevada, North Carolina, North Dakota, Oregon, South Carolina, Tennessee, Texas, Utah, Washington, Wyoming	Maryland, New Hampshire, Washington
1972	Indiana, Kentucky	Connecticut, Kansas, South Carolina, Vermont
1973	District of Columbia, New Mexico	Nevada, Texas
1974	New Jersey, Puerto Rico	Montana, North Carolina, Puerto Rico
1975	—	Nebraska, New Mexico, Oregon
1976	—	Virginia
1977	Arizona, Arkansas	Arizona, Idaho, Minnesota, West Virginia
1978	—	Indiana, Kentucky
1979	—	Florida, Hawaii, Pennsylvania, Utah
1980	Oklahoma	Illinois
1981	Alabama	Georgia, Oklahoma
1982–86	—	Delaware, Michigan, Alabama, North Dakota, Maine, Mississippi, Rhode Island, Massachusetts
1987–91	—	Iowa, Missouri, Arkansas, Ohio, South Dakota, Tennessee, Alaska, Wyoming, California, Colorado, Louisiana, New Jersey
1992	—	District of Columbia

Source: Standard and Poor's Insurer Solvency Review, Property/Casualty ed. (1996–97), pp. xxxvi–xxxix; Standard and Poor's Insurer Solvency Review, Life/Health ed. (1997–98), pp. xxxvi–xxxix.

when Congress passed the McCarran-Ferguson Act, the federal government had promised to leave insurance regulation to the states, a promise that only reconfirmed a division of authority regarding insurance that had been well accepted by both legislatures and courts since at least the mid-nineteenth century.[58] But now, in the 1960s, it appeared that some in Congress were becoming increasingly uncomfortable with the arrangement.

Frustrated that many automobile owners—and particularly those in America's inner cities—were forced to buy coverage from high-risk insurers, Senator Thomas Dodd sponsored a bill in 1966 that would have created a federal guaranty fund covering claims against insolvent automobile insurers. The proposed legislation came in the aftermath of Senate hearings on the subject as well as a flurry of news stories spotlighting the tragic plight of accident victims whose legitimate claims went unpaid as a result of insurance company failures.[59] Dodd charged that under these circumstances, "citizens could have no peace of mind knowing that their suffering might go uncompensated and their families would not be secure."[60]

With pressure rapidly mounting for federal action, the National Association of Insurance Commissioners (NAIC) worked with industry leaders to defuse the crisis by radically expanding both the availability and the scope of the so-called "uninsured motorist" endorsement. Such an endorsement, which became mandatory in numerous states, assured each potential accident victim that her own insurance company would compensate her losses in the event that the guilty motorist was himself uninsured or that his insurance company became insolvent before it could pay the claim.[61] But this was obviously only a partial solution. It did little to protect an insured motorist against the insolvency of her own insurance company, and it applied exclusively to automobile policies.

Aware of these problems, Senator Warren Magnuson called for the creation of a comprehensive Federal Insurance Guaranty Corporation in 1969. Although he and several of his allies in Congress repeatedly insisted that they had no interest in usurping state regulatory authority over the insurance industry, almost no one seemed to believe them.[62] Clearly threatened, the NAIC began working furiously to secure the rapid enactment of guaranty fund legislation at the state level, once again with the hope of preempting federal action. In a memorandum to members dated December 31, 1969, NAIC executive secretary Jon Hanson asserted that immediate passage of state guaranty fund laws was probably the only way to avoid federal intervention. "It is anticipated that S. 2236 will reach the Senate floor for a vote by early spring," he wrote in the memorandum. "The indication is strong that such a bill would pass in the absence of prompt and widespread enactment of the model (or comparable) state insolvency legislation at the forthcoming state legislative sessions."[63]

Earlier in 1969, lawmakers in Wisconsin had created the very first comprehensive guaranty fund, which covered all lines of insurance other than variable annuities and variable life policies. Besides offering nearly universal coverage, the Wisconsin law was also distinctive because it relied on post-assessments for financing. Prior guaranty fund laws had provided only narrow coverage (addressing isolated lines of insurance such as workers' compensation or automobile liability) and generally required pre-funding through regular premium payments. The Wisconsin law thus marked a major change from previous experiments. Drafted by Kimball, it was quickly adopted by the NAIC as the basis for its new model guaranty fund bill.[64]

The NAIC's model bill differed from the Wisconsin law in only one major respect: it was limited mainly to property and casualty insurance. Otherwise, its key provisions closely resembled those that Kimball had originally drafted for Wisconsin. All carriers writing any of the designated lines of insurance within the state were required to join an insurance guaranty association. Members were authorized to select the association's board of directors, but all such appointments required the approval of the state's insurance commissioner. Significantly, no contributions to the association were required unless and until a member insurance company actually failed. In the event of an insolvency, each solvent member would then be assessed annually up to 2 percent of premiums in the designated lines to cover unpaid claims. While covered workers' compensation claims were always to be paid in full, other covered claims were capped at $300,000 per claimant, and the repayment of unearned premiums was capped at $10,000 per policy. Significantly, the model law permitted member companies to recoup all assessments through subsequent premium increases.[65]

Variations on this model bill were enacted with remarkable speed over the next several years. Four states had already created property and casualty guaranty funds by the end of 1969. All but eight states had done so by the end of 1971; and the remaining ones—plus the District of Columbia and Puerto Rico—fell into line over the next decade (see Table 9.1). The NAIC, meanwhile, had introduced another model guaranty fund bill for life and health insurance policies in 1970. Although much of the insurance industry opposed this new initiative (perhaps because there was no longer any imminent threat of congressional action), industry representatives still proved influential in shaping the model bill. In the end, the main difference from the property and casualty proposal was that considerable emphasis was now placed not only on the payment of covered claims but also on the continuation of coverage, which was viewed as essential to assuring personal security in the life and health lines.[66] As shown in Table 9.1, thirteen states (plus Puerto Rico) established life and health guaranty funds by the end of 1974, and twenty-eight by the conclusion of the decade. New Jersey was the last state to adopt such a fund, in 1991, and the District of Columbia finally rounded out the list the following year.

Insurers' Insurance: A Special Sort of Risk Management

From a risk management perspective, the main objective of all this legislation was to protect individual policyholders by spreading insurance insolvency risk as broadly as possible. The NAIC subcommittee on guaranty funds concluded in 1970 that the "enactment of insolvency fund legislation . . . should not be viewed in the context of good companies subsidizing the bad." Rather, the subcommittee suggested, these laws should be seen as providing "a mechanism by which each policyholder, through a slightly increased cost, purchases protection for himself against the insolvency of his insurer. This is another form of risk spreading."[67]

Indeed, this was precisely the reason why the NAIC's model property and casualty bill permitted insurers to recoup assessments through slightly increased premiums. Many states also ended up allowing insurers to recoup assessments through tax offsets. Either way, the goal was to *spread* risk widely—in one case across the consuming public and in the other across the taxpaying public. The NAIC subcommittee acknowledged that an alternative approach would have been to try to *reduce* or even eliminate the risk of insolvency through exceedingly strict regulation. But it concluded that such a strategy "might well be so highly onorous [sic] as to be unacceptable to our free enterprise–competitive system. Thus, there is and there will continue to be a need for insolvency fund legislation."[68]

Though undoubtedly strong, this commitment to broad-based risk spreading was ultimately not strong enough to overcome demands for a state-level solution. No one could deny that the federal government was capable of spreading risk more broadly than the individual states, but opponents of the federal approach insisted that state funds would be administered more efficiently and that they would provide both insurers and regulators with stronger incentives for prevention than would a unified federal fund.[69] Overall, relatively little attention was devoted to the inherent vulnerability of state funds to massive disasters. Officials at the NAIC, it seems, were far more concerned about the prospect of isolated insurance failures than about the remote threat of systematic failure within any given state.[70]

A related question that sparked considerably more debate, particularly in Congress, was whether the Federal Deposit Insurance Corporation constituted a good model for guaranteeing insurance policies. Senator Magnuson and his allies insisted that it did, while representatives of the insurance industry and the insurance commissioners argued vehemently that it did not. The Nixon administration, meanwhile, staked out an intermediary position. Administration officials endorsed state-level regulation, the establishment of state guaranty programs (rather than Magnuson's Federal Insurance Guaranty Fund), and the concept of post-assessment financing. But they also favored the creation of some sort of federal agency, financed exclusively out of post-assessments, to serve as a backstop if and when the states proved incapable of managing particular insurance insolvencies on their own.[71]

At the Senate hearings in early 1970, spokesmen for the administration argued that post-assessment financing—whether at the state or the federal level—would provide the strongest possible incentives for controlling moral hazard. A pre-funded, FDIC-style system, they maintained, would invite regulatory laxity by making insurance bailouts seem relatively painless. But "by levying a postinsolvency assessment on the companies doing business in the State of domicile of the failing company, there would be a very substantial incentive for them to press for not only sound insurance laws in that State, but also reasonably good administration of that law." When an amazed Senate staffer asked whether the administration expected "the regulated industry [to be] urging better regulation upon itself," a high-level official from the Department of Transportation, Paul Cherington, answered in the affirmative. "Yes, sir," he said, implicitly resurrecting the old Wisconsin school argument about the preventive power of carefully targeted risk shifting.[72]

As it turned out, concerns about moral hazard were so great that many policymakers favored not only post-assessments (ostensibly to keep insurers and regulators on their toes) but also a gag rule to minimize consumer complacency in the selection of insurers. The NAIC's model property and casualty bill suggested in a "general comments" section that state lawmakers ought to consider "the addition of a section specifically permitting or prohibiting advertisements by member insurers which include reference to coverage of the insurance guaranty association."[73] Large insurance companies generally supported a complete prohibition on such advertising, seeking to prevent weaker insurers from converting mandatory membership in a state guaranty association into a source of competitive advantage. Sensitive to industry pressure and apparently concerned that public knowledge about insurance guaranties might further compromise consumer monitoring of insurers, the NAIC later endorsed a near-total prohibition on advertising in its model life and health bill. For their part, most state legislators ended up adopting similar gag rules in their respective guaranty laws.[74]

What all this suggested is that the ultimate policy goal in establishing guaranty funds was not to protect the financial system (as was the case with deposit insurance), but rather to protect consumers *after* insurer insolvency while introducing as little moral hazard as possible. Proponents sometimes claimed that the existence of guaranty funds would strengthen the whole insurance system—that it would bolster "public confidence and hence the value of the insurance institution, whose very existence is the result of the public's desire and need to be and feel secure from risk."[75] But policymakers generally placed much greater emphasis on the idea of protecting the individual consumer than on safeguarding the insurance industry or stabilizing the broader financial system. Certainly the inclusion of a gag rule indicates that public confidence building was not a central objective.

The contrast with deposit insurance came into particularly sharp relief during the Senate hearings in early 1970. Frustrated with the administration's vague proposals for state funds, federal backstops, and post-assessments, Senator Philip Hart pointedly asked Harold Passer of the Department of Commerce whether he would recommend the same disjointed system for guaranteeing bank deposits: "If we had no Federal insurance of bank deposits and you were now coming up here to suggest how we respond to what once was a very acute problem of losses because of bank failures, would you recommend structuring the bank deposit insurance system the way you are recommending structuring the insurance guarantee fund? If you could do it over again, would you put in the form you are urging us to put the insurance fund in?"[76]

Acknowledging that this was a "very probing question," Passer carefully explained that the reasons for guaranteeing bank deposits were fundamentally different from those for guaranteeing insurance policies. Banks, he maintained, "are suppliers of and participators in the money supply system in the United States, and this is part of the lifeblood of commerce and not just a business meeting a special need. Therefore, I think there is some basis for looking at it as a kind of a special situation." To drive home the point, Passer added that "the confidence that you need in a system which creates money is, I think, a different order of magnitude from a system for any other kind of ordinary business service."[77]

Apparently unconvinced, Senator Hart continued to press his witness. If Passer was admitting that the FDIC approach generated greater public confidence, Hart asked, why not apply it to insurance as well as deposits? Because, Passer replied calmly, public confidence was not nearly as important in the insurance context. "We are not talking about the means of payment. . . . We are talking about a service. There are many, many services and they all are important and this is one service among many, whereas the money supply is unique."[78]

Deposit insurance, in other words, was a Phase I risk management policy designed to protect and promote a strategic sector in the economy—the monetary system. Well-publicized consumer protection was essential in order to maintain public confidence in the means of payment, "part of the lifeblood of commerce." Insurance guaranties, by comparison, constituted a Phase III risk management policy in which consumer protection was an end in itself. Indeed, as will become clear in the next section, consumer protection was consistently heralded as the raison d'être for insurance guaranty funds. The analogy to deposit insurance thus quickly fell apart.

Focus on the Consumer

The consumer orientation of the insurance guaranty idea was abundantly evident at every step of the policymaking process. Even Senator Magnuson, who was perhaps the strongest proponent of the FDIC analogy, opened his committee hearings in late 1969 by stressing the vital need for additional consumer protection in the insurance industry. "So, we will begin hearings on S. 2236," he said, "which . . . [will] provide, we hope, American consumers protection against property and casualty insurance company insolvencies. Given the hardships which these insolvencies impose upon American policyholders and claimants, it is imperative that this committee provide a means of insuring American consumers against the loss of their insurance."[79]

Naturally, Erma Angevine of the Consumer Federation of America agreed, declaring that "the American consumer has a vital stake in the industry affected by this bill."[80] But so too did Harold Passer, representing the administration, even though he was officially on record as opposing the bill under consideration. After Passer outlined the administration's counterproposal, Senator Frank Moss asked, "Do I gather from that statement that you believe protection of the consumer should be the touchstone, the primary focus, of any Federal bill?" Passer replied forcefully: "Yes, Senator. We certainly agree that the consumer needs to be fully and completely protected in this area. As you noted, we are in complete agreement that Federal legislation is needed to insure that this protection does in fact exist."[81]

State-level policymakers consistently highlighted the very same objective. The NAIC's subcommittee on guaranty fund legislation noted at the end of 1970 that ever since the "June 1969 meeting . . . the commissioners have been vitally interested in developing a model bill *to protect consumers across the country* against the insolvency of property and liability insurers."[82] In fact, the Wisconsin law that served as the basis for the NAIC's model bill was itself known unofficially as the "Insurance Consumers Protection Act of 1969."[83]

Consumers were thought to require special protection not only because of their extreme financial vulnerability (being easily devastated by the nonpayment of insurance claims), but also because of their supposed inability to assess insurer insolvency risk on their own. According to the NAIC, individual consumers were "entitled to protection" because they "purchased their insurance relying on the insurance industry's integrity and good faith in performing contractual obligations."[84] The state, in other words, had an obligation to protect these trusting souls.

Perhaps not surprisingly, highly sophisticated claimants were treated differently as a result of this logic. The NAIC's model property and casualty bill explicitly excluded the claims of insurers and reinsurers on the grounds that "coverage should [not] be extended to elements of the insurance industry which know or reasonably can be expected to know the financial condition of the various companies."[85] As Kimball observed, "insurers are peculiarly able to protect themselves."[86] By this same reasoning, Kimball and the NAIC subsequently sought to exclude large commercial policyholders from guaranty fund coverage, since sizable companies were presumably capable of assessing and monitoring insurers without government assistance.[87]

Guaranty funds were thus created mainly for the purpose of shielding naïve, incompetent, or simply unlucky policyholders from the risk of insurer insolvency. A rash of insurance company failures in the mid-1960s served as a catalyst for federal proposals, and this in turn provoked action at the state level. As one insurance expert explained, "the insolvencies that occurred during the 1960s affected policyholders who were believed to be unable to protect themselves from financially weak insurers because they lacked the ability to compare the financial condition of potential insurers."[88]

Of course, insurer insolvency was not a new phenomenon in the 1960s. Within the life insurance industry alone, fifty-seven firms had collapsed between 1840 and 1900, wreaking havoc upon unsuspecting policyholders all across the country.[89] Yet the victims of these early failures received no special assistance from the state. The difference was that in the nineteenth century, consumer protection had not yet emerged as a dominant social priority. Once it had by the late 1960s, a brief upturn in insurance company failures was now capable of precipitating a dramatic legislative response.[90] Without a doubt, the rise of the state guaranty funds constituted an impressive display of Phase III policymaking in action.

An Explosion in Environmental Liability

No survey of Phase III would be complete without at least a brief examination of the dramatic increase in environmental liability that American business began to face after 1960. Although producers had always been potentially liable in court for environmental damage, a number of common law developments gradually expanded that liability in the second half of the twentieth century. More striking still was the enactment of major environmental statutes—particularly at the federal level—that imposed massive new liability on firms for a wide range of environmental hazards. The change was so extreme that most insurance companies began limiting environmental liability coverage in the 1970s, and many eliminated it altogether in the 1980s.

The biggest environmental liability law of all was the Comprehensive Environmental Response, Compensation, and Liability Act (CERCLA), first passed in 1980 and commonly referred to as Superfund. The extent to which this legislation constituted pure risk management policy is open to doubt, since its authors appear to have focused more on ex post cost allocation than on ex ante risk shifting in fashioning its liability provisions. But there is no doubt about what lawmakers were trying to accomplish. Their goal was to improve environmental safety and security for all citizens while imposing the inevitable costs—and risks—on American business. As will become clear, these environmental policymakers were truly testing the boundaries of Phase III.

Environmental Liability at Common Law

Even in the nineteenth century, producers had faced a modest amount of environmental liability. This is because victims of environmental damage could pursue a variety of common law remedies. As we saw in the last chapter, property damage sometimes arose out of environmental accidents, such as the sudden release of water from a faulty storage tank or converted mine shaft. In these cases, victims were entitled to sue under accident law. Although plaintiffs normally had to prove negligence to recover, the famous *Rylands* decision of 1868 made clear that recovery was sometimes possible even in the absence of negligence. Where abnormally dangerous conditions or processes were involved, defendants were often held strictly liable for any injuries that resulted.[91]

Accidents were by no means the only source of environmental damage, however. Many enterprises polluted the air and water in their regular course of business. When injury to another party resulted, negligence or strict liability might still constitute grounds for recovery, depending on the specific circumstances involved. Yet plaintiffs were far more likely to seek relief under nuisance law. Deeply rooted in English history, the law of nuisance had been employed as early as the thirteenth century to adjudicate disputes concerning lime-pit smoke and other common annoyances.[92] As the famous eighteenth-century legal commentator William Blackstone explained, "[i]f one does any other act, in itself lawful, which yet being done in that place necessarily tends to the damage of another's property, it is a nuisance [sic]: for it is incumbent on him to find some other place to do that act, where it will be less offensive."[93] Proof of negligence was not required.

Consistent with Blackstone's declaration that offenders would have to "find some other place to do that act," nuisance law permitted victims to obtain relief through injunction instead of (or in addition to) compensation. A successful plaintiff could thus force a defendant to terminate his injurious activity altogether, even if this meant forcing the defendant out of business. Yet precisely because this remedy was so extreme, it became increasingly common in the early twentieth century for American judges to award monetary damages in lieu of injunctive relief, particularly when the latter remedy was expected to destroy more social value than it conserved.[94]

In 1904, for example, the Supreme Court of Tennessee decided a case involving several small farmers who sought injunctive relief against two smoke-producing copper plants. The smoke had not only compromised the health of one plaintiff's spouse, but also severely damaged all the plaintiffs' timber and crops and generally prevented them "from using and enjoying their farms and homes as they did prior to the inauguration of these enterprises." While acknowledging that the farmers' injuries were real and disturbing, the Tennessee court nonetheless concluded that the costs of injunctive relief would far outweigh the benefits. The copper plants in question employed well over a thousand workers in the community, and an injunction would likely force them to shut down operations, compelling "thousands of people . . . to wander forth to other localities to find shelter and work." Under these circumstances, the court determined that the only just result was to hold the defendants liable for the costs of their nuisance, but not to enjoin them from continuing their productive activity.[95]

Although nuisance was probably the most frequent cause of action in nineteenth- and early twentieth-century environmental cases, the law of trespass created yet another source of environmental liability prior to the 1960s. Though typically associated with personal intrusion onto another's property, trespass did not have to involve a defendant's body. An individual could just as easily trespass "by casting material upon another's land, by discharging water, soot, or carbon, by allowing gas or oil to flow underground into someone else's land."[96] The Supreme Court of Pennsylvania ruled in 1901 that coal dirt floating away from a coal mine and ultimately impairing the works of a downstream flour mill constituted a "continuous trespass." According to the court, this justified not only compensatory damages against the mine owner but also a perpetual injunction to prevent him "from polluting the waters of Panther creek."[97]

As this last case makes clear, standard common law remedies sometimes emerged as surprisingly powerful environmental tools. Focusing particularly on nineteenth-century nuisance law, Morton Horwitz acknowledged that while "other areas of the law were changing to accommodate the growth of American industry, the law of nuisances for the longest time appeared on its face to maintain the pristine purity of a preindustrial mentality."[98] In practice, however, the range of environmental hazards that could be controlled through these common law devices proved rather limited, particularly as the nation's courts erected one obstacle after another impeding environmental suits.

By the second half of the nineteenth century, developers working on publicly authorized projects enjoyed immunity from most nuisance suits.[99] The New York Court of Appeals reasoned in 1850 that although a strict interpretation of nuisance (which applied to public as well as private projects) had long been attractive to the state's judges, it was no longer tenable since it would inevitably constrain economic development. "A city could never be built under such a doctrine," the court concluded.[100] A related obstacle blocked private parties from obtaining relief for public nuisances. Unlike a private nuisance, which adversely affected an individual property holder, a public nuisance affected a large number of people in a roughly equal manner. In most cases, only public officials enjoyed standing to file such suits; and they often declined to do so.

Horwitz emphasized that the railroads, in particular, benefited enormously from this public-private nuisance distinction in the latter nineteenth century.[101]

Nor were these the only major obstacles. The high transaction costs involved in going to trial undoubtedly discouraged a great many victims of environmental hazards—especially those sustaining only modest injuries—from filing suits in the first place. Judges, moreover, retained considerable discretion in deciding all those nuisance cases that did go to trial. Under most circumstances the defendant would prevail, unless the court determined that he had used his property in an "unreasonable" manner and that the resulting injury was "substantial"—two highly subjective judgments, to be sure.[102]

Perhaps most important of all, individuals who sustained personal injuries as a result of environmental hazards typically found little relief in the courts. Not only were the environmental causes of disease poorly understood, particularly before the second half of the twentieth century, but causation was often difficult or impossible to prove in specific cases. Equally problematic for potential plaintiffs, strict statutes of limitations frequently barred legal redress before a victim was even aware of an injury or its source in the environment.[103] Most successful environmental hazard suits thus revolved mainly around property damages rather than personal injuries during the nineteenth and early twentieth centuries.

Judges and legislators finally began scaling back a variety of these barriers beginning in the 1960s. Although environmental liability law experienced nothing like the doctrinal revolution that transformed product liability law at this time, a series of smaller changes probably did produce a modest expansion of common law liability for environmental hazards. The public-private distinction in nuisance law, which had previously represented a major obstacle for countless victims, was eased considerably in the 1970s.[104] At about the same time, growing acceptance of class action suits brought large numbers of plaintiffs into the fold who would have been unlikely to file suits on their own. In 1979, for example, over a thousand residents of a town in Alabama sued the Olin Corporation for exposure to DDT, which the company had allegedly dumped into the Tennessee River years earlier. After a settlement was reached in 1981 (under which each plaintiff received $10,000), about thirteen thousand more residents from surrounding areas soon joined a class action suit that was ultimately settled for $15 million.[105]

Yet another factor that facilitated environmental injury suits was a significant change in the treatment of statutes of limitations. Whereas the clock had traditionally started ticking from the moment the defendant committed his injurious act, numerous jurisdictions began adopting a so-called discovery rule in the 1960s, which started the clock only after the plaintiff discovered her injury. Particularly since relevant statutes of limitations were often of very short duration (typically under five years), this change made a huge difference for the victims of latent environmental injuries, including cancer and other diseases that were slow to manifest. Thirty-nine states had adopted the discovery rule by the early 1980s (mostly through judicial action), and Congress ultimately federalized the rule in 1986.[106]

Together, these assorted changes strengthened the hands of plaintiffs in environmental damage suits. Perhaps even more fundamentally, growing awareness about environmental risks likely heightened the sensitivity of judges while simultaneously expanding the pool of persons who might conceivably see themselves as environmental victims. Public recognition of the dangers of DDT, for example, suddenly burst forth with a vengeance after Rachel Carson published her 1962 best-seller, *Silent Spring*.[107]

At present, it is impossible to determine the exact extent to which common law liability for environmental hazards increased in the years after 1960—or even whether it increased at all. While some scholars have claimed that "[e]nvironmental tort litigation appears to be burgeoning," others have remained skeptical.[108] The one point on which they all seem to agree is that the expansion of common law environmental liability—whatever its magnitude—has been dwarfed by a far more spectacular rise in statutory liability, the topic to which we now turn.

The Revolutionary Expansion of Statutory Environmental Liability

Throughout the twentieth century, but mainly after 1960, federal lawmakers engaged in an ongoing campaign against environmental hazards. The main legislative landmarks through 1990 are listed in Table 9.2. In most cases, the purpose of this legislation was to *reduce* environmental risk through direct regulation. The Toxic Substance Control Act of 1976, for example, authorized the Environmental Protection Agency (EPA) to take all necessary action—up to and including prohibition—to control

Table 9.2   Major federal environmental legislation, 1899–1990

Year	Legislation
1899	Refuse Act
1924	Oil Pollution Act
1947	Federal Insecticide, Fungicide, and Rodenticide Act (FIFRA)
1948	Federal Water Pollution Control Act
1963	Clean Air Act
1965	Water Quality Act
1965	Solid Waste Disposal Act
1970	Environmental Protection Agency (EPA) created by executive order
1970	National Environmental Policy Act (NEPA)
1970	Water Quality Improvement Act
1970	Clean Air Act Amendments
1972	Federal Water Pollution Control Act, or Clean Water Act (CWA)
1972	Federal Insecticide, Fungicide, and Rodenticide Act Amendments
1974	Safe Drinking Water Act
1975	Hazardous Materials Transportation Act
1976	Toxic Substances Control Act (TOSCA)
1976	Resource Conservation and Recovery Act (RCRA)
1977	Clean Air Act Amendments
1977	Clean Water Act Amendments
1978	Hazardous Materials Transportation Act Amendments
1980	Comprehensive Environmental Response, Compensation, and Liability Act (CERCLA)
1984	Resource, Conservation, and Recovery Act Amendments
1986	Superfund Amendments and Reauthorization Act (SARA)
1987	Water Quality Act Amendments
1988	Federal Insecticide, Fungicide, and Rodenticide Act Amendments
1990	Clean Air Act Amendments
1990	Oil Pollution Act
1990	Pollution Prevention Act

Source: Richard H. K. Vietor, Forest Reinhardt, and Jackie Prince Roberts, *Note on Contingent Environmental Liabilities,* no. 9-794-098 (Boston: Harvard Business School, 1994), pp. 18–20; Kevin Madonna, "Federal Environmental Statutes," *Pace Environmental Law Review,* 13 (Spring 1996), 1171–1206.

the production and distribution of chemical substances that presented "an unreasonable risk of injury to health or the environment."[109] Not surprisingly, these risk-reduction measures proved very costly for the firms involved. Even before passage of the Clean Air Act Amendments of 1990, the EPA estimated that compliance with federal environmental regulations cost about $90 billion annually—with the Clean Air and Clean Water Acts each accounting for about a third of the total.[110] By the end of the decade, the Office of Management and Budget estimated that the total "monetized" cost of federal environmental regulations ranged somewhere between $120 and $170 billion per year.[111]

Although risk-reducing regulation proliferated rapidly after 1960, this was not the only method of environmental risk management that federal lawmakers employed. A number of prominent legislative initiatives also harnessed the power of *risk shifting* by imposing substantial liability on environmental wrongdoers. In some sense, nearly all environmental legislation expanded the legal liability of American firms. This is because statutory violations typically constituted "per se" negligence under common law and because violations frequently triggered civil or criminal penalties specified in the statutes themselves.[112] Only a relatively small fraction of these laws, however, purposefully and aggressively utilized liability as an environmental tool. The most prominent example was the Comprehensive Environmental Response, Compensation, and Liability Act of 1980, but there were a number of earlier examples as well.[113]

Congress inaugurated the risk-shifting strategy in 1970 when it passed the Water Quality Improvement Act. This law authorized the federal government to recover costs for the cleanup of oil spills in navigable waters. Although the parties responsible were held strictly liable under the statute, their liability was also explicitly limited, except in cases of willful negligence or misconduct. Vessel liability was capped at $100 per gross registered ton or $14 million, whichever was less; and the liability of each onshore facility was capped at $8 million. The only legitimate defenses against government suits of this kind involved acts of God, acts of war, government negligence, and acts or omissions of third parties. Two years later, the Federal Water Pollution Control Act extended this liability regime to cover not just oil but hazardous substances of all kinds. Subsequent amendments in 1977 increased the vessel liability cap to $150 per gross ton, completely eliminated the $14 million ceiling on vessel liability, and increased the liability limit for onshore facilities from $8 to $50 million.[114]

Congress continued to experiment with environmental risk shifting throughout the 1970s. The Trans-Alaska Pipeline Authorization Act of 1973, the Deepwater Port Act of 1974, and the Outer Continental Shelf

Lands Act Amendment of 1978 all imposed strict liability for oil spills within specified areas.[115] Beyond the problem of oil spills, however, Congress relied mainly on standard risk-reduction (command-and-control) measures to implement environmental policy through the end of the decade. The Toxic Substance Control Act of 1976, the Resource Conservation and Recovery Act of 1976, and the Clean Air Amendments of 1977 all fit this traditional model. Even the Clean Water Amendments of 1977—while increasing liability for hazardous spills and emissions in the nation's waters—still dealt primarily with regulatory issues and the regulatory authority of the EPA.[116]

Liability finally began to occupy a position of strategic importance in federal environmental policy with the passage of CERCLA in 1980. Signed into law after President Carter had already lost the election to Ronald Reagan at the end of the year, CERCLA created a fund (commonly known as Superfund) for the cleanup of hazardous waste. Congress approved an initial appropriation of $1.6 billion, to be financed mainly out of new taxes on petroleum and certain chemicals. But the most striking thing about the new law was that it held just about everyone connected in any way with the transport, treatment, or disposal of hazardous substances both strictly and jointly and severally liable for all necessary cleanup costs and natural resource damage. Liability extended not only to the current owners of the property in question but also to all previous owners who knew at the time that waste was being stored there. And because the liability was joint and several, federal officials could go after any or all of these parties for the full cleanup costs. The statute's reach was simply breathtaking.[117]

Congress had already passed the Resource Conservation and Recovery Act (RCRA) four years earlier, establishing an elaborate permit system and "cradle-to-grave" tracking of hazardous wastes. But RCRA was designed to deal only with existing and future waste sites, not defunct ones. The infamous revelations about Love Canal in 1978 exposed RCRA's deficiencies in graphic detail and helped provoke federal lawmakers to develop a new policy for addressing abandoned and inactive sites.[118] The result was Superfund. As the House Committee on Interstate and Foreign Commerce explained in a report on the impending law in 1980: "Deficiencies in RCRA have left important regulatory gaps. . . . [RCRA] is prospective and applies to past sites only to the extent that they are posing an imminent hazard. . . . It is the intent of the Committee in this legislation [Superfund] to initiate and establish a comprehensive response and financing mechanism to abate and control the vast problems associated with abandoned and inactive hazardous waste disposal sites."[119]

The bill's liability provisions were surely its most striking feature. In theory, a company that had once helped to transport a single truckload of hazardous waste to a site twenty years earlier could now be forced to pay for the entire cleanup of the abandoned site at a cost of tens—or even hundreds—of millions of dollars. While non-cleanup damages were capped at $50 million, liability for cleanup costs remained unlimited.[120] Lawmakers viewed these provisions as constituting an extremely powerful tool for recovering cleanup costs and for punishing those associated with hazardous waste for the terrible (even if unanticipated) consequences of their handiwork. In fact, the original Senate draft of the bill (S. 1480) would have imposed even more extensive liability, forcing responsible parties not only to cover cleanup costs and natural resource damage but also to compensate those injured through exposure to hazardous substances. Although this additional liability for personal injuries was ultimately excised from the bill, the surviving liability provisions remained formidable, to say the least.[121]

Liability-based environmental policy continued to evolve after the creation of Superfund, at both the state and federal levels. Numerous states enacted their own hazardous waste laws, some even tougher than the relevant federal statutes.[122] Congress also expanded a number of existing laws. The original RCRA legislation of 1976 had permitted the EPA to sue for injunctive relief "upon receipt of evidence that . . . hazardous waste is presenting an imminent and substantial endangerment to health or the environment."[123] But after Congress broadened RCRA in 1984, judges now interpreted the statute to permit both the EPA and private citizens to sue for cleanup costs at abated sites.[124] The Superfund Amendments and Reauthorization Act (SARA) of 1986 not only sharply increased appropriations for Superfund but also modestly expanded the original act's liability provisions and expressly permitted citizen suits.[125] Finally, in response to the massive *Exxon Valdez* disaster in 1989, Congress passed new liability legislation for oil spills. The Oil Pollution Act of 1990 held responsible parties strictly liable for all spills in navigable waters and on adjoining shorelines. The act's liability provisions covered not only cleanup costs but also compensation for damages to natural resources, real or personal property, subsistence use, public revenues, profits and earning capacity, and public services.[126] Even after these various expansions, however, Superfund still remained by far the largest single source of environmental liability in the United States.

Superfund: Testing the Limits of Phase III

Superfund certainly had all the trappings of a Phase III risk management policy. It addressed a set of risks facing all citizens while shifting enormous (and highly unpredictable) costs onto producers. This combination would have seemed terribly out of place in the nineteenth or early twentieth century. Even in 1980, two fierce critics of the bill, Representatives Thomas Loeffler and David Stockman, characterized it as embodying "an anti-industrial, zero-discharge mentality." The goal, they insisted, was not "the conventional notion of protection of public safety, but an ideological goal of zero-discharge, zero risk."[127]

"Zero risk" for citizens, that is. Business risk soon spiraled upward. In fact, environmental liability grew so rapidly over the first half of the 1980s that the vast majority of insurers soon intensified their ongoing efforts to reduce environmental exposure. They began by explicitly eliminating coverage for government-imposed cleanup costs and, in 1986, completely removed pollution coverage from their comprehensive general liability policies.[128] Although some insurers introduced special environmental endorsements to fill the void, many decided to get out of the environmental liability market altogether. The result was that most companies involved with hazardous waste now found it exceedingly difficult, if not impossible, to obtain adequate insurance coverage.[129] Their environmental risks thus loomed even larger than the authors of CERCLA might have expected.

One of the traditional justifications for publicly mandated risk shifting was that it would encourage responsible parties to try to prevent (or at least diminish) the underlying hazard; and this argument certainly came into play in the battle to enact Superfund. Congressman Albert Gore, Jr., of Tennessee observed in a House committee report that although "the press and public have primarily focused on the 'superfund' provisions of the bill, the liability sections are also important in addressing the existing problem and creating a strong incentive to ensure that a high standard of care is observed by future generators, handlers and disposers of hazardous wastes."[130] Similarly, House sponsor James Florio of New Jersey emphasized that the bill's liability provisions would not only ensure that costs were "borne by those responsible," thereby replenishing the government fund, but also create "a strong incentive both for prevention of [hazardous] releases and voluntary cleanup of releases by responsible parties."[131] Over in the Senate, Robert T. Stafford of Vermont emphasized that for three years he and his colleagues had been working on a bill "that would respond to emergencies caused by chemical poisons, and . . . seek to discourage the release of those chemicals into the environment."[132]

Phillip Cummings, who served as chief counsel to the Senate Committee on Environment and Public Works when CERCLA was drafted, later insisted that "liability-based deterrence" was the central concept. "The main purpose of CERCLA," he explained in a 1990 article, "is to make spills or dumping of hazardous substances less likely through liability, enlisting business and commercial instincts for the bottom line in place of traditional regulation. It was a conscious intention of the law's authors to draw lenders and insurers into this new army of quasi-regulators, along with corporate risk managers and boards of directors."[133] John R. Commons would have been delighted that the risk management reasoning he first utilized in the campaigns for workers' compensation and unemployment insurance at the beginning of the century was still very much alive.[134]

But the truth is that CERCLA was not a standard risk-shifting policy. In fact, the standard arguments for risk shifting constituted only a relatively small part of the original case for the law's liability provisions. The most common justifications given at the time were that the liability provisions would help offset government cleanup costs and that they would place the burden where it belonged, on those originally responsible. Although the provisions' possible deterrent effects on future behavior were highlighted from time to time, policymakers placed far more emphasis on the benefits of ex post cost allocation than on those of ex ante risk shifting. Certainly, the standard of joint and several liability was more consistent with pure cost recovery than with risk-based deterrence, since it implied that liability would not be apportioned according to blameworthiness. Even Representative Gore, who had noted the bill's deterrent value back in May, was unequivocal on the House floor in September 1980 that the Superfund legislation was mainly backward-looking. "[T]he prospective dumping will be addressed in a regulatory program to take effect later this fall pursuant to the mandate of the Resource Conservation and Recovery Act," he now conceded. "What we are addressing in this [Superfund] legislation is the dumping that occurred in the past."[135]

As many proponents claimed at the time, retroactive liability had the potential to induce current operators to clean up their own sites voluntarily.[136] But the idea of preventing or limiting hazardous dumping itself was something else entirely. Regardless of how much retroactive liability was imposed, it was obviously impossible to "deter" dumping that had already occurred. Since the main goal in 1980 was to clean up inactive and abandoned sites, the logic of deterrence through risk shifting could hardly have been a central motivation.[137]

As it turned out, however, the promise of liability-based deterrence loomed much larger in later years, particularly as concerns mounted about the slow pace of hazardous site cleanup under Superfund. By 1991 (more than a decade after the law's enactment), the EPA had commenced cleanups at about four hundred sites but had completed action on only thirty-three of the more than twelve hundred sites then on its national priorities list. The average cost for cleaning up a site was approximately $50 million, of which about 44 percent was allegedly consumed in litigation and other transaction costs.[138] "As far as cleaning up existing toxic waste goes, Superfund is a super failure," environmental consultant Jon Elliott declared in 1991. The one bright spot, in his view, was liability-based deterrence: "Where the program is doing well is in deterrence—it is scaring companies away from committing future abuses."[139] Critics naturally interpreted the impact of Superfund's liability provisions quite differently, emphasizing a "chilling effect" on economic development rather than a deterrent effect on environmental misdeeds. But all sides seemed to agree that the potentially massive environmental liability arising out of Superfund was significantly affecting business behavior, whether for good or for ill.[140]

In spite of the above-mentioned caveats about original intent, therefore, the enactment of Superfund in 1980 should be classified as a Phase III risk management policy. At root, it increased citizen security against environmental risks at business expense. Although the traditional logic of risk shifting was not particularly relevant to the original legislative goal of cleaning up abandoned sites, the law's authors nonetheless chose a cost-recovery mechanism—strict, joint, and several liability—which was closely associated with risk shifting and thus invited the traditional logic. The promise of preventing environmental hazards by shifting the attendant financial risk onto those responsible was certainly highlighted at the time of enactment, and it ultimately emerged as a central justification (and arguably *the* central justification) for Superfund's severe liability provisions over the next decade.[141] Policy strategy, in other words, ultimately followed policy structure, as risk-based deterrence finally took its place alongside direct (risk-reducing) regulation as one of the twin pillars of American environmental policy.

Conclusion

Both this chapter and the previous one have focused on an especially novel attribute of risk management policy after 1960—namely, the increasing emphasis on the security of the average citizen, rather than just the businessperson or the worker, as in earlier periods. Whether in the form of strict manufacturer liability for product injuries, federal coverage of disaster losses, state insurance guaranties, or statutory liability for polluters, Phase III risk management policies marked a major departure in terms of both specific objectives and larger social priorities.

But the new accent on citizen security was in fact only one of the distinctive features of public risk management in the latter part of the twentieth century. Equally striking was just how extensively the risk management tool was used during this period—often to promote citizen security, but by no means always for this purpose. As Table 9.3 makes clear, new Phase I and Phase II policies were also enacted at this time. In passing the Price-Anderson Act of 1957, for example, Congress sought to promote the development of nuclear energy by capping the potential liability of private nuclear facilities. Just over a decade later, Congress chartered the Federal National Mortgage Association (Fannie Mae), which fostered the development of a vibrant secondary mortgage market by buying, guaranteeing, and bundling residential mortgages for resale. Both programs helped private parties manage investment risk and thus

Table 9.3   Major risk management policies after 1960

Phase I (business security)	Phase II (worker security)	Phase III (citizen security)
Nuclear energy liability caps (Price-Anderson Act of 1957)	Occupational safety and health regulation (esp. OSHA)	Transformation of liability law (esp. strict manufacturer liability in product injury cases)
Guaranties for secondary mortgage market (Fannie Mae and Freddie Mac)	Pension regulation and insurance (ERISA, PBGC)	Consumer safety regulation (e.g., Consumer Product Safety Act of 1972)
Company bailouts (Lockheed, Chrysler)		Federal disaster relief
		State insurance guaranty funds
Country bailouts (Mexico, Korea, etc.)		Environmental regulation and environmental liability (esp. Clean Air Act, Clean Water Act, RCRA, and CERCLA)
		Mandatory federal insurance (esp. Medicare)
		Voluntary federal insurance (esp. flood insurance)
		Credit card liability caps
		Expansion of consumer bankruptcy law

fit neatly into Phase I, although the latter also benefited homeowners by slightly subsidizing mortgage interest rates. The creation of the Pension Benefit Guaranty Corporation (PBGC) in 1974, meanwhile, clearly constituted a Phase II policy since it guaranteed private sector defined-benefit pension plans for American workers. The establishment of the Occupational Safety and Health Administration in 1970 marked yet another major Phase II initiative to advance worker security.[142]

The point is that beginning around 1960, policymakers not only demonstrated unprecedented interest in addressing a wide range of risks facing the average citizen but also revealed a new affinity for risk management policies of all kinds. Financial guaranty programs—ranging from Fannie Mae (Phase I) to the PBGC (Phase II) to the state insurance guaranty funds (Phase III)—proved especially popular with American lawmakers. By the late 1990s, the federal government alone estimated that it had assumed over $6 trillion in contingent liabilities.[143] Whether this love affair with public risk management had begun to sour in the 1990s is a question that lies beyond the scope of this book. For now, though, it is enough to recognize that the love affair existed and that it profoundly influenced both the tenor and the reach of American public policy in the second half of the twentieth century.

The Foundations of American Risk Management Policy

As the historical record makes clear, risk management has never been an entirely private affair in the United States. Lawmakers have frequently intervened, striving to reduce some types of risk outright and to reallocate numerous others. One of the main objectives of the preceding chapters has been to highlight just how pervasive these sorts of interventions have been over the past two hundred years, ranging from the enactment of limited liability laws in the early nineteenth century to the creation of state insurance guaranty funds in the latter part of the twentieth.

At a conceptual level, the central proposition of this book is that risk management constitutes one of the fundamental ways in which government policymakers solve problems. The origins of this idea go back a long way. Writing more than two thousand years ago, Cicero posited that the primary purpose of the state was to *reduce* risk by securing private property rights. "[N]othing is to be maintained in a state with such care as the civil law," he counseled. "In truth, if this is taken away, there is no possibility of any one feeling certain what is his own property or what belongs to another."[1] Eminent political philosophers regularly returned to this interpretation in later years, including Thomas Hobbes in the seventeenth century and John Stuart Mill in the nineteenth. Poorly enforced property rights, Mill wrote, "means uncertainty whether they who sow shall reap, whether they who produce shall consume, and they who spare to-day shall enjoy tomorrow."[2]

In recent times, a growing body of scholarship has looked beyond property rights, exploring how the regulatory apparatus of the state has been used to *reduce* a broad array of risks that threaten personal health and safety. Policymakers can reduce risk directly by prohibiting or otherwise constraining activities that are themselves hazardous, such as driving an automobile over sixty-five miles per hour or handling a deadly toxin on the job. According to Supreme Court Justice Stephen Breyer, "[r]egulators try to make our lives safer by eliminating or reducing our exposure to certain potentially risky substances or even persons (unsafe food additives, dangerous chemicals, unqualified doctors)."[3] Economists and lawyers, including Justice Breyer himself, commonly refer to this sort of policy as "risk regulation."[4]

But the fact is that risk-reduction strategies, whether in the form of regulation or enforceable property rights, are not the government's only means for managing risk. Policymakers have also frequently sought to reallocate risk, either by *shifting* it from one party to another or by *spreading* it across a large number of people. Risk management policy, in other words, encompasses all three of the classic risk management tools: shifting, spreading, and reduction. Remarkably, this simple—yet novel—insight allows us to bring a large number of seemingly disparate public policies, including all of those listed in the table of contents, under a common analytic roof.[5]

Although none of the policymakers discussed in these pages ever went so far as to characterize risk management as a general function of government, most did characterize their own initiatives as necessary responses to risk. Whether it was Governor Levi Lincoln of Massachusetts calling for the protection of passive investors against the "risk of utter ruin" or Justice Roger Traynor of California contemplating how best to protect consumers against "the risk of injury," American lawmakers have long recognized the public significance of private risks.[6] As Chapter 4 on money demonstrates, moreover, legislators were intuitively aware at least since the early antebellum period that shifting, spreading, and reduction policies could serve as alternative ways of addressing a single risk management problem.

The notion of public risk management, in other words, has deep roots in actual problems, debates, and decisions, which is why it yields so readily to historical analysis. Broadly speaking, the findings that emerge from this exercise in historical political economy can be summarized in three basic arguments.

First, the historical record reveals risk management to have been an exceedingly flexible policy tool, used to address a wide range of social problems and to serve a diverse set of social objectives. During the nineteenth century, lawmakers adopted risk management policies such as limited liability and bankruptcy to promote business development and economic growth (Phase I). But as the nineteenth century gave way to the twentieth, new policymakers increasingly targeted risks facing the nation's workers through the enactment of workers' compensation laws and other forms of social insurance (Phase II). Eventually, during the second half of the twentieth century, judges and legislators changed focus yet again, fashioning risk management policies—such as strict manufacturer liability and expansive federal disaster relief—designed to safeguard the consumer and, indeed, the citizen at large (Phase III). Reflecting a profound transformation in public priorities since the founding of the Republic, these three phases testify to the remarkable plasticity—and endurance—of risk management policy as a mode of social problem solving.

Second, the historical record reveals a remarkable degree of economic sophistication in the way leading policymakers thought about risk and about the government's role in managing it. One manifestation of this was that many lawmakers, over both the nineteenth and twentieth centuries, proved deeply suspicious of the market's capacity to solve certain risk-related problems on its own. The idea that markets for risk are far from perfect is familiar to many modern economists. As noted in the introduction, Kenneth Arrow and Robert Lind observed more than thirty years ago that "the inherent difficulty in establishing certain markets for insurance" constitutes "one of the strongest criticisms of a system of freely competitive markets."[7] What the history of risk management policy demonstrates is that public officials were implicitly aware of this problem from a very early time and that they devoted considerable energy to addressing it. It also indicates that they looked well beyond asymmetric information problems such as adverse selection and moral hazard in explaining risk-related failures in the private sector. Systematic risk, risk-based externalities, and (most intriguing of all) prevalent cognitive biases appear to have been of particular concern.

A closely related question concerned the government's own weaknesses as a risk manager. Critics consistently argued that government meddling with private sector risks would make matters worse, severely distorting incentives and inviting personal irresponsibility. They claimed that the availability of a discharge in bankruptcy, for example, would induce debtors to engage in wild speculation. According to the critics, the amount of moral hazard that well-meaning legislators could unleash through the enactment of risk management policies was simply staggering. Proponents countered these arguments by emphasizing the power of risk monitoring. In the case of bankruptcy discharge, a number of congressmen insisted that wild speculation would be unlikely since creditors themselves could be expected to keep a close eye on those to whom they lent money. In advancing such arguments about moral hazard and risk monitoring, lawmakers seem to have intuitively grasped two of the central concepts of modern risk management theory. Although such piercing insights surfaced only occasionally in each of the various debates, the fact that they surfaced at all should be of great interest to students of political economy and policy history alike.

Finally, the historical record helps us understand why public intervention in markets for risk was so prevalent in the United States, despite the country's reputation as a bastion of laissez-faire. American historians have long debated whether the nation's reputed commitment to free-market principles was in fact consistent with its record of government involvement in the economy. The history of public risk management offers a valuable new perspective on this question, suggesting at least one means by which Americans reconciled their philosophical hostility to government (and their faith in the market) with their practical inclination to use the state to address social problems. Apparently willing to suspend their belief in laissez-faire when addressing certain types of risk, many policy advocates took comfort in their ability to cast risk-reallocation policies—from limited liability to social insurance—within the familiar rhetoric of contract and markets. To put it simply, public risk management seems to have constituted a peculiarly attractive form of statism for anti-statists.

The remainder of this chapter elaborates on each of these three arguments: that lawmakers employed risk management policy to achieve a broad range of social objectives, which themselves evolved over time; that these policymakers often proved surprisingly sophisticated in their economic treatment of risk and of the government's role as a risk manager; and that they perceived particular forms of public risk management as being unusually consistent with their anti-statist and free-market principles. Above all, this chapter aims to reinforce the proposition that risk management has long served policymakers in their role as public problem solvers and that it is indeed a critical function of government.

Evolving Social Objectives: The Three Phases of Risk Management Policy

As much as anything else, perhaps, the history of public risk management in the United States conveys a sense of pragmatic policymaking, with many lawmakers appearing to have been genuinely interested in identifying and ultimately solving pressing social problems.[8] One of the most remarkable things about risk management policy is just how flexible it turned out to be, permitting policymakers to address an extraordinary array of needs under enormously varied circumstances.

Today, in the midst of Phase III, it is common for casual observers to view virtually all government involvement with risk as bound up with some sort of liberal social agenda that privileges individual security over economic growth. Accounts in the popular press tend to corroborate this interpretation, with regular reports on massive product injury awards, ballooning federal disaster payments, dysfunctional workplace safety regulations, and the like. But the truth is that risk management as a governmental function is neither liberal nor conservative, since it can be—and indeed has been—employed to serve widely divergent policy objectives.

As we have seen, risk management policy passed through three broad phases over the nation's history. Under Phase I, which lasted until about 1900, lawmakers generally sought to enhance security for business, seeking to promote trade and investment. Risk management policy thus exhibited a clear bias in favor of economic growth. Limited liability, bank regulation and insurance, and bankruptcy law were three of the most important Phase I policies. While limited liability was enacted at the state level to help mobilize equity capital, particularly for manufacturing, bankruptcy law was adopted at the federal level to help rehabilitate precious entrepreneurial talent (human capital) in the aftermath of failure. Banking policy, meanwhile, which was pursued in various forms at both the state and federal levels, aimed to facilitate all types of transactions by cultivating a private money supply that was both plentiful and secure. Other Phase I policies from the nineteenth century included a decidedly pro-business liability regime, which shielded firms against the cost of accidents, as well as a fixed exchange rate, which sharply reduced uncertainty for those engaged in international trade and investment.

Although many of these policies remained in place in the twentieth century, the direction of American risk management policy was already showing signs of change toward the end of the nineteenth. State lawmakers had begun scaling back employer defenses against worker injury suits in the 1880s and 1890s; and they proceeded to enact the nation's first form of social insurance, workers' compensation, in the 1910s. Phase II reached its peak two decades later when Congress inaugurated public old age and unemployment insurance as part of the landmark Social Security Act of 1935. Worker security had now clearly emerged as a dominant social priority. As President Roosevelt himself declared in a message to Congress in 1934, "These three great objectives—the security of the home, the security of livelihood, and the security of social insurance—are, it seems to me, a minimum of the promise that we can offer to the American people. They constitute a right which belongs to every individual and every family willing to work."[9]

The boundaries of public risk management underwent another dramatic expansion beginning in the 1960s, as lawmakers sought to provide greater security for the consumer and for the citizen at large. Although Phase III proved more diffuse than either of its antecedents and encompassed a much wider array of programs, the change in emphasis was still abundantly evident. The transformations of product liability law, consumer safety regulation, environmental protections, and even federal disaster relief all pointed in the same direction. Security against catastrophic loss was fast approximating a new right of citizenship under Phase III.[10]

Like most attempts at historical classification, this one is far from perfect. Meaningful historical developments rarely come in neat chronological packets. Certainly, there are plenty of exceptions to the three-phases framework presented here. Foreign investment insurance, for example, was first enacted in the mid-twentieth century, despite its status as a Phase I policy.[11] Similarly, the Meat Inspection and the Pure Food and Drug acts were both passed in 1906, fully a half-century before the rapid proliferation of other Phase III consumer protection policies in the

Table 10.1 The three phases of risk management policy in the United States

Period	Phase I: Creating a secure environment for business	Phase II: Creating a secure environment for workers	Phase III: Creating a secure environment for all citizens
Prior to 1900	Property rights Common internal currency Deposit insurance (I) Limited liability Bankruptcy law Enterprise liability law Fixed exchange rate		[National defense] [Local poor relief]
1900–1960	Deposit insurance (II)* Crop insurance* Foreign investment insurance	Workplace safety regulation Workers' compensation Old age insurance Unemployment insurance Macroeconomic stabilization policy* Disability insurance	Product safety laws (esp. foods and drugs) Federally insured mortgages (FHA and VA)
Since 1960	Company bailouts Country bailouts (Mexico etc.)	Occupational safety and health regulation Pension regulation and insurance	Dramatic expansion of: Federal disaster relief* Health, safety, and environmental regulation Federal insurance* Other federal financial guaranties* Means-tested "welfare" programs State insurance guaranty funds Product liability law Environmental liability law

1960s and 1970s. As Table 10.1 illustrates, there are numerous other exceptions as well.

Still, this tripartite periodization reveals more than it conceals. Most of the key policy initiatives appear in the shaded diagonal region in Table 10.1; and the exceptions stand out as precisely that—exceptions. In a number of cases, the sequential transformations from one phase to another are apparent not only across policies but actually within specific policy areas. The metamorphosis of enterprise liability law constitutes the most striking example of this phenomenon. Throughout most of the nineteenth century, American liability law exhibited a strong pro-business bias in accidental injury cases. But this bias, so typical of Phase I, was progressively reversed over the twentieth century. State legislators extended special protection to workers with the enactment of workers' compensation laws in the 1910s (Phase II). And the nation's judges subsequently extended protection to consumers as well with the adoption of strict manufacturer liability in the 1960s and 1970s (Phase III).

Providing an excellent illustration of the three phases of risk management policy, the progressive transformation of business liability for accidents also exemplifies both the adaptability of risk management as a policy tool and the close substitutability of alternative risk management strategies. As reformers searched for ways to protect the nation's labor force against workplace hazards in the late nineteenth and early twentieth centuries, proposals to alter the rules of legal liability gradually evolved into plans for compulsory accident insurance (workers' compensation). In fact, an expansive strategy of health and safety regulation was also scaled back during the Progressive period in favor of experience-rated social insurance.[12] As John Andrews of the American Association for Labor Legislation noted in 1918, "Gradually we realized that the best way to protect health in industry was not to attempt to forbid a shifting catalog of specific acts [through regulation], but . . . to bring pressure to bear upon the employers [through compulsory, experience-rated insurance] so as to make them personally keen to keep down sickness."[13]

Similarly, when legal reformers began contemplating new ways of safeguarding consumers some years later, they once again viewed insurance, liability, and regulation as alternative vehicles toward the same objective—each with varying strengths and weaknesses. Although the product safety regime that ultimately emerged came to rest on a combination of strict manufacturer liability (risk shifting) and consumer safety regulation (risk reduction), some of the earliest advocates of strict liability had actually viewed it as a steppingstone to comprehensive social insurance against accidents of all types (risk spreading). "The full blessings of distribution," the legal scholar and reformer Fleming James wrote in 1941, "can best be attained by comprehensive social insurance."[14]

As this extended example demonstrates, policymakers always had a variety of tools at their disposal for managing accident risk. Liability rules facilitated risk shifting (as well as some risk spreading when liability was imposed on large firms). Insurance fostered the broadest possible spreading of risk (as well as a limited amount of risk shifting when premiums were experience rated). And regulation permitted direct risk reduction by constraining hazardous behavior. American policymakers eventually employed all of these tools in service to an evolving set of social objectives: security for business in the nineteenth century, security for workers in the early twentieth, and security for citizen-consumers in the late twentieth. This much is clear.

What is less clear is why social priorities—and thus the risk management policies that served them—evolved in this way. There are a number of possible explanations. Although it is not currently possible to determine whether job-related risks actually increased for the average worker with the coming of the second industrial revolution in the late nineteenth century, this was widely believed to be true at the time. Accident rates were especially high in the railroad and coal mining industries, and the ups and downs of the business cycle were thought to have intensified with the increased pace and scale of modern industry. Social insurance, the centerpiece of Phase II, was thus regarded as a necessary response to the increased vicissitudes of industrial life.

Another common argument in the early twentieth century was that the state needed to play a greater role in protecting workers because traditional family support networks had broken down in the face of rapid urbanization. Whereas the extended family could often do a reasonable job of spreading risk among its members, the smaller size of the nuclear family rendered it far less effective in this capacity. A related argument was that as the scale of industrial enterprises grew ever larger, fewer and fewer workers continued to enjoy personal relationships with their employers, which might once have provided at least a minimal cushion against adversity. The nation's workers had become "but parts of a great impersonal mechanism," lamented William F. Willoughby, a prominent Progressive Era reformer and professor of economics at Princeton.[15] Comparable arguments about the growing distance between consumers and producers were subsequently introduced in the struggle for strict manufacturer liability in the 1960s, though in this case the relevant economic transformation had actually begun many years before.

Yet another possible explanation for the onset of Phases II and III relates to the rapid growth of organized labor around the turn of the century and the rise of a vibrant consumer movement in the 1960s. But this sort of interest-oriented approach turns out to be less persuasive than it first appears. As far as Phase II is concerned, the interpretation is greatly complicated by the fact that the leadership of the American Federation of Labor, including Samuel Gompers himself, opposed every form of social insurance other than workers' compensation until the onset of the Great Depression. And even then, the influence of organized labor does not appear to have been decisive in the enactment of Social Security. The rapid emergence of a consumer movement in the 1960s, moreover, only begs the question of why long-standing consumer risks suddenly arose as such a salient political issue at this particular moment in time.

Perhaps the most compelling explanation from an economic standpoint is that the public's interest in financial and personal security progressively increased with rising affluence. A standard assumption among economists—one of their so-called stylized facts—is that relative risk aversion increases with wealth, which implies that individuals are likely to buy ever more insurance against major losses as they grow richer. If so, then it would stand to reason that an electorate might demand more public insurance as it grew richer. The prodigious expansion of national income and wealth in the United States (and all throughout the industrialized world) may therefore have helped to drive the growing prominence of economic security as a social and political objective. The main problem with this explanation, however, is that it lacks specificity, offering relatively little insight into either the precise timing of the phases or, for that matter, the reason why workers received special protection from the state several decades before consumers.

Fortunately, the underlying historical trends are clear enough, even if the necessary explanatory logic is not. American risk management policy underwent dramatic changes in the twentieth century. Personal security against potentially devastating hazards increasingly rivaled economic growth as a national objective, first with regard to employment and ultimately with regard to just about everything else. The implications of this progressive shift in social priorities were simply breathtaking—transforming the government's role in the economy, the cost structure of virtually every firm, and even the economic function of the family unit itself. The three phases of risk management policy thus reflected profound changes in the very nature and workings of American society, while at the same time revealing the enormous flexibility of risk management as a policy tool.

Economic Rationale: The Conceptual Foundations of Public Risk Management

From an economic standpoint, the most striking impression one derives from reviewing the legislative history of American risk management policy is that proponents tended to view risk-related market imperfections as relatively obvious facts of life. The idea that private markets could always be trusted to shift risks to those best able to manage them carried remarkably little weight.[16] Although these private failures were often just taken for granted, policymakers occasionally tried to specify where they came from—sometimes in ways that were broadly consistent with the formal economic concept of market failure but even more often in ways that were not. In any case, their attempts at specification reflect a surprising degree of economic sophistication. They also offer precious insight into the true economic foundations of American risk management policy.

Explaining Risk-Related Failures in the Private Sector

Admittedly, the subject of risk-related failures in the private sector can prove puzzling, since risk management is simultaneously one of the greatest strengths and one of the greatest weaknesses of our free-market system. Modern financial markets exhibit unparalleled efficiency and present a multitude of opportunities for productive transfers of risk. The commodity markets, for instance, make hedging against sudden fluctuations in the price of oil almost as easy as buying a barrel. But despite a plethora of such markets, there are still countless others that are either incomplete or missing altogether. Though we can hedge the price of oil, we cannot hedge the price of labor or (without government help) the overall price level.[17] In earlier times, of course, such deficiencies were even more prevalent than they are now.

As we saw in Chapter 2, the main sources of risk-related failure can be divided into four categories: information problems, perception problems, commitment problems, and externalization problems. American policymakers rarely employed these exact terms. But over the course of the nation's history, they appealed—or at least alluded—to all of these problems in justifying government intervention.

INFORMATION PROBLEMS

Within academic circles, an especially popular explanation why markets for risk sometimes fall short has to do with information deficiencies. Vital information may be distributed asymmetrically among parties to a transaction, available to one side but not the other. Or critical information may be prohibitively expensive for anyone to obtain or simply unavailable at any price. Either individually or in combination, these sorts of information deficiencies have the potential to infect and debilitate otherwise healthy markets for risk.

Economists have paid particular attention to the problem of asymmetric information—so much, in fact, that it is sometimes cast as virtually the only relevant obstacle to successful risk management in the private sector. Although we have to be careful not to exaggerate the significance of asymmetric information problems for policymaking, the fascination with these problems within the economics profession is certainly understandable. After all, they are potentially applicable in a wide range of contexts and are amenable to exquisite mathematical modeling.

The two most conspicuous asymmetric information problems, adverse selection and moral hazard, threaten to weaken or even destroy insurance markets whenever those who are obtaining insurance know more about the risks in question than those doing the insuring. Adverse selection becomes an issue when individuals know in advance of buying insurance that they are more or less likely than average to collect benefits. High-risk individuals will tend to buy a lot of insurance (at the average premium) and low-risk individuals much less, thus skewing the insurance pool. Moral hazard comes into play once insurance has already been purchased. Knowing they are insured, individuals tend to act less responsibly, which increases the likelihood of loss.

As economics textbooks are quick to point out, adverse selection and moral hazard constitute critical sources of market failure. To the extent that vital information about risk and risk taking remains opaque to insurers, private insurance markets will suffer and are even liable to disappear altogether. Given this, it may come as some surprise that, in practice, adverse selection and moral hazard have only rarely emerged as significant justifications for government intervention.

To be sure, moral hazard has frequently been cited by critics as a reason *not* to enact risk management policies. But its use as an affirmative rationale for intervention remains far more limited. In the early twentieth century, supporters of public unemployment insurance argued that one of the reasons private insurers refused to cover joblessness was that insured workers could easily fake or engineer their own unemployment in order to collect benefits.[18] Government officials were presumably in a better position to prevent this sort of immoral behavior by requiring beneficiaries to search for jobs through publicly run employment agencies. Outside of the debate over unemployment insurance, however, references to moral hazard have come almost entirely from opponents—rather than proponents—of public risk management.

Direct references to adverse selection, meanwhile, have rarely been articulated by either side, though the idea may have played an implicit role in a number of debates. During the discussions of federal old age insurance in the 1930s, opponents of the so-called Clark Amendment (which would have allowed firms with sufficiently generous pension plans to opt out of Social Security) claimed that such a provision would siphon off all the good risks, leaving the public program to contend with all the bad ones.[19] Key advocates of federal old age insurance might also have had an adverse selection argument in mind when they dismissed private insurance annuities as outrageously expensive and thus of little practical use.[20] But these remained rare exceptions. The truth is that champions of public risk management hardly ever relied on adverse selection and moral hazard arguments, even though both concepts had been well understood at least since the mid-nineteenth century.

Other sorts of information problems were cited with somewhat greater frequency. For example, concerns about the near impossibility of small depositors' collecting reliable credit risk information on their banks arose during debates over federal deposit insurance in 1933.[21] Similarly, concerns about the difficulties consumers faced in determining product risk information played a significant role in the advent of strict manufacturer liability in product injury law several decades later.[22] In both cases it was the potential victim, rather than the potential insurer, who was thought to suffer from inadequate or inferior information—precisely the opposite of the standard asymmetric information problem highlighted in the economics literature. There is also some evidence to suggest that the issue of Knightian uncertainty (unquantifiable risk) may have factored into discussions of federal disaster policy in the 1990s.[23] Significantly, though, these sorts of information problems— where potential victims faced prohibitive costs in obtaining accurate information about risk or where reliable historical data were simply unavailable at any price—were often treated by policy advocates as close cousins to problems of risk perception.

PERCEPTION PROBLEMS

Over the years, behavioral psychologists and economists have documented a large number of systematic biases that adversely affect the way most of us perceive and interpret risk. These range from misapplications of simple heuristics, such as anchoring and framing, to more complex behavioral patterns, such as optimistic bias and illusions of control. Some of these biases even have links to the phenomenon of Knightian uncertainty. Because all of these so-called perception problems were discussed in Chapter 2, there is no need to review them in any detail here.[24] It is worth emphasizing, however, that a variety of perception problems—and particularly optimistic bias—frequently factored into the debates over key risk management policies.

To begin with, bankruptcy discharge was implicitly justified in the nineteenth century on the grounds that gifted entrepreneurs typically overestimated their odds of success and thus devoted too little effort to protecting their own human capital. Only by forcing them to buy what amounted to mandatory insurance against default (in the form of a discharge in bankruptcy) could the survival of their socially precious human capital be assured in the aftermath of failure.[25] Similarly, some of the key proponents of workers' compensation laws in the early twentieth century claimed that workers failed to negotiate compensating wage differentials for hazardous work because they were overly optimistic about their own chances of escaping injury. As Henry Seager put it, each worker "thinks of himself as having a charmed life."[26]

As for old age insurance, supporters insisted during the 1930s that many workers were simply too myopic to save adequately for their own retirement and that those who did save often vastly overestimated their future returns. A generation later, some of the leading advocates of strict manufacturer liability in product injury cases resurrected Seager's "charmed life" hypothesis, suggesting that consumers were perhaps unable to manage product risks themselves because they underestimated their odds of getting hurt. "Such things always happen to 'the other guy,'" wrote Guido Calabresi in his seminal work on accident law, "and no amount of statistical information can convince an individual that they could happen to him."[27] Even in the realm of federal disaster policy, perception problems seem to have played a role, since widespread underinsurance against catastrophes was sometimes blamed on a common human tendency to round extremely small probabilities to zero.[28] Lawmakers may also have been attempting to exploit another perception problem—what I have termed the lottery impulse—in the enactment of limited liability laws during the nineteenth century, though the available evidence on this point is far from conclusive.[29]

Not surprisingly, there has been some debate within the academic community about the actual extent of these sorts of perception problems and whether they truly justify government intervention.[30] Several prominent scholars of liability law have even concluded, for example, that consumers *over*estimate (rather than underestimate) product risks and that strict liability is therefore counterproductive.[31] Our primary concern here, however, is that perception problems have frequently been cited—whether rightly or wrongly—as important justifications for government intervention in private markets for risk. On this point the historical record is clear. Although these biases do not constitute market failures in the strict sense of the term, they have nonetheless been advanced as powerful arguments for government paternalism.[32]

COMMITMENT PROBLEMS

Yet another potential source of risk-related failure in the private sector stems from commitment problems, of which there are two basic types. On the one hand, private risk management may become unstable or break down altogether when no private party can credibly commit to cover a particular risk—in most cases because the risk is systematic. To take an extreme example, no private insurance company could ever credibly promise to cover either life or property losses stemming from a nuclear war. Any insurer that did write such coverage would, in all likelihood, be doing little more than defrauding its customers. On the other hand, private risk management may also break down when government officials prove unable to commit *not* to intervene in the event of a particular hazard. No rational farmer would ever purchase flood insurance if intense public pressure always forced federal lawmakers to bail out uninsured farmers in the aftermath of floods.[33]

Commitment problems of both varieties have helped to motivate the enactment of numerous risk management policies. As we have seen, private financial institutions face potential commitment problems whenever there exists a threat of systematic (highly correlated) losses. This helps to explain the government's role in backing bank money, whether in the form of nineteenth-century bank notes or modern-day demandable deposits (checking accounts). Clearly, no bank is capable of surviving a massive run on its cash reserves without insurance, and no private insurer of bank deposits would ever be capable of surviving a simultaneous run on all banks—a banking panic—without state support. This is why public backing has long been regarded as necessary to ensure the credibility of the "private" money supply. Although concerns about contagion risk and credible commitment often remained implicit during antebellum debates over banking policy, they ultimately surfaced in far more explicit form during the campaign to enact federal deposit insurance in 1933.[34]

The dual problem of systematic risk and credible commitment also proved salient in a number of other prominent policy debates. Early twentieth-century social reformers frequently attributed the near absence of private unemployment insurance to this problem. Given a sufficiently severe economic downturn, any company writing such insurance could easily find itself overwhelmed with claims. Depression-era reformers and policymakers sounded similar warnings about the vulnerabilities of private pension plans, many of which collapsed amidst the unprecedented financial turmoil of the 1930s. And concerns about systematic risk and credible commitment surfaced again in discussions of federal disaster policy and state insurance guaranty funds in the final third of the twentieth century. The recognition that sufficiently large systematic losses—arising, for example, from massive natural catastrophes—could wipe out even some of the largest and best-managed insurance companies ended up reinforcing demands for a significant government role.

Naturally, the state could not be expected to intervene every time private financial commitments were determined to be less than perfectly secure, since this standard would require public involvement in virtually every financial transaction. But when the potential losses were likely to be financially devastating for large numbers of people (as with natural disasters and insurance company failures) or threatened to disrupt the economic system itself (as with bank failures), policymakers often felt obliged to provide government guaranties. This obligation was felt with particular intensity where the victims were thought to be exceptionally vulnerable. As the leading advocates of federal old age insurance repeatedly insisted, public coverage of retirement risk was essential because the elderly victims of failed private pension funds (unlike most other victims of financial collapses) typically had no means of escape, having already depleted their lifetime earning power—their human capital.

Ironically, it was precisely this sense of public obligation that tended to trigger the other major commitment problem, the government's inability to say no. This issue of non-credible government commitment has been particularly evident in assessments of federal disaster policy. As Representative Fred Grandy of Iowa observed in 1993, "We're basically telling people, 'We want you to buy insurance, but if you don't, we'll bail you out anyway.'"[35] The same basic problem, though perhaps in less extreme form, also lingered in the background of discussions involving numerous other risk management policies, from old age insurance to deposit insurance. Knowing that they would likely be forced to bail out victims of financial crises in any case, lawmakers sometimes concluded that they might as well establish permanent insurance programs, which would at least generate "premiums" (in the form of earmarked tax revenues) in the meantime.

Once major programs like Social Security and federal deposit insurance were enacted, moreover, commitment problems loomed even larger for anyone interested in scaling them back. One of the strongest critiques of recent proposals to invest a portion of Social Security funds in the stock market is that federal lawmakers might feel compelled to bail out participants in the event of a major market downturn.[36] If true, the federal government's commitment problem—that is, its inability to commit *not* to provide such a bailout in the future—would leave policy-makers with little choice but to maintain the current Social Security program, at least until public expectations themselves could be thoroughly reformed.

EXTERNALIZATION (AND FEEDBACK) PROBLEMS

A fourth problem plaguing private markets for risk—and the final one to be considered here—comes under the heading of externalization. As noted in Chapter 2, an externality is a generic source of market failure, not one that is limited exclusively or even mainly to risk-related scenarios. The classic example is pollution. In the absence of government oversight, polluters are able to impose (i.e., externalize) costs on others without having to bear the consequences. One potential solution is for the government to levy a tax on every unit of pollution, effectively "internalizing" the externality.[37]

Within the realm of risk management policy, externalities (or at least close approximations) have factored into the debate in a number of different contexts. During the first two decades of the twentieth century, social reformers claimed that employers did little to prevent ghastly industrial hazards because they were effectively shielded from the financial consequences. The best solution, the reformers believed, was experience-rated social insurance, which would force employers to internalize the risks of on-the-job accidents, occupational disease, and even unemployment. According to this logic, well-designed social insurance programs would not only ease the financial burden that befell the victims, but also actually help to prevent the hazards themselves by appropriately aligning employer incentives. John Commons once described workers' compensation "as a kind of social pressure brought to bear upon all employers in order to make them devote as much attention to the prevention of accidents and to the speedy recovery from accidents as they do to the manufacture and sale of the products."[38]

The analogy to environmental policy was obvious, even at the time. Commons himself frequently characterized social insurance as a "tax" on industrial hazards and as a means of promoting "conservation of the nation's human resources."[39] Yet workplace hazards differ from environmental hazards in one very important respect. Whereas the victims of environmental hazards are typically independent third parties, the victims of workplace hazards are employees who have entered into contractual relationships with their employers. Strictly speaking, therefore, workplace hazards are not externalities because workers have the opportunity to exact a price for these risks as part of the wage bargain. But Progressive Era reformers maintained that this was far too strict a reading of the problem. They dismissed the fabled employment contract (in which workers were said to have voluntarily assumed responsibility for all job-related risks) as a mere abstraction, a "legal fiction" with "no basis in fact." In their view, precious few industrial laborers were able to exact sufficient wage premiums for hazardous work.[40] Indeed, this was precisely the context in which Henry Seager emphasized that workers were severely handicapped by their own excessive optimism—by their faith in a "charmed life."

Seager's reasoning suggested that perception problems such as optimistic bias have the potential to facilitate risk externalization, even within formal contractual relationships. Since the recipients of the risk (in this case, workers) remain largely oblivious to the costs being imposed on them, these costs are effectively externalized (by their employers). Significantly, the very same line of reasoning was employed again in the second half of the twentieth century to justify strict manufacturer liability in product injury suits. Even though consumers theoretically could demand lower prices for unusually hazardous products, some legal reformers claimed that they generally failed to do so, given their propensity to underestimate product injury risks. According to these reformers, strict liability promised to internalize the resulting externality by shifting uncompensated risk back onto the manufacturers who originally generated it and profited by it.

The logic of externalization was occasionally taken in even more novel directions. During debates over deposit insurance and unemployment insurance in the 1930s, a number of policymakers claimed that under very special circumstances, risk spreading could actually reduce aggregate risk by tempering a particularly vicious externality. (This was an extraordinary claim since, as we have seen, risk spreading is generally thought either to exert no effect on aggregate risk or, more likely, to increase it as a result of moral hazard. It has been said, for instance, that automobile insurance is likely to increase accident rates, since insured motorists tend to be a bit less careful behind the wheel.) Reformers nonetheless argued that individual anxiety about potential bank failures or unemployment could itself provoke behavior that might increase the overall level of risk. Nervous depositors might try to withdraw their funds, which would increase the odds of bank failure; and nervous workers might decide to reduce their consumption, which could exacerbate unemployment by depressing overall demand for goods and services.

In each case, public insurance promised to weaken or even eliminate this insidious feedback loop, reducing aggregate risk by reducing individual insecurity. As the economist and lawmaker Paul Douglas explained with regard to unemployment insurance: "The provision of self-respecting unemployment benefits would diminish the fears which the employed workers would entertain towards the prospect of unemployment and hence would lessen their frantic personal savings at such times. . . . There would be a better balance between spending and saving and less unemployment would be created."[41] Though unusually abstract for a political argument, Douglas's careful reasoning about externalized risk and the power of a public solution ultimately achieved some currency in the depths of the Great Depression.

Balancing Public Strengths and Weaknesses: The Critical Issue of Monitoring

What should now be clear is that the appeal of public risk management is at least partly attributable to enduring doubts about the efficacy of *private* risk management. While many policy advocates simply took risk-related market weaknesses for granted, some actually tried to specify how and why the market mechanism went awry. As we have seen, they paid particular attention to perception problems as well as commitment, externalization, and information problems.

Naturally, though, it was not enough simply to identify deficiencies in the market. Proponents must also have believed that government could succeed where the private market had failed. The state clearly enjoyed certain advantages as a risk manager. Foremost among these were its powers of compulsion, including its power to tax and to impose legal liability.[42] At the same time, however, lawmakers had long recognized that risk-reallocation policies tended to distort incentives, often tempting beneficiaries to act irresponsibly. In critiquing proposals for new risk management programs, opponents almost always devoted disproportional attention to the dangers of moral hazard, warning that public involvement with private risks would create dreadful inducements for lax or even fraudulent behavior.

Many of the policymakers who authored major risk management policies actually shared this concern, though in less extreme form. It was for this reason that they often attempted to identify effective risk monitors, who could be expected to remain vigilant about spotting and disciplining moral hazard. The issue of monitoring ultimately factored into almost every debate over a risk management policy in one way or another, and occasionally even emerged as a central issue, as in the case of public deposit insurance. Drawing a comparison between public risk management and conventional insurance, Table 10.2 specifies the implicit risk monitors in most of the major policy initiatives examined over the preceding chapters. Sometimes the government itself has filled this role, but not always.

Consider the case of limited liability, for example. Limited liability shifts a portion of corporate default risk from shareholders to creditors. When the nation's first limited liability laws were being debated in the early nineteenth century, critics warned of a deluge of reckless investment once shareholders realized they had everything to gain and little to lose from undertaking high-stakes gambles with their creditors' money. But some of the most insightful proponents of limited liability disagreed, insisting that creditors were well positioned—and perhaps ideally positioned—to monitor corporate activities. In retrospect, it appears that these proponents were largely correct. Limited liability corporations have not, as a general rule, degenerated into reckless risk takers. Most students of the subject agree that this is because creditors have typically functioned as competent risk monitors, establishing guidelines for appropriate levels of corporate risk taking and closely tracking performance.

A far more controversial case involves product liability law. The early advocates of strict manufacturer liability claimed that producers were not only better suited than consumers to bear (or spread) the cost of accidents, but also better positioned to monitor the underlying risk. After all, manufacturers are perfectly situated to investigate design flaws and defect rates in their own production processes. Yet, as so many critics have pointed out, manufacturers are often incapable of monitoring how consumers actually use their products. It is precisely this tension that has generated much of the public debate over product liability law, stemming from difficult cases like the McDonald's hot coffee dispute. Was the coffee "defective" because it was too hot, or did the woman who spilled it on herself exercise inadequate care? The answer to this question has significant implications for determining who is the optimal risk monitor and thus where liability should ultimately fall.

As for the government itself, its record as a risk monitor is mixed. As we have seen, the introduction of public deposit insurance (first in New York State in 1829 and ultimately at the federal level in 1933) necessitated the creation of a regulatory apparatus that could effectively monitor the riskiness of insured banks. While the federal government has generally earned high marks for the quality of its bank supervision, there have been some notable lapses. The central cause of the savings and loan fiasco, it appears, was that lawmakers had negligently deregulated the industry in the early 1980s, forgetting that insured institutions would inevitably act recklessly if effective monitoring (by federal regulators) was sufficiently suppressed.[43] Similarly, in the case of federal disaster policy, it appears that lawmakers have gradually been creating a significant moral hazard problem by covering losses ex post without adequately monitoring risky behavior ex ante.

Perhaps the most intriguing case of all involves federal old age insurance, enacted as part of Social Security in 1935. At the time, lawmakers sought to manage a wide range of risks associated with retirement, from longevity risk to market risk. Luckily for them, moral hazard was not a problem across the board. In the case of longevity risk, for example, Social Security's monthly annuity payments created a strong incentive for recipients to try to live longer. But this posed little cause for concern since it seemed unimaginable that individual retirees could *intentionally* extend their life spans, regardless of how financially advantageous it was to do so. A more practical concern was that the existence of Social Security might affect workers' savings habits, leading them to take greater risks with their savings or simply to save less overall. But since the size of a worker's annuity payment was not tied to his wealth (or level of need) at retirement, there was in fact little reward for risky savings behavior. So, once again, the moral hazard involved was relatively slight.

Work-duration risk was an altogether different matter, however. In an ideal world, the lawmakers who crafted Social Security would have liked to insure workers against premature depletion of their human capital (that is, involuntary early retirement). The problem, of course, is that it

Table 10.2   Risk management policy as implicit insurance: the pivotal role of the risk monitor

	Private fire insurance (for comparison only)	Limited liability law	Bank note and deposit insurance	Bankruptcy discharge	Workers' compensation
Covered risk	Fire damage to a structure	Corporate default	Bank failure	Personal default	Workplace accidents
Shift	Property owners ↓ Insurance company	Shareholders ↓ Creditors (voluntary and involuntary)	Bank creditors (note holders, depositors) ↓ Govt. fund	Debtors (entrepreneurs) ↓ Creditors (voluntary and involuntary)	Workers ↓ Employer (and often th onto insurer
Premium	Standard insurance premium	Implicit risk premium embedded in interest rate on corporate loans	Explicit premium banks must pay to govt. fund	Implicit risk premium embedded in interest rate on loans	Reduced compensating way differentials; increased price final goods
Moral hazard	Less precautionary behavior or vigilance on part of insured property holders	Increased shareholder appetite for risky corporate investment	Decreased monitoring by insured creditors and increased risk taking by bank shareholders	Increased debtor appetite for risky investments	Increased carelessness in the workplace; fraudulent reporting job-related accidents
Risk monitor	Insurance company (requirements regarding smoke alarms, distance from fire hydrants, etc.)	Voluntary creditor (through contractual covenants, etc.)	Government (regulatory arm of bank insurance fund)	Voluntary creditor (through contractual covenants, etc.)	Employer (installs safety equipment, requires safety routines, etc.)
Social objectives	Encourage home ownership and increase owners' sense of security by reducing burden on individual fire victims	Encourage equity investment in corporate enterprises by reducing financial threat to individual investor	Increase security of money supply and bolster public willingness to use banks by reducing riskiness of deposits, etc.	Provide "fresh start" and source of relief for failed debtors; conserve human capital by reducing ex post burden on entrepreneurs	Increase work security and reduce poverty among working families by spreading risk workplace accidents and creating incentives prevention

mployment rance	Old age insurance	Strict manufacturer liability	Federal disaster policy	State insurance guaranty funds	Environmental liability law (e.g., Superfund)
oluntary unem-yment	Inadequate income in old age	Product-related injuries	Disaster-related losses	Insurance company failures (unpaid claims)	Environmental risks to health and property
Workers ↓ te unemployment nsurance funds	Workers ↓ Federal govt. trust funds	Consumers ↓ Producers (and often onto insurers)	Citizens / homeowners ↓ Federal government	Citizens who carry insurance ↓ State insurance guaranty funds	Citizens ↓ Industry
licit govt. pre-m (tax) on em-yers; reduced ge differentials for ual work; etc.	Explicit govt. premium (tax) on employers and employees	Implicit risk premium embedded in price of product	Implicit premium embedded in federal taxes	Explicit post-assessment premium on surviving insurance companies	Implicit premiums embedded in price of products
reased worker lingness to forgo ployment; fraud-nt unemployment ms	Increased worker willingness to retire earlier than necessary and reduced willingness to save for retirement	Increased consumer carelessness in use of products; fraudulent reporting of accidents	Increased citizen willingness to live in hazardous areas, under-insure, etc.	Decreased monitoring by insurance company clients and increased risk taking by insurers	Decreased monitoring of potential environmental hazards by citizens; fraudulent claims
vernment (work-rch requirements,)	Government (?)	Manufacturer (well positioned to detect defects in design and production, but not consumer misuse of products)	Government (in theory, could prohibit construction in hazardous areas, etc.)	Government (regulation of insurance industry, capital requirements, etc.)	Industry (careful monitoring and tracking of all hazardous substances, etc.)
rease worker se-ity and reduce erty by spreading mployment risk, ating incentives prevention, and intaining pur-sing power	Increase worker security and reduce poverty among elderly by spreading retirement risks (longevity risk, investment risk, etc.)	Increase manufacturer incentives to produce safe products; spread burden of injuries that cannot be prevented	Increase citizen security by spreading catastrophic risk in the broadest possible fashion	Increase citizen security by broadly spreading the burden of insurance company failures	Increase industry incentives not to contaminate the environment; spread burden of environmental damage that cannot be prevented

was virtually impossible to verify whether a laborer who claimed he could no longer work had truly depleted his human capital or was merely faking it. Facing a major moral hazard problem and no meaningful way to monitor it, New Deal lawmakers recognized they had little choice but to adopt a rigid retirement age (sixty-five), thus abandoning their desire to insure work-duration risk.[44]

The lesson to be taken from this last example is that even the staunchest proponents of public risk management did not view government intervention as a perfect solution to every risk management problem. Economic realism worked in both directions. As we have seen, policymakers were often surprisingly quick to highlight risk-related deficiencies in the private sector, including information, perception, commitment, and externalization problems. In so doing, they raised serious questions about the social desirability of market allocations of risk, and they spotlighted the promise of public policy responses, particularly given the government's inherent strengths as a risk manager. Yet many of the most thoughtful policymakers also recognized how vital it was to identify and harness effective risk monitors so as to control the moral hazard that risk management policy was prone to create.

Even in the realm of public risk management, in other words, there was considerable uncertainty about how government interventions would turn out. Basic economic reasoning helped expose potential opportunities and pitfalls. But, in the end, the question of whether and how to intervene depended on much more than economic logic alone. As should become clear in the next section, prevailing ideas about the role of government were also of profound importance in shaping policy outcomes.

The Unusual Appeal of Public Risk Management: Statism for Anti-Statists?

Historians and social scientists have long debated the supposed distinctiveness of American political culture. The provocative notion of "American exceptionalism" was first inspired by Alexis de Tocqueville's observation that the "position of the Americans is . . . quite exceptional" and later reinforced by Werner Sombart's famous question, "Why is there no socialism in the United States?"[45] Although the debate continues even now, allusions to American distinctiveness remain pervasive in both scholarly and popular treatments of American institutions, and nowhere is this more true than in explorations of America's political economy.[46] Writes Seymour Martin Lipset, "America began and continues as the most anti-statist, legalistic, and rights-oriented nation."[47]

There can be little doubt that Americans have traditionally harbored deep anti-statist sentiments. Writing in the late nineteenth century, that keen British observer of America, James Bryce, estimated "that nine men out of ten would tell a stranger that both the Federal and the State governments interfered little, and would ascribe the prosperity of the country to this non-interference as well as to the self-reliant spirit of the people. So far as there can be said to be any theory on the subject in a land which gets on without theories, *laissez aller* has been the orthodox and accepted doctrine in the sphere both of Federal and State legislation."[48]

Even now, most public opinion polls confirm the notion that American citizens are considerably less comfortable with government than their counterparts in other developed countries. A cross-national survey conducted in 1996 found that Americans were dramatically more likely to think that government had "too much power" and dramatically less likely to think that it is "the responsibility of the government to reduce . . . differences in income."[49] (See Table 10.3.)

An American Paradox

Although relatively few historians have tried to refute the notion that anti-statist sentiments run deep in the United States, many have questioned the extent to which such sentiments actually constrained public policy. Bryce himself suggested that the nation's ostensible commitment to laissez-faire meant little in practice. "The new democracies of America are just as eager for state interference as the democracy of Britain," he insisted, "and try their experiments with even more light-hearted promptitude."[50] Similarly, the professional journalist and political economist Albert Shaw wrote in the late nineteenth century of the "average" American's "unequaled capacity for the entertainment of legal fictions and kindred delusions."[51]

In fact, a long line of policy historians has struggled to debunk the myth of laissez-faire, documenting the broad use of state power in the United States through both the nineteenth and twentieth centuries.[52] Writing in 1943, Oscar Handlin characterized the belief that there was a

Table 10.3   Attitudes about the role of government in five industrialized countries, 1996

Issue	United States	France	Germany	Japan	Sweden
Does the government have too much or too little power? Percent saying:					
Too much	66	44	34	21	27
About right	30	41	41	13	52
Too little	4	16	11	47	21
Is it the responsibility of the government to reduce differences in income? Percent saying:					
Yes	33	71	53	44	59
"Mixed feelings"	24	13	17	23	20
No	43	16	21	26	21

Source: 1996 International Social Survey Project (ISSP), as cited in *Public Perspective,* 9, no. 2 (February/March 1998), 32.

"continuous laissez-faire bent to policy in the United States" as a "common misconception of American economic thought, as of American economy."[53] More recently, the historian William Novak has joined the fray, leading one of the broadest assaults so far. "In its weak version," he acknowledges, "there is a grain of tired truth in the stateless thesis. But in its more common, strong rendition, implying a substantive absence of power or activity on the part of public officials [in the nineteenth century], the myth of American statelessness is *groundless.*"[54]

Strangely, though, no matter how carefully they have orchestrated their attacks, nor how fiercely they have executed them, these historians have never quite managed to finish the job. The "myth" of a minimalist American state has survived, particularly with respect to the pre–New Deal era. Part of the reason may be that the notion comports so well with how Americans view themselves and want to remember their past. As Albert Shaw observed, an emotional commitment to laissez-faire and to a small state flourished in America because it seemed "to harmonize with the self-relying, independent character of the American citizen-sovereign, whose personal freedom and self-directed activities are his dearest boast."[55] Perhaps also, however, the myth survived because there is at least some truth to it. In the United States, as the historian Morton Keller has put it, "traditional American values—hostility to the active, centralized state, deep commitments to social individualism and economic competition—had a continuing influence on twentieth century regulatory policy."[56] Whatever the case, there can be no question that the tension between anti-statist sentiments on the one hand and the reality of persistent state action on the other remains one of the central paradoxes of American political economy.

The history of public risk management offers a valuable new perspective on this paradox. To be sure, it reinforces the findings of historical revisionists like Handlin and Novak by documenting a surprisingly vigorous use of government power in the United States well before the New Deal. Already in the early nineteenth century, policymakers were actively managing a wide range of private sector risks—in banking, insurance, manufacturing, and beyond. Even in accident law, the nation's judges often acted as aggressive risk managers, consciously tipping the legal balance to serve objectives that they believed to be in the public interest. In defining the assumption-of-risk doctrine, for example, which made it so difficult for injured workers to collect damages from their employers, Justice Lemuel Shaw acknowledged in 1842 that the rule stemmed "from considerations as well of justice as of policy."[57]

More intriguing still, the history of public risk management suggests several ways in which Americans seemed to reconcile their laissez-faire and anti-statist sentiments with their pragmatic inclination to employ state power to solve social problems. For one thing, Americans have long demonstrated a remarkable willingness to suspend their free-market principles in the face of major risk-related problems, as if certain risks simply fell outside the bounds of laissez-faire philosophy. It is surely no coincidence that two of the earliest industries to be regulated in this country, insurance and banking, both revolved fundamentally around risk. Confirming the quasi-public nature of these industries, the U.S. Supreme Court declared in a 1951 decision that in both insurance and banking "the power of the state is broad enough to take over the whole business, leaving no part for private enterprise."[58] It is hard to imagine such a statement being applied to many other, non–risk-based industries: perhaps public utilities and a few well-known public goods such as education and road building, but not much beyond that.

As recently as the summer of 2000, the discovery that certain Firestone tires were far riskier than previously thought—potentially the cause of dozens or even hundreds of fatal accidents—led to a profusion of demands for new regulations and new liability designed to limit this sort of risk in the future. What was most remarkable about these demands is that they came not just from the most liberal members of Congress but also from many of its most conservative members, who were well known for championing smaller government and deference to the market. Republican senator Arlen Specter introduced a bill designed to criminalize the manufacture and sale of products that were "dangerous to human life and limb beyond the reasonable and accepted risk with such or similar products lacking such a flaw."[59] In cases like these, traditional anti-statist sentiments seemed not to apply.

Equally important, the historical record suggests that risk-reallocation policies (though not risk-reduction policies) may have proved particularly appealing in the United States because they tended to require little in the way of invasive bureaucracy and could easily be cast in the rhetoric of contract. Risk-shifting policies such as limited liability and bankruptcy law, for example, required no bureaucracy whatsoever other than the courts themselves. The same can be said of product liability law. Even social insurance programs, which currently absorb about 10 percent of U.S. GDP, were originally sold to the public as close analogues to private insurance that conformed to market principles and were deeply rooted in the logic of contract.

As we have seen, New Dealers—like their predecessors in the Progressive period—went to great lengths to emphasize the analogy to private insurance in promoting Social Security, working on the assumption that it would make the plan "acceptable to a society which was dominated by business ethics and which stressed individual economic responsibility."[60] Indeed, program administrators highlighted the insurance analogy at every opportunity, aggressively downplaying notions of redistribution. A 1940 pamphlet put out by the Social Security Board reassured workers that "[y]our Social Security Card . . . shows that you have an insurance account with the U.S. Government–Federal old-age and survivors insurance." Social Security was a "national insurance plan," the pamphlet explained, and "taxes are like the premium on any other kind of insurance."[61] Three years earlier, another pamphlet had emphasized that unemployment compensation was "like other types of insurance," that it was "not charity or relief but a means of preventing need for relief."[62]

The contractual nature of social insurance—or at least the illusion of contract—was obviously of great importance. And though social insurance required more bureaucratic infrastructure than risk-shifting policies like limited liability, it still proved remarkably lean from an administrative standpoint. Under Social Security, the ratio of administrative costs to total expenditures was just 6 percent in 1950, and it had fallen to an astoundingly small 0.5 percent by 1999.[63]

It is even conceivable that one of the main reasons why compulsory health insurance was never adopted in the United States was the expectation that, unlike other forms of social insurance, public health insurance would require deep public involvement in the provision of health care services.[64] In the 1910s, many doctors feared that with the adoption of compulsory health insurance, the physician would "professionally cease to be an individualist and will be but a cog in a great medical machine."[65] During subsequent campaigns, particularly in the 1940s and 1990s, opponents of universal health insurance commonly charged that it would amount to a "government takeover" of the whole industry.[66] Although this obviously remains an open question, there is plenty of evidence to suggest that Americans harbor a distinctive aversion to the idea of public ownership or control of health care. When asked in 1996 whether hospitals "should mainly be run by private organizations or companies, or by government," only 26 percent of Americans said government, as compared to 71 percent in France, 63 percent in Germany, 35 percent in Japan, and 94 percent in Sweden.[67]

A Distinctively American Approach?

Whether American "exceptionalism" ultimately produced a distinctive "American approach" to public risk management is, unfortunately, impossible to say with much confidence at this point. Certainly, every government in the world has utilized a wide range of risk management policies, and most of the industrialized nations have witnessed policy shifts roughly analogous to our three phases. Yet the United States does seem to stand out as at least a bit different in a number of respects. Elsewhere around the world, more activist states have often chosen to integrate risk management tools into broader and more aggressive policy undertakings, including programs of industrial targeting and far-reaching income redistribution, while such undertakings have remained relatively rare in the United States.

During the early nineteenth century, American policymakers at both the state and federal levels experimented with a wide range of industrial policy interventions, from protective tariffs to direct public financing of preferred investment projects. But while federal tariff and land policies remained remarkably aggressive throughout the century, state lawmakers increasingly relied on the limited liability corporation—rather than the public purse—to finance highly risky industrial investments. Exemplifying this transition, New York lawmakers drafted a new state constitution in 1846 that simultaneously authorized the enactment of a limited liability general incorporation statute, sharply constrained all forms of public borrowing, and specifically prohibited any further extensions of public credit to private business corporations. As the historian Ronald Seavoy writes: "State aid continued to be substantial but its form changed. Increasingly, the aid was favorable [general incorporation] statutes that equalized the opportunities of individuals and geographic areas to mobilize capital and credit in a society composed of a large number of small capitalists."[68]

General incorporation with limited liability protection was eventually adopted in every industrializing nation, but it rarely constituted as pivotal a policy tool for capital mobilization as in the United States. Perhaps the most striking example of an alternative approach was Japanese industrial policy after World War II, which also relied heavily on public risk management but of a very different sort. Japanese officials guided private funds to targeted sectors through a relatively small number of large banks. Although most of these banks were privately held, they were nonetheless willing to take direction from above in return for implicit government guaranties on industrial lending. Japanese planners thus used public risk absorption as a lever for a much broader policy of industrial targeting and finance.[69]

In Europe, methods of capital mobilization were by no means uniform during the period of industrialization; but there appears to have been a much stronger tendency toward centralized financial authority on the Continent than in either Britain or the United States. In Germany after unification, a handful of universal banks occupied a commanding position atop the nation's financial system and played a decisive role in guiding heavy industrialization. The state's influence over the universal banks has often been exaggerated. Nevertheless, German political leaders seem to have viewed the great banks as quasi-public entities that were particularly well positioned to help achieve domestic economic and foreign policy goals. Throughout the late nineteenth century and much of the twentieth, German officials maintained exceedingly close relationships with the nation's top universal banks and may even have extended implicit guaranties of various sorts.[70]

The state played an even larger role in mobilizing capital and guiding investment in France—especially during the mid-nineteenth century, during and after World War I, and again after World War II. As the economic historian Charles Kindleberger notes, the state "drew on the savings of France" to finance "public works, to guarantee railroad bonds, to assist urban construction and agricultural improvement, and to assist industry to re-equip in the face of British competition." It also proved pivotal in supporting reconstruction after the two world wars—through a combination of large-scale public financing and, after 1945, indicative state planning and extensive government ownership as well.[71] Public risk absorption thus figured prominently in the mobilization of capital in France; and, once again, it was often linked with a broader policy of industrial targeting and oversight that was largely absent in the United States.

In fact, financial authority in the United States was decentralized as a matter of policy, a consequence of widespread prohibitions on branch and interstate banking and ultimately the legal separation of commercial from investment banking during the New Deal. Although federal deposit insurance did not arise until 1933, New York's Joshua Forman had suggested as early as 1829 that a combination of small unit banks and public risk pooling constituted a distinctively American solution to the problem of money risk. In his view, such an approach would ensure a secure money supply while at the same time avoiding the centralization of financial decision making that would inevitably accompany a system of branch or state banking.[72] Significantly, government absorption of bank risk was almost never associated with activist industrial policy in the United States in either the nineteenth or the twentieth century.

There is also some evidence of a distinctive American approach to public risk management in the realm of social policy, though only at a rather high level of generality. Not only did the United States begin adopting social insurance considerably later than most of its counterparts in Europe, but its programs, once enacted, tended to involve smaller benefits, little if any financing out of general revenues, and (in many but not all cases) less of a redistributive tilt.[73] The United States was also the only major industrial country never to adopt compulsory health insurance for its working population.

Conclusion

Clearly there is something to the idea of American distinctiveness, and it is useful to think about the development of risk management policy in this way. But we must also be careful not to push this sort of analysis too far. Risk management policy does not exist in the United States merely because it sometimes requires little in the way of bureaucracy. Even several of the nation's popular public insurance programs are associated with substantial regulation, designed to control the problem of moral hazard. The Federal Deposit Insurance Corporation, for example, boasts a powerful regulatory arm that closely monitors and supervises all the banks it insures.

More striking still, state and federal lawmakers have fashioned a dense web of health, safety, and environmental regulations that are designed to reduce risk straightaway. And they have done so with broad popular support.[74] Although such regulation (direct risk reduction) stands outside the scope of this book, there is no question that it constitutes an important form of public risk management.[75] There is also no question that many of these regulations have required substantial government bureaucracies and have involved a considerable degree of interference in, and control over, private sector activities.

Significantly, though, the vast majority of our health, safety, and environmental regulations are of fairly recent vintage, most having been established no earlier than the 1960s. The fact that these regulations exist at all in the United States indicates that the public's interest in controlling risk—and in using the government for this purpose—is powerful in its own right, apparently strong enough to overcome some fairly substantial apprehensions about the dangers of "big government." Perhaps public support for this sort of extensive risk-reducing regulation could only have developed after favorable experiences with less invasive forms of public risk management, such as those commonly employed in the nineteenth and early twentieth centuries. Even now, the United States relies far more than other industrialized countries on product and environmental liability as market-conforming complements to protective regulation.[76] American distinctiveness, in other words, remains relevant, though perhaps less so than in earlier times.

In the end, there is simply no denying that risk management policy has come to play a very prominent role in American life in all its various forms. Lawmakers have employed their power to reallocate and even reduce risk to serve a wide range of social objectives, which have steadily evolved over time. Relative to their counterparts in other countries, they have shown considerable deference to the market, frequently choosing risk management policies that either augmented or simply mimicked standard contractual relationships. Relative to their reputation as champions of laissez-faire, however, they have intervened in private market transactions both often and easily, convinced that private mechanisms for allocating risk were far from perfect.

Werner Sombart asked why there was no socialism in the United States. But the more relevant question here is how, in the absence of socialism, Americans have harnessed the power of the state to address social problems. Public risk management turns out to be an important part of the answer. Instead of redistributing income or capital as good socialists would, U.S. lawmakers have actively redistributed risk, carving out a distinctive economic role for the state within the crucible of American capitalism.

Epilogue: Risk, Knowledge, and the Veil of Ignorance

At the dawn of the twenty-first century, public risk management remains a live issue, in both economic and political terms. The "new economy" has produced plenty of new risks to be managed. At the same time, new (or resurgent) ideas about the role of government and the responsibility of the individual citizen have generated powerful demands for the reform of existing risk management policies, from bankruptcy law to Social Security.

In most cases, the pivotal economic issues are what they have always been: market imperfections on the one hand and monitoring arrangements on the other. But this is not universally true. In at least one area, health care financing, the traditional logic of public risk management seems not to apply. An increasingly potent rationale for the public management of health risk is not that private markets are functioning poorly, but rather that they promise to function all too well, dividing us into ever smaller risk pools in the face of a torrent of genetic information about our own personal predispositions to illness.

The remainder of this epilogue, therefore, is divided into two parts. The first briefly identifies a number of current policy challenges that can be productively understood as new variations on old risk management problems. The second, by contrast, examines a looming policy challenge in the health care arena that is considerably less familiar but that raises provocative new questions about the future of public risk management in an age of seemingly limitless information.

326

The More Things Change, the More They Stay the Same

To be sure, many of the risks that have emerged in the new economy bear a striking resemblance to risks that have been with us for years. Sometimes the connection is so strong that existing risk management policies have proved perfectly sufficient to address them. Consider, for example, the way in which a little-known risk management policy enacted well before the introduction of the personal computer has come to facilitate the explosive growth of retail sales on the Internet.

Back in 1970, Congress passed a law to protect consumers against credit card fraud, capping their liability for unauthorized use at just $50. At the time, the primary objective was to safeguard citizens against losses stemming from the interception of live unsolicited credit cards sent through the mail.[1] No one could have imagined that this policy might someday play a pivotal role in liberating the commercial potential of something called the Internet. But that is exactly what appears to have happened a little over two decades later. This simple risk management device—the credit card liability cap—succeeded in boosting the confidence of on-line shoppers in the 1990s, if for no other reason than because the American media were free of horror stories about stolen card numbers and devastating losses. By shifting the risk of loss onto card issuers like Visa and Mastercard, which were optimally positioned to monitor credit card use, this little-noticed federal policy helped fashion an ideal means of payment for the wiles of the Internet.[2]

Existing risk management policies have not always proved sufficient to address new problems, however. One of the most astonishing economic developments of the late twentieth century (stemming once again from the revolution in communication and information technology) was the internationalization of money risk, which wreaked havoc across much of the developing world, from Mexico to Malaysia. Just as lawmakers of the nineteenth and early twentieth centuries had to worry about contagious panics bringing down their banks, modern lawmakers—particularly in developing countries—had to worry about contagious panics devastating their currencies. In fact, the underlying logic of a currency crisis is almost identical to that of a bank run. Yet the solution that American lawmakers ultimately settled on to address the domestic bank run problem, public deposit insurance, was not easily transferable to an international context. This is because sovereign governments could not be monitored and regulated in the same way as domestic banks, a fact that threatened to make the moral hazard that international deposit insurance would inevitably spawn all but impossible to control.

Globalization, in other words, had added a vexing new twist to an age-old risk management problem, and this new twist revolved fundamentally around a deficiency in monitoring. Although the United States and the International Monetary Fund committed several hundred billion dollars in bailout funds to stem a series of currency crises during the 1990s, relatively little progress was made toward developing a permanent framework for addressing these sorts of risks in the future.[3] The internationalization of money risk thus seemed destined to become a critical testing ground for public risk management in the new global economy of the twenty-first century.

Returning closer to home, we find mounting pressure not only for the creation of new institutions of public risk management but also for the reform of existing ones. Of particular interest are proposals for the partial privatization of Social Security, which would require an unprecedented contraction, rather than expansion, of federal risk bearing. Given the impending retirement of the baby boomers, combined with the increasing availability of sophisticated financial instruments, proponents of partial privatization claim that the time is ripe for letting individual workers assume greater responsibility for their own retirement planning. More specifically, they have proposed allowing citizens to divert a portion of their Social Security taxes into private, individual investment accounts.

Whether the introduction of private accounts would yield higher rates of return than Social Security itself, as many proponents of privatization contend, remains a hotly debated subject.[4] But as the historical record makes clear, an equally important question is whether individual workers would be capable of managing the additional risk on their own—something about which the original authors of Social Security were profoundly skeptical. While it is true that private investment options (including mutual funds and annuities) have expanded dramatically in recent years, typical investment strategies for retirement continue to expose individuals to considerable risk.[5] In fact, two concerns that figured in the original debates remain remarkably current today.

First, many lawmakers concluded in 1935 that countless citizens who had saved for retirement had pursued sub-optimal or unduly risky investment strategies. As Senator George Norris of Nebraska observed, "[I]t could be said, as an objection to [Social Security], 'If you would let me handle the money, I would have made more out of it.' Sometimes that would be true, but we all know, from our own experience that, as a general rule, it has not been so."[6] Similarly, Senator Robert Wagner of New York protested that the average worker "is not an actuary. He is not a mathematician. He is just a plain worker."[7]

Second, members of Congress were well aware in the mid-1930s that a financial catastrophe—like the one they had just recently experienced—threatened virtually everyone, including those who had proved reasonably cautious in their investment strategies.[8] These congressmen also recognized that in the aftermath of such a catastrophe, citizens would inevitably turn to the government for assistance. Indeed, this is why New Deal lawmakers resisted proposals to allow some firms to opt out of Social Security, fearing that the federal government would inevitably have to bail out these firms' private pension plans in the event of failure.[9]

Not surprisingly, current critics of Social Security privatization have raised almost precisely the same objections. They claim that a great many investors would fail to achieve expected returns, whether because of bad management or bad luck, and that federal lawmakers would likely feel compelled to bail out losers in the event of a major market downturn. As presidential candidate Al Gore put it during the 2000 campaign, "If we turn the Social Security system into a system of winners and losers, we will be jeopardizing retirement security for too many Americans, and in the end we will all have to pay to make up the differences."[10]

All this is not to say that partial privatization of Social Security is necessarily a bad idea. The point is simply that a frank discussion of risk—and who should bear it—must inevitably factor into the public debate. An honest look back at the historical record reveals that federal old age insurance was originally conceived, in large measure, as a risk management device, designed to minimize risk rather than to maximize expected returns on retirement savings. Both perception and commitment problems loomed large in justifying government involvement. Current proposals for privatizing Social Security, therefore, ought to be evaluated with this in mind. After all, privatization can make sense only if the program's original risk management logic had been flawed in the first place or had somehow become obsolete in later years.

A complete survey of how risk management policy is evolving at the present time lies well beyond the scope of this book. Such a discussion would require a volume of its own, or perhaps several. New economic conditions and shifting social priorities have placed almost every facet of public risk management back on the political agenda in one way or another. At the time of this writing, American lawmakers are actively considering, in addition to the proposals already discussed, a variety of reforms that would tighten discharge provisions for consumer debtors, limit product liability awards to injured plaintiffs, expand Medicare coverage to include prescription drugs, and assist private insurance carriers in covering natural catastrophe losses.

In most cases, the traditional logic of public risk management remains highly relevant. Current policymakers, like their predecessors, find themselves wrestling with risk-related imperfections in the private marketplace and searching for effective risk monitors whenever they actually choose to reallocate a risk. In at least one major policy area, however, something quite new has emerged—a risk management problem based, strangely, on the existence of *too much* information about what hazards are most likely to strike us in the future. This is the problem to which we now turn.

Conjuring an Illusion of Ignorance

Ironically, in the midst of the so-called information age, we have begun to relearn an old truth: that the revelation of hidden information often proves to be a mixed blessing. This is certainly true of genetic research. Today, at a time of extraordinary scientific progress along a wide variety of fronts, many observers have characterized the ongoing effort to "break" the human genetic code as the most extraordinary development of all. In the words of the eminently quotable Lester Thurow, "The human genome project is Newton and Einstein rolled together."[11] Indeed, rapid advances in genetic science appear to hold enormous promise, particularly for the practice of medicine. But they also threaten to fracture the nation's health insurance system by revealing information that could render broad-based risk spreading impossible to sustain. Since health care currently consumes almost 14 percent of U.S. GDP and touches the life of every single American, any potential shock to our health care financing regime is obviously an issue of substantial economic and social significance.

In recent years, numerous experts have predicted a revolution in genetics and genetic applications. Francis Collins, the director of the National Human Genome Research Institute, declared that genetic "revelations hold within them the promise of a true transformation of medical practice."[12] It is, of course, altogether possible that future developments will prove less dramatic than expected. At the dawn of the atomic age, it was common for analysts to speculate about virtually costless energy, envisioning a world in which cheap nuclear dynamos powered everything from automobiles to spaceships. Current predictions at the dawn of the "genetics age" could prove equally fantastic.[13] At this point, however, the skeptics appear distinctly in the minority.[14]

Assuming that optimists like Collins have offered a reasonably accurate picture of the future, then advances in genetics are bound to revolutionize not only health care delivery but health care financing as well. This is because genetic testing could allow unprecedented precision in individual risk stratification, effectively piercing the "veil of ignorance" that makes broad-based insurance possible.[15] In an unfettered private market, insurers would seek to divide us into an ever-larger number of progressively smaller pools, always aiming to group together individuals with comparable levels of risk. The healthiest would end up in one pool, the sickest in another, and so forth. Although this sort of market segmentation would make perfect economic sense (with insurers utilizing all available information in determining rates), it might seriously undercut the *social* appeal of private health insurance. For one thing, it could place adequate health coverage beyond the means of those who needed it most—namely, our friends and neighbors who turned out to be most genetically predisposed to disease. As Dr. Collins himself acknowledged, "Genetic information can be used as the basis for insidious discrimination."[16]

So far the only legislative strategy for addressing this problem has been to prohibit insurance companies from making use of genetic information. As of September 2000, thirty-seven states had enacted a range of restrictions and prohibitions that limited the ability of insurers to employ genetic information in setting rates or curtailing coverage. Twenty-four states had acted to prohibit genetic discrimination in the workplace. At the federal level, the 1996 Health Insurance Portability and Accountability Act blocked group health plans and insurers (though not individual insurance plans) from utilizing genetic information in establishing premiums or denying coverage. President Clinton, moreover, issued an executive order in early 2000 barring any government agency from engaging in genetic discrimination.[17]

From an economic standpoint, this strategy of information suppression appears profoundly misguided. After all, a public policy that prohibits insurers from making use of genetic test results actually *creates* a market failure by enforcing an information asymmetry between buyers and sellers of insurance. It boils down to government-mandated adverse selection. Individuals who discover (through medical tests) that they are genetically predisposed to serious illness will want to buy large amounts of life and health insurance, particularly if their insurers are legally barred from discriminating against them. This will inevitably skew the insurance pool, drawing in the worst risks and driving the best ones away. Achim Wambach, an economist at the University of Munich, has warned that "[n]on-disclosure of genetic-test results could spell the end of the life-insurance market."[18] In fact, nondisclosure rules could ultimately decimate the health insurance market as well.

One has to wonder, moreover, whether such precious information will truly remain suppressed for very long. Insurance companies have, for some time, been prohibited from taking race into account in extending coverage and setting rates. But given the pace and direction of recent advances in genetic science, the consequences of suppressing genetic information are likely to be of considerably greater economic significance. At a minimum, insurers will face intense competitive pressure to find ways of circumventing the law.

But regardless of whether the current strategy of information suppression ultimately succeeds or fails, its very existence underscores the powerful social appeal of maintaining the pretense of equality. Upon signing his executive order, President Clinton declared, "We must never allow these discoveries to change the basic belief upon which our Government, our society, our system of ethics is founded, that all of us are created equal, entitled to equal treatment under the law."[19] Similarly, in July 2000, Dr. Collins spoke of the necessity of putting "in place public policies reflective of our core American values that prevent the unjust, unfair, and discriminatory use of genetic information."[20]

This appeal to enlightened social blindness—if I might call it that—rests on a solid intellectual foundation. The philosopher John Rawls defined a just institution as one that would be chosen by members of a community who had no knowledge of their own special strengths and weaknesses as individuals. "The principles of justice are chosen behind a veil of ignorance," he wrote. "Since all are similarly situated and no one is able to design principles to favor his particular condition, the principles of justice are the result of a fair agreement or bargain. . . . The original position is, one might say, the appropriate initial status quo, and thus the fundamental agreements reached in it are fair."[21]

The beauty of broad-based insurance is that it is fundamentally a collective decision about resource allocation made from behind a veil of ignorance. We buy insurance precisely because we do not know what will happen to us in the future. As long as we all remain ignorant of our own personal probabilities of falling victim to a given hazard, we all have an interest in purchasing insurance at an average premium. Such broad-based risk spreading, organized on a voluntary basis, proves exceedingly attractive from a social standpoint because it means that we have all agreed to funnel resources to those who will ultimately end up most in need.

New knowledge, however, threatens to destroy this voluntary method of reallocating resources. And most of us intuitively oppose its dismantling. Although we rarely object when insurers penalize us for risk factors within our own control (such as heavy smoking or drinking), we instinctively object when they discriminate on the basis of risk factors that are innate (such as race, gender, or other genetic attributes). The latter form of discrimination strikes us as profoundly unfair. And this is precisely why it has become official policy in the United States to try to prohibit insurance companies from utilizing genetic information in setting rates or limiting coverage. The fear, to draw on a biblical metaphor, is that our happy community will be torn asunder—that we will be driven from our Garden of Eden—should we dare to eat from the forbidden Tree of Knowledge.[22]

Part of the allure of public risk management must be that it promises to promote the ideal of a just and cohesive society, in which resources are allocated from behind a veil of ignorance. Ideally, such an allocation could be achieved through private insurance—on the basis of consensual and broad-based risk pooling. But when the private market proves unable to deliver this result on its own, policymakers have the ability to mimic what the private market might have done were all citizens equally at risk and thus all in it together. Although not explicitly expressed by leading policy advocates at the time, this may well have been one of the implicit—perhaps even unconscious—justifications for mandating workers' compensation, unemployment insurance, old age insurance, strict liability in product injury suits, extensive federal disaster relief, and the like. By fashioning remedies of this sort, which emulate broad-based risk pooling, American policymakers were able to redistribute resources in a socially acceptable manner, drawing on the legitimacy of private insurance as an allocative mechanism.[23]

The current strategy for dealing with genetic information—that is, prohibiting insurers from making use of it—aims to achieve the same basic objective, only in a less invasive way than compulsory insurance. Ideally, such a strategy would ensure broad-based risk pooling, since private insurers would be barred from dividing the pool along genetic lines. As we have seen, however, the basic economics of this strategy raise serious doubts about its long-term viability.

Were the strategy of information suppression ultimately to fail at some point in the future, policymakers would then face considerable pressure to mimic the veil of ignorance in some other way. The most obvious solution—though by no means the most welcome one for many Americans—would be to make health insurance compulsory and to set premiums at some average actuarial rate (through community rating). This would come close to replicating the outcome one might expect from the private market if we all remained in the dark about who would stay healthy and who would fall sick in the future. Compulsory community-rated insurance, which has long been the norm in most other developed economies, would prevent not only market fragmentation along genetic lines but also market breakdown as a result of adverse selection (since no one would be allowed to opt out). Carrying this logic to its ultimate conclusion, Andrew Sullivan argued in the *New York Times* that ongoing genetic advances make "socialized medicine . . . all but inevitable."[24]

Of course, the introduction of compulsory insurance would not actually solve the underlying problem. Once done, the damage that new knowledge does to the veil of ignorance cannot be undone. But with the help of government coercion, a society can attempt to behave *as if* the veil were still intact—precisely the result that compulsory health insurance would be designed to achieve. There is no denying that Americans have long resisted such a policy, having rejected major proposals for compulsory health insurance about a half-dozen times throughout the twentieth century. What this analysis suggests, however, is that dramatic advances in genetic science may someday undercut the economic viability of broad-based risk pooling and could thus generate increasing pressure for the government to get further involved in the supervision and perhaps even the provision of health insurance.

Clearly, public risk management remains an evolving project, shaped not only by economic conditions and social values but also by the state of scientific knowledge, which seems to be developing more rapidly than ever. To be sure, the "new economy" has brought with it new risks to be managed, ranging from credit card fraud on the Internet to contagious currency crises in the international economy. But potentially even more important than these new risks are new forms of knowledge that, despite their enormous promise, threaten to debilitate many of the institutions of risk management that we hold dear.[25]

For all of our individual aversion to risk, the existence of risk (ironically) helps us to act justly by imposing upon us a veil of ignorance. As new knowledge cuts through that veil with scalpel-like precision, American lawmakers seem determined to conjure an *illusion of ignorance*—whether through a policy of information suppression or, perhaps someday, compulsory insurance. No one can know the future. But as we come to know more about what the future may bring, the importance of government's role as a risk manager may very well increase, reflecting society's solemn struggle to act justly, even from behind its tattered veil.

Notes

Preface

1. Anna C. Brackett, *The Technique of Rest* (New York: Harper and Brothers, 1892), p. 112.
2. "U.S. Securities and Insurance Industries: Keeping the Promise," Hearing of the House Financial Services Committee, 107th Cong., 1st sess., September 26, 2001.
3. Alan Cowell with Edmund L. Andrews, "European Converts to Laissez-Faire See the Rush to Intervene as Heresy," *New York Times,* October 25, 2001, pp. C1, C8.

1. Introduction

1. The most relevant studies have typically focused on either government risk bearing or direct risk reduction, both of which are subsets of the more general category of public risk management. On government risk bearing, see esp. Mark S. Sniderman, ed., *Government Risk Bearing: Proceedings of a Conference Held at the Federal Reserve Bank of Cleveland, May 1991* (Boston: Kluwer Academic Publishers, 1993); Mark R. Greene, "The Government as an Insurer," *Journal of Risk and Insurance,* 43 (1976), 393–407; Mark R. Greene, "A Review and Evaluation of Selected Government Programs to Handle Risk," *Annals of the American Academy of Political and Social Sciences* (1979), 129–144. On direct risk reduction (or "risk regulation"), see esp. Stephen Breyer, *Breaking the Vicious Circle: Toward Effective Risk Regulation* (Cambridge, Mass.: Harvard University Press, 1993); W. Kip Viscusi, "The Value of Risks to Life and Health," *Journal of Economic Literature,* 31, no. 4 (December 1993), 1912–46; W. Kip Viscusi, *Fatal Tradeoffs: Public and Private Responsibilities for Risk* (New York: Oxford University Press, 1992); Cass R. Sunstein, *After the Rights Revolution: Reconceiving the Regulatory State* (Cambridge, Mass.: Harvard University Press, 1990).
2. "Impact of Government Shutdown on American Workers," transcript of

news conference with Secretary of Labor Robert Reich, Federal News Service, January 3, 1996. Three decades earlier the economist Paul Samuelson had articulated a remarkably similar point, though at a broader conceptual level, during a meeting of the American Economic Association. "One can look at much of government," he suggested, "as primarily a device for mutual reinsurance." See "Discussion," *American Economic Review,* 54, no. 3 (May 1964), Papers and Proceedings, 96.

3. Henry Fairlie, "Fear of Living: America's Morbid Aversion to Risk," *New Republic,* January 23, 1989, p. 14.

4. Debra Saunders, "The Coffee's Hot, Stupid," *Atlanta Journal and Constitution,* September 13, 1994, p. A6. For a broader critique of government attempts to create a "no-risk society," see Yair Aharoni, *The No-Risk Society* (Chatham, N.J.: Chatham House Publishers, 1981).

5. See esp. Ann Kallman Bixby, "Public Social Welfare Expenditures, Fiscal Year 1995," *Social Security Bulletin,* 62, no. 2 (1999), 86–94; *Economic Report of the President, 1999* (Washington, D.C.: Government Printing Office [hereafter GPO], 1999).

6. *Analytical Perspectives: Budget of the United States Government, Fiscal Year 1999* (Washington, D.C.: GPO, 1998), p. 165.

7. "The 1991 Budget: Excerpts from Darman; Darman Conducts a Tour of Wonderland: The Federal Budget," *New York Times,* January 27, 1990, sec. 1, p. 12. See also Aharoni, *No-Risk Society,* pp. 4–6, 35–36, 98–107.

8. Gerald Celente, "Capitalism for Cowards," *New York Times,* October 16, 1998, p. A27.

9. Kenneth J. Arrow and Robert C. Lind, "Uncertainty and the Evaluation of Public Investment Decisions," *American Economic Review,* 60, no. 3 (June 1970), 374.

10. Kenneth J. Arrow, "Uncertainty and the Welfare Economics of Medical Care," *American Economic Review,* 53, no. 5 (December 1963), 961.

11. "Governor's Message," in *Resolves of the General Court of the Commonwealth of Massachusetts,* January 6–March 13, 1830, pp. 229–230.

12. Paul Halpern, Michael Trebilcock, and Stuart Turnbull, "An Economic Analysis of Limited Liability in Corporation Law," *University of Toronto Law Journal,* 20 (1980), 126.

13. John Hicks, "Limited Liability: The Pros and Cons," in Tony Orhnial, ed., *Limited Liability and the Corporation* (London: Croom Helm, 1982), pp. 11, 12.

14. *Appendix to the Congressional Globe,* 26th Cong., 1st sess., May 1840, p. 544.

15. At first glance, property rights hardly appear to be a risk management tool. Yet without clear and well-enforced property rights, all capital investment and indeed all economic transactions would represent dangerous gambles.

John Stuart Mill observed that insecure property "means uncertainty whether they who sow shall reap, whether they who produce shall consume, and they who spare to-day shall enjoy tomorrow." John Stuart Mill, *Principles of Political Economy* (London: Longmans, Green, Reader, and Dyer, 1871), bk. 5, chap. 8, p. 531. The enforcement of contracts—and property rights more generally—thus reduces risks that otherwise would affect all economic activity and, in particular, every economic transaction. Theodore Lowi has identified law and order, protection of property, and contract enforcement as three essential "presuppositions," without which "few people will habitually take risks to improve on what they have." Theodore J. Lowi, "Risks and Rights in the History of American Governments," *Daedalus*, 119, no. 4 (Fall 1990), 17–40, esp. 20–26.

16. John R. Commons, "Industrial Relations," address at the International Convention of Government Labor Officials, Park Hotel, Madison, Wisc., June 3, 1919, p. 4, in *Microfilm Edition of the John R. Commons Papers*, reel 17, fr. 818. On Commons's influence, see, e.g., Kenneth E. Boulding, "A New Look at Institutionalism," *American Economic Review*, 47, no. 2 (May 1957), 7.

17. Franklin D. Roosevelt, "A Social Security Program Must Include All Those Who Need Its Protection," radio address on the third anniversary of the Social Security Act, August 15, 1938.

18. Ralph Easley to Olga Halsey, April 25, 1916, in *The Microfilm Edition of the Papers of the American Association for Labor Legislation, 1905–1945* (Glen Rock, N.J.: Microfilming Corporation of America, 1973), reel 17.

19. Mark A. Daly circular letter "To All Members," February 23, 1918, ibid., reel 18.

20. *Congressional Record* (House), 74th Cong., 1st sess., April 13, 1935, p. 5583.

21. David A. Moss, "Courting Disaster: The Transformation of Federal Disaster Policy since 1803," in Kenneth A. Froot, ed., *The Financing of Catastrophe Risk* (Chicago: University of Chicago Press, 1999), pp. 327–328.

22. Herbert Hoover, *The Memoirs of Herbert Hoover: The Cabinet and the Presidency, 1920–1933*, vol. 2 (New York: Macmillan, 1952), p. 126.

23. See, e.g., William Proxmire, *Hearings before the Subcommittee on Financial Institutions of the Committee on Banking and Currency, United States Senate*, December 1969, p. 1.

24. Roger J. Traynor, "The Ways and Meanings of Defective Products and Strict Liability," *Tennessee Law Review*, 32, no. 3 (Spring 1965), 363.

25. On the absence of markets for "macro" risks, see Robert J. Shiller, *Macro Markets: Creating Institutions for Managing Society's Largest Economic Risks* (Oxford: Clarendon Press, 1993).

26. Henry R. Seager, "Outline of a Program of Social Reform" (1907), re-

printed in *Labor and Other Economic Essays by Henry R. Seager,* ed. Charles A. Gulick, Jr. (New York: Harper and Brothers, 1931), pp. 82–83. See also David A. Moss, *Socializing Security: Progressive-Era Economists and the Origins of American Social Policy* (Cambridge, Mass.: Harvard University Press, 1996), pp. 60–65.

27. Guido Calabresi, *The Costs of Accidents: A Legal and Economic Analysis* (New Haven: Yale University Press, 1970), pp. 56–57.

28. For an exception, see Bertrand Villeneuve, "The Insurers as the Informed Party: A Solution to Three Insurance Puzzles," Document de Travail 76, Institut d'Economie Industrielle, March 1998.

29. James Willard Hurst, *Law and the Condition of Freedom in the Nineteenth-Century United States* (Madison: University of Wisconsin Press, 1956), pp. 22–23.

30. Historical data on per capita gross domestic product may be found in Angus Maddison, *Dynamic Forces in Capitalist Development: A Long-Run Comparative View* (New York: Oxford University Press, 1991), esp. tables 1.1, A.2, B.4, and B.7. Maddison based cross-country rankings on per capita GDP adjusted for purchasing power parity. More recent GDP data and price deflators (to adjust for inflation) may be found in the *Economic Report of the President, 2001* (Washington, D.C.: GPO, 2001), esp. tables B-3 and B-31. For poverty-line data, see Joseph Dalaker and Bernadette D. Proctor, *Poverty in the United States: 1999* (Washington, D.C.: Bureau of the Census, September 2000), table 1 (Consumer Population Reports, Consumer Income, P60–210).

31. See Kenneth Arrow, *Aspects of the Theory of Risk-Bearing* (Helsinki: Yrjo Jahnssonin, 1965), lecture 2 ("The Theory of Risk Aversion"), pp. 28–44.

32. See Herman E. Kroos and Martin R. Blyn, *A History of Financial Intermediaries* (New York: Random House, 1971), pp. 35, 109–111, 165; *Historical Statistics of the United States* (Washington, D.C.: GPO, 1975), pt. 2, ser. X-880, X-882, and X-885, p. 1056; Crystal Eastman, *Work Accidents and the Law* (New York: Arno, 1969 [1910]), pp. 190–206, 145; I. M. Rubinow, *Social Insurance* (New York: Henry Holt and Company, 1916 [1913]), pp. 136–139.

33. John Kenneth Galbraith, *Economics in Perspective: A Critical History* (Boston: Houghton Mifflin, 1987), p. 290. On the relationship between national income and social welfare policy, see also Harold L. Wilensky, *The Welfare State and Equality: Structural and Ideological Roots of Public Expenditures* (Berkeley: University of California Press, 1975), esp. pp. 15–49.

34. A critical feature of Japan's much-lauded postwar strategy, for example, was the government's implicit absorption of investment risk. Powerful government officials targeted key sectors such as steel and chemicals for

rapid growth, and then effectively promised to back big banks that lent liberally to leading firms in these industries. A good deal of investment risk was thus shifted onto the government via the banks, dramatically lowering the cost of capital in preferred sectors and fueling Japan's economic miracle. All this was done, moreover, with no apparent effect on the government budget. Public guarantees rarely cost anything at the moment they are issued.

35. Seymour Martin Lipset, *American Exceptionalism: A Double-Edged Sword* (New York: W. W. Norton, 1996), p. 98.

36. See, e.g., Sheila Jasanoff, "American Exceptionalism and the Political Acknowledgment of Risk," in Edward J. Burger, Jr., ed., *Risk* (Ann Arbor: University of Michigan Press, 1993), pp. 61–81.

37. In the extreme, one could even argue that something as seemingly unrelated to risk management as new school construction could be conceived as a risk-reduction policy, since new buildings are often thought to be safer than old ones. For our purposes, however, a law, regulation, or judicial ruling will be classified as a risk management policy only when risk reduction or risk reallocation figures as a *primary objective or consequence* of the policy. Clearly, something like new school construction would fall outside the confines of this definition in most cases. Yet even if we limit the field in this way, the number of risk-reduction policies that have been introduced over the years remains remarkably large.

38. For a list of several particularly prominent contributions to the literature on risk regulation, see note 1.

39. A number of scholars have explored the relative strengths of liability law and regulation as alternative devices for managing specific hazards. See esp. Steven Shavell, "Liability for Harm versus Regulation of Safety," *Journal of Legal Studies,* 13 (June 1984), 357–374; William M. Landes and Richard A. Posner, "Tort Law as a Regulatory Regime for Catastrophic Personal Injuries," *Journal of Legal Studies,* 13 (August 1984), 417–434; W. Kip Viscusi, "Product Liability and Regulation: Establishing the Appropriate Institutional Division of Labor," *American Economic Review,* 78, no. 2 (May 1988), Papers and Proceedings, 300–304; W. Kip Viscusi, "Toward a Diminished Role for Tort Liability: Social Insurance, Government Regulation, and Contemporary Risks to Health and Safety," *Yale Journal on Regulation,* 6 (Winter 1989), 65–107. There is also a small literature on the important phenomenon of government risk bearing (see note 1). But until now there has been no systematic attempt to look across a broad range of policies whose primary objective or consequence involves the reallocation of risk.

40. Indeed, it might be argued that increased workers' compensation benefits

could conceivably serve as a substitute for the complex web of workplace safety regulations put out by the Occupational Safety and Health Administration, a federal agency established in 1970.

41. Where possible, an attempt has been made to examine at least one policy from each set of policies designed to deal with a major category of risks. For example, quite a number of important risk-reallocation policies address risks associated with retirement, such as old age insurance (Social Security), Medicare, and the Employee Retirement Income Security Act (ERISA), which created the Pension Benefit Guaranty Corporation (PBGC). While Medicare and ERISA are not taken up in detail in subsequent chapters, the advent of old age insurance is examined in considerable depth in Chapter 7.

42. This distinction between policies that reallocate risk and those that redistribute income or wealth adds another potential category (or at least additional nuance) to Theodore Lowi's now classic characterization of the three functions of government: distribution, regulation, and redistribution. See Theodore J. Lowi, "American Business, Public Policy, Case-Studies, and Political Theory," *World Politics*, 16, no. 4 (July 1964), 677–715. Significantly, the historian Peter Baldwin has found within a European context that risk-based policies (primarily social insurance) engender a distinctive political dynamic. See Peter Baldwin, *The Politics of Social Solidarity: Class Bases of the European Welfare State, 1875–1975* (New York: Cambridge University Press, 1990). Of course, if one abstracted away from what is known about existing differences between individuals and imagined that policy were made from behind a Rawlsian "veil of ignorance," then the distinction between income redistribution and risk reallocation would disappear. See, e.g., Mancur Olson, "Why Some Welfare-State Redistribution to the Poor Is a Great Idea," in Charles K. Rowley, ed., *Democracy and Public Choice: Essays in Honor of Gordon Tullock* (New York: Basil Blackwell, 1987), esp. pp. 217–218.

2. A Primer on Risk and Its History

1. L. E. Maistrov, *Probability Theory: A Historical Sketch*, trans. and ed. Samuel Kotz (New York: Academic Press, 1974), p. 18; Isaac Todhunter, *A History of the Mathematical Theory of Probability from the Time of Pascal to That of Laplace* (New York: Chelsea Publishing Company, 1949 [1865]), p. 2; F. N. David, "Dicing and Gaming (A Note on the History of Probability)," in E. S. Pearson and M. G. Kendall, eds., *Studies in the History of Statistics and Probability* (Darien, Conn.: Hafner Publishing Co., 1970), pp. 12–13; Peter L. Bernstein, *Against the Gods: The Remarkable Story of Risk* (New York: John Wiley & Sons, 1996), pp. 50–52.

2. Ian Hacking, *The Emergence of Probability: A Philosophical Study of Early Ideas about Probability, Induction, and Statistical Inference* (New York: Cambridge University Press, 1975), pp. 54, 56.
3. Ibid., p. 96.
4. Blaise Pascal, *Thoughts*, trans. W. F. Trotter (New York: P. F. Collier & Son, 1910), sec. 3 ("Of the Necessity of the Wager"), esp. pp. 84–89; William James, *The Will to Believe and Other Essays in Popular Philosophy* (Cambridge, Mass.: Harvard University Press, 1979 [1897]), pp. 16–17; James W. Tankard, Jr., *The Statistical Pioneers* (Cambridge, Mass.: Schenkman Publishing Company, 1984), p. 15. For a fascinating discussion of an early antecedent to Pascal's reasoning (from the fourth century A.D.), see Vincent T. Covello and Jeryl Mumpower, "Risk Analysis and Risk Management: An Historical Perspective," *Risk Analysis*, 5, no. 2 (1985), 104.
5. Daniel Bernoulli, "Exposition of a New Theory on the Measurement of Risk" (1738), trans. Louise Sommer, *Econometrica*, 22, no. 1 (January 1954), 23–36.
6. Adapted from ibid., p. 31.
7. Ibid., p. 29.
8. For an intriguing critique of this standard view of risk aversion, see Matthew Rabin and Richard H. Thaler, "Anomalies: Risk Aversion," *Journal of Economic Perspectives*, 15, no. 1 (Winter 2001), 219–232.
9. See, e.g., Milton Friedman and L. J. Savage, "The Expected-Utility Hypothesis and the Measurability of Utility," *Journal of Political Economy*, 60, no. 6 (December 1952), 463–474; John Von Neumann and Oskar Morgenstern, *Theory of Games and Economic Behavior* (Princeton: Princeton University Press, 1947 [1944]).
10. See, e.g., D. E. W. Gibb, *Lloyd's of London: A Study in Individualism* (New York: St. Martin's Press, 1957).
11. Howard P. Dunham, *The Business of Insurance: A Textbook and Reference Work Covering All Lines of Insurance* (New York: Ronald Press Co., 1912), 1:31; W. S. Holdsworth, "The Early History of the Contract of Insurance," *Columbia Law Review*, 17, no. 2 (February 1917), 109.
12. *Insurance Markets of the World* (Zurich: Swiss Reinsurance Company, 1964), p. 294.
13. C. F. Trennery, *The Origin and Early History of Insurance, Including the Contract of Bottomry* (London: P. S. King & Son, 1926), pp. 4–6. Although Trennery dates the Hammurabi Code to 2250 B.C., ca. 1780 B.C. is probably correct.
14. See Bernstein, *Against the Gods*, p. 92; W. R. Vance, "The Early History of Insurance Law," *Columbia Law Review*, 8, no. 1 (January 1908), 6; Holdsworth, "Early History," p. 86. See also Covello and Mumpower, "Risk Analysis," pp. 108–109.

15. Edwin W. Patterson, *The Insurance Commissioner in the United States: A Study in Administrative Law and Practice* (Cambridge, Mass.: Harvard University Press, 1927), p. 514; Frederick Hoffman, *Insurance: Science and Economics* (New York: Spectator Company, 1911), p. 143.

16. Vance, "Early History of Insurance Law," p. 1; Trennery, *Origin and Early History of Insurance*, pp. 13–14.

17. Bernstein, *Against the Gods*, p. 92; Vance, "Early History of Insurance Law," p. 2; Trennery, *Origin and Early History of Insurance*, pp. 15–16.

18. Vance, "Early History of Insurance Law," p. 2; Lorraine Daston, *Classical Probability in the Enlightenment* (Princeton: Princeton University Press, 1988), p. 116; Hacking, *Emergence of Probability*, p. 111.

19. Bernstein, *Against the Gods*, p. 92; Vance, "Early History of Insurance Law," pp. 3–5.

20. Holdsworth, "Early History," p. 86; Vance, "Early History of Insurance Law," pp. 4–5.

21. Quoted in Vance, "Early History of Insurance Law," p. 15.

22. Quoted in Stephen M. Stigler, *The History of Statistics: The Measurement of Uncertainty before 1900* (Cambridge, Mass.: Harvard University Press, 1986), p. 65.

23. This example was broadly inspired by a similar one offered in Scott P. Mason, "The Allocation of Risk," in Dwight B. Crane et al., *The Global Financial System: A Functional Perspective* (Boston: Harvard Business School Press, 1995), esp. pp. 168–172.

24. Since each merchant faces a 20% chance of losing his shipment, the probability that both merchants will lose their shipments is 20% × 20%, or 4%. Since each merchant faces an 80% chance of his shipment arriving safely, the probability that both shipments will arrive safely is 80% × 80%, or 64%. Finally, for just one shipment to arrive safely, the other shipment must be lost. Since there are two ways for this to occur, the probability of just one ship arriving safely is (80% × 20%) + (20% × 80%), or 32%.

25. Shepard B. Clough, *A Century of American Life Insurance: A History of the Mutual Life Insurance Company of New York, 1843–1943* (New York: Columbia University Press, 1946), p. 4.

26. See, e.g., Robert M. Townsend, "Consumption Insurance: An Evaluation of Risk-Bearing Systems in Low-Income Economies," *Journal of Economic Perspectives*, 9, no. 3 (Summer 1995), 83–102.

27. Trennery, *The Origin and Early History of Insurance*, p. 249.

28. Ibid., pp. 253–254.

29. Andrew Cornford, "Some Recent Innovations in International Finance: Different Faces of Risk Management and Control," *Journal of Economic Issues*, 30, no. 2 (June 1996), 495.

30. Quoted in Richard Ehrenberg, *Capital and Finance in the Age of the Renaissance: A Study of the Fuggers and Their Connections,* trans. H. M. Lucas (Fairfield, N.J.: Augustus M. Kelley Publishers, 1985 [1928]), pp. 243–244.

31. Henry Crosby Emery, *Speculation on the Stock and Produce Exchanges of the United States* (New York: Columbia University, 1896), p. 33.

32. J. Duncan LaPlante, "Growth and Organization of Commodity Markets," in Perry Kaufman, ed., *Handbook of Futures Markets* (New York: John Wiley and Sons, 1984), pp. 6–7; Cornford, "Some Recent Innovations in International Finance," p. 495.

33. Emery, *Speculation on the Stock and Produce Exchanges,* pp. 34–37.

34. Ehrenberg, *Capital and Finance,* p. 357; Richard J. Teweles and Frank J. Jones, *The Futures Game: Who Wins? Who Loses? Why?* (New York: McGraw-Hill, 1987), pp. 6–7.

35. In economics, a socially optimal outcome is commonly defined as one in which no person can be made better off without making someone else worse off. This is known as Pareto optimality, named after the Italian economist Vilfredo Pareto (1848–1923).

36. Kenneth J. Arrow, "The Role of Securities in the Optimal Allocation of Risk-Bearing," *Review of Economic Studies,* 31, no. 2 (April 1964), 91–96 [original French version, 1953]; Gerard Debreu, *Theory of Value: An Axiomatic Analysis of General Equilibrium* (New Haven: Yale University Press, 1959), chap. 7.

37. Kenneth J. Arrow, "Political and Economic Evaluation of Social Effects and Externalities," in Julius Margolis, ed., *Analysis of Public Output* (New York: Columbia University Press, 1970), p. 6.

38. Miles Menander Dawson, "Effects of Free Surrender and Loan Privileges in Life Insurance," *Publications of the American Statistical Association,* 4, no. 28/29 (December 1894–March 1895), 84.

39. On potential strategies for addressing the problem of adverse selection without government intervention, see Michael Rothschild and Joseph Stiglitz, "Equilibrium in Competitive Insurance Markets: An Essay on the Economics of Imperfect Information," *Quarterly Journal of Economics,* 90, no. 4 (November 1976), 629–649; Howard Kunreuther and Richard J. Roth, Sr., *Paying the Price: The Status and Role of Insurance against Natural Disasters in the United States* (Washington, D.C.: Joseph Henry Press, 1998), pp. 35–36.

40. Arthur C. Ducat, *The Practice of Fire Underwriting,* 4th ed. (1865), quoted in Tom Baker, "On the Genealogy of Moral Hazard," *Texas Law Review,* 75 (December 1996), 249n44.

41. Baker, "Genealogy of Moral Hazard," pp. 248–249.

42. John Haynes, "Risk as an Economic Factor," *Quarterly Journal of Economics*, 9, no. 4 (July 1895), 412.

43. Baker, "Genealogy of Moral Hazard."

44. See esp. Mark V. Pauly, "The Economics of Moral Hazard: Comment," *American Economic Review*, 58, no. 3, pt. 1 (June 1968), 531–537. Devices that private insurers employ to limit the problem of moral hazard include deductibles and coinsurance (535–536).

45. *Congressional Globe*, 27th Cong., 1st sess., August 11, 1841, p. 324.

46. *Appendix to the Congressional Globe*, 27th Cong., 1st sess., July 1841, p. 206.

47. Kenneth J. Arrow, "Uncertainty and the Welfare Economics of Medical Care," *American Economic Review*, 53, no. 5 (December 1963), 941–973.

48. George A. Akerlof, "The Market for 'Lemons': Quality Uncertainty and the Market Mechanism," *Quarterly Journal of Economics*, 84, no. 3 (August 1970), 488–500.

49. Dawson, "Effects of Free Surrender," p. 85.

50. See David A. Moss, "Courting Disaster? The Transformation of Federal Disaster Policy since 1803," in Kenneth A. Froot, ed., *The Financing of Catastrophe Risk* (Chicago: University of Chicago Press, 1999), pp. 335–339. Cognizant of the limits of historical averages, private insurers have devoted considerable resources to trying to improve their estimates of expected catastrophe losses through the use of sophisticated computer modeling. See, e.g., Paul R. Kleindorfer and Howard C. Kunreuther, "Challenges Facing the Insurance Industry in Managing Catastrophic Risks," in Froot, *Financing of Catastrophe Risk*, pp. 149–189.

51. Frank H. Knight, *Risk, Uncertainty, and Profit* (Chicago: University of Chicago Press, 1971 [1921]), p. 233. See also John Maynard Keynes, "The General Theory of Employment," *Quarterly Journal of Economics*, 51, no. 2 (February 1937), 213–214.

52. Presented here as a perception problem, Knightian uncertainty also qualifies as an information problem, since it stems from the absence of empirical information about particular probabilities.

53. See esp. Leonard J. Savage, *The Foundations of Statistics* (New York: Wiley, 1954); Milton Friedman and Leonard J. Savage, "The Utility of Choices Involving Risk," *Journal of Political Economy*, 56, no. 4 (August 1948), 279–304; Kenneth Arrow, "Alternative Approaches to the Theory of Choice in Risk-Taking Situations," *Econometrica*, 19, no. 4 (October 1951), 404–437, esp. 417; Jack Hirshleifer and John G. Riley, *The Analytics of Uncertainty and Information* (Cambridge: Cambridge University Press, 1992), p. 10.

54. Leonard J. Savage, *The Foundations of Statistics* (New York: Wiley, 1954);

Frank P. Ramsey, *The Foundations of Mathematics* (New York: Harcourt Brace, 1931).

55. Daniel Ellsberg, "Risk, Ambiguity, and the Savage Axioms," *Quarterly Journal of Economics*, 75, no. 4 (November 1961), 643–669. See also William Fellner, "Distortion of Subjective Probabilities as a Reaction to Uncertainty," *Quarterly Journal of Economics*, 75, no. 4 (November 1961), 670–689.

56. Ellsberg, "Risk, Ambiguity, and the Savage Axioms," p. 654.

57. Howard Raiffa, "Risk, Ambiguity, and the Savage Axioms: Comment," *Quarterly Journal of Economics*, 75, no. 4 (November 1961), 691. On Savage's apparent violation of the Savage Axioms, see Ellsberg, "Risk, Ambiguity, and the Savage Axioms," p. 656.

58. Ellsberg, "Risk, Ambiguity, and the Savage Axioms," p. 656.

59. Ibid., p. 669. For an even broader critique of the standard economic model of human decision making, based on the phenomenon of Knightian uncertainty, see esp. Jens Beckert, "What Is Sociological about Economic Sociology? Uncertainty and the Embeddedness of Economic Action," *Theory and Society*, 25, no. 6 (December 1996), 802–840.

60. For an early survey of empirical tests of the expected utility model, see Paul J. H. Schoemaker, "The Expected Utility Model: Its Variants, Purpose, Evidence, and Limitations," *Journal of Economic Literature*, 20, no. 2 (June 1982), esp. 541–552.

61. George A. Akerlof and Janet L. Yellen, "Rational Models of Irrational Behavior," *American Economic Review*, 77, no. 2 (May 1987), Papers and Proceedings, 140.

62. Amos Tversky and Daniel Kahneman, "Judgment under Uncertainty: Heuristics and Biases," reprinted from *Science* (185 [1974], 1124–31) in Peter Diamond and Michael Rothschild, eds., *Uncertainty in Economics: Reading and Exercises* (New York: Academic Press, 1978), p. 19. See also Herbert A. Simon, "A Behavioral Model of Rational Choice," *Quarterly Journal of Economics*, 69, no. 1 (February 1955), 99–118; Herbert A. Simon, "Theories of Decision-Making in Economics and Behavioral Science," *American Economic Review*, 49, no. 3 (June 1959), 253–283; Herbert A. Simon, "Rationality as Process and as Product of Thought," *American Economic Review*, 68, no. 2 (May 1978), Papers and Proceedings, pp. 1–16.

63. Tversky and Kahneman, "Judgment under Uncertainty," p. 26.

64. See esp. Ola Svenson, "Are We All Less Risky and More Skillful Than Our Fellow Drivers?" *Acta Psychologica*, 47 (1981), 143–148.

65. Neil D. Weinstein, "Optimistic Biases about Personal Risks," *Science*, 246, no. 4935 (December 8, 1989), 1232–33; Neil D. Weinstein, "Why It Won't Happen to Me: Perceptions of Risk Factors and Susceptibility," *Health Psy-*

chology, 3, no. 5 (1984), 431–457; A. J. Rothman, W. M. Klein, and N. D. Weinstein, "Absolute and Relative Biases in Estimations of Personal Risk," *Journal of Applied Social Psychology*, 26, no. 14 (July 16, 1996), 1213–36; Neil D. Weinstein, "Unrealistic Optimism about Susceptibility to Health Problems: Conclusions from a Community-Wide Sample," *Journal of Behavioral Medicine*, 10, no. 5 (October 1987), 481–500.

66. Adam Smith, *An Inquiry into the Nature and Causes of the Wealth of Nations* (Chicago: University of Chicago Press, 1976 [1776]), bk. 1, pp. 119–120.

67. Amos Tversky and Daniel Kahneman, "The Framing of Decisions and the Psychology of Choice," *Science*, 211 (January 1981), 453–458. For the earliest empirical treatment of so-called preference reversals, see Sarah Lichtenstein and Paul Slovic, "Reversals of Preferences between Bids and Choices in Gambling Decisions," *Journal of Experimental Psychology*, 89 (January 1971), 46–55. On the related concept of loss aversion, which suggests that people value losses more than equal-sized gains (relative to a given reference point), see also Daniel Kahneman and Amos Tversky, "Prospect Theory: An Analysis of Decision under Risk," *Econometrica*, 47, no. 2 (March 1979), esp. 279–280; Daniel Kahneman, Jack L. Knetsch, and Richard H. Thaler, "Anomalies: The Endowment Effect, Loss Aversion, and Status Quo Bias," *Journal of Economic Perspectives*, 5, no. 1 (Winter 1991), esp. 199–203; Amos Tversky and Daniel Kahneman, "Loss Aversion in Riskless Choice: A Reference-Dependent Model," *Quarterly Journal of Economics*, 106, no. 4 (November 1991), 1039–61.

68. Kahneman and Tversky, "Prospect Theory," p. 283.

69. See esp. Howard Kunreuther, "Ambiguity and Government Risk-Bearing for Low-Probability Events," in Mark S. Sniderman, ed., *Government Risk-Bearing: Proceedings of a Conference Held at the Federal Reserve Bank of Cleveland, May 1991* (Boston: Kluwer Academic Publishers, 1993), pp. 21–41; Colin F. Camerer and Howard Kunreuther, "Decision Processes for Low Probability Events: Policy Implications," *Journal of Policy Analysis and Management*, 8, no. 4 (1989), 565–592.

70. See esp. Kenneth J. Arrow, "Risk Perception in Psychology and Economics," *Economic Inquiry*, 20 (January 1982), 1–9. A useful compilation of articles on behavioral anomalies and the perception of risk is Daniel Kahneman and Amos Tversky, eds., *Choices, Values, and Frames* (Cambridge: Cambridge University Press, 2000). See also Paul Slovic, *The Perception of Risk* (Sterling, Va.: Earthscan Publications, 2000); W. Kip Viscusi and Wesley A. Magat, *Learning about Risk: Consumer and Worker Responses to Hazard Information* (Cambridge, Mass.: Harvard University Press, 1987).

71. Dani Rodrik and Richard Zeckhauser, "The Dilemma of Government Re-

sponsiveness," *Journal of Policy Analysis and Management,* 7, no. 4 (1988), 601–620. See also Robert C. Merton and Zvi Bodie, "On the Management of Financial Guarantees," *Financial Management,* 21, no. 4 (Winter 1992), esp. 103 (regarding the "paradox of power"); Finn E. Kydland and Edward C. Prescott, "Rules Rather Than Discretion: The Inconsistency of Optimal Plans," *Journal of Political Economy,* 85, no. 3 (June 1977), esp. 474, 477.

72. Quoted in Bob Benenson, "Insurance Finds Few Takers," *Congressional Quarterly,* 51, no. 29 (July 17, 1993), 1861. For a closely related argument in the economics literature, see Stephen Coate, "Altruism, the Samaritan's Dilemma, and Government Transfer Policy," *American Economic Review,* 85, no. 1 (March 1995), 46–57.

73. When an individual files for bankruptcy, his creditors are entitled to most of his tangible assets, such as his car, his bank account, and his stocks and bonds. But his creditors are not entitled to his human capital—that is, his future stream of income. At the end of the bankruptcy proceedings, the judge will grant him a discharge, denying his creditors any claim on his future earnings.

74. Robert C. Merton, "On the Role of Social Security as a Means for Efficient Risk Sharing in an Economy Where Human Capital Is Not Tradable," in Zvi Bodie and John B. Shoven, eds., *Financial Aspects of the United States Pension System* (Chicago: University of Chicago Press, 1983), pp. 325–358.

75. J. E. Stiglitz, "On the Relevance or Irrelevance of Public Financial Policy: Indexation, Price Rigidities, and Optimal Monetary Policies," in Rudiger Dornbush and Mario Henrique Simonsen, eds., *Inflation, Debt, and Indexation* (Cambridge, Mass.: MIT Press, 1983), p. 186. See also Stanley Fischer, "Welfare Aspects of Government Issue of Indexed Bonds," in Dornbush and Simonsen, *Inflation, Debt, and Indexation,* pp. 229–230.

76. Stiglitz, "On the Relevance or Irrelevance of Public Financial Policy," p. 186.

77. See, e.g., Lewis, *Congressional Record* (House), 74th Cong., 1st sess., July 17, 1935, p. 11337, reading Murray W. Latimer, *Industrial Pension Systems in the United States and Canada* (New York: Industrial Relations Counselors, 1932), p. 106; Shipstead, *Congressional Record* (Senate), 74th Cong., 1st sess., June 18, 1935, p. 9523; Frances Perkins's testimony, *Economic Security Act: Hearings before the Committee on Ways and Means on H.R. 4120,* House of Representatives, 74th Cong., 1st sess., p. 179.

78. Milton Friedman, *A Program for Monetary Stability* (New York: Fordham University Press, 1960), p. 6.

79. A. C. Pigou, *Wealth and Welfare* (London: Macmillan, 1912), pp. 162–165. Although Pigou was not the first scholar to identify the problem of exter-

nalities, he offered a more careful and systematic treatment than anyone else had before. Perhaps the first expression of the concept dates back to 1887, when the British political economist Henry Sidgwick briefly noted the potential for divergence between individual and social utility. See Henry Sidgwick, *The Principles of Political Economy* (London: Macmillan, 1887), p. 410.

80. See, e.g., Richard J. Zeckhauser and W. Kip Viscusi, "The Risk Management Dilemma," *Annals of the American Academy of Political and Social Science*, 545 (May 1996), esp. 144–146.

81. If anything, this example is overly optimistic regarding the effect of pooling on aggregate risk, since it excludes even the possibility of moral hazard. In reality, risk pooling might very well *increase* aggregate risk by tempting merchants and their ship captains to take fewer precautions in preparing for their voyages and to exercise less care while out on the high seas.

82. One important disadvantage of trying to address adverse selection by compelling coverage at an average premium is that it will inevitably make some low-risk individuals worse off (by forcing them to pay more for the coverage than they were willing to pay in the absence of compulsion). Policy enthusiasts might argue that this is but a minor complication, since lawmakers could still make *everyone* better off simply by taxing the biggest winners (high-risk individuals) and transferring the proceeds to the biggest losers (low-risk individuals). Unfortunately, the essence of the underlying asymmetric-information problem is that outsiders, including the government itself, cannot distinguish high-risk from low-risk people. A policy of redistribution from winners to losers would thus be impossible. Compulsory insurance, in other words, can help to address the primary symptom of adverse selection (i.e., the disintegration of insurance pools) but not the disease itself (i.e., asymmetric information). It is conceivable, however, that the existence of a compulsory insurance regime might dampen complaints from those in the low-risk category by discouraging individual participants from trying to determine their own risk status. To be sure, such information would be less valuable to them under a compulsory than under a voluntary insurance regime. As Ronald Coase has suggested (in a somewhat different context), "[i]nformation needed for transactions which cannot be carried out will not be collected." See R. H. Coase, *The Firm, the Market, and the Law* (Chicago: University of Chicago Press, 1988), p. 178.

83. On information provision as a strategy for addressing systematic biases in risk estimation, see, e.g., Paul R. Kleindorfer, Howard C. Kunreuther, and Paul J. H. Schoemaker, *Decision Sciences: An Integrative Perspective* (Cam-

bridge: Cambridge University Press, 1993), pp. 361–367. See also Viscusi and Magat, *Learning about Risk.*

84. Merton, "Role of Social Security," esp. p. 328.

3. Limited Liability

1. Quoted in Henry Winthrop Ballantine, *Ballantine on Corporations* (Chicago: Callaghan and Company, 1927), p. 6n11.
2. Nicholas Murray Butler, *Why Should We Change Our Form of Government? Studies in Practical Politics* (New York: Charles Scribner's Sons, 1912), p. 82.
3. "Limited or Unlimited Liability," *Economist,* July 1, 1854, p. 698. Although the editors expected that a limited liability statute would have little effect, they did not oppose its enactment since it would bring the law into line with practice and since "no national misfortune or loss can arise" (p. 699).
4. "The Ownership of British Industrial Capital," *Economist,* December 18, 1926, p. 1053.
5. See, e.g., Roger E. Meiners, James S. Mofsky, and Robert D. Tollison, "Piercing the Veil of Limited Liability," *Delaware Journal of Corporate Law,* 4 (1979), 351–367; Phillip I. Blumberg, "Limited Liability and Corporate Groups," *Journal of Corporation Law* (Summer 1986), 574–631; David W. Leebron, "Limited Liability, Tort Victims, and Creditors," *Columbia Law Review,* 91 (November 1991), 1565–1650; Henry Hansmann and Reinier Kraakman, "Toward Unlimited Shareholder Liability for Corporate Torts," *Yale Law Journal,* 100 (1991), 1879–1934.
6. U.S. Department of Commerce, *Historical Statistics of the United States, Colonial Times to 1970* (Washington, D.C.: GPO, 1975), pt. 2, ser. U-190–196, p. 886. See also Jeffrey A. Frankel, "The 1807–1809 Embargo against Britain," *Journal of Economic History,* 42, no. 2 (June 1982), 291–308.
7. Ronald E. Seavoy, *The Origins of the American Business Corporation, 1784–1855* (Westport, Conn.: Greenwood Press, 1982), pp. 62–66.
8. E. Merrick Dodd, "The Evolution of Limited Liability in American Industry: Massachusetts," *Harvard Law Review,* 61 (1948), 1355. See also George Heberton Evans, Jr., *Business Incorporations in the United States, 1800–1943* (New York: National Bureau of Economic Research, 1948), esp. chap. 3 ("The Period of the Special Charter"), pp. 10–30.
9. L. Ray Gunn, *The Decline of Authority: Public Economic Policy and Political Development in New York State, 1800–1860* (Ithaca, N.Y.: Cornell University Press, 1988), p. 99. See also Charles Sellers, *The Market Revolution: Jacksonian America, 1815–1846* (New York: Oxford University Press, 1991). "Nowhere," writes Sellers, "had market relationships evolved more

fully than in New York. . . . Nowhere had the market's explosive expansion made people so conscious of the linkage between public policy and economic consequences" (pp. 108–109).

10. Seavoy, *Origins of the American Business Corporation*, pp. 62–66; Gunn, *Decline of Authority*, pp. 100–101.

11. Act of March 22, 1811, New York Laws, 1811, ch. 67, pp. 151–152. General incorporation statutes for public service organizations (such as religious congregations and educational institutions) had been enacted in many states in the late eighteenth century. Some states had also enacted general incorporation laws for turnpike and canal companies. North Carolina enacted an incorporation statute for canal companies as early as 1795. But New York's 1811 statute was apparently the first general incorporation law for manufacturing firms. See Phillip I. Blumberg, "Limited Liability and Corporate Groups," *Journal of Corporation Law*, 11 (Summer 1986), 593n133; Seavoy, *Origins of the American Business Corporation*, esp. pp. 9–38, 282; Pauline Maier, "The Revolutionary Origins of the American Corporation," *William and Mary Quarterly*, 3d ser., 50, no. 1 (January 1993), 56–57; Margaret G. Myers, *A Financial History of the United States* (New York: Columbia University Press, 1970), p. 103. On manufacturing promotion and the 1811 statute, see also Ronald E. Seavoy, "Laws to Encourage Manufacturing: New York Policy and the 1811 General Incorporation Statute," *Business History Review*, 46, no. 1 (Spring 1972), 85–95.

12. W. C. Kessler, "A Statistical Study of the New York General Incorporation Act of 1811," *Journal of Political Economy*, 48, no. 6 (December 1940), 879, table 1; Victor S. Clark, *History of Manufactures in the United States* (New York: McGraw-Hill, 1929), 1:266–267. On the number of incorporations across states, see also Evans, *Business Incorporations in the United States, 1800–1943*, esp. p. 12, table 6; William C. Kessler, "Incorporation in New England: A Statistical Study, 1800–1875," *Journal of Economic History*, 8, no. 1 (May 1948), 46–47, tables 1 and 2; Clive Day, "The Early Development of the American Cotton Manufacture," *Quarterly Journal of Economics*, 39, no. 3 (May 1925), 460; Edwin Merrick Dodd, *American Business Corporations until 1860, with Special Reference to Massachusetts* (Cambridge, Mass.: Harvard University Press, 1954), pp. 400–401 and n29.

13. Stewart Kyd, *A Treatise on the Law of Corporations* (London: Printed for J. Butterworth, 1793), 1:13.

14. *Trustees of Dartmouth College v. Woodward*, 17 U.S. 518, 636 (1819). On the changing conception of the corporation over time, see Herbert Hovenkamp, "The Classical Corporation in American Legal Thought," *Georgetown Law Journal*, 76 (June 1988), 1593–1689.

15. Act of March 22, 1811, New York Laws, ch. 57, sec. 7, p. 152.

16. Quoted from *Slee v. Bloom*, 19 Johns 456, 473–474 (1822), in Stanley E.

Howard, "Stockholders' Liability under the New York Act of March 22, 1811," *Journal of Political Economy*, 46 (August 1938), 508, emphasis added.

17. Although at least two other students of the subject have come to the same conclusion—that Spencer's words seemed to suggest limited liability—one could certainly read Spencer's ambiguous language the other way (i.e., as a statement of double, rather than single, liability). See esp. Howard, "Stockholders' Liability," pp. 508–510; Seavoy, *Origins of the American Business Corporation*, pp. 69–71.

18. *Briggs v. Penniman*, 8 Cowen (N.Y. Com. Law) 387, 392 (1826).

19. Ibid., 396. See also Howard, "Stockholders' Liability," pp. 508–514. On John C. Spencer, see L. B. Proctor, *The Bench and Bar of New York* (New York: Diossy & Company, 1870), pp. 304–353.

20. Evans, *Business Incorporations*, p. 12, table 6; Kessler, "Incorporation in New England," p. 46, table 1; Clark, *History of Manufactures*, pp. 266–267; Day, "Early Development of the American Cotton Manufacture," p. 460; Gunn, *Decline of Authority*, pp. 44–46.

21. Shaw Livermore, "Unlimited Liability in Early American Corporations," *Journal of Political Economy*, 43, no. 5 (October 1935), 685.

22. Caroline F. Ware, *The Early New England Cotton Manufacture* (Boston: Houghton Mifflin, 1931), p. 301.

23. Act of March 3, 1809, Massachusetts Laws, 1806–1809, ch. 65, p. 464.

24. *Tippets v. Walker*, 4 Mass. 595 (1808); *Commonwealth v. Blue-Hill Turnpike Corporation*, 5 Mass. 420 (1809); *Spear v. Grant*, 16 Mass. 9 (1819); *Wood v. Dummer*, 3 Mass. 308 (1824). See also Joseph K. Angell and Samuel Ames, *A Treatise on the Law of Private Corporations Aggregate* (New York: Arno Press, 1972 [1832]), p. 349; Dale A. Oesterle, "Formative Contributions to American Corporate Law by the Massachusetts Supreme Judicial Court from 1806 to 1810," in Russell K. Osgood, ed., *The History of the Law in Massachusetts: The Supreme Judicial Court, 1692–1992* (Boston: Supreme Judicial Court Historical Society, 1992), pp. 148–149; Dodd, "Evolution of Limited Liability," pp. 1358–59.

25. Dodd, *American Business Corporations*, pp. 392–393 and n2; Clark, *History of Manufactures*, pp. 529–577.

26. Clark, *History of Manufactures in the United States*, esp. pp. 39–44 ("Land Grants, Loans, and Lotteries in Aid of Manufactures"). See also Oscar Handlin and Mary Flug Handlin, *Commonwealth: A Study of the Role of Government in the American Economy: Massachusetts, 1774–1861* (New York: New York University Press, 1947), chap. 3 ("To Encourage Industry and Economy"), pp. 53–92.

27. See A. R. Spofford, "Lotteries in American History," American Historical Association *Annual Report* (1892), 173–174; Ronald Rychlak, "Lotteries,

Revenues, and Social Costs: A Historical Examination of State-Sponsored Gambling," *Boston College Law Review,* 34 (December 1992), 24.

28. Handlin and Handlin, *Commonwealth,* pp. 73–74.

29. Blumberg, "Limited Liability and Corporate Groups," pp. 588–589; Seavoy, *Origins of the American Business Corporation,* esp. chap. 2 ("Internal Improvement Corporations"), pp. 39–52; E. Merrick Dodd, "The Evolution of Limited Liability in American Industry: Massachusetts," *Harvard Law Review,* 61 (1948), esp. 1353–54; Oscar and Mary Handlin, "Origins of the American Business Corporation," *Journal of Economic History,* 5 (May 1945), esp. 8–9.

30. Ware, *Early New England Cotton Manufacture,* chap. 3 ("Embargo and War"), pp. 39–59; Benjamin W. Labaree, "The Search for Recovery: New England Outports after the War of 1812: Newburyport as a Case Study," in Conrad Edick Wright, ed., *Massachusetts and the New Nation* (Boston: Massachusetts Historical Society, 1992), esp. pp. 57–59.

31. *Remarks Made in the Senate upon the Manufacturing Bill by Hon. Messrs Hastings & Pickering* (1830), pamphlet, p. 9.

32. Ware, *Early New England Cotton Manufacture,* p. 60; Jonathan Prude, *The Coming of Industrial Order: Town and Factory Life in Rural Massachusetts, 1810–1860* (New York: Cambridge University Press, 1983), p. 51.

33. Quoted in Ware, *Early New England Cotton Manufacture,* pp. 62–63.

34. Seavoy, *Origins of the American Business Corporation,* pp. 97–98.

35. Dodd, *American Business Corporations until 1860,* esp. pp. 392n1, 398–399, 399n23, 409, and 419–420. See also *Remarks Made in the Senate upon the Manufacturing Bill by Hon. Messrs Hastings & Pickering,* p. 6.

36. On Levi Lincoln, Jr.'s, life, see esp. *A Memorial of Levi Lincoln, the Governor of Massachusetts from 1825 to 1834* (Boston: J. E. Farwell & Company, 1868); Emory Washburn, *Memoir of Hon. Levi Lincoln* (Cambridge, Mass.: J. Wilson, 1869).

37. "Governor's Speech," June 2, 1825, in *Resolves of the General Court of the Commonwealth of Massachusetts,* May 25–June 18, 1825, pp. 192–194.

38. Ibid., p. 194.

39. On New York's early experiment with proportional liability, see Livermore, "Unlimited Liability in Early Corporations," p. 683.

40. Act of March 10, 1827, Massachusetts Laws, 1827, ch. 137, p. 547.

41. *Reasons for Repealing the Laws of Massachusetts, Which Render the Members of Manufacturing Companies Personally Liable for Their Debts,* pamphlet (Boston: Dutton and Wentworth Printers, 1830), p. 5. In 1830, $8 million represented a significant amount of manufacturing capital for Massachusetts to lose. As of 1840, the total capital invested in all cotton textile production across the United States totaled only $51 million, and (according to one estimate) the total capital invested in all manufacturing operations

totaled only $268 million. See J. Leander Bishop, *A History of American Manufactures from 1608 to 1860* (Philadelphia: Edward Young & Co., 1868), 2:419.

42. *Remarks Made in the Senate upon the Manufacturing Bill by Hon. Messrs Hastings & Pickering*, p. 6.

43. "Governor's Message," in *Resolves of the General Court of the Commonwealth of Massachusetts*, January 6–March 13, 1830, p. 230.

44. See *Bank of Augusta v. Earle*, 38 U.S. 519, 588–589 (1839); Dodd, *American Business Corporations*, pp. 46–57; Hovenkamp, "Classical Corporation," p. 1649; Ballantine, *Ballantine on Corporations*, p. 846.

45. *Remarks Made in the Senate upon the Manufacturing Bill by Hon. Messrs Hastings & Pickering*, p. 9.

46. "Governor's Speech" (1825), pp. 193–194.

47. *Andover and Medford Turnpike Corporation v. Gould*, 5 Mass. 40, 44–45 (1809), as cited in Oesterle, "Formative Contributions to American Corporate Law," p. 151.

48. *Petition of the Directors of the "Salem Mill-Dam Corporation,"* May 31, 1826, handwritten petition in the Massachusetts State Archives.

49. "Governor's Message" (1830), pp. 229–230.

50. "Substance of Mr. Lowell's Remarks," *Boston Daily Advertiser*, February 20, 1830.

51. "Remarks by Mr. Brooks of Bernardston, on the subject of individual liability in Manufacturing Corporations," *Boston Daily Advertiser*, February 25, 1830. On the related notion that corporations themselves "were particularly well suited to republics," see Maier, "Revolutionary Origins of the American Corporation," p. 75.

52. *Reasons for Repealing the Laws of Massachusetts*, pp. 5–6. See also, e.g., *Remarks Made in the Senate upon the Manufacturing Bill by Hon. Messrs Hastings & Pickering*, p. 12.

53. *Remarks Made in the Senate upon the Manufacturing Bill by Hon. Messrs Hastings & Pickering*, p. 18.

54. "Governor's Message" (1830), p. 229.

55. *Remarks Made in the Senate upon the Manufacturing Bill by Hon. Messrs Hastings & Pickering*, p. 11.

56. On the economic downturn of 1829–30, see Clark, *History of Manufactures in the United States*, pp. 545, 566–567; Ware, *Early New England Cotton Manufacture*, pp. 147–148.

57. "Substance of Mr. Lowell's Remarks," February 20, 1830. See also "Remarks by Mr. Brooks," February 25, 1830.

58. *Remarks Made in the Senate upon the Manufacturing Bill by Hon. Messrs Hastings & Pickering*, p. 4.

59. "Mr. Sturgis' Speech on the Bill Defining the General Powers and Duties of

Manufacturing Corporations," *Boston Daily Advertiser,* March 3, 1830. On Representative Sturgis's personal holdings of manufacturing shares, see "Remarks of William Sturgis," *Boston Daily Advertiser,* February 27, 1830.

60. "Mr. Sturgis' Speech," March 3, 1830.

61. Act of February 23, 1830, Massachusetts Laws, 1830, ch. 53, Manufacturing Corporations Act, pp. 325, 328. As the quoted passage suggests, the 1830 law did qualify the grant of limited liability in a number of ways. Two qualifications stand out as especially important. Under the law, shareholders remained jointly and severally liable until the whole capital stock had been paid in (p. 328); and, even more striking, directors would remain jointly and severally liable for all debts that exceeded the paid-in capital stock (p. 329).

62. Act of February 17, 1848, New York Laws, 1848, ch. 40.

63. Seavoy, *Origins of the American Business Corporation,* p. 195.

64. See esp. Maier, "Revolutionary Origins of the American Corporation," p. 76; Seavoy, *Origins of the American Business Corporation,* pp. 180–181.

65. Act of May 15, 1851, An Act Relating to Joint Stock Companies, Massachusetts Laws, 1851, ch. 133, p. 633; Act of July 7, 1866, New Hampshire Laws, 1866, ch. 4224, p. 3246.

66. See especially Dodd, *American Business Corporations,* pp. 391–437; Stephen Goldfarb, "Laws Governing the Incorporation of Manufacturing Companies Passed by Southern State Legislatures before the Civil War," *Southern Studies,* 24, no. 4 (Winter 1985), esp. 410–411, table 2.

67. Blumberg, "Limited Liability and Corporate Groups," pp. 597–599.

68. See, e.g., New York Laws of 1970, ch. 974, sec. 1; "Shareholder Liability in Professional Legal Corporations: A Survey of the States," *University of Pittsburgh Law Review,* 47 (Spring 1986), 817; Jerome Medalie, "Supreme Judicial Court Rule 3:18: Incorporation of Attorneys," *Massachusetts Law Quarterly,* 55 (1970), 153.

69. See esp. Susan Pace Hamill, "The Origins behind the Limited Liability Company," *Ohio State Law Journal,* 59 (1998), 1459–1522.

70. Dodd, *American Business Corporations,* pp. 400–402, 406–407. See also Kevin F. Forbes, "Limited Liability and the Development of the Business Corporation," *Journal of Law, Economics, and Organization,* 2 (1986), esp. 168–170. Using regression analysis, Forbes has found a positive correlation between the existence of limited liability law in Massachusetts and the number of incorporations in that state's textile industry over the period 1811–1842.

71. Phillip I. Blumberg, "The Corporate Entity in an Era of Multinational Corporations," *Delaware Journal of Corporate Law,* 15 (Spring 1990), 294–295 and n25.

72. On the role of merchants in financing early American manufacturing corporations, see esp. Lance E. Davis, "Stock Ownership in the Early New England Textile Industry," *Business History Review,* 32 (Summer 1958), 204–222.

73. Although scholars have found it difficult to document the precise impact of limited liability law on early industrialization in the United States, attempts have been made to assess the impact elsewhere. See esp. Stephen Haber, "The Efficiency Consequences of Institutional Change: Financial Market Regulation and Industrial Productivity Growth in Brazil, 1866–1934," in John H. Coatsworth and Alan M. Taylor, eds., *Latin America and the World Economy since 1800* (Cambridge, Mass.: Harvard University Press, 1998), pp. 275–322, which suggests that the introduction of limited liability law played an important role in promoting Brazilian textile production during the late nineteenth and early twentieth centuries.

74. Dodd, "Evolution of Limited Liability," pp. 1378–79.

75. For an early statement of this view, see Arthur T. Hadley, *Railroad Transportation: Its History and Its Laws* (New York: G. P. Putnam's Sons, 1900), esp. pp. 43–47.

76. Herman E. Krooss and Martin R. Blyn, *A History of Financial Intermediaries* (New York: Random House, 1971), p. 86.

77. John Hicks, "Limited Liability: The Pros and Cons," in Tony Orhnial, ed., *Limited Liability and the Corporation* (London: Croom Helm, 1982), p. 12. See also, e.g., *Anderson v. Abbott,* 321 U.S. 359, 362 (1944).

78. Butler, *Why Should We Change Our Form of Government,* p. 82.

79. *Commonwealth v. Blue-Hill Turnpike Corporation,* 5 Mass. 420 (1809). See also Oesterle, "Formative Contributions to American Corporate Law," pp. 148–149; Dodd, "Evolution of Limited Liability," pp. 1358–59.

80. Oesterle, "Formative Contributions to American Corporate Law," p. 148.

81. Lawrence M. Friedman, *A History of American Law* (New York: Simon and Schuster, 1985), p. 299. See also Gary T. Schwartz, "The Character of Early American Tort Law," *UCLA Law Review,* 36 (April 1989), 641–718.

82. *State v. Minnesota Thresher Manuf'g Co.,* 40 Minn. 213, 222 (1889).

83. "Report of the Committee on Revision of the Corporation Laws," *California State Bar Journal,* 3, no. 3 (September 1928), 15.

84. Minutes of the California State Bar Committee on Revision of the Corporation Laws, June 25 and July 9, 1928.

85. See also Fabius M. Clarke, *California Corporation Law Governing Ordinary Business Corporations* (San Francisco: Bender-Moss Company, 1916), esp. pp. 359–414; D.S.C., "Corporations: Limited Liability: Amendments of the California Constitution and Code," *California Law Review,* 17 (1928–29), 276–281; William H. Gorrill, "What the State Legislature Did for Corpora-

tion Law Revision," *California State Bar Journal,* 3 (June 1929), 262–264; Henry Winthrop Ballantine, "Major Changes in California Corporation Law," *California State Bar Journal,* 6 (July 1931), 159–164; Henry Winthrop Ballantine, "Questions of Policy in Drafting a Modern Corporation Law," *California Law Review,* 19, no. 5 (July 1931), 465–485. For an alternative view of the introduction of limited liability in California, which suggests that the change may have had less effect than expected, see Mark I. Weinstein, "Limited Liability in California: 1928–1931," unpublished paper, September 15, 2000.

86. D.S.C., "Corporations: Limited Liability," p. 277.

87. "Governor's Speech" (1825), pp. 193–194.

88. Although interpersonal utilities are not technically comparable, the general conclusion that gains to shareholders are likely to outweigh losses to creditors (even if unprovable) seems eminently reasonable from a practical standpoint.

89. Alexander Hamilton, "Idea Concerning a Lottery," in *The Papers of Alexander Hamilton,* ed. Harold C. Syrett, vol. 13 (November 1792–February 1793) (New York: Columbia University Press, 1967), p. 518.

90. "The Lottery," *Ladies Companion,* 7 (June 1837), 81. Also quoted in John Samuel Ezell, *Fortune's Merry Wheel: The Lottery in America* (Cambridge, Mass.: Harvard University Press, 1960), p. 216. On the notion that "most gambling is . . . due to a taste for adventure or a failure to know or comprehend the odds," see, e.g., Mancur Olson, "Why Some Welfare-State Redistribution to the Poor Is a Great Idea," in Charles K. Rowley, ed., *Democracy and Public Choice: Essays in Honor of Gordon Tullock* (New York: Basil Blackwell, 1987), esp. pp. 209–210.

91. Adam Smith, *An Inquiry into the Nature and Causes of the Wealth of Nations* (Chicago: University of Chicago Press, 1976 [1776]), bk. 1, pp. 120–121.

92. Stanley Elkins and Eric McKitrick, *The Age of Federalism* (New York: Oxford University Press, 1993), esp. p. 262; Joseph Stancliffe Davis, *Essays in the Earlier History of American Corporations* (Cambridge, Mass.: Harvard University Press, 1917), essay 3 ("The 'S.U.M.': The First New Jersey Business Corporation"); "An ACT to incorporate the Contributors to the Society for establishing useful Manufactures, and for the further Encouragement of the said Society," November 22, 1791, Acts of the General Assembly of the State of New Jersey, ch. 346, sec. 6, p. 732, and sec. 25, p. 741. Although the charter itself was silent on the issue of shareholder liability, the corporation scholar Joseph S. Davis concluded that limited liability was implied. See John W. Cadman, Jr., *The Corporation in New Jersey: Business and Politics, 1791–1875* (Cambridge, Mass.: Harvard University Press, 1949), p. 39. On Hamilton's use of the term "adventurers," see Ham-

ilton, "Idea Concerning a Lottery," p. 518; Cadman, *The Corporation in New Jersey*, p. 39.

93. Krooss and Blyn, *History of Financial Intermediaries*, p. 76; Rychlak, "Lotteries," p. 30; Ezell, *Fortune's Merry Wheel*, p. 84.

94. John Maynard Keynes, *The General Theory of Employment, Interest, and Money* (New York: Harcourt Brace Jovanovich, 1964 [1936]), p. 150. See also Smith, *Wealth of Nations*, bk. I, chap. 10, pt. 1, p. 124; Frank Knight, Discussion, *American Economic Review*, 44, no. 2 (May 1954), Papers and Proceedings of the Sixty-sixth Annual Meeting of the American Economic Association, 63.

95. Milton Friedman and L. J. Savage, "The Utility Analysis of Choices Involving Risk," *Journal of Political Economy*, 56, no. 4 (August 1948), 286. See also Adolf A. Berle, "The Impact of the Corporation on Classical Economic Theory," *Quarterly Journal of Economics*, 79, no. 1 (February 1965), 38.

96. Gerard Baker, "Greenspan Says Internet Stocks Have the Appeal of a Lottery," *Financial Times*, January 29, 1999, sec. 1, p. 1; Alan Greenspan, Hearing of the Senate Committee on the Budget, Federal News Service, January 28, 1999.

97. See esp. David W. Leebron, "Limited Liability, Tort Victims, and Creditors," *Columbia Law Review*, 91, no. 7 (November 1991), 1565–1650; Henry Hansmann and Reinier Kraakman, "Toward Unlimited Shareholder Liability for Corporate Torts," *Yale Law Journal*, 100 (1991), 1879–1934.

98. See esp. Michael C. Jensen and William H. Meckling, "Theory of the Firm: Managerial Behavior, Agency Costs, and Ownership Structure," *Journal of Financial Economics*, 3 (1976), 331.

99. See Dodd, "Evolution of Limited Liability," p. 1379; Alfred D. Chandler, Jr., *The Visible Hand: The Managerial Revolution in American Business* (Cambridge, Mass.: Harvard University Press, 1977), pp. 92–93. See also Davis, "Stock Ownership in the Early New England Textile Industry," pp. 214–215.

100. See esp. Henry G. Manne, "Our Two Corporation Systems: Law and Economics," *Virginia Law Review*, 53 (March 1967), esp. 262; Janet Cooper Alexander, "Unlimited Shareholder Liability through a Procedural Lens," *Harvard Law Review*, 106 (December 1992), 387–445.

101. In 1998, for example, households and nonprofit organizations in the United States held individual stocks worth $6.3 trillion. Their holdings of mutual fund shares, most of which were likely diversified, totaled only $2.5 trillion. Involvement in pension funds has certainly helped the cause of diversification. By 1998, pension fund reserves totaled $8.7 trillion. *Flow of Funds Accounts of the United States: Annual Flows and Outstandings,*

1991–1998 (Washington, D.C.: Board of Governors of the Federal Reserve System, June 11, 1999), p. 54, table L.100.

102. See esp. Daniel Kahneman and Amos Tversky, "Prospect Theory: An Analysis of Decision under Risk," *Econometrica*, 47, no. 2 (March 1979), 283; Howard Raiffa, "Preferences for Multi-Attributed Alternatives," Memorandum RM-5868-DOT/RC (Santa Monica: Rand Corporation, April 1969), esp. pp. 81–95; Milton C. Weinstein and Robert J. Quinn, "Psychological Considerations in Valuing Health Risk Reductions," *Natural Resources Journal*, 23 (July 1983), esp. 665–673. For a discussion of the "rational" outcome, see Milton C. Weinstein, Donald S. Shepard, and Joseph S. Pliskin, "The Economic Value of Changing Mortality Probabilities: A Decision-Theoretic Approach," *Quarterly Journal of Economics*, 94, no. 2 (March 1980), esp. 382–385.

103. "Limited or Unlimited Liability," *Economist*, July 1, 1854, p. 698. There is also evidence from eighteenth-century Britain on the existence of all-equity firms, which effectively limited the liability of shareholders by forgoing debt and thus eliminating any possibility of default (except on obligations to involuntary creditors). See esp. Margaret Patterson and David Reiffen, "The Effect of the Bubble Act on the Market for Joint Stock Shares," *Journal of Economic History*, 50, no. 1 (March 1990), 167–168.

104. *Commonwealth v. Blue-Hill Turnpike Corporation*, 5 Mass. 420 (1809).

105. In fact, there is limited evidence that voluntary creditors were actually given preference over involuntary ones in the enactment and adjudication of liability law. See esp. *Heacock v. Sherman*, 14 Wend. (N.Y.) 58 (1835); *Chase v. Curtis & Another*, 113 U.S. 452, 462–463 (1885); Hovenkamp, "Classical Corporation," p. 1657; Ballantine, *Ballantine on Corporations*, pp. 702–703.

106. Roger E. Meiners, James S. Mofsky, and Robert D. Tollison, "Piercing the Veil of Limited Liability," *Delaware Journal of Corporate Law*, 4 (1979), 364.

107. Ibid., p. 352. For the conceptual basis of this claim, see R. H. Coase, "The Problem of Social Cost," *Journal of Law and Economics*, 3 (October 1960), esp. 10, 13.

108. The existence of transaction costs would only strengthen this effect. Even relatively mild transaction costs associated with opting out of limited liability (through pledges of personal security) would now give shareholders a good excuse for not wanting to do so.

109. See, e.g., "Governor's Message" (1830), pp. 228–229; "Remarks by Mr. Brooks of Bernardston, on the subject of individual liability in Manufacturing Corporations," *Boston Daily Advertiser*, February 25, 1830.

110. Hansmann and Kraakman, "Toward Unlimited Shareholder Liability," p. 1883.

4. Money

1. Governor DeWitt Clinton, *Journal of the Senate of the State of New York,* 42nd sess. (Albany: J. Buel, 1819), p. 11.
2. Quoted in Samuel Rezneck, "The Depression of 1819–1822: A Social History," *American Historical Review,* 39, no. 1 (October 1933), 30.
3. By the end of 1819, the value of bank notes held by the public, estimated at $47 million, was nearly ten times as large as the value of specie held by the public, estimated between $4.9 and $5.2 million. See Milton Friedman and Anna Jacobson Schwartz, *Monetary Statistics of the United States* (New York: National Bureau of Economic Research, 1970), pp. 218–219, table 13.
4. The notion of banks as insurers was first formalized in Douglas W. Diamond and Philip H. Dybvig, "Bank Runs, Deposit Insurance, and Liquidity," *Journal of Political Economy,* 91, no. 3 (June 1983), 401–419.
5. Civis, *An Appeal to the Honorable the Members of the Senate and the House of Assembly, of the State of New York* (New York, 1816), p. 6.
6. Milton Friedman, *A Program for Monetary Stability* (New York: Fordham University Press, 1960), p. 4.
7. Adam Smith, *An Inquiry into the Nature and Causes of the Wealth of Nations* (Chicago: University of Chicago Press, 1976 [1776]), bk. 1, chap. 4, p. 29.
8. C. A. E. Goodhart, *Money, Information, and Uncertainty* (New York: Harper and Row, 1975), p. 3. See also Karl Brunner and Allan H. Meltzer, "The Uses of Money: Money in the Theory of an Exchange Economy," *American Economic Review,* 61, no. 5 (December 1971), 787, 804.
9. See Diamond and Dybvig, "Bank Runs, Deposit Insurance, and Liquidity."
10. Henry Thornton, *An Enquiry into the Nature and Effects of the Paper Credit of Great Britain* (New York: Farrar & Rinehart, 1939 [1802]), p. 171.
11. F. M. Taylor, "The Objects and Methods of Currency Reform in the United States," *Quarterly Journal of Economics,* 12, no. 3 (April 1898), 340.
12. Message from Governor William H. Seward, January 7, 1840, *Journal of the Assembly of the State of New York,* 63rd sess. (Albany: E. Croswell, 1840), p. 20.
13. Annual Message of the Governor, January 6, 1829, *Journal of the Senate of the State of New York,* 52nd sess. (Albany: E. Croswell, 1829), p. 10.
14. See, e.g., *Report of the Committee on Banks and Insurance Companies, made to the Assembly, February 13, 1829* [commonly known as the Paige Report] (Albany: Croswell & Van Benthuysen, 1829), p. 14. See also David Ricardo, *Proposals for an Economical and Secure Currency: With Observations on the Profits of the Bank of England, as They Regard the Public and the Proprietors of Bank Stock,* 2nd ed. (London: J. Murray, 1816), pp. 35–36.

15. *Journal of the Assembly of the State of New York,* 52nd sess. (Albany: E. Croswell, 1829), p. 176. See also Sister Mary Grace Madeleine, *Monetary and Banking Theories of Jacksonian Democracy* (Philadelphia: Dolphin Press, 1943), esp. pp. x–xi, 145, 152.

16. *Journal of the Assembly, 1829,* p. 176. See also Michael D. Bordo and Anna J. Schwartz, "Money and Prices in the Nineteenth Century: An Old Debate Rejoined," *Journal of Economic History,* 40, no. 1 (March 1980), 61–67. The British monetary expert Henry Thornton implicitly agreed with Forman's assessment. See Thornton, *An Enquiry into the Nature and Effects of the Paper Credit of Great Britain,* esp. pp. 199–200, 247–249.

17. See, e.g., *Journal of the Assembly, 1829,* pp. 174, 176. On the common practice of effectively converting short-term debt into long-term debt, see Bray Hammond, "Long and Short Term Credit in Early American Banking," *Quarterly Journal of Economics,* 49, no. 1 (November 1934), 89–90.

18. See Neil Wallace, "Narrow Banking Meets the Diamond-Dybvig Model," *Quarterly Review,* Federal Reserve Bank of Minneapolis (Winter 1996), 9.

19. Hammond, "Long and Short Term Credit in Early American Banking," p. 102.

20. Charles Sellers, *The Market Revolution: Jacksonian America, 1815–1846* (New York: Oxford University Press, 1991), p. 45.

21. Naomi Lamoreaux, *Insider Lending: Banks, Personal Connections, and Economic Development in Industrial New England* (Cambridge: Cambridge University Press, 1994), p. 82. Because capital stock often accounted for more than a third (and in some cases up to two-thirds) of a bank's total liabilities, Lamoreaux has characterized these early banks as "investment clubs," which "enabled small savers to buy shares in a diversified portfolio of investments" (p. 82).

22. Guido Calabresi and John Hirschoff, "Toward a Test for Strict Liability in Torts," *Yale Law Journal,* 81 (1972), 1083.

23. John Jay Knox, *A History of Banking in the United States* (New York: Bradford Rhodes & Company, 1903), p. 393.

24. John Cleaveland, *The Banking System of the State of New York* (New York: John S. Voorhies, 1857), pp. xv–xvi.

25. Knox, *History of Banking in the United States,* p. 398. On comparable rules in other states, see J. Van Fenstermaker, *The Development of American Commercial Banking, 1782–1837* (Kent, Ohio: Kent State University, 1965), pp. 21–22.

26. Knox, *History of Banking in the United States,* p. 391.

27. L. Carroll Root, "New York Bank Currency: Safety Fund vs. Bond Security," *Sound Currency,* 2, no. 5 (February 1895), 3.

28. See Robert E. Chaddock, *The Safety Fund Banking System in New York, 1829–1866,* National Monetary Commission, 61st Cong., 2nd sess., Senate Document 581, pp. 244–245.

29. See U.S. Department of Commerce, Bureau of the Census, *Historical Statistics of the United States, Colonial Times to 1970* (Washington, D.C.: GPO, 1975), ser. U-196 (merchandise trade deficit), E-52 (wholesale prices), and E-135 (consumer prices); Milton Friedman and Anna Jacobson Schwartz, *Monetary Statistics of the United States* (New York: National Bureau of Economic Research, 1970), pp. 218–219 (gold stock).

30. Quoted in Donald H. Kagin, "Monetary Aspects of the Treasury Notes of the War of 1812," *Journal of Economic History,* 44, no. 1 (March 1984), 79.

31. See William M. Gouge, *A Short History of Paper-Money and Banking in the United States,* 2nd ed. (New York: B & S Collins, 1835), p. 19; Fenstermaker, *Development of American Commercial Banking,* p. 111; *Historical Statistics of the United States,* ser. X-561 (which offers slightly different numbers than Fenstermaker); Friedman and Schwartz, *Monetary Statistics of the United States,* pp. 218–219.

32. See esp. Arthur Nussbaum, *A History of the Dollar* (New York: Columbia University Press, 1957), pp. 70–71; John Watt Kearny, *Sketch of American Finances, 1789–1835* (New York: G. P. Putnam's Sons, 1887), pp. 107–108; Kagin, "Monetary Aspects of the Treasury Notes of the War of 1812," pp. 81–86.

33. For wholesale and consumer price indices, see *Historical Statistics of the United States,* ser. E-52 and E-135. Discount rates on state bank notes surged almost everywhere except New England, where strict laws (including a 12 percent annual penalty for nonpayment of notes) apparently prevented depreciation relative to specie. See "Report on the Causes and Extent of the Present General Distress, read January 29th, 1820," Pennsylvania Senate Committee, quoted in Gouge, *Short History of Paper-Money and Banking in the United States,* p. 19; Knox, *History of Banking in the United States,* p. 361.

34. Albert Gallatin, "Considerations on the Currency and Banking System of the United States" (1831), reprinted in *The Writings of Albert Gallatin,* ed. Henry Adams (New York: Antiquarian Press, 1960), 3:363.

35. Margaret G. Myers, *A Financial History of the United States* (New York: Columbia University Press, 1970), p. 83; William J. Shultz, *Financial Development of the United States* (New York: Prentice-Hall, 1937), p. 181.

36. See *Journal of the Assembly of the State of New York,* 41st sess. (Albany: J. Buel, 1818), p. 15; Restraining Act of 1818, Laws of 1818, p. 242, secs. 1

and 3, reprinted in Cleaveland, *Banking System of the State of New York,* pp. 237–238.

37. Clinton, *Journal of the Senate, 1819,* p. 11. On the "embarrassed state of [the] currency," see also *Journal of the Senate, 1819,* pp. 66, 69.

38. Root, "New York Bank Currency," p. 3.

39. Knox, *History of Banking in the United States,* p. 398. See also Bray Hammond, *Banks and Politics in America from the Revolution to the Civil War* (Princeton: Princeton University Press, 1957), p. 579.

40. Jabez Hammond, *The History of Political Parties in the State of New York* (Albany: C. Van Benthuysen, 1843), 1:337, quoted in Bray Hammond, "Free Banks and Corporations: The New York Free Banking Act of 1838," *Journal of Political Economy,* 44, no. 2 (April 1936), 190. See also Hammond, *Banks and Politics in America,* pp. 578–579; Robert E. Wright, "Banking and Politics in New York, 1784–1829," Ph.D. diss. (State University of New York at Buffalo, 1996), pp. 940–941.

41. Root, "New York Bank Currency," p. 3. On the increased restrictions in bank charters, see Ralph W. Marquis and Frank P. Smith, "Double Liability for Bank Stock," *American Economic Review,* 27, no. 3 (September 1937), 493; Chaddock, *Safety Fund Banking System,* pp. 245–246; Cleaveland, *Banking System of the State of New York,* pp. xxvii–xxviii.

42. Cleaveland, *Banking System of the State of New York,* pp. xxix–xxxix; Root, "New York Bank Currency," p. 3; William H. Dillistin, *Historical Directory of the Banks of the State of New York* (New York: New York State Bankers Association, 1946), p. 105; DeWitt Clinton, *Journal of the Assembly of the State of New York,* 50th sess. (Albany: E. Croswell, 1827), p. 16; Chaddock, *Safety Fund Banking System,* p. 252.

43. Marquis and Smith, "Double Liability for Bank Stock," p. 493. By this time, New Hampshire, Pennsylvania, Massachusetts, and Rhode Island had already begun experimenting with excess liability provisions for bank shareholders. See Davis R. Dewey, *State Banking before the Civil War,* National Monetary Commission, 61st Cong., 2nd sess., Senate Document 581, pp. 117–119.

44. Marquis and Smith, "Double Liability for Bank Stock," p. 493.

45. Revised Statutes, ch. 18, pt. 1, title 2, art. 1, sec. 16, reprinted in Cleaveland, *Banking System of the State of New York,* p. 12.

46. See esp. Marquis and Smith, "Double Liability for Bank Stock," pp. 491–493.

47. For a contemporary recitation of this logic (to justify an 1825 proposal to allow individuals to engage in private banking with unlimited liability), see *Journal of the Senate of the State of New York,* 48th sess. (Albany: E. Croswell, 1825), pp. 102–103.

48. For an alternative view, see Gary Gorton, "Reputation Formation in Early Bank Note Markets," *Journal of Political Economy*, 104, no. 2 (1996), 346–397.

49. Benjamin C. Esty, "The Impact of Contingent Liability on Commercial Bank Risk-Taking," *Journal of Financial Economics*, 47 (1998), 189–218.

50. *Albany Argus and City Gazette*, February 26, 1827, p. 2. See also Representative J. Van Beuren in *Albany Argus*, March 4, 1829, p. 2.

51. Root, "New York Bank Currency," p. 3.

52. On Barker, see esp. J. T. W. Hubbard, *For Each, the Strength of All: A History of Banking in the State of New York* (New York: New York University Press, 1995), pp. 70–71. Strangely, although the Bank of Washington and Warren is widely described as having failed in 1825, its notes continued to circulate near par until 1830. See *New-York American*, bank note tables, 1825–1830.

53. Ronald Seavoy, *The Origins of the American Business Corporation, 1784–1855* (Westport, Conn.: Greenwood Press, 1982), p. 117. See also *Albany Argus*, April 4, 16, and 17, 1828.

54. *Journal of the Senate, 1829*, p. 8.

55. Martin Van Buren, *The Autobiography of Martin Van Buren*, ed. John C. Fitzpatrick (Washington, D.C.: GPO, 1920), p. 221.

56. See esp. Hubbard, *For Each, the Strength of All*, pp. 57–78.

57. *Journal of the Assembly, 1829*, p. 175.

58. Ibid., p. 174.

59. Ibid., p. 10, emphasis added.

60. Ralph C. H. Catterall, *The Second Bank of the United States* (Chicago: University of Chicago Press, 1960 [1902]), esp. pp. 96–98; Peter Temin, *The Jacksonian Economy* (New York: W. W. Norton, 1969), esp. pp. 49–53.

61. Arthur Fraas, "The Second Bank of the United States: An Instrument for an Interregional Monetary Union," *Journal of Economic History*, 34, no. 2 (June 1974), 448.

62. See esp. Hammond, *Banks and Politics in America*, p. 560; Nathaniel P. Tallmadge, *Speech of Hon. N. P. Tallmadge, Delivered in the Senate of the State of New-York, February, 1832, on the Resolution against Renewing the Charter of the Bank of the United States* (Albany: Packard and Van Bethuysen, 1832), pp. 31–33.

63. *Journal of the Assembly, 1829*, p. 177.

64. Ibid., p. 184.

65. Fritz Redlich, *The Molding of American Banking: Men and Ideas* (New York: Johnson Reprint Company, 1968), 1:92.

66. *Journal of the Assembly, 1829*, pp. 176–177, 181–182.

67. Bray Hammond, *Banks and Politics in America from the Revolution to the Civil War* (Princeton: Princeton University Press, 1957), p. 558.

68. *Journal of the Senate, 1829,* p. 9.

69. *Journal of the Assembly, 1829,* p. 178.

70. *Report of the Committee on Banks and Insurance Companies* (Paige Report, 1823), pp. 19–20, 22–23.

71. Erastus Root, "The Speeches of General Erastus Root, on the Resolution of Mr. Clayton, of Georgia, Proposing a Committee of Visitation to the Bank of the United States, delivered on the 7th, 8th, and 14th days of March, 1832, in the House of Representatives" (1832), p. 11.

72. *Albany Argus,* February 28, 1829, p. 2. See also Chaddock, *Safety Fund Banking System in New York,* pp. 264–266.

73. *Albany Argus,* February 28, 1829, p. 2.

74. *Albany Argus,* March 2, 1829, p. 2.

75. Chaddock, *Safety Fund Banking System in New York,* pp. 241–242, 267.

76. *Journal of the Assembly, 1829,* p. 923.

77. "An Act to Create a Fund for the Benefit of Certain Moneyed Corporations, and for other purposes: Passed April 2, 1829," reprinted in Cleaveland, *Banking System of the State of New York,* pp. 29–38; *Journal of the Assembly, 1829,* p. 755.

78. See, e.g., *Niles' Register,* April 11, 1829, p. 102; Root, "New York Bank Currency," p. 7. The Middle District Bank failed within months of renewing its charter in 1829 and is thus not counted as a member of the Safety Fund system. On the entry of the city banks, which involved considerable negotiation, see Chaddock, *Safety Fund Banking System in New York,* pp. 270–271; *An Examination of Some of the Provisions of the "Act to Create a Fund for the Benefit of the Creditors of Certain Monied Corporations, and for other Purposes." Passed April 1829,* By a Stockholder (1829); R. K. Moulton, *Legislative and Documentary History of the Banks of the United States* (New York: G. & C. Carvill & Co., 1834), p. 71; Redlich, *Molding of American Banking,* 1:95.

79. Redlich, *Molding of American Banking,* 1:230; Knox, *History of Banking in the United States,* pp. 355–356; Carter H. Golembe, "The Deposit Insurance Legislation of 1933: An Examination of Its Antecedents and Its Purposes," *Political Science Quarterly,* 75, no. 2 (June 1960), 182–186; Carter H. Golembe and Clark Warburton, *Insurance of Bank Obligations in Six States* (Washington, D.C.: Federal Deposit Insurance Corporation, 1958).

80. Root, "New York Bank Currency," pp. 3 and 7; Fenstermaker, *Development of American Commercial Banking,* p. 111, table A-1.

81. Root, "New York Bank Currency," p. 3; Dillistin, *Historical Directory,* p. 105.

82. See, e.g., *Annual Report of the Bank Commissioners, January 31, 1832*, Assembly Document 70, 1832, p. 10.
83. *Annual Report of the Bank Commissioners, January 31, 1833*, Assembly Document 69, 1833, pp. 5–6.
84. Chaddock, *Safety Fund Banking System in New York*, p. 276.
85. *Journal of the Assembly, 1829*, p. 184.
86. Although most bank loans in antebellum New York were for terms of not more than 90 (or, in the extreme, 180) days, it was common for such loans to be granted on the understanding that they would be rolled over again and again. Hammond described this practice as "a convenient mask for advances of long term credit." See Hammond, "Long and Short Term Credit," p. 89. See also George Tucker, *The Theory of Money and Banks Investigated* (Boston: Charles C. Little and James Brown, 1839), pp. 165–167.
87. Root, "New York Bank Currency," p. 7. The charters granted in 1834 appear to have limited note-to-capital ratios to only 1.5. Schultz, *Financial Development of the United States*, p. 206.
88. Reprinted in the *Daily Albany Argus*, March 14, 1837, p. 2.
89. See, e.g., Carl Degler, "The Locofocos: Urban 'Agrarians,'" *Journal of Economic History*, 16, no. 3 (September 1956), 322–333.
90. For descriptions of public meetings advocating this position, see *Daily Albany Argus*, March 17, 18, 28, and 31, 1837, and for reprints of editorials on this issue, *Daily Albany Argus*, March 14 and 20, 1837.
91. Reprinted in the *Daily Albany Argus*, March 14, 1837, p. 2.
92. Senate Document 55, 1837, pp. 19, 11, 12.
93. Chaddock, *Safety Fund Banking System in New York*, p. 376; Assembly Document 303, 1837, p. 9. On a related bill, see also *Daily Albany Argus*, March 20, 1837, p. 2.
94. Assembly Document 318, 1838, pp. 2–3; Root, "New York Bank Currency," p. 8; Chaddock, *Safety Fund Banking System in New York*, pp. 300–301; Knox, *History of Banking in the United States*, p. 408.
95. *Annual Report of the Comptroller, January 11, 1843*, Assembly Document 10, 1843, p. 53.
96. *Annual Report of the Bank Commissioners, January 24, 1838*, Assembly Document 71, 1838, p. 13; Root, "New York Bank Currency," p. 8. Although the Buffalo banks made it through the immediate crisis intact, all three subsequently failed in the early 1840s.
97. Early in the legislative debates over free banking, the Assembly rejected an amendment that would have incorporated free banks into the safety fund. See *Daily Albany Argus*, February 20, 1838.
98. Although the Safety Fund survived for nearly thirty more years, the panic of 1837 marked the beginning of a long decline. No new Safety Fund

banks were chartered after 1836, and the failure of eleven banks in 1840–1842 overwhelmed the resources of the fund. To ease the pressure, the legislature removed the guarantee on deposits in April 1842; but between November 1841 and April 1845, the comptroller was still unable to redeem notes regularly because the Safety Fund remained effectively insolvent. The state finally solved the problem in 1845 by issuing a stock mortgaging all future contributions to the Safety Fund, after which the notes of failed banks were soon redeemed. The Safety Fund subsequently suffered five more failures—one in 1848, one in 1854, and three in 1857. Meanwhile, the total number of participating banks continued to dwindle as Safety Fund banks steadily converted to free banks. The last Safety Fund charters expired in 1866, and with that the system quietly came to an end. Although the fund did ultimately make good on all of its commitments, many note holders of failed banks had been forced to suffer long delays and depreciation before receiving appropriate reimbursement. See Chaddock, *Safety Fund Banking System in New York,* pp. 328, 360–367; *Annual Report of the Comptroller, December 30, 1848,* Assembly Document 5, 1849, pp. 51–52; Root, "New York Bank Currency," pp. 7–10. The Safety Fund's profound weakness, which first became apparent in the early 1840s, can be attributed to various defects in the original legislation. Perhaps the most severe flaw was that mandatory contributions to the fund were based on bank capital rather than on bank liabilities (notes and deposits), which were the items being insured. See esp. Chaddock, *Safety Fund Banking System in New York,* pp. 350–354, 358–359, 387; Root, "New York Bank Currency," pp. 14–15; Knox, *History of Banking in the United States,* pp. 412–413. See also Howard Bodenhorn, "Zombie Banks and the Demise of New York's Safety Fund," *Eastern Economic Journal,* 22, no. 1 (Winter 1996), 26.

99. The constitutionality of free banks was contested in New York until a new state constitution was adopted in 1846. See Hammond, *Banks and Politics in America,* pp. 585–592. The very first free banking law in the United States was enacted in Michigan in 1837, just one year before the New York statute. On Whig ideas regarding credit, currency, and incorporation, see Glyndon G. Van Deusen, "Some Aspects of Whig Thought and Theory in the Jacksonian Period," *American Historical Review,* 63, no. 2 (January 1958), esp. 310–315.

100. An Act to Authorize the Business of Banking [Free Banking Act], New York Laws of 1838, ch. 260, p. 245, sec. 15.

101. The 1838 law required that at least half of the backing be in the form of government bonds, which were then referred to as "stock." Originally, almost all state and federal bonds qualified, but this was subsequently narrowed solely to New York State and federal bonds (thus excluding the

bonds of other states). The other half of note backing could take the form of low-risk mortgages. See Laws of 1838, ch. 260, p. 245, secs. 2, 7, and 8; Laws of 1840, ch. 363, p. 306, sec. 1; Laws of 1844, ch. 41, p. 35, sec. 1; Laws of 1848, ch. 340, p. 462, secs. 2 and 3; Laws of 1849, ch. 313, p. 455, sec. 1; Laws of 1851, ch. 164, p. 309, sec. 10; and Root, "New York Bank Currency," pp. 16–17. All of these sections are reprinted in Cleaveland, *Banking System of State of New York,* pp. 83–184. Unlike state and federal bonds, mortgages were not easily tradable on secondary markets. See esp. Margaret G. Myers, *The New York Money Market* (New York: Columbia University Press, 1931), 1:293–294; D. M. Frederiksen, "Mortgage Banking in America," *Journal of Political Economy,* 2, no. 2 (March 1894), esp. 222–223. The state's banking regulators explicitly acknowledged this problem on numerous occasions. See, e.g., *Annual Report of the Superintendent of the Banking Department,* Assembly Document 10, January 5, 1855, p. 14.

102. New York Laws of 1838, ch. 260, secs. 4, 11, and 29. The 14 percent penalty was increased to 20 percent in 1840 and then reduced to 7 percent in 1851.

103. *Daily Albany Argus,* April 4, 1838, p. 1.

104. See Madeleine, *Monetary and Banking Theories,* pp. 140, 159; Smith, *An Inquiry into the Nature and Causes of the Wealth of Nations,* bk. 2, chap. 2, pp. 323–326; Abraham H. Venit, "Isaac Bronson: His Banking Theory and the Financial Controversies of the Jacksonian Period," *Journal of Economic History,* 5, no. 2 (November 1945), 203–204; John McVickar, *Hints on Banking in a Letter to a Gentleman in Albany by a New Yorker* (New York: Vanderpool & Cole, 1827), p. 39. See also Redlich, *Molding of American Banking,* 1:194.

105. Over the years 1838 to 1863, only 34 of 449 free banks incorporated in New York State ever failed to redeem their notes at par. On average, the customers of these 34 banks lost an average of about 26 cents per dollar on bank notes in circulation. Looking across all 449 free banks, the average loss on bank notes in circulation was less than two-tenths of a cent on the dollar. See Arthur J. Rolnick and Warren E. Weber, "New Evidence on the Free Banking Era," *American Economic Review,* 73, no. 5 (December 1983), 1085 (table 2), 1088 (table 4), and 1089 (table 5).

106. Isaac Bronson, "Letter from Issac Bronson, Esq., to a Member of Congress, New York, 1832," *Financial Register of the United States* (Philadelphia: Adam Waldie, July 1838), 2, no. 1, 11–12.

107. *Journal of the Senate, 1829,* pp. 81–84. Although there were thirty-eight chartered banks as of 1828, only twenty-one were included in the 1829 legislative report.

108. Diamond and Dybvig, "Bank Runs, Deposit Insurance, and Liquidity," p. 405.

109. Eddie George, "Are Banks Still Special?" *Bank of England Quarterly Bulletin* (February 1997), 113.

110. As Naomi Lamoreaux has so convincingly demonstrated with respect to New England banks, this was not the only (or perhaps even the primary) function of antebellum banks. See Lamoreaux, *Insider Lending,* pp. 3, 64–65, 82. At that time, capital accounted for a much larger proportion of bank liabilities than it does now, meaning that banks were less dependent on bank notes and deposits for loanable funds. Capital was often an equally important source. Nonetheless, intermediation between liquid notes and deposits and illiquid loans still represented a very important bank function, even if not the only or dominant one. For a discussion of how banks in New York and Pennsylvania differed from those in New England during this period, see Robert E. Wright, "Bank Ownership and Lending Patterns in New York and Pennsylvania, 1781–1831," *Business History Review,* 73, no. 1 (Spring 1999), 40–60.

111. *Annual Report of the Bank Commissioners,* Assembly Document 29, January 26, 1842, pp. 88–90; *Annual Report of the Superintendent of the Banking Department,* Assembly Document 4, January 6, 1862, pp. 63–73. The years 1841 and 1860 were chosen for these comparisons because they cover almost the full range of free banking experience before the Civil War, because they exclude free banking's volatile start-up years, and because detailed state data (by bank type) were available for these years. Free bank deposits continued to surge after 1860, reaching $248 million at the end of 1864, yielding a deposit-to-note ratio of about 9. *Annual Report of the Superintendent of the Banking Department* (1866), pp. 82–90. All of the deposit figures cited in the text exclude interbank (and, where possible, government) deposits.

112. *Annual Report of the Bank Commissioners* (1842), p. 90; *Annual Report of the Superintendent* (1862), pp. 63–73. Non-free banks include chartered banks and Safety Fund banks.

113. *Annual Report of the Comptroller of the Currency in the Second Session of the Forty-fourth Congress of the United States,* December 4, 1876 (Washington, D.C.: GPO, 1876), p. xxv.

114. *Annual Report of the Superintendent of the Banking Department,* State of New York, Assembly Document 3, January 3, 1860.

115. *Annual Report of the Comptroller of the Currency* (1876), pp. xlv and ciii. The comptroller's report presents data for the beginning of January of each year. Because the annual data presented here reflect end-of-year values (unless otherwise noted), the comptroller's annual figures have all been shifted back by one year.

116. Quoted in Harry E. Miller, *Banking Theories in the United States before 1860* (Cambridge, Mass.: Harvard University Press, 1927), p. 110.

117. *Annual Report of the Bank Commissioners, January 25, 1841,* Assembly Document 64, 1841, p. 16, in which the commissioners claimed that coverage of deposits in the Safety Fund law was simply a mistake. Redlich asserts, by contrast, that Forman and other framers of the Safety Fund legislation had always intended to cover deposits as well as notes. Redlich, *Molding of American Banking,* 1:264n21. About the ongoing confusion regarding the monetary function of demand deposits, see also Charles F. Dunbar, "Deposits as Currency," *Quarterly Journal of Economics,* 1, no. 4 (July 1887), 402.

118. Assembly Document 2, 1858, p. 2. See also *Annual Report of the Superintendent of the Banking Department,* State of New York, Assembly Document 3, January 3, 1860, p. 15; Samuel Rezneck, "The Influence of Depression upon American Opinion, 1857–1859," *Journal of Economic History,* 2, no. 1 (May 1942), 3.

119. Rezneck, "Influence of Depression," p. 2. See also Charles W. Calomiris and Larry Schweikart, "The Panic of 1857: Origins, Transmission, and Containment," *Journal of Economic History,* 51, no. 4 (December 1991), 807–834; William Graham Sumner, *A History of Banking in the United States* (New York: Journal of Commerce and Commercial Bulletin, 1896), pp. 426–428.

120. Root, "New York Bank Currency," pp. 3, 7, 19.

121. Louisiana presents an interesting point of comparison. Although its legislature did not pass a general incorporation law until 1853, it separated liquidity creation from credit creation more than ten years earlier. The Louisiana Bank Act of 1842 required banks to hold specie reserves equal to one-third of liquid liabilities and back the other two-thirds with short-term (ninety-day) commercial paper. Long-term lending was limited to loans on capital since both notes and deposits were included in the definition of liquid liabilities. There were no bank failures under this Louisiana system after 1842, leading some scholars to herald the legislation as a great success. But safety represents only one side of the equation. Over the next twenty years, loans and discounts in Louisiana remained relatively stagnant, despite significant growth in the country at large. See Hammond, *Banks and Politics in America,* pp. 676–686; Knox, *History of Banking in the United States,* pp. 613–614; Sumner, *History of Banking in the United States,* pp. 387–391, 434–437; Rockoff, "Varieties of Banking," p. 163; *Annual Report of the Comptroller,* pp. cxii–cxiii (for Louisiana bank balance sheets); George D. Green, "Louisiana, 1804–1861," in Rondo Cameron, ed., *Banking and Economic Development* (New York: Oxford University Press, 1972), pp. 216–220.

122. Double liability was readopted at the New York constitutional convention of 1846, but it was not put into effect until the beginning of 1850. See art. 8, sec. 7 of the Constitution of 1846, printed in *Report of the Debates and Proceeding of the Convention for the Revision of the Constitution of the State of New York,* 1846, p. 13.

123. See John Wilson Million, "The Debate on the National Bank Act of 1863," *Journal of Political Economy,* 2, no. 2 (March 1894), 251–80; James Willard Hurst, *A Legal History of Money in the United States, 1774–1970* (Lincoln: University of Nebraska Press, 1973), p. 79; John A. James, *Money and Capital Markets in Postbellum America* (Princeton: Princeton University Press, 1978), pp. 27–29, 74–78; Thomas Wilson, *The Power "To Coin" Money: The Exercise of Monetary Powers by the Congress* (Armonk, N.Y.: M. E. Sharpe, 1992), pp. 156–160.

124. Golembe, "Deposit Insurance Legislation of 1933," p. 187.

125. *Annual Report of the Comptroller of the Currency,* December 1, 1890 (Washington, D.C.: GPO, 1890), 1:22–24. See also *Annual Report of the Comptroller of the Currency,* December 5, 1892 (Washington, D.C.: GPO, 1892), 1:31–32.

126. Quoted in Henry Parker Willis, "The Federal Reserve Act," *American Economic Review,* 4, no. 1 (March 1914), 4. See also Representative Carter Glass, *Congressional Record* (House), 63rd Cong., 1st sess., September 10, 1913, pp. 4642–51.

127. See, e.g., Carter Glass, *Congressional Record* (House), September 10, 1913, p. 4642; Benjamin J. Klebaner, *American Commercial Banking: A History* (Boston: Twayne Publishers, 1990), pp. 111–112.

128. On the various state-level initiatives in the early twentieth century, see esp. four articles by Thornton Cooke, "The Insurance of Bank Deposits in the West," *Quarterly Journal of Economics,* 24, no. 1 (November 1909), 85–108; "The Insurance of Bank Deposits in the West: II," *Quarterly Journal of Economics,* 24, no. 2 (February 1910), 327–391; "Four Years More of Deposit Guaranty," *Quarterly Journal of Economics,* 28, no. 1 (November 1913), 69–114; and "The Collapse of Bank-Deposit Guaranty in Oklahoma and Its Position in Other States," *Quarterly Journal of Economics,* 38, no. 1 (November 1923), 108–139; also Eugene Nelson White, "State-Sponsored Insurance of Bank Deposits in the United States, 1907–1929," *Journal of Economic History,* 41, no. 3 (September 1981), 537–557; Golembe, "Deposit Insurance Legislation of 1933," esp. pp. 187–188; Charles W. Calomiris, "Is Deposit Insurance Necessary? A Historical Perspective," *Journal of Economic History,* 50, no. 2 (June 1990), esp. 288–293; *A Brief History of Deposit Insurance in the United States* (Washington, D.C.: Federal Deposit Insurance Corporation, 1998), pp. 12–19.

129. Steagall, *Congressional Record* (House), 73rd Cong., 1st sess., May 20, 1933, p. 3835.

130. Ibid., pp. 3839–40.

131. Luce, ibid., May 22, 1933, p. 3917.

132. Steagall, ibid., May 20, 1933, p. 3837.

133. Bacon, ibid., May 22, 1933, p. 3959.

134. Bulkley, *Congressional Record* (Senate), May 8, 1933, p. 3008. See also Bacon, *Congressional Record* (House), May 22, 1933, p. 3960.

135. Bacon, *Congressional Record* (House), May 22, 1933, p. 3960.

136. Bulkley, *Congressional Record* (Senate), May 8, 1933, p. 3008. See also Carter Glass, ibid., May 19, 1933, p. 3728; Bacon, *Congressional Record* (House), May 22, 1933, p. 3960; Arthur Vandenberg, *Congressional Record* (Senate), May 26, 1933, p. 4240. Anticipating the possibility that weak banks might try to lure insured depositors with higher than normal interest rates, the authors of the legislation strictly limited the payment of interest on bank deposits, thereby "eliminat[ing] the most unsound method of competition for deposit accounts." Bulkley, *Congressional Record* (Senate), May 8, 1933, p. 3008. See also Albert H. Cox, "Regulation of Interest on Deposits: An Historical Overview," *Journal of Finance,* 22, no. 2 (May 1967), 274–296.

137. Bacon, *Congressional Record* (House), May 22, 1933, p. 3959.

138. Glass, *Congressional Record* (Senate), May 19, 1933, p. 3728.

139. Steagall, *Congressional Record* (House), May 20, 1933, p. 3838. It was also suggested during the debates that one of the reasons state insurance plans had failed was that banking losses were essentially uninsurable as a result of Knightian uncertainty. See, e.g., Bacon, *Congressional Record* (House), May 22, 1933, pp. 3960–61. The argument was not explicitly made, however, that the federal government was better positioned than the states to deal with such uncertainty.

140. Frederick Sisson, *Congressional Record* (House), May 22, 1933, p. 3924. See also Dondero, ibid., May 23, 1933, p. 4058.

141. See, e.g., Glass, *Congressional Record* (Senate), May 19, 1933, pp. 3726–29.

142. See, e.g., interchange between Senators King and Glass, ibid., p. 3729.

143. In fact, the reasons given for ending double liability in 1933 were almost identical to those given in 1829: that excess shareholder liability did little to increase reimbursement of creditor losses and that it seemed to attract speculators into the banking business. On the 1933 versions of these arguments, see esp. Luce, *Congressional Record* (House), May 22, 1933, p. 3917; Bacon, ibid., p. 3961.

144. Frustrated that some representatives viewed his deposit insurance proposal as a threat to small unit banks, Representative Steagall argued force-

fully (and with considerable credibility) that the real purpose was just the opposite. "No man is more concerned about preserving the independent community banks . . . than I am," Steagall declared. "This bill will preserve independent, dual banking in the United States to supply community credit, community service, and for the upbuilding of community life. That is what this bill is intended to do. That is the purpose of this bill; that is what the measure will accomplish." Steagall, *Congressional Record* (House), May 23, 1933, p. 4033.

145. Keller, ibid., May 22, 1933, p. 3913.
146. In 1829, for example, Joshua Forman declared that since "banks have powers . . . so deeply affecting the interests of community, they ought to be considered and treated as public institutions, intended as much for the public good, as the profit of the stockholders." *Journal of the Assembly, 1829,* p. 176.
147. Even with these policies in place, however, continued vigilance has proved essential. The savings and loan debacle in the 1980s testified to the dangers of regulatory laxity, particularly against the backdrop of a federal deposit insurance system.
148. Hastings, *Congressional Record* (House), May 22, 1933, p. 3924.
149. See esp. Golembe, "Deposit Insurance Legislation of 1933," pp. 189–195.

5. Bankruptcy

1. Quoted in Samuel Rezneck, "The Social History of an American Depression, 1837–1843," *American Historical Review,* 40, no. 4 (July 1935), 662–687.
2. See, e.g., Milton Brown, *Appendix to the Congressional Globe* (House), 27th Cong., 1st sess., August 1841, p. 482.
3. Tallmadge, *Appendix to the Congressional Globe* (Senate), 27th Cong., 1st sess., July 1841, p. 468.
4. Buchanan, *Congressional Globe* (Senate), 27th Cong., 1st sess., July 24, 1841, p. 206.
5. Daniel Webster, "A Uniform System of Bankruptcy," U.S. Senate, May 18, 1840, reprinted in *The Great Speeches and Orations of Daniel Webster* (Boston: Little, Brown, 1879), p. 471.
6. Richard Posner, "The Rights of Creditors of Affiliated Corporations," *University of Chicago Law Review,* 43 (1976), 503.
7. Thomas H. Jackson, "The Fresh-Start Policy in Bankruptcy Law," *Harvard Law Review,* 98 (May 1985), 1400. Although Jackson identifies limited liability as one potentially useful analogy in analyzing bankruptcy discharge, he does not limit his analysis to this one analogy.

8. Douglas G. Baird, *The Elements of Bankruptcy* (Westbury, N.Y.: Foundation Press, 1993), p. 33.
9. Trumbull, *Congressional Globe* (House), 27th Cong., 1st sess., August 11, 1841, p. 324.
10. Peter J. Coleman, *Debtors and Creditors in America: Insolvency, Imprisonment for Debt, and Bankruptcy, 1607–1900* (Madison: State Historical Society of Wisconsin, 1974), p. 133.
11. Ibid., pp. 45–46, 113, 179–184. See also F. H. Buckley, "The American Fresh Start," *Southern California Interdisciplinary Law Journal,* 4 (Fall 1994), 94, 96.
12. Coleman, *Debtors and Creditors in America*, pp. 39–40, 191–192, 203–205.
13. Quoted in Samuel Eliot Morison, Henry Steele Commager, and William E. Leuchtenburg, *The Growth of the American Republic* (New York: Oxford University Press, 1969), 1:239.
14. Charles Warren, *Bankruptcy in United States History* (Cambridge, Mass.: Harvard University Press, 1935), pp. 146–148; Coleman, *Debtors and Creditors in America*, pp. 73, 80–81, 203–205.
15. See William G. Anderson, *The Price of Liberty: The Public Debt of the American Revolution* (Charlottesville: University Press of Virginia, 1983), pp. 3–32. Madison is quoted in James W. Ely, Jr., *The Guardian of Every Other Right: A Constitutional History of Property Rights* (New York: Oxford University Press, 1992), p. 37.
16. Steven R. Boyd, "The Contract Clause and the Evolution of American Federalism, 1789–1815," *William and Mary Quarterly*, 3rd ser., 44, no. 3 (July 1987), 533–534.
17. Ibid., p. 534.
18. See Warren, *Bankruptcy in United States History*, p. 147.
19. See Bernard Bailyn et al., *The Great Republic: A History of the American People* (Lexington, Mass.: D. C. Heath and Company, 1977), 1:329; Ely, *Guardian of Every Other Right*, pp. 39–40; Coleman, *Debtors and Creditors in America*, p. 73.
20. Quoted in Morison, Commager, and Leuchtenburg, *Growth of the American Republic*, 1:242. On the "almost universal expression of indignation and regret" that state debtor-protection laws produced, see also *Adams v. Storey*, 1 Federal Cases 141, 145–146 (1817).
21. Warren, *Bankruptcy in United States History*, p. 146.
22. Quoted in Boyd, "Contract Clause," p. 534.
23. Ibid., pp. 537–540.
24. Ibid., pp. 540–541.
25. *Sturges v. Crowninshield*, 4 Wheat. 122, 208, 17 U.S. 122, 208 (1819).
26. *Ogden v. Saunders*, 12 Wheat. 213, 25 U.S. 213 (1827). On *Sturges* and

Ogden, see also Guy C. H. Corliss, "Discharge under State Insolvent Law," *Albany Law Journal,* 29 (March 8, 1884), 186–189; Charles Jordan Tabb, "The Historical Evolution of the Bankruptcy Discharge," *American Bankruptcy Law Journal,* 65 (1991), 348–349.

27. Quoted in Rezneck, "Social History of an American Depression," p. 676.

28. Ibid., p. 682.

29. John Forster, *The Life of Charles Dickens* (Boston: Estes and Lauriat Publishers, 1890[?]), 1:24; Robert Langton, *The Childhood and Youth of Charles Dickens* (London: Hutchinson & Co., 1891), p. 70. Whereas Forster dates John Dickens's year in prison to 1822, Langton dates it to 1824. On the infamous Marshalsea debtors' prison, see also Charles Dickens, *Little Dorrit* (London: Macmillan, 1899).

30. Warren, *Bankruptcy in United States History,* pp. 174–175 and n8.

31. Coleman, *Debtors and Creditors in America,* p. 117, quoting Helen L. Sumner.

32. Edwin T. Randall, "Imprisonment for Debt in America: Fact and Fiction," *Mississippi Valley Historical Review,* 39, no. 1 (June 1952), 89–102. See also Bruce H. Mann, "Tales from the Crypt: Prison, Legal Authority, and the Debtors' Constitution in the Early Republic," *William and Mary Quarterly,* 51, no. 2 (April 1994), 183–202.

33. Dickens wrote that his father was "as kindhearted and generous a man as ever lived in the world. Everything I can remember of his conduct . . . is beyond all praise. . . . He never undertook any business, charge or trust, that he did not zealously, conscientiously, punctually, honourably discharge." Quoted in Forster, *Life of Charles Dickens,* 1:18.

34. Coleman, *Debtors and Creditors in America,* pp. 41, 44–45, 51–52, 119; Warren, *Bankruptcy in United States History,* p. 52; Rhett Frimet, "The Birth of Bankruptcy in the United States," *Commercial Law Journal,* 96 (1991), 175.

35. Coleman, *Debtors and Creditors in America,* p. 255.

36. Warren, *Bankruptcy in United States History,* p. 146.

37. Paul Goodman, "The Emergence of Homestead Exemption in the United States: Accommodation and Resistance to the Market Revolution, 1840–1880," *Journal of American History,* 80, no. 2 (September 1993), 477.

38. Ibid., p. 472.

39. *Adams v. Storey,* 1 Federal Cases 141, 145–146, 151 (1817). See also Boyd, "Contract Clause," p. 547.

40. Goodman, "Emergence of Homestead Exemption," pp. 477–478.

41. *Trawick v. Harris,* 8 Tex. 312, 316 (1852). Also quoted in part in Goodman, "Emergence of Homestead Exemption," p. 478.

42. See esp. Douglas G. Baird, "A World without Bankruptcy," in Jagdeep S.

Bhandari and Lawrence A. Weiss, eds., *Corporate Bankruptcy: Economic and Legal Perspectives* (Cambridge: Cambridge University Press, 1996), p. 29.

43. Coleman, *Debtors and Creditors in America,* pp. 45, 179, 181–182, 218, 109, 91–94.

44. Art. 1, sec. 8.

45. See, e.g., James Bayard, *History of Congress* (House), 5th Cong., 3rd sess., January 1799, pp. 2656–57. See also *Adams v. Storey,* 1 Federal Cases 141, 142 (1817).

46. See, e.g., Trumbull, *Congressional Globe* (House), 27th Cong., 1st sess., August 11, 1841, p. 324.

47. Robert Waln, *History of Congress* (House), 5th Cong., 3rd sess., January 1799, p. 2577.

48. Harrison Otis, *History of Congress* (House), 5th Cong., 3rd sess., January 1799, p. 2674.

49. Ibid.

50. Bankruptcy Act of 1800, 6th Cong., 1st sess., ch. 19, 2 Stat. 19, sec. 36.

51. Pinckney, *History of Congress* (House), 5th Cong., 3rd sess., January 1799, p. 2582.

52. *History of Congress* (House), 8th Cong., 1st sess., November 1803, p. 618.

53. Act of August 16, 1841, ch. 9, sec. 1, 5 Stat. 440, 441–442.

54. Warren, *Bankruptcy in United States History,* pp. 81–85.

55. Act of March 2, 1867, ch. 176, secs. 11, 36, 37, 39, 14 Stat. 517, 521–522, 534–536.

56. Warren, *Bankruptcy in United States History,* p. 127.

57. Quoted in Tabb, "The Historical Evolution of the Bankruptcy Discharge," p. 365.

58. Burke, *Congressional Record* (House), 55th Cong., 2nd sess., February 16, 1898, p. 1801.

59. Act of July 1, 1898, ch. 541, sec. 4, 30 Stat. 544.

60. The most critical component of modern bankruptcy law that remained absent by 1900 was provision for corporate reorganization, which ultimately emerged in the twentieth century. It was not until the 1933 and 1934 amendments to the 1898 act that section 77B codified the principles and processes of corporate reorganization under the umbrella of the federal bankruptcy law. Section 77B was succeeded by chapter 10 of the Chandler Act of 1938, which in turn was rewritten as chapter 11 of the Bankruptcy Act of 1978. See Act of June 7, 1934, ch. 424, secs. 77–77B, 48 Stat. 912–25; Act of June 22, 1938, ch. 575, 52 Stat. 840 et seq.; Act of November 6, 1978 (P.L. 95–598), 92 Stat. 2549–2644 (1978).

61. Charles Tabb has observed that "the United States may well have the most

liberal discharge laws in the world." See Charles Jordan Tabb, "The Historical Evolution of the Bankruptcy Discharge," *American Bankruptcy Law Journal*, 65 (Spring 1991), 325.

62. See, e.g., Warren, *Bankruptcy in United States History*, p. 9.

63. Ibid., pp. 10–18; Frimet, "The Birth of Bankruptcy in the United States," pp. 166–169. On Duer and Morris, see also Stanley Elkins and Eric McKitrick, *The Age of Federalism: The Early American Republic, 1788–1800* (New York: Oxford University Press, 1993), pp. 272–276, 278, 179, and 459.

64. For contemporary characterizations of the economic crisis, see, e.g., *Congressional Record* (House), 55th Cong., 2nd sess., February 18, 1898, p. 1911 (Rep. James Lloyd); February 17, 1898, pp. 1850–51 (Rep. Stephen Sparkman).

65. See, e.g., Elijah Lewis, *Congressional Record* (House), 55th Cong., 2nd sess., February 18, 1898, p. 1909. See also February 16, 1898, p. 1793 (Rep. William Terry).

66. Tallmadge, *Appendix to the Congressional Globe* (Senate), 27th Cong., 1st sess., July 1841, p. 468.

67. Fessenden, *Appendix to the Congressional Globe* (House), 27th Cong., 1st sess., August 1841, p. 470.

68. Bell, *Congressional Record* (House), 55th Cong., 2nd sess., February 16, 1898, p. 1797.

69. See also, e.g., De Alva Stanwood Alexander, ibid., February 17, 1898, p. 1840.

70. Ibid., February 18, 1898, p. 1890.

71. Ibid., February 16, 1898, p. 1793.

72. Ibid.

73. Ibid., February 17, 1898, p. 1852.

74. *History of Congress* (House), 8th Cong., 1st sess., November 1803, p. 620.

75. Whitman, ibid., 15th Cong., 1st sess., February 1818, pp. 1017–18. Whitman highlighted price risk and political risk as especially problematic for the merchant.

76. See, e.g., Richard Young, *Appendix to the Congressional Globe* (Senate), 27th Cong., 2nd sess., January 1842, p. 97.

77. Howard, *Appendix to the Congressional Globe* (House), 27th Cong., 1st sess., August 1841, p. 493. See also Smith, *Appendix to the Congressional Globe* (Senate), 26th Cong., 1st sess., May 1840, p. 837.

78. Strange, *Appendix to the Congressional Globe* (Senate), 26th Cong., 1st sess., May 1840, p. 544.

79. See, e.g., remarks of Representative Richard Parker of New Jersey, *Congressional Record* (House), 55th Cong., 2nd sess., February 17, 1898, p. 1852.

80. Lewis, ibid., February 18, 1898, pp. 1908–9.

81. Marshall Field to Mr. Lawrence, February 9, 1895, quoted ibid., p. 1902.

Field's critics charged that his opposition to a federal bankruptcy law was entirely self-serving. Marshall Field & Co. had such a well-developed legal department, the critics claimed, that the company could almost always prevail over rival creditors in collection efforts pursued under state law. See, e.g., ibid., pp. 1898–1904.

82. *Appendix to the Congressional Globe* (Senate), 26th Cong., 1st sess., May 1840, p. 837. See also, e.g., Daniel Barnard, *Appendix to the Congressional Globe* (House), 27th Cong., 1st sess., August 1841, p. 499.

83. Robert Burke, *Congressional Record* (House), 55th Cong., 2nd sess., February 16, 1898, p. 1802.

84. Nisbet, *Appendix to the Congressional Globe* (House), 27th Cong., 1st sess., August 1841, p. 479.

85. Fessenden, ibid., p. 469.

86. Sulzer, *Congressional Record* (House), 55th Cong., 2nd sess., February 18, 1898, p. 1890.

87. Underwood, ibid., February 16, 1898, p. 1793.

88. See Ray, ibid., February 18, 1898, p. 1914.

89. In all of the congressional bankruptcy debates, which stretched across the entire century, only a handful of statements advancing this sort of argument truly stand out. See, e.g., ibid.

90. Fessenden, *Appendix to the Congressional Globe* (House), 27th Cong., 1st sess., August 1841, pp. 469–471.

91. John Haynes, "Risk as an Economic Factor," *Quarterly Journal of Economics*, 9, no. 4 (July 1895), 433. See also, e.g., Frank H. Knight, Comments, *American Economic Review*, 44, no. 2 (May 1954), Papers and Proceedings of the Sixty-sixth Annual Meeting of the American Economic Association, 63.

92. See, e.g., Barnard, *Appendix to the Congressional Globe* (House), 27th Cong., 1st sess., August 1841, p. 498.

93. Jackson, "Fresh-Start Policy in Bankruptcy Law," esp. 1414. Based on entrepreneurs' high level of risk taking, one might also conclude that they were risk lovers. If so, then establishing a nonwaivable right to discharge, which essentially forced them to buy default insurance from creditors at the cost of higher interest rates, would have reduced the utility they derived from their otherwise risky ventures.

94. See *Mr. Berrien, of Georgia on the Bill to Repeal the Bankrupt Law. Delivered in the Senate of the United States, January 26, 1842* (Washington, D.C.: National Intelligencer Office, 1842), p. 23. Speaking in January 1842, Senator Berrien was attempting to block an effort to repeal the Bankruptcy Act of 1841. See also, e.g., Elisha Hunt Allen, *Appendix to the Congressional Globe* (House), August 1841, p. 478.

95. Many failed debtors likely reduced their *official* but not their *actual* work

effort by earning new income under assumed names in the hope of hiding it from their creditors.

96. Ball, *Congressional Record* (House), 55th Cong., 2nd sess., February 18, 1898, p. 1885. See also David Henderson, ibid., February 16, 1898, pp. 1788–89. Supporters of discharge also emphasized on occasion that the promise of a legal discharge might reduce the pressure on embarrassed debtors to engage in rash and excessive risk taking on the eve of default, since the adverse consequences of insolvency would be considerably lessened. See, e.g., Robert Hayne, *Gales and Seaton's Register of Debates in Congress,* 19th Cong., 1st sess., U.S. Senate, May 1, 1826, p. 651.

97. Nisbet, *Appendix to the Congressional Globe* (House), 27th Cong., 1st sess., August 1841, p. 479.

98. Ray, *Congressional Record* (House), 55th Cong., 2nd sess., February 18, 1898, p. 1914.

99. Tallmadge, *Appendix to the Congressional Globe* (House), 27th Cong., 1st sess., July 1841, p. 468.

100. On the implications of rendering human capital nontradable, see esp. David Mayers, "Nonmarketable Assets and Capital Market Equilibrium under Uncertainty," in Michael C. Jensen, ed., *Studies in the Theory of Capital Markets* (New York: Praeger, 1972), pp. 223–248; Robert C. Merton, "On the Role of Social Security as a Means for Efficient Risk Sharing in an Economy Where Human Capital Is Not Tradable," in Zvi Bodie and John B. Shoven, eds., *Financial Aspects of the United States Pension System* (Chicago: University of Chicago Press, 1983), pp. 325–358.

101. *Sturges v. Crowninshield,* 4 Wheat. 122, 17 U.S. 122 (1819).

102. Connolly, *Congressional Record* (House), 55th Cong., 2nd sess., February 18, 1898, p. 1893.

103. Burke, ibid., February 16, 1898, p. 1801.

104. Quoted by Representative Samuel McCall, ibid., February 17, 1898, p. 1847.

105. The issue of debt servitude arose again in the 1930s, when policymakers were debating what would become chapter 13 of the bankruptcy code. Adopted in 1938, chapter 13 allows the debtor to retain more of his assets (as compared to a traditional chapter 7 proceeding), but it also entitles creditors to attach some of the debtor's future earnings. Policymakers chose to make the choice of chapter 13 voluntary (i.e., at the discretion of the debtor) because of concerns that a mandatory chapter 13 would be perceived as bordering on debt servitude. See David A. Moss and Gibbs A. Johnson, "The Rise of Consumer Bankruptcy: Evolution, Revolution, or Both," *American Bankruptcy Law Journal,* 73 (Spring 1999), 319–320, 320n45.

106. See esp. Thomas K. Finletter, *The Law of Bankruptcy Reorganization* (Charlottesville: The Michie Company, 1939); John Gerdes, "Corporate Reorganization: Changes Effected by Chapter X of the Bankruptcy Act," *Harvard Law Review*, 52 (November 1938), 1–39. See also note 60.

6. Workers' Insurance

1. John R. Commons, *Social Reform and the Church* (New York: Thomas Y. Crowell, 1894), pp. 37–38. Portions of this chapter draw heavily from David A. Moss, *Socializing Security: Progressive-Era Economists and the Origins of American Social Policy* (Cambridge, Mass.: Harvard University Press, 1996).
2. See, e.g., Henry R. Seager, "Outline of a Program of Social Legislation with Special Reference to Wage-Earners," in *American Association for Labor Legislation: Proceedings of the First Annual Meeting* (Madison, April 1908), pp. 85–86.
3. Ibid., p. 86.
4. John B. Andrews to Harrington Emerson, November 24, 1915, in *Microfilm Edition of the Papers of the American Association for Labor Legislation, 1905–1945* (Glen Rock, N.J.: Microfilming Corporation of America, 1973), reel 15 (hereafter AALL Papers).
5. Circular letter from Louis H. Fibel, President, Great Eastern Casualty Company, "To Our New York Agents" [copy], January 27, 1916, AALL Papers, reel 16. See also identical circular letter on Great Eastern letterhead, February 17, 1916, AALL Papers, reel 16.
6. See, e.g., *Commission to Study Social Insurance and Unemployment*, Hearings before the Committee on Labor, House of Representatives, 64th Cong., 1st sess. [on H.J. Res. 159], April 6 and 11, 1916, p. 153; Samuel Gompers, "Not Even Compulsory Benevolence Will Do," in *Compulsory Health Insurance*, Annual Meeting Addresses, National Civic Federation, January 22, 1917 (New York, 1917), pp. 9–10; Samuel Gompers, "Labor vs. Its Barnacles," *American Federationist*, 23, no. 4 (April 1916), 268–274.
7. *Congressional Record* (House), 74th Cong., 1st sess., April 13, 1935, p. 5583.
8. See, e.g., Charles Richmond Henderson, *Industrial Insurance in the United States* (Chicago: University of Chicago Press, 1909), p. 41.
9. Henry R. Seager, "Outline of a Program of Social Reform" [February 1907], in *Labor and Other Economic Essays by Henry R. Seager*, ed. Charles A. Gulick, Jr. (New York: Harper and Brothers, 1931), p. 79; Seager, "Outline of a Program of Social Legislation," p. 91.
10. See, e.g., H. Roger Grant, *Insurance Reform: Consumer Action in the Progres-*

sive Era (Ames: Iowa State University Press, 1979), pp. 5–6; Morton Keller, *The Life Insurance Enterprise, 1885–1910* (Cambridge, Mass.: Harvard University Press, 1963), p. 9; Shepard B. Clough, *A Century of American Life Insurance: A History of the Mutual Life Insurance Company of New York, 1843–1943* (New York: Columbia University Press, 1946), pp. 3–4.

11. Don D. Lescohier, "Industrial Accidents, Employer's Liability, and Workmen's Compensation in Minnesota," *Publications of the American Statistical Association,* 12, no. 94 (June 1911), 648.

12. Gustavus Myers, "A Study of the Causes of Industrial Accidents," *Publications of the American Statistical Association,* 14, no. 111 (September 1915), 686–687. On the higher mortality rates in industrial as compared to agricultural districts in England and Wales in 1890–1892, see Frederick L. Hoffman, "Problems of Social Statistics and Social Research," *Publications of the American Statistical Association,* 11, no. 82 (June 1908), 128.

13. Willard C. Fisher, "The Field of Workmen's Compensation in the United States," *American Economic Review,* 5, no. 2 (June 1915), 268. See also Henderson, *Industrial Insurance,* pp. 55–56.

14. I. M. Rubinow, "Labor Insurance," *Journal of Political Economy,* 12, no. 3 (June 1904), 370. See also, e.g., *Report to the Legislature of the State of New York by the Commission Appointed under Chapter 518 of the Laws of 1909 to Inquire into the Question of Employers' Liability and Other Matters,* 1st report, March 19, 1910 (Albany: J. B. Lyon Company, 1910), p. 5 (hereafter *First Wainwright Report*).

15. See, e.g., Frederick L. Hoffman, "Industrial Accidents and Industrial Diseases," *Publications of the American Statistical Association,* 11, no. 88 (December 1909), 567–603.

16. Adna F. Weber, "Employers' Liability and Accident Insurance," *Political Science Quarterly,* 17, no. 2 (June 1902), 257.

17. Ibid. See also Hoffman, "Industrial Accidents and Industrial Diseases," esp. p. 570.

18. William F. Willoughby, "The Problem of Social Insurance: An Analysis," *American Labor Legislation Review* 3, no. 2 (June 1913), 156–157 (hereafter ALLR). See also Henderson, *Industrial Insurance,* pp. 44, 52. Modern historical treatments of this phenomenon include David Montgomery, *Workers' Control in America: Studies in the History of Work, Technology, and Labor Struggles* (New York: Cambridge University Press, 1979); David Montgomery, *The Fall of the House of Labor: The Workplace, the State, and American Labor Activism, 1865–1925* (New York: Cambridge University Press, 1987); Herbert G. Gutman, *Work, Culture, and Society in Industrializing America: Essays in American Working-Class and Social History* (New York: Knopf, 1976).

19. Weber, "Employers' Liability and Accident Insurance," p. 279.

20. See, e.g., *New York Central Railroad v. White*, 243 U.S. 188, 197 (1917).

21. Crystal Eastman, *Work-Accidents and the Law* (New York: Charities Publication Committee, 1910), pp. 86–87. The sum of the figures identifying responsibility for accidents exceeds the total number of accidents because responsibility was assigned when a party was found to be either *partly or solely* responsible, allowing for overlap in blame.

22. William Hard, "Unemployment as a Coming Issue," *ALLR*, 2, no. 1 (February 1912), 95, 94. See also, e.g., John B. Andrews, "A Practical Program for the Prevention of Unemployment in America," first released as a pamphlet in 1914 and reprinted in *ALLR*, 5, no. 2 (June 1915), 173.

23. See, e.g., John B. Andrews, "Introductory Note," *ALLR*, 5, no. 3 (November 1915), 469. William H. Beveridge published *Unemployment: A Problem of Industry* in 1909.

24. See esp. Irwin Yellowitz, "The Origins of Unemployment Reform in the United States," *Labor History*, 9, no. 3 (Fall 1968), 360.

25. Alexander Keyssar, *Out of Work: The First Century of Unemployment in Massachusetts* (Cambridge: Cambridge University Press, 1986), esp. pp. 3–4 and 262–263. See also Robert H. Bremner, *From the Depths: The Discovery of Poverty in the United States* (New York: New York University Press, 1964), chap. 1; Robert Bremner, "'Scientific Philanthropy,' 1873–93," *Social Service Review*, 30, no. 2 (June 1956), 273.

26. U.S. Department of Commerce, Bureau of the Census, *Historical Statistics of the United States, Colonial Times to 1970* (Washington, D.C.: GPO, 1975), ser. X-885 and X-889, pp. 1056–57; Frederick L. Hoffman, "Problems of Social Statistics and Social Research," *Publications of the American Statistical Association*, 11, no. 82 (June 1908), 127. See also Henderson, *Industrial Insurance*, esp. pp. 149–174; C. F. Trenerry, *The Origin and Early History of Insurance* (London: P. S. King & Son, 1926); Keller, *Life Insurance Enterprise*, pp. 9–11; *The Documentary History of Insurance, 1000 B.C.–1875 A.D.* (Newark: Prudential Press, 1915); Herman E. Kroos and Martin R. Blyn, *A History of Financial Intermediaries* (New York: Random House, 1971), pp. 110–111.

27. Louise Bolard More, *Wage-Earners' Budgets: A Study of Standards and Cost of Living in New York City* (New York: Henry Holt and Company, 1907), pp. 55, 267–270; Robert Coit Chapin, *The Standard of Living among Workingmen's Families in New York City* (New York: Charities Publication Committee, 1909), pp. 191–197, 245–250; B. S. Warren, "Sickness Insurance: A Preventive of Charity Practice," *Journal of the American Medical Association*, 65, no. 24 (December 11, 1915), 2057; [New York City] Bureau of Standards, *Report on the Cost of Living for an Unskilled Laborer's Family in*

New York City (1915), pp. 6, 11, 15, 41; Hoffman, "Problems of Social Statistics," p. 125.

28. Henderson, *Industrial Insurance,* esp. chaps. 2–8.
29. Ibid., p. 158.
30. Ibid., p. 42.
31. See, e.g., Rubinow, "Labor Insurance," p. 378.
32. John R. Commons and A. J. Altmeyer, "The Health Insurance Movement in the United States," in Ohio Health and Old Age Insurance Commission, *Health, Health Insurance, Old Age Pensions* (Columbus: F. J. Heer Printing Co., 1919), p. 295.
33. Henry R. Seager, "Plan for Health Insurance Act," *ALLR,* 6, no. 1 (1916), 21.
34. Henderson, *Industrial Insurance,* pp. 1–40; Weber, "Employers' Liability and Accident Insurance," esp. pp. 267–276; Peter A. Köhler and Hans F. Zacher, eds., *The Evolution of Social Insurance, 1881–1981: Studies of Germany, France, Great Britain, Austria, and Switzerland* (New York: St. Martin's Press, 1982).
35. Rubinow, "Labor Insurance," p. 377.
36. Weber, "Employers' Liability and Accident Insurance," p. 258. See also Henderson, *Industrial Insurance,* p. 56.
37. See, e.g., Willoughby, "The Problem of Social Insurance," p. 158; Edward T. Devine, "Pensions for Mothers," *ALLR,* 3, no. 2 (June 1913), 193, 196–197; Theda Skocpol and John Ikenberry, "The Political Formation of the American Welfare State in Historical and Comparative Perspective," *Comparative Social Research,* 6 (1983), esp. 134–139.
38. Henry R. Seager, "The Constitution and Social Progress in the State of New York," reprinted in *Labor and Other Economic Essays,* pp. 262, 260.
39. John R. Commons and John B. Andrews, *Principles of Labor Legislation,* 4th rev. ed. (New York: Augustus M. Kelley Publishers, 1967 [1936, 1916]), pp. 236–237.
40. *Ives v. South Buffalo Railway Company,* 201 N.Y. 271, 317 (1911).
41. The competitive disadvantage problem could obviously have been solved through the passage of federal legislation. But it was widely believed at the time—at least until the 1930s—that the federal government lacked the constitutional authority to enact social insurance laws applying to anyone other than workers engaged in interstate commerce, federal employees, and laborers located in the American territories.
42. Henderson, *Industrial Insurance,* p. 59. See also Moss, *Socializing Security,* esp. pp. 10–11, 95–96, 128–129, 156–157, 165–170.
43. John Nelson, "New Menace of Higher Manufacturing Costs," *The Iron Age,*

98, no. 2 (July 13, 1916), 87. See also Edson S. Lott, "Fallacies of Compulsory Social Insurance," *American Industries*, 17, no. 6 (January 1917), 18; "Health Insurance Now a Practical Issue," *The Survey*, 35, no. 24 (March 11, 1916), 691; *Commission to Study Social Insurance and Unemployment*, Hearings before the Committee on Labor, House of Representatives, 64th Cong., 1st sess. [on H.J. Res. 159], April 6 and 11, 1916 (Washington, D.C.: GPO, 1918), pp. 44–45; Joseph L. Cohen, *Insurance against Unemployment* (London: P. S. King & Son, 1921), pp. 461–462.

44. On the role of the AALL, see esp. Moss, *Socializing Security*. See also Richard Martin Lyon, "The American Association for Labor Legislation and the Fight for Workmen's Compensation Laws, 1906–1942," M.S. thesis (Cornell University, 1952); Lloyd F. Pierce, "The Activities of the American Association for Labor Legislation in Behalf of Social Security and Protective Labor Legislation," Ph.D. diss. (University of Wisconsin, 1953); Roy Lubove, *The Struggle for Social Security, 1900–1935* (Pittsburgh: University of Pittsburgh Press, 1986 [1968]); Daniel Nelson, *Unemployment Insurance: The American Experience, 1915–1935* (Madison: University of Wisconsin Press, 1969); Theda Skocpol, *Protecting Soldiers and Mothers: The Political Origins of Social Policy in the United States* (Cambridge, Mass.: Harvard University Press, 1992).

45. Hoffman, "Industrial Accidents and Industrial Diseases," p. 570.

46. Ibid., p. 603, table 19.

47. Lawrence M. Friedman, "Civil Wrongs: Personal Injury Law in the Late Nineteenth Century," *American Bar Foundation Research Journal*, 1987, nos. 2 and 3 (Spring–Summer 1987), 369. For a more favorable view of worker recovery in the nineteenth century, see esp. Peter Karsten, *Heart versus Head: Judge-Made Law in Nineteenth-Century America* (Chapel Hill: University of North Carolina Press, 1997).

48. *Farwell v. Boston & Worcester Railroad Corporation* (1842), 45 Mass. 49, p. 57.

49. Henry R. Seager, "The Compensation Amendment to the New York Constitution," in *Labor and Other Economic Essays*, pp. 155–157.

50. See Weber, "Employers' Liability and Accident Insurance," pp. 259–260.

51. *Crispin v. Babbit*, 81 N.Y. 516, 528 (1880). Earl went on to characterize the traditional public policy objective in classic Phase I terms: "As most of the enterprises of modern times, which contribute to human progress and the welfare of society, must be carried on by numerous servants working to the same end under common masters, it has been supposed that it would cast upon a master too much responsibility to hold him liable for injuries, against which he could by no possibility guard, sustained by one

servant from the negligence of a co-servant, and that the servants would be better protected if they were obliged to rely upon their own care and vigilance rather than those of the master" (pp. 528–529).

52. See esp. *Farwell v. Boston & Worcester Railroad Corporation* (1842), 45 Mass. 49, p. 57.

53. Weber, "Employers' Liability and Accident Insurance," p. 258.

54. *Crispin v. Babbit*, 81 N.Y. 516, 529 (1880).

55. *First Wainwright Report*, p. 13.

56. Hoffman, "Industrial Accidents and Industrial Diseases," p. 599, table 13.

57. Commons and Andrews, *Principles of Labor Legislation*, p. 232.

58. Eastman, *Work-Accidents and the Law*, p. 192. See also, e.g., Seager, "Compensation Amendment to the New York Constitution," p. 156; *First Wainwright Report*, pp. 19–33.

59. Price V. Fishback and Shawn E. Kantor, "The Adoption of Workers' Compensation in the United States, 1900–1930," *Journal of Law and Economics*, 41, no. 2, pt. 1 (October 1998), 305–341.

60. On the long-standing (and very American) tradition of poverty prevention, see David A. Moss, "The Political Economy of Insecurity: The American Association for Labor Legislation and the Crusade for Social Welfare Reform in the Progressive Era," Ph.D. diss. (Yale University, November 1992), chap. 2, pp. 54–96.

61. John R. Commons, "Industrial Relations," address delivered at the International Convention of Government Labor Officials, Park Hotel, Madison, June 3, 1919, in *The Wisconsin Progressives: The Papers of John R. Commons* (Teaneck, N.J.: Chadwyck-Healey, 1985), reel 17, fr. 820 (hereafter Commons Papers). See also Alpheus H. Snow, "Social Insurance," *University of Pennsylvania Law Review and American Law Register*, 59, no. 5 (February 1911), 288–289.

62. John R. Commons, "Social Insurance and the Medical Profession," *Wisconsin Medical Journal*, 13 (January 1915), 303.

63. Seager, "Outline of a Program of Social Reform," p. 83. See also, e.g., Henderson, *Industrial Insurance*, pp. 243–244.

64. Adam Smith, *An Inquiry into the Nature and Causes of the Wealth of Nations* (Chicago: University of Chicago Press, 1976), bk. 1, chap. 10, pt. 1, p. 112.

65. Henry R. Seager, "Outline of a Program of Social Legislation with Special Reference to Wage Earners," in *American Association for Labor Legislation: Proceedings of the First Annual Meeting*, pp. 92–93.

66. On the existence of compensating wage differentials for hazardous and otherwise disagreeable work during the late nineteenth and early twentieth centuries in the United States, see Price V. Fishback and Shawn Everett Kantor, "'Square Deal' or Raw Deal? Market Compensation for

Workplace Disamenities, 1884–1903," *Journal of Economic History,* 52, no. 4 (December 1992), 826–848; Seung-Wook Kim and Price V. Fishback, "Institutional Change, Compensating Differentials, and Accident Risk in American Railroading, 1892–1945," *Journal of Economic History,* 53, no. 4 (December 1993), 796–823; Price V. Fishback, "Liability Rules and Accident Prevention in the Workplace: Empirical Evidence from the Early Twentieth Century," *Journal of Legal Studies,* 16, no. 2 (June 1987), 305–328; Price V. Fishback, "Workplace Safety during the Progressive Era: Fatal Accidents in Bituminous Coal Mining, 1912–1923," *Explorations in Economic History,* 23, no. 3 (July 1986), 269–298; Timothy J. Hatton and Jeffrey G. Williamson, "Unemployment, Employment Contracts, and Wage Differentials: Michigan in the 1890s," *Journal of Economic History,* 51, no. 3 (September 1991), 605–632.

67. *First Wainwright Report,* p. 7. See also, e.g., Eastman, *Work-Accidents and the Law,* pp. 269–270; Eugene Wambaugh, "Workmen's Compensation Acts: Their Theory and Their Constitutionality," *Harvard Law Review,* 25 (1911), 129; Edward Ewing Pratt, "Lead Poisoning in New York City," *ALLR,* 2, no. 2 (June 1912), 275.

68. Seager, "The Constitution and Social Progress in the State of New York," p. 264. See also, e.g., Samuel Harper, "Workmen's Compensation in Illinois," *Illinois Law Review,* 6 (1911), 181.

69. Seager, "Outline of a Program of Social Legislation," pp. 92–93. On the problems of inadequate information and shortsightedness, see also, e.g., "Report of Commissioners John R. Commons and Florence J. Harriman," in *Final Report of the Commission on Industrial Relations* (Washington, D.C., 1915), p. 391; Commons and Andrews, *Principles of Labor Legislation,* 225; John R. Commons, *Industrial Goodwill* (New York: McGraw-Hill, 1919), p. 56; Sumner H. Slichter, review, *"The Worker in Modern Economic Society," Journal of Political Economy,* 34, no. 1 (February 1926), esp. 106–110.

70. Henry R. Seager, "Outline of a Program of Social Reform" (1907), in *Labor and Other Economic Essays,* pp. 82–83.

71. Henry Rogers Seager, *Social Insurance: A Program of Social Reform* (New York: Macmillan, 1910), p. 57.

72. John R. Commons, discussion at meeting of American Association for Labor Legislation, *City Club Bulletin* (1909), 378, Commons Papers, reel 16, fr. 837.

73. Andrews to Olga Halsey, January 27, 1915, AALL Papers, reel 13; Moss, *Socializing Security,* chap. 4, pp. 59–76.

74. Seager, "The Constitution and Social Progress," p. 260.

75. On the enactment of elective laws in 1911, see Moss, *Socializing Security,*

pp. 125–126. Washington State was the only state to enact a *compulsory* workers' compensation law in 1911 that was upheld in the courts. See "Employers' Liability, Workmen's Compensation and Insurance," *ALLR*, 1, no. 3 (October 1911), 96–114.

76. Seager, "Compensation Amendment to the New York Constitution," p. 165.

77. See, e.g., Moss, *Socializing Security*, esp. pp. 119, 129–131; Roy Lubove, "Workmen's Compensation and the Prerogatives of Voluntarism," *Labor History*, 8, no. 3 (Fall 1967), 258–259.

78. Andrews, circular letter to New York Members, December 17, 1913, AALL Papers, reel 10.

79. *Matter of Jensen v. Southern Pacific Co.*, 215 N.Y. 514, 526 (1915). See also *Mountain Timber Company v. Washington* (1917), 243 U.S. 219, esp. 244–245; *New York Central Railroad Co. v. White*, 243 U.S. 188 (1917). The deposit insurance case was *Noble State Bank v. Haskell*, 219 U.S. 104 (1911).

80. Price V. Fishback and Shawn Everett Kantor, "The Durable Experiment: State Insurance of Workers' Compensation Risk in the Early Twentieth Century," *Journal of Economic History*, 56, no. 4 (December 1996), 810.

81. Lyon, "American Association for Labor Legislation and the Fight for Workmen's Compensation Laws," pp. 21, 21a; Lubove, *Struggle for Social Security*, pp. 53–61; Moss, *Socializing Security*, pp. 126–129.

82. "General Discussion," *ALLR*, 7, no. 1 (March 1917), 125.

83. John R. Commons, "Unemployment—Prevention and Insurance," in Lionel D. Edie, ed., *The Stabilization of Business* (New York: Macmillan, 1923), p. 190.

84. "Memorial on Occupational Diseases," *ALLR*, 1, no. 1 (January 1911), 127–128.

85. See esp. David A. Moss, "Kindling a Flame under Federalism: Progressive Reformers, Corporate Elites, and the Phosphorous Match Campaign of 1909–12," *Business History Review*, 68, no. 2 (Summer 1994), 244–275; Moss, *Socializing Security*, chap. 5, pp. 77–96.

86. See "Introductory Note," *ALLR*, 2, no. 4 (December 1912), 534; "Prevention of Occupational Diseases with Special Reference to Lead Poisoning," *ALLR*, 2, no. 4 (December 1912), 537–546.

87. See esp. John B. Andrews, "A Practical Program for the Prevention of Unemployment in America," *ALLR*, 5, no. 2 (June 1915), 175, 182–184, 189–191; John R. Commons, *Industrial Goodwill* (New York: McGraw-Hill, 1919), p. 65.

88. Andrews to J. Hopkins, September 5, 1918, AALL Papers, reel 18.

89. Andrews to Eugene L. Fisk, November 16, 1915, AALL Papers, reel 15.

90. John R. Commons, "Bringing about Industrial Peace," December 13, 1919,

Commons Papers, reel 17, frs. 863–902, p. 14. See also Andrews to William P. Capes, December 4, 1915, AALL Papers, reel 15; "Unemployment Survey," *ALLR*, 5, no. 3 (November 1915), 582–588.

91. Commons and Andrews, *Principles of Labor Legislation*, pp. 225, 226.

92. On Commons's preference for prevention over compensation (and, by implication, risk shifting over risk spreading), see, e.g., John R. Commons, "Health Programs," address at fifteenth annual meeting of the National Tuberculosis Association, Atlantic City, June 16, 1919, Commons Papers, reel 17, frs. 842–843: "There is, of course, also a philanthropic purpose in [compulsory health insurance], but that philanthropic purpose is really secondary. The main purpose is the business purpose of making sickness-prevention profitable."

93. John B. Andrews, "Social Insurance," n.d., AALL Papers, reel 62. See also, e.g., John B. Andrews, "Secretary's Report, 1915," *ALLR*, 6, no. 1 (1916), 104.

94. "Report of the General Administrative Council Meeting of the AALL," Chicago, April 10, 1909, AALL Papers, reel 61.

95. *Historical Statistics of the United States*, ser. D-85, p. 135; "Unemployment Survey," *ALLR*, 5, no. 3 (November 1915), 479.

96. Moss, *Socializing Security*, p. 226n9.

97. Ibid., pp. 135–136.

98. Ibid., p. 136.

99. See, e.g., Henry R. Seager, "Plan for Health Insurance Act," *ALLR*, 6, no. 1 (1916), 21.

100. I. M. Rubinow, "Standards of Sickness Insurance: I," *Journal of Political Economy*, 23, no. 3 (March 1915), 226–227; Commons and Andrews, *Principles of Labor Legislation*, p. 225; Henderson, *Industrial Insurance*, pp. 183–189.

101. "Public Hearing before the [Massachusetts] Special Commission on Social Insurance," October 3, 1916, AALL Papers, reel 62, p. 55. See also Paul Starr, *The Social Transformation of American Medicine* (New York: Basic Books, 1982), p. 236.

102. Moss, *Socializing Security*, p. 138. See also I. M. Rubinow, "Standards of Sickness Insurance: I–III," *Journal of Political Economy*, 23, nos. 3–5 (March, April, and May 1915), 221–251, 327–364, and 437–464; Seager, "Plan for Health Insurance Act," p. 24.

103. "Health Insurance—Tentative Draft of an Act," *ALLR*, 6, no. 2 (June 1916), 239–268; Seager, "Plan for Health Insurance Act," pp. 21–25.

104. Transcript of the New York State Senate Judiciary Committee Hearing on the Mills Health Insurance Bill (Senate Bill no. 236), March 14, 1916, reprinted in "Hearing on Mills Health Insurance Bill Brings out Much Oppo-

sition from Both Employer and Employee," *Monitor,* 2, no. 10 (March 1916), 28, 32.

105. "Public Hearing before the [Massachusetts] Special Commission on Social Insurance," p. 120.

106. Moss, *Socializing Security,* pp. 139–141.

107. Frederick R. Green to Andrews, November 11, 1915, AALL Papers, reel 15.

108. I. M. Rubinow, "Health Insurance through Local Mutual Funds," *ALLR,* 7, no. 1 (March 1917), 70. On the legislative developments through 1916 and 1917, see Dorothy Ketcham, "Health Insurance," *American Political Science Review,* 13, no. 1 (February 1919), 89–92; Moss, *Socializing Security,* pp. 142–144. Ketcham claimed that health insurance bills had been introduced in fifteen states in 1917, but did not name the states.

109. I. M. Rubinow, *The Quest for Security* (New York: Henry Holt, 1934), pp. 210, 214.

110. Transcript of the New York State Senate Judiciary Committee Hearing on the Mills Health Insurance Bill (Senate Print no. 365), March 7, 1917, reprinted in "Convincing and Effective Opposition to Health Insurance Bill Takes Proponents off Their Feet," *Monitor,* 3, no. 10 (March 1917), 16.

111. Transcript of the New York State Senate Judiciary Committee Hearing on the Mills Health Insurance Bill, pp. 22–23.

112. Transcript of the New York State Senate Judiciary Committee Hearing on Senator Nicoll's Health Insurance Bill, March 26, 1918, reprinted in "Health Insurance Hearing," *Monitor,* 4, no. 11 (April 1918), 21.

113. John B. Andrews, "Progress toward Health Insurance," n.d., AALL Papers, reel 18, p. 11.

114. Quoted from the Insurance Economics Society of America, *Bulletin,* no. 2, in Odin W. Anderson, "Health Insurance in the United States, 1910–1920," *Journal of the History of Medicine and Allied Sciences,* 5 (Autumn 1950), 384.

115. See, e.g., Frederick L. Hoffman, *Facts and Fallacies of Compulsory Health Insurance* (Newark: Prudential Press, 1917), p. 83.

116. Only data on total industrial life insurance in force (not premiums) are available for 1917. For 1876–1904, however, years in which full data were available, the ratio of premiums to insurance in force equaled 4.53 percent. Since total industrial life insurance in force for 1917 was $5.026 billion, a reasonable estimate of industrial life insurance premiums in 1917 is 4.53 percent of that figure, or $227.7 million. Henderson, *Industrial Insurance,* p. 158; *Historical Statistics of the United States,* ser. X-885, p. 1056.

117. Rubinow, *Quest for Security,* p. 213.

118. See esp. William E. Forbath, *Law and the Shaping of the American Labor Movement* (Cambridge, Mass.: Harvard University Press, 1991); Henderson, *Industrial Insurance,* p. 61.

119. On the unions' preference for voluntary over compulsory insurance, see, e.g., *Report of Proceedings of the Thirty-sixth Annual Convention of the American Federation of Labor* (Washington, D.C.: Law Reporter Printing Co., 1916), p. 145; Gompers, "Labor vs. Its Barnacles," esp. p. 270.

120. "Mr. Gompers Opposes Enemies of Labor Legislation," *Legislative Labor News*, 4, no. 86 (June 1915), [5]; Milton Fairchild to Henry Seager, ca. June 1915, AALL Papers, reel 14.

121. "New York Federation of Labor Is Back of Health Insurance Bill to Be Urged at Present Session of the Legislature," *Monitor*, 4, no. 9 (February 1918), 1–3; *Health Insurance: Official Endorsement of the New York State Federation of Labor, with Report of Its Committee on Health* (New York State Federation of Labor, 1918), esp. pp. 3, 5, 6, and 16.

122. "Labor and Health Insurance," *Monitor*, 4, no. 9 (February 1918), 10.

123. Extract of Governor Alfred E. Smith's January 1, 1919, message to the New York legislature, reprinted in "Health Insurance Will Conserve Human Life," *ALLR*, 9, no. 2 (June 1919), 225.

124. "Health Insurance Bill Passes New York State Senate," *ALLR*, 9, no. 2 (June 1919), 232–237.

125. "The Legislature," *Monitor*, 5, no. 11 (April 1919), 20.

126. Arthur J. Viseltear, "Compulsory Health Insurance in California, 1915–1918," *Journal of the History of Medicine and Allied Sciences*, 24, no. 2 (April 1969), 181.

127. "More Testimony," *Monitor*, 7, no. 6 (November 1920), 16.

7. Social Security

1. Presidential statement signing the Social Security Act, August 14, 1935.

2. Ibid. See also, e.g., Doughton, *Congressional Record* (House), 74th Cong., 1st sess., April 11, 1935, p. 5468; Wagner, *Congressional Record* (Senate), 74th Cong., 1st sess., June 14, 1935, p. 9283; Sirovich, *Congressional Record* (House), April 16, 1935, p. 5790 ("Before the intense centralization of industry arrived in the large cities, homesteads were kept and there was always room for grandpa and grandma at the fireside").

3. *Report to the President of the Committee on Economic Security* (Washington, D.C.: GPO, 1935), p. 2. See also Henry R. Seager, "Outline of a Program of Social Legislation with Special Reference to Wage-Earners," in *American Association for Labor Legislation: Proceedings of the First Annual Meeting* (Madison, April 1908), pp. 85–103; Henry Rogers Seager, *Social Insurance: A Program of Social Reform* (New York: Macmillan, 1910).

4. U.S. Department of Commerce, Bureau of the Census, *Historical Statistics of the United States, Colonial Times to 1970* (Washington, D.C.: GPO, 1975), pt. 1, ser. D-8 and D-9, p. 126.

5. John R. Commons, "Unemployment—Prevention and Insurance," in Lionel D. Edie, ed., *The Stabilization of Business* (New York: Macmillan, 1923), p. 181. See also "To Prevent Unemployment," *New York Times,* October 10, 1921, Commons Papers, reel 19, fr. 246.

6. John R. Commons and John B. Andrews, *Principles of Labor Legislation,* 4th rev. ed. (New York: Augustus M. Kelley Publishers, 1967 [1936, 1916]), p. 293n101.

7. Daniel Nelson, *Unemployment Insurance: The American Experience, 1915–1935* (Madison: University of Wisconsin Press, 1969), pp. 118–128; Saul J. Blaustein, *Unemployment Insurance in the United States* (Kalamazoo, Mich.: W. E. Upjohn Institute for Employment Research, 1993), pp. 117–118; Commons and Andrews, *Principles of Labor Legislation,* pp. 308–309; "Wisconsin Unemployment Compensation Act of 1931," reprinted in Paul H. Douglas, *Standards of Unemployment Insurance* (Chicago: University of Chicago Press, 1932), app. A, pp. 200–218.

8. For a spirited defense of the Groves-Raushenbush approach, see Harold M. Groves and Elizabeth Brandeis, "Economic Bases of the Wisconsin Unemployment Reserves Act," *American Economic Review,* 24, no. 1 (March 1934), 38–52.

9. John R. Commons, "Unemployment Insurance," Economic Series Lecture no. 24, delivered April 9, 1932, over a nationwide network of the National Broadcasting Company, reprinted in Commons Papers, reel 21, frs. 490–491. See also several articles in the *American Labor Legislation Review* [*ALLR*], 22, no. 1 (March 1932): Harold M. Groves, "Compensation for Idle Labor in Wisconsin," 7; John R. Commons, "The Groves Unemployment Reserves Law," 8–10; Paul A. Raushenbush, "Wisconsin's Unemployment Compensation Act," 11–18.

10. Paul H. Douglas, *Social Security in the United States: An Analysis and Appraisal of the Federal Social Security Act* (New York: Whittlesey House, 1936), pp. 15–16. See also Report of the Interstate Commission on Unemployment Insurance, reprinted in Douglas, *Standards of Unemployment Insurance,* app. B, p. 220.

11. See Paul H. Douglas, "Two Problems of Unemployment Insurance," *Journal of the American Statistical Association,* 30, no. 189 (March 1935), esp. 215–217; Walter A. Morton, "The Aims of Unemployment Insurance with Especial Reference to the Wisconsin Act," *American Economic Review,* 23, no. 3 (September 1933), esp. 409–410; Abraham Epstein, *Insecurity: A Challenge to America,* 2nd rev. ed. (New York: Agathon Press, 1968 [1938, 1933], esp. p. 312; Paul H. Douglas, reviews of Abraham Epstein's *Insecurity: A Challenge to America* and John B. Ewing's *Job Insurance, American Political Science Review,* 27, no. 5 (October 1933), 835–836. Even Andrews

once expressed concern that benefits would be too low under the reserves approach. See John Andrews to Paul Raushenbush, January 15, 1931, AALL Papers, reel 43, also cited in Roy Lubove, *The Struggle for Social Security, 1900–1935* (Pittsburgh: University of Pittsburgh Press, 1986 [1968]), pp. 169 and 267n92.

12. Douglas, *Social Security*, pp. 13–14. See also Nelson, *Unemployment Insurance*, p. 149.

13. Blaustein, *Unemployment Insurance*, p. 119; Nelson, *Unemployment Insurance*, p. 184 and apps. 1 and 2, pp. 225–236; Douglas, *Social Security*, p. 17; Carter Goodrich, "An Analysis of American Plans for State Unemployment Insurance," *American Economic Review*, 21, no. 3 (September 1931), 399–415. The Ohio commission's model bill is reprinted in Douglas, *Standards of Unemployment Insurance*, app. C, pp. 226–242.

14. Nelson, *Unemployment Insurance*, app. 2 ("Excerpts from the Report of the Ohio Commission, 1932"), p. 232.

15. Ibid., p. 184.

16. Quoted ibid.

17. Douglas, *Social Security*, pp. 17–18; Nelson, *Unemployment Insurance*, p. 189.

18. Donald M. Smith, "A Comparison of State Unemployment Insurance Measures, 1930–1935," M.A. thesis (University of Chicago, 1935), p. 4, cited in Douglas, *Social Security*, p. 18. For slightly different estimates, see Katherine Baicker, Claudia Goldin, and Lawrence Katz, "A Distinctive System: Origins and Impact of U.S. Unemployment Compensation," in Michael D. Bordo, Claudia Goldin, and Eugene N. White, eds., *The Defining Moment: The Great Depression and the American Economy in the Twentieth Century* (Chicago: University of Chicago Press, 1998), p. 238.

19. David A. Moss, *Socializing Security: Progressive-Era Economists and the Origins of American Social Policy* (Cambridge, Mass.: Harvard University Press, 1996), pp. 160–161; Lubove, *The Struggle for Social Security*, pp. 138–143; Nelson, *Unemployment Insurance*, pp. 152, 194–196; Leotto Louis, "Abraham Epstein and the Movement for Old Age Security," *Labor History*, 16, no. 3 (1975), 359–377.

20. Quoted in Nelson, *Unemployment Insurance*, p. 195.

21. Ibid., p. 184. See also, e.g., Paul H. Douglas, "Discussion," *American Economic Review*, 23, no. 1 (March 1933), Papers and Proceedings, 52–54; E. M. Burns, "The Economics of Unemployment Relief," *American Economic Review*, 23, no. 1 (March 1933), Papers and Proceedings, 31–43.

22. Douglas, "Discussion," p. 53.

23. I. M. Rubinow, "Labor Insurance," *Journal of Political Economy*, 12, no. 3 (June 1904), 374–375.

24. I. M. Rubinow, "Subsidized Unemployment Insurance," *Journal of Political Economy*, 21, no. 5 (May 1913), 413.

25. Paul H. Douglas, *Standards of Unemployment Insurance* (Chicago: University of Chicago Press, 1932), p. 164.

26. See Michael Rappaport, "The Private Provision of Unemployment Insurance," *Wisconsin Law Review*, 61 (January–February 1992), 65n8; Paul Monroe, "Insurance against Non-Employment," *American Journal of Sociology*, 2, no. 6 (May 1897), 771–785; Marquis James, *The Metropolitan Life: A Study in Business Growth* (New York: Viking Press, 1947), p. 432n41. On the legal tolerance of private unemployment insurance in Michigan, see Bryce M. Stewart, *Unemployment Benefits in the United States: The Plans and Their Settings* (New York: Industrial Relations Counselors, 1930), pp. 98, 573.

27. James, *Metropolitan Life*, pp. 201, 226–231, 336–337; Rappaport, "Private Provision of Unemployment Insurance," pp. 66–68.

28. The counterfactual argument regarding the feasibility of private unemployment insurance is put forth by Rappaport, "Private Provision of Unemployment Insurance," esp. pp. 62–72.

29. Ibid., pp. 67–68. The New York State legislature, desperate to do something about record unemployment, finally did pass the long-awaited authorization bill in 1931; but Governor Roosevelt, still awaiting the results of his interstate commission on unemployment insurance, immediately vetoed it. Nelson, *Unemployment Insurance*, p. 166. On Roosevelt's veto, see also Bernard Bellush, *Franklin D. Roosevelt as Governor of New York* (New York: AMS Press, 1968), pp. 187–188; Franklin D. Roosevelt, veto message regarding Assembly bill, Int. no. 2096, Pr. no. 2421, "An Act to amend the insurance law, in relation to unemployment insurance corporations," April 14, 1931, in *Public Papers of Franklin D. Roosevelt, Forty-eighth Governor of the State of New York, Second Term, 1931* (Albany, J. B. Lyon Company, 1937), pp. 237–238.

30. Quoted in Rappaport, "Private Provision of Unemployment Insurance," p. 67.

31. Louis I. Dublin, *A Family of Thirty Million: The Story of the Metropolitan Life Insurance Company* (New York: Metropolitan Life Insurance Company, 1943), p. 93.

32. See esp. Roderic Olzendam, *Memorandum Presented by Roderic Olzendam, Social Insurance Research Director of the Metropolitan Life Insurance Company, at the Invitation of the Joint Legislative Committee on Unemployment of the State of New York*, pamphlet (New York, December 1, 1932). Speaking before the Joint Legislative Committee on Unemployment in 1932, Olzendam of Metropolitan Life asserted: "As far as I am informed, there are

no insurance companies today which would advocate any change in the law which would make it permissible for them to experiment with unemployment insurance. So far as our own Company is concerned, we have definitely concluded that, on the basis of our studies, during the past two years, we certainly would not now be willing to undertake such an experiment" (p. 4).

33. Rubinow, "Subsidized Unemployment Insurance," p. 416.
34. Harry Malisoff, "The Emergence of Unemployment Compensation, I," *Political Science Quarterly,* 54, no. 2 (June 1939), 239n4, 240n8.
35. Douglas, *Standards of Unemployment Insurance,* p. 33.
36. Commons and Andrews, *Principles of Labor Legislation,* p. 293. For an almost identical indictment, see Epstein, *Insecurity,* p. 349.
37. See esp. Industrial Relations Counselors, *An Historical Basis for Unemployment Insurance* (Minneapolis: University of Minnesota Press, 1934), pp. 68, 240–247; Douglas, *Standards of Unemployment Insurance,* p. 38.
38. Rubinow, "Subsidized Unemployment Insurance," p. 418.
39. Rappaport, "Private Provision of Unemployment Insurance," pp. 65–66.
40. Malisoff, "Emergence of Unemployment Compensation, I," pp. 239n5, 240n8.
41. Groves and Brandeis, "Economic Bases of the Wisconsin Unemployment Reserves Act," p. 45n6.
42. Lubove, *Struggle for Social Security,* p. 169; Malisoff, "Emergence of Unemployment Compensation, I," p. 247.
43. Paul A. Raushenbush and Elizabeth Brandeis Raushenbush, *Our "U.C." Story, 1930–1967* (Madison, Wisc., 1979), pp. 38–39; *Florida v. Mellon,* 273 U.S. 12 (1927). On Congress's intentions in creating the tax-offset scheme in 1926, see Thomas H. Eliot's discussion in Katie Louchheim, ed., *The Making of the New Deal: The Insiders Speak* (Cambridge, Mass.: Harvard University Press, 1983), pp. 160–161.
44. Statement of Thomas H. Eliot in Louchheim, *Making of the New Deal,* pp. 160–161; Raushenbush and Raushenbush, *Our "U.C." Story,* pp. 38–39. See also Wilbur J. Cohen, "The Development of the Social Security Act of 1935: Reflections Some Fifty Years Later," *Minnesota Law Review,* 68, no. 2 (December 1983), 401–402; Nelson, *Unemployment Insurance,* p. 199.
45. Nelson, *Unemployment Insurance,* pp. 134–135, 198–204; "New Federal Plan for Unemployment Compensation Legislation," *ALLR,* 24, no. 1 (March 1934), 7–8; John B. Andrews, "A National Challenge," *ALLR,* 24, no. 1 (March 1934), 3; "Administration Job Insurance Bill 'Side-Tracked' at Washington," *ALLR,* 24, no. 2 (June 1934), 53–56.
46. "The Initiation of Studies to Achieve a Program of National Social and Economic Security," Executive Order no. 6757, June 29, 1934, reprinted in

The Report of the Committee on Economic Security of 1935, and Other Basic Documents Relating to the Development of the Social Security Act, Fiftieth Anniversary ed. (Washington, D.C.: National Conference on Social Welfare, 1985), p. 140.

47. Ibid.

48. Arthur J. Altmeyer, The Formative Years of Social Security (Madison: University of Wisconsin Press, 1968), p. viii.

49. Edwin Witte, "What to Expect of Social Security," American Economic Review, 34, no. 1 (March 1944), 214. Witte also noted that in "its present connotation, the term social security does not seem to go back further than 1933, when the late Dr. Abraham Epstein expanded his Association for Old Age Security into the Association for Social Security."

50. Altmeyer, Formative Years, p. 13. See also J. Douglas Brown, An American Philosophy of Social Security: Evolutions and Issues (Princeton: Princeton University Press, 1972), pp. 8–9; Ann Shola Orloff, The Politics of Pensions: A Comparative Analysis of Britain, Canada, and the United States, 1880–1940 (Madison: University of Wisconsin Press, 1993), p. 291.

51. Interview with Barbara Nachtrieb Armstrong, conducted December 19, 20, and 22, 1965, by Peter A. Corning, Social Security Administration Project, Oral History Research Office, Columbia University, pp. 31, 183–184 (hereafter Armstrong oral history interview). On Armstrong's concern that Perkins and Witte were overly concerned with passing state-level unemployment insurance and basically uninterested in old age insurance, see esp. pp. 54, 78, 85.

52. Congressional Record (House), April 11, 1935, p. 5476.

53. Committee on Economic Security, The Report to the President of the Committee on Economic Security (Washington, D.C.: GPO, 1935), pp. 37–40.

54. Armstrong oral history interview, p. 215. See also Edwin E. Witte, The Development of the Social Security Act (Madison: University of Wisconsin Press, 1963), p. 112; Blaustein, Unemployment Insurance, p. 135.

55. Frances Perkins, The Roosevelt I Knew (New York: Viking, 1946), pp. 291–292; Douglas, Social Security, pp. 33–34. See also Altmeyer, Formative Years, pp. 14–15; Wilbur J. Cohen, "The Development of the Social Security Act of 1935: Reflections Some Fifty Years Later," Minnesota Law Review, 68, no. 2 (December 1983), 399. When Secretary Perkins turned to Justice Harlan Fiske Stone in 1934 for some advice about how best to satisfy the Court in constructing an unemployment insurance system, the avuncular justice told her, "The taxing power of the Federal Government, my dear; the taxing power is sufficient for everything you want and need." Perkins, The Roosevelt I Knew, p. 286.

56. Quoted in Nelson, Unemployment Insurance, p. 206.

57. Frances Perkins, *Economic Security Act: Hearings before the Committee on Finance on S. 1130* (Senate), 74th Cong., 1st sess., p. 101. She did acknowledge, however, "that certain parts of the seasonal unemployment, of that due to technical improvements, and of that due to the practice of industries in keeping large numbers of men partially attached to the industry for use in rush periods or peak loads are due to an inadequate social conception of the employer of the problem which is before him."

58. Committee on Economic Security, *Report to the President*, p. 14. See also Perkins, *The Roosevelt I Knew*, p. 285. On the connection between the purchasing power argument and pooling, see, e.g., Douglas, "Discussion," p. 52.

59. Committee on Economic Security, *Report to the President*, pp. 15–23.

60. On business support for the Wisconsin approach, see esp. Nelson, *Unemployment Insurance*, p. 208.

61. Committee on Economic Security, *Report to the President*, pp. 7–10; Perkins, *Economic Security Act: Hearings before the Committee on Finance* (Senate), pp. 119–120.

62. Committee on Economic Security, *Report to the President*, pp. 7, 10.

63. Walter Lippmann to J. M. Keynes, January 9, 1935, Walter Lippmann Collection, Yale University, Group 326, ser. 3, box 82, folder 1217.

64. Witte, *Development of the Social Security Act*, p. 77.

65. Donald S. Howard, *The WPA and Federal Relief Policy* (New York: Russell Sage Foundation, 1943), pp. 563–565.

66. Cohen, "Development of the Social Security Act," p. 380n4.

67. On the shorter workweek proposal, see esp. Truax, *Congressional Record* (House), April 15, 1935, p. 5691; Barkley, *Congressional Record* (Senate), June 19, 1935, p. 9626. On the legal right to work, see Lewis, *Congressional Record* (House), April 15, 1935, p. 5687; Keller, *Congressional Record* (House), April 12, 1935, p. 5551. Significantly, John R. Commons first proposed a legal right to work in the 1890s, but subsequently backed away from the idea. See John R. Commons, *The Distribution of Wealth* (New York: Macmillan, 1893), pp. 80, 82–83; John R. Commons, "The Right to Work," *Arena*, 21, no. 2 (February 1899), 131–142. On the "technotax," see Hoeppel, *Congressional Record* (House), April 13, 1935, pp. 5589–90, April 19, 1935, pp. 6054–55. The CES apparently considered a similar proposal but decided against it; see Frances Perkins, *Economic Security Act: Hearings before the Committee on Ways and Means on H.R. 4120* (House), 74th Cong., 1st sess., p. 205.

68. Social Security Act, August 14, 1935, Public Law no. 271, 74th Cong., Titles III, VIII, IX.

69. *Congressional Record* (Senate), June 14, 1935, p. 9283.

70. The very same problems were again emphasized by the courts once the constitutionality of the Social Security Act and the resulting state unemployment laws began to be challenged. See esp. *W. H. H. Chamberlin, Inc. v. Andrews*, 159 Misc. 124, 145, 286 N.Y.S. 242, 270 (1936); *Steward Mach. Co. v. Davis*, 301 U.S. 548, 588 (1937).

71. *Congressional Record* (House), April 11, 1935, p. 5468. See also Committee on Economic Security, *Report to the President*, p. 15 ("unemployment insurance has . . . in all countries provided a self-respected method of support, far superior to relief").

72. According to the CES, "[t]he primary purpose of unemployment compensation is to socialize the losses resulting from unemployment, but it should also serve the purpose of decreasing rather than increasing unemployment." Committee on Economic Security, *Report to the President*, p. 22. Echoing these sentiments in Congress, Representative Doughton insisted, "The social-security program . . . is an attempt to mitigate and to prevent the distress and suffering which so frequently arise from our industrial economy." *Congressional Record* (House), April 11, 1935, p. 5468.

73. See *Congressional Record* (House), April 19, 1935, pp. 6059–60.

74. See, e.g., Doughton, ibid., April 11, 1935, pp. 5476, 5468; Healey, ibid., April 16, 1935, p. 5813.

75. Perkins, *Economic Security Act: Hearings before the Committee on Finance* (Senate), p. 115. See also Perkins, *Economic Security Act: Hearings before the Committee on Ways and Means* (House), pp. 184–185.

76. Nelson, *Unemployment Insurance*, p. 218.

77. *Congressional Record* (Senate), June 15, 1935, pp. 9359–61.

78. Ibid., June 14, 1935, p. 9284.

79. See, e.g., Harrison, ibid., p. 9271; Wagner, ibid., p. 9284.

80. Nelson, *Unemployment Insurance*, p. 218.

81. Malisoff, "Emergence of Unemployment Compensation, I," p. 252.

82. Blaustein, *Unemployment Insurance*, pp. 160–161. See also William Haber and Merrill G. Murray, *Unemployment Insurance in the American Economy* (Homewood, Ill.: Richard D. Irwin, 1966), p. 120.

83. Committee on Economic Security, *Report to the President*, pp. 23–24. See also *Social Security in America: The Factual Background of the Social Security Act as Summarized from Staff Reports to the Committee on Economic Security* (Washington, D.C.: GPO, 1937), pp. 139–142, 149–154.

84. *Congressional Record* (Senate), June 14, 1935, pp. 9288–90, 9285–86. See also *Social Security in America*, pp. 167–178.

85. *Congressional Record* (Senate), June 14, 1935, p. 9285.

86. The one exception was a compulsory old age insurance program for federal employees, which was enacted in 1920. The nation's first compulsory,

contributory program applying to private workers came into being when Congress passed the Railroad Retirement Act in 1934. See Commons and Andrews, *Principles of Labor Legislation*, pp. 283–284.

87. Simply put, neither old age nor old age dependency was a hazard that employers could reasonably be expected to prevent. No matter how much of the burden was shifted onto employers via experience-rated insurance premiums, they could not possibly "prevent" their workers from growing old. Employers could conceivably have held on to their older workers longer, thus delaying the termination of earnings and the onset of dependency. But persuading employers to do this would have been exceedingly difficult, since older workers were typically seen as less productive. See esp. Moss, *Socializing Security,* p. 170. See also, e.g., Eveline M. Burns, "Social Insurance in Evolution," *American Economic Review,* 34, no. 1 (March 1944), Papers and Proceedings, p. 210.

88. Commons and Andrews, *Principles of Labor Legislation,* p. 285.

89. See, e.g., Henry Seager, "Old Age Pensions" (1908), reprinted in *Labor and Other Economic Essays by Henry R. Seager,* ed. Charles A. Gulick, Jr. (New York: Harper and Brothers Publishers, 1931), pp. 149–154. See also Frederick L. Hoffman, "State Pensions and Annuities in Old Age," *Publications of the American Statistical Association,* 11, no. 85 (March 1909), esp. 371.

90. Commons and Andrews, *Principles of Labor Legislation,* pp. 278, 284–285; Lubove, *Struggle for Social Security,* pp. 135–137; Mark H. Leff, "Taxing the 'Forgotten Man': The Politics of Social Security Finance in the New Deal," *Journal of American History,* 70, no. 2 (September 1983), 360. See also *Social Security in America,* pp. 156–167.

91. Armstrong oral history interview, p. 31.

92. Committee on Economic Security, *Report to the President,* pp. 25, 33. This argument was also highlighted frequently during the congressional debates. See, e.g., Wagner, *Congressional Record* (Senate), June 14, 1935, pp. 9285, 9286. On the reasons for the CES's apparent conversion to the insurance approach, see Armstrong oral history interview, pp. 81–83, 154–155; Brown, *American Philosophy of Social Security,* p. 21.

93. Committee on Economic Security, *Report to the President,* p. 25.

94. Ibid., pp. 26–29.

95. Ibid., p. 25. On the notion of payroll taxes as insurance premiums, see, e.g., Perkins, *Economic Security Act: Hearings before the Committee on Finance* (Senate), p. 106.

96. Most of these modifications were relatively minor, but a few were not. For example, the final legislation excluded agricultural workers and household employees from the insurance program (Social Security Act, sec. 210b), removed the $250 monthly earnings cut-off for non-manual work-

ers (sec. 210), and set the combined payroll tax rate at 6 rather than 5 percent (Social Security Act, sec. 801). It also eliminated a CES proposal that would have had the federal government sell supplementary annuities to the public on a voluntary basis. Committee on Economic Security, *Report to the President,* pp. 34–35. On the controversy over the exclusion of agricultural and domestic workers, see esp. Perkins, *The Roosevelt I Knew,* pp. 297–298; Armstrong oral history interview, pp. 129–130.

97. See, e.g., Witte, *Development of the Social Security Act,* pp. 76–79; Thomas H. Eliot, "The Legal Background of the Social Security Act," address delivered at a general staff meeting at Social Security Administration headquarters, Baltimore, February 3, 1961.

98. Social Security Act, August 14, 1935, Public Law no. 271, 74th Cong., Titles II and VIII; *Helvering v. Davis,* 301 U.S. 619 (1937); Eliot, "Legal Background of the Social Security Act"; Armstrong oral history interview, pp. 131–133.

99. On these two arguments, see esp. *Social Security in America,* p. 137; Armstrong oral history interview, pp. 255–256, 261–262; Wilbur J. Cohen, *Retirement Policies under Social Security* (Berkeley: University of California Press, 1957), p. 19; Wagner, *Congressional Record* (Senate), June 14, 1935, p. 9286; Murray Latimer, *Economic Security Act: Hearings before the Committee on Ways and Means* (House), pp. 220–225; Perkins, *Economic Security Act: Hearings before the Committee on Ways and Means* (House), p. 180. On the philosophy of removing older workers from the labor force, see also William Graebner, *A History of Retirement: The Meaning and Function of an American Institution, 1885–1978* (New Haven: Yale University Press, 1980), esp. pp. 18–53, 181–214.

100. *Congressional Record* (Senate), June 14, 1935, p. 9286.

101. Barbara Nachtrieb Armstrong, *Insuring the Essential: Minimum Wage Plus Social Insurance—A Living Wage Program* (New York: Macmillan, 1932), p. 381.

102. *Congressional Record* (Senate), June 14, 1935, p. 9292. See also, e.g., Wagner, ibid., p. 9285; Sirovich, *Congressional Record* (House), April 16, 1935, p. 5790.

103. Committee on Economic Security, *Report to the President,* pp. 31, 30.

104. Leff, "Taxing the 'Forgotten Man,'" pp. 368–370.

105. Social Security Act, August 14, 1935, Public Law no. 271, 74th Cong., secs. 202, 801, 804.

106. Leff, "Taxing the 'Forgotten Man,'" p. 369.

107. Armstrong oral history interview, p. 264. See also, e.g., Epstein, *Insecurity,* pp. 780, 783.

108. See esp. Social Security Act Amendments, August 10, 1939, Public Law no.

379, 76th Cong., secs. 202, 203, 601, 604; Robert M. Ball, "The 1939 Amendments to the Social Security Act and What Followed," in *Report of the Committee on Economic Security of 1935*, pp. 165–167. According to Leff, the 1939 amendments significantly undermined the president's "strict insurance model." "Taxing the 'Forgotten Man,'" p. 371. On the program's alleged redistributive inadequacy, see esp. Jerry R. Cates, *Insuring Inequality: Administrative Leadership in Social Security, 1935–54* (Ann Arbor: University of Michigan Press, 1983), chap. 1, pp. 5–21.

109. J. Douglas Brown, *Economic Security Act: Hearings before the Committee on Ways and Means* (House), pp. 245–246.

110. Ibid., p. 203. See also Henry Morgenthau, ibid., p. 900.

111. On Social Security's old age insurance program as a "lifetime compulsory saving framework," see also Alicia H. Munnell, *The Future of Social Security* (Washington, D.C.: Brookings Institution, 1977), pp. 92–93.

112. *Congressional Record* (Senate), June 14, 1935, p. 9292.

113. *Social Security in America*, p. 138.

114. *Congressional Record* (Senate), June 18, 1935, p. 9526.

115. *Historical Statistics of the United States*, pt. 1, ser. B-107.

116. U.S. Department of Labor, *Care of Aged Persons in the United States*, Bulletin of the United States Bureau of Labor Statistics no. 489 (Washington, D.C.: GPO, October 1929), p. 296. For an early treatment of the problem of myopic decision making and the potential role of government in addressing it, see A. C. Pigou, *The Economics of Welfare* (London: Macmillan, 1932), pp. 23–30.

117. Benjamin M. Friedman and Mark J. Warshawsky, "The Cost of Annuities: Implications for Saving Behavior and Bequests," *Quarterly Journal of Economics*, 105, no. 1 (February 1990), 136, 140.

118. Rubinow, *Quest for Security*, p. 293.

119. Committee on Economic Security, *Report to the President*, p. 29.

120. Though sold in significant quantities in the 1920s, disability insurance fell out of favor among private insurers in the 1930s as a result of very large payouts. Apparently, many insured workers who lost their jobs successfully claimed disability during the depression. See Edward Berkowitz and Kim McQuaid, "Businessman and Bureaucrat: The Evolution of the American Social Welfare System, 1900–1940," *Journal of Economic History*, 38, no. 1 (March 1978), 137–138.

121. On work-duration risk, see esp. Peter A. Diamond, "A Framework for Social Security Analysis," *Journal of Public Economics*, 8, no. 3 (December 1977), 280–281.

122. *Social Security in America*, p. 139.

123. Brown, *American Philosophy of Social Security*, p. 125.

124. On the legislative changes, see esp. Geoffrey Kollmann, "Summary of Major Changes in the Social Security Cash Benefits Program, 1935–1996," *CRS Report for Congress* (Congressional Research Service, Library of Congress, December 20, 1996), pp. 1, 6–7, 8, 12. On the implications for work-duration risk, see Diamond, "Framework for Social Security Analysis," pp. 276–277, 280–281.

125. *Economic Security Act: Hearings before the Committee on Ways and Means* (House), p. 220.

126. *Congressional Record* (Senate), June 14, 1935, p. 9285.

127. See, e.g., Committee on Economic Security, *Report to the President,* p. 29.

128. *Congressional Record* (House), April 16, 1935, p. 5789.

129. See esp. Robert C. Merton, "On the Role of Social Security as a Means for Efficient Risk Sharing in an Economy Where Human Capital Is Not Tradable," in Zvi Bodie and John B. Shoven, eds., *Financial Aspects of the U.S. Pension System* (Chicago: University of Chicago Press, 1983), pp. 325–358. Merton argues that one potential justification for public old age insurance is that it redistributes human capital (via the payroll tax) from the young (who typically have too much human capital in their portfolios) to the old (who typically have too little human capital in their portfolios). This sort of portfolio diversification cannot be accomplished privately because human capital is not legally tradable in the marketplace as a result of constitutional prohibitions on slavery and the availability of a discharge in bankruptcy.

130. *Congressional Record* (Senate), June 14, 1935, p. 9292; *Congressional Record* (House), April 16, 1935, p. 5790.

131. Beiter, *Congressional Record* (House), April 16, 1935, p. 5768.

132. *Congressional Record* (Senate), June 18, 1935, p. 9525.

133. Ibid., p. 9520.

134. See, e.g., in *Congressional Record* (House), Crawford, April 15, 1935, pp. 5708–9; Beiter, April 16, 1935, p. 5768; Colden, April 16, 1935, p. 5804; Young, April 13, 1935, p. 5594; Sirovich, April 16, 1935, p. 5789; Fuller, April 17, 1935, p. 5858; Kenney, April 13, 1935, p. 5605; also Latimer, *Economic Security Act: Hearings before the Committee on Ways and Means* (House), p. 221; Brown, ibid., p. 241; *Social Security in America,* p. 153; Rubinow, *Quest for Security,* esp. pp. 33, 230, 235, 297.

135. *Economic Security Act: Hearings before the Committee on Ways and Means* (House), pp. 179, 241, 1011.

136. *Congressional Record* (Senate), June 17, 1935, p. 9442, and June 18, 1935, pp. 9510–12.

137. See, e.g., ibid., June 18, 1935, pp. 9511, 9515, 9516, 9518, 9527, 9531. See also Douglas, *Social Security,* pp. 121–122.

138. Ann Shola Orloff, *The Politics of Pensions: A Comparative Analysis of Britain, Canada, and the United States, 1880–1940* (Madison: University of Wisconsin Press, 1993), p. 293; Douglas, *Social Security,* pp. 124–125.

139. *Congressional Record* (House), July 17, 1935, p. 11342. See also, e.g., Wagner, *Congressional Record* (Senate), June 18, 1935, p. 9525 ("I am firmly convinced that if this amendment were adopted we should find the Government holding the bag for the older men"); Harrison, *Congressional Record* (Senate), June 18, 1935, pp. 9521–23.

140. Brown, *American Philosophy of Social Security,* p. 65. See also Harrison, *Congressional Record* (Senate), June 18, 1935, pp. 9521–23.

141. *Congressional Record* (Senate), June 18, 1935, p. 9521.

142. Shipstead, ibid., p. 9523. See also, e.g., ibid., July 17, 1935, pp. 1136–37 (Hill), 11341 (Sauthoff), 11342 (Dockweiler).

143. Ibid., June 18, 1935, p. 9525.

144. Colden, *Congressional Record* (House), April 16, 1935, p. 5804.

145. On the concept of intergenerational risk spreading, see, e.g., J. E. Stiglitz, "On the Relevance or Irrelevance of Public Financial Policy: Indexation, Price Rigidities, and Optimal Monetary Policies," in Rudiger Dornbush and Mario Henrique Simonsen, eds., *Inflation, Debt, and Indexation* (Cambridge, Mass.: MIT Press, 1983), esp. pp. 183, 186; Stanley Fischer, "Welfare Aspects of Government Issue of Indexed Bonds," ibid., esp. pp. 229–230, 233.

146. Committee on Economic Security, *Report to the President,* p. 32.

147. Some economists at the Treasury Department did seek to establish a "pension geared to the business cycle," which would be stepped up in a slump and cut back in an inflationary boom; but even here the logic of intergenerational risk spreading does not appear to have been explicitly laid out. See Altmeyer, *Formative Years,* pp. 109–110.

148. Even today, inflation risk is very difficult to manage, except through the purchase of inflation-indexed government bonds, which were introduced for the first time in 1997.

149. On the problem of inflation risk, see esp. Armstrong, *Insuring the Essentials,* pp. 385–386; *Social Security in America,* p. 153; Dirksen, *Congressional Record* (House), April 16, 1935, p. 5812: "The Department of Agriculture tells us that the retail price of food has gone up about 29 percent since 1933. . . . In other words, a $50 pension in 1933 would only be a $35 pension in 1935. . . . [I]f we are going to be consistent in our attack on the 50-cent dollar, we must make proper allowance for that fact in computing pensions." Dirksen seemed to be proposing the indexation of old age benefits, but the idea failed to catch on in 1935.

150. The ratio was 36.1 percent in 1940, 21.3 in 1950, 33.7 in 1960, 29.4 in

1970, 35.3 in 1980, 29.2 in 1990, and 29.7 in 1996. Significantly, the average annual Social Security retirement benefit has risen sharply as a fraction of the average annual earnings of production and nonsupervisory workers, increasing from 23.4 percent in 1960 to 40.2 percent in 1996. See *Social Security Bulletin: Annual Statistical Supplement* (1997), table 6.A2; *Historical Statistics of the United States,* ser. F-2; *Economic Report of the President* (1997), tables B-29 and B-45.

151. President Franklin D. Roosevelt, Message to Congress Reviewing the Broad Objectives and Accomplishments of the Administration, June 8, 1934. Of course, there were also those who objected to this approach. Said Representative Charles Eaton during the Social Security debates in Congress, "This is a crazy notion, as expressed in a lot of this new-deal legislation, and accepted by increasing numbers of our people, that somehow . . . the Government of the United States can make it impossible and unnecessary for any of its citizens to face any difficulty, to run any risk. . . . The thing is absolutely absurd." *Congressional Record* (House), April 13, 1935, p. 5580.

152. Committee on Economic Security, *Report to the President,* pp. 1, 2. See also Perkins, *Economic Security Act: Hearings before the Committee on Finance* (Senate), pp. 102–103.

153. It was incomplete in other ways as well. Perhaps most important of all, the compulsory insurance programs established under Social Security explicitly excluded several categories of workers, especially agricultural laborers and household employees, who together constituted a large fraction of the nation's black workforce.

154. Altmeyer, *Formative Years,* p. 267. See also Arthur J. Altmeyer, Statement before the Senate Special Committee on Old Age Security, July 21, 1941, Social Security Administration Historical Archives, www.ssa.gov/history/aja741.html; Arthur J. Altmeyer, "Desirability of Expanding the Social Insurance Program Now," *Social Security Bulletin,* 5, no. 11 (November 1942), 5–9.

155. See esp. Witte, *Development of the Social Security Act,* p. 181.

156. Perkins, *The Roosevelt I Knew,* p. 289; Witte, *Development of the Social Security Act,* p. 174; Arthur Altmeyer, oral history interview with Peter A. Coming, Social Security Administration Project, Oral History Research Office, Columbia University, interview no. 2, March 23, 1966; President Franklin D. Roosevelt, Address to the Advisory Council of the Committee on Economic Security of the Problems of Economic and Social Security, November 14, 1934.

157. Witte, *Development of the Social Security Act,* pp. 187–189. See also "Report to the President of the Committee on Economic Security: Final Report on

Risks to Economic Security Arising Out of Ill Health," preliminary draft, March 7, 1935, Social Security Administration Historical Archives; "Letter of Transmittal and Summary of Major Recommendations on Health Insurance from the Committee on Economic Security to the President," November 6, 1935, reprinted in Witte, *Development of the Social Security Act,* app. 3, pp. 205–210.

158. Kollmann, "Summary of Major Changes in the Social Security Cash Benefits Program: 1935–1996," pp. 6–10, 12.

159. Remarkably, the enactment of ERISA indicated that one of the original objections to the Clark Amendment—that public monitoring of government-guaranteed private pension plans would never work—had finally been cast aside. On the origins of ERISA, see James A. Wooten, "Regulating the 'Unseen Revolution': A Political History of the Employee Retirement Income Security Act of 1974," draft Ph.D. diss. (Yale University, 2001).

8. Product Liability Law

1. Peter W. Huber, *Liability: The Legal Revolution and Its Consequences* (New York: Basic Books, 1990), p. ix.

2. *Winterbottom v. Wright,* 10 M. & W. 109 (1842). On the far-reaching impact of this British decision on American law, see, e.g., W. Page Keeton et al., *Products Liability and Safety: Cases and Materials* (Westbury, N.Y.: Foundation Press, 1989), p. 40.

3. *Winterbottom v. Wright,* 10 M. & W. 109, 114, 115, 116–117 (1842).

4. See, e.g., *Roddy v. Missouri Pacific Railway Co.,* 104 Mo. 234 (1891): "The right of a third party to maintain an action for injuries resulting from a breach of contract between two contracting parties has been denied by the overwhelming weight of authority of the state and federal courts of this country, and the courts of England" (p. 245).

5. *Lester Tompkins v. Quaker Oats Co.,* 239 Mass. 147, 149 (1921). In most cases the intermediaries themselves were similarly insulated. See, e.g., *Pitman v. Lynn Gas & Electric Co.,* 241 Mass. 322 (1922), esp. 325.

6. *Priestly v. Fowler,* 3 M. & W. 1, 150 Reprint 1030, 1032 (1837).

7. *Farwell v. Boston & Worcester Railroad Corporation,* 4 Metc. 49 (1842), esp. 57.

8. Lawrence M. Friedman, *History of American Law,* 2nd ed. (New York: Simon and Schuster, 1985), p. 302.

9. Oliver Wendell Holmes, *The Common Law* (Boston: Little, Brown, 1963 [1881]), p. 76. Holmes went on to speculate that the "state might conceivably make itself a mutual insurance company against accidents, and distribute the burden of its citizens' mishaps among all its members." But he

cautioned against any such development, insisting that the state should intervene only when a "clear benefit" could be expected. "Universal insurance, if desired, can be better and more cheaply accomplished by private enterprise," he wrote (p. 77).

10. *Farwell v. Boston & Worcester Railroad Corporation*, 4 Metc. 49 (1842): "[L]ike similar losses from accidental causes, [this loss] must rest where it fell" (p. 59).

11. *Thomas v. Winchester*, 6 N.Y. 397 (1852).

12. *Elkins, Bly, & Co. v. McKean*, 79 Pa. 493 (1876), esp. 502, 503.

13. *Heizer v. Kingsland & Douglass Mfr. Co.*, 110 Mo. 605, 612 (1892).

14. *Huset v. J. I. Case Threshing Mach. Co.*, 120 F. 865 (1903), esp. 870–872. The California case cited is *Lewis v. Terry*, 111 Cal. 39 (1896). Note that the reference to *Lewis* in *Huset* mistakenly characterizes the plaintiff as Mr. Apperson's wife rather than his tenant. Either way, however, the victim would have lacked privity if she had not purchased the bed herself. For a critique of Sanborn's reasoning, see Francis H. Bohlen, "Liability of Manufacturers to Persons Other than Their Immediate Vendees," *Law Quarterly Review*, 45 (July 1929), esp. 353–360.

15. Gary T. Schwartz, "Tort Law and the Economy in Nineteenth-Century America: A Reinterpretation," *Yale Law Review*, 90 (July 1981), 1720; Peter Karsten, *Heart vs. Head: Judge-Made Law in Nineteenth-Century America* (Chapel Hill: University of North Carolina Press, 1997), p. 95. See also William Novak, *The People's Welfare: Law and Regulation in Nineteenth-Century America* (Chapel Hill: University of North Carolina Press, 1996); Nathan Honson, "Iowa Tort History, 1839–1869: Subsidization of Enterprise or Equitable Allocation of Liability," *Iowa Law Review*, 81 (March 1996), 811–832.

16. *Huset v. J. I. Case Threshing Mach. Co.*, 120 F. 865, 867–870 (1903).

17. *Curtin v. Somerset*, 140 Pa. 70, 80 (1891).

18. *Lebourdrais v. Vitrified Wheel Co.*, 194 Mass. 341, 343 (1907). In 1873, Justice Robert Earl of the New York Court of Appeals had reached even beyond the limits of privity in articulating the logic of Phase I, proclaiming: "We must have factories, machinery, dams, canals and railroads. They are demanded by the manifold wants of mankind, and lay at the basis of all our civilization. If I have any of these upon my lands, and they are not a nuisance and are not so managed as to become such, I am not responsible for any damage they accidentally and unavoidably do my neighbor. He receives his compensation for such damage by the general good, in which he shares, and the right which he has to place the same things upon his lands." *Losee v. Buchanan et al.*, 51 N.Y. 476, 484–485 (1873).

19. *Huset v. J. I. Case Threshing Mach. Co.*, 120 F. 865, 867 (1903).

20. Willard Hurst, *Law and the Conditions of Freedom in the Nineteenth-Century United States* (Madison: University of Wisconsin Press, 1956), p. 20.

21. Friedman, *History of American Law*, pp. 468–469.

22. Ibid., p. 473.

23. Morton J. Horwitz, *The Transformation of American Law, 1780–1860* (Cambridge, Mass.: Harvard University Press, 1977), pp. 99–100. Schwartz and others have characterized Horwitz's formulation as the "subsidy thesis." See, e.g., Gary T. Schwartz, "The Character of Early American Tort Law," *UCLA Law Review*, 36 (1989), esp. 641–642.

24. Friedman seems to have paid more attention to the exceptions than the others, however, noting at one point that the "law of torts was never quite so harsh and unyielding as its formal rules may have made it appear. Almost from the very first, juries, judges, and legislatures took away with their left hand some of what had been built up with the right." Friedman, *History of American Law*, p. 302n47.

25. The dominance of the privity rule was evident not only in judicial decisions but also in the leading treatises of the day. See, e.g., Thomas G. Shearman and Amasa A. Redfield, *Treatise on the Law of Negligence* (New York: Baker, Voorhis, and Co., 1870), pp. 64–65.

26. William O. Douglas, "Vicarious Liability and Administration of Risk I," *Yale Law Journal*, 38, no. 5 (March 1929), 591.

27. Roy Lubove, *The Struggle for Social Security, 1900–1935* (Pittsburgh: University of Pittsburgh Press, 1986 [1968]), p. 51.

28. Mary Coate Houtz, "The Insurance Response to a Shifting Caveat," in American Bar Association, *Report of the Proceedings of the Section of Insurance Law* (September 1944), 304.

29. Ibid. See also p. 303: "[I]nsurers began to write products liability insurance almost concurrently with the general widening of producers' responsibility."

30. *MacPherson v. Buick Motor Company*, 217 N.Y. 382 (1916).

31. Ibid., 382, 385.

32. Ibid., 382, 391, 389, 396, 390.

33. *Atkins v. American Motors Corp.*, 335 So. 2d 134, 138 (1976). Similarly, according to the *Carter v. Yardley* decision, "[t]he *MacPherson* case caused the exception to swallow the asserted general rule of nonliability, leaving nothing upon which that rule could operate." 319 Mass. 92, 103 (1946). See also, e.g., Eugene Wollan and Robert L. Horkitz, "Products Liability in the United States," *Best's Review* (Property-Casualty Insurance ed.), 85 (July 1984), 48 (in which the authors characterize *MacPherson* as "the fountainhead of American products liability law" and suggest that it marked the dawning of a "new era").

34. Not until 1946, for example, did the Supreme Court of Massachusetts definitively abandon the privity rule. See *Carter v. Yardley,* 319 Mass. 92 (1946): "The time has come for us to recognize that that asserted general rule [of nonliability without privity] no longer exists. In principle it was unsound. It tended to produce unjust results. It has been abandoned by the great weight of authority elsewhere. We now abandon it in this Commonwealth" (p. 104).

35. *Atkins v. American Motors Corp.,* 335 So. 2d 134, 138 (1976).

36. *Escola v. Coca Cola Bottling Company,* 24 Cal. 2d 453, 461–462 (1944).

37. John Maynard Keynes, *The General Theory of Employment, Interest, and Money* (New York: Harcourt Brace Jovanovich, 1964 [1936]), p. 383.

38. See, e.g., L. W. Feezer, "Capacity to Bear Loss as a Factor in the Decision of Certain Types of Tort Cases," *University of Pennsylvania Law Review,* 78, no. 7 (May 1930), 813; Fowler V. Harper and Fleming James, Jr., *The Law of Torts* (Boston: Little, Brown, 1956), 2:751–752; Dix W. Noel, "Manufacturers of Products: The Drift toward Strict Liability," *Tennessee Law Review,* 24, no. 7 (Spring 1957), 1011; Fleming James, Jr., "Tort Law in Midstream: Its Challenge to the Judicial Process," *Buffalo Law Review,* 8 (1959), 316–317.

39. Francis H. Bohlen, "The Basis of Affirmative Obligations in the Law of Tort," *American Law Register,* 44 [54 o.s.], no. 6 (June 1905), 355.

40. Charles O. Gregory, "Trespass to Negligence to Absolute Liability," *Virginia Law Review,* 37, no. 3 (April 1951), 365, 368.

41. *Farwell v. Boston & Worcester Railroad Corporation,* 4 Metc. 49 (1842).

42. Harper and James, *Law of Torts,* p. 752. Appealing to a recognized authority, they cited Oliver Wendell Holmes, who wrote in *The Common Law* that "the public generally profits by individual activity. As action cannot be avoided, and tends to the public good, there is obviously no policy in throwing the hazard of what is at once desirable and inevitable upon the actor."

43. Guido Calabresi, "Some Thoughts on Risk Distribution and the Law of Torts," *Yale Law Journal,* 70, no. 4 (March 1961), 517. Although the specific context for the quoted passages was a discussion of worker injuries rather than worker and consumer injuries, Calabresi explicitly stressed the applicability of this logic to both worker and consumer injuries in a lengthy footnote (p. 515n43).

44. Roger J. Traynor, "The Ways and Meanings of Defective Products and Strict Liability," *Tennessee Law Review,* 32, no. 3 (Spring 1965), 363.

45. See, e.g., Noel, "Manufacturers of Products," pp. 1009–10; Cornelius W. Gillam, "Products Liability in a Nutshell," *Oregon Law Review,* 37, no. 2 (February 1958), 146–147.

46. Feezer, "Capacity to Bear Loss," p. 808 (including p. 808n4).

47. Harper and James, *Law of Torts*, p. 1535; William L. Prosser, "The Assault upon the Citadel (Strict Liability to the Consumer)," *Yale Law Journal*, 69, no. 7 (June 1960), 1142. As of 1991, Prosser's article ranked as the second most frequently cited article ever published in the *Yale Law Journal*. Calabresi's "Some Thoughts on Risk Distribution and the Law of Torts" ranked seventh. See Fred R. Shapiro, "The Most-Cited Articles from *The Yale Law Journal*," *Yale Law Journal*, 100 (March 1991), table 1.

48. K. N. Llewellyn, "The Effect of Legal Institutions upon Economics," *American Economic Review*, 15, no. 4 (December 1925), 665, 678, 680.

49. Douglas, "Vicarious Liability and Administration of Risk I," 584–604; "Vicarious Liability and Administration of Risk II," *Yale Law Journal*, 38, no. 6 (April 1929), 720–745.

50. Douglas, "Vicarious Liability and Administration of Risk, I," pp. 587–588.

51. Ibid., pp. 598–602, 603–604.

52. Fleming James, Jr., "General Products—Should Manufacturers Be Liable without Negligence?" *Tennessee Law Review*, 24 (1957), 923.

53. Many of the most powerful arguments for extending strict liability beyond workplace injuries, which ultimately helped to reshape product injury law, were first rehearsed within the realm of automobile accident liability law, particularly during the 1920s. See esp. David A. Moss and Michael R. Fein, "'Pure Accidents' and the Evolving Bias of American Liability Law," mimeographed, December 29, 2000: "By mid-century, proponents of compulsory, no-fault automobile accident insurance had successfully introduced the economic logic of strict liability into the legal profession. In the wake of *Escola*, these economic arguments gained still greater currency among legal scholars" (p. 41).

54. Quoted in Noel, "Manufacturers of Products," p. 1010. See also John B. Clutterbuck, "Karl N. Llewellyn and the Intellectual Foundations of Enterprise Liability," *Yale Law Journal*, 97 (1988), esp. 1138, 1132.

55. James, "General Products," p. 923.

56. Guido Calabresi and Jon T. Hirshoff, "Toward a Test for Strict Liability in Torts," *Yale Law Journal*, 81, no. 6 (May 1972), 1060.

57. *Farwell v. Boston & Worcester Railroad Corporation*, 4 Metc. 49, 59 (1842).

58. Ezra Ripley Thayer, "Liability without Fault," *Harvard Law Review*, 29, no. 8 (June 1916), 802.

59. George L. Priest, "The Invention of Enterprise Liability: A Critical History of the Intellectual Foundations of Modern Tort Law," *Journal of Legal Studies*, 14 (December 1985), 463.

60. Llewellyn, "Effect of Legal Institutions upon Economics," p. 681.

61. Harper and James, *Law of Torts*, pp. 753, 756. With regard to the capacity

of "large groups and enterprises" to prevent accidents, they maintain that "recent studies emphasize the extent to which large units (such as transportation companies, the government, insurance companies, and the like) are in a strategic position to reduce accidents" (p. 756). See also James, "Tort Law in Midstream," pp. 330–331; Fleming James, Jr., and John J. Dickinson, "Accident Proneness and Accident Law," *Harvard Law Review,* 63 (1950), 769–795.

62. Quoted in Noel, "Manufacturers of Products," p. 1010.

63. Gregory, "Trespass to Negligence to Absolute Liability," pp. 383–384.

64. Prosser, "Assault upon the Citadel," pp. 1120, 1119.

65. Fleming James, Jr., "Contribution among Joint Tortfeasors: A Pragmatic Criticism," *Harvard Law Review,* 54 (1941), 1156.

66. Ibid., p. 1157. See also James, "General Products," pp. 923–924; Fleming James, Jr., "Accident Liability Reconsidered: The Impact of Liability Insurance," *Yale Law Journal,* 57 (1948), 550; Harper and James, *Law of Torts,* pp. 762–763; Priest, "Invention of Enterprise Liability," pp. 470–483.

67. Calabresi, "Some Thoughts on Risk Distribution," p. 530.

68. Ibid., pp. 518–519.

69. Ibid., p. 518.

70. See, e.g., ibid., pp. 502, 514.

71. Ibid., p. 518. On the inherent tension between risk allocation and risk distribution, see also, e.g., Douglas, "Vicarious Liability," p. 603.

72. Calabresi, "Some Thoughts on Risk Distribution," p. 530.

73. Ibid., p. 531.

74. Ibid., p. 505. On the economic "irrelevance" of legal liability rules, see R. H. Coase, "The Problem of Social Cost," *Journal of Law and Economics,* 3 (October 1960), esp. 10, 13.

75. James, "Tort Law in Midstream," pp. 329–330. See also, e.g., Gregory, "Trespass to Negligence to Absolute Liability," p. 384. See also Calabresi, "Some Thoughts on Risk Distribution," p. 506, where he suggests that part of the reason for underinsurance on the part of individuals may have been that accident insurance was simply more expensive for individuals than for firms.

76. Friedrich Kessler, "Contracts of Adhesion: Some Thoughts about Freedom of Contract," *Columbia Law Review,* 43 (1943), esp. 632–633. See also Priest, "Invention of Enterprise Liability," pp. 494–496.

77. Calabresi, "Some Thoughts on Risk Distribution," p. 506. See also, e.g., Harper and James, *Law of Torts,* esp. p. 1545. Arguing along similar lines, Justice Traynor maintained in his famous concurring opinion in *Escola* that the "consumer no longer has the means or skill enough to investigate

for himself the soundness of a product. . . . Consumers no longer approach products warily but accept them on faith, relying on the reputation of the manufacturer or the trade mark." *Escola v. Coca Cola Bottling Company,* 24 Cal. 2d 453, 467 (1944).

78. Calabresi, "Some Thoughts on Risk Distribution," p. 506.

79. Henry R. Seager, "Outline of a Program of Social Reform," in *Labor and Other Economic Essays by Henry R. Seager,* ed. Charles A. Gulick, Jr. (New York: Harper and Brothers, 1931), 82–83.

80. Guido Calabresi, *The Costs of Accidents: A Legal and Economic Analysis* (New Haven: Yale University Press, 1970), esp. pp. 56–57. See also pp. 148–149, 206–208, as well as Guido Calabresi, "Fault, Accidents, and the Wonderful World of Blum and Kalven," *Yale Law Journal,* 75 (1965), 224. Nearly identical arguments—that is, regarding the pervasive belief that product-related accidents always happen to "the other guy"—may be found in numerous discussions of product safety during this period. See, e.g., National Commission on Product Safety, *Hearings* (New York: Law-Arts Publishers, 1970), 7:176 (comments of Arnold B. Elkind, chairman of the National Commission on Product Safety, reprinted from National Association of Manufacturers meeting transcript, October 9, 1969), and pp. 212–214 (Statement of Virginia Knauer, Special Assistant to the President for Consumer Affairs, October 1, 1969). For a summary of more recent work on the apparent tendency of consumers to underestimate product risks, see, e.g., Jon D. Hanson and Douglas A. Kysar, "Taking Behavioralism Seriously: The Problem of Market Manipulation," *New York University Law Review,* 74 (June 1999), 696–704. On the opposite problem of overestimation, see pp. 704–714. For an early theoretical perspective on this problem, see also Michael Spence, "Consumer Misperceptions, Product Failure and Producer Liability," *Review of Economic Studies,* 44, no. 3 (October 1977), 561–572.

81. Calabresi, *Costs of Accidents,* pp. 135–140, 144–150.

82. Harper and James, *Law of Torts,* p. 747.

83. *Rylands v. Fletcher,* L.R. 3 H.L. 330 (1868).

84. *Rylands v. Fletcher,* 3 Hurl. & C. 774 (1865).

85. *Rylands v. Fletcher,* L.R. 3 H.L. 330, 341 (1868).

86. Harper and James, *Law of Torts,* pp. 788, 795–870. Strict liability was also occasionally imposed by statute. An 1804 Massachusetts law, for example, held that a turnpike corporation "shall be liable to pay all damages which may happen to any person from whom toll is demandable, for any damages which shall arise from defect of bridges, or want of repair of said turnpike road." According to Justice Shaw, the statute was "founded on the

consideration, that the toll is an adequate compensation for the risk assumed, and that by throwing the risk upon those who have the best means of taking precautions against it, the public will have the greatest security against actual damage and loss." See *Yale v. Hampden & Berkshire Turnpike Corp.*, 35 Mass. 357, 359 (1836).

87. *Exner v. Sherman Power Const. Co.*, 54 F.2d 510, 512–513 (1931), emphasis added. See also Gregory, "Trespass to Negligence to Absolute Liability," pp. 391–395.

88. See esp. William L. Prosser, "The Implied Warranty of Merchantable Quality," *Minnesota Law Review*, 27, no. 2 (January 1943), 117–168; Harper and James, *Law of Torts*, pp. 1569–70, 1599–1601.

89. Harper and James, *Law of Torts*, pp. 1078, 1075–1107; Prosser, "Assault upon the Citadel," pp. 1114–15; G. Edward White, *Tort Law in America: An Intellectual History* (New York: Oxford University Press, 1985), p. 171.

90. Gillam, "Products Liability in a Nutshell," p. 147. See also Harper and James, *Law of Torts*, pp. 1570–71, 1606; Prosser, "Assault upon the Citadel," pp. 1117–18.

91. Prosser, "Assault upon the Citadel," pp. 1115–17; White, *Tort Law in America*, p. 171.

92. Harper and James, *Law of Torts*, pp. 1571–72. See also pp. 1605–6.

93. James, "General Products," p. 925.

94. Prosser, "Assault upon the Citadel," p. 1126.

95. Ibid., pp. 1133–34.

96. For an earlier criticism of the implied warranty approach, see, e.g., Gregory, "Trespass to Negligence to Absolute Liability," pp. 384–385, 395.

97. *Henningsen v. Bloomfield Motors, Inc.*, 32 N.J. 358 (1960). On the timing of the release and arrival of Prosser's article, see Priest, "Invention of Enterprise Liability," p. 506n292.

98. *Henningsen v. Bloomfield Motors, Inc.*, 32 N.J. 358, 364–369 (1960).

99. Ibid. For examples of cites to Harper and James, see, e.g., pp. 373, 380, 381, 383, 391, 400, 415. For cites to other prominent legal scholars, including Feezer, Kessler, and Prosser (though not Prosser's 1960 article, since it had not yet appeared), see pp. 379, 381, 389, 391, 400, 407.

100. Ibid., 379–380.

101. William L. Prosser, "The Fall of the Citadel (Strict Liability to the Consumer)," *Yale Law Journal*, 50 (1966), 791.

102. *Greenman v. Yuba Power Products, Inc.*, 59 Cal. 2d 57, 62 (1963).

103. Ibid., 63.

104. Ibid., 64.

105. Ibid., 63.

106. On the evolution of section 402A drafts, see *Putnam v. Erie City Mfg. Co.*,

338 F.2d 911, 918–919 (5th Cir. 1964); Priest, "Invention of Enterprise Liability," pp. 512–514.

107. American Law Institute, Restatement (Second) of Torts (1965), sec. 402A, Special Liability of Seller of Product for Physical Harm to User or Consumer.

108. Priest, "Invention of Enterprise Liability," p. 512. Perhaps not surprisingly, Prosser obtained the advice of Fleming James, Roger Traynor, and other prominent legal minds in preparing section 402A.

109. Prosser, "Fall of the Citadel," pp. 794–797.

110. Priest, "Invention of Enterprise Liability," p. 518.

111. Marc Galanter, "The Day after the Litigation Explosion," *Maryland Law Review*, 46 (Fall 1986), 23, table 3; Theodore Eisenberg and James A. Henderson, Jr., "Inside the Quiet Revolution in Products Liability," *UCLA Law Review*, 39 (April 1992), 798, table A-3. The data on total civil filings are for the years 1975–1985. Civil cases filed rose from 112,308 to 273,670 (a 144 percent increase) over that period.

112. Gary T. Schwartz, "New Products, Old Products, Evolving Law, Retroactive Law," *New York University Law Review*, 58 (October 1983), 812.

113. Priest, "Invention of Enterprise Liability," pp. 461, 462.

114. See esp. George L. Priest, "Strict Products Liability: The Original Intent," *Cardozo Law Review*, 10 (1989), 2304; W. Kip Viscusi, "Product and Occupational Liability," *Journal of Economic Perspectives*, 5, no. 3 (Summer 1991), 74–75.

115. *McCormack v. Hankscraft Co.*, 278 Minn. 322 (1967); Priest, "Invention of Enterprise Liability," p. 524.

116. *Grimshaw v. Ford Motor Co.*, 119 Cal. App. 3d 757 (1981). For a general discussion of the difficulty of defining the meaning of "defective product," see esp. Traynor, "Ways and Meanings of Defective Products and Strict Liability," pp. 363–376.

117. Priest, "Strict Products Liability: The Original Intent," pp. 2301–27. For an early discussion of design defects, see esp. Harper and James, *Law of Torts*, pp. 1540–57. See also Traynor, "Ways and Meanings of Defective Products and Strict Liability," pp. 368, 372–373.

118. Priest, "Strict Products Liability: The Original Intent," pp. 2326–27: "[T]he evolution of standards in both design and warning cases have been strongly directed by the concepts of risk distribution and cost internalization."

119. *Browning-Ferris Industries v. Kelco, Inc.*, 492 U.S. 257, 282 (1989).

120. Michael Rustad and Thomas Koenig, "Historical Continuity of Punitive Damage Awards: Reforming the Tort Reformers," *American University Law Review*, 42 (1993), 1287–90, 1299–1300 (quoting Greenleaf).

121. Rustad and Koenig, "Historical Continuity of Punitive Damage Awards," 1302–7, 1309, 1328–30. On the legal rule that defendant behavior must be reprehensible to justify punitive damages, see also A. Mitchell Polinsky and Steven Shavell, "Punitive Damages: An Economic Analysis," *Harvard Law Review*, 111, no. 4 (February 1998), 905; *BMW of North America, Inc. v. Gore*, 517 U.S. 559, 575–576 (1996).

122. *Liebeck v. McDonald's Restaurants*, No. CV-93—2419, 1995 WL 360309 (N.M. Dist. 1994); *BMW of North America, Inc. v. Gore*, 517 U.S. 559 (1996).

123. Michael Rustad, "In Defense of Punitive Damages in Products Liability: Testing Tort Anecdotes with Empirical Data," *Iowa Law Review*, 78 (October 1992), 38, table 3. On misconceptions regarding punitive damages (and the tort system generally), see also Marc Galanter, "Real World Torts: An Antidote to Anecdote," *Maryland Law Review*, 55, no. 4 (October 1996), esp. 1126–40.

124. Michael L. Rustad, "Unraveling Punitive Damages: Current Data and Further Inquiry," *Wisconsin Law Review* (1998), 20, 37, 67, 38. See also *Penzoil Co. v. Texaco Inc.*, 481 U.S. 1 (1987).

125. Rustad, "Unraveling Punitive Damages," pp. 20–23, 25, 28–30, 39–40; Theodore Eisenberg et al., "The Predictability of Punitive Damages," *Journal of Legal Studies*, 26 (June 1997), 634–635 and table 1.

126. U.S. Department of Justice, Office of Justice Programs, "Civil Jury Cases and Verdicts in Large Counties" (Civil Justice Survey of State Courts, 1992), *Bureau of Justice Statistics Special Report*, July 1995, tables 1, 2, 6, and 8.

127. See Rustad, "Unraveling Punitive Damages," pp. 17–56.

128. Eisenberg et al., "Predictability of Punitive Damages," esp. pp. 637–639; Rustad, "Unraveling Punitive Damages," pp. 22–23, 31, 40–44. See also Evan Osborne, "Courts as Casinos? An Empirical Investigation of Randomness and Efficiency in Civil Litigation," *Journal of Legal Studies*, 28, no. 1 (January 1999), 187–203.

129. Frank Swoboda and Caroline E. Mayer, "A $4.9 Billion Message: Jury Hits GM with Historic Crash Verdict," *Washington Post*, July 10, 1999, p. A1; William Glaberson, "The $2.9 Million Cup of Coffee: When the Verdict Is Just a Fantasy," *New York Times*, June 6, 1999, sec. 4, p. 1; Andrea A. Curcio, "Painful Publicity: An Alternative Punitive Damage Sanction," *DePaul Law Review*, 45 (Winter 1996), 385–386; Polinsky and Shavell, "Punitive Damages," p. 901.

130. Rustad, "In Defense of Punitive Damages in Products Liability," esp. pp. 38–39; Rustad, "Unraveling Punitive Damages," pp. 23, 30.

131. James, "General Products," pp. 926–927.
132. Traynor, "Ways and Meanings of Defective Products and Strict Liability," p. 367.
133. See, e.g., Barnaby J. Feder, "Asbestos Injury Suits Mount, with Severe Business Impact," *New York Times,* July 3, 1981, p. A1; "Victim Compensation," *Chemical Week,* March 9, 1983, pp. 32–38; Barnaby J. Feder, "Dow Corning in Bankruptcy over Lawsuits," *New York Times,* May 16, 1995, p. A1.
134. See esp. United States General Accounting Office, *Liability Insurance: Effects of Recent Crisis on Business and Other Organizations* (Washington, D.C., July 1988); Ralph A. Winter, "The Liability Insurance Market," *Journal of Economic Perspectives,* 5, no. 3 (Summer 1991), 115–136.
135. Michael J. Miller, "Strict Liability, Negligence, and the Standard of Care for Transfusion-Transmitted Disease," *Arizona Law Review,* 36 (Summer 1994), 488–494. Even before these statutes were enacted, moreover, courts in most states had already found ways to exempt blood suppliers from strict liability (pp. 482–488). In New Jersey, one of the two states in which no statute was passed (the other was Vermont), the New Jersey Supreme Court "held that blood suppliers are not subject to strict liability" (p. 490n117).
136. See, e.g., Stacy Shapiro, "Tort Costs Hurt Aircraft Manufacturers," *Business Insurance,* June 10, 1991, pp. 34–35; Patrick J. Shea, "Solving America's General Aviation Crisis: The Advantages of Federal Preemption over Tort Reform," *Cornell Law Review,* 80 (March 1995), esp. 765–768; General Aviation Revitalization Act of 1994, Pub. L. no. 103–298, 108 Stat. 1552. See also Edward H. Phillips, "GA Rebounding after Liability Reform," *Aviation Week and Space Technology,* 151, no. 11 (September 13, 1999), 40.
137. For a description of the various rules in the fifty states, see esp. U.S. Department of Justice, "Civil Jury Cases," p. 6. By the mid-1990s, twenty-seven states had "modified comparative negligence" rules that bar recovery if the plaintiff is more negligent than (or, in nine states, at least as negligent as) the defendant. Thirteen states had a pure comparative negligence rule, where plaintiff recovery of actual damages is proportionately reduced according to his own degree of negligence. Six states had pure contributory negligence rules, prohibiting plaintiff recovery altogether whenever the plaintiff's negligence contributed to the injury in any way. Finally, four states had mixed rules.
138. See S. Reed Morgan, "McDonald's Burned Itself," *Legal Times,* September 19, 1994, p. 26.
139. U.S. Department of Justice, "Civil Jury Cases," p. 6.

140. *Farwell v. Boston & Worcester Railroad Corporation*, 4 Metc. 49, 59 (1842). See esp. Moss and Fein, "'Pure Accidents' and the Evolving Bias of American Liability Law."

141. *Farwell v. Boston & Worcester Railroad Corporation*, 4 Metc. 49, 59 (1842). See also Holmes, *Common Law*, pp. 76–77.

9. Security for All

1. Henry Fairlie, "Fear of Living: America's Morbid Aversion to Risk," *New Republic*, January 23, 1989, p. 14.

2. This section draws heavily on David A. Moss, "Courting Disaster? The Transformation of Federal Disaster Policy since 1803," in Kenneth A. Froot, ed., *The Financing of Catastrophe Risk* (Chicago: University of Chicago Press, 1999), pp. 307–355; David A. Moss and Julie Rosenbaum, "The Great Mississippi Flood of 1993," Harvard Business School Case Study no. 797–097 (February 10, 1997).

3. See *Congressional Record* (House), 81st Cong., 2nd sess., August 7, 1950, pp. 11900–902.

4. Whereas between 1803 and 1947 the federal government provided disaster relief, on average, less than once per year, between 1977 and 1993 the federal government provided assistance, on average, for thirty-four disasters per year. See *Federal Disaster Assistance: Report of the Senate Task Force on Funding Disaster Relief* (Washington, D.C.: GPO, 1995), table 1.1, p. 5.

5. See President Cleveland's veto statement, February 16, 1887, Ex. Doc. no. 175, 49th Cong., 2nd sess., *House Executive Documents*, 24. See also Clara Barton to Grover Cleveland, February 19, 1887, Grover Cleveland Papers, microfilm edition (Washington, D.C.: Library of Congress, 1958), ser. 2, reel 41.

6. See Charles Hurd, *The Compact History of the American Red Cross* (New York: Hawthorn Books, 1959), pp. 111–112.

7. On the legislative history of federal disaster relief, see esp. Peter J. May, *Recovering from Catastrophes: Federal Disaster Relief Policy and Politics* (Westport, Conn.: Greenwood Press, 1985), pp. 17–47; Roy S. Popkin, "The History and Politics of Disaster Management in the United States," in Andrew Kirkby, ed., *Nothing to Fear: Risks and Hazards in American Society* (Tucson: University of Arizona Press, 1990), pp. 101–129; *Federal Disaster Assistance*, pp. 99–102; Office of Emergency Preparedness, *Report to Congress: Disaster Preparedness* (Washington, D.C.: GPO, January 1972), 1:167–173; Howard Kunreuther, *Recovery from Natural Disasters: Insurance or Federal Aid* (Washington, D.C.: American Enterprise Institute, 1973), pp. 3–21.

8. See Office of Emergency Preparedness, *Report to Congress: Disaster Preparedness,* 1:168–170.

9. Douglas Dacy and Howard Kunreuther, *The Economics of Natural Disasters: Implications for Federal Policy* (New York: Free Press, 1969), p. 32, table 2.1. In calculating total federal spending on disasters in 1953 and 1965, a subsidy rate on SBA loans of 33 percent was assumed.

10. "Message from the President Relative to Disaster Assistance," House Document no. 91–323, 91st Cong., 2nd sess. (1970), p. 6.

11. Ibid., p. 1.

12. On the economic and political impact of Hurricane Camille, see "Federal Disaster Assistance," in *Congressional Quarterly Almanac,* vol. 26 (1970), esp. 754–755; Committee on Public Works, United States Senate, *Disaster Assistance,* Report no. 91–1157, 91st Cong., 2nd sess., August 31, 1970, esp. pp. 2–3.

13. On legislative developments through 1974, see the sources cited in note 9 as well as the key federal acts: P.L. 81–875 (1950), 89–769 (1966), 91–79 (1969), 91–606 (1970), and 93–288 (1974). On the dramatic change in federal disaster relief since the mid-1960s, see also Cramer, *Congressional Record* (House), 89th Cong., 2nd sess., October 17, 1966, p. 27096.

14. On the origins of FEMA, see *Federal Disaster Assistance,* pp. 94–97.

15. Senate Committee on Public Works, *Disaster Assistance,* p. 2.

16. *Disaster Assistance Legislation: Hearings before the Subcommittee on Flood Control of the Committee on Public Works on H.R. 17518 and Related Bills,* House of Representatives, 91st Cong. (July 1970), p. 20.

17. *The Mississippi Valley Flood Disaster of 1927: Official Report of the Relief Operations* (Washington, D.C.: American National Red Cross, [1929]), pp. 10, 120–21, 146; Pete Daniel, *Deep'n As It Come: The 1927 Mississippi River Flood* (New York: Oxford University Press, 1977), p. 10. There is some dispute over the number of flood-related fatalities in 1927. At the time officials reported fewer than ten, but Daniel has since estimated the number at between 250 and 500. See also Robert L. Koenig, "Upper Mississippi Lacks Coordination of Flood Control," *St. Louis Post-Dispatch,* August 29, 1993, p. 1A.

18. *The Great Flood of 1993: National Disaster Survey Report* (Washington, D.C.: National Oceanic and Atmospheric Administration, February 1994), pp. 1.4, 1.5; *Facts on File World News Digest,* August 26, 1993, p. 624 E3; Steven Phillips, *The Soil Conservation Service Responds to the 1993 Midwest Floods* (Washington, D.C.: U.S. Department of Agriculture, November 1994), p. 18; William Freivogel, "Flood of Money: Federal Aid Is Sometimes Uncoordinated and Arbitrary," *St. Louis Post-Dispatch,* September 26,

1993, p. 1B; Ken Sheets, "After the Flood," *Kiplinger's Personal Finance Magazine*, 47, no. 10 (October 1993), 67; *Sharing the Challenge: Floodplain Management into the Twenty-first Century: Report of the Interagency Floodplain Management Review Committee* (Washington, D.C.: GPO, June 1994), p. 16.

19. Quoted in *Mississippi Valley Flood Disaster of 1927*, p. 13.

20. See Bruce Alan Lohof, "Hoover and the Mississippi Valley Flood: A Case Study of the Political Thought of Herbert Hoover," Ph.D. diss. (Syracuse University, 1968), esp. pp. 122, 169–170, 185; *Mississippi Valley Flood Disaster of 1927*, pp. 10–13. The affected states added roughly another $10 million in relief appropriations.

21. Quoted in *Mississippi Valley Flood Disaster of 1927*, p. 145.

22. Herbert Hoover, *The Memoirs of Herbert Hoover: The Cabinet and the Presidency, 1920–1933* (New York: Macmillan, 1952), 2:126.

23. See esp. Moss, "Courting Disaster," pp. 309–311.

24. Quoted in Helen Dewar, "For Senate Foes of Spending, Flood Disaster Spells Relief," *Washington Post*, August 5, 1993, p. A19.

25. Quoted in Bob Benenson, "Insurance Finds Few Takers," *Congressional Quarterly*, 51, no. 29 (July 17, 1993), 1861. See also, e.g., Representative Patricia Schroeder of Colorado, *Congressional Record* (House), 103rd Cong., 1st sess., July 19, 1993, p. H4760: "As we watch this tremendously awful flood scene unravel in the Midwest . . . and we look at the terrific debt, we are going to have to make some very difficult choices. One of the main choices will be: Do we help those who took responsibility, got flood insurance, put up levees, tried to do everything they could; or do we help those who did not do that, who risked it all and figured if all fails, the Federal Government will bail them out?"

26. Quoted in Susan Hegger, "Carnahan, Edgar, Four Other Governors Press Clinton for Relief," *St. Louis Post-Dispatch*, July 28, 1993, p. 9A.

27. Quoted in Tony Freemantle, "'Flood Summit' Centers on Aid: Clinton Asked for Funds, Not Troops," *Houston Chronicle*, July 18, 1993, p. A1.

28. Representative Albert R. Wynn of Maryland, quoted in Clifford Krauss, "The Midwest Flooding; House Approves Flood Relief after Fight on Deficit," *New York Times*, July 28, 1993, p. A1.

29. The House of Representatives passed the emergency supplemental appropriations bill by a vote of 400 to 27 on July 27. The bill was then favorably reported to the full Senate by a unanimous 29–0 vote of the Senate Appropriations Committee on July 30. The full Senate passed the bill by a voice vote on August 4, and President Clinton signed it into law (P.L. 103–75) eight days later.

30. On this transformation, see also Kunreuther, *Recovery from Natural Disas-*

ters, esp. chap. 1 ("The Changing Federal Role in Disaster Relief"), pp. 3–26.

31. In none of these disasters were privately insured losses as a fraction of total estimated losses very large. The ratio of privately insured to total losses was 0.6 percent in the case of Hurricane Diane in 1955, virtually zero in the case of the Pacific Northwest floods of 1964, and 4.9 percent in the case of Tropical Storm Agnes in 1972. These particular disasters were selected in part to allow a comparison of federal coverage across time for events in which private insurance coverage was low. See Dacy and Kunreuther, *Economics of Natural Disasters,* pp. 46 and 35, tables 2.4 and 2.2; Kunreuther, *Recovery from Natural Disasters,* p. 16, table 3. The estimated federal coverage rate for Tropical Storm Agnes in 1972 (48.3 percent) likely understates the actual coverage rate since it is based on the generic assumption that the subsidy on SBA loans equaled one-third of their face value. Yet because the interest rate on SBA loans in 1972–73 was unusually low (only 1 percent), the actual subsidy was probably considerably higher. See Moss, "Courting Disaster," pp. 328–329, figure 8.2; Kunreuther, *Recovery from Natural Disasters,* pp. 10–11, table 1.

32. For example, several important forms of relief for private recipients (including grants, heavily subsidized loans, and favorable tax treatment of losses) were no longer as generous in 1993 as in the aftermath of Tropical Storm Agnes in 1972. By contrast, federal assistance for the repair and reconstruction of public facilities at the state and local levels was more generous, with the federal government now covering an even larger share of public sector losses. See Paul K. Freeman and Howard Kunreuther, *Managing Environmental Risk through Insurance* (Boston: Kluwer Academic Publishers, 1997), pp. 7–8; Kunreuther, *Recovery from Natural Disasters,* pp. 12–13, 29–35; Moss, "Courting Disaster," pp. 328–333.

33. For federal disaster expenditures from 1977 to 1993, see *Federal Disaster Assistance,* p. 5, table 1.1. A detailed treatment of how federal appropriations for the Midwest flood of 1993 were allocated can be found in Moss, "Courting Disaster," pp. 328–331, esp. p. 330, table 8.7. According to this source, three-quarters of total federal disaster spending on the 1993 flood went to recipients in the private sector. The other quarter helped to cover losses in the public sector. Of the funds dedicated to private recipients, by far the largest share went to farmers, who suffered massive losses in the form of crop destruction, soil erosion, and structural damage to buildings and equipment.

34. *Congressional Record* (House), 89th Cong., 2nd sess., October 17, 1966, pp. 27096–97.

35. Barry K. Goodwin and Vincent H. Smith, *The Economics of Crop Insurance*

and Disaster Aid (Washington, D.C.: AEI Press, 1995), esp. chap. 3 ("History of Federal Multi-Peril Crop Insurance"), pp. 33–65.

36. Quoted in Alfred Manes, *Insurance: Facts and Problems* (New York: Harper & Brothers, 1938), chap. 12, reprinted in Kailin Tuan, ed., *Modern Insurance Theory and Education* (Orange, N.J.: Varsity Press, 1972), 1:308.

37. William G. Hoyt and Walter B. Langbein, *Floods* (Princeton: Princeton University Press, 1955), p. 104.

38. Saul Jay Singer, "Flooding the Fifth Amendment: The National Flood Insurance Program and the 'Takings' Clause," *Boston College Environmental Affairs Law Review,* 17 (Winter 1990), 334–335. On Truman's abortive proposal, see also W. B. Langbein, "Flood Insurance," *Land Economics,* 29, no. 4 (November 1953), 328–329.

39. Committee on Banking and Currency, U.S. Senate, *National Flood Insurance Act of 1967,* 90th Cong., 1st sess., Senate Report no. 459 (August 29, 1967), p. 4.

40. *Federal Disaster Assistance,* p. 63; Singer, "Flooding the Fifth Amendment," pp. 335–336.

41. For the insurance industry perspective, see esp. National Flood Insurers Association, *A History of the National Flood Insurance Program* (n.d.).

42. Dacy and Kunreuther, *Economics of Natural Disasters,* p. 235.

43. *Congressional Record* (Senate), 93rd Cong., 2nd sess., February 26, 1974, p. 4166.

44. Ibid.

45. On the proposal for a Natural Disaster Insurance Corporation in the 1990s, see Moss, "Courting Disaster," pp. 341–343.

46. See, e.g., Bill Emerson and Ted Stevens, "Natural Disasters: A Budget Time Bomb," *Washington Post,* October 31, 1995, p. A13.

47. Spencer L. Kimball, "History and Development of the Law of State Insurer Delinquency Proceedings: Another Look after Twenty Years," *Journal of Insurance Regulation,* 5 (September 1986), 8.

48. Spencer L. Kimball, *Insurance and Public Policy: A Study in the Legal Implementation of Social and Economic Public Policy, Based on Wisconsin Records, 1835–1959* (Madison: University of Wisconsin Press, 1960), esp. chap. 4 ("Protecting the Integrity of the Insurance Fund against Dissipation"), pp. 129–208; Robert H. Jerry II, *Understanding Insurance Law,* 2nd ed. (New York: Matthew Bender & Co., 1996), pp. 51–57; Edwin Wilhite Patterson, *The Insurance Commissioner in the United States: A Study in Administrative Law and Practice* (Cambridge, Mass.: Harvard University Press, 1927), pp. 519–537; Alfred C. Bennett, "Liquidations of Insurance Companies," in Charles C. Center and Richard M. Heins, eds., *Insurance and Government* (New York: McGraw-Hill, 1962), p. 199; Richard M.

Heins, "Liquidations of Insurance Companies," in Center and Heins, *Insurance and Government,* pp. 239–240; Kimball, "History and Development," pp. 6, 12.

49. Jerry, *Understanding Insurance Law,* pp. 52–53.

50. Ibid., pp. 51–54.

51. See, e.g., Patterson, *Insurance Commissioner,* p. 521.

52. Kimball, *Insurance and Public Policy,* p. 129.

53. Bennett, "Liquidations of Insurance Companies," pp. 213–214.

54. Douglas G. Olson, "Property and Casualty Guaranty Funds before 1970: Lessons for the 1980s," *Journal of Insurance Regulation,* 4, no. 4 (1986), 134; Bennett, "Liquidations of Insurance Companies," p. 211.

55. Bennett, "Liquidations of Insurance Companies," pp. 214–217; Kimball, "History and Development," p. 27n83.

56. Bennett, "Liquidations of Insurance Companies," pp. 211–213; Olson, "Property and Casualty Guaranty Funds before 1970," p. 134.

57. Olson, "Property and Casualty Guaranty Funds before 1970," pp. 133–134; Kimball, "History and Development," p. 27.

58. See esp. *Paul v. Virginia,* 75 U.S. 168 (1869). The Supreme Court had called this division into question with *United States v. South-Eastern Underwriters Association,* 322 U.S. 533 (1944), thus motivating passage of the McCarran Act the next year.

59. Paul G. Roberts, "Insurance Company Insolvencies and Insurance Guaranty Funds: A Look at the Nonduplication of Recovery Clause," *Iowa Law Review,* 74 (May 1989), 932–933; Olson, "Property and Casualty Guaranty Funds before 1970," pp. 136–139.

60. Quoted in Roberts, "Insurance Company Insolvencies," p. 933.

61. Olson, "Property and Casualty Guaranty Funds before 1970," pp. 138–139; statement of Andre Maisonpierre, vice president, American Mutual Insurance Alliance, *Federal Insurance Guaranty Corporation: Hearings before the Committee on Commerce . . . on S. 2236,* U.S. Senate, 91st Cong., 1st sess. (1970), p. 69.

62. Opening hearings on his bill, Senator Magnuson declared: "The authors of S. 2236 in no way intend to supplant state regulation through proposed Federal insurance guaranty corporations. Our intention is the opposite. We want to give the State regulators assistance in performing as well as possible their roles." *Federal Insurance Guaranty Corporation: Hearings before the Committee on Commerce . . . on S. 2236,* p. 2. For strong opposing views, see esp. pp. 37, 70, 276.

63. "Memorandum on the NAIC State Post Assessment Insurers Guaranty Association Model Bill," December 31, 1969, reprinted in National Association of Insurance Commissioners, *Proceedings of the National Association of*

Insurance Commissioners, 1970 Regular Meeting (Raleigh, N.C.: Commercial Printing Co., 1970), 2:1099.

64. Insurance Security Fund, Wisconsin Session Laws, ch. 646 (1969); NAIC, *Proceedings of the National Association of Insurance Commissioners, 1970 Regular Meeting*, 2:1088; Christopher J. Wilcox, "The U.S. Guaranty Association Concept at Twenty-Five: A Quarter-Century Assessment," *Journal of Insurance Regulation*, 14, no. 3 (Spring 1996), 370–372; Kimball, "History and "Development," p. 27.

65. "Synopsis of the NAIC State Post Assessment Insurance Guaranty Association Model Bill," in NAIC, *Proceedings of the National Association of Insurance Commissioners*, 2:1100–1101; "Post-Assessment Property and Liability Insurance Guaranty Association Model Act," reprinted in Thomas A. Harnett and Sol Schreiber, eds., *Insolvency and Solidity of Insurance Companies* (New York: Practicing Law Institute, 1987), pp. 95–112.

66. Jon S. Hanson, *Regulation of the Life Insurance Business* (Bryn Mawr, Pa.: American College, 1996), pp. 80–81; Richard Bromley, "A History of the Development of the Life and Health Insurance Guaranty Association Model Act," in American Bar Association, National Institute on Insurer Insolvency, *Law and Practice of Insurance Company Insolvency* (Chicago, June 7–8, 1986), pp. 621–634, 618.

67. National Association of Insurance Commissioners, *Proceedings of the National Association of Insurance Commissioners, 1971 Regular Meeting* (Raleigh, N.C.: Commercial Printing Co., 1971), 1:158–159. See also "Possible Objections to State Post Assessment Guaranty Funds and Responses Thereto," in NAIC, *Proceedings of the National Association of Insurance Commissioners, 1970 Regular Meeting*, 2:1101: "Under the model bill, insurers simply advance funds in the form of assessment payments for the payment of claims against insolvent insurers. Subsequently the companies would recoup such amounts through appropriate premium loadings. The burden ultimately falls on the policyholders, not the companies, and hence is spread among those who enjoy the security against insolvent insurers."

68. NAIC, *Proceedings of the National Association of Insurance Commissioners, 1971 Regular Meeting*, 1:159.

69. "Possible Objections to State Post Assessment Guaranty Funds and Responses Thereto," in NAIC, *Proceedings of the National Association of Insurance Commissioners*, 2:1102. See also, e.g., statement of Maisonpierre, *Federal Insurance Guaranty Corporation: Hearings before the Committee on Commerce . . . on S. 2236*, pp. 72–73.

70. See, e.g., memorandum from NAIC executive secretary Jon S. Hanson, October 3, 1969, reprinted in *Proceedings of the National Association of Insurance Commissioners, 1970 Regular Meeting*, 1:262: "The NAIC has taken the position that although the magnitude of the insolvency problem is not

great when viewed on a national basis, nevertheless the consequences can be quite severe for those individuals involved." See also Insurance Security Fund, Wisconsin Session Laws, ch. 646, Preliminary Comments, p. 270: "No funding that is reasonable in amount could ever be adequate for a catastrophic rash of insolvencies." For congressional expressions of concern about the disaster problem, see, e.g., Sen. Moss, *Federal Insurance Guaranty Corporation: Hearings before the Committee on Commerce . . . on S. 2236*, p. 297.

71. See *Federal Insurance Guaranty Corporation: Hearings before the Committee on Commerce . . . on S. 2236*, pp. 274–299, esp. p. 288: "We [in the administration] are assuming that [a successful guaranty system] is feasible in most states, and what we really need is a Federal backup in those few cases where it isn't."

72. Ibid., pp. 286–287. See also p. 298.

73. "Post-Assessment Property and Liability Insurance Guaranty Association Model Act," reprinted in Harnett and Schreiber, *Insolvency and Solidity of Insurance Companies*, p. 111.

74. Bromley, "A History of the Development of the Life and Health Insurance Guaranty Association Model Act," pp. 632, 658–659; Hanson, *Regulation of the Life Insurance Business*, p. 83.

75. "Memorandum on the NAIC State Post Assessment Insurers Guaranty Association Model Bill," p. 1098. See also Insurance Security Fund, Wisconsin Session Laws, ch. 646.01(2), p. 271.

76. *Federal Insurance Guaranty Corporation: Hearings before the Committee on Commerce . . . on S. 2236*, p. 284.

77. Ibid.

78. Ibid., p. 285. See also esp. Passer's comments, p. 289.

79. Ibid., p. 1.

80. Ibid., p. 255.

81. Ibid., p. 278.

82. Memorandum to Members of the NAIC, December 14, 1970, reprinted in *Proceedings of the National Association of Insurance Commissioners, 1971 Regular Meeting*, 1:156, emphasis added.

83. Kimball, "History and Development," p. 27.

84. Quoted in Bromley, "A History of the Development of the Life and Health Insurance Guaranty Association Model Act," p. 635.

85. "Post-Assessment Property and Liability Insurance Guaranty Association Model Act," reprinted in Harnett and Schreiber, *Insolvency and Solidity of Insurance Companies*, p. 98.

86. Quoted in Wilcox, "U.S. Guaranty Association Concept at Twenty-five," p. 390.

87. See esp. ibid., p. 389. See also, e.g., Cosmo Macero, Jr., "Protection Sought

for State Emergency Claims Fund," *Boston Herald,* February 24, 1998, p. 36; "Massachusetts Lawmakers Weigh Changes to Guaranty Fund," *BestWire,* May 17, 1999.

88. Olson, "Property and Casualty Guaranty Funds before 1970," p. 145.

89. Frederick L. Hoffman, "Fifty Years of American Life Insurance Progress," *Publications of the American Statistical Association,* 12, no. 95 (September 1911), 716, table 4.

90. On insurance company failures from 1958 to 1969, see *Federal Insurance Guaranty Corporation: Hearings before the Committee on Commerce . . . on S. 2236,* p. 112.

91. *Rylands v. Fletcher,* L.R. 3 H.L. 330 (1868). On the evolution of strict liability in environmental cases, see Superfund Section 301(e) Study Group, *Injuries and Damages from Hazardous Wastes: Analysis and Improvement of Legal Remedies,* Report to Congress (Washington, D.C.: GPO, 1982), pt. 1, pp. 95–109.

92. Tom Kuhnle, "The Rebirth of Common Law Actions for Addressing Hazardous Waste Contamination," *Stanford Environmental Law Journal,* 15 (January 1996), 193.

93. Quoted in Louise A. Halper, "Untangling the Nuisance Knot," *Boston College Environmental Affairs Law Review,* 26 (Fall 1998), 100.

94. See esp. ibid., pp. 109–114.

95. *Madison v. Ducktown Sulphur, Copper & Iron Co.,* 113 Tenn. 331, 337–338, 340–345, 366–369 (1904): "Shall the complainants be granted, in the way of damages, the full measure of relief to which their injuries entitle them, or shall we go further, and grant their request to blot out two great mining and manufacturing enterprises, destroy half of the taxable values of a county, and drive more than 10,000 people from their homes? We think there can be no doubt as to what the true answer to this question should be" (p. 366).

96. J. Gordon Arbuckle et al., *Environmental Law Handbook* (Rockville, Md.: Government Institutes, 1991), p. 17.

97. *Keppel v. Lehigh Coal & Navigation Co.,* 200 Pa. 649, 651, 652 (1901).

98. Morton J. Horwitz, *The Transformation of American Law, 1780–1860* (Cambridge, Mass.: Harvard University Press, 1977), p. 74.

99. H. Marlow Green, "Common Law, Property Rights, and the Environment: A Comparative Analysis of Historical Developments in the United States and England and a Model for the Future," *Cornell International Law Journal,* 30 (1997), 549; Horwitz, *Transformation of American Law,* p. 76. See also *Radcliff's Executors v. Mayor of Brooklyn,* 4 N.Y. 195 (1850).

100. *Radcliff's Executors v. Mayor of Brooklyn,* 4 N.Y. 195, 203 (1850).

101. Horwitz, *Transformation of American Law,* pp. 76–78. See also Roger

Meiners and Bruce Yandle, "Common Law and the Conceit of Modern Environmental Policy," *George Mason Law Review,* 7 (Summer 1999), 927–928.

102. See, e.g., *McCarty v. Natural Carbonic Gas Company,* 189 N.Y. 40, 49 (1907). See also *Village of Euclid v. Ambler Realty Co.,* 272 U.S. 365, 388 (1926): "A nuisance may be merely a right thing in the wrong place,—like a pig in the parlor instead of the barnyard." See also Kuhnle, "Rebirth of Common Law Actions," pp. 197–200.

103. Mark D. Seltzer, "Personal Injury Hazardous Waste Litigation: A Proposal for Tort Reform," *Boston College Environmental Affairs Law Review,* 10 (Spring 1982), 827–833; "Development in the Law—Toxic Waste Litigation: IX. Common Law Personal Injury Recovery," *Harvard Law Review,* 99 (May 1986), 1602–9, 1617–25. See also Superfund Section 301(e) Study Group, *Injuries and Damages from Hazardous Wastes,* pp. 28–30.

104. Meiners and Yandle, "Common Law and the Conceit of Modern Environmental Policy," pp. 927–928.

105. Deborah R. Hensler and Mark A. Peterson, "Understanding Mass Personal Injury Litigation: A Socio-Legal Analysis," *Brooklyn Law Review,* 59 (Fall 1993), 1006–7; Francis E. McGovern, "The Defensive Use of Federal Class Actions in Mass Torts," *Arizona Law Review,* 39 (Summer 1997), 607–610. On mass torts, see Peter Schuck, "Mass Torts: An Institutional Evolutionist Perspective," *Cornell Law Review,* 80 (May 1995), 941–989.

106. "Development in the Law—Toxic Waste Litigation," pp. 1605–6; Michael D. Green, "The Paradox of Statutes of Limitations in Toxic Substances Litigation," *California Law Review,* 76 (October 1988), 979n65. See also Superfund Section 301(e) Study Group, *Injuries and Damages from Hazardous Wastes,* pp. 28–30.

107. See, e.g., John Carlucci, "Reforming the Law on Pesticides," *Virginia Environmental Law Journal,* 14 (Fall 1994), 192–193.

108. Troyen A. Brennan, "Environmental Torts," *Vanderbilt Law Review,* 46 (January 1993), 2 (a list of relevant cases appears at 2n1). See also Kuhnle, "Rebirth of Common Law Actions," p. 191; Peter S. Menell, "The Limitations of Legal Institutions for Addressing Environmental Risks," *Journal of Economic Perspectives,* 5, no. 3 (Summer 1991), esp. 93–94, 97–102.

109. Toxic Substances Control Act of 1976, P.L. 94–469, sec. 6(a).

110. Paul R. Portney, "Economics and the Clean Air Act," *Journal of Economic Perspectives,* 4, no. 4 (Autumn 1990), 174.

111. U.S. Office of Management and Budget, *Report to Congress on the Costs and Benefits of Federal Regulations, 1998* (Washington, D.C., January 1999), table 3.

112. On per se negligence in environmental cases, see, e.g., Superfund Section

301(e) Study Group, *Injuries and Damages from Hazardous Wastes*, pp. 76–79.

113. Phillip T. Cummings, "Completing the Circle," *Environmental Forum*, 7, no. 6 (November–December 1990), 11–12; Sidney A. Wallace and Temple L. Ratcliffe, "Water Pollution Laws: Can They Be Cleaned Up?" *Tulane Law Review*, 57 (June 1983), 1342–51.

114. Water and Environmental Quality Improvement Act of 1970, P.L. 91–224; "Comprehensive Water Pollution Control Act Cleared," *Congressional Quarterly Almanac, 91st Congress, 2nd Session . . . , 1970*, 26 (Washington, D.C., 1970), 175–178; Federal Water Pollution Control Act Amendments of 1972, P.L. 92–500; "Clean Water: Congress Overrides Presidential Veto," *Congressional Quarterly Almanac, 92nd Congress, 2nd Session . . . , 1972*, 28 (Washington, D.C., 1972), 708–722; Clean Water Act of 1977, P.L. 95–217. See also Wallace and Ratcliffe, "Water Pollution Laws," pp. 1344–46; Robert L. Glicksman, "Pollution on the Federal Lands, II: Water Pollution Law," *UCLA Journal of Environmental Law and Policy*, 12 (1993), 104. An important precedent for all of these water pollution laws was the Rivers and Harbors Act (or Refuse Act) of 1899, which made it a crime "to throw, discharge, or deposit . . . any refuse matter of any kind or description whatever other than that flowing from streets and sewers and passing therefrom in a liquid state, into any navigable water of the United States" without a permit from the secretary of war. See Rivers and Harbors Act of 1899, 55th Cong., 3rd sess., ch. 425, 1899, sec. 13, p. 1152 (33 U.S.C.S. §407 [1999]).

115. Wallace and Ratcliffe, "Water Pollution Laws," pp. 1346–48; Trans-Alaska Pipeline Authorization Act of 1973, P.L. 93–153, sec. 204; Deepwater Port Act of 1974, P.L. 93–627, sec. 18; Outer Continental Shelf Lands Act Amendment of 1978, P.L. 95–372, secs. 303–304.

116. Toxic Substances Control Act of 1976, P.L. 94–469; Resource Conservation and Recovery Act of 1976, P.L. 94–580; Clean Air Act Amendments of 1977, P.L. 95–95; Clean Water Act of 1977, P.L. 95–217.

117. Comprehensive Environmental Response, Compensation, and Liability Act of 1980, P.L. 95–510. See esp. secs. 104 (Response Authorities), 107 (Liability), 111 (Uses of Fund), 211 (Imposition of Taxes), 221 (Establishment of Hazardous Substance Response Trust Fund), 303 (Expiration, Sunset Provision). Although the standard of strict, joint, and several liability appeared explicitly in the original Senate bill, it remained only implicit in the final legislation. As Cummings explains ("Completing the Circle," pp. 15–16): "The committee staff had argued that strict, joint, and several liability . . . was not radical but was the standard of liability under §311 of the [Clean Water Act]. Alan Simpson (R.-Wyoming) was skeptical; if

that were so, he countered, why not just say that. The committee staff agreed. . . . The committee staff appears to have been right about the standard of liability under §311; responsible parties have in fact been held strictly, jointly, and severally liable under CERCLA."

118. See Cummings, "Completing the Circle," p. 12.

119. Committee on Interstate and Foreign Commerce, House of Representatives, *Hazardous Waste Containment Act of 1980*, House Report no. 96–1016 (May 16, 1980), p. 22.

120. Comprehensive Environmental Response, Compensation, and Liability Act of 1980, P.L. 95–510, sec. 107(c).

121. Cummings, "Completing the Circle," pp. 13–16.

122. Linda K. Breggin, James McElfish, and John Pendergrass, "State Superfund Programs: An Overview of the Environmental Law Institute's (ELI's) 1998 Research," *Albany Law Environmental Outlook*, 4 (Winter 1999), esp. 2–4, 6–7; Ruth Gastel, "Environmental Pollution: Insurance Issues," *III Insurance Issues Update* (May 1999).

123. Resource Conservation and Recovery Act of 1976, P.L. 94–580, sec. 7003.

124. L. Neal Ellis, Jr., and Charles D. Case, *Toxic Tort and Hazardous Substance Litigation* (Charlottesville: Michie Butterworth Law Publishers, 1995), pp. 323–324.

125. Superfund Amendments and Reauthorization Act of 1986, P.L. 99–499.

126. Oil Pollution Act of 1990, P.L. 101–380, esp. secs. 1002–4. See also Antonio Rodriguez and Paul A. C. Jaffe, "The Oil Pollution Act of 1990," *Maritime Lawyer*, 15 (Fall 1990), 1–28.

127. Committee on Interstate and Foreign Commerce, *Hazardous Waste Containment Act of 1980*, pp. 70, 74.

128. Jordan S. Stanzler and Charles A. Yuen, "Coverage for Environmental Cleanup Costs: History of the Word 'Damages' in the Standard Form Comprehensive General Liability Policy," *Columbia Business Law Review* (1990), esp. 489–490; Jim L. Julian and Charles L. Schlumberger, "Insurance Coverage for Environmental Clean-Up Costs under Comprehensive General Liability Policies," *University of Arkansas at Little Rock Law Journal*, 19 (Fall 1996), esp. 57–59.

129. On the reduced availability of environmental liability insurance, see, e.g., U.S. General Accounting Office, *Hazardous Waste: The Cost and Availability of Pollution Insurance*, GAO/PEMD-89-6 (Washington, D.C., 1988), pp. 3–5; U.S. General Accounting Office, *Hazardous Waste: An Update on the Cost and Availability of Pollution Insurance*, GAO/PEMD-94-16 (Washington, D.C., 1994), p. 24, fig. 2.5. By 1986, 55 percent of hazardous waste companies polled by the General Accounting Office reported being "unable to find" environmental liability coverage. Five years later, 87 percent of those

polled indicated that it was "very difficult or nearly impossible" to obtain an "adequate amount of pollution liability insurance." On the connection between Superfund's enactment and the subsequent liability insurance crisis, see, e.g., George Clemon Freeman, Jr., "Tort Law Reform: Superfund/RCRA Liability as a Major Cause of the Insurance Crisis," *Tort and Insurance Law Journal,* 21 (Summer 1986), 517–542.

130. Committee on Interstate and Foreign Commerce, *Hazardous Waste Containment Act of 1980,* p. 63.

131. *Congressional Record* (House), 96th Cong., 2nd sess., September 19, 1980, p. 26338.

132. *Congressional Record* (Senate), 96th Cong., 2nd sess., November 18, 1980, p. 30113.

133. Cummings, "Completing the Circle," p. 11.

134. The risk management logic underlying Superfund's liability provisions was also deeply rooted in the campaign for strict liability in product injury suits, which had been waged mainly by law professors. On the analogy to product liability law, see, e.g., Superfund Section 301(e) Study Group, *Injuries and Damages from Hazardous Wastes: Analysis and Improvement of Legal Remedies,* Report to Congress (Washington, D.C.: GPO, 1982), pt. 1, pp. 96–99.

135. *Congressional Record* (House), 96th Cong., 2nd sess., September 19, 1980, p. 26342.

136. See esp. Committee on Interstate and Foreign Commerce, *Hazardous Waste Containment Act of 1980,* p. 33. According to the House report, the "purpose" of the liability provisions was "to provide a mechanism for prompt recovery of monies expended for the [cleanup of hazardous substances] from persons responsible therefor and to induce such potentially liable persons to pursue appropriate environmental response actions voluntarily."

137. On the characterization of the Superfund law as mainly (though not exclusively) for the purpose of cleaning up existing and especially abandoned sites, see, e.g., *Congressional Record* (House), 96th Cong., 2nd sess., September 19, 1980, pp. 26338 (Florio), 26339 (Staggers), 26342 (Gore); *Congressional Record* (Senate), 96th Cong., 2nd sess., November 18, 1980, p. 30113 (Stafford). See also, e.g., Frederick R. Anderson, "Natural Resource Damages, Superfund, and the Courts," *Boston College Environmental Affairs Law Journal,* 16 (Spring 1989), 409n7. Sure enough, the bill's critics in Congress were quick to argue that its retroactive use of legal liability was highly irregular. "The bill addresses past externalities," Representatives Loeffler and Stockman maintained, "not current or future ones in which sound policy principles would dictate that users absorb control

costs. The general treasury should bear the expense of correcting hazards resulting from inadequacies in past legal structures and policies." A related criticism, put forward by five representatives (including Loeffler and Stockman), was that the proposed law "blurs the distinction between a welfare system and a tort law system." See Committee on Interstate and Foreign Commerce, *Hazardous Waste Containment Act of 1980*, pp. 74, 68.

138. Frank Viviano, "Superfund Costs May Top S&L Bailout: U.S. Toxics Cleanup Mired in Lawsuits," *San Francisco Chronicle*, May 29, 1991, p. A1. For more recent data on the Superfund cleanups and costs, see David G. Wood, "Superfund: Information on the Program's Funding and Status," *GAO Reports*, October 29, 1999 (GAO/RCED-00–25).

139. Quoted in Viviano, "Superfund Costs May Top S&L Bailout," p. A1. See also Sam Atwood, "Superfund: Boon or Bust? Debate Rages On," *USA Today*, April 22, 1991, p. 9E.

140. On Superfund's "chilling effect," see, e.g., Eric Harrison, "Wichita Rescues Redevelopment by Paying for Toxic Cleanup," *Los Angeles Times*, November 6, 1991, p. A5; Philip R. Sellinger and Avery Chapman, "EPA's Plan to Reassure Lenders Doesn't Go Far Enough," *American Banker*, January 22, 1992, p. 4; Neal R. Peirce, "Cleaning Up the Urban 'Brownfields,'" *Baltimore Sun*, March 13, 1995, p. 7A; Amy L. Edward and David Kahn, "Cleaning Up Your Act," *Legal Times*, October 14, 1996, pp. S44–S45; "Prepared Statement by Mayor James P. Perron, Elkhart, Indiana, on Behalf of the U.S. Conference of Mayors before the Senate Environment and Public Works Committee," *Federal News Service*, September 4, 1997. See also Susan R. Poulter, "Cleanup and Restoration: Who Should Pay?" *Journal of Land, Resources, and Environmental Law*, 18 (1998), 89–90.

141. On the rise of deterrence-based arguments, see, e.g., Adam Babich, "Understanding the New Era in Environmental Law," *South Carolina Law Review*, 41 (1990), 733–764; Mary E. S. Raivel, "CERCLA Liability as a Pollution Prevention Strategy," *Maryland Journal of Contemporary Legal Issues*, 4 (Winter 1992–93), 131–151; Joan Glickman, "A Superfund Retrospective: Past, Present, and . . . ," *Public Management*, 76, no. 2 (February 1994), esp. 6.

142. On these various programs, see David A. Moss, "Government, Markets, and Uncertainty: An Historical Approach to Public Risk Management in the United States," Harvard Business School Working Paper no. 97–025 (October 1996), esp. pp. 40–53. Significantly, even in the case of Price-Anderson, which has been characterized here as a Phase I policy, the pressures of Phase III were eventually felt. When the program was extended in 1975, Congress seemed to grant an implicit guaranty of unknown proportions by strongly suggesting that the federal government would ultimately

cover damages in excess of the legislation's $560 million liability cap were a major nuclear accident to occur. As part of a subsequent extension in 1988, Congress dramatically increased the maximum liability facing a pool of the nation's private nuclear operators to about $7 billion (per incident). In these ways, federal lawmakers effectively wrapped an anachronistic Phase I policy in the now familiar garb of Phase III. See *Duke Power Co. v. Carolina Environmental Study Group*, 438 U.S. 59, 66–67 (1978); Cheryl D. Block, "Overt and Covert Bailouts: Developing a Public Bailout Policy," *Indiana Law Journal*, 67 (Fall 1992), 975; "Increase Voted in Insurance for Nuclear Accident," *New York Times*, March 19, 1988, sec. 1, p. 6; "Congress Passes Fifteen-Year Extension of Price-Anderson Act," *BNA Federal Contracts Reports*, 50, no. 6 (August 8, 1988), 290.

143. *Analytical Perspectives, Budget of the United States Government, Fiscal Year 1999* (Washington, D.C.: GPO, 1998), p. 165.

10. The Foundations of American Risk Management Policy

1. "The Oration of M. T. Cicero in Behalf of Aulus Caecina" [*Pro Caecina*], chap. 25, in *The Orations of Marcus Tullius Cicero*, vol. 2, trans. C. D. Yonge (London: George Bell and Sons, 1891), p. 63. See also ibid., chap. 26; Neal Wood, *Cicero's Social and Political Thought* (Berkeley: University of California Press, 1988), esp. chaps. 6 ("Private Property and Its Accumulation"), pp. 105–119, and 7 ("The Idea of the State"), pp. 120–142.

2. John Stuart Mill, *Principles of Political Economy* (London: Longmans, Green, Reader, and Dyer, 1871), bk. 5, chap. 8, p. 531. See also Thomas Hobbes, *Leviathan* (New York: Collier, 1962 [1651]), esp. chap. 24, para. 5, pp. 185–186.

3. Stephen Breyer, *Breaking the Vicious Circle: Toward Effective Risk Regulation* (Cambridge, Mass.: Harvard University Press, 1993), p. 3.

4. On risk regulation, see esp., all by W. Kip Viscusi, *Risk by Choice: Regulating Health and Safety in the Workplace* (Cambridge, Mass.: Harvard University Press, 1983); *Fatal Tradeoffs: Public and Private Responsibilities for Risk* (New York: Oxford University Press, 1992); "The Value of Risks to Life and Health," *Journal of Economic Literature*, 31, no. 4 (December 1993), 1912–46; "Economic Foundations of the Current Regulatory Reform Efforts," *Journal of Economic Perspectives*, 10, no. 3 (Summer 1996), 119–134; and "Are Risk Regulators Rational? Evidence from Hazardous Waste Cleanup Decisions," *American Economic Review*, 89, no. 4 (September 1999), 1010–27; also Robert A. Pollak, "Regulating Risks," *Journal of Economic Literature*, 33, no. 1 (March 1995), 179–191; Walter Y. Oi, "Safety at What Price?" *American Economic Review*, 85, no. 2 (May 1995),

67–71; Cass R. Sunstein, *After the Rights Revolution: Reconceiving the Regulatory State* (Cambridge, Mass.: Harvard University Press, 1990); Peter Huber, "The Old-New Division in Risk Regulation," *Virginia Law Review*, 69 (September 1983), 1025–1106.

5. Although this notion has received surprisingly little attention from students of public policy and has never been articulated this way, it has not been ignored altogether. See esp. Steven Shavell, "Liability for Harm Versus Regulation of Safety," *Journal of Legal Studies*, 13 (1984), 357–374, which compares risk-reduction with risk-shifting strategies in the context of product safety.

6. "Governor's Speech," June 2, 1825, in *Resolves of the General Court of the Commonwealth of Massachusetts, May 25–June 18, 1825*, pp. 193–194; *Escola v. Coca Cola Bottling Company*, 24 Cal. 2d 453, 461–462 (1944).

7. Kenneth J. Arrow and Robert C. Lind, "Uncertainty and the Evaluation of Public Investment Decisions," *American Economic Review*, 60, no. 3 (June 1970), 374.

8. To be sure, highly fluid political interests and alliances played a significant role in all of the legislative campaigns highlighted over the preceding chapters. Growing public hostility to the so-called Albany Regency, for example, helped to influence the evolution of banking policy in antebellum New York; and deeply rooted tensions between North and South were never far from the surface in congressional debates over bankruptcy law. An unusual alliance of union and employer groups, moreover, was largely responsible for the defeat of compulsory health and unemployment insurance bills in many states in the 1910s. Yet it is impossible to identify any single political dynamic or coalition that consistently shaped the policymaking process across all of the various experiments with public risk management. One can find evidence of capture in the enactment of workers' compensation laws in the early twentieth century, since employers sometimes played a significant role in shaping the final legislation. But one would be hard-pressed to find substantial evidence of capture in the making of modern product liability law or federal disaster relief. For the most part, policymakers were distinguished by their interest in actual problem solving, rather than in the diversion of rents or some other nefarious motive. On capture theory, which suggests that government regulation is typically fashioned in the interests of the regulated, whose political power allows them to "capture" policymaking and regulatory processes, see esp. George J. Stigler, "The Theory of Economic Regulation," *Bell Journal of Economics and Management Science*, 2, no. 1 (Spring 1971), 3–21; Sam Pelzman, "Toward a More General Theory of Regulation," *Journal of Law and Economics*, 19, no. 2 (August 1976), 211–248.

9. "Message to Congress Reviewing the Broad Objectives and Accomplishments of the Administration," June 8, 1934, in *The Public Papers and Addresses of Franklin D. Roosevelt*, vol. 3, *The Advance of Recovery and Reform* (New York: Random House, 1938), pp. 287–293.

10. For a broader (comparative) discussion of producer versus consumer orientation in national economic strategy, see Bruce R. Scott, "Economic Strategy and Economic Performance," Harvard Business School Case Study no. 792–086 (November 24, 1992), esp. pp. 51–55.

11. Soon after World War II, Congress established the Investment Guaranty Program, which insured U.S. investors against noncommercial risks in war-torn Europe. The program was expanded in the late 1950s to cover investment in less-developed countries. In 1969, Congress turned political risk insurance over to the newly authorized Overseas Private Investment Corporation (OPIC), which continues to operate today. See Patricia McKinsey Robin, "The Bit Won't Bite: The American Bilateral Investment Program," *American University Law Review*, 33 (Summer 1984), 936–937. Interestingly, foreign investment insurance may reasonably be viewed as a proxy for enforceable property rights in the international sphere. As Cicero recognized as early as the first century B.C., the domestic enforcement of property rights directly reduces risks of theft and expropriation facing the owners of property. The problem in the case of foreign direct investment is that the U.S. government cannot itself enforce private property rights in other sovereign nations, except through the application of military force. Foreign investment insurance offers a reasonable alternative, *spreading* the risk of property infringement abroad rather than directly *reducing* it.

12. At a conceptual level, a liability regime *shifts* risk, insurance *spreads* risk, and regulation *reduces* risk. In practice, however, a liability regime that shifts risk onto large entities (such as major corporations) will also tend to spread risk, since large entities are able to break their risks into small pieces and pass them on to shareholders and consumers. Insurance that is experience rated, moreover, succeeds in spreading a large portion of risk across all policyholders but also shifts part of it onto those policyholders with the worst records of insured losses. Finally, to the extent that either a liability regime or an insurance program shifts risk onto firms or individuals, it will *indirectly* promote risk reduction by creating favorable incentives for hazard prevention. As John Andrews once told a colleague at the American Association for Labor Legislation, "I know that Prof. Commons and I in all of the work we have done together have thought first of prevention [i.e., shifting] and second of relief [i.e., spreading] in dealing with each form of social insurance in this country." See John Andrews to Olga Halsey, January 27, 1915, AALL Papers, reel 13.

13. John Andrews to J. Hopkins, September 5, 1918, AALL Papers, reel 18.

14. Fleming James, Jr., "Contribution among Joint Tortfeasors: A Pragmatic Criticism," *Harvard Law Review,* 54 (1941), 1157.

15. William F. Willoughby, "The Problem of Social Insurance: An Analysis," *American Labor Legislation Review,* 3, no. 2 (June 1913), 157.

16. Under optimal market conditions, of course, risk should always seek those best able to manage it. Either implicitly or explicitly, poor risk managers should pay better risk managers to assume their risks. To some extent this actually happens in practice. Most of us pay insurance companies to absorb a wide range of risks, from fire and theft to accident and illness. Many of us also buy and sell stocks in the marketplace. Though less transparent than insurance, stocks are at least as important in the realm of risk management because each share represents a claim on a risky stream of earnings. From this perspective, organized stock markets constitute elaborate markets for risk. Forward contracts, futures contracts, puts, calls, and every other type of tradable option are also fundamentally risk management devices. But regardless of what vehicle is used, an efficient market should always allocate risk to those best positioned to reduce it, spread it, or simply bear it themselves.

17. See, e.g., Robert J. Shiller, *Macro Markets: Creating Institutions for Managing Society's Largest Economic Risks* (New York: Oxford University Press, 1993), esp. pp. 1–16.

18. See esp. I. M. Rubinow, "Labor Insurance," *Journal of Political Economy,* 12, no. 3 (June 1904), 374–375; I. M. Rubinow, "Subsidized Unemployment Insurance," *Journal of Political Economy,* 21, no. 5 (May 1913), 413; and Paul H. Douglas, *Standards of Unemployment Insurance* (Chicago: University of Chicago Press, 1932), p. 164.

19. See, e.g., Doughton, *Congressional Record* (House), 74th Cong., 1st sess., July 17, 1935, p. 11342; Wagner, *Congressional Record* (Senate), 74th Cong., 1st sess., June 18, 1935, p. 9525; Harrison, *Congressional Record* (Senate), June 18, 1935, pp. 9521–22, 9522–23.

20. In more recent years, adverse selection has frequently been cited as a possible culprit for the narrowness of private annuity markets and thus as a potential argument for government compulsion. See, e.g., Benjamin M. Friedman and Mark J. Warshawsky, "The Cost of Annuities: Implications for Saving Behavior and Bequests," *Quarterly Journal of Economics,* 105, no. 1 (February 1990), 136, 140.

21. See, e.g., Bulkley, *Congressional Record* (Senate), 73rd Cong., 1st sess., May 8, 1933, p. 3006.

22. See esp. *Escola v. Coca Cola Bottling Company,* 24 Cal. 2d 453, 467 (1944). See also Gary T. Schwartz, "Foreword: Understanding Products Liability," *California Law Review,* 67, no. 3 (May 1979), 452–454.

23. On Knightian uncertainty and disaster policy, see David A. Moss,

"Courting Disaster? The Transformation of Federal Disaster Policy since 1803," in Kenneth A. Froot, ed., *The Financing of Catastrophe Risk* (Chicago: University of Chicago Press, 1999), pp. 307–355; Howard Kunreuther, "Ambiguity and Government Risk-Bearing for Low-Probability Events," in Mark S. Sniderman, ed., *Government Risk-Bearing* (Boston: Kluwer Academic Publishers, 1993), esp. pp. 24–30, 35–37. Knightian uncertainty may also have played a role in a number of other government forays into risk management, including several varieties of war risk insurance and foreign investment insurance. But no firm conclusions can be drawn at this point in the absence of further research on the subject. On war risk and foreign investment insurance, see esp. Virginia Haufler, *Dangerous Commerce: Insurance and the Management of International Risk* (Ithaca, N.Y.: Cornell University Press, 1997). According to Knight, insurance companies and other bureaucratic organizations—while well suited to manage quantifiable risk—are ill suited to manage uncertainty (i.e., unquantifiable risk). See esp. Frank H. Knight, *Risk, Uncertainty, and Profit* (Chicago: University of Chicago Press, 1971 [1921]), pp. 233, 247.

24. For an excellent (and very readable) summary of many of these biases, see esp. Daniel Kahneman and Mark W. Riepe, "Aspects of Investor Psychology: Beliefs, Preferences, and Biases Investment Advisors Should Know About," *Journal of Portfolio Management*, 24, no. 4 (Summer 1998), 52–65.

25. Significantly, this nineteenth-century view of entrepreneurs as overoptimists finds corroboration in recent research on entrepreneurship. See esp. Lowell W. Busenitz, "Entrepreneurial Risk and Strategic Decision Making," *Journal of Applied Behavioral Science*, 35, no. 3 (September 1999), 325–340.

26. Henry R. Seager, "Outline of a Program of Social Reform" (1907), in *Labor and Other Economic Essays by Henry R. Seager*, ed. Charles A. Gulick, Jr. (New York: Harper and Brothers, 1931), pp. 82–83.

27. Guido Calabresi, *The Costs of Accidents: A Legal and Economic Analysis* (New Haven: Yale University Press, 1970), esp. pp. 56–57. By 1991, a report for the American Law Institute concluded, "[t]he principal assumption in the literature supporting a role for legal liability is that consumers underestimate product defect risks and, as a consequence, put insufficient market pressure on firms to produce safety." See *Reporters' Study on Enterprise Responsibility for Personal Injury* (Philadelphia: American Law Institute, 1991), 1:230.

28. Howard Kunreuther et al., *Disaster Insurance Protection: Public Policy Lessons* (New York: John Wiley & Sons, 1978), pp. 236–237, 240–241.

29. The evidence linking lotteries and limited liability, though only suggestive, is presented in Chapter 3. If antebellum lawmakers did indeed have the

lottery impulse in mind when they enacted limited liability laws, then this represented an unusual twist in risk management policy, since the typical objective was to remedy perception problems rather than exploit them.

30. For a review of this literature, see John D. Hanson and Douglas A. Kysar, "Taking Behavioralism Seriously: The Problem of Market Manipulation," *New York University Law Review,* 74, no. 3 (June 1999), esp. 643–721.

31. See, e.g., W. Kip Viscusi, "Individual Rationality, Hazard Warnings, and the Foundations of Tort Law," *Rutgers Law Review,* 48 (Spring 1996), esp. 639–650.

32. See Hanson and Kysar, "Taking Behavioralism Seriously," p. 745, where it is suggested that systematic irrationality should be conceived as a form of market failure.

33. On this latter commitment problem, see esp. Dani Rodrik and Richard Zeckhauser, "The Dilemma of Government Responsiveness," *Journal of Policy Analysis and Management,* 7, no. 4 (1988), 601–620.

34. See, e.g., Bulkley, *Congressional Record* (Senate), May 8, 1933, p. 3006.

35. Quoted in Bob Benenson, "Insurance Finds Few Takers," *Congressional Quarterly,* 51, no. 29 (July 17, 1993), 1861.

36. See, e.g., Richard W. Stevenson, "Benefits and Drawbacks to Bush and Gore Proposals for Overhauling Social Security," *New York Times,* May 19, 2000, p. A23; Paul Krugman, "Unhappy Returns?" *New York Times,* May 17, 2000, p. A23; James Dao and Alison Mitchell, "Gore Denounces Bush Social Security Plan as Too Risky," *New York Times,* May 17, 2000, p. A20.

37. For a critique of the traditional (Pigouvian) view that the "tax should be equal to the damage done and should therefore vary with the amount of the harmful effect," see R. H. Coase, "The Problem of Social Cost," *Journal of Law and Economics,* 3 (October 1960), esp. 41. For an early critique of Coase's critique, see William J. Baumol, "On Taxation and the Control of Externalities," *American Economic Review,* 62, no. 3 (June 1972), 307–322.

38. John R. Commons, "Social Insurance and the Medical Profession," *Wisconsin Medical Journal,* 13 (January 1915), 303.

39. David A. Moss, *Socializing Security: Progressive-Era Economists and the Origins of American Social Policy* (Cambridge, Mass.: Harvard University Press, 1996), pp. 64–65, 73, 201n18; John R. Commons, *Industrial Goodwill* (New York: McGraw-Hill, 1919), p. 129.

40. See, e.g., Adna F. Weber, "Employers' Liability and Accident Insurance," *Political Science Quarterly,* 17, no. 2 (June 1902), 258–259.

41. Paul H. Douglas, "Discussion," *American Economic Review,* 23, no. 1 (March 1933), Papers and Proceedings, 53. In a less pronounced way, similar arguments were also employed in support of federal bankruptcy law, since the bankruptcy process was expected to eliminate the bank run psy-

chology that sometimes led nervous creditors to destroy otherwise healthy debtors. But as Chapter 5 on bankruptcy made clear, creditor provisions like these almost always took a back seat to the more prominent issue of discharge in nineteenth-century debates over bankruptcy law.

42. At a conceptual level, the government's greatest strengths as a risk manager stem from three basic attributes: its ability to compel participation in risk management programs, even *after* a hazard has occurred; its near-perfect credit rating, based on its power to tax and to print money; and its unparalleled monitoring capabilities, rooted in its police, regulatory, and subpoena powers. No private actor can match the government on any one of these dimensions, let alone all three.

43. See, e.g., Robert C. Merton and Zvi Bodie, "On the Management of Financial Guarantees," *Financial Management*, 21, no. 4 (Winter 1992), 106.

44. Revealing their intense interest in work-duration risk, the authors of the Social Security Act did restrict benefits to those who continued working past sixty-five, on the grounds that these workers had obviously not depleted their human capital. And in subsequent years, Congress adopted federal disability insurance and ultimately permitted early retirement at the age of sixty-two (in return for a discounted annuity). Although these steps addressed part of the problem, work-duration risk remains largely uninsurable to this day.

45. Alexis de Tocqueville, *Democracy in America* (New York: Knopf, 1948), 2:36–37; Werner Sombart, *Why Is There No Socialism in the United States?* trans. P. M. Hocking and C. T. Husbands (London: Macmillan, 1976 [1906]).

46. On the prevalence of this notion among comparativist historians, see esp. Michael Kammen, "The Problem of American Exceptionalism: A Reconsideration," *American Quarterly*, 45, no. 1 (March 1993), 22: "I find increasingly that when scholars function comparatively they are struck, in one way or another, with the [American] state's *relatively* decentralized or noninterventionist nature."

47. Seymour Martin Lipset, *American Exceptionalism: A Double-Edged Sword* (New York: W. W. Norton, 1996), p. 20.

48. James Bryce, *The American Commonwealth*, 3rd ed. (New York: Macmillan, 1895), 2:540–541.

49. 1996 International Social Survey Project (ISSP), as cited in *Public Perspective*, 9, no. 2 (February–March 1998), 32.

50. Bryce, *American Commonwealth*, 2:541.

51. Albert Shaw, "The American State and the American Man," *Contemporary Review*, 51 (1887), 695–696.

52. See esp. J. Allen Smith, *The Spirit of American Government: A Study of the Constitution, Its Origin, Influence, and Relation to Democracy* (New York:

Macmillan, 1907); Charles Beard, *Public Policy and the General Welfare* (New York: Farrar and Rinehart, 1941); Oscar and Mary Flug Handlin, *Commonwealth: A Study of the Role of Government in the American Economy, Massachusetts, 1774–1861* (New York: New York University Press, 1947); Louis Hartz, *Economic Policy and Democratic Thought: Pennsylvania, 1776–1860* (Cambridge, Mass.: Harvard University Press, 1948); George Rogers Taylor, *The Transportation Revolution, 1815–1860* (New York: Rinehart, 1951); Milton Heath, *Constructive Liberalism: The Role of the State in Economic Development in Georgia to 1860* (Cambridge, Mass.: Harvard University Press, 1954); Carter Goodrich, *Government Promotion of American Canals and Railroads, 1800–1890* (New York: Columbia University Press, 1960); Harry N. Scheiber, *Ohio Canal Era: A Case Study of Government and the Economy, 1820–1861* (Athens: Ohio University Press, 1969); Frank Bourgin, *The Great Challenge: The Myth of Laissez-Faire in the Early Republic* (New York: George Braziller, 1989); L. Ray Gunn, *Decline of Authority: Public Economic Policy and Political Development in New York State, 1800–1860* (Ithaca, N.Y.: Cornell University Press, 1988); William J. Novak, *The People's Welfare: Law and Regulation in Nineteenth-Century America* (Chapel Hill: University of North Carolina Press, 1996).

53. Oscar Handlin, "Laissez-Faire Thought in Massachusetts, 1790–1880," *Journal of Economic History,* 3 (December 1943), 55.

54. Novak, *People's Welfare,* p. 3.

55. Shaw, "American State and the American Man," pp. 695–696.

56. Morton Keller, "The Pluralist State: American Economic Regulation in Comparative Perspective, 1900–1930," in Thomas K. McCraw, ed., *Regulation in Perspective: Historical Essays* (Cambridge, Mass.: Harvard University Press, 1981), p. 65. See also, e.g., Stephen Skowronek, *Building a New American State: The Expansion of National Administrative Capacities, 1877–1920* (Cambridge: Cambridge University Press, 1982); Charles Bright, "The State in the Nineteenth Century," in Charles Bright and Susan Harding, eds., *Statemaking and Social Movements: Essays in History and Theory* (Ann Arbor: University of Michigan Press, 1984), esp. pp. 121, 139; Gaston Rimlinger, *Welfare Policy and Industrialization in Europe, America, and Russia* (New York: John Wiley and Sons, 1971); Herbert Hovenkamp, *Enterprise and American Law, 1836–1937* (Cambridge, Mass.: Harvard University Press, 1991).

57. *Farwell v. Boston and Worcester Railroad Corporation,* 45 Mass. 49, 57 (1842).

58. *California State Automobile Association v. Maloney,* 341 U.S. 105, 110 (1951).

59. Quoted in Dick Thornburgh, "Sue, but Don't Prosecute," *New York Times,* September 20, 2000, p. A27. See also Paul Magnusson and Lorraine

Woellert, "Ford/Firestone: An Election-Year Double Whammy," *Business Week*, September 25, 2000, p. 59; Cindy Skrzycki, "Forward Momentum: Tire Recalls Propel Stalled Safety Legislation," *Washington Post*, September 19, 2000, p. E1.

60. Eveline M. Burns, "Social Insurance in Evolution," *American Economic Review*, 34, no. 1 (March 1944), 199. See also Herbert McClosky and John Zaller, *The American Ethos: Public Attitudes toward Capitalism and Democracy* (Cambridge, Mass.: Harvard University Press, 1984), pp. 275–277; Robert Y. Shapiro and John T. Young, "Public Opinion and the Welfare State: The United States in Comparative Perspective," *Political Science Quarterly*, 104, 1 (Spring 1989), 71.

61. Quoted in Jerry R. Cates, *Insuring Inequality: Administrative Leadership in Social Security, 1935–54* (Ann Arbor: University of Michigan Press, 1983), p. 33.

62. *Why Social Security?* (Washington, D.C.: Social Security Board, 1937). Recent studies of the Social Security program suggest that it involves only modest redistribution of income. See, e.g., Julia Lynn Coronado, Don Fullerton, and Thomas Glass, "Distributional Impacts of Proposed Changes to the Social Security System," National Bureau of Economic Research (NBER) Working Paper no. 6989, March 1999; Alan L. Gustman and Thomas L. Steinmeier, "How Effective Is Redistribution under the Social Security Benefit Formula?" NBER Working Paper no. 7597, March 2000.

63. *Social Security Bulletin: Annual Statistical Supplement, 2000*, table 4.A1 (Old Age and Survivors' Insurance, 1937–1999).

64. One possible explanation for this fear relates to the issues of moral hazard and monitoring. It has often been said that health insurance invites an unusually large amount of moral hazard. If so, then the monitoring requirements associated with health insurance would also be unusually great. This would help to explain why a government that provides health insurance might also be expected to demand considerable control over health care provision, that is, as a means of monitoring and controlling a formidable moral hazard problem.

65. Transcript of the New York State Senate Judiciary Committee Hearing on the Mills Health Insurance Bill (Senate Print no. 365), March 7, 1917, pp. 22–23.

66. See, e.g., Karen Tumulty and Edwin Chen, "Congress Reaches Its D-Day, as in Debate, on Health Bill," *Los Angeles Times*, August 9, 1994, p. A4: "'Am I willing to use every power I have as a member of the U.S. Senate to stop a *government takeover* of health care in America?' asked [Senator] Gramm, who is one of the most tenacious opponents of the alternatives being offered by the Democrats. 'The answer is yes, and I'm going to do it proudly'"

(emphasis added). On the struggle over compulsory health insurance in the 1940s, see esp. Paul Starr, *The Social Transformation of American Medicine* (New York: Basic Books, 1982), pp. 280–289. Significantly, though, Starr concludes that the "opponents did not win because their views were more deeply rooted in American culture than those of the supporters" (p. 287).

67. 1996 ISSP, p. 32. See also Shapiro and Young, "Public Opinion and the Welfare State," pp. 78–80; Hazel Erskine, "The Polls: Health Insurance," *Public Opinion Quarterly*, 39, no. 1 (Spring 1975), esp. 134–143; Stanley L. Payne, "Some Opinion Research Principles Developed through Studies of Social Medicine," *Public Opinion Quarterly*, 10, no. 1 (Spring 1946), 93–98.

68. Ronald E. Seavoy, *The Origins of the American Business Corporation, 1784–1855* (Westport, Conn.: Greenwood Press, 1982), pp. 266–267. As L. Ray Gunn explains, delegates to the 1846 convention had originally contemplated imposing proportional liability on New York corporations. But after exemptions were proposed for insurance companies and public utilities, the delegates ultimately chose to remain silent on the issue, which meant that "limited liability . . . remained in force." Gunn, *Decline of Authority*, pp. 231–232.

69. See esp. Chalmers Johnson, *MITI and the Japanese Miracle: The Growth of Industrial Policy, 1925–1975* (Stanford: Stanford University Press, 1982), pp. 200–207.

70. Richard Tilly, "Germany," in Richard Sylla and Gianni Toniolo, eds., *Patterns of European Industrialization: The Nineteenth Century* (New York: Routledge, 1991), esp. pp. 181–184, 190–191; Wilfried Feldenkirchen, "Banking and Economic Growth: Banks and Industry in Germany in the Nineteenth Century and Their Changing Relationship during Industrialization," in W. R. Lee, ed., *German Industry and German Industrialization: Essays in German Economic and Business History in the Nineteenth and Twentieth Centuries* (New York: Routledge, 1991), pp. 116–147.

71. Charles P. Kindleberger, *Economic Growth in France and Britain, 1851–1950* (Cambridge, Mass.: Harvard University Press, 1964), pp. 41–44, 185–190. See also David A. Landes, *The Unbound Prometheus: Technological Change and Industrial Development in Western Europe from 1750 to the Present* (Cambridge: Cambridge University Press, 1969), esp. p. 400; John H. McArthur and Bruce R. Scott, *Industrial Planning in France* (Boston: Division of Research, Graduate School of Business Administration, Harvard University, 1969).

72. See esp. *Journal of the Senate of the State of New York*, 52nd sess. (Albany: E. Croswell, 1829), p. 178.

73. As one of the main authors of the Social Security Act, Edwin E. Witte later stated: "Only to a very minor degree does [the old age insurance program]

modify the distribution of wealth and it does not alter at all the fundamentals of our capitalistic and individualistic economy. Nor does it relieve the individual of primary responsibility for his own support and that of his dependents." Quoted in Cates, *Insuring Inequality,* p. 24. An important reason for this, which Witte alluded to in 1955, was that Social Security established "completely self-financed social insurance programs, without Government contributions, which to this day is a distinctive feature of social insurance in this country." Edwin E. Witte, "Reflections on the Beginnings of Social Security," remarks delivered at observance of the twentieth anniversary of the Social Security Act by the Department of Health, Education and Welfare, Washington, D.C., August 15, 1955. On welfare state regimes, see also Gøsta Esping-Andersen, *The Three Worlds of Welfare Capitalism* (Princeton: Princeton University Press, 1990); Robert E. Goodin, Bruce Heady, Ruud Muffels, and Henk-Jan Dirven, *The Real Worlds of Welfare Capitalism* (Cambridge: Cambridge University Press, 1999); Gaston V. Rimlinger, *Welfare Policy and Industrialization in Europe, America, and Russia* (New York: Wiley, 1971).

74. On public support for consumer protection regulation in the 1960s and 1970s (when many of these regulations were first put in place), see Robert Y. Shapiro and John M. Gilroy, "The Polls: Regulation, Part II," *Public Opinion Quarterly,* 48, no. 3 (Autumn 1984), esp. 669–671.

75. On the relative advantages and disadvantages of risk-reallocation versus direct risk-reduction strategies, see Steven Shavell, "Liability for Harm versus Regulation of Safety," *Journal of Legal Studies,* 13 (June 1984), 357–74.

76. One indication of the nation's greater reliance on liability as a risk management tool is the fact that liability insurance premiums account for a far larger percentage of GDP in the United States than anywhere else in the developed world. In 1994, liability premiums accounted for 2.2 percent of GDP in the United States, 0.8 percent in the United Kingdom, 0.8 percent in France, 1.3 percent in Germany, and 0.5 percent in Japan. See Tillinghast–Towers Perrin, *Tort Cost Trends: An International Perspective* (Philadelphia, 1995).

Epilogue

1. See, e.g., William Proxmire, *Hearings before the Subcommittee on Financial Institutions of the Committee on Banking and Currency,* United States Senate, December 1969, p. 1.

2. In France, by contrast, where no comparable cardholder protections had been put in place, horror stories abounded, and consumers expressed intense anxiety about giving out their credit card numbers on-line. Aware of this problem in France and other member nations, European Union of-

ficials issued a directive in 1997 urging all member states to adopt strict limitations on cardholder liability. Such action, they predicted, would "contribute to the advent of the information society and, in particular, electronic commerce by promoting customer confidence in and retailer acceptance of [electronic payment] instruments." Directive 97/7/EC of the European Parliament and of the Council of May 20, 1997, on the Protection of Consumers in Respect of Distance Contracts; Commission Recommendation 97/489/EC of July 30, 1997, Concerning Transactions by Electronic Payment Instruments and in Particular the Relationship between Issuer and Holder.

3. See, e.g., David E. Sanger, "Big Powers Plan a World Economic Bailout Fund," *New York Times,* June 8, 1995, p. D1.

4. Part of the difficulty in comparing returns is that the effective yield on Social Security contributions appears low at the present time because of the heavy burden of existing obligations to current and future retirees, including the baby boomers themselves. Since these obligations will likely have to be paid regardless of whether Social Security is privatized, standard returns on stock portfolios (typically in the neighborhood of 7 percent per year) cannot be said to represent an accurate basis for estimating returns on a "privatized" Social Security system. See esp. John Geanakoplos, Olivia S. Mitchell, and Stephen P. Zeldes, "Would a Privatized Social Security System Really Pay a Higher Rate of Return?" in R. Douglas Arnold, Michael J. Graetz, and Alicia H. Munnell, eds., *Framing the Social Security Debate: Values, Politics, and Economics* (Washington, D.C.: National Academy of Social Insurance, 1998), pp. 137–157.

5. For a strong critique of the argument that stocks are not particularly risky when held for the long run, see Zvi Bodie, "On the Risk of Stocks in the Long Run," *Financial Analysts Journal,* 51, no. 3 (May–June 1995), 18–22.

6. *Congressional Record* (Senate), 74th Cong., 1st sess., June 14, 1935, p. 9292.

7. *Congressional Record* (Senate), 74th Cong., 1st sess., June 18, 1935, p. 9525.

8. In 1935, Senator Royal Copeland of New York bemoaned the plight of "thousands of families, I suppose millions, who thought they had prepared for the rainy day, but by reason of the depression, and the circumstances involved in it, they have come to be almost as bad off as many who were born and have lived all their lives in poverty." See *Congressional Record* (Senate), June 18, 1935, p. 9520.

9. See, e.g., Harrison, *Congressional Record* (Senate), June 18, 1935, p. 9521; Shipstead, *Congressional Record* (Senate), June 18, 1935, p. 9523; Hill, *Congressional Record* (Senate), July 17, 1935, pp. 1136–37; Wagner, *Congressional Record* (Senate), June 18, 1935, p. 9525.

10. Quoted in Alison Mitchell, "Bush Presents Social Security as Crucial Test," *New York Times,* May 16, 2000, p. A1. Although concerns about investment risk have tended to figure most prominently in critiques of recent privatization proposals, critics have highlighted a number of other problems as well. Again like the original authors of Social Security, a number of current critics of privatization have questioned how effectively citizens would manage longevity risk on their own—wondering whether citizens would choose to annuitize their nest eggs at retirement and, if so, whether private (voluntary) annuities would prove more costly than expected as a result of adverse selection. A related concern is whether inflation-indexed annuities would be available in the private marketplace and, if they were, whether citizens would voluntarily choose to purchase them at retirement. Critics have also expressed concern about the potential impact of partial privatization of old age insurance on related public insurance programs (especially disability insurance) as well as about the sizable transaction costs that might well be associated with individualized retirement accounts. See, e.g., Alicia H. Munnell, "Reforming Social Security: The Case against Individual Accounts," *National Tax Journal,* 52, no. 4 (December 1999), 803–817; Peter A. Diamond, "The Economics of Social Security Reform," in Arnold, Graetz, and Munnell, *Framing the Social Security Debate,* pp. 38–64; and Jonathan Chait, "Bold Over: Bush versus Social Security," *New Republic,* May 29, 2000, pp. 20–23.

11. Don Bauder, "Cheney Scored on IPO Windfall; Thurow's Age of Intellectualism," *San Diego Union-Tribune,* October 27, 2000, p. C1.

12. Prepared testimony of Francis S. Collins, M.D., Ph.D., director, National Human Genome Research Institute, National Institutes of Health, before the Senate Committee on Health, Education, Labor and Pensions, *Federal News Service,* July 20, 2000.

13. See, e.g., Neil A. Holtzman and Theresa M. Marteau, "Will Genetics Revolutionize Medicine?" *New England Journal of Medicine,* 343, no. 2 (July 13, 2000), 141–144.

14. See, e.g., Richard Saltus, "Doctor Warns of 'Hype' in Genome Decoding in N. E. Journal, Questions Raised on Real Medical Value," *Boston Globe,* July 13, 2000, p. A9.

15. On the "veil of ignorance" and Rawlsian justice, see esp. John Rawls, *A Theory of Justice* (Cambridge, Mass.: Harvard University Press, 1971), esp. pp. 12, 136–142; Ronald Dworkin, "What Is Equality? Part 2: Equality of Resources," *Philosophy and Public Affairs,* 10, no. 4 (1981), 283–345.

16. Prepared testimony of Francis S. Collins, July 20, 2000. See also Francis Collins, *Health Insurance in the Age of Genetics* (Washington, D.C.: Department of Health and Human Services, July 1997); Kathy L. Hudson et al., "Genetic Discrimination and Health Insurance: An Urgent Need for Re-

form," *Science,* 270, no. 5235 (October 20, 1995), 391–393; Elizabeth Cooper, "Testing for Genetic Traits: The Need for a New Legal Doctrine of Informed Consent," *Maryland Law Review,* 58 (1999), esp. 349–350; "Insurance in the Genetic Age," *Economist,* October 21, 2000, p. 23.

17. "Health Insurance Discrimination," National Human Genome Research Institute, *Issue Update* (September 2000), pp. 1–4; "Employment Discrimination," National Human Genome Research Institute, *Issue Update* (September 2000), p. 3; Ann Scott Tyson, "Lawmakers Play Catch-up to Genetic Science," *Christian Science Monitor,* August 10, 2000, p. 3. Although Congress had yet to enact a law focusing exclusively on genetic information and insurance, there was mounting interest in doing so. The most popular bill of this sort was the Genetic Information Nondiscrimination in Health Insurance Act, also known as the Slaughter-Snowe Act.

18. Quoted in "Testing Times," *Economist,* October 21, 2000, p. 93. See also David J. Christianson, "Genetic Testing: Risk Classification and Adverse Selection," *Journal of Insurance Regulation,* 15, no. 1 (Fall 1996), 75–79.

19. President William Jefferson Clinton, "Remarks on Signing an Executive Order to Prohibit Discrimination in Federal Employment Based on Genetic Information," February 8, 2000, Pres. Doc. 241, in *Weekly Compilation of Presidential Documents,* vol. 36, no. 6, pp. 233–289.

20. Prepared testimony of Francis S. Collins, July 20, 2000.

21. Rawls, *Theory of Justice,* p. 12.

22. As the biblical story makes clear, the temptation to uncover and use new information can be unbearably strong. Then "your eyes shall be opened," the serpent told Eve in Genesis 3:5, "and you shall be as gods, knowing good and evil." But, of course, new information is not always a blessing. After Eve and Adam had eaten the forbidden fruit, "the eyes of them both were opened, and they knew that they were naked" (3:7). God sent them "forth from the Garden of Eden" (3:23) and cursed the ground beneath them, declaring that "in sorrow shalt thou eat of it all the days of thy life" (3:17).

23. In fact, this logic may offer an additional reason why American lawmakers have rarely cited adverse selection in the private marketplace as a justification for risk management policy. Acknowledgment of an adverse selection problem would represent a tacit admission that all risks were not distributed equally and that a compulsory solution would necessarily involve some redistribution of wealth, rather than risk alone.

24. Andrew Sullivan, "Promotion of the Fittest," *New York Times,* July 23, 2000, sec. 6, p. 16.

25. See Pierre Rosanvallon, *The New Social Question: Rethinking the Welfare State,* trans. Barbara Harshav (Princeton: Princeton University Press, 2000), esp. chap. 1 ("The Decline of the Insuring Society"), pp. 11–26.

Acknowledgments

In writing this book, I have received assistance from many quarters. Peter Leight, Bruce Scott, Lou Wells, and Jim Wooten read and critiqued every chapter, sometimes through multiple drafts. To each of them, I am and will remain profoundly grateful for their incisive comments, their willingness to talk through difficult problems (at almost any hour of the day or night), and their unwavering support and friendship.

Many others read and commented on individual chapters, influencing the book in a great many ways, both large and small. Knowing that an acknowledgment of this sort is never sufficient, I nonetheless wish to express my gratitude to Rawi Abdelal, Sam Abrams, Lisa Adams, Michael Aronson, Tom Baker, Ed Balleisen, Sven Beckert, Zvi Bodie, Alex Dyck, Willis Emmons, Ben Esty, Walter Friedman, Ken Froot, Marjorie Girth, Jerry Green, Morton Horwitz, Meg Jacobs, Carl Kester, Reinier Kraakman, Howard Kunreuther, George Lodge, Bruce Mann, John Melissinos, Erwann Michel-Kerjan, Daniel Nelson, Ken Oye, Huw Pill, Forest Reinhardt, Moses Rischin, Dave Robertson, Julio Rotemberg, Harvey Sapolsky, Steve Sass, Rosemary Stevens, Steve Van Evera, Dick Vietor, Kip Viscusi, Elizabeth Warren, Eugene Wedoff, and Bert Westbrook for their suggestions, insights, and guidance.

I have also benefited from outstanding research assistance, which was very generously supported by Harvard Business School's Division of Research. Javed Ahmed, Sarah Brennan, My Do, Michael Fein, J. P. Gownder, Gibbs Johnson, Marian Lee, Emily Richman, Julie Rosenbaum, and Wendy Smith each did a wonderful job hunting down articles and sifting through voluminous primary records. Sarah, Michael, and Julie deserve special acknowledgment for their extended work on specific chapters. The book would undoubtedly have been thinner (both literally and figuratively) had any one of them not participated so energetically in the project.

Although I have obviously assumed many debts in writing this book, by far the largest is to my family: my wife, Abby, my daughters, Julia and Emily, my parents and parents-in-law, and my siblings. Without their love and their undying patience and support, I could not possibly have brought this project to fruition—a project that I first conceived, not coincidentally, at a family gathering in Pittsburgh in 1995. My family has always provided the inspiration for my work. I can only hope they know the true depth of my gratitude and my admiration for who they are.

Finally, I must express my appreciation to several publishers for allowing me to use copyrighted material in various chapters. Chapter 4 draws heavily from David A. Moss and Sarah Brennan, "Managing Money Risk in Antebellum New York: From Chartered Banking to Free Banking and Beyond," *Studies in American Political Development,* 15, no. 2 (Fall 2001). Assorted excerpts—as well as Tables 4.1, 4.3, and 4.5 (drawn from Table 1 in the article), Table 4.2, Table 4.4, and Figure 4.1—are reprinted with the permission of Cambridge University Press. Portions of Chapter 9, including Figure 9.1, first appeared in David A. Moss and Julie Rosenbaum, *The Great Mississippi Flood of 1993,* case no. 9-797-097 (Boston: Harvard Business School, 1997), and are reprinted with the permission of Harvard Business School Publishing. Chapter 9 also draws in part on David A. Moss, "Courting Disaster? The Transformation of Federal Disaster Policy since 1803," in Kenneth A. Froot, ed., *The Financing of Catastrophe Risk* (Chicago: University of Chicago Press, 1999), © 1999 by the National Bureau of Economic Research. Assorted excerpts as well as a modified version of Table 10.1 are reprinted with the permission of University of Chicago Press.

Index